KV-635-916

M&E PROFESSIONAL STUDIES

Written by a team of practising lecturers and prepared under the Series Editorship of a leading partnership of London accountancy tutors, the *M&E Professional Studies* series has been specially designed to meet the course needs of professional students in virtually all the examined subjects at appropriate professional, degree and diploma levels.

With carefully structured and thoroughly up-to-date contents, most titles include end-of-chapter progress tests based on the text, a large number of practice examination questions and suggested answers, a glossary of the more difficult key terms, and a very comprehensive index. An extensive programme of classroom testing, student surveys and independent assessment has been completed in relation to this series prior to publication.

With twenty substantial texts in the series, *M&E Professional Studies* constitutes a major contribution to business education, and will enable students throughout the English-speaking world to gain the syllabus-related depth of knowledge and practice necessary to ensure a successful examination result.

M&E Professional Studies titles currently available

Advanced Accounting Practice
Advanced Auditing and Investigations
Advanced Financial Accounting
Advanced Taxation
Auditing
Company Law
Costing
Economics
Executorship and Trust Law and Accounts
Financial Management
Foundation Accounting
Law
Management Accounting
Managerial Economics
Numerical Analysis and Data Processing
Organisation and Management
Quantitative Analysis
The Regulatory Framework of Accounting
Systems Analysis and Design
Taxation

M&E PROFESSIONAL STUDIES

ADVANCED AUDITING AND INVESTIGATIONS

Second Edition

Emile Woolf

Series Editors
Emile Woolf FCA FCCA FBIM
Suresh Tanna BSc(Hons) FCA
Karam Singh BTech MBA FCA

Pitman Publishing Limited
128 Long Acre, London WC2E 9AN

A Longman Group Company

© Emile Woolf 1986

First published 1985
Second Edition 1986

British Library Cataloguing in Publication Data
Woolf, Emile
  Advanced auditing and investigations.–
  2nd ed.–(M & E professional studies
  series, ISSN 0266-8475)
  1. Corporations–Great Britain–
  Auditing
I. Title
  657′.45′0941   HF5686.C7
ISBN 0-7121-0686-3

All rights reserved. No part of this publication may be reproduced,
stored in a retrieval system, or transmitted, in any form or by any
means, electronic, mechanical, photocopying, recording and/or otherwise,
without the prior written permission of the publishers. This book may
not be lent, resold, hired out or otherwise disposed of by way of trade
in any form of binding or cover other than that in which it is published,
without the prior consent of the publishers.

Typeset by Avocet Marketing Services, Bicester, Oxfordshire
Printed and bound in Great Britain
at The Bath Press, Avon

Preface

This new edition fully reflects the requirements made by certified and chartered examiners in recent years following the introduction of revised (and more demanding) examination syllabi in relation to advanced auditing.

The new legislation, introduced in the *Companies Acts 1980* and *1981*, now incorporated in the *Companies Act 1985* is far-reaching in its consequences and its effect on auditors is more pervasive than is generally appreciated. All these changes are analysed and thoroughly discussed in Chapter 7.

Recent years have seen the proliferation of new Auditing Guidelines, whose purpose is to elucidate and explain the import of the original 1980 Standards. All of these Guidelines have been included in this book in the appropriate chapters together with appropriate commentaries and explanatory extracts from the APC publication *True & Fair*. All major APC full and draft Guidelines issued in 1985 have also been included.

Small company audits and the feasibility of introducing "review assignments", analytical reviews of financial statements, and investigations under the Companies Act, are also discussed in detail. The chapter on the use of statistical sampling techniques (Chapter 9) reflects the increasing use made by auditors of *monetary unit sampling* on audits of all sizes, and a concise yet comprehensive explanation is given of the underlying mathematical principles. Chapter 10 (on auditors' liability) takes into account the recent dramatic extension of potential claims against auditors by third parties.

The appendices of selected examination questions and answers indicate the very latest trends in setting examinations in auditing at the higher level. As an aid to students seeking reference to specific topics a detailed index is included at the end of the manual, whilst Chapter 4 contains a short but invaluable glossary explaining auditing concepts and terms.

For this edition the book has been comprehensively revised to reflect not only the far-reaching effects of the long-awaited *Companies Act 1985* consolidation, but also the APC Guidelines and draft guidelines on "going concern" considerations affecting auditors; reliance on other specialists; reliance on other auditors; quality control in auditing; changes in a professional appointment; letters to management; reliance on

management assurances; and letters of engagement. The most up-to-date guidance
statements and reviews of accounting standards, with special reference to depreciation,
extraordinary items, deferred taxation and goodwill, have also been included.

I must take this opportunity to acknowledge the considerable assistance I have had
from the immensely authoritative yet practical *Auditing & Accounting Newsletter*,
issued internally by my "old firm" Deloitte, Haskins & Sells for the guidance of their
partners, managers and staff on matters of current importance. I am similarly indebted
to the Auditing Practices Committee (APC) of the CCAB for their kind permission to
include extracts from *True & Fair* and from the 1980 Auditing Standards and
subsequent guidelines; and to the Chartered Association of Certified Accountants for
permission to include past examination questions and published answers at the end of
the text.

I would like to record my gratitude to Lorraine Rottondo of the EW FACT College
in London for her considerable assistance in preparing this edition and checking the
proofs; and to the ever-patient Julia Henderson, also with the College, for her tireless
devotion to the detailed matters which have made this Professional Studies Series so
successful.

My final acknowledgment is to the vast (but unrecorded) number of students who
have attended my lectures, listened to my cassettes, and read my articles and texts over
the past twenty years in so many parts of the world, thereby forcing me to keep abreast
with auditing and related developments, as and when they arise. Long may this practice
continue (although, it is hoped, not always involving the same students)!

Emile Woolf
May 1986

Contents

List of Abbreviations

Throughout the text reference is necessarily made to the official titles of professional bodies, committees, government agencies, etc., and their official pronouncements. Although these titles are spelt out in full on the first occasion they appear in the text, it may nevertheless be useful to have an alphabetical glossary to which quick reference may be made when required.

AICPA   American Institute of Certified Public Accountants
AISG   Accountants International Study Group
APC   Auditing Practices Committee
ASC   Accounting Standards Committee
CA   Companies Act
CCAB   Consultative Committee of Accountancy Bodies
CIPFA   Chartered Institute of Public Finance and Accountancy
ED   Exposure Draft
FASB   Financial Accounting Standards Board
IASC   International Accounting Standards Committee
ICAEW   Institute of Chartered Accountants in England and Wales
ICMA   Institute of Cost and Management Accountants
SE   Stock Exchange
SEC   Securities and Exchange Commission
SSAP   Statement of Standard Accounting Practice

Table of Cases

Note: Abbreviations used below include: AC=Appeal Cases; All ER=All England Reports; Ch=Chancery Division; HL=House of Lords; KB=King's Bench; QB=Queen's Bench; WLR=Weekly Law Reports; WN=Weekly Notes.
[   ] Indicates date essential for discovering case.
(   ) Indicates date case was reported.

Table of Statutes

Table of Statements of Standard Accounting Practice and Auditing Guidelines

CHAPTER ONE
Introduction to Auditing

1.0 WHAT IS AUDITING?

"Audit" is a Latin word, meaning "he hears". It is derived in this way since, in ancient times, the accounts of an estate, domain or manor were checked by having them called out by those who had compiled them, to those in authority (the auditors).

In its modern sense, an audit is a process (carried out by suitably qualified "auditors") whereby the accounting records of a business entity (including charities, trusts and professional firms) are subjected to scrutiny in such detail as will enable the auditors to form an opinion as to their truth, fairness and accuracy. This opinion is then embodied in an "audit report", addressed to those interested parties who commissioned the audit, or to whom the auditors are responsible under statute.

2.0 BACKGROUND TO MODERN AUDITING

Auditing, in some form, has existed for as long as men have found it necessary to account for their transactions; but auditing, as it is now understood, has its roots two to three hundred years ago, in the first division of interests between those engaged in a business undertaking (the entrepreneurs), and those who made the finance available without necessarily becoming directly involved with its management.

Although the immediate concern is with the legal provisions and the techniques which govern the practice of auditing today, an appreciation of the current auditing "scene" is immeasurably enhanced by troubling to understand its earlier origins and, in particular, the economic conditions which led gradually but inexorably to the establishment of an auditing profession, with a vital role and heavy responsibilities. A cursory backward glance is therefore opportune.

Such a glance will also make the subject more *interesting*—a subject reputed, through successive generations of students, to be insufferably boring, to be tolerated purely as a necessary evil and a means towards an end. This view is largely a product of the way in which the subject of auditing has, by and large, been taught.

The sixteenth and seventeenth centuries witnessed a great expansion in exploration and international trade, involving Europe in dealings with the East and the Americas. The adventurers who undertook these exploits rarely possessed the necessary financial means, and they consequently depended heavily on outside backing from wealthy merchants, bankers, and even royalty, as in the case of Christopher Columbus. In England, Queen Elizabeth I gave active assistance to a number of such foreign ventures.

It became a common feature in the coffee-houses of the City of London for information on prospective foreign undertakings to be passed round, and syndicates formed with a view to providing the necessary funds. Information of this nature was usually embodied in a "prospectus", to which syndicate members and other "backers" would append their names. As might be expected, prospectus details were often painted in terms more glowing than the circumstances genuinely justified, and several massive frauds—such as the famous "South Sea Bubble"—drew attention to the need for some form of control.

It was in this way that a body of legislation gradually developed, whose aim was the protection of investors against unscrupulous attempts by promoters to divest them of their funds. The latest in this long statutory line is the Prevention of Fraud (Investments) Act 1958, which prescribes severe penalties not only for wilful deceit, but also for criminal "recklessness" *not* involving fraud. This, however, will be discussed fully in a later section.

Prior to the eighteenth century the concept of "limited liability" was unknown, all participants in a venture (whether as active or sleeping partners) being fully liable, jointly and severally, for the full amount of the debts of the enterprise. A number of factors combined, however, to alter this situation:

(a) Outside assistance was needed on an unprecedented scale to finance increasingly ambitious projects, and the full liability of non-active backers would have entailed prohibitive risks for them.

(b) Successive waves of land enclosures laid the foundations of a "landlord economy". This increased hazards of enterprise and initiative owing to the ability of the new landowners to demand higher rents from entrepreneurs, or to foreclose.

(c) The scientific inventiveness of the eighteenth and nineteenth centuries led to the Industrial Revolution, whose fruits required an economic investment of vast dimensions and, of course, entailed equally vast economic hazards to the investors.

Adaptability has always been the genius of the people of these islands; the new situation created new problems which, in turn, called for new solutions. The immense impetus of the Industrial Revolution in this country (and the foundations of capitalism to which it gave birth) are attributable to the relative ease with which these solutions were found.

Every student of elementary economics is aware that, for production to thrive, three factors—land, labour and capital—are needed. These requirements, in nineteenth century Britain, were largely met by two main expedients: firstly, by dispossessing (albeit by Act of Parliament!) the "Commons" of their land, which had the dual effect of (a) making *land* available for the new industries, and (b) providing a *labouring* "workforce" of men, women and children, now dispossessed and thus forced to work in the locations and conditions imposed on them—or face the consequences!

The second expedient referred to was the establishment of the limited liability ("joint stock" in the early days) company, since this step enormously facilitated the provision of necessary *capital*. Under the rules of limited liability, no participator can be called upon to settle debts of the undertaking over and above the amount of capital he has already agreed to subscribe (known as his "share"). In this way, therefore, shareholders were able to measure precisely the extent of the risk which their investment entailed.

As the practical advantages of this split between the "operators" and "owners" of enterprises were experienced, the incorporation of limited liability companies grew apace, and it became clear that legislation was needed which would

(a) effectively protect the interests of the non-active shareholders from the extravagance, inefficiency, ineptitude, vagaries and, in some cases, deceit of their stewards (who, in time, became known as "directors"); and

(b) force the latter to *account* for the results of all transactions by them, on the company's behalf, during their period of stewardship.

A series of Companies Acts, commencing in 1844, therefore developed for the above purposes, and in time incorporated requirements that these "stewardship" accounts should be subjected to audit by independent experts, who would then report the results of their findings to the shareholders, normally annually.

3.0   AUDIT PRACTICE TODAY: STATUTORY AND PRIVATE AUDITS

The practice of auditing today can still be conveniently split into two main areas, which may be respectively labelled "statutory" and "private". The former category arises under the succession of Companies Acts mentioned above, as a result of which it has become a statutory obligation for every limited company to have a duly qualified auditor. A "private" audit, on the other hand, is one undertaken at the behest of an interested party (e.g. a sole trader) or parties (e.g. partners in a partnership), even though there is no legal obligation for an audit to be carried out.

In the case of private audits the *scope* of the audit may be determined as narrowly or broadly as the proprietor client wishes, according to his requirements; statutory audits, on the other hand, have their scope and depth largely determined by the governing legislation, which neither the directors nor shareholders of the client company have authority to alter. Note that private audits have nothing to do with private companies. *All* limited companies, public or private, require a statutory audit at the present time, although consideration is currently being given to the substitution of a "review" in place of a full audit for those private companies whose directors and shareholders are the same people. This matter is considered further in Chapter 3.

4.0   STATUTORY AUDITS: THE RELATIONSHIPS INVOLVED

It has been established for over eighty years that a limited company possesses a separate corporate identity, or legal personality, irrespective of what befalls its officers and shareholders; and it is therefore able to enter into contracts and business relationships in its own right (*Salomon* v. *Salomon & Co Ltd* (1897)). In practical terms, of course, this is done through the agency of its officers.

A company's relationship with its auditor is similarly governed by contract, and it is important to understand, from the start, that the contract is between the *auditor* and the *company* (*not* its shareholders, directors or other officers). Under contract law valuable consideration must move *from* the contracting parties, irrespective of where such consideration goes, and the consideration in context is as shown in Fig. 1.

So it is seen that shareholders, directors and other officers of a company stand in a *third party* relationship to the company's auditor, outside of contract; this has important implications for the question of the auditor's liability, which will be discussed in detail in a later section.

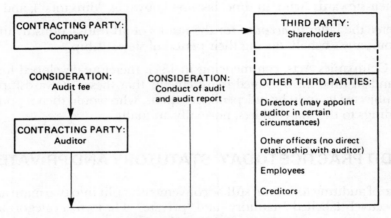

Fig. 1 *Contractual basis of auditing.*

It should, however, be remembered throughout a study of the subject that the execution of audit duties and responsibilities must be performed with that nebulous but vital quality, "reasonable care and skill". Any charge of dereliction of duty or negligence will invariably be tested in the courts by reference to that criterion, even though what constitutes "reasonable" is subject to change, in step with changes in legislation and standards of professional work in general.

5.0   AUDITING AND ACCOUNTANCY

Strictly speaking, an audit can commence only when the necessary accounting work has been completed. In practice, however, especially in the case of a smaller company (and other) clients, the distinction between audit and accountancy work is not clearly appreciated. This confusion usually arises because of the limited book-keeping capabilities of those involved in running small businesses, and it is always tempting to "leave things to the auditor" to complete. It should be clearly understood, however, that in such a case the completion of the accounts is *not* part of the audit; it has even been variously argued, with some justification, than an independent audit is impossible if the auditor has been closely involved in preparing the accounts being audited.

Thus, although many practising accountants readily undertake both accounting and audit work (as well as handling all the client's tax affairs), these tasks are respectively undertaken with "different hats on", and a separate fee for each is normally negotiated.

6.0 DEVELOPMENT OF PROFESSIONAL BODIES

Following the developments which have already been described, it was clear that the work of accounting and auditing was far too important to be left to the haphazard and inept meddlings of persons who possessed no suitable training or experience in these fields. A number of nationally based professional bodies were therefore established in the latter half of the last century, commencing with the Institute of Chartered Accountants in Scotland. The Institute of Chartered Accountants in England and Wales (ICAEW) and its counterpart in Ireland were set up shortly after. Three other eminent accounting bodies, viz. (now) the Chartered Association of Certified Accountants (ACCA), the Institute of Cost and Management Accountants (ICMA), and the Chartered Institute of Public Finance and Accounting (CIPFA), also possess royal charters.

Each body has its own specialist expertise in the fields in which it operates, and is independently governed by an elected council of members, with the support of a full-time secretariat. Although their specialisms vary, there have been powerful attempts to effect a total integration of the accountancy profession, but this has so far failed to win the necessary support. It is likely, however, that some integration (possibly limited to the three Chartered Institutes and the Association) will be achieved within the next decade.

7.0 PROFESSIONAL "PRONOUNCEMENTS"

All the professional accounting bodies have an established publishing tradition. Much of the dynamic growth and development of accounting theory can undoubtedly be attributed to the works published under the auspices of these bodies over several decades. Since auditing, as considered in this text, is traditionally practised by members of the Institutes of Chartered Accountants and the Chartered Association of Certified Accountants, most auditing pronouncements stem from these sources. It is therefore important at this stage to acknowledge these sources as contributing, in large measure, both to established auditing theory and to practice. In particular the most prolific source of such material was the ICAEW series entitled *Statements on Auditing*, issued periodically for the guidance of members, and incorporated in the Members' Handbook. During the mid-1970s, however, responsibility for issuing these statements was taken over by the Auditing Practices Committee (APC) of the Consultative Committee of Accountancy Bodies (CCAB), comprising representatives of *all* major UK accountancy bodies. The APC issued, in May 1980, a set of three new Auditing Standards (based upon earlier Discussion Drafts), and these now constitute essential reading for all students. They will be discussed later in this chapter, and also in Chapter 8.

Apart from these statements, students preparing for advanced auditing examinations may wish to refer to certain other appropriate sources, especially:

(a) The published findings of the Accountants International Study Group

(AISG), which comprises representatives of the UK and Canadian Chartered Institutes, and the American Institute of Certified Public Accountants (AICPA).

(b) The pronouncements of the Accounting Standards Committee (ASC), in the form of Exposure Drafts (EDs) and Statements of Standard Accounting Practice (SSAPs). The aim of this committee, which has been active since 1969, is to reduce the number of ways in which transactions executed in the same or similar circumstances may be treated for accounting purposes, by laying down "Accounting Standards" which must be strictly observed. The ASC members include representatives of the three Chartered Institutes, ACCA, ICMA and CIPFA.

(c) The pronouncements of the International Accounting Standards Committee (IASC), whose purpose is essentially similar to that of UK ASC, but intended rather to operate in the international sphere.

(d) The professional accountancy press. This, of course, is extensive, but the considerable quantity of material which is published regularly should not deter students from actively keeping abreast of developments within the profession—especially since, in 1977, the Institute (ICAEW) declared *Accountancy* its official journal, to be required reading for members. The pages containing essential, official and semi-official material are marked with coloured borders. Each of the main professional bodies publishes its own monthly journal, and students should obviously read, on a regular basis, the journals issued by the body whose examinations they intend to sit, apart from any others which may be recommended. Table 1 may be of some use to those students of auditing who have not yet established an efficient reading pattern.

Reading newspapers and periodicals efficiently is an art. It is essential to be selective in what is read and, ideally, to maintain files in which useful articles are kept in subject order. Although Table 1 may appear forbidding, it should be remembered that items of news and current interest (such as a new Exposure Draft, the heavily qualified audit report of a public company, or a résumé of a Department of Trade and Industry Inspectors' Report) will invariably be featured in several journals at the same time; the study of just one such report is all that is needed, provided it is comprehensive.

8.0 LETTERS OF ENGAGEMENT

The task of the auditor today is at once more onerous and more complex than ever before, as well as being subject to greater risk of liability. It is therefore essential that both client and auditor should be "of one mind" as to the work which the auditor is undertaking. For many years it has been the practice of professional firms to issue letters to their clients at the time of being engaged to undertake professional work, in which they set out in broad terms:

(a) what they understand the engagement to involve;

(b) the way in which they would normally set about the work, including the assistance and co-operation which they would expect from the client;

(c)   the basis on which fees would be calculated; and

(d)   a brief description of the other services which the firm is able to provide, if called upon to do so by the client.

In connection with (b) above, the letter should state that the audit will include a critical review of the system of internal control, and that tests carried out on the basis of that review will be in accordance with what the *auditor* thinks necessary. Some letters, at this point, refer to specific tests such as physical verification of stocks and circularisation of debtors.

Some engagement letters, as they are called, are detailed and specific while others are drafted more loosely, depending upon the preference of the firm in question; although a particular firm would normally standardise the form of engagement letters to be issued by it in differing circumstances. It is normal practice to send two copies of the letter, together with a request that one be signed by the client as an acknowledgment of his agreement as to terms, and immediately returned to the auditor for filing.

An APC Guideline (May 1985) was designed to assist members with the preparation of the engagement letter. It stresses that two main matters are to be clearly stated:

Table 1: Suggested reading

Essential	Strongly recommended	Additionally useful
MONTHLY:	MONTHLY:	MONTHLY
Accountancy (for all students of auditing— available at student rates)	*The Accountant* (by subscription at student rates)	*Management Today*
		Journal of Accountancy (AICPA)
The Certified Students' Newsletter (for certified students)	*The Certified Accountant* (Certified members)	
		The Accountants' Magazine (Scottish Institute)
WEEKLY:	WEEKLY:	
The business news section of *The Sunday Times* *The Sunday Telegraph*, or *The Observer.*	*Accountancy Age*	
	Financial Weekly	
DAILY:		
The Financial Times or the city and business pages of *The Daily Telegraph* *The Times,* or *The Guardian*	*The Economist*	

    (a)   the functions of the auditor are quite distinct from the provision of accountancy, tax or other services; and

    (b)   it is not the *main* purpose of the audit to discover defalcations, irregularities and errors in the client's records, and the audit should not be relied upon for these purposes. (The question of fraud is dealt with in Chapters 5 and 10.)

On the other hand, in the case of statutory audits, the letter should set out the requirements imposed by statute, which *cannot* be varied by either client or auditor.

Engagement letters relating to non-statutory assignments (e.g. work requested by sole traders, partnerships or unincorporated associations such as social clubs) should carefully delineate the work involved as specifically as possible, since any subsequent dispute or negligence charge (possibly leading to litigation) would be decided largely on the questions of:

    (a)   the scope, and

    (b)   the depth of work, defined at the time of engagement.

Many court cases in the past could have been avoided if more attention had been paid to this matter, and in most of these cases the courts took the view that the onus was on the auditor, as the professional party to the contract, to take the necessary steps *ab initio* to avoid a misunderstanding as to the work (and hence the extent of responsibilities) undertaken.

With statutory engagements there is less risk of the relationship between client and auditor being misconstrued by the client, since so much of this relationship is governed by companies legislation. An engagement letter is none the less strongly advisable and the APC Guideline stressed that the letter should embody the contractual terms which subsist between the auditor and his client. The text of the Guideline follows below, and section 8.2 gives a specimen letter of engagement based on the Guideline and demonstrates its function in the case of one small company appointment.

8.1   APC Guideline: Engagement Letters

Responsibilities and scope of the audit
The letter should explain the principal statutory responsibilities of the client and the statutory and professional responsibilities of the auditor.

In the case of a company, it should be indicated that it is the statutory responsibility of the client to maintain proper accounting records, and to prepare financial statements which give a true and fair view and comply with the Companies Acts and other relevant legislation. It should also be indicated that the auditor's statutory responsibilities include making a report to the members stating whether in his opinion the financial statements give a true and fair view and whether they comply with the Companies Acts.

It should be explained that the auditor has an obligation to satisfy himself whether or not the directors' report contains any matters which are inconsistent with the audited financial statements. Furthermore, it should be indicated that the auditor has a professional responsibility to report if the financial statements do not comply in any material respect with Statements of Standard Accounting Practice, unless in his opinion the non-compliance is justified in the circumstances.

The scope of the audit should be explained. In this connection, it should be pointed out that the audit will be conducted in accordance with approved Auditing Standards and have regard to relevant Auditing Guidelines. It should be indicated that:

(a) the auditor will obtain an understanding of the accounting system in order to assess its adequacy as a basis for the preparation of the financial statements;

(b) the auditor will expect to obtain relevant and reliable evidence sufficient to enable him to draw reasonable conclusions therefrom;

(c) the nature and extent of the tests will vary according to the auditor's assessment of the accounting system and, where he wishes to place reliance upon it, the system of internal control;

(d) the auditor will report to management any significant weaknesses in, or observations on, the client's systems which come to his notice and which he thinks should be brought to management's attention.

Where appropriate, reference should be made to recurring special arrangements concerning the audit. These could include arrangements in respect of internal auditors, divisions, overseas subsidiaries, other auditors and (in the case of a small business managed by directors who are the major shareholders) significant reliance on supervision by the directors.

Representations by management
Where appropriate it should be indicated that, prior to the completion of the audit, the auditor may seek written representations from management on matters having a material effect on the financial statements.

Irregularities and fraud
The responsibility for the prevention and detection of irregularity and fraud rests with management and this responsibility is fulfilled mainly through the implementation and continued operation of an adequate system of internal control. The engagement letter should make this clear. Furthermore, it should explain that the auditor will endeavour to plan his audit so that he has a reasonable expectation of detecting material mis-statements in the financial statements resulting from irregularities or fraud, but that the examination should not be relied upon to disclose irregularities and frauds which may exist. If a special examination for irregularities or fraud is required by the client, then this should be specified in the engagement letter, but not in the audit section.

Accounting and taxation services
The auditor may undertake, for the company, services in addition to carrying out his responsibilities as auditor. An engagement letter should adequately describe the nature and scope of those services. In the case of accounting services, the letter should distinguish the accountant's and the client's responsibilities in relation to them and to the day-to-day book-keeping, the maintenance of all accounting records and the preparation of financial statements. Preferably this should be done in a separate letter but such services may form the subject of a section in the audit engagement letter.

In the case of the provision of taxation services, the responsibilities for the various procedures such as the preparation of tax computations and the submission of returns to the relevant authorities should be clearly set out, either in a section of the main letter or in a separate letter.

Where accounting, taxation or other services are undertaken on behalf of an audit client, information may be provided to members of the audit firm other than those engaged on the audit. If this is the case, it may be appropriate for the audit engagement letter to indicate that the auditor is not to be treated as having notice, for the purposes of his audit responsibilities, of the information given to such people.

Fees

Mention should normally be made of fees and of the basis on which they are computed, rendered and paid.

Agreement of terms

The engagement letter should include a request to management that they confirm in writing their agreement to the terms of the engagement. It should be clearly understood that when agreed the letter will give rise to contractual obligations, and its precise content must therefore be carefully considered. In the case of a company, the auditor should request that the letter of acknowledgment be signed on behalf of the board.

8.2   Illustration: Example of an engagement letter

This form of letter is generally appropriate for an incorporated client, but it can also be used as the basis of an engagement letter to the unincorporated client.

Warrington, Minge & Co
Chartered/Certified Accountants
29 Corporation Street
Watford
Herts

The Directors
Boxwood Timber Co Ltd
Ivy Lane   Date
Berkhamsted
Herts

Gentlemen:

APPOINTMENT AS AUDITORS

The purpose of this letter is to set out the basis on which we (are to) act as auditors of the company (and its subsidiaries) and the respective areas of responsibility of the company and of ourselves.

1.   Audit

1.1   As directors of the above company, you are responsible for maintaining proper accounting records and preparing financial statements which give a true and fair view and comply with the Companies Acts. You are also responsible for making available to us, as and when required, all the company's accounting records and all other records and related information, including minutes of all management and shareholders' meetings.

1.2   We have a statutory responsibility to report to the members whether in our opinion the financial statements give a true and fair view of the state of the company's affairs and of the profit or loss for the year and whether they comply with the Companies Act 1985. In arriving at our opinion, we are required to consider the following matters, and to report on any in respect of which we are not satisfied:

(a)   whether proper accounting records have been kept by the company and proper returns adequate for our audit have been received from branches not visited by us;

(b)   whether the company's balance sheet and profit and loss account are in agreement with the accounting records and returns;

(c)   whether we have obtained all the information and explanations which we think necessary for the purpose of our audit; and

(d)   whether the information in the directors' report is consistent with that in the audited financial statements.

In addition, there are certain other matters which, according to the circumstances, may need to be dealt with in our report. For example, where the financial statements do not give full details of directors' remuneration or of transactions with the company, the Companies Act requires us to disclose such matters in our report.

1.3   We have a professional responsibility to report if the financial statements do not comply in any material respect with Statements of Standard Accounting Practice, unless in our opinion the non-compliance is justified in the circumstances.

1.4   Our audit will be conducted in accordance with the Auditing Standards issued by the accountancy bodies and will have regard to relevant Auditing Guidelines. Furthermore, it will be conducted in such a manner as we consider necessary to fulfil our responsibilities and will include such tests of transactions and of the existence, ownership and valuation of assets and liabilities as we consider necessary. We shall obtain an understanding of the accounting system in order to assess its adequacy as a basis for the preparation of the financial statements and to establish whether proper accounting records have been maintained. We shall expect to obtain such relevant and reliable evidence as we consider sufficient to enable us to draw reasonable conclusions therefrom. The nature and extent of our tests will vary according to our assessment of the company's accounting system, and where we wish to place reliance on it the system of internal control, and may cover any aspect of the business operations. We shall report to you any significant weaknesses in, or observations on, the company's systems which come to our notice and which we think should be brought to your attention.

1.5   As part of our normal audit procedures, we may request you to provide written confirmation of oral representations which we have received from you during the course of the audit.

1.6   In order to assist us with the examination of your financial statements, we shall request sight of all documents or statements, including the chairman's statement and the directors' report, which are due to be issued with the financial statements. We are also entitled to attend all general meetings of the company and to receive notice of all such meetings.

1.7 (*Where appropriate*) We appreciate that the present size of your business renders it uneconomic to create a system of internal control based on the segregation of duties for different functions within each area of the business. In the running of your company we understand that the directors are closely involved with the control of the company's transactions. In planning and performing our audit work we shall take account of this supervision. Further, we may ask additionally for confirmation in writing that all the transactions undertaken by the company have been properly reflected and recorded in the accounting records, and our audit report on your company's financial statements may refer to this confirmation.

1.8 **The responsibility for the prevention and detection of irregularities and fraud rests with yourselves. However, we shall endeavour to plan our audit so that we have a reasonable expectation of detecting material misstatements in the financial statements or accounting records resulting from irregularities or fraud, but our examination should not be relied upon to disclose irregularities and frauds which may exist.**

1.9 (*Where appropriate*) We shall not be treated as having notice, for the purposes of our audit responsibilities, of information provided to members of our firm other than those engaged on the audit (e.g. information provided in connection with accounting, taxation and other services).

(*Where appropriate*) Accounting and other services, and taxation services (either included here or set out in a separate letter)

It was agreed that we should carry out the following services as your agents and on the basis that you will make full disclosure to us of all relevant information.

2.   (*Where appropriate*) Accounting and other services

We shall:

2.1 prepare the financial statements based on accounting records maintained by yourselves;

2.2 provide assistance to the company secretary by preparing and lodging returns with the Registrar of Companies;

2.3 investigate irregularities and fraud upon receiving specific instructions.

3.   (*Where appropriate*) Taxation services

3.1 We shall in respect of each accounting period prepare a computation of profits, adjusted in accordance with the provisions of the Taxes Acts, for the purpose of assessment to corporation tax. Subject to your approval, this will then be submitted to the Inspector of Taxes as being the company's formal return. We shall lodge formal notice of appeal against excessive or incorrect assessments to corporation tax where notice of such assessments is received by us. Where appropriate, we shall also make formal application for postponement of tax in dispute and shall advise as to appropriate payments on account.

3.2 You will be responsible, unless otherwise agreed, for all other returns, more particularly: the returns of advance corporation tax and income tax deducted at source as required on Forms CT61, returns relating to employee taxes under PAYE and returns of employee expenses and benefits on Forms P11D. Your staff will deal with all returns and other requirements in relation to value added tax.

3.3 We shall be pleased to advise you on matters relating to the company's corporation tax liability, the implications of particular business transactions and on other taxation matters which you refer to us, such as national insurance, income tax deducted at source, employee benefits, development land tax, value added tax and capital transfer tax.

4. Fees

Our fees are computed on the basis of the time spent on your affairs by the partners and our staff, and on the levels of skill and responsibility involved. Unless otherwise agreed, our fees will be charged separately for each of the main classes of work described above, will be billed at appropriate intervals during the course of the year and will be due on presentation.

5. Agreement of terms

Once it has been agreed, this letter will remain effective, from one audit appointment to another, until it is replaced. We shall be grateful if you could confirm in writing your agreement to the terms of this letter, or let us know if they are not in accordance with your understanding of our terms of appointment.

Yours faithfully,

9.0 THE RANGE OF PROFESSIONAL SERVICES

Professional accountants, in practice as such, undertake many assignments other than auditing. Although these assignments are immensely varied, and no two are ever exactly the same, it is nevertheless possible to provide a rough analysis of the routine work of many practising offices, as shown in Table 2.

Table 2: Professional services

Category	Outline nature of work
Auditing	Records and accounts produced by client
Accountancy	Writing up books of account from source documents provided
	Preparing final accounts from books

Taxation	Advising on most beneficial method of organising client's affairs, from the tax point of view Preparing tax computations from accounts adjusted for tax purposes Dealing with tax assessments levied on client, including tax appeals Handling all correspondence with the Inland Revenue authorities Dealing with Customs & Excise officials over VAT
Share registration	Maintaining statutory registers of shareholders and debenture holders
Management consultancy	Advising on systems of general internal control Costing Budgets Documentation Internal audit New accounting machines Computers
Financial consultancy	Providing advice on optimum avenues of investment Raising finance in short, medium and long term Monitoring client company's profitability and liquidity Establishing optimum levels of readily realisable assets such as stocks, debtors and investments
Investigations	Alleged fraud Under the Companies Act, at the instigation of the Department of Trade and Industry Prospectus reports for new issues of shares or debentures Valuation work: purchase of a business; share in a partnership; shares in a limited company (minority or majority holdings) Prospective loans to a third party
Liquidations, receiverships and trusts	Realising the best return on the assets of a company being wound up, as expeditiously as possible, in order to settle the claims of its creditors and for the benefit of its shareholders Acting as receiver for the debenture holders of a company being wound up or defaulting on the terms of its debenture trust deed Acting as trustee
Miscellaneous	Preparing or certifying claims for subsidy, grant or rebate Compiling reports for submission to government departments, containing figures relating to quotas, levies

or subscriptions; or for statistical purposes; or confirming
solvency

Reporting on profit forecasts, in accordance with the City
Code on Takeovers and Mergers

10.0   INDEPENDENCE RULES

The auditor's independence may be mildly or severely undermined in a variety of ways.
Yet, without his independence, the auditor is like an ornament, a cosmetic effect; just for
show. The condensed history (2.0 above) has demonstrated how the need for a totally
independent review arose in the first place, and this need has in no way diminished with
the passage of years. Indeed, in times of economic difficulty a disinterested audit takes
on an especially vital role.

Limited independence rules have worked satisfactorily for many years in other
countries such as the USA, although it should be mentioned that in the USA such rules
are determined and laid down by a federal body which has recourse to powerful
sanctions, known as the Securities and Exchange Commission (SEC), which acts quite
independently of the AICPA.

In the UK there is no equivalent of the SEC (although it has been seriously advocated
for some years), and the devising of suitable independence rules is thus largely
incumbent on the profession itself. The penalty of failure will undoubtedly be the
imposition of state-determined rules.

Considering the wide range of professional work undertaken as a matter of course, it
is not surprising that allegations are heard to the effect that an auditor's independence
may effectively be undermined when he undertakes one or more unconnected
assignments in addition to the audit work. Quite apart from the very real question of
whether it is possible for an auditor to objectively audit the accounts and records which
he, in his capacity as accountant, has himself prepared, a loss of independence may arise
when the fees receivable for the "other work" undertaken far exceed the fee for the
"pure" audit.

The most recent CCAB guidance statement on professional ethics lists the ways in
which independence may be lost, and provides guidelines on compromising situations
which should be avoided. The following possible compromising situations are listed
and dealt with in more detail later in this section:

(a)   Recurring fees receivable from any one source make up an unduly heavy
      proportion of the auditor's total fee income: the ethics document suggests a
      limit of 15%.

(b)   The auditor is a shareholder or debenture holder of the company whose
      accounts he is auditing: this and situations (c) and (d) below should be
      avoided.

(c)   The auditor is a blood relation of one or more of the client company's officers.

(d)   The auditor is financially involved, personally, with one or more of the client
      company's officers.

(e) The auditor, in his capacity as financial adviser of the company in severe financial difficulties, is searching for ways of keeping the company "afloat", yet knows the heavily qualified audit report which is appropriate in the circumstances will render all attempts to salvage the company useless: this situation is an example of the problem described in the fourth paragraph of this section.

Notes

(a) Auditors are permitted to hold shares in a non-beneficial capacity (e.g. as trustee) provided the holding does not exceed 10% of the trust itself, nor 10% of the class of shares held.

(b) Many firms of accountants operate "independence" rules internally, e.g. forbidding audit staff to deal in the shares of client companies, whether or not they are personally engaged on the audit work. The Companies Act 1985 now forbids this under "insider" legislation.

(c) It is most important to appreciate that the question of independence is also affected by factors quite outside of the auditor's control. For example, as will be seen when the rights, powers and duties of the statutory auditor are considered, it is permissible for directors with a controlling influence to remove the auditor without good cause (possibly with bad cause), against which act the auditor possesses little effective recourse. Until the auditor is adequately protected against unwarranted dismissal it is difficult to envisage complete independence.

10.1 Professional discipline and independence

Although the topics selected for the first published Auditing Standards (see 17.0 below) required definitive treatment in the manner chosen, many commentators would argue that more appropriate themes on which to launch new standards would have related to standards of training and competence, and standards of independence. Although it is expected that these matters will be covered in due course, the question of independence represents a recurring problem.

So far as small companies are concerned, it is often argued that the independence of auditors is both impossible and unnecessary in view of the fact that shareholders and directors are often the same people.

In recent years, the professional accounting bodies have revised their ethical guidelines with a view to enhancing audit independence—at least so far as the public image is concerned—as an important aspect of the self-regulatory process. In essence, disciplinary supervision now extends to instances of sub-standard work, as well as to the more usual areas of misconduct (e.g. failure to attend promptly to correspondence, etc), and a number of instances have been publicised in the professional press concerning, for example, the issue by auditors of clean reports in circumstances where qualification (on doubts concerning stock valuation, non-compliance with SSAPs, failure to provide a funds statement, to name a few issues) was thought to be more appropriate.

Apart from publication of names of those censured, which may include the firm as well as the individual concerned, fines of up to £1,000 may be levied; practising certificates may be withdrawn for a specified period; and exclusion of membership always exists as an ultimate possibility in severe cases.

Also within the broad context of self-regulation may be seen the specific rules on independence of auditors. Those now preclude all forms of financial and personal entanglement arising from shareholdings, loans, relationships in a personal or advisory capacity with company officers, and a situation in which more than 15% of a firm's gross recurring fees are derived from one client source, groups of companies being treated as one for this purpose. Although the initial draft of this guide forbade all shareholdings, the version finally approved permits auditors to act in a non-beneficial trustee capacity as shareholders of public companies, provided the shares held do not exceed 10% of the class of shares issued, and do not exceed more than 10% in value of the total trust fund.

While the establishment of these rules is both timely and necessary, it is most important that students of the subject should not overlook the greatest of all impediments to audit independence—the audit fee itself. This remains true irrespective of whether that fee is more or less than 15% of the total. This is not to suggest, however, as some commentators believe, that self-regulation is ultimately impossible and that all audits should be a function of the state, exercised through the offices of the Department of Trade and Industry; such a change would involve no improvement in the quality of audits, which would additionally be hamstrung by the usual impost of bureaucratic processes to which all state-sector activities are subject.

There can be no objection to auditors working for a fee, and there is no need for this fee in any way to compromise the auditors' independence; but under the present arrangements it is the power of the directors to threaten the auditors with removal (in circumstances where, perhaps, they are doing too good a job) that creates the independence problem. There have been far too many cases arising over the past ten years in which it was obvious that, as a result of such threats, spoken or unspoken, auditors have allowed accounts to be published in which there is less than adequate disclosure of all the reservations in the auditors' minds. It is therefore clear that the next step in the enhancement of audit independence must be on the statutory level, in such manner as will allow auditors a right of appeal to an independent body, e.g. incorporating Department of Trade and Industry officials as well as members of the professional institutes, in any circumstances where their proposed removal can be attributed to unworthy motives of the kind alluded to above.

10.2 Statement on Professional Independence

The full statement on professional independence is as follows.

General

1. It is the duty of an accountant to present or report on information objectively. That duty is the essence of professionalism and is appropriate to all accountants in public practice, in commerce, in industry and in the public service.

2. In the Guidance that follows, paras 3 to 31 concern largely, but not exclusively, members in practice. Para 32 deals exclusively with the position of members who are not in practice.

Responsibility of members in public practice

3. It is the responsibility of practising members to use their best endeavours to ensure

that the guidance given in paras 4 to 31 below is followed in their practices. The specific responsibility of practising members does not in any way detract from the general responsibilities of all members towards their professional body.

Fees

4. It is undesirable that a practice should derive too great a part of its professional income from one client or group of connected clients. A practice, therefore, should endeavour to ensure that the recurring fees paid by one client or group of connected clients do not exceed 15% of the gross fee of the practice or, in the case of a member practising part-time, 15% of his gross earned income. It is recognised that a new practice seeking to establish itself or an old practice running itself down may well not, in the short term, be able to comply with this criterion.

5. In circumstances where a member is dependent for his income on the profits of any one office within a practice and the gross income of that office is regularly dependent on one client or group of connected clients for more than 15% of its gross fees, a partner from another office of the practice should take final responsibility for any report made by the practice on the affairs of that client.

Personal relationships

6. Personal relationships can affect objectivity. There is a particular need, therefore, for a practice to ensure that its objective approach to any assignment is not endangered as a consequence of any personal relationship. By way of example, problems may arise where the same partner or senior staff member works for a number of years on the same audit or where anyone in the practice has a mutual business interest with an officer or employee of a client or has an interest in a joint venture with a client. Such problems can also exist in cases of close friendship or relationship by blood or marriage or where work is being done for a company dominated by one individual.

Financial involvement with or in the affairs of clients

GENERAL

7. Financial involvement with a client may affect objectivity. Such involvement can arise in a number of ways of which a shareholding in a company upon which the practice is retained to report is a typical example.

BENEFICIAL SHAREHOLDINGS—AUDIT CLIENTS

8. A practice should ensure that it does not have as an audit client a company in which a partner in the practice, the spouse or minor child of such a partner, is the beneficial holder of shares, nor should it employ on the audit any member of staff who is a beneficial holder of such shares.

9. (a) Shares in an audit client may be involuntarily acquired as where, for example, a partner inherits such shares or marries a shareholder or in a take-over situation. In such cases the shares should be disposed of at the earliest practicable date, being a date at which the transaction would not amount to insider dealing. Similar action should be taken where shares are held in a company becoming an audit client.

(b) Where a provision in an Act of Parliament requires the auditor of a company to be a shareholder therein the auditor should hold no more than the minimum number of shares necessary to comply with that provision.

(c) Where a provision in the articles of association of a client company requires an auditor to be a shareholder therein the auditor should hold no more than the minimum number of shares necessary to comply with that provision in the articles as it stood on 31st December 1977.

(d) Shares held under this para should be disclosed in the accounts or in the directors' report or, if not so disclosed, in the audit report, except that any insignificant shareholding to which sub-para (a) applies need not be disclosed.

BENEFICIAL SHAREHOLDINGS—CLIENTS UPON WHICH A PRACTICE REPORTS OTHER THAN AS AUDITOR

10. Where a practice is asked to report on a company other than as auditor, every effort should be made to ensure that no partner or member of staff engaged on the assignment, or the spouse or minor child of such a partner, has any beneficial interest in the company. If it is discovered that such is the case immediate steps should be taken to remove from the assignment as soon as possible the partner or staff member concerned.

BENEFICIAL SHAREHOLDINGS—GENERAL EXCEPTIONS

11. The guidance given in paras 8, 9 and 10 is not intended to preclude a beneficial holding in an authorised unit trust, listed investment trust or Lloyd's syndicate which holds shares in a client company, except where the unit or investment trust or syndicate is itself a client on which the practice reports. Nor is it intended to preclude personal savings in a client building society or industrial or provident society, except where such savings are of an amount significant in relation to the assets of the saver.

TRUSTEE SHAREHOLDINGS—PUBLIC COMPANIES

12. A practice should not have as an audit client a public company if a partner in the practice, or the spouse of a partner, is a trustee of a trust holding shares in that company and the holding is in excess of 10% of the issued share capital of the company or of the total assets comprised in the trust. In other cases, unless the trust is an approved charity, a partner who is trustee or is the spouse of the trustee should not personally take part in the audit and the shareholding should be disclosed in the accounts or in the directors' report, or if not so disclosed, in the audit report. Where more than one trust is involved it is sufficient that the number of trusts and aggregate holding is disclosed. Where a practice is asked to report on a company other than as auditor, the principles set out in para 10 apply.

TRUSTEE SHAREHOLDINGS—PRIVATE COMPANIES

13. Where a practice is retained to report as auditor or otherwise on a private company, shares of which are held by a trust of which a partner or the spouse of a partner in the practice is a trustee, the shareholding should be disclosed in the accounts or in the directors' report, or if not so disclosed, in the report made by the practice. Where

possible a review of the files in such a case should be undertaken by another partner.

CORPORATE TRUSTEES

14. Similar considerations to those set out in paras 12 and 13 apply when a partner or spouse of a partner is a director or employee of a trust company which acts as trustee, other than a mere custodian trustee, or a trust holding shares in a company on which the practice reports.

VOTING ON AUDIT APPOINTMENTS

15. Where any shares are held in an audit client company they should not be voted at any general meeting of the company in relation to the appointment or remuneration of auditors.

BENEFICIARIES' INTERESTS IN TRUSTS

16. A partner should not personally take part in the audit of a client company if he, his spouse or minor child, is a beneficiary drawing income or entitled to accumulated income from a trust which, to his knowledge, holds shares in the company. Similar principles apply where a practice is asked to report on a company other than as auditor.

NOMINEE SHAREHOLDINGS

17. Similar considerations to those set out in para 12 apply to nominee shareholdings in public companies on which the practice reports.

LOANS TO AND FROM CLIENTS—PRACTICE LOANS

18. (a) A practice should not make a loan to a client, nor guarantee a client's borrowings, nor for the future accept a loan from a client or have borrowings guaranteed by a client. This guidance does not preclude a practice from having a current account in credit or a deposit account with a client clearing bank or similar banking institution.

LOANS TO AND FROM CLIENTS—INDIVIDUAL LOANS

18. (b) Neither a partner in a practice nor the spouse or minor child of a partner, should make a loan to a client, or guarantee a client's borrowings, or for the future accept a loan from a client or have borrowings guaranteed by a client. This guidance is not intended to preclude loans between close relations such as may be regarded as a normal consequence of family life. In the context of this sub-paragraph, the word "loan" does not include a current or deposit account with a clearing bank or similar banking institution, nor does it include a loan or overdraft from a clearing bank.

(c) A loan from or overdraft with a clearing bank does not preclude a member from being appointed by that bank to be a receiver.

GOODS AND SERVICES

19. Acceptance of goods or services from a client may be a threat to independence. These should not be accepted by a partner, his spouse or minor child or by the staff

of the practice save on terms no more favourable than those available to the generality of the employees of the client. Acceptance of undue hospitality poses a similar threat.

COMMISSION

20. Where advice given to a client is such that, if acted upon, it will result in commission being earned by the practice or anyone in it, special care should be taken that the advice is in fact in the best interests of the client. The client should be informed, in writing, both of the fact that commission will be received and, as soon as practicable, of the amount and terms of such commission.

Conflicts of interest

GENERAL

21. (a) In cases where conflicts of interest arise there should be a full and frank explanation to those involved, coupled with any action necessary to disengage from one or both positions, the conflicting interests of which have occasioned the difficulty. Conflicts should, so far as possible, be avoided by not accepting any appointment or assignment in which conflict seems likely to occur.

COMPETING CLIENTS

21. (b) As an example, a practice which advises a company upon the figures on which it bases a tender for a contract should avoid the conflict of interest which would arise if it knowingly became involved in advising a rival company tendering for the same contract.

CLIENTS IN DISPUTE

21. (c) Another example is where a practice which is financial adviser to a company also deals with the personal affairs of its directors and there is a dispute between the company and one of those directors. In such a case a practice should select which of its clients it is to advise. It should not advise both and it may well be preferable that it advises neither although it may, if asked by both clients, put forward proposals for settling the dispute. Similar considerations apply in the case of a partnership dispute.

PROVISION OF OTHER SERVICES TO AUDIT CLIENTS

22. Whilst it is right that members should provide, for audit clients, other services beyond performing the audit, nevertheless care must be taken not to perform executive functions or to make executive decisions. These are the duties of management. This theme runs through the examples given in paras 23–30 below. In particular members should beware lest, in providing such services, they drift into a situation in which they step across the border line of what is proper.

PREPARATION OF ACCOUNTING RECORDS

23. (a) A practice should not participate in the preparation of the accounting records of a public company audit client save in exceptional circumstances.

(b) In the case of a private company audit client, it is frequently necessary to provide a much fuller service than would be appropriate in the case of a public company audit client and this may include participation in the preparation of accounting records.

(c)   In all cases in which a practice is concerned in the preparation of accounting records of an audit client particular care must be taken to ensure that the client accepts full responsibility for such records and that objectivity in carrying out the audit is not impaired.

CURRENT APPOINTMENT IN A COMPANY REPORTED ON

24.   A practice, wherever it may be situated, should not report on a company, even if the law of the country in which the company is registered would so permit, if a partner or employee of the practice is an officer or employee of the company. Nor should a practice report on a company if a company associated with the practice fills the appointment of secretary to the client. It should be particularly noted that this guidance is applicable to members whether they are within or without the United Kingdom and whether they are in practice or not.

PREVIOUS APPOINTMENT IN A COMPANY REPORTED ON

25.   No one should personally take part in the exercise of the reporting function on a company if he has, during the period upon which the report is to be made, or at any time in the two years prior to the first day thereof, been an officer (other than auditor) or employee of that company.

LIQUIDATIONS FOLLOWING RECEIVERSHIPS

26.   Where a partner in or an employee of a practice is, or in the previous two years has been, receiver of any of the assets of a company, no partner in or employer of the practice should accept appointment as liquidator of the company.

LIQUIDATIONS GENERALLY

27.   Where a practice or a partner in or an employee of a practice has, or during the previous two years has had, a continuing professional relationship (as to which see para 29) with a company, no partner or employee of the practice should accept appointment as liquidator of the company if the company is insolvent. Where the company is solvent such appointment should not be accepted without careful consideration being given to the implications of acceptance in that particular case.

RECEIVERSHIPS

28.   Where a practice or a partner in or an employee of a practice has, or during the previous two years has had, a continuing professional relationship (as to which see para 29) with a company, no partner in or employee of the practice should accept appointment as receiver or as receiver and manager of that company.

CONTINUING PROFESSIONAL RELATIONSHIP

29.   Such "continuing professional relationship" as is referred to in paras 27 and 28 above does not arise where the relationship is one which springs from the appointment of the practice by, or at the instigation of, a creditor or other party having an actual or potential financial interest in the company to investigate, monitor or advise on its affairs.

AUDIT FOLLOWING RECEIVERSHIP

30. Where a partner in or an employee of a practice has been receiver of any of the assets of a company, neither the practice nor any partner in or employee of the practice should accept appointment as auditor of the company, or of any company which was under the control of the receiver, for any accounting period during which the receiver acted or exercised control.

NEW CLIENTS

31. Whenever a practice is asked to accept an appointment, consideration will need to be given to whether acceptance might give rise to a situation in which independence may be compromised whether by a prospective conflict of interest or otherwise. All reasonable steps should be taken to establish that acceptance is unlikely to threaten independence.

Responsibility of members not in practice

32. As is said in para 3 of the statement, members who are not in practice have a duty to be objective in carrying out their professional work, whether or not the appearance of independence may be attainable. Thus a member performing professional work in commerce, industry or the public service should recognise the problems created by personal relationships or financial involvements which by reason of their nature or degree might threaten his objectivity in respect of his work, for he, like the member in practice, must observe the high standards of conduct and integrity expected of the membership of the profession.

10.3   Audit committees as an aid to independence

Some may ask whether the independence issue is worth all the fuss, whether it is really so essential. To that there is a simple answer: the concept of the auditor and the concept of independence are the twin sides of the same coin. The auditor who has lost his independence has lost his *raison d'être*, he has become dependent, and a "dependent auditor" is a contradiction in terms.

Those situations which have the effect of undermining the auditor's independence are many and various. Most, however, have one distinguishing feature in common; they are all situations in which there is an implicit temptation on the part of the auditor to avoid incurring the displeasure of those able to sack him.

A current proposal which merits serious attention advocates the establishment, initially for all listed companies, of an independent "audit committee", chiefly comprising *non-executive* officers of the company, appointed to view the company's position in a detached and dispassionate light, and to liaise effectively between its main board and its external auditors. Since the final form and function of such a committee is still a matter for debate, it would be quite misleading to attempt too close a definition; the following activities have, however, been associated with it:

(a) to formally and regularly review the financial results shown by both management accounts and those presented to shareholders;

(b) to make recommendations for the improvement of management control;

(c) to assist external auditors in obtaining all the information they require and in resolving any difficulties experienced by them in pursuing their independent examination;

(d)   to deal with any material reservations of the auditors regarding the company's management, its records and its final accounts, including the manner in which significant items are presented therein;

(e)   to facilitate a satisfactory working relationship between the management and auditors, and between the internal and external audit functions;

(f)   to ensure that there are adequate procedures for reviewing "rights" circulars, interim statements, forecasts, and other financial information prior to distribution to shareholders.

It is often the case that what in the UK is considered to be a novel development is in fact something which the North Americans have debated long and hard for years, even decades; and the question of audit committees is no exception. Both the Securities and Exchange Commission (SEC) and the New York Stock Exchange (NYSE) first recommended the institution of audit committees in 1940. This recommendation was followed by several companies, but only gained real momentum in 1967, when the American Institute of Certified Public Accountants acted positively by recommending that "publicly owned corporations appoint committees composed of outside directors to nominate the independent auditors . . . and to discuss the auditor's work with them".

In 1972 and 1973, in the wake of the Equity Funding fraud scandal, both the SEC and NYSE put further pressure on company boards to appoint audit committees, culminating in the requirement that (since 1st January 1978) all public companies must have audit committees, as a condition of listing.

Many believe that there is a clear need for such committees in the UK, and that, apart from the matters listed above, they should:

(a)   be responsible for the appointment of external auditors, as well as fixing their remuneration;

(b)   be available for consultation with the auditors at all times, if necessary without the presence of management;

(c)   regularly discuss and review the procedures employed by the auditors;

(d)   be concerned with all matters relating to the disclosure by the accounts of a true and fair view for the benefit of all users.

Counter-arguments

Against the persuasive arguments set out above, the following should also be borne in mind.

(a)   There is in the UK very little definition given to the optimum constitution and function of an audit committee, and those public companies who have voluntarily appointed such committees have done so on a variety of bases. Furthermore, there is little collective experience upon which to base an evaluation of their usefulness and effectiveness, either as an aid to the independence of external auditors, or as a means of controlling the excesses of senior corporative executives. It may therefore be validly argued that at least ten more years of experience on an experimental basis are needed before the concept of audit committees should be given statutory support.

(b) Many parliamentary attempts to introduce audit committees have been based on a concept somewhat different from that normally adopted. The chief aim in such cases appears to be to appoint "watchdog" shareholder committees, whose purpose would be to maintain a watching brief over the activities of the main board, and would probably incorporate an audit of corporate objectives and achievements. The more usual concept of audit committees is clearly rather different, and it may be that these legislative efforts (including the use of the name "audit committee") may turn out to have been counter-productive in hastening the adoption of this idea.

(c) The wider experience of audit committees on the North American continent is itself inconclusive, in so far as the audit committee is supposed to monitor and control the conduct of dominating company directors; certainly, external auditors appear to be no better protected by the presence of such committees against threats of removal every time they appear to make a stand on questions of disclosure and accounting treatment. Doubts therefore remain concerning the independence of the audit committee itself, and whether it can ever, on a part-time, non-executive basis, exercise the degree of influence over senior full-time directors for which its presence is created in the first place.

(d) Justifiable fears also exist that a powerful audit committee may serve to hamper executive flair which, by its very nature, will always appear to contravene accepted norms. As in any other area of human activity, innovation and experimentation are vital to successful commercial enterprise, in the face of which a non-executive audit committee (whose members are concerned to avoid risks and keep low profiles) may be more akin to a millstone than a spur.

11.0 QUALITIES OF THE AUDITOR

Although the audit is predominantly concerned with a client organisation's accounts (and hence its underlying accounting records and documentation), the auditor needs to maintain the widest possible view of the client's circumstances. Each individual business transaction takes place within a somewhat broader context, and the truly skilled auditor has a view which includes seemingly insignificant details and their place in relation to the mainstream of the client's business activity, at one and the same time.

A set of final accounts, after all, is simply a financial photograph, seemingly motionless, with a tinge of inevitability about it; yet that photograph might be taken with a wide- or narrow-angle lens; it might be "touched up" for effect, dramatised, or distorted; it might be explicit, or merely suggestive, leaving the final impression to the perceptive observer to discern. It is the task of the auditor to consider and to report on that impression, the picture which that financial photograph conveys. Successive Companies Acts have searched for the formulation which most effectively sums up the impression which accounts *ought* to convey: "true and correct", "fairly", "true and fair" have all been tried. Each such formulation has certain inherent virtues as well as inherent limitations. Under present company law the accounts are required to give a "true and fair" view, and it is thus clear that in expressing his own opinion on those accounts, the auditor needs to consider far more than merely whether each and every individual transaction is accurately reflected therein. It is quite conceivable, for instance, that a set of accounts might "accurately" be prepared from the records of a concern on the verge of bankruptcy, and yet give no hint of the impending disaster. The auditor of those accounts has a clear duty to "spell it out" in terms which cannot reasonably be misconstrued.

12.0   GENERAL ADVANTAGES OF AN AUDIT

It is often believed, mistakenly, that a genuine need for an external, independent audit arises only in the case of large and complex organisations, or where the interests of outside non-executive shareholders must be protected. Quite apart from such situations there are a number of inherent advantages in having accounts audited, even where there is no statutory provision for this to be done. By way of example, consider the case of the independent audit of a business partnership. The following advantages may readily be cited:

(a)   Disputes between partners regarding the accounts may be largely avoided, especially where complicated profit-sharing arrangements subsist.

(b)   The admission of a new partner is facilitated if sets of audited historical accounts are available for examination.

(c)   Any partnership change (e.g. death or retirement, or alteration of profit-sharing ratios) will require to be reflected in the accounts, and it is usual for the partnership assets, including goodwill, to be revalued at such a time. Since such revaluations directly affect the respective shares of each partner, it is advisable to have the post-change accounts audited.

(d)   Applications to banks and other outside parties for the purpose of raising funds are greatly enhanced by the availability of audited accounts.

(e)   Audited accounts (albeit adjusted) submitted to the Inland Revenue for tax assessment purposes carry greater authority than accounts which have not been audited.

(f)   The presence of a qualified auditor is useful because of the variety of other capacities in which he is able to assist—see section 9.0 above. Additionally, a number of partnership and other agreements incorporate a provision for the auditor to act as *arbitrator* in the event of dispute on specified issues.

13.0   "OPINIONS" AND "CERTIFICATES"

The number of individual transactions undertaken by the majority of business concerns in the course of a financial year makes any attempt at an exhaustive check virtually impossible. From a practical point of view, therefore, the auditor's task is limited to the expression of an opinion (as opposed to guarantee) on the view presented by the accounts of the business unit which he has audited. Companies legislation is quite clear on this point, containing the words "in his opinion" with reference to the auditor's duties.

For this reason the word "certificate" should be avoided in this context, since there is obviously a very great difference between certifying the correctness of figures presented, and merely expressing an opinion on them. Auditors in the USA still refer to their "certificate", but in the UK it is correctly titled the "auditor's report". The only occasions on which the auditor actually *certifies* would arise when he has checked that a set of accounts has been correctly drawn up in a form prescribed for a particular purpose, e.g. when claiming a government grant.

It should not, however, be imagined that the general requirement for the auditor simply to express an opinion on accounts (instead of certifying their correctness) in any way lightens his burden. On the contrary, it should be obvious that the risks involved are much greater when an authoritative opinion has to be based upon a less than exhaustive enquiry, since the question inevitably arises as to how extensive a check is warranted in varying circumstances. Exposure to potential liability accompanies every audit assignment and instances of liability which have arisen in the past are most commonly attributable to the failure (in the opinion of the court) of the auditor to execute a sufficiently extensive examination in the particular circumstances obtaining.

14.0 FORM OF THE AUDIT

Although all genuine audits will have precisely the same *objective*, viz. to report to the interested parties on the results of the audit investigation undertaken, within the context of the engagement, it is nevertheless true that the way in which the audit is conducted will depend largely on the size and circumstances of the client concerned.

For the audit objective to be achieved a systematic approach to the task is vitally important. Although all aspects of audit work are closely interrelated, it is convenient to distinguish the *essential phases* through which the audit develops, as follows:

(a) to make a critical review of the system of book-keeping, accounting and internal control;

(b) to make such tests and enquiries as the auditors consider necessary to form an opinion as to the reliability of the records as a basis for the preparation of accounts;

(c) to compare the profit and loss account and balance sheet with the underlying records in order to see whether they are in accordance therewith;

(d) to make a critical review of the profit and loss account and the balance sheet in order that a report may be made to the members stating whether, in the opinion of the auditors, the accounts are presented, and the items are described, in such a way that they show not only a true but also a fair view and give, in the prescribed manner, the information required by the Companies Acts.

Items (a) to (d) set out above represent a framework which embraces virtually the whole of normal audit work. It should therefore be used by the student to give perspective to any individual aspect of the subject which is being studied. Subsequent chapters deal with these phases in detail.

It should be clear from what has so far been said that the quantity, range and depth of audit work undertaken in any given set of circumstances will depend upon the auditor's own assessment of the system which produces, in the first place, the record which he is required to audit. Since the quality and reliability of systems are almost infinitely variable, the length of time taken to conduct an audit, and the number and level of audit personnel required to do so, are equally variable. It is nevertheless possible to draw up broad classifications, as shown in Table 3.

Table 3. Classification of audit work

Audit type	Description
Complete, or final	Usually applies to smaller concerns where the volume and complexity of transactions do not require the auditor to attend more than once each year. This visit normally takes place as soon as possible after the business's financial year-end and continues until it has been completed and the audit report signed.
Interim *and* final	In the case of larger clients the auditor will often find it necessary to conduct the audit on an interim basis, in view of the increased volume of testing which it is necessary for him and his staff to undertake. Interim audits, always by arrangement with the client, may be bi-annual, quarterly, or even monthly depending upon the volume of audit work considered necessary. Interim audits possess the advantage of leaving the final audit relatively free for the verification of year-end accounts, the assessment of the system and most detailed checking of underlying books and documents having already been carried out.
Continuous	Where the client's system displays certain fundamental and material weaknesses the auditor will feel obliged to check a higher proportion of transactions than would otherwise be the case, and in exceptional circumstances it may therefore be necessary for members of the audit team to execute checking work continuously, throughout the year, to which the accounts relate.

15.0 ACCOUNTING SUBJECTIVITY AND THE AUDITOR

Quite apart from the practical reasons for the auditor's report to express an opinion rather than a certificate it should be remembered that total objectivity in accounting is probably an idealist's dream. Even if it were physically practicable for the auditor to examine, in detail, every single shred of documentary evidence relating to the transactions of a large company throughout its financial year, it would still not be possible to certify more than the arithmetic and book-keeping accuracy. Accounting (as opposed to book-keeping) involves the exercise of judgment and there is thus every chance that two auditors of equal skill and experience will view a particular circumstance differently, even at a fundamental level.

Views, which some may regard as cynical, have been raised suggesting that modern accounting, being necessarily complex, may all too easily be subjectively manipulated in pursuit of unworthy motives. In times of economic difficulty certain managements may be tempted to present their accounts in a way which seeks to hide the problems they face, and the auditor, as guardian of the interests of shareholders and (indirectly) other outsiders, has the clear duty to insist that appropriate amendments be made or else to qualify his own report explicitly.

There are accounting areas which are traditionally susceptible to a variety of interpretations (and hence presentations), such as treatment of deferred taxation; depreciation; research and development expenditure; goodwill; leasing; government grants; extraordinary items; post balance sheet events; prior-year adjustments; currency conversion differences; unrealised capital surpluses; and many others. The work of the ASC is essentially aimed at the standardisation, so far as is possible, of the accounting treatments of the above items in the context of similar sets of circumstances.

16.0   AUDIT WORKING PAPERS

16.1   Object

The main object of the auditor's working papers is to record and demonstrate the steps which have been taken by the auditors to enable them to form an opinion on the accounts upon which they are required to report. To achieve this object the working papers should provide:

(a)   a means of controlling the current year's audit work and the basis on which to plan the following year's audit;

(b)   evidence of the work carried out by the auditors;

(c)   schedules in support of the accounts additional to, or summarising, the detail in the client's books;

(d)   information about the business whose accounts have been audited, including its recent history.

16.2   Form

It is not practicable to specify the precise form that working papers should take. They should be designed so as to achieve the object set out above, according to the auditors' own requirements and the particular circumstances of each audit, and should be comprehensible in themselves. It should also be noted that it may be possible to use copies of certain of the client's accounting papers for some of the schedules required by the auditors.

The subdivision of the working papers between current and permanent files will, in practice, be a matter of convenience and the suggested allocation, given below, should be interpreted in this light.

16.3 Current file

The current year's file, which will relate primarily to the set of accounts or statement being audited, should normally contain the following:

(a) A *copy of the accounts* or statement on which the auditors are reporting, authenticated by directors' signatures or otherwise.

(b) *An index* covering all the working papers, unless they are cross-referenced to the relevant items in the accounts.

(c) (i) An *internal control questionnaire* or other record, including flow-chart if appropriate, designed to ascertain the adequacy of the system of internal control, and

    (ii) an *audit programme* supplemented by particulars and dates of the work carried out and precise details of audit tests and their results.

These two documents are often combined, as the results disclosed by the one should determine the work to be carried out on the other. Any weaknesses discovered and resulting action should be recorded. Where the rotation of the more detailed tests from year to year is the practice, a separate schedule should be kept showing details of the particular tests carried out in the current year.

(d) A *schedule for each item in the balance sheet*, preferably including comparative figures, showing its make-up and how existence, ownership and value or liability have been verified. These schedules should be cross-referenced to documents arising from external verification such as bank letters and the results of circularisation of debtors and attendance at physical stocktaking.

(e) A *schedule supporting each item in the statutory profit and loss account*, preferably including comparative figures, and such other items in the trading or subsidiary accounts as may be necessary.

(f) A *check-list* concerning compliance with statutory disclosure provisions.

(g) A *record showing queries raised during the audit and their disposal*, with notes where appropriate for attention the following year. Queries not cleared at the time should be entered on to a further schedule for the attention of the person reviewing the audit and for reference to the client if necessary. Material queries, which cannot be settled satisfactorily by immediate reference to the client, may require a qualification of the auditors' report and should be fully documented and supported by a note of all discussions with the client and any explanations given.

(h) A *schedule of important statistics or working ratios*, comparative figures being included where appropriate. Useful ratios may include:

    (i) gross profit percentages;

(ii) current assets to current liabilities;

(iii) stock to turnover;

(iv) trade debtors and creditors—average period of credit;

(v) profit to capital employed

Significant variations in the above ratios will need to be explained and may have to be examined over a period of years to indicate important variations in the company's accounts. A reference in the working papers to the facts disclosed in the client's management information may provide useful evidence of the reasons for significant variations.

(i) A *record or extract of minutes of meetings of the directors and shareholders.* These should be cross-referenced where relevant to the auditor's working schedules.

(j) *Copies of letters to the client setting out any material weaknesses* or matters with which the auditors are dissatisfied in respect of the accounts or control procedures. Such letters should be sent where the particular matter has been discussed informally with one or more of the company's officials.

(k) *Letters of representation,* i.e. written confirmation by the client of information and opinions expressed in respect of matters such as stock values and amounts of current and contingent liabilities.

Matters which, while not of permanent importance, will require attention during the subsequent year's audit should be listed, with reference to the relevant working papers, and this note should be transferred to the next current file when opened.

16.4   Permanent file

Matters of continuing importance affecting the company or the audit should be kept in a separate file, suitably indexed, and these should normally include:

(a) *memorandum and articles of association* and other appropriate statutory or legal regulations;

(b) *copies of other documents and minutes of continuing importance;*

(c) *a short description of the type of business carried on and the places of business;*

(d) *listes of accounting records and responsible officials and a plan of the organisation;*

(e) *statements showing a note of any accounting matters of importance* such as a record of reserves and bases of accounting adopted, e.g. for the valuation of stock and work in progress, depreciation and the carrying forward and writing off of expenditure ultimately chargeable to revenue;

(f) *the client's internal accounting instructions and internal audit instructions,* including where appropriate stocktaking instructions.

Steps should be taken to ensure that the permanent file is brought up to date at appropriate times. In the case of a non-statutory audit the permanent file should also contain the client's instructions as to the scope of the work to be performed.

17.0   THE AUDITING STANDARDS AND GUIDELINES OF 1980

As mentioned in section 7.0 above, the APC issued in 1980 a set of standards laying down basic auditing principles, accompanied by guidelines explaining their detailed application. The format of these standards is indicated in 17.1 below, and the full text of the Operational Standard and its guidelines then follows. The two standards dealing with audit reports are to be found in Chapter 8.

At this early stage in your studies you should not attempt to master the detail of the standards and guidelines, but you will need to refer back to them constantly as you work through the manual.

17.1   The format of the standards and guidelines

Standards	Guidelines
The auditor's operational standard	Planning, controlling and recording Accounting systems Audit evidence Internal controls Review of financial statements
The audit report Qualifications in audit reports	Audit report examples

17.2   The Auditor's Operational Standard

1.   This auditing standard applies whenever an audit is carried out.

Planning, controlling and recording
2.   The auditor should adequately plan, control and record his work.

Accounting systems
3.   The auditor should ascertain the enterprise's system of recording and processing transactions and assess its adequacy as a basis for the preparation of financial statements.

Audit evidence
4.   The auditor should obtain relevant and reliable audit evidence sufficient to enable him to draw reasonable conclusions therefrom.

Internal controls
5.   If the auditor wishes to place reliance on any internal controls, he should ascertain and evaluate those controls and perform compliance tests on their operation.

Review of financial statements
6.   The auditor should carry out such a review of the financial statements as is

sufficient, in conjunction with the conclusions drawn from the other audit evidence obtained, to give them a reasonable basis for his opinion on the financial statements.

17.3 Guidelines: Planning, Controlling and Recording

Introduction

1. Paragraph 2 of the Auditing Standard "The Auditor's Operational Standard" states that: "The auditor should adequately plan, control and record his work." This Auditing Guideline, which gives·guidance on how that paragraph may be applied, should be read in conjunction with the Explanatory Foreword to Auditing Standards and Guidelines including the Glossary of Terms.

2. In order to ensure that an audit is carried out effectively and efficiently, the work needs to be planned, controlled and recorded at each stage of its progress. Planning, controlling and recording are considered separately below although they are not mutually exclusive.

3. The need to plan, control and record audit work exists regardless of the size of the enterprise concerned. Although all of the procedures described in this Guideline need to be considered by the auditor, in the case of smaller enterprises the work involved in implementing them will be less.

(a) Planning

BACKGROUND

4. The form and nature of the planning required for an audit will be affected by the size and complexity of the enterprise, the commercial environment in which it operates, the method of processing transactions and the reporting requirements to which it is subject. In this context, the auditor should aim to provide an effective and economic service within an appropriate time-scale.

5. Adequate audit planning:

    (a) establishes the intended means of achieving the objectives of the audit;

    (b) assists in the direction and control of the work;

    (c) helps to ensure that attention is devoted to critical aspects of the audit; and

    (d) helps to ensure that the work is completed expeditiously.

6. In order to plan his work adequately the auditor needs to understand the nature of the business of the enterprise, its organisation, its method of operating and the industry in which it is involved, so that he is able to appreciate which events and transactions are likely to have a significant effect on the financial statements.

PROCEDURES

7. The auditor should consider the outline audit approach he proposes to adopt, including the extent to which he may wish to rely on internal controls and any aspects of the audit which need particular attention. He should also take into

account in his planning any additional work which he has agreed to undertake.

8.   Preparatory procedures which the auditor should consider include the following:

(a)   reviewing matters raised in the audit of the previous year which may have continuing relevance in the current year;

(b)   assessing the effects of any changes in legislation or accounting practice affecting the financial statements of the enterprise;

(c)   reviewing interim or management accounts where these are available and consulting with the management or staff of the enterprise: matters which should be considered include current trading circumstances, and significant changes in:

(i)   the business carried on,

(ii) the enterprise's management;

(d)   identifying any significant changes in the enterprise's accounting procedures, such as a new computer-based system.

9.   The auditor should also consider:

(a)   the timing of significant phases of the preparation of the financial statements;

(b)   the extent to which analyses and summaries can be prepared by the enterprise's employees;

(c)   the relevance of any work to be carried out by the enterprise's internal auditors.

10.   The auditor will need to determine the number of audit staff required, the experience and special skills they need to possess and the timing of their audit visits. He will need to ensure that all audit staff are briefed regarding the enterprise's affairs and the nature and scope of the work they are required to carry out. The preparation of a memorandum setting out the outline audit approach may be helpful.

11.   On joint audits there should be consultation between the joint auditors to determine the allocation of the work to be undertaken and the procedures for its control and review.

(b) Controlling

BACKGROUND

12.   Management structures vary between firms of auditors and this Auditing Guideline should be interpreted in the context of the particular structure within each firm. The Guideline has, however, been written on the basis that the audit is carried out by a reporting partner and his staff.

13.   The reporting partner needs to be satisfied that on each audit the work is being performed to an acceptable standard. The most important elements of control of

an audit are the direction and supervision of the audit staff and the review of the work they have done. The degree of supervision required depends on the complexity of the assignment and the experience and proficiency of the audit staff.

PROCEDURES

14. The nature of the procedures needed to control an audit and the extent to which they need to be formalised cannot be precisely specified as they depend on the organisation of the audit firm and the degree of delegation of the audit work. The procedures established should be designed and applied to ensure the following:

(a) work is allocated to audit staff who have appropriate training, experience and proficiency;

(b) audit staff at all levels clearly understand their responsibilities and the objectives of the procedures which they are expected to perform. Audit staff should be informed of any matters identified during the planning stage that may affect the nature, extent or timing of the procedures they are to perform. They should be instructed to bring to the attention of those to whom they are responsible any significant accounting or auditing problems that they encounter;

(c) the working papers provide an adequate record of the work that has been carried out and the conclusions that have been reached;

(d) the work performed by each member of the audit staff is reviewed by more senior persons in the audit firm. This is necessary to ensure that the work was adequately performed and to confirm that the results obtained support the audit conclusions which have been reached.

15. The final stages of an audit require special attention. At this time, when pressures are greatest, control of the audit work is particularly required to ensure that mistakes and omissions do not occur. The use of an audit completion checklist, with sections to be filled in by the reporting partner and his staff, will help to provide such control.

16. Where matters of principle or contentious matters arise which may affect the audit opinion the auditor should consider consulting another experienced accountant. This accountant may be a partner, a senior colleague, or another practitioner. If another practitioner is consulted, confidentiality of the client's affairs must be maintained.

17. The auditor should also consider how the overall quality of the work carried out within the firm can best be monitored and maintained.

(c) Recording

BACKGROUND

18. Reasons for preparing audit working papers include the following:

(a) The reporting partner needs to be able to satisfy himself that work delegated by him has been properly performed. The reporting partner can generally do this only by having available to him detailed working papers prepared by the audit staff who performed the work.

(b)   Working papers provide, for future reference, details of problems encountered together with evidence of work performed and conclusions drawn therefrom in arriving at the audit opinion.

(c)   The preparation of working papers encourages the auditor to adopt a methodical approach.

PROCEDURES

19.   *Contents of working papers.* [See more detailed exposition at 16.0 above.] Audit working papers should always be sufficiently complete and detailed to enable an experienced auditor with no previous connection with the audit subsequently to ascertain from them what work was performed and to support the conclusions reached. Audit working papers should be prepared as the audit proceeds so that details and problems are not omitted.

20.   Audit working papers should include a summary of all significant matters identified which may require the exercise of judgment, together with the auditor's conclusions thereon. If difficult questions of principle or of judgment arise, the auditor should record the relevant information received and summarise both the management's and his conclusions. It is in such areas as these that the auditor's judgment may subsequently be questioned, particularly by a third party who has the benefit of hindsight. It is important to be able to tell what facts were known at the time the auditor reached his conclusions and to be able to demonstrate that, based on those facts, the conclusion was reasonable.

21.   Audit working papers will typically contain:

(a)   information which will be of continuing importance to the audit (e.g. memorandum and articles of association);

(b)   audit planning information;

(c)   the auditor's assessment of the enterprise's accounting system and, if appropriate, his review and evaluation of its internal controls;

(d)   details of the audit work carried out, notes of errors or exceptions found and action taken thereon, together with the conclusions drawn by the audit staff who performed the various sections of the work;

(e)   evidence that the work of the audit staff has been properly reviewed;

(f)   records of relevant balances and other financial information, including analyses and summaries supporting the financial statements;

(g)   a summary of significant points affecting the financial statements and the audit report, showing how these points were dealt with.

22.   *Standardisation of working papers.* The use of standardised working papers may

improve the efficiency with which they are prepared and reviewed. Used properly they help to instruct audit staff and facilitate the delegation of work while providing a means to control its quality.

23. However, despite the advantages of standardising the routine documentation of the audit (e.g. checklists, specimen letters, standard organisation of the working papers), it is never appropriate to follow mechanically a "standard" approach to the conduct and documentation of the audit without regard to the need to exercise professional judgment.

24. *Ownership and custody of working papers.* Working papers are the property of the auditor and he should adopt appropriate procedures to ensure their safe custody and confidentiality.

17.4 Guidelines: Accounting Systems

Introduction

1. Paragraph 3 of the Auditing Standard "The Auditor's Operational Standard" states that: "The auditor should ascertain the enterprise's system of recording and processing transactions and assess its adequacy as a basis for the preparation of financial statements." This Auditing Guideline, which gives guidance on how that paragraph may be applied, should be read in conjunction with the Explanatory Foreword to Auditing Standards and Guidelines including the Glossary of Terms.

Background

2. As part of his audit planning, in particular in determining the nature of his audit tests, the auditor will need to consider the overall design of the accounting system and the adequacy of the accounting records from which the financial statements are prepared.

3. The auditor will often have a separate and distinct responsibility to form an opinion as to the adequacy of the accounting records for the purpose of complying with the legislation or regulations to which the enterprise may be subject. The Companies Act 1976 sets out the requirements concerning accounting records for companies incorporated in Great Britain. Auditors of enterprises such as building societies or trade unions which are subject to separate legislation will need to consider their specific duties relating to accounting records.

4. The management of an enterprise requires complete and accurate accounting and other records to assist it in:

   (a) controlling the business;

   (b) safeguarding the assets;

   (c) preparing financial statements;

   (d) complying with legislation.

5.   An accounting system should provide for the orderly assembly of accounting information and appropriate analyses to enable financial statements to be prepared. What constitutes an adequate accounting system will depend on the size, nature and complexity of the enterprise. In its simplest form for a small business dealing primarily with cash sales and with only a few suppliers the accounting system may need to consist of only an analysed cash book and a list of unpaid invoices. In contrast, a company manufacturing several different products and operating through a number of dispersed locations may need a complex accounting system to enable information required for financial statements to be assembled.

6.   Depending upon the size and nature of the business concerned an accounting system will frequently need to incorporate internal controls to provide assurance that:

   (a)   all the transactions and other accounting information which should be recorded have in fact been recorded;

   (b)   errors or irregularities in processing accounting information will become apparent;

   (c)   assets and liabilities recorded in the accounting system exist and are recorded at the correct amounts.

7.   The evaluation of the internal controls referred to in paragraph 6 is dealt with in a separate auditing guideline but in practice the auditor will probably carry out the work concurrently with his assessment of the accounting system.

Procedures

8.   The auditor will need to obtain an understanding of the enterprise as a whole and how the accounting system reflects assets and liabilities and transactions.

9.   The auditor will need to ascertain and record the accounting system in order to assess its adequacy as a basis for the preparation of financial statements. The extent to which the auditor should record the enterprise's accounting system and the method used will depend on the complexity and nature of the system and on the degree of reliance he plans to place on internal controls. Where the auditor plans to rely on internal controls, the accounting system needs to be recorded in considerable detail so as to facilitate the evaluation of the controls and the preparation of a programme of compliance and substantive tests. The record may take the form of narrative notes, flow-charts, or checklists or a combination of them.

10.   As an aid to recording the accounting system, the auditor should consider tracing a small number of transactions (possibly one or two of each type) through the system. This procedure (often known as "walk-through checks") will confirm that there is no reason to suppose that the accounting system does not operate in the manner recorded. The procedure is particularly appropriate where the enterprise has itself prepared the record of the system which the auditor is to use.

11.   In addition to making an assessment of the adequacy of the accounting system the auditor needs to confirm that the system has operated as laid down throughout the period. Evidence of this may be obtained by means of the compliance tests that the auditor carries out when he chooses to rely on internal controls. Alternatively the evidence may be obtained indirectly from his substantive testing.

17.5   Guidelines: Audit Evidence

Introduction
1.   Paragraph 4 of the Auditing Standard "The Auditor's Operational Standard" states that: "The author should obtain relevant and reliable audit evidence sufficient to enable him to draw reasonable conclusions therefrom." This Auditing Guideline, which gives evidence on how that paragraph may be applied, should be read in conjunction with the Explanatory Foreword to Auditing Standards and Guidelines including the Glossary of Terms.

Background
2.   *The nature of audit evidence.* Audit evidence is information obtained by the auditor in arriving at the conclusions on which he bases his opinion on the financial statements. Sources of audit evidence include the accounting systems and underlying documentation of the enterprise, its tangible assets, management and employees, its customers, suppliers and other third parties who have dealings with, or knowledge of, the enterprise or its business.

3.   The sources and amount of evidence needed to achieve the required level of assurance are questions for the auditor to determine by exercising his judgment in the light of the opinion called for under the terms of his engagement. He will be influenced by the materiality of the matter being examined, the relevance and reliability of evidence available from each source and the cost and time involved in obtaining it. Often the auditor will obtain evidence from several sources which, together, will provide him with the necessary assurance.

4.   *Sufficiency.* The auditor can rarely be certain of the validity of the financial statements. However, he needs to obtain sufficient, relevant and reliable evidence to form a reasonable basis for his opinion thereon. The auditor's judgment as to what constitutes sufficient, relevant and reliable audit evidence is influenced by such factors as:

   (a)   his knowledge of the business of the enterprise and the industry in which it operates;

   (b)   the degree of risk of mis-statement through errors or irregularities: this risk may be affected by such factors as:

      (i)   the nature and materiality of the items in the financial statements;

      (ii)   the auditor's experience as to the reliability of the management and staff of the enterprise and of its records;

      (iii)   the financial position of the enterprise;

       (iv) possible management bias;

    (c)   the persuasiveness of the evidence.

5.   *Relevance.* The relevance of the audit evidence should be considered in relation to the overall audit objective of forming an opinion and reporting on the financial statements. To achieve this objective the auditor needs to obtain evidence to enable him to draw reasonable conclusions in answer to the following questions:

BALANCE SHEET ITEMS

    (a)   Have all the assets and liabilities been recorded?

    (b)   Do the recorded assets and liabilities exist?

    (c)   Are the assets owned by the enterprise and are the liabilities properly those of the enterprise?

    (d)   Have the amounts attributed to the assets and liabilities been arrived at in accordance with the stated accounting policies, on an acceptable and consistent basis?

    (e)   Have the assets, liabilities and capital and reserves been properly disclosed?

PROFIT AND LOSS ACCOUNT ITEMS

    (f)   Have all income and expenses been recorded?

    (g)   Did the recorded income and expense transactions in fact occur?

    (h)   Have the income and expenses been measured in accordance with the stated accounting policies, on an acceptable and consistent basis?

    (i)   Have income and expenses been properly disclosed where appropriate?

6.   *Reliability.* Although the reliability of audit evidence is dependent upon the particular circumstances, the following general presumptions may be found helpful:

    (a)   documentary evidence is more reliable than oral evidence;

    (b) evidence obtained from independent sources outside the enterprise is more reliable than that secured solely from within the enterprise;

    (c)   evidence originated by the auditor by such means as analysis and physical inspection is more reliable than evidence obtained from others.

7.   The auditor should consider whether the conclusions drawn from differing types of evidence are consistent with one another. When audit evidence obtained from one source appears inconsistent with that obtained from another, the reliability of each remains in doubt until further work has been done to resolve the inconsistency. However, when the individual items of evidence relating to a particular matter are all consistent, then the auditor may obtain a cumulative degree of assurance higher than that which he obtains from the individual items.

Procedures

8. *Obtaining audit evidence.* Audit evidence is obtained by carrying out audit tests which may be classified as "substantive" or "compliance" according to their primary purpose. Both such purposes are sometimes achieved concurrently. Substantive tests are defined as those tests of transactions and balances, and other procedures such as analytical review, which seek to provide audit evidence as to the completeness, accuracy and validity of the information contained in the accounting records or in the financial statements. Compliance tests are defined as those tests which seek to provide audit evidence that internal control procedures are being applied as prescribed.

9. The auditor may rely on appropriate evidence obtained by substantive testing to form his opinion, provided that sufficient of such evidence is obtained. Alternatively, he may be able to obtain assurance from the presence of a reliable system of internal control, and thereby reduce the extent of substantive testing. The audit procedures which are appropriate when the auditor wishes to place reliance on the enterprise's internal controls are set out in the Auditing Guideline "Internal Controls".

Techniques of audit testing

10. Techniques of audit testing fall into the following broad categories:

(a) *Inspection*—reviewing or examining records, documents or tangible assets. Inspection of records and documents provides evidence of varying degrees of reliability depending upon their nature and source (see paragraph 6(b) above). Inspection of tangible assets provides the auditor with reliable evidence as to their existence, but not necessarily as to their ownership, cost or value.

(b) *Observation*—looking at an operation or procedure being performed by others with a view to determining the manner of its performance. Observation provides reliable evidence as to the manner of the performance at the time of observation, but not at any other time.

(c) *Enquiry*—seeking relevant information from knowledgeable persons inside or outside the enterprise, whether formally or informally, orally or in writing. The degree of reliability that the auditor attaches to evidence obtained in this manner is dependent on his opinion of the competence, experience, independence and integrity of the respondent.

(d) *Computation*—checking the arithmetical accuracy of accounting records or performing independent calculations.

11. *Analytical review procedures.* In addition to the above techniques, there are analytical review procedures, referred to in paragraph 8 above. These procedures include studying significant ratios, trends and other statistics and investigating any unusual or unexpected variations. The precise nature of these procedures and the manner in which they are documented will depend on the circumstances of each audit.

12. The comparisons which can be made will depend on the nature, accessibility and relevance of the data available. Once the auditor has decided on the comparisons which he intends to make in performing his analytical review, he should determine what variations he expects to be disclosed by them.

13. Unusual or unexpected variations, and expected variations which fail to occur, should be investigated. Explanations obtained should be verified and evaluated by the auditor to determine whether they are consistent with his understanding of the business and his general knowledge. Explanations may indicate a change in the business of which the auditor was previously unaware, in which case he should reconsider the adequacy of his audit approach. Alternatively they may indicate the possibility of mis-statements in the financial statements; in these circumstances the auditor will need to extend his testing to determine whether the financial statements do include material mis-statements.

17.6   Internal Controls

Introduction

1. Paragraph 5 of the Auditing Standard "The Auditor's Operational Standard" states that: "If the auditor wishes to place reliance on any internal controls he should ascertain and evaluate those controls and perform compliance tests on their operation." This Auditing Guideline, which gives guidance on how that paragraph may be applied, should be read in conjunction with the Explanatory Foreword to Auditing Standards and Guidelines including the Glossary of Terms.

Background

2. At an early stage in his work the auditor will have to decide the extent to which he wishes to place reliance on the internal controls of the enterprise. As the audit proceeds, that decision will be kept under review and, depending on the results of his examination, he may decide to place more or less reliance on these controls.

MANAGEMENT RESPONSIBILITY FOR INTERNAL CONTROL

3. An internal control system is defined as being "the whole system of controls, financial and otherwise, established by the management in order to carry on the business of the enterprise in an orderly and efficient manner, ensure adherence to management policies, safeguard the assets and secure as far as possible the completeness and accuracy of the records. The individual components of an internal control system are known as 'controls' or 'internal controls'."

4. It is a responsibility of management to decide the extent of the internal control system which is appropriate to the enterprise. The nature and extent of controls will vary between enterprises and also from one part of an enterprise to another. The controls used will depend on the nature, size and volume of the transactions, the degree of control which members of management are able to exercise personally, the geographical distribution of the enterprise and many other factors. The choice of controls may reflect a comparison of the cost of operating individual controls against the benefits expected to be derived from them.

5.   The operating procedures and methods of recording and processing transactions used by small enterprises often differ significantly from those of large enterprises. Many of the internal controls which would be relevant to the larger enterprises are not practical, appropriate or necessary in the small enterprise. Managements of small enterprises have less need to depend on formal internal controls for the reliability of the records and other information, because of their personal contact with, or involvement in, the operation of the enterprise itself.

LIMITATION ON THE EFFECTIVENESS OF INTERNAL CONTROLS

6.   No internal control system, however elaborate, can by itself guarantee efficient administration and the completeness and accuracy of the records; nor can it be proof against fraudulent collusion, especially on the part of those holding positions of authority or trust. Internal controls depending on segregation of duties can be avoided by collusion. Authorisation controls can be abused by the person in whom the authority is vested. Management is frequently in a position to override controls which it has itself set up. Whilst the competence and integrity of the personnel operating the controls may be ensured by selection and training, these qualities may alter due to pressure exerted both within and without the enterprise. Human error due to errors of judgment of interpretation, to misunderstanding, carelessness, fatigue or distraction may undermine the effective operation of internal controls.

THE AUDITOR'S USE OF INTERNAL CONTROLS

7.   The auditor's objective in evaluating and testing internal controls is to determine the degree of reliance which he may place on the information contained in the accounting records. If he obtains reasonable assurance by means of compliance tests that the internal controls are effective in ensuring the completeness and accuracy of the accounting records and the validity of entries therein, he may limit the extent of his substantive testing.

8.   Because of the inherent limitations in even the most effective internal control system, it will not be possible for the auditor to rely solely on its operation as a basis for his opinion on the financial statements.

9.   In some enterprises the auditor may be unable to determine whether all the transactions have been reflected in the accounting records unless there are effective internal controls.

10.   The types of internal controls on which the auditor may seek to rely vary widely. An appendix contains a description of some of the main types of internal controls which the auditor may find and on which he may seek to place some degree of reliance.

Procedures

AUDIT PROCEDURES IN RELATION TO INTERNAL CONTROLS

11.   The auditor will need to ascertain and record the internal control system in order

to make a preliminary evaluation of the effectiveness of its component controls and to decide the extent of his reliance thereon. This recording will normally be carried out concurrently with the recording of the accounting system. As indicated in the Guideline on accounting systems the auditor may find it helpful to trace one or two transactions through the system.

12.   The evaluation of internal controls will be assisted by the use of documentation designed to help identify the internal controls on which the auditor may wish to place reliance. Such documentation can take a variety of forms but might be based on questions asking either:

(a)   whether controls exist which meet specified overall control objectives; or

(b)   whether there are controls which prevent or detect particular specified errors or omissions.

13.   Where this preliminary evaluation indicates that there are controls which meet the objective which the auditor has identified, he should design and carry out compliance tests if he wishes to rely on them. Where, however, the preliminary evaluation discloses weaknesses in, or the absence of, internal controls, such that material error or omission could arise in the accounting records or financial statements, the auditor will move directly to designing and carrying out substantive tests.

14.   *Compliance tests.* The auditor is not entitled to place any reliance on internal controls based solely on his preliminary evaluation. He should carry out compliance tests to obtain reasonable assurance that the controls on which he wishes to rely were functioning both properly and throughout the period. It should be noted that it is the control which is being tested by a compliance test, and not the transaction which may be the medium used for the test. For this reason the auditor should record and investigate all exceptions revealed by his compliance testing, regardless of the amount involved in the particular transaction. (An "exception" in the context is an occurrence where a control has not been operated correctly whether or not a quantitative error has occurred.)

15.   If compliance tests disclose no exceptions the auditor may reasonably place reliance on the effective functioning of the internal controls tested. He can, therefore, limit his substantive tests on the relevant information in the accounting records.

16.   If the compliance tests have disclosed exceptions which indicate that the control being tested was not operating properly in practice, the auditor should determine the reasons for this. He needs to assess whether each exception is only an isolated departure or is representative of others, and whether it indicates the possible existence of errors in the accounting records. If the explanation he receives suggests that the exception is only an isolated departure, then he must confirm the validity of the explanation, for example by carrying out further tests. If the explanation or the further tests confirm that the control being tested was not operating properly

throughout the period, then he cannot rely on that control. In these circumstances the auditor is unable to restrict his substantive testing unless he can identify an alternative control on which to rely. Before relying on that alternative control he must carry out suitable compliance tests on it.

TIMING AND SCOPE OF THE REVIEW AND TESTING OF INTERNAL CONTROLS

17. If reliance is to be placed on the operation of controls, the auditor should ensure that there is evidence of the effectiveness of those controls throughout the whole period under review. Compliance tests carried out at an interim date prior to the year end need, therefore, to be supplemented by tests of controls for the remainder of the year; alternatively, the auditor will need to carry out other procedures to enable him to gain adequate assurance as to the reliability of the accounting records during the period which has not been subject to compliance tests. In determining the alternative procedures which are necessary he should consider:

(a) the results of earlier compliance tests;

(b) whether, according to enquiries made, controls have remained the same for the remaining period;

(c) the length of the remaining period;

(d) the nature and size of the transactions and account items involved; and

(e) the substantive tests which he will carry out irrespective of the adequacy of controls.

18. Where the internal control system has changed during the accounting period under review, the auditor will have to evaluate and test the internal controls on which he wishes to rely, both before and after the change.

RELIANCE ON INTERNAL AUDIT

19. Internal audit is an element of the internal control system set up by management. The extent to which the external auditor is able to take account of the work of the internal auditor will depend on his assessment of the effectiveness of the internal audit function. In making this assessment, the external auditor will be concerned with:

(a) the degree of independence of the internal auditor from those whose responsibilities he is reviewing;

(b) the number of suitably qualified and experienced staff employed in the internal audit function;

(c) the scope, extent, direction and timing of the tests made by the internal auditor;

(d) the evidence available of the work done by the internal auditor and of the review of that work;

(e) the extent to which management takes action based upon the reports of the internal audit function.

20.   Provided that relevant internal audit work has been carried out effectively, the external auditor may be able to reduce the level of his tests.

REPORTING TO MANAGEMENT ON INTERNAL CONTROLS

21.   It is important that the auditor should report, as soon as practicable, significant weaknesses in internal controls which come to his attention during the course of an audit to an appropriately senior level of management of the enterprise. Any such report should indicate that the weaknesses notified are only those which have come to the attention of the auditor during the course of his normal audit work and are not necessarily, therefore, all the weaknesses which may exist.

22.   The fact that the auditor reports weaknesses in internal controls to management does not absolve:

(a)   management from its responsibility for the maintenance of an adequate internal control system; or

(b)   the auditor from the need to consider the effect of such weaknesses on the extent of his audit work and on his audit opinion.

Appendix: types of internal controls

The following is a description of some of the types of controls which the auditor may find in many enterprises and on some or a combination of which he may seek to place some degree of reliance.

1.   *Organisation.* Enterprises should have a plan of their organisation, defining and allocating responsibilities and identifying lines of reporting for all aspects of the enterprise's operations, including the controls. The delegation of authority and responsibility should be clearly specified.

2.   *Segregation of duties.* One of the prime means of control is the separation of those responsibilities or duties which would, if combined, enable one individual to record and process a complete transaction. Segregation of duties reduces the risk of intentional manipulation or error and increases the element of checking. Functions which should be separated include those of authorisation, execution, custody, recording and, in the case of a computer-based accounting system, systems development and daily operations.

3.   *Physical.* These are concerned mainly with the custody of assets and involve procedures and security measures designed to ensure that access to assets is limited to authorised personnel. This includes both direct access and indirect access via documentation. These controls assume importance in the case of valuable, portable, exchangeable or desirable assets.

4.   *Authorisation and approval.* All transactions should require authorisation or approval by an appropriately responsible person. The limits for these authorisations should be specified.

5.   *Arithmetical and accounting.* These are the controls within the recording function

which check that the transactions to be recorded and processed have been authorised, that they are all included and that they are correctly recorded and accurately processed. Such controls include checking the arithmetical accuracy of the records, the maintenance and checking of totals, reconciliations, control accounts and trial balances, and accounting for documents.

6. *Personnel.* There should be procedures to ensure that personnel have capabilities commensurate with their responsibilities. Inevitably, the proper functioning of any system depends on the competence and integrity of those operating it. The qualifications, selection and training as well as the innate personal characteristics of the personnel involved are important features to be considered in setting up any control system.

7. *Supervision.* Any system of internal control should include the supervision by responsible officials of day-to-day transactions and the recording thereof.

8. *Management.* These are the controls exercised by management outside the day-to-day routine of the system. They include the overall supervisory controls exercised by management, the review of management accounts and comparison thereof with budgets, the internal audit function and other special review procedures.

17.7 Guidelines: Review of Financial Statements

Introduction
1. Paragraph 6 of the Auditing Standard "The Auditor's Operational Standard" states that: "The auditor should carry out such a review of the financial statements as is sufficient, in conjunction with the conclusions drawn from the other audit evidence obtained, to give him a reasonable basis for his opinion on the financial statements." This Auditing Guideline, which gives guidance on how that paragraph may be applied, should be read in conjunction with the Explanatory Foreword to Auditing Standards and Guidelines including the Glossary of Terms.

Background
2. The auditor is required to form an opinion on the enterprise's financial statements as a whole. Having accumulated audit evidence about individual items or groups of items, he should therefore carry out an overall review to determine whether in his opinion:

 (a)   the financial statements have been prepared using acceptable accounting policies which have been consistently applied and are appropriate to the enterprise's business;

 (b)   the results of operations, state of affairs and all other information included in the financial statements are compatible with each other and with the auditor's knowledge of the enterprise;

 (c)   there is adequate disclosure of all appropriate matters and the information contained in the financial statements is suitably classified and presented;

(d)   the financial statements comply with all statutory requirements and other regulations relevant to the constitution and activities of that enterprise; and ultimately whether:

(e)   the conclusions drawn from the other tests which he has carried out, together with those drawn from his overall review of the financial statements, enable him to form an opinion on the financial statements.

3.   Throughout the review the auditor needs to take account of the materiality of the matters under review and the confidence which his other audit work has already given him in the accuracy and completeness of the information contained in the financial statements.

4.   Skill and imagination are required to recognise the matters to be examined in carrying out an overall review and sound judgment is needed to interpret the information obtained. Accordingly the review should not be delegated to someone lacking the necessary experience and skill.

5.   An overall review of the financial statements based on the auditor's knowledge of the business of the enterprise is not of itself a sufficient basis for the expression of an audit opinion on those statements. However, it provides valuable support for the conclusions arrived at as a result of his other audit work. In addition, apparent inconsistencies could indicate areas in which material errors, omissions or irregularities may have occurred which have not been disclosed by other auditing procedures.

Procedures

ACCOUNTING POLICIES

6.   The auditor should review the accounting policies adopted by the enterprise to determine whether such policies:

(a)   comply with Statements of Standard Accounting Practice or, in the absence thereof, are otherwise acceptable;

(b)   are consistent with those of the previous period;

(c)   are consistently applied throughout the enterprise;

(d)   are disclosed in accordance with the requirements of Statement of Standard Accounting Practice No. 2 "Disclosure of Accounting Policies".

7.   When considering whether the policies adopted by management are acceptable the auditor should have regard, *inter alia*, to the policies commonly adopted in particular industries and to policies for which there is substantial authoritative support.

GENERAL REVIEW

8.   The auditor should consider whether the results of operations and the state of affairs of the enterprise as reported in the financial statements are consistent with

his knowledge of the underlying circumstances of the business.

9. In addition to any analytical review procedures carried out during the course of the audit, the auditor should carry out an overall review of the information in the financial statements themselves and compare it with other available data. For such a review to be effective the auditor needs to have sufficient knowledge of the activities of the enterprise and of the business which it operates to be able to determine whether particular items are abnormal. This background information should be available in the auditor's working papers as a result of his planning and earlier audit procedures.

PRESENTATION AND DISCLOSURE

10. The auditor should consider the information in the financial statements in order to ensure that the conclusions which a reader might draw from it would be justified and consistent with the circumstances of the enterprise's business. In particular, he should bear in mind the need for the financial statements to reflect the substance of the underlying transactions and balances and not merely their form. He should consider also whether the presentation adopted in the financial statements may have been unduly influenced by management's desire to present facts in a favourable or unfavourable light.

11. The auditor should also consider whether the financial statements adequately reflect the information and explanations obtained and conclusions reached on particular aspects of the audit.

12. The auditor should consider whether his review has disclosed any new factors which affect the presentation or accounting policies adopted. For example it may become apparent, as a result of his review of the financial statements as a whole, that the enterprise has liquidity problems and the auditor should consider whether or not the financial statements should have been prepared on a going concern basis.

COMPLIANCE WITH REGULATIONS

13. In reviewing the financial statements to ensure compliance with the requirements of statutes, Statements of Standard Accounting Practice and other applicable regulations, the auditor may find it helpful to use a checklist or other aide-memoire.

18.0 QUALITY CONTROL

In 1984 the APC issued a guideline entitled "Quality Control" which expands on the original 1980 Guideline "Planning, Controlling and Recording". The text is as follows in section 18.1.

18.1   Auditing Guideline: Quality Control

Preface

Para 2 of the Auditing Standard "The Auditor's Operational Standard" states that the auditor "should adequately plan, control and record his work." The Auditing Guideline "Planning, Controlling and Recording" gives guidance on how that paragraph may be applied and describes the quality control measures necessary in respect of individual audits. However, para 17 of that guideline states that the auditor "should also consider how the overall quality of the work carried out within the firm can best be monitored and maintained".

This guideline is therefore intended to provide guidance on those quality control procedures that relate to audit practices in general and is drafted so as to apply to firms or organisations of all sizes. Without prejudice to the powers of the public sector audit organisations, the principles contained in this guideline apply to all organisations carrying out independent audits whether in the private or the public sector. The word "firm" has been used throughout simply for ease of reference.

Introduction

1.   The principles of quality control are applicable not only to auditing but to the entire range of professional services provided by a firm. For the purposes of this guideline, however, quality control is the means by which a firm obtains reasonable assurance that its expression of audit opinions always reflects observance of approved Auditing Standards, any statutory or contractual requirements and any professional standards set by the firm itself. Quality control should also promote observance of the personal standards relevant to the work of an auditor, which are described in the ethical statements published by the Accountancy Bodies.

Procedures

2.   The objectives of quality control procedures are the same for all firms. At the beginning of subsequent paragraphs, therefore, a specific objective of quality control, which is considered to be universally applicable, is highlighted. This is followed by a brief description of the procedures that firms may adopt to meet this objective. For each firm the exact nature and extent of the procedures needed will depend on its size and the nature of its practice, the number of its offices and its organisation.

3.   *Each firm should establish procedures appropriate to its circumstances and communicate them to all partners and relevant staff, and to other professionals employed by the firm in the course of its audit practice.* This should normally involve putting them in writing, although it is recognised that oral communication may be effective in the small closely controlled firm.

The following paragraphs describe the objectives and the basic procedures applicable to each firm.

ACCEPTANCE OF APPOINTMENT AND REAPPOINTMENT AS AUDITOR
4.   *Each firm should ensure that, in making a decision to accept appointment or*

reappointment as auditor, consideration is given to the firm's own independence and its ability to provide an adequate service to the client. The firm should determine what information is needed to evaluate prospective clients, and whether the decision to accept appointment or reappointment should be taken by the firm as a whole or by a designated partner or committee.

PROFESSIONAL ETHICS

5.   *There should be procedures within the firm to ensure that all partners and professional staff adhere to the principles of independence, objectivity, integrity and confidentiality, set out in the ethical statements issued by the Accountancy Bodies.* These procedures include providing guidance, particularly to those staff who are not members of the Accountancy Bodies, resolving questions on the above principles, and monitoring compliance with them. For larger firms in particular, it may be appropriate that the task of guiding staff in these areas should be allotted to a particular partner. If, for example, the firm does not permit staff to hold shares in client companies, the designated partner should ensure that staff are aware of such a policy.

SKILLS AND COMPETENCE

6.   *The firm's partners and staff should have attained the skills and competence required to fulfil their responsibilities.* This involves procedures relating to:

(a)   recruitment (para 7);

(b)   technical training and updating (para 8);

(c)   on-the-job training and professional development (para 9).

Staff should be informed of the firm's procedures, for example by means of manuals and standardised documentation or programmes. The firm's procedures should be regularly updated.

7.   Effective recruitment of personnel with suitable qualifications, including any necessary expertise in specialised areas and industries, involves both planning for staffing needs and determining criteria for recruitment based on such needs. Such criteria should be designed to ensure that cost considerations do not deter the firm from recruitment of audit staff with the experience and ability to exercise the appropriate judgment.

8.   All partners and staff should be required to keep themselves technically up to date on matters that are relevant to their work. The firm should assist them to meet this requirement. Such assistance should include:

(a)   circulating digests or full texts, where appropriate, of professional publications and relevant legislation;

(b)   maintaining a technical library;

(c)   issuing technical circulars and memoranda on professional developments as they affect the firm;

(d)   encouraging attendance at professional courses;

(e)   maintaining appropriate training arrangements.

The methods of implementing the above procedures may vary according to the size of the firm. For example, a smaller firm can ensure that it has copies of essential reference books relevant to its practice where a fuller technical library would be impracticable. Also manuals and standardised documentation do not need to be produced internally by the smaller firm but can be acquired from various professional bodies and commercial sources; and co-operative arrangements with other firms can help meet training needs.

9.   The Auditing Guideline "Planning, Controlling and Recording" relates staff assignment to the needs of the particular audit visit but, in the context of quality control generally, a further factor in staff assignment should be the opportunity for on-the-job training and professional development. This should provide staff with exposure to different types of audit and with the opportunity to work with more experienced members of the team who should be made responsible for the supervision and review of the work of junior staff. It is important that the performance of staff on audits is evaluated and that the results of these assessments are communicated to the staff concerned, giving the opportunity for staff to respond to comments made and for any action to be agreed.

CONSULTATION

10.   *There should be procedures for consultation.* These will include a structured approach to audit file review (so that the review procedures recommended in the Auditing Guideline "Planning, Controlling and Recording" are effective for every audit); reference of technical problems to designated specialists within the firm; and procedures for resolving matters of judgment. For smaller firms, and particularly for sole practitioners, consultation at the appropriate professional level within the firm may not be possible. Consultation with another practitioner or with any relevant professional advisory service may be a suitable alternative, providing confidentiality of the client's affairs is maintained. To provide opportunities for such consultations, practitioners in smaller firms will find it helpful to develop links with other practitioners or with relevant professional associations.

Monitoring the firm's procedures

11.   *The firm should monitor the effectiveness of its application of the quality control procedures outlined above.* This monitoring process should provide reasonable assurance that measures to maintain the professional standards of the firm are being properly and effectively carried out.

12.   This process should include periodic review of a sample of the firm's audit files by independent reviewers from within the firm. The firm should:

(a)   have procedures for selection of particular audits for review, and for the frequency, timing, nature and extent of reviews;

(b)   set the levels of competence for the partners and staff who are to participate in review activities;

(c)   establish procedures to resolve disagreements which may arise between the reviewers and audit staff.

It should be borne in mind that the purpose of this independent review is to provide an assessment of the overall standards of the firm, and so it is quite separate from the purpose of the earlier review procedures referred to in para 10, which are carried out by members of the audit team to provide control over the individual audit.

13.   Where, in the smaller firm, independent review within the firm is not possible, attendance at professional courses and communication with other practitioners can provide the opportunity of comparison with the standards of others, thereby identifying potential problem areas. Alternatively, an independent and objective basis for monitoring the effectiveness of quality control procedures can be achieved by reference to professional practice advisory services, where available.

14.   Whatever action is taken by the firm to monitor the effectiveness of quality control procedures, the firm should ensure that any recommendations for improvement that arise are implemented.

PROGRESS TEST 1

1.   Does the statutory auditor have a contractual relationship with the company? (4.0)

2.   To what extent might the letter of engagement act as a disclaimer in respect of responsibility for fraud? (8.0)

3.   What are the advantages of an audit? (12.0)

4.   Set out the main ingredients of the Operational Standard. (17.0)

CHAPTER TWO
Internal Control

1.0 INTRODUCTION

From what has been said in Chapter 1 it should be clear that the respective qualities and defects inherent in any system will be instrumental in determining the volume of audit work necessary. Every system will incorporate controls and these, collectively, are referred to as the "internal control"/"internal control system"/"system of internal control", or other variants.

The guideline to Standard No. 1 defines internal control quite explicitly, as follows:

"the whole system of controls, financial and otherwise, established by the management in order to carry on the business of the enterprise in an orderly and efficient manner, ensure adherence to management polices, safeguard the assets and secure as far as possible the completeness and accuracy of the records. The individual components of an internal control system are known as 'controls' or 'internal controls'."

The striking thing about the definition is its all-embracing nature, and it is clear that internal control is concerned with the controls operative in every area of corporate activity, as well as with the way in which individual controls interrelate.

"Internal check" and "internal audit" are both important aspects of internal control.

2.0 INTERNAL CHECK

"Internal check" concerns those detailed administrative aspects of an organisation which are designed purely for the purposes of prevention or early detection of errors and fraud. As such, internal check will include the allocation of book-keeping and other clerical duties in such a way as to ensure:

(a) that no single task is carried out from its beginning to its conclusion by only one person; and

(b)   that the work of each clerk engaged upon a task is subject to independent check in the course of another's duties.

Examples of internal check abound, but the following two adequately illustrate its purpose and the operation of (a) and (b) above, respectively:

(a)   The wages office of an industrial company employing a large number of staff (who are paid in cash) may employ a system which ensures the clerical separation of the following functions:

    (i)   collection and sorting of time cards;

    (ii)   calculation of standard and overtime hours worked;

    (iii)   calculation of gross pay by reference to independently held personnel records;

    (iv)   entering gross pay, deductions and calculation of net pay on payroll;

    (v)   cast and cross-cast of payroll;

    (vi)   independent double check of (v) above;

    (vii)   obtaining wages cheque upon production of completed payroll;

    (viii)   going to the bank for the money, accompanied by an assistant;

    (ix)   insertion of cash in envelopes against duplicate payslips;

    (x)   payment of wages, accompanied by an assistant, and obtaining receipt from each employee paid;

    (xi)   returning receipt signatures and unclaimed wages to chief of wages office for special action (e.g. re-banking, locking in safe, posting to absent employee, etc.).

Note: The above list indicates the main clerical tasks in an industrial wages department. Although eleven stages are listed, this does not necessarily require the employment of eleven clerks, since one clerk may perform a number of functions, provided they are not too closely related. Organisational skill is obviously required in this direction. Certain overall wages controls will also normally operate, such as the independent retention by the chief accountant of an "establishment roll" with which each payroll may be compared, taking into account the list of the new staff and leavers, also independently compiled (in the personnel—not wages— department).

(b)   A large retail store may employ a system which is designed to ensure that:

    (i)   no member of its sales staff handles cash; and

    (ii)   the cashiers have no contact with customers other than to take cash or issue receipts.

Sales staff issue the customer with a detailed docket describing the goods, and extending the price. The salesman wraps the goods while the customer pays the amount shown on the docket to the cashier, who in turn provides a receipt; on seeing the receipt the salesman then releases the goods to the customer.

Note: There is an independent check on the cashier if the salesman retains copies of the dockets (which he would normally have to do for commission purposes anyway). The daily list of dockets represents the cash which should be in the till. The till, of course, should be kept locked, only the manager of the shop having a key.

3.0   INTERNAL AUDIT

The objectives of internal and external auditing are similar, except that the internal auditors are employees of the company and are responsible to its management. They consequently lack the independence with which the external auditor's position is endowed.

With the growth in size and complexity of many companies in recent years, the importance of the internal audit has correspondingly increased so that it is today a major factor in assessing a company's internal control, and its development has made a considerable contribution to contemporary auditing practice. The *Institute of Internal Auditors* is an independent professional body which is well established on both sides of the Atlantic, and the importance of the role which its members now play within commerce and industry is gaining increased recognition.

Obviously only larger organisations have both the need and the means to support a full-scale internal audit department, but where such departments do operate the statutory auditor will pay particular attention to the activities of its members, since these activities will have a direct bearing on the scope and depth of his own work.

3.1   Relationship between internal and external auditors

On accounting matters the internal auditor and the independent auditor operate largely in the same field and they have a common interest in ascertaining that there is:

(a)   an effective system of internal check to prevent or detect errors and fraud and that it is operating satisfactorily;

(b)   an adequate accounting system to provide the information necessary for preparing true and fair financial statements.

Although the two forms of audit have a common interest in the important matters mentioned in the preceding paragraph, there are some fundamental differences:

(a)   *Scope.* The extent of the work undertaken by the internal auditor is determined by the management, whereas that of the independent auditor arises from the responsibilities placed on him by statute.

(b)   *Approach.* The internal auditor's approach is with a view to ensuring that the accounting system is efficient, so that the accounting information presented to management throughout the period is accurate and discloses material facts. The independent auditor's approach, however, is governed by his duty to satisfy himself that the accounts to be presented to shareholders show a true and fair view of the profit or loss for the financial period and of the state of the company's affairs at the end of that period.

(c) *Responsibility.* The internal auditor's responsibility is to the management, whereas the independent auditor is responsible directly to the shareholders. It follows that the internal auditor, being a servant of the company, does not have the independence of status which the independent auditor possesses.

Notwithstanding these important differences, the work of both the internal auditor and the independent auditor, on accounting matters, is carried out largely by similar means, such as:

(a) examination of the system of internal check, for both soundness in principle and effectiveness in operation;

(b) examination and checking of accounting records and statements;

(c) verification of assets and liabilities;

(d) observation, inquiry, the making of statistical comparisons and other such measures as may be judged necessary.

3.2   Co-operation between independent and internal auditor

It will be evident from the preceding paragraphs that the similarity between the means by which the independent auditor and the internal auditor carry out their respective duties is such that without co-operation between them there could be unnecessary duplication of work.

Because of his experience acquired in public practice, the independent auditor may be of assistance in an advisory capacity in connection with the installation and subsequent operation of an internal audit, and in carrying out his duties he may derive much assistance from the internal auditor's intimate knowledge of the accounting system and technical knowledge of the business, particularly in connection with stock-in-trade, the physical existence of fixed assets, depreciation charges, the ascertainment of liabilities and the risks of fraud or misappropriation.

There also exists considerable scope for mutual assistance between the two auditors in the planning of their respective audits. Where the independent auditor is satisfied that the internal auditor has adequately covered part of the work which the independent auditor would otherwise do he may be able to reduce the extent of his examination of detail; and consultation between the two auditors may enable the internal auditor to refrain from carrying out work which he would otherwise do but which, having regard to the examination which the independent auditor considers he must make in any event, would result in duplication. Examples of specific ways in which the work of the two auditors may be co-ordinated are:

(a) the independent auditor may be able to rely to a large extent on the internal auditor in determining whether the system of internal check is operating satisfactorily and in assessing the general reliability of the accounting records;

(b) the programme of the internal auditor may include, by agreement, work which has the effect of giving direct assistance to the independent auditor by participating during the accounting period in matters such as cash counts and visits to branches, made either by the internal auditor alone or jointly with the independent auditor;

(c) the internal auditor may arrange his programme at the end of the accounting period so that assistance is given to the independent auditor in connection with matters such as the confirmation of customer's accounts, verification of assets such as stock-in-trade and the preparation of audit working schedules required by the independent auditor for his records.

The internal auditor's responsibility is to the management and he is in no sense a servant of the independent auditor. It follows therefore that the extent to which the internal auditor can so arrange his work as to be of specific assistance to the independent auditor will depend upon decisions of the management on the scope of the internal audit and the number of staff employed thereon. Consultation between the two auditors, and where necessary with the management, should however ensure that so far as is practicable the fullest possible assistance is available to the independent auditor.

3.3   Assessment of the internal audit

The usual scope of internal audit work may be conveniently classified into four main interlocking capacities:

(a) advisory;

(b) executive (or implementive);

(c) reporting;

(d) routine testing.

It is therefore necessary for the external auditor to discover the effectiveness of the internal audit operation in each of these capacities before relying on it to the extent of materially reducing the volume of his own normal procedural tests in important areas.

The following are the most important questions which would need to be answered in relation to each of the above capacities:

(a) *Advisory role:*

(i) To what extent is the internal audit department required to recommend improvements in the system currently in operation?

(ii) If so requested, to which level of management are the recommendations directed?

(iii) Are such recommendations made as a matter of course, or in response to specific instructions?

(iv) What evidence is there that such recommendations made in the past have been acknowledged/read/studied/partially implemented/wholly implemented?

(b) *Executive role:*

(i) What part is the internal audit department expected to play in implementing its own proposals?

(ii) To what extent is it involved in the planning and phasing-in of new systems, e.g. new computer applications?

(iii) Is it required to monitor the functioning and output of systems recently instituted?

(c) *Reporting role:*

   (i) What is the department's brief regarding management reports? In particular are, say, monthly reports on routine matters required, or are reports prepared only when special matters are under investigation?

  (ii) Do internal audit reports contain a considerable amount of detailed information, running to unmanageable lengths, or do they follow normal "exception" reporting practices, i.e. referring only to matters of immediate concern? (The danger is that reports which are produced regularly, mechanically following an established pattern, risk being equally mechanically ignored!)

(d) *Routine testing role:*

   (i) Is the system which the internal auditors are testing clearly laid down in a procedures manual or flow-charting series?

  (ii) Do they normally report all deviations from standard practice which they discover during testing?

 (iii) What objective evidence of their testing routines exists?

  (iv) Do they work strictly to an audit programme; if so, how often is the programme reviewed?

   (v) Do they operate a system of rotation testing to ensure that the whole of the work under their purview is surveyed at reasonable (but irregular) intervals?

  (vi) Does their programme include surprise visits to observe the wages distribution, and any other unscheduled checks of this nature?

The answers to the above questions would normally be ascertained by including an internal audit section in the standard internal control questionnaire. The questions themselves should be put to the member of the board to whom the chief internal auditor is responsible.

Other, more general, questions which are also important would be concerned with the professional qualifications (if any) of the senior members of the internal audit department; their length of service with the company; whether they were required to work initially in other departments to familiarise themselves with the routines operated prior to joining the internal audit department; and a realistic appraisal of the extent of their independence of the staff in other senior and junior management positions whose work they may be required to check.

In this way the statutory auditor discovers whether the internal audit is operating in name only (many internal auditor departments do anything from market research to factory maintenance—anything barring internal auditing that is!), or whether its work makes a useful and independent contribution to effective management control.

3.4   APC Guidelines, October 1983

Preface

This guideline gives guidance on the matters that need to be considered and the procedures that need to be followed by external auditors when placing reliance on internal audit. It should be read in conjunction with "The Auditor's Operational Standard", its related auditing guidelines and the Explanatory Foreword to the Auditing Standards and Guidelines.

In certain circumstances the external auditor may have a responsibility to form an opinion on the internal audit function. Guidance is not given in respect of the forming of such an opinion, but many of the principles and procedures described in this guideline will also apply in these circumstances.

Introduction

1. Internal audit is an element of the internal control system set up by the management of an enterprise to examine, evaluate and report on accounting and other controls on operations. It exists either voluntarily or in certain circumstances because of a statutory requirement.

2. Certain of the objectives of internal audit may be similar to those of external audit, and procedures similar to those carried out during an external audit may be followed. Accordingly, the external auditor should make a general assessment of the internal audit function in order to be able to determine whether or not he wishes to place reliance on the work of internal audit. An external auditor may be able to place reliance on internal audit as a means of reducing the work he performs himself in:

    (a) gathering information on accounting systems and internal controls;

    (b) compliance and substantive testing.

3. The scope of internal audit's work will generally be determined in advance and a programme of work will be prepared. Where reliance is placed on the work of internal audit, the external auditor will need to take into account this programme of work and amend the extent of his own work accordingly. In addition, the external auditor may agree with management that internal audit may render him direct assistance by performing certain of the procedures necessary to accomplish the objectives of the external audit but under the control of the chief internal auditor. A decision to provide direct assistance by substituting the work of internal audit could affect internal audit's own work programme and should involve an assessment of the relative costs of using internal and external audit.

4. This guideline does not deal with those cases where internal audit staff are seconded to work under the direct supervision and control of the external auditor. This is because there are no special considerations which distinguish the use of seconded internal audit staff from that of the external auditor's own staff.

Background

THE INTERNAL AUDIT FUNCTION

5. The scope and objectives of internal audit vary widely and are dependent upon the responsibilities assigned to it by management, the size and structure of the enterprise, and the skills and experience of the internal auditors. Normally, however, internal audit operates in one or more of the following broad areas:

(a) review of accounting systems and related internal controls;

(b) examination of financial and operating information for management, including detailed testing of transactions and balances;

(c) review of the economy, efficiency and effectiveness of operations and of the functioning of non-financial controls;

(d) review of the implementation of corporate policies, plans and procedures;

(e) special investigations.

6. Where internal audit staff carry out routine tasks such as authorisation and approval of day-to-day arithmetical and accounting controls, these tasks do not form part of the internal audit function and are not dealt with in this guideline; this is because they are recognised as other types of internal controls by the appendix to the auditing guideline "Internal Controls".

THE RELATIONSHIP BETWEEN EXTERNAL AND INTERNAL AUDIT

7. Unlike the internal auditor who is an employee of the enterprise, the external auditor is independent, usually having a statutory responsibility to report on the financial statements giving an account of management's stewardship.

8. Although the extent of the work of the external auditor may be reduced by placing reliance on the work of internal audit, the responsibility to report is that of the external auditor alone, and therefore is indivisible and is not reduced by this reliance.

9. As a result, all final judgments relating to matters which are material to the financial statements or other aspects on which he is reporting, must be made by the external auditor.

Procedures

PLANNING

10. Before any decision is taken to place reliance on internal audit, it is necessary for the external auditor to make a general assessment of the likely effectiveness and the relevance of the internal audit function. The criteria for making this general assessment should include the following:

(a) *The degree of independence.* Although an internal auditor is an employee of the enterprise and cannot therefore be independent of it, he should be able to plan and carry out his work as he wishes and have access to the highest level of management. He should also be free of any operating responsibility which may create a conflict of interest when he attempts to discharge his internal audit function, or of a situation where middle management on whom he is reporting is responsible for his or his staff's appointment, promotion or remuneration. Furthermore, an internal auditor should be free to communicate fully with the external auditor, who should be able to receive copies of all internal audit reports that he requires. Any constraints or restrictions placed upon internal audit should be carefully evaluated by the external auditor.

(b) *The scope and objectives of the internal audit function.* The external auditor should examine the internal auditor's formal terms of reference and should ascertain the scope and objectives of internal audit assignments. In most circumstances, the external auditor will regard assignments as likely to be relevant where they are carried out in the areas described in para 5(a) and (b) above. He will also be interested in internal audit's role in respect of the areas described in paras 5(c), (d) and (e) above, when it has an important bearing on the reliability of the financial statements or other matters being reported on.

(c) *Due professional care.* The external auditor should consider whether the work of internal audit generally appears to be properly planned, controlled, recorded and reviewed. Examples of the exercise of due professional care by internal audit are the existence of an adequate audit manual, general internal audit plans, procedures for controlling individual assignments, and satisfactory arrangements for reporting and follow-up.

(d) *Technical competence.* The external auditor should ascertain whether the work of internal audit is performed by persons having adequate training and proficiency as auditors. Indicators of technical competence may be membership of an appropriate professional body or the possession of relevant practical experience.

(e) *Internal audit reports.* The external auditor should consider the quality of reports issued by internal audit and ascertain whether management considers, responds to and where appropriate acts upon internal audit reports, and whether this is evidenced.

11. The external auditor's general assessment of the likely effectiveness and the relevance of the internal audit function will influence his judgment as to whether he wishes to place reliance on internal audit. Consequently the external auditor should document his assessment and conclusions in this respect and should update his assessment year by year. He should also inform management in writing of any significant weaknesses in the internal audit function which came to his attention.

12. Where the external auditor decides that he can place reliance on internal audit, he should consider in determining the extent of that reliance:

(a) the materiality of the areas or the items to be tested or of the information to be obtained;

(b) the level of audit risk inherent in the areas or items to be tested or in the information to be obtained;

(c) the level of judgment required;

(d) the sufficiency of complementary audit evidence;

(e) specialist skills possessed by internal audit staff.

13. The external auditor should be involved in the audit of all material matters in the financial statements particularly in those areas where there is significant risk of mis-statement. High audit risk does not preclude placing some reliance on internal audit, but the external auditor should ensure that the extent of his involvement is sufficient to enable him to form his own conclusions.

14. Having decided to place reliance on the work of internal audit, the external auditor should discuss with the chief internal auditor the timing of internal audit work, test levels, sample selection and the form of documentation to be used.

15. The extent to which the external auditor places reliance on internal audit, and the reasons for deciding that extent, should be fully set out in an audit planning memorandum. Furthermore, the external auditor should also consider sending a letter to management in order to confirm the overall arrangements that have been agreed.

CONTROLLING

16. Where the external auditor places reliance on the work of internal audit, he should review the work of internal audit and satisfy himself that it is being properly controlled. In this connection, the external auditor should:

(a) consider whether the work has been properly supervised and reviewed in detail when it has been completed;

(b) compare the results of the work with those of the external auditor's staff on similar audit areas or items, if any;

(c) satisfy himself that any exceptions or unusual matters that have come to light as a result of the work have been properly resolved;

(d) examine reports relating to the work produced by internal audit and management's response to those reports;

(e) from time to time, determine whether internal audit will be able to complete the programme that it has agreed to undertake and, if it will not, make appropriate alternative arrangements;

(f) at the conclusion of the audit, review the effectiveness of the basis of working and discuss with the chief internal auditor the significant findings and any means of improving the approach.

RECORDING

17. The external auditor will need to ensure that all work relating to his audit, whether

performed by internal audit or the external auditor, is properly recorded. He should satisfy himself that the working papers relating to the work of internal audit upon which he is placing reliance are up to an acceptable standard. Consideration should be given to the method of recording so that relevant working papers are available and are of use to both the external auditor and internal audit.

AUDIT EVIDENCE

18.   Where the external auditor places reliance on internal audit, whether by means of direct assistance or otherwise, he should satisfy himself that sufficient evidence is obtained to afford a reasonable basis for the conclusions reached by internal audit, and that those conclusions are appropriate to the circumstances and are consistent with the results of the work performed. This may involve him in performing supplementary procedures. The extent of these procedures will depend on his general assessment of the internal audit function, the materiality of the area or item to be tested, and the risk of mis-statement in the financial statements (see para 13). The procedures may include re-examining transactions or balances that internal audit have tested, examining similar transactions or balances, or the performance of analytical review procedures.

INTERNAL CONTROLS

19.   Where the work of internal audit reveals weaknesses in internal controls, the external auditor should consider whether it is enough to draw management's attention to a report from internal audit or whether he should also report to management himself, particularly where he considers management response to internal audit reports is inadequate or where the weaknesses are significant. The external auditor should consider whether his own programme should be amended because of those weaknesses.

REVIEW OF FINANCIAL STATEMENTS

20.   The external auditor should perform the procedures described in the Auditing Guideline "Review of Financial Statements".

4.0   THE ESSENTIALS OF INTERNAL CONTROL

In very broad terms, a commercial system may be said to comprise three elements, from the auditor's viewpoint:

   (a)   *initiation* of contractual obligations;

   (b)   *recording* the consequences of the initiation of contractual obligations;

   (c)   *custody and handling* of assets whose movement is recorded under (b) above.

As a general guide internal control may be regarded, in a nutshell, as being the system which ensures, so far as is practicable, *separation* of (a), (b) and (c) above.

   As an exercise, the student is recommended to envisage essentials (a), (b) and (c) in relation to any aspect of an organised system. This will demonstrate the comprehensive nature of internal control.

5.0   THE CLIENT ORGANISATION

Although most of the auditor's direct dealings with the client organisation will take place within, or through, its *accounting section* he should be aware of the nature of the activities of all fields of activity, and how these are evidenced in the records. Most large industrial companies, for example, will incorporate several "departments", and Table 4 is included to impart a sense of scale:

Table 4. Client organisation structure

Main departments	Sub-departments
Accounts	Ledgers
	Invoicing
	Machine accounting
	Cashiers
	Wages
	Budgets
	Taxation
	Divisional accounting
	Product costing/pricing
Personnel	Employee files
	Staff welfare
	Trade union relations
Sales	Customer relations
	Advertising
	Technical
	Market research
	After-sales servicing
	Filing/documentation
	Analysis/statistics
	Internal liaison
Buying	Ordering
	Supplier records
	Production liaison
Production	Inspection/quality control
	Production scheduling
	Plant maintenance
	Production records
	Plant registers
	Work in progress costing
	Warehouse
	Stock recording
	Despatch control
	Goods inwards control
	Requisitions/re-ordering

The above list is by no means exhaustive, and could easily have been extended to include the departments which deal with:

(a) estates development, buying, selling and leasing;

(b) vehicles;

(c) research and development (sometimes part of production);

(d) organisation and methods;

(e) overseas liaison;

(f) internal audit.

6.0 PRACTICAL APPLICATIONS OF INTERNAL CONTROL

Before attempting to form an opinion on the effectiveness of the system of internal control in a particular client organisation, the auditor should be aware, in general terms, of the way in which the principles of internal control find their practical application in the areas which most companies have in common. These areas, apart from the *general* financial arrangements, may be summarised thus:

(a) cash and cheques (received, paid and balances in hand);

(b) wages and salaries;

(c) purchases and trade creditors;

(d) sales and trade debtors;

(e) stocks and work in progress;

(f) fixed assets and investments.

The practical application of internal control principles to the above areas will include the following:

6.1 General financial arrangements

These consist of:

(a) devising an appropriate and properly integrated system of accounts and records;

(b) determining the form of general financial supervision and control by management, using such means as budgetary control, regular interim accounts of suitable frequency, and special reports;

(c) ensuring that adequate precautions are taken to safeguard (and if necessary to duplicate and store separately) important records;

(d) engaging, training and allocating to specific duties management and staff competent to fulfil their responsibilities; arranging for rotation of duties as necessary; and deputing responsibilities during staff absences.

6.2 Cash and cheques received (including cash and bank balances)

Receipts by post and cash sales

Considerations involved in dealing with cash and cheques received by post include:

(a) instituting safeguards to minimise the risk of interception of mail between its receipt and opening;

(b) wherever possible, appointing a responsible person, independent of the cashier, to open, or supervise the opening of, mail;

(c) ensuring that cash and cheques received are

  (i) adequately protected (for instance, by the restrictive crossing of all cheques, money orders and the like on first handling) and

  (ii) properly accounted for (for instance, by the preparation of post-lists of moneys received for independent comparison with subsequent records, book entries and paying-in slips).

In establishing an adequate system of control over cash sales and collection it should be decided:

(a) who is to be authorised to receive cash and cash articles (i.e. whether such items are to be received only by cashiers or may be accepted by sales assistants, travellers, roundsmen, or others);

(b) how sales and the receipt of cash and cash articles are to be evidenced, and what checks may usefully be adopted as regards such transactions (for instance, by the use of serially numbered receipt forms or counterfoils, or cash registers incorporating sealed till rolls).

Custody and control of money received

Considerations involved include:

(a) the appointment of suitable persons to be responsible at different stages for the collection and handling of money received, with clearly defined responsibilities;

(b) how, by whom, and with what frequency cash registers are to be cleared;

(c) what arrangements are to be made for agreeing cash collection with cash and sales records (preferably this should be carried out by a person independent of the receiving cashier or employee);

(d) according to the nature of the business, what arrangements are to be made for dealing with, recording and investigating any cash shortages or surpluses.

Recording

Considerations involved include:

(a) who is to be responsible for maintaining records of money received;

(b) what practicable limitations may be put on the duties and responsibilities of the receiving cashier, particularly as regards dealing with such matters as other books of account, other funds, securities and negotiable instruments, sales invoices, credit notes and cash payments;

(c) who is to perform the receiving cashier's functions during his absence at lunch, on holiday, or through sickness;

(d) in what circumstances, if any, receipts are to be given; whether copies are to be retained; the serial numbering of receipt books and forms; how their issue and use are to be controlled; what arrangements are to be made, and who is to be responsible, for checking receipt counterfoils against (i) cash records and (ii) bank paying-in slips; and how alterations to receipts are to be authorised and evidenced.

Payments into bank

Considerations involved include:

(a) how frequently payments are to be made into the bank (preferably daily);

(b) who is to make up the bank paying-in slips (preferably this should be done by a person independent of the receiving and recording cashier) and whether there is to be any independent check of paying-in slips against post-lists, receipt counterfoils and cash book entries;

(c) who is to make payments into the bank (preferably not the person responsible for preparing paying-in slips);

(d) whether all receipts are to be banked intact; if not, how disbursements are to be controlled.

Cash and bank balances

Questions to be decided in connection with the control of cash balances include:

(a) what amounts are to be retained as cash floats at cash desks and registers, and whether payments out of cash received are to be permitted;

(b) what restrictions are to be imposed as to access to cash registers;

(c) rules regarding the size of cash floats to meet expenses, and their methods of reimbursement;

(d) the frequency with which cash floats are to be checked by independent officials;

(e) what arrangements are to be made for safeguarding cash left on the premises outside business hours;

(f) whether any special insurance arrangements (such as fidelity guarantee and cash insurance) are judged desirable having regard to the nature of the business, the sums handled, and the length of time they are kept on the premises;

(g) what additional independent checks on cash may usefully be operated (for instance, by periodic surprise cash counts);

(h) what arrangements are to be made for the control of funds held in trust for employees, both those which are the legal responsibility of the company and, as necessary, those which are held by nominated employees independent of the company's authority (for instance, sick funds or holiday clubs).

6.3 Cheque and cash payments

The arrangements for controlling payments will depend to a great extent on the nature of business transacted, the volume of payments involved, and the size of the company.

Cheque payments

Amongst the points to be decided in settling the system for payments by cheque are the following:

(a) what procedure is to be adopted for controlling the supply and issue of cheques for use, and who is to be responsible for their safe-keeping;

(b) who is to be responsible for preparing cheques;

(c) what documents are to be used as authorisation for preparing cheques, rules as to their presentation to cheque signatories as evidence in support of payment, and the steps to be taken to ensure that payment cannot be made twice on the strength of the same document;

(d) the names, number and status of persons authorised to sign cheques; limitations as to their authority; the minimum number of signatories required for each cheque; if only one signatory is required, whether additional independent authorisation of payments is desirable; if more than one signatory is required, how it is to be ensured that those concerned will operate effective independent scrutiny (for instance, by prohibiting the signing by any signatory of blank cheques in advance); limitations, if any, as to the amount permissible to be drawn on one signature; whether cheques drawn in favour of persons signing are to be prohibited;

(e) safeguards to be adopted if cheques are signed mechanically or carry printed signatures;

(f) the extent to which cheques issued should be restrictively crossed; and the circumstances, if any, in which blank or bearer cheques may be issued;

(g) arrangements for the prompt despatch of signed cheques and precautions against interception;

(h) arrangements for obtaining paid cheques; whether they are to be regarded as sufficient evidence of payment or whether receipts are to be required; and the procedure to be followed in dealing with paid cheques returned as regards examination and preservation;

(i) the arrangements to be made to ensure that payments are made within discount periods.

Cash payments

Factors to be considered include the following:

(a) nomination of a responsible person to authorise expenditure, the means of indicating such authorisation and the documentation to be presented and preserved as evidence;

(b) arrangements to ensure that the vouchers supporting payments cannot be presented for payment twice;

(c) whether any limit is to be imposed as regards amounts disbursed in respect of individual payments;

(d) rules as to cash advances to employees and officials, IOUs, and the cashing of cheques.

6.4 Wages and salaries

Considerations involved include:

(a) who may authorise the engagement and discharge of employees;

(b) who may authorise general and individual changes in rates of pay;

(c) how notifications of changes in personnel and rates of pay are to be recorded and controlled to prevent irregularities and errors in the preparation and payment of wages and salaries;

(d) how deductions from employees' pay other than for income tax and national insurance are to be authorised;

(e) what arrangements are to be made for recording hours worked (in the case of hourly-paid workers) or work done (in the case of piece workers) and for ensuring that the records are subject to scrutiny and approval by an appropriate official before being passed to the wages department; special supervision and control arrangements may be desirable where overtime working is material;

(f) whether advances of pay are to be permitted; if so, who may authorise them, what limitations are to be imposed, how they are to be recovered;

(g) how holiday pay is to be dealt with;

(h) who is to deal with pay queries.

Preparation of payroll

The procedure for preparing the payroll should be clearly established. Principal matters for consideration include the following:

(a) what records are to be used as bases for the compilation of the payroll and how they are to be authorised;

(b) who is to be responsible (i) for preparing pay sheets, (ii) for checking them and (iii) for approving them (preferably separate persons), and by what means individual responsibility at each stage is to be indicated;

(c) what procedures are to be laid down for notifying and dealing with non-routine circumstances such as an employee's leaving at short notice in the middle of a pay period.

Payment of wages and salaries

Where employees are paid in cash the following matters are amongst those that require decision:

(a) what arrangements are to be made to provide the requisite cash for paying out (e.g. by encashment of a cheque for the total amount of net wages) and what steps are to be taken to safeguard such moneys during collection and transit and until distributed;

(b) what safeguards against irregularities are to be adopted (e.g. by arranging for pay packets to be filled by persons other than those responsible for preparing pay sheets, providing them with the exact amount of cash required, and forbidding their access to other cash), and what particulars are to be given to payees;

(c) who is to pay cash wages over to employees (preferably a person independent of those engaged in the preparation of pay sheets and pay packets); how payees' identities are to be verified; what officials are to be in attendance; and how distribution is to be recorded (e.g. by recipient's signature or by checking off names on the list);

(d) what arrangements are to be made for dealing with unclaimed wages.

Where wages and salaries are paid by cheque or bank transfer the matters to be decided include:

(a) which persons are (i) to prepare and (ii) to sign cheques and bank transfer lists (preferably those persons should be independent of each other and of those responsible for preparing pay sheets);

(b) whether a separate wages and salaries bank account is to be maintained, what amounts are to be transferred to it from time to time (preferably on due dates the net amount required to meet pay cheques and transfers), and who is to be responsible for its regular reconciliation (preferably someone independent of those responsible for maintaining pay records).

Additional checks on pay arrangements

In addition to the routine arrangements and day-to-day checks referred to above, use may be made, as judged desirable, of a number of independent overall checks on wages and salaries. Amongst those available may be listed the following:

(a) the maintenance, separate from wages and salaries departments, of employees' records, with which pay lists may be compared as necessary;

(b) the preparation of reconciliations to explain changes in total pay and deductions between one pay day and the next;

(c) surprise counts of cash held by wages and salaries departments;

(d) the comparison of actual pay totals with independently prepared figures such as budget estimates of standard costs and the investigation of variances;

(e) the agreement of gross earnings and total tax deducted for the year with PAYE returns to the Inland Revenue.

6.5 Purchases and trade creditors

The three separate functions into which accounting controls may be divided clearly appear in the considerations involved in purchase procedures. They are buying ("authorisation"), receipt of goods ("custody") and accounting ("recording").

Buying
Factors to be considered include:

(a) the procedure to be followed when issuing requisitions for additions to and replacements of stocks, and the persons to be responsible for such requisitions;

(b) the preparation and authorisation of purchase orders (including procedures for authorising acceptance where tenders have been submitted or prices quoted);

(c) the institution of checks for the safe-keeping of order forms and safeguarding their use;

(d) as regards capital items, any special arrangements as to authorisations required (for a fuller description of this aspect see the section dealing with fixed assets below).

Goods inwards
Factors to be considered include:

(a) arrangements for examining goods inwards as to quantity, quality and condition, and for evidencing such examination;

(b) the appointment of a person responsible for accepting goods, and the procedure for recording and evidencing their arrival and acceptance;

(c) the procedure to be instituted for checking goods inwards records against authorised purchased orders.

Accounting
Factors to be considered include:

(a) the appointment of persons so far as possible separately responsible for:

  (i) checking suppliers' invoices;
  (ii) recording purchases and purchase returns;
  (iii) maintaining suppliers' ledger accounts or similar records;
  (iv) checking suppliers' statements;
  (v) authorising payment;

(b) arrangements to ensure that before accounts are paid:

(i) the goods concerned have been received, accord with the purchase order, are properly priced and correctly invoiced;

(ii) the expenditure has been properly allocated; and

(iii) payment has been duly authorised by the official responsible;

(c) the establishment of appropriate procedures in connection with purchase returns, special credits and other adjustments;

(d) arrangements to ensure that liabilities relating to goods received during an accounting period are properly brought into the accounts of the period concerned (i.e. cut-off procedures);

(e) the establishment of arrangements to deal with purchases from companies or branches forming part of the same group;

(f) arrangements to deal with purchases made for employees under special terms;

(g) regular independent checking of suppliers' accounts against current statements, or direct verification with suppliers;

(h) the institution of a purchases control account and its regular checking by an independent official against suppliers' balances.

6.6 Sales and trade debtors

The separation of authorisation, custodian and recording functions described above in respect of purchases and trade creditors applies similarly to sales and trade debtors.

Sales
Considerations include the following:

(a) what arrangements are to be made to ensure that goods are sold at their correct prices, and to deal with and check exchanges, discounts and special reductions including those in connection with cash sales;

(b) who is to be responsible for, and how control is to be maintained over, the granting of credit terms to customers;

(c) who is to be responsible for accepting customers' orders, and what procedure is to be adopted for issuing production orders and despatch notes;

(d) who is to be responsible for the preparation of invoices and credit notes and what controls are to be instituted to prevent errors and irregularities (for instance, how selling prices are to be ascertained and authorised, how the issue of credit notes is to be controlled and checked, what checks there should be on the prices, quantities, extensions and totals shown on invoices and credit notes, and how such documents in blank or completed are to be protected against loss or misuse);

(e) what special controls are to be exercised over the despatch of goods free of charge or on special terms.

Goods outwards

Factors to be considered include:

(a) who may authorise the despatch of goods and how such authority is to be evidenced;

(b) what arrangements are to be made to examine and record goods outwards (preferably this should be done by a person who has no access to stocks and has no accounting or invoicing duties);

(c) the procedure to be instituted for agreeing goods outwards records with customers' orders, despatch notes and invoices.

Accounting

So far as possible sales ledger staff should have no access to cash, cash books or stocks, and should not be responsible for invoicing and other duties normally assigned to sales staff. The following are amongst matters which should be considered:

(a) the appointment of persons as far as possible separately responsible for:

    (i) recording sales and sales returns;

    (ii) maintaining customers' accounts;

    (iii) preparing debtors' statements;

(b) the establishment of appropriate control procedures in connection with sales returns, price adjustments and similar matters;

(c) arrangements to ensure that goods despatched but not invoiced (or vice versa) during an accounting period are properly dealt with in the accounts of the period concerned (i.e. cut-off procedures);

(d) the establishment of arrangements to deal with sales to companies or branches forming part of the same group;

(e) what procedures are to be adopted for the preparation, checking and despatch of debtors' statements and for ensuring that they are not subject to interference before despatch;

(f) how discounts granted and special terms are to be authorised and evidenced;

(g) who is to deal with customers' queries arising in connection with statements;

(h) what procedure is to be adopted for reviewing and following up overdue accounts;

(i) who is to authorise the writing off of bad debts, and how such authority is to be evidenced;

(j) the institution of a sales control account and its regular checking, preferably by an independent official against customers' balances on the sales ledger.

6.7 Stocks (including work in progress)

Amongst the main considerations may be listed the following:

(a) what arrangements are to be made for receiving, checking and recording goods inwards;

(b) who is to be responsible for the safeguarding of stocks and what precautions are to be taken against theft, misuse and deterioration;

(c) what arrangements are to be made for controlling stocks (through maximum and minimum stock limits) and recording stocks (e.g. by stock ledgers, independent control accounts and continuous stock records such as bin cards);

(d) how movements of stock out of store (or from one process or department to another) are to be authorised, evidenced and recorded, and what steps are to be taken to guard against irregularities;

(e) what arrangements are to be made for dealing with and accounting for returnable containers (both suppliers' and own);

(f) what arrangements are to be made for dealing with and maintaining accounting control over company stocks held by others;

(g) what persons are to be responsible for physically checking stocks, at what intervals such checks are to be carried out, and what procedures are to be followed;

(h) what bases are to be adopted for computing the amount at which stocks are to be stated in the accounts;

(i) what arrangements are to be made for the periodic review of the conditions of stocks, how damaged, slow-moving and obsolete stocks are to be dealt with, and how write-offs are to be authorised;

(j) what steps are to be taken to control and account for scrap and waste, and receipts from the disposal of such items.

6.8   Fixed assets and investments

Fixed assets

Some of the principal matters to be decided in connection with controls relating to fixed assets are as follows:

(a) who is to authorise capital expenditure and how such authorisation is to be evidenced;

(b) who is to authorise the sale, scrapping or transfer of fixed assets, how such authorisation is to be evidenced, and what arrangements are to be made for controlling and dealing with receipts from disposals;

(c) who is to maintain accounting records in respect of fixed assets and how it is to be ensured that the proper accounting distinction is observed between capital and revenue expenditure;

(d) what arrangements are to be made for keeping plant and property registers and how frequently they are to be agreed with the relevant accounts and physically verified;

(e)   what arrangements are to be made to ensure that fixed assets are properly maintained and applied in the service of the company (e.g. by periodic physical checks as to their location, operation and condition);

(f)   where fixed assets are transferred between branches or members of the same group, what arrangements in respect of pricing, depreciation and accounting are to be made;

(g)   how depreciation rates are to be authorised and evidenced, and which persons are to be responsible for carrying out and checking the necessary calculations.

Investments

Arrangements for dealing with investments will involve, *inter alia*, determining:

(a)   who is to be responsible for authorising purchases and sales of investments, and how such authorisations are to be evidenced (those responsible should preferably have no concern with cash or the custody of documents of title);

(b)   what arrangements should be made for maintaining a detailed investment register; and who should be responsible for agreeing it periodically with the investment control account and physically verifying the documents of title;

(c)   what arrangements are to be made for checking contract notes against authorised purchase of sale instructions and for ensuring that charges are correctly calculated; for dealing with share transfers; and for ensuring that share certificates are duly received or delivered and that bonuses, rights, capital repayments and dividends or interest are received and properly accounted for.

PROGRESS TEST 2

1.   How should the external auditor assess the quality of internal audit? (3.3)

2.   What matters require consideration in the practical application of internal control principles to payment of wages? (6.4)

3.   Set out that section of an ICQ which relates to sales and trade debtors. (6.6)

CHAPTER THREE

Assessment of Internal Control and Small Company Audit Problems

1.0 INTRODUCTION

Previous chapters have established that the volume of detailed checking carried out by the auditor in any area will bear a direct correspondence with the respective strengths and weaknesses inherent in the system operated in that area. Clearly, such strengths and weaknesses that exist may not be readily apparent from a superficial examination and the first task of the auditor, especially in relation to a new client, is thus to investigate the functioning of the system of internal control with such an assessment in mind.

Although this task is considerably more straightforward if the client is in a compact unit, with a simple organisation employing a small number of staff whose designated functions are abundantly clear, it should never be imagined that in such "easy" situations there is no need to be concerned with the system, or that one can "go straight into the audit". The audit has four essential features:

(a) to make a critical review of the system of book-keeping, accounting and internal control;

(b) to make such tests and enquiries as the auditors consider necessary to form an opinion as to the reliability of the records as a basis for the preparation of accounts;

(c) to compare the profit and loss account and balance sheet with the underlying records in order to see whether they are in accordance therewith;

(d) to make a critical review of the profit and loss account and the balance sheet in order that a report may be made to the members stating whether, in the opinion of the auditors, the accounts are presented, and the items are described, in such a way that they show not only true but also a fair view and give, in the prescribed manner, the information required by the Companies Acts.

These features are inescapable if an intelligent standard of auditing, free of the risk of liability, is to be achieved.

The means of assessing qualities and defects in a system may vary according to circumstances, but certain generally applicable techniques have been developed over the past two decades, most of which are now well established. Ensuing sections of this chapter describe those techniques most commonly used in practice today.

2.0 INTERNAL CONTROL QUESTIONNAIRES

This is the longest established of all assessment techniques. It is, of course, used only in those situations where such use is cost-effective. In small companies, where internal control is rudimentary, it is often more practical for the auditor to conduct procedures which assume no reliance on internal control (see section 7.0 of this chapter). The questionnaire is a standard document, designed by the firm using it, and comprises a series of questions, each of which raises an enquiry on internal control. It is divided into sections which roughly correspond with the client organisation's divisions. Any sections which are inapplicable (e.g. the cash receipts section in the case of a mail order company) are obviously ignored.

The following points should be noted:

(a) A blank ICQ would normally be completed in the case of a new client only if its size and complexity justified this; internal control in smaller organisations can usually be assessed by:

    (i) raising relevant questions and carefully noting the replies; and

    (ii) observations of procedures.

(b) A completed ICQ should have an effective "life" of three to five years during which time only updating would be necessary. It is sound policy, however, to appraise the system "from scratch" once the original ICQ is clearly out of date. The completion of a new ICQ would be necessary in any event if a radical change in the system (e.g. the transfer from manual to mechanised data processing) had taken place.

(c) The ICQ should be completed by a senior member of the audit staff after putting the questions to the appropriate client company officers during a series of interviews specially arranged for the purpose. It is obviously important also to note instances where the officer concerned is clearly unaware of the workings of that part of the system for which he is nominally responsible.

(d) The answer to ICQ questions must be corroborated by members of the audit staff, on a test observation basis. This will ensure that the view presented by the ICQ accurately reflects the procedures that operate from day to day. These tests, designed to ensure that the system is accurately portrayed in the audit files, are known by various titles, but are usually called "walk-through" tests. It is most important to remember that they do *not* constitute part of the *audit programme*, which can be performed only *after* the internal control system has been satisfactorily assessed and appraised.

(e) The questions in a well-drafted ICQ will facilitate a rapid assessment of the system. This is normally achieved by formulating questions in which:

    (i) the relevant internal control criteria are implicit, so that no more than a "yes/no" answer is required to indicate compliance or lack, as the case may be; and

    (ii) compliance with the particular control is always indicated by the answer "yes", and weakness correspondingly indicated by the answer "no". This degree of simplicity is not possible in the case of every question, of course; for example, where the names of executive officers authorised to sign cheques are sought, or where the upper monetary limit of authority to authorise expenditure is to be recorded.

2.1   The form of the ICQ

This may differ substantially between one auditing firm and another, although the purpose in each case is the same. For the purpose of illustration a model ICQ, published by the Institute of Chartered Accountants in England and Wales for the guidance of members whose firms have not already adopted a particular form, has been selected. It has, however, been slightly modified for instructional purposes, and only four key areas of the ICQ are included:

(a)   purchases and trade creditors;

(b)   sales and trade debtors;

(c)   stocks and work in progress;

(d)   industrial wages.

Although several other major areas are not presented here (e.g. acquisition and disposal of fixed assets) the four sections shown adequately demonstrate the optimum functioning of the ICQ in practice. Each of the sections includes between 13 and 16 questions of particular significance, specially selected from a much longer series in the ICAEW model referred to above.

Illustration: specimen internal control questionnaire

Notes:

(a)   Answers should be based on replies given by senior client personnel and on your own tests and observations.

(b)   Wherever the "no" column is ticked an explanatory note should be included in the current working paper file, and cross-reference to the internal control (i/c) letter should be made at the completion of that phase of the audit.

(c)   At the completion of the full audit the ICQ should be carefully examined to ensure its accuracy in the light of the audit experience just gained in relation to the particular client in question.

	Tick as appropriate			Ref. to I/C letter ("no" answers)	Date
	Yes	No	Not applic		

Section: purchases and trade creditors

(a) Are official orders issued showing names of suppliers, quantities ordered and prices?

(b) Are copies of orders retained for file?

(c) Who authorises orders and what are their authority limits?
Specify:
Name   Position   Authority limit

. . . .

(d) Are the above persons independent of those who issue requisitions?

(e) Is a record kept of orders placed but not executed?

(f) If the answer to (e) is "yes", how is this record compiled? Specify:

(g) Are goods from suppliers inspected on arrival as to quantity and quality?

(h) How is the receipt of supplies recorded (e.g. by means of goods inwards notes)? Specify:

(i) Are these records prepared by a person independent of those responsible for:

  (i) ordering functions?

  (ii) processing and recording of invoices?

(j) Are all invoices received:

  (i) compared with copy orders?
  (ii) compared with goods inwards records?
  (iii) checked for prices?

	Tick as appropriate			Ref. to I/C letter ("no" answers)	Date
	Yes	No	Not applic		
(iv) checked for calculations, extensions and additions?					
(k) Are the above functions (see (j) above) carried out by a person independent of those responsible for:					
(i) ordering functions?					
(ii) receipt and control of goods?					
(l) Are bought ledger personnel independent of those responsible for:					
(i) approving invoices and credit notes?					
(ii) cheque payment functions?					
(m) Is the control account function independent of bought ledger personnel?					
Section: sales and trade debtors					
(a) How are sales orders recorded, including those received other than by post? Specify:					
(b) Are orders from customers approved before acceptance by the sales department?					
(c) If answer to (b) is "yes", how is approval evidenced?					
(d) Are customers' credit limits checked against their balances before orders are accepted?					
(e) Is this function carried out by a person independent of the sales department?					

	Tick as appropriate			Ref. to I/C letter ("no" answers)	Date
	Yes	No	Not applic		
(f) What record is kept of orders received but not yet executed, and how is that record compiled? Specify:					

(g) Are records of goods despatched prepared independently of:
  (i) the sales department?
  (ii) the processing of invoices?					

(h) Are goods despatched records regularly reviewed for items against which no invoices have been issued?					

(i) Are sales invoices prepared by a person independent of those responsible for:
 	
  (i) accepting orders?
  (ii) control and despatch of goods?
  (iii) cash receipt functions?					

(j) Are sales invoices compared with:
 	
  (i) sales orders?
  (ii) goods despatched notes?
  (iii) receipted advice/delivery notes?					

(k) Is this function carried out by a person independent of those who:
 	
  (i) record despatches?
  (ii) prepare invoices?					

(l) Are sales ledger personnel independent of cash receipt functions?					
(m) Are statements of account regularly sent to customers (e.g. monthly)?					

	Tick as appropriate			Ref. to I/C letter ("no" answers)	Date
	Yes	No	Not applic		

(n) Are statements checked before despatch to customers by persons independent of:

   (i) the sales ledger personnel?
   (ii) cash receipt functions?

Section: stock and work in progress

(a) Is the storage accommodation adequate to provide protection against:

   (i) deterioration?
   (ii) access by unauthorised persons?
   (iii) any other local hazards?

(b) Are issues from stores made only on properly authorised requisitions?

(c) Who are authorised to sign requisitions?
Specify: ....
....

(d) Are bin cards or similar records maintained at stores locations?

(e) Are continuous stock records maintained for:

   (i) raw materials?
   (ii) bought out components?
   (iii) consumable stores?
   (iv) finished goods?
   (v) stocks held on behalf of third parties?
   (vi) stocks in hands of third parties?

(f) Are these records maintained:

   (i) in quantity only?
   (ii) in value only?
   (iii) in both quantity and value?

| | Tick as appropriate | | | | |
	Yes	No	Not applic	Ref. to I/C letter ("no" answers)	Date
(g) Are stores records maintained by a person independent of:					
(i) the stores keepers?					
(ii) those responsible for physically counting or checking stocks?					
(h) Are independently maintained control accounts kept for each category of stock set out in (e) above?					
(i) Is the costing system fully integrated with the financial records?					
(j) If not, are totals of various categories of costs (including overheads) regularly reconciled with the actual costs in the financial records?					
(k) Are works orders issued:					
(i) against specific customers' orders?					
(ii) on the basis of predetermined production targets?					
(iii) on some other basis? Describe:					
(l) How are works orders authorised? Specify:					
(m) On what basis are materials, labour and other direct costs charged to work in progress accounts? Specify:					
(n) Are overheads clearly divided into fixed and variable overheads?					
(o) What is the basis of allocation of overheads to costs and what overheads are recovered in this way? Specify:					

	Tick as appropriate			Ref. to I/C letter ("no" answers)	Date
	Yes	No	Not applic		

(p) Does the system ensure that excess or abortive costs are written off and not carried forward in work in progress?

Section: industrial wages

(a) Are the duties of the wages staff rotated periodically?

(b) Are personnel files kept for each member of staff, independently of the wages department?

(c) What are the normal working hours? Specify:

(d) On what basis is overtime paid? Specify:

(e) Who authorises overtime and how is it evidenced? Specify:

(f) Does the system provide for independent periodic checking with personnel records of:

    (i) names on payroll?
    (ii) rates of pay and deductions?

(g) Once completed in ink or other permanent form is the payroll finally approved for payment by a person independent of all other payroll functions?

(h) Is the wages cheque compared by the cheque signatory with the payroll summary?

(i) Is the number of names on the payroll independently checked against an official establishment roll, maintained outside wages department?

	Tick as appropriate			Ref. to I/C letter ("no" answers)	Date
	Yes	No	Not applic		
(j) If net pay is shown in envelopes, are envelope figures totalled and agreed with net amount of payroll?					
(k) Are persons responsible for wages pay-out independent of the preparation of the payroll?					
(l) Are surprise attendances periodically made at pay-outs by a responsible official independent of the wages department?					
(m) What records are maintained of unclaimed wages? Specify:					
(n) How long after pay-out are unclaimed wages broken down and rebanked? Specify:					
(o) Is an authority required before an employee can collect unclaimed wages on behalf of another?					

3.0 THE ORGANISATION CHART

From the above it will be clear that answers to ICQ questions should be obtained only from those in authority. One of the first tasks of the auditor, therefore, is to ascertain the chain of authority and delegation which provides the backbone of the organisation. This is conveniently depicted in the form of an "organisation chart", which should then be placed on file as a permanent record, and periodically brought up to date. Figs. 2 and 3 show two examples of organisation charts applicable to:

(a) accounting and office services; and

(b) production.

It should be clear from these that such charts may conveniently be prepared to illustrate the broad structure of the company or group as a whole, or any department/division within the entity.

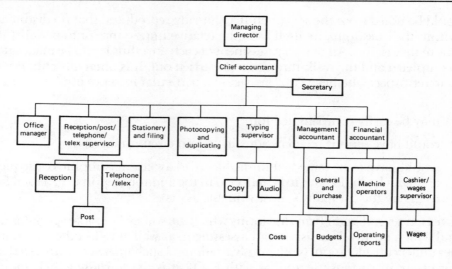

Fig. 2. *Organisation chart—accounting and office services.*

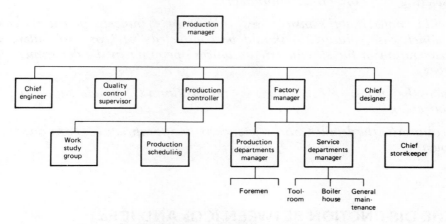

Fig. 3. *Organisation chart—production.*

4.0   INTERNAL CONTROL EVALUATION

ICQs are by no means the only way of recording and assessing the client's system of internal control. In some cases, where the client company has a "procedures manual" which is both comprehensive and explicit, this may be adequate for audit purposes as well.

It should be noted from the specimen ICQ already reproduced that no distinction is made within the questionnaire itself as to the relative importance or materiality of the questions in themselves. An overall assessment of each area thus has to be made after the ICQ is completed and the walk-through tests carried out. It is often difficult, however, to assess in retrospect whether a "no" answer in a particular instance implies a weakness which:

(a) may be easily compensated for;

(b) could have serious repercussions in certain circumstances; or

(c) would have to be remedied immediately to avoid catastrophic consequences, and which would have to be reflected in the auditor's report (e.g. a total failure to insure the company's most valuable assets).

For this reason several audit firms use forms which are somewhat more specialised than ICQs and which positively assist overall assessment, as well as reflect the materiality of the issues under consideration. Numerous variations of such *internal control evaluation* (ICE) forms are in current use and, as with ICQs, it is the *purpose* which should be grasped rather than the mere form. A specimen ICE is shown in Fig. 4.

Notes:

(a)   *The checklist in column (2) should be carefully studied and each item ticked before answering "yes" or "no" in column (4).*

(b)   *It will be noted that the answer "yes" in column (4) indicates potential weakness, in which case column (5) should be completed "yes" or "no" after careful consideration of the specific circumstances operating in the department under survey.*

(c)   *Where the answer in column (4) is "no", column (5) should show "n/a" (not applicable).*

(d)   *In column (6) the detailed cross-reference to the appropriate ICQ section should be shown.*

5.0   THE DISTINCTION BETWEEN ICQs AND ICEs

Students are often confused as to the distinction between ICQs and ICEs and the following points ought therefore to be carefully noted:

(a) The overall objective in both instances is to assess the reliability of the client organisation's own internal control system, so that the audit programme may be scientifically (as opposed to haphazardly) planned.

(b) The ICQ incorporates a large number of detailed questions but does *not* attempt to distinguish their relative materiality *inter se*. The ICE, by contrast, isolates (in the form of the *"control question"*) the main control objective within the area under review.

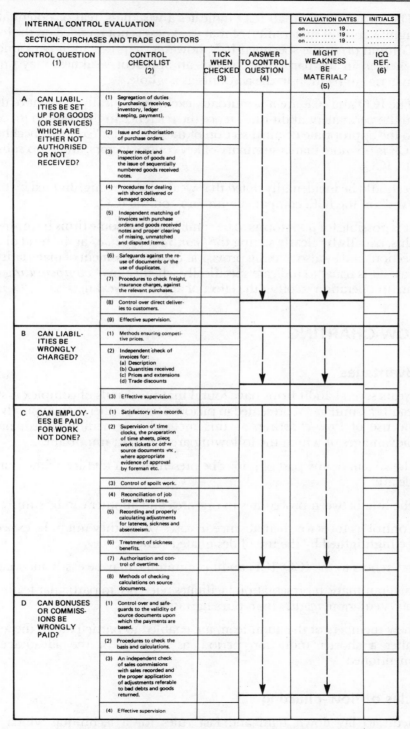

INTERNAL CONTROL EVALUATION				EVALUATION DATES	INITIALS
				on .... 19... on .... 19... on .... 19...	....
SECTION: PURCHASES AND TRADE CREDITORS					
CONTROL QUESTION (1)	CONTROL CHECKLIST (2)	TICK WHEN CHECKED (3)	ANSWER TO CONTROL QUESTION (4)	MIGHT WEAKNESS BE MATERIAL? (5)	ICQ REF. (6)
A CAN LIABILITIES BE SET UP FOR GOODS (OR SERVICES) WHICH ARE EITHER NOT AUTHORISED OR NOT RECEIVED?	(1) Segregation of duties (purchasing, receiving, inventory, ledger keeping, payment).				
	(2) Issue and authorisation of purchase orders.				
	(3) Proper receipt and inspection of goods and the issue of sequentially numbered goods received notes.				
	(4) Procedures for dealing with short delivered or damaged goods.				
	(5) Independent matching of invoices with purchase orders and goods received notes and proper clearing of missing, unmatched and disputed items.				
	(6) Safeguards against the re-use of documents or the use of duplicates.				
	(7) Procedures to check freight, insurance charges, against the relevant purchases.				
	(8) Control over direct deliveries to customers.				
	(9) Effective supervision.				
B CAN LIABILITIES BE WRONGLY CHARGED?	(1) Methods ensuring competitive prices.				
	(2) Independent check of invoices for: (a) Description (b) Quantities received (c) Prices and extensions (d) Trade discounts				
	(3) Effective supervision				
C CAN EMPLOYEES BE PAID FOR WORK NOT DONE?	(1) Satisfactory time records.				
	(2) Supervision of time clocks, the preparation of time sheets, piece work tickets or other source documents and, where appropriate evidence of approval by foreman etc.				
	(3) Control of spoilt work.				
	(4) Reconciliation of job time with rate time.				
	(5) Recording and properly calculating adjustments for lateness, sickness and absenteeism.				
	(6) Treatment of sickness benefits.				
	(7) Authorisation and control of overtime.				
	(8) Methods of checking calculations on source documents.				
D CAN BONUSES OR COMMISSIONS BE WRONGLY PAID?	(1) Control over and safeguards to the validity of source documents upon which the payments are based.				
	(2) Procedures to check the basis and calculations.				
	(3) An independent check of sales commissions with sales recorded and the proper application of adjustments referable to bad debts and goods returned.				
	(4) Effective supervision				

Fig. 4. *Specimen internal control evaluation form (see Notes on p. 88).*

(c) The answer "no" in an ICQ indicates a weakness, real or potential, but the significance (or materiality) of that weakness is not revealed on the form itself. Column (5) in the specimen ICE, however, requires audit personnel to state whether, in the particular context, an apparent weakness may prove to be material in relation to the accounts as a whole.

(d) The ICQ and ICE are *not* mutually exclusive—ideally, both have their place in the permanent audit file. Hence the reference in the column (6) of the ICE to the appropriate detailed section of the ICQ. The "control checklist" in the ICE is no more than a summary of key control factors, and is no substitute for the ICQ.

(e) It should be incidentally noted that weaknesses are highlighted by the answer "yes" on the ICE, compared with "no" on the ICQ.

(f) It is possible for *both* forms to be combined, and some firms have already done this, usually by clearly stating the *"control objective"* at the head of each ICQ section, and by also making provision for an assessment of materiality. In such cases it is usual to indicate specifically whether any *"compensating controls"* are in operation to offset the effect of apparent weaknesses.

6.0 FLOW-CHARTING

6.1 Advantages

In recent years several audit firms have found that the details of complex systems may be more readily assimilated if presented in pictorial form, rather than in purely narrative terms. The use of flow-charting, as this method is generally called, has certain practical advantages of which the following are the most important.

(a) the system or any part of it may be presented as a totality, without any loss of detail;

(b) the link between procedures in one area and another can be simply depicted;

(c) control features (or their absence in cases where they might be expected) may be highlighted by the use of designated symbols;

(d) references to the ICQ/ICE/audit programme may be easily incorporated;

(e) diagrammatic representation facilitates reference to particular features within a system more readily than pure narrative;

(f) new members of the audit team are enabled to participate in the audit work after a shorter induction period, as a result of the advantages already mentioned.

6.2 Rules of flow-charting

It is difficult to lay down hard and fast rules for a technique which has been independently developed by a number of firms working without any effective co-ordination. As a result, a wide variety of symbols proliferates at present; flow-lines move in vertical, diagonal and horizontal directions. In fact there is little uniformity on matters of detail. Some years ago the British Standards Institute issued a standard on flow-charting symbols, and these have been adopted almost in their entirety by the computer industry; the accounting profession has not followed this example, however.

Despite the variety of techniques in operation, it is possible to list the rules which are most generally observed in practice, as follows:

(a) The direction of flow adopted should be followed consistently. Except in the case of a "loop" ("sub-routine" where computers are involved), which depicts the continuous repetition of an operation until a specified occurrence takes place, the flow direction should never be reversed.

(b) Unless BSI symbols are used, a key should always be provided.

(c) A specially designed template should always be used—freehand flow-charting is rarely acceptable.

(d) The chart should not be cramped—use a continuity symbol and begin a new page.

(e) If it is necessary to refer to a document a second (or third etc.) time on the same chart, the outline on successive occasions should be broken (or "ghosted").

(f) Remember what is being charted: the diagram represents a series of events in *time* (as opposed to *space*). The *sequence* is therefore all important.

(g) The chart must reflect the system—weaknesses included. It is often tempting to assume that the sensible procedure is always adopted in practice by the client's staff, but it is the actual procedure that must be drawn.

(h) Activities often involve the production of a *document*—always *separate* the symbols for activity and document respectively.

(i) Avoid the cross of flow lines if possible. If unavoidable, use the device shown in Fig. 5.

(j) Marginal notes may be included in the chart, using a "dotted" flow line and a marginal bracket, thus:

6.3   The use of symbols

In Fig. 6 the symbols from the current IBM computer template are reproduced. These, incidentally, conform with British Standards symbols. Relatively few of the symbols given are needed by auditors, as explained below. Computer symbols are shown because flow-charting is the common language of computer programming, and familiarity with these symbols is becoming increasingly important for auditors.

Of all the symbols shown, audit purposes (other than computer audits) normally require the use of only:

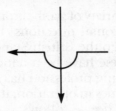

Fig. 5. *Flow-chart symbol—cross flow lines.*

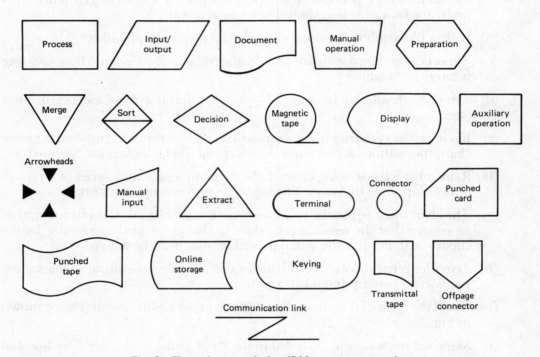

Fig. 6. *Flow-chart symbols—IBM computer template.*

(a) manual operation;

(b) document;

(c) decision;

(d) merge;

(e) terminal;

(f) arrowheads (on flow lines).

Additionally, the symbol shown in Fig. 7 may be used to indicate "file", with a code letter in the bottom section of the triangle, thus:

P   permanent
T   temporary
D   date sequence
A   alphabetic sequence

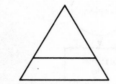

Fig. 7. *Flow-chart symbol—file.*

6.4   Flow-charting in the examination

When working under pressure of time it is preferable to avoid the necessity of preparing a rough plan of the systems flow-chart before commencing the final version. The simplest approach for those without considerable flow-charting experience is to use the full width and chart progressively down the page until reaching the concluding event or document. Fig. 8 demonstrates this method. It should be possible, for example, to follow with ease the routine functions which the flow-chart in Fig. 8 is describing. (*The chart is based on a typical examination question.*)

6.5   Flow-charting in practice

When the constraints of time are less severe than in the examination room, flow-charting of a more ambitious nature may be undertaken. Many firms which have adopted flow-charting as a regularly applied technique for all larger clients list the steps depicted, in abbreviated narrative form, in the left-hand column of the page—numbered sequentially. The remainder of the page is divided into further columns, one for each department in which the charted activities take place. Lateral flow lines therefore indicate the flow from one department to another, although the fundamental direction remains vertical, from top to bottom.

Figure 9, which illustrates this method, employs a set of symbols now used by several firms, and which are obviously different from the BSI symbols used in the previous illustration. This method has the obvious advantages of:

(a) keeping the charts clear of narrative and directional "signposts";

(b) indicating in which section or department of the organisation the activity is taking place;

(c) retaining a concise but clear summary of activities in narrative form, in the actual sequence in which they take place;

(d) highlighting control features by the use of the small diamond-shaped symbol, which represents a check, or inspection.

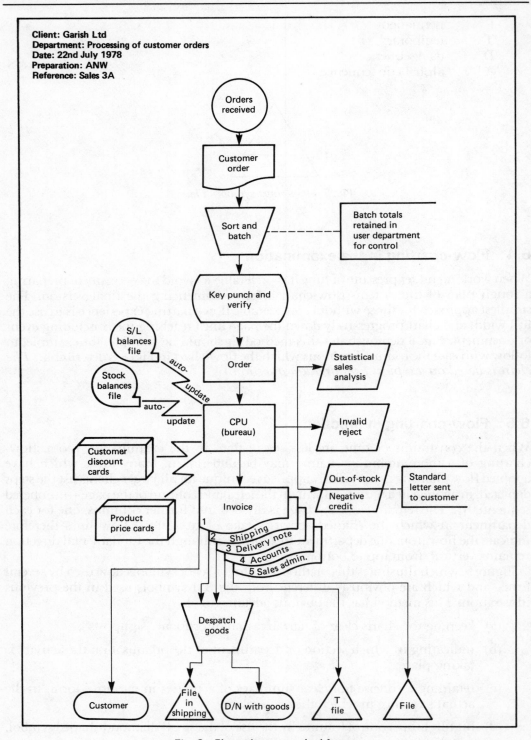

Client: Garish Ltd
Department: Processing of customer orders
Date: 22nd July 1978
Preparation: ANW
Reference: Sales 3A

Fig. 8. *Flow-chart—vertical format.*

6.6   Conclusion

It has been noted that, although no two firms employ identical flow-charting methods, the technique itself is now established as a fact of auditing life. It has proved to be of immense value in providing a "ready reference" to each detail lying hidden within a mountain of complexity. There are certainly no absolute "rights" and "wrongs" in the drawing of the charts—indeed, clearly labelled rectangles and circles can be almost as effective as the symbols. Any chart drafted by a student is "right" if:

(a)   it is neat;

(b)   it is clear and explicit;

(c)   it is well-spaced;

(d)   it is accurate.

Finally, there is only one way of becoming a flow-charting expert—practice!

7.0   AUDIT PRACTICE IN RELATION TO SMALLER COMPANIES

The techniques of internal control assessment already described take on full significance in the context of the audit of large companies. In the case of smaller companies, however, the audit objectives are unchanged but the absence of normal internal control criteria will often necessitate a different approach to the audit work. This subject is briefly dealt with in the new Auditing Standards, both in the explanatory notes and in the Guidelines—with particular reference to specimen report No. 6, reproduced in Chapter 8.

Prior to the adoption (in the form of the Companies Act 1985) of the EEC Fourth Directive, the question of whether small companies require a full audit was hotly debated. Although there is now some relaxation of small company filing regulations, the audit requirement persists.

In reality, of course, what passes as an audit for many such companies generally comprises the preparation of the accounts by the auditor, clearly acting in an accounting capacity. The question which always arises is whether this arrangement is satisfactory, and whether a formal audit, in such cases, can be realistically attempted at all. One is also left with the question of how far it is possible for a set of accounts to be independently audited by the person who has prepared them. The notes which follow summarise this continuing debate, a favourite theme for professional examiners.

The application of auditing standards to the audit of small companies managed and owned by substantially the same people is a subject the Auditing Practices Committee has under continuous consideration. A fundamental question in this context is whether the value derived from the audit of such a company is commensurate with the cost of carrying it out.

From the point of view of the *proprietor* there is clearly an advantage in having accounts properly prepared, but the additional advantage of having them audited is marginal. The same applies to the other *shareholders* who are usually small in number and closely connected with the proprietor.

The *creditor* derives some benefit but, since accounts are often filed many months after a company's year end, those providing credit more often resort to trade sources for

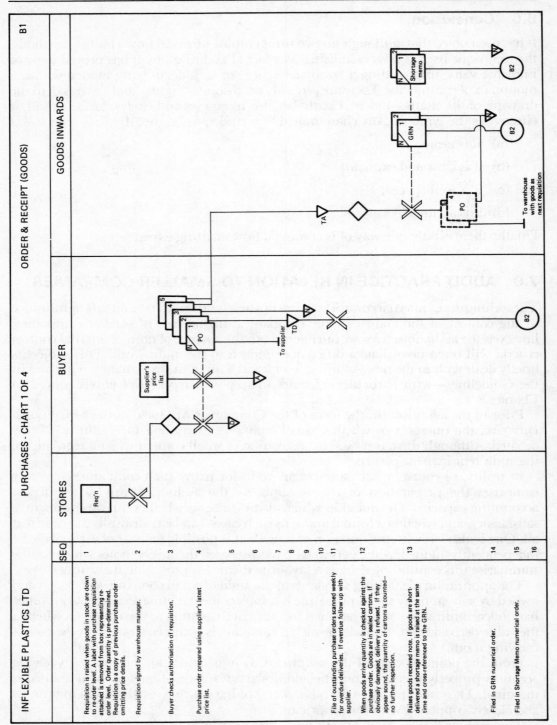

Fig. 9. *Flow-chart—columnar format.*

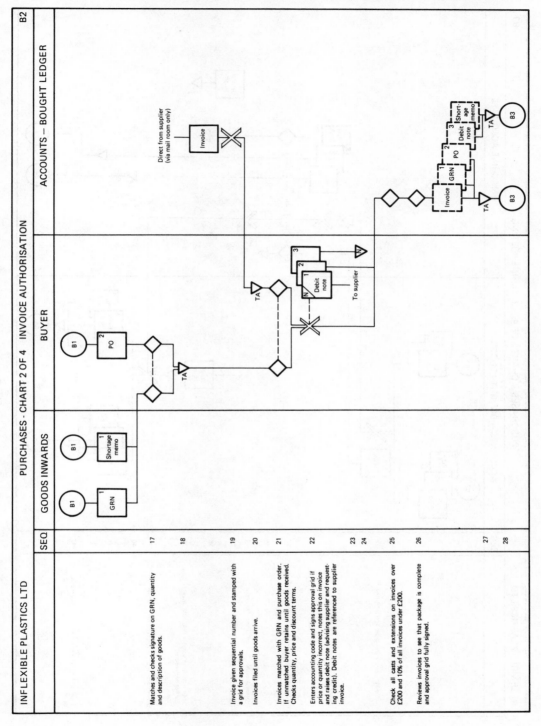

Fig. 9—*continued*

Fig. 9—*continued*

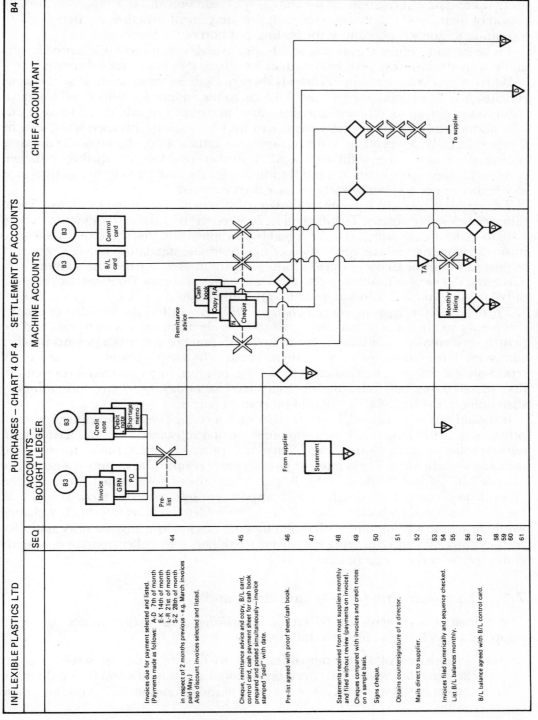

Fig. 9—*continued*

more up-to-date information on the company's creditworthiness. *Employees* also, by reason of their small number and the simple management structure, are frequently in a position to guess reasonably at the trading position of the business.

These are some of the arguments which lead to a view that there is less need for the audit of small *proprietary* companies than for others. (See below for definition.)

When it comes to auditing standards there are other factors leading to the same conclusions. The proprietor will usually look to his auditor for help in all financial matters: tax, preparation of accounts, assistance in negotiating additional finance, etc. The auditor, in examining these areas, will thus be auditing his own work; can he therefore be truly independent? If the accountant and the auditor should not be the same person the cost of the audit increases. A further problem is whether sufficient corroborative evidence exists in a small company for the auditor to form an opinion as to whether or not all the transactions have been recorded.

The problem could be resolved by allowing *different audit standards* to be applied to different types of company. To differentiate between the two, the auditor's report would have to make it clear which standards had been applied and this could quickly lead to misunderstanding and the application of inappropriate standards. The law presently requires auditors of all companies to form an opinion as to whether the accounts give a true and fair view without regard to the relative sizes of clients. Dual standards are not only far from an ideal solution, but also arguably illegal.

There is therefore a strong case for *changing the law* to allow shareholders of smaller companies to choose whether they wish to have their companies' accounts audited (which incidentally would not be out of step with practice and developments in other countries). If they so choose there would still need to be a requirement for some form of report (in less stringent terms than at present) to be given by a qualified accountant so that the accounts may have the necessary level of authority to creditors, minority shareholders, the Inland Revenue and other third parties.

It should not be imagined, however, that such a change would be applicable to all private companies; many private companies are of a substantial size and have several outside interests in the form of trade creditors, providers of long-term finance, and minority shareholders. These interests would clearly continue to require the assurance provided by an independent audit. But a change may be warranted in the case of "proprietary" companies, which for this purpose may be regarded as those in which *all the directors are shareholders, and all the shareholders are directors*. Such a change would bring the UK into line with most other nations in requiring statutory audits for public companies only, leaving the matter discretionary for smaller companies, usually at the option of their shareholders.

7.1 The arguments for and against an audit

The principal arguments in favour of *abolishing* audit requirements for small companies may be summarised as follows:

    (a) Proprietors of such companies tend to require financial services (book-keeping, tax advice, etc.) from professional accountants, and regard the audit aspect of the work as part of the price of incorporation, but of no immediate value.

    (b) Since (in proprietary companies) the shareholders and directors are the same people, there is something ludicrous about the spectacle of "directors" supplying information to the auditor so that the latter is then in a position to report back to them with their "shareholder hats" on.

(c) There is no legal requirement for outside interests to be served by the auditor and, in any case, such outsiders make no contribution to the audit fee.

(d) Many outside interests such as banks are well protected by personal guarantees from directors and charges against company assets. They are therefore not dependent on the audit for protection.

(e) Creditors are able to make little use of the audit since the accounts and audit report are filed many months after credit is given and such accounts, even if fully understood, would therefore provide little indication of the risks involved.

The arguments in favour of *retaining* the audit, on the other hand, may be summarised as follows:

(a) Outside interests do in fact pay a price for dealing with limited liability companies in that the shareholders/directors may select their moment for putting the company into liquidation at little or no cost to themselves, and to the exclusive detriment of unprotected trade creditors. The possibility of such an action represents the supreme privilege of incorporation, and the audit therefore represents a vital safeguard against its abuse.

(b) Although the law fails to acknowledge any duty of care to outsiders on the part of the auditor, such a duty may reasonably be inferred from the requirement under the Companies Act 1985 that all companies previously exempt from so doing are required to publish their audited accounts, together with their annual return, by filing them at Companies House. There is thus a clear inference that outsiders may rely upon such filed accounts for any reasonable purpose, and recent case law on auditors' liability to third parties seems to confirm this (see Chapter 10).

(c) Although the arguments concerning late filing are appreciated, it is quite incorrect to equate the value of the audit as a whole with the value of the audit report—often regarded as a formality and of academic interest. It is the audit *presence* which imposes a major discipline on corporate conduct, and which constitutes one of the most significant safeguards of the interests of all those who do business with incorporated entities. It is therefore likely that delinquency and mismanagement would, to an unquantifiable degree, result from a complete removal of the audit discipline.

7.2   The audit as a safeguard

The mere audit presence acts as a moral check upon the client's staff and on the procedures they follow. The knowledge that the records are subsequently to be subjected to an independent check, the timing and extent of which remain largely unknown to staff and officers alike, acts as a far more powerful spur to the honest, industrious and accurate performance of managerial and clerical tasks than we within the profession perhaps realise.

Directors of client companies, moreover, are constrained in some measure by the stipulations of company law on capital preservation, the maintenance and retention of up-to-date records, filing of accounts and annual returns, conduct of meetings and recordings of proceedings in formal minutes, and a host of other equally important matters, which collectively impose a discipline on the conduct of business affairs. The auditor, indirectly perhaps, ensures wherever possible that these disciplines are observed.

It is fashionable to be cynical these days, and point to the innumerable instances where the incompetent or delinquent behaviour of corporate officers has passed unhampered by auditors and all the other regulatory measures provided by law and by custom, thereby suggesting that their ineffectiveness should signal their own demise. Yet of one thing we may be certain: without an audit presence such abuses would be greater, and failures vastly more common—the rule, even, rather than the exception. And the prime sufferers when a company collapses, let us remind ourselves, are invariably the unsecured trade creditors.

For all those who would trade with incorporated entities, the audit requirement should therefore continue to afford a measure of assurance that they are not embarking on a one-way ride to financial loss. And such assurance should be provided irrespective of who reads or heeds the audit report.

7.3   Review or audit?

Although there has been much discussion concerning the substitution of a "review" for a full-scale audit, no clear definition has been given of what such a review would entail. If the Canadian system is followed, a review would comprise a rigorous investigation of the company's published accounts with special reference to comparisons with earlier periods and with other businesses in the same trade, including an analysis of ratios, trends and forecasts. A review would, however, normally exclude many basic verification procedures covering inspection of physical stocks, plant and machinery and other tangible assets; inspection of basic documentary evidence, so far as this may reasonably be made available, would nevertheless normally be expected.

Under the terms of the Canadian approach, as formulated by the Canadian Institute of Chartered Accountants, the aim of the review is to establish no more than the plausibility (or otherwise) of the financial statements of the enterprise. The question of whether a comprehensive review of the accounts and records should be substituted for a full-scale audit for proprietary companies in the UK will no doubt continue to be debated in the years to come, but the Companies Act 1985, temporarily at least, settled the immediate issue.

The transatlantic version of a review involves principally an examination of:

(a)   comparative data;

(b)   ratio analysis;

(c)   trend analysis.

It does not involve normal audit verification procedures, such as tests on accuracy of records, inspection of physical assets, or direct confirmation. No audit opinion is therefore offered, and the reviewers' report will usually:

(a) summarise the engagement terms and work done;

(b) state that an audit has not been performed; and

(c) provide negative assurance, i.e. that nothing was revealed to suggest that the financial statements are misleading or materially inaccurate.

7.4 An independent view

Following an invitation by the APC to express views on this subject, one international firm responded substantially as follows:

Should mandatory audits continue for small companies?

1. It is our view that because the directors of small companies exercise "proprietorial" control, usually little value is gained by members from an independent audit opinion. The original aim of the audit function was to give the members of a company comfort regarding the management's stewardship of their company during the period under review. When, as is generally so in small companies, the proprietors also manage the company we doubt whether there is any value in an independent audit opinion that is addressed to members.

2. It is often impossible for auditors to obtain adequate assurance on internal control or documentary evidence to verify transactions, particularly those that involve cash. Consequently, following the introduction of auditing standards, it is likely that many auditor's reports on small companies will need to be qualified. We believe that the plethora of qualified accounts that would then result would be unhelpful, and so we consider that the financial statements of small companies should not be subject to a statutory requirement for audit. This view is held by a majority of partners in our firm.

3. We believe that, in practice, many small companies would choose to continue to have their financial statements audited. Many boards of directors would desire to have an independent opinion, and debenture holders, mortgagees and bankers would also require the assurance of an audit opinion (even though on occasions that opinion might be qualified).

4. We believe, also, that an audit should be conducted if the holders of more than a specified percentage of the company's share capital request it. If that percentage were set at 10% the rights of the minority shareholders would be afforded reasonable protection.

5. We consider that, at the date of the annual general meeting at which the financial statements of the previous period are considered, the members of the company should decide whether or not the financial statements for the current period are to be audited. Shareholders should, however, have the right to convene an extraordinary meeting at a later date for the purpose of requesting an audit on the financial statements of a current period.

6. We are of course aware that where the members of a company request an audit, and

where the financial statements of the previous financial period have not been audited, the auditor may not be able to express an unqualified opinion on the profit and loss account for the current period. This is because he may not be able to obtain audit satisfaction on the opening balances for the period on which he is reporting.

Should small company financial statements be reviewed?

7.   If the mandatory audit requirements were removed, we do not consider that review procedures offer a practicable alternative. To obtain the required level of assurance, the reviewer's approach would not be materially different from the auditor's approach. He would be required to apply standards which tested the truth and fairness of the accounts and, in so doing, he would perform substantially the same tests as he would if he were performing a statutory audit. We consider that a review would not be practicable because:

(a)   it would be difficult to define the level of assurance that would result from such a review;

(b)   by definition, a review must contain qualifications, and these reduce its value;

(c)   it would be difficult to avoid misleading the public as to the status of review. Inevitably, it would in time, take on the status of a statutory audit.

This view is almost unanimous within our firm.

Definition of a "small company"

8.   It has been suggested that the bottom tier of companies as defined by the Companies Act 1985 should be the criteria that should be used for defining the small company for audit purposes. We agree with this suggestion in principle.

General

The following additional points were made by many of our partners:

(a)   If the requirement for a mandatory audit were removed, directors should be required to make a positive statement that, in their opinion, the accounts give a true and fair view.

(b)   It should be made easier for companies to revert to unlimited status without causing them difficulties as regards administration and taxation.

8.0   LETTERS OF WEAKNESS

Usually, at the conclusion of the interim audit, after the review of the client's system has been carried out, auditors will bring to the attention of management weaknesses in the system of internal control. "Letters of weakness" (sometimes referred to as "management letters", or "internal control letters") are addressed to the management and refer to those weaknesses in the system which could lead to fraud or errors (or both), and which should therefore be remedied without delay.

These letters generally distinguish between matters which are of vital importance, and those which are of secondary importance.

The letter of weakness is intended as a constructive item of management advice, which not only reports weaknesses and defects in the system of internal control, but also suggests methods of correcting or overcoming those weaknesses. The weakness reported to management should be followed up during subsequent audits, and if it is found that they have not been remedied, it is customary for a second letter to be written. If management continually fails to rectify the points in question, the auditor will have no option but to consider qualifying his audit report.

8.1   Specimen letter of weakness

1010 Chesterford Square
London WC1 4DN

1st October 1985

Confidential

D. Gasworthy Esq
Financial Director
Toxic Gases Ltd
1 Exchange Street
London EC1 4DX

Dear Sir,

Internal control
During our interim audit for the year ending 31st December 1985 we examined certain aspects of your company's system of internal control. Accompanying this letter is a memorandum containing recommendations on possible ways in which the system could be improved to overcome weaknesses in control which came to our notice during the examination.

The memorandum is submitted as part of our usual practice, and follows one prepared during last year's interim audit and sent to you on 10th September 1984. We are pleased to note that the recommendations included in that memorandum have now been adopted.

The matters dealt with in this memorandum came to our notice during the conduct of our normal audit procedures which are designed primarily with a view to the expression of our opinion on the accounts of the company, and therefore our comments cannot be expected to include all possible improvements in internal control.

Recommendations for improving internal control are set out in Section 1 and other matters dealt with in Section 2 of the attached memorandum.

We have discussed the contents of the memorandum with Mr K. Wick, your chief accountant, and other company officials, who in general accept the recommendations. We look forward to receiving your comments in due course.

We take this opportunity to express our gratitude to all members of the company's staff who have assisted us in carrying out our work.

Yours faithfully,

Woody, Allen & Co

8.2 Memorandum to letter of weakness

Section 1—internal control

CASH AND BANK BALANCES

1. *Monthly bank reconciliations should be checked by an official outside the cash office.* At present the cashier prepares bank reconciliations each month and reports cash book balances to the company secretary. No independent check of the bank reconciliations is made. An independent review of the reconciliation would help ensure that prompt action is taken to clear any long outstanding items on the reconciliation and result in a stronger system of internal control over cash.

DEBTORS AND SALES

2. *Credit limits should be set for all customers and strictly observed.* Our audit tests revealed that credit limits were not set for all customers, and even where set they had been exceeded in some cases for prolonged periods; in a number of cases this was due to the slow payment of their accounts by the customers. If this recommendation is adopted the company's credit control will be improved and risk of loss through bad debts reduced.

WAGES

3. *Duties in the wages department should be changed to prevent the clerk who calculates wages and makes up wage packets from also paying the wages.* Under the present system, the wages are paid out by the wages clerk who calculates wage payments and also makes up wage packets. If a person outside the wages department is responsible in future for paying wages, the internal control will be improved and defalcations would be possible only by collusion. We wish to stress that our audit tests have given no cause to doubt the integrity of personnel at present employed in the wages department, and that our recommendation is made with a view to improving the present system.

STOCKS

4.   *Procedures should be set up for a regular review of stocks to ensure that slow moving and obsolete stocks and those in excess of production requirements are regularly identified and reported to management.* Our audit work revealed a number of stock items which had to be written down because they were obsolete or surplus to requirements. Under the present system, the function of reviewing stocks for slow moving and obsolete items rests with the factory manager, but with the increase in his other responsibilities he now has had less time to devote to this aspect of control. We recommend that a system of regular scrutiny of stock levels and of regular reporting to management should be instituted, which will enable action to be taken to dispose of surplus or obsolete stock which will release storage space and reduce funds invested in stocks.

5.   *Records of differences between physical and book stocks revealed by the continuous stocktaking should be reported regularly to management.* The factory manager, who authorises adjustments to stock records for discrepancies disclosed by the stocktaking, does not report these adjustments to management. The amounts by which the stock records have been adjusted during the last six months have been much greater than in the previous six months, and monthly reports to management would enable closer control to be maintained.

Section 2—other matters

FIXED ASSETS
We recommend that existing depreciation rates be reviewed to ensure that they are still adequate. Expenditure on plant and machinery is at present written off by the company over a period of ten years. We are of the opinion that the more advanced types of machinery, which have recently been bought, may well be obsolete in a shorter period. It is suggested that company officials review the recent plant additions and consider whether the rate of depreciation used in previous years is adequate in the present circumstances.

PROGRESS TEST 3

1.   What is the difference between an ICQ and an ICE? (5.0)

2.   What are the principal advantages of flow-charting? (6.1)

3.   What are the arguments in favour of abolishing the audit of small companies? (7.1)

4.   Specify the purposes of a letter of weakness. (8.0)

CHAPTER FOUR
Auditing Procedures — Terminology

1.0 INTRODUCTION

It is necessary to reconsider, in a little more detail, the essential features of every audit, large or small. These are:

(a) A review of the system of internal control, including internal check, internal audit (if any), and accounting.

(b) An execution of detailed audit tests, based on the results of enquiries made at phase (a) above, and normally incorporated in what is termed the "audit programme". The object of this phase is to examine the records in sufficient depth to determine their reliability as a basis for the preparation of financial statements.

(c) A comparison between the underlying records examined at phase (b) above and the final accounts presented for audit, to ensure that the accounts are in agreement with the records audited. In this context it is useful to bear in mind that the auditor is obliged under the Companies Act 1985 to qualify his report if, in his opinion, the accounts and underlying records are not in agreement.

(d) A critical review of the final accounts themselves, to determine whether:

  (i) they show a true and fair view;

  (ii) they are presented in accordance with the disclosure requirements of the Companies Act;

  (iii) they comply with best accounting practice and the Statements of Standard Accounting Practice in force at the time;

  (iv) any qualification of the audit report would be appropriate;

  (v) a comparison between the current and previous period's accounts reveals any discrepancies requiring further investigation.

This latter phase (d) of the audit would commence with the verification of assets and liabilities included in the balance sheet, and would end with the signing of the audit report, whether "clean" or qualified. During this phase the auditor would closely review his own working papers, including ICQ, ICE, charts and systems notes, "weakness" letters (sent to management highlighting systems weaknesses already discovered during phase (a) above), and would ensure:

(a) that all outstanding queries had been dealt with satisfactorily;

(b) that no steps in the audit programme—often conducted by employees of the auditor—had been inadvertently omitted; and

(c) that the effect on the final accounts of material weaknesses had been quantified so far as possible.

Before proceeding with this digest of terminology, it is advisable to revise the auditor's Operational Standard (see Chapter 1, section 17.0), with special reference to audit evidence.

2.0 TERMINOLOGY OF AUDIT TESTING

It is useful at this stage to summarise some of the terminology associated with the audit tests which feature at different stages of the audit. Students should be warned, however, never to adopt a rigid attitude towards terminology since, as with flow-charting techniques, different firms develop their own terms for these tests, and conflict is by no means unknown.

The glossary which follows gives the meanings which are at present most generally attributed to the terms:

Vouching

Not to be confused with "verification" (see below). Vouching takes place at phase (b) of the audit—see section 1.0 of this chapter. Vouching may be defined as the inspection of all available documentary evidence, in support of transactions purported to have taken place during the period under review, the most important objectives being the ascertainment of *cost* and *authority*. In examining a purchase invoice, for example, the auditor would ascertain, *inter alia*, whether:

(a) the transaction took place within the period under review;

(b) the goods or services acquired appear to be compatible with the company's normal trading activities, i.e. acquired in the ordinary course of business;

(c) the casts, calculations, extensions, discounts, etc. are arithmetically accurate;

(d) the expenditure has been correctly allocated, and that effect has been given to the distinction between capital and revenue expenditure, i.e. correct determination of *cost*;

(e) there is evidence (e.g. initials) of the document having already been checked internally and authorised for payment.

It is important to remember that vouchers supporting all transactions during the period must stand a chance of being selected for examination. In the case of larger expenditures the vouchers will be examined in any event.

As far as *authority* is concerned, it should be noted that this is required at all levels, from the company's own procedures, through its articles and memorandum, to the law itself.

Verification

Not to be confused with "vouching" (see above). Verification is the first step of phase (d) of audit—see section 1.0 of this chapter. It is concerned with the company's situation at only one precise moment in time, i.e. close of business on balance sheet date. For this reason assets and liabilities are verified, but transactions are vouched. The transactions vouched may or may not result in assets or liabilities, which may then be verified. Verification involves *valuation*, *existence* and *ownership*, at the balance sheet date, as well as adequate *presentation* of the information to be conveyed.

Compliance testing

These tests take place during phase (a) of the audit and are designed to test whether the controls alleged to be in operation are in fact being followed. The completion of ICQs etc. is usually facilitated by information from the company's senior executives—the purpose of compliance tests is to establish independently the accuracy of the information. The tests should therefore cover *typical* transactions, but they do not require to be numerically *representative* (in the statistical sense). These tests are defined in the Auditing Standards as "those tests which seek to provide audit evidence that internal control procedures are being applied as prescribed".

Substantive testing

These tests take effect at phases (b) to (d) given in section 1.0 of this chapter, and include mainly:

(a) the vouching of transactions;

(b) the checking of postings;

(c) the checking of casts, extensions and calculations;

(d) the reconciliation of bank accounts and personal ledger control accounts;

(e) the verification by appropriate means of all account balances;

(f) analytical review of the final accounts.

The extent of the substantive tests in the audit programme bears a direct correspondence with the auditor's overall assessment of the system of internal control, at the conclusion of phase (a).

It is vital that the substantive tests carried out should be statistically representative of all transactions in the area being tested, since otherwise there is a risk that unjustifiable conclusions will be deduced from the examination of company records. (There is, of course, the attendant risk in such circumstances that the auditor may become personally liable for negligence should any financial loss become traceable to his failure to carry out an adequate examination.)

The Auditing Standards define substantive tests as "those tests of transactions and balances, and other procedures such as analytical review, which seek to provide audit evidence as to the completeness, accuracy and validity of the information contained in the accounting records or in the financial statements".

Weakness tests

This is a term given to any additional tests which the auditor deems necessary in view of the number of errors or weaknesses which become apparent during the execution of substantive tests (see above) under the audit programme. The "weakness tests" thus amount to an extension of the work originally planned under the programme, after it becomes clear that a higher proportion of errors exists than was first anticipated.

Rotational tests

A variety of meanings have been attributed to this term, but these fall basically into two types:

(a) Where the system of internal control is known to be good, and the sample of items tested is correspondingly small, it is considered sound practice to carry out a series of additional tests in a particular area (such as wages, sales, stores records, etc.) over and above those which are scheduled in the programme. The area to be probed is not disclosed in advance, and this practice has the dual effect of:

(i) acting as a moral check on staff working within a basically sound system, in which complacency can all too easily set in; and

(ii) making quite sure that the system is operating fully as effectively in day-to-day practice as the auditor believes. This is known correctly as "rotation of audit emphasis".

(b) Where the client company has a large number of branches, depots, warehouses, etc., it will be impracticable, if not impossible, for the auditor to test procedures at all of these in the course of one cycle of audit tests; in such a case visits and tests may be devised on a rotational basis, thus giving an acceptable spread of testing over a longer period of time.

With all forms of rotational tests it is important to select the object of the tests on a random basis each time (i.e. each department or branch stands an equal chance of selection on the occasion of each audit, irrespective of the time elapsed since it was last selected, unless special emphasis needs to be given to any high-value or error-prone items).

Depth tests

This term simply describes the method by which substantive tests (see above) may be conducted. The tests commence with the inception of a transaction, and trace its threads through every department affected by it, to its conclusion. A purchase of goods may commence when a predetermined re-order level has been reached. The ensuing stages may be summarised thus:

(a) requisition: pre-printed, pre-numbered and authorised;

(b) official company order, also sequentially pre-numbered and authorised—placed with approved suppliers only;

   (c) receipt of supplier's invoice;

   (d) receipt of supplier's statement;

   (e) entries in purchases day book;

   (f) postings to purchase ledger and purchase ledger control account;

   (g) cheque in settlement;

   (h) entry on bank statement and returned "paid" cheque (if requested);

   (i) cash book entry;

   (j) postings from cash book to ledger and control account, taking in any discounts;

   (k) receipt of goods, together with delivery/advice note;

   (l) admission of goods to stores;

   (m) indication, by initials or rubber stamp on internal goods inwards note, of compliance with order regarding specification, quantity and quality;

   (n) entries in stores records.

It should be noted that the above list is not necessarily comprehensive, nor do its constituent stages inevitably take place in the sequence suggested. The important point to note is that from the moment it was realised that re-order level had been reached, a chain of events was put in motion, together leaving what may be termed an "audit trail".

Each item selected for testing must be traced meticulously, and although sample sizes need not be large, they must, of course, be representative.

Depth tests do not need to begin with the first in a series of events—in fact it is important that a proportion of items tested should be traced in reverse order: the tracing of the stages whereby a duly authorised requisition becomes goods on the warehouse shelf does *not* establish that the other goods on that shelf arrived there by equally legitimate means. The only way to establish correct functioning in this respect, therefore, is to trace a representative sample of these goods back to the ordering stage. This is similar to what is sometimes known as "directional testing".

It is acceptable practice to check a slightly smaller number of transactions at each successive stage within a depth test, on the mathematical grounds (based on probability theory) that the optimum sample size decreases as the auditor's "level of confidence" concerning the functioning of the system increases.

Depth testing has found an indispensable place in modern auditing practice and, if intelligently conducted, its reconstruction of the audit trail reveals more about the functioning (or malfunctioning) of the client's system in practice than the haphazard and mechanical approach to testing, slavishly following what was always done before (for no reason other than that it was done before), which for so many years has blighted the practice of auditing.

"Walk-through" tests

Similar to depth tests, although normally conducted at phase (a) specified in section 1.0 to this chapter. They assist the auditor's ascertainment of how the system functions. It will therefore be seen that compliance tests (see above) may be conducted in this way. A "walk-through" test, as its title suggests, involves the tracing of each step within the area being assessed.

"Vouching audit"

The term "vouching audit" has been given to the audit situation in which there is a virtual absence of internal control, as a result of which it is necessary for the auditor to check in detail a substantial proportion of all documentary evidence before reaching his conclusions and compiling his report. It is not uncommon in such a situation for the checking of even 40% or 50% of all transactions to be considered necessary. The reason for this is usually that the firm's organisation is haphazard in both conception and execution, there being few regular procedures upon which the auditor may rely.

Judgment sampling

Unlike statistical sampling, this method of sampling is based exclusively upon the auditor's judgment of an audit situation. Clearly, he will bring to bear on his decision all he has gathered about the operation of the system of internal control, as applied to the recording of day-to-day transactions, but no matter how skilful his assessment of appropriate sample sizes, this judgment is necessarily subjective and hence devoid of any mathematical accuracy. In situations in which a relatively small number of transactions is under review, judgment sampling is largely unavoidable.

"Balance sheet audit" or analytical review

The following are the principal steps to be included in the programme for a balance sheet audit, after the completion of the basic verification of assets and liabilities, with special reference to documents of title, agreements, correspondence and valuation:

(a) Compare each item in the final accounts with the corresponding item for the previous year and ascertain the reasons for any material variations.

(b) Consider whether increases or decreases in charges for wages, materials consumed and other variable expenses appear to be proportionate to the increase or decrease in turnover. Ascertain the quantities of turnover where the monetary value thereof has been inflated or deflated by price changes, alterations in rates of VAT, or customs duties.

(c) Obtain a satisfactory explanation for any material change in the rate of gross profit shown.

(d) Scrutinise any exceptional transactions or items of a non-recurring nature which have resulted in charges or credits of a material amount to the revenue of the period under review.

(e) Consider the changes in the position disclosed by the balance sheet; for example, does this reveal increased liquidity, a proportionate reduction in capital or long-term liabilities, or increases in fixed assets?

(f) Compare the value of stocks on hand with the cost of sales and enquire into any material change in this ratio, which indicates the average rate at which stocks have been turned round in the year. Compare the values of stocks with those adopted for insurance purposes.

(g) Examine the schedules showing the composition of each item in the balance sheet, and compare such items with the corresponding figures for the previous period.

(h) Compare the total due by trade debtors to turnover and compare this ratio with the corresponding figures for the previous year. If it is found that longer credit appears to have been taken by customers, pay particular attention to the provisions for bad and doubtful debts, and the possibility that remittances have not been accounted for. If sales of an exceptional amount are recorded towards the end of the period, make certain that the sales in question are properly attributable to that period, and examine the returns for the following period.

(i) Consider, in a similar way, the total due to trade creditors in relation to the purchases for the period, the value of stocks on hand and the period of credit normally taken.

(j) Compare the schedules of provisions, accruals and prepayments with those for the previous period and enquire into any material changes.

(k) Scrutinise the directors' minute books for references to matters affecting the accounts, e.g. capital commitments, pending litigation, sums payable under service agreements, capital and loan issues, etc.

(l) Consider the values placed on current assets, with particular reference to the basis of valuation of stock and work in progress.

(m) Consider the reasonableness of provisions made for depreciation and the adequacy of further sums set aside for the increased cost of replacing the assets concerned.

(n) Ascertain whether there have been any changes in the basis of accounting which have resulted in a material increase or decrease in recorded profit.

(o) Determine the amounts and nature of any contingent liabilities and commitments for capital expenditure not provided for in the accounts, and ascertain the extent of any contracts for forward purchases or sales. In cases of forward contracts, consider whether any provision for anticipated losses is required at the balance sheet date.

(p) Where appropriate, compare with the accounts concerned the figures shown by certificates and returns made to trade associations, insurance companies and government departments in respect of wages and salaries paid, declarations for insurance purposes, returns to the Customs and Excise authorities and similar documents.

(q) Check that the requirements of the Companies Act on disclosure have been complied with in every detail.

(r) Ensure that

  (i) Stock Exchange requirements for listed companies, and

  (ii) Statements of Standard Accounting Practice, have been closely observed, failing which it may be necessary to consider an appropriate qualification to the audit report unless the directors agree to make the necessary amendments.

(An example of significant accounting ratios is given in Fig. 10, as an excerpt from the analytical review process.)

The operations audit

ALTERNATIVE TITLES: "MANAGEMENT AUDIT", "EFFICIENCY AUDIT"

This is a total audit of every area of operation, not necessarily carried out by the statutory auditor. It is an investigation to ascertain whether every level of management and staff is functioning at its optimum, and a set of recommendations is issued to the board after every review. The operations audit team will set criteria for efficiency, as well as the more usual targets and goals for sales and budgets; standard OA techniques also incorporate the means of assessing and monitoring performance against these objectives.

Social audit

ALTERNATIVE TITLE: "SOCIAL RESPONSIBILITY AUDIT"

This audit takes into account the relationship of a company's activities to:

(a) its employees;

(b) the community/the public;

(c) customers;

in the context of social considerations.

(a) *Employees:* social audit will review facilities for recreation and welfare as well as direct incentives, bonuses, retirement arrangements, etc.

(b) *The community and the public:* social audit will consider the environment, pollution, ecology and other factors of the company's activities in both the immediate, medium-term and long-term. It will also include less momentous matters of social conscience such as whether, for example, goods are being persistently delivered on the pavement, thereby endangering and inconveniencing passers-by; or whether the company has alternatively allocated and constructed a special delivery bay, at considerable expense, in order to avoid such a situation.

(c) *Customers:* The social audit will, in this context, review:

(i) pricing policy;

(ii) quality control over products sold;

(iii) method of handling guarantees, correspondence and complaints;

(iv) accuracy of advertising;

(v) terms of payment and methods of debt collection.

SIGNIFICANT ACCOUNTING RATIOS	PRIOR YEARS			CURRENT YEAR		Yardstick ratios
	19 . . .	19 . . .	19 . . .	Interim	Final	
FINANCIAL STATEMENTS FIGURES	000	000	000	. . ./. . ./. . .		
Credit sales			103,248		204,791	
Total sales			103,248		204,791	
Cost of sales			66,476		137,943	
Gross profit			36,772		66,848	
Net profit			4,565		14,848	
Stocks and work in progress			9,556		30,310	
Debtors			31,816		65,217	
Liquid assets			100		100	
Current assets			41,472		95,627	
Current liabilities			41,795		97,010	
Net current assets			(323)		(1,383)	
Fixed assets			31,299		80,838	
Total assets			72,711		176,465	
Total liabilities			54,706		141,752	
Capital employed			30,976		79,455	
Shareholders' funds			18,065		34,713	
PROFIT RATIOS						
Gross profit to total sales			36%		33%	
Net profit to total sales			4.4%		7.3%	
Net profit to capital employed			15%		19%	
TRADING RATIOS						
Total sales to capital employed			3.3:1		2.6:1	
Total sales to net current assets						
Cost of sales to stocks and work in progress			7.0:1		4.6:1	
SOLVENCY RATIOS						
Current assets to current liabilities			1:1		1:1	
Liquid assets to current liabilities						
Credit sales to debtors			3.2:1		3.1:1	
CAPITAL RATIOS						
Shareholders' funds to total assets			0.2:1		0.2:1	
Current liabilities to shareholders' funds			2.3:1		2.8:1	
Gearing/total liabilities to shareholders' funds			3.0:1		4.1:1	
Other						

Fig. 10. *Significant accounting ratios.*

PROGRESS TEST 4

1. Distinguish between compliance and substantive testing. (2.0)
2. List ten matters to be included within the scope of analytical review. (2.0)
3. State the steps to be included in a depth test of purchases. (2.0)

CHAPTER FIVE

Verification of Assets and Liabilities (1) — Basic Aspects

1.0 INTRODUCTION

Correct use of terminology is important in examinations. Broadly speaking, when we speak of "vouching" we are referring to the method by which the auditor ensures that transactions have been correctly recorded in a company's books. For this purpose he will invariably examine documentary evidence to support the entries in those books. It is therefore in the nature of vouching that it will be primarily concerned with *income and expenditure.*

"Verification", on the other hand, is concerned with the company's situation at close of business on the balance sheet date (referred to in the Companies Act 1985 as the "accounting reference date"). As such we would accept that verification procedures are designed to ensure that the assets and liabilities (and hence the residual equity interests) are reliably valued and presented in the balance sheet, i.e. at one point in time.

While it is perfectly possible for the bulk of *vouching* work to be accomplished during an interim audit, only a limited amount of *verification* work can be performed prior to the final audit—and even this will be largely designed to ensure that the controls relating to specific areas of activity are functioning properly. For example, interim verification work might involve the testing of physical stocks against the balances shown in the company's memorandum stock records; similarly, a circularisation of debtors may be performed at this stage, as well as a test count of the company's investments, cash on the premises, and specific assets listed in, say, the plant register.

Work of this nature will provide the auditor with a measure of assurance (or lack of it) concerning the *quality of the controls* in force, and the *reliability of the records* in the area concerned. It is always worth remembering that "reliability", when applied to records, refers to:

(a) completeness;

(b) accuracy;

(c) whether the records are up to date; and

    (d) validity, e.g. whether the transaction recorded validly took place on behalf of the company. (Perhaps "authenticity" conveys the intended meaning more clearly.)

(NB: records which are ostensibly *up to date* may not, in fact, be complete; major liabilities, for example, might have been entirely omitted.)

2.0 "COST" AND "AUTHORITY"

Verification procedures need not extend to

    (a) the correct determination of "cost" or

    (b) establishment of "authority",

unless the items concerned were acquired during the accounting period under review. It is obvious that if they were acquired in earlier periods, this work will have been done in the year of acquisition. The examiners do not always make this clear, in which event it is usually safest to assume (and to state the assumption) that the assets were acquired *within* the period, thus requiring you to incorporate in your answer the procedures needed to establish (a) and (b) above.

    Such procedures will obviously be designed to ensure that adequate distinction has been made between "revenue cost" and "capital cost". These distinctions are, to some extent, artificial since most assets (with the exception of freehold land, investments, goodwill etc.) will eventually be written off to revenue. The point is really that we are simply applying the "accruals concept" of accounting—as explained in SSAP 2. For convenience we tend to treat expenditure whose corresponding benefit is absorbed within the *current* period as *"revenue"* costs, while those items charged to revenue (e.g. via depreciation charges) over a period of several years are regarded as "capital expenditure". Items which do not fall neatly into one category or the other, like research and development expenditure, are often described as items of "deferred revenue expenditure".

    When considering "authority" it is important to remember that auditors should be concerned with more than simply ensuring that the appropriate signature appears on a cheque or a voucher. It is, of course, vital that authority levels within the organisation should be regularised and observed in practice, and for this purpose the auditor will find that (a) the client's procedural manual and (b) the detailed organisation chart are invaluable.

    But authority extends further to incorporate the provisions of the company's memorandum and articles of association—e.g. whether the company has sufficient borrowing powers to finance its activity levels at any time, not to mention the ultimate authority, as embodied in company law. For example, there can be no authority for loans to directors which are in breach of section 330 of the Companies Act 1985.

3.0 OTHER VERIFICATION OBJECTIVES

There are more specific verification objectives which concern:

(a) valuation;

(b) existence; and

(c) ownership.

3.1 Valuation

The auditor must be satisfied that assets appear in the balance sheet at a fair value which may, of course, be rather different from their original cost. (He is also concerned that liabilities are fairly "valued"—i.e. stated at their correct amount.) It is therefore important, in relation to assets, for the auditor to ensure that, apart from the correct determination of cost, depreciation or any other fall in value due to, say, obsolescence, has been fully taken into account on an acceptable basis, consistent with that adopted in previous years. In the case of assets other than fixed assets, such as investments, or stocks of goods, any fall in value must also be taken into account:

(a) if it is material, and

(b) if it is regarded as permanent.

It is appropriate to mention at this point that in times of rapid price increases depreciation charges based on historical cost (HC) fail to achieve one of the objectives of making such a charge in the first place. While HC depreciation charges do spread the original cost over the period which benefits from the use of the asset, they may well fail to ensure the retention in the business of sufficient funds to replace the asset when this becomes necessary. For this reason current cost accounting (CCA) is now generally advocated since this requires depreciation to be calculated in terms of the values consumed expressed in *current* terms and would therefore, for all practical purposes, be based on the replacement cost of the assets concerned.

3.2 Existence

The auditor should rely upon physical verification procedures wherever practicable and appropriate. This is specially relevant in cases where the physical assets may be directly compared by the auditor with the company's own records, for example:

Asset	Record to be compared
(a) Cash balances	Petty cash books, vouchers, etc.
(b) Stocks of raw materials, finished goods and work in progress	Stores records, bin cards, work in progress schedules, costing schedules
(c) Investments	Investments ledger
(d) Vehicles, plant and machinery	Vehicle registers, plant registers

Such physical tests should be carried out on a carefully planned random selection basis (which may, if appropriate, be part of a statistical sampling scheme) and a record retained describing the nature, extent and findings of each test executed. It is an obvious, but none the less often overlooked, fact that a great deal of information can be derived from physical observation by the auditor or his agents. A factory building included in the accounts on the basis that it is "substantially complete" can be *seen* to be so (or not so) at an audit inspection arranged for the purpose. (The importance of physical inspection is dealt with in section 14.0 below with reference to four major fraud cases.)

3.3 Ownership

Existence is one thing, ownership quite another. It is impossible to lay down hard and fast rules on methods of establishing that the client is in fact the beneficial owner of the assets concerned (or that the liabilities concerned are in fact required to be met by the client), since much depends upon the circumstances prevailing. In simple cases it will be possible to verify ownership by reference to documents, such as deeds or leases in relation to property, but in other cases it may be necessary to rely upon corroborative evidence or the representations of outside parties.

If the use of the asset in question gives rise to a *benefit* or an *expense* (or both), the vouching of the benefit/expense will probably provide sufficient corroborative evidence of both the ownership and the existence of the underlying asset in cases where it is impracticable to verify these features directly. For example, a hotel owned abroad should produce a verifiable income, regularly remitted, as well as identifiable outgoings on maintenance, repairs and general upkeep. From a close examination of these items the auditor might reasonably infer:

(a) that the hotel exists, and

(b) that it is beneficially owned by the client company.

Circumspection is still needed, however, as many major frauds have depended not only upon the creation of fictitious documentation, but also upon the contrived appearance of income and expenditure. (The *McKesson and Robins* (1938) and *Equity Funding* (1973) cases are but two USA classics in this particular genre.) On occasion, therefore, the auditor may well believe that there is no substitute for direct audit work to be carried out in the location in question, in which case the usual procedure would be to request his associate audit firm in the area to undertake the examination, details of which he will clearly specify in advance. It may, of course, be necessary for him specially to appoint an associate for the purpose. This is becoming a widespread audit practice today.

4.0 AUDIT EVIDENCE

The guideline to the Operational Standard on the subject of audit evidence is reproduced in Chapter 1, section 17.2, and this should now be thoroughly revised before proceeding further.

5.0 THE USE BY THE AUDITOR OF EXTERNAL CONFIRMATION

The instances in which auditors may regard requests for external confirmation as appropriate are too many and too varied to be dealt with exhaustively. The principles involved were established in case law, in *Re City Equitable Fire Insurance Co*, explained in section 4.0 of Chapter 10. Table 5 provides a few examples of assets and liabilities whose verification may be facilitated by such confirmation.

Table 5. External confirmations

Assets	Liabilities	Confirming third party
Bank balances Securities	Overdrafts Loans Contingent liabilities Accrued interest	Bank
Debtor balances	Creditor balances	Individual debtors/ suppliers
Staff loans		Individual members of staff
	Mortgages Advances Secured loans Accrued interest	Finance house
Valuation of property Valuation of specialised stocks, e.g. gems		Acknowledged/qualified valuation experts
Assets held abroad	Liabilities repayable abroad	Overseas agents Associate firms
Goods sent to agents, on consignment and out on sale-or-return basis		Agents, consignees and sale-or-return holders
Information pertaining to investments in subsidiary companies		Auditors of subsidiaries
Goods held in bond or in warehouse		Harbour board Warehouse company
Goods held in field-warehouse*		Field-warehousing company
Leased premises— insurance of		Landlord of leased premises

Assets	Liabilities	Confirming third party
	Pending litigation, possible damages, costs and legal fees outstanding	Solicitors

*Field-warehousing: a long-established financial practice whereby a company's goods are held in the independent custody of a field-warehousing company, thus enabling finance to be raised on the collateral of those goods, as certified by the "warehouse receipts" issued by the field-warehousing company. The warehouse receipts therefore become negotiable securities. Warehouse receipts, incidentally, formed the basis of the "crime of the century", the "Great Salad Oil Swindle" in the USA discovered in 1963.

6.0 THE USE BY THE AUDITOR OF STATISTICAL EVIDENCE

Audit work on the final accounts involves a good deal more than the direct or indirect verification of specific assets and liabilities. It is equally important that the accounts, in themselves, should be seen by the auditor to "make sense". This is a gradual process, and the auditor's confidence in the view conveyed by the accounts builds up steadily as his verification work proceeds. Towards the closing stages of the review of the accounts the auditor may find that the "decision-type" flow-diagram shown in Fig. 11 assists in determining what further evidence of a statistical nature may be needed in reaching the audit opinion to be embodied in the report. This stage of the audit falls within the scope of the Analytical Review (see Chapter 4, section 11.0), itself a part of substantive testing procedures.

The flow-chart suggests that (a) the existence of available statistical evidence and (b) the creation or procurement of evidence by the auditor himself may be viewed as alternatives. In practice, where both appropriate and practicable, the auditor will in fact make use of both sources of evidence.

The flow-chart makes reference to "checklists of internally and externally generated statistical evidence". The terms "internally" and "externally" should be taken to relate respectively to evidence created *within* the client organisation and that which has been independently generated (including evidence compiled by the auditor himself). The precise form and content of such checklists will vary considerably from one audit firm to another, but the following table provides a clear picture of the nature of evidence envisaged:

Examples of the auditor's use of statistical evidence

Examples of evidence generated within client organisation (Internal)	Examples of evidence generated independently (External)	
	(i) by auditor	(ii) by outside organisations
Cash budgets/forecasts	Comparisons of material items	Returns to trade federations
Departmental expenditure budgets	(a) previous years; (b) other companies in same trade.	Interfirm comparisons

Divisional/company/group profit forecasts		Published government statistics for the particular industry/trade
Divisional results (e.g. monthly)	Trends in accounting ratios, e.g.:	Information supplied to insurance companies
	(a) closing stock: cost of sales;	
	(b) debtors: sales;	
	(c) purchases: creditors;	
Internal management ratios, e.g.:	(d) gross profit: sales;	
	(e) net profit: sales;	
(a) profitability;	(f) current assets: current liabi-lities;	
(b) efficiency;		
(c) liquidity;	(g) fixed assets: shareholders' equity.	Returns to Customs and Excise and other government agencies
(d) other performance indicators;		
(e) product/sales mix;		
(f) marketing expenditure and sales;		Comparisons with other businesses in the same type of trade or industry
(g) sales and R & D expenditure.		
Standard costing records:	Age analysis:	
(a) fixed cost recovery rates;	(a) stocks;	
(b) variance analysis;	(b) debtors.	
(c) adjustments to standards;		
(d) pricing analysis.	Other analytical tests (see Chapter 4, section 2.0, Fig. 10).	
Board minutes		
Letter of representation		
Internal audit reports		

The auditor should assess the extent to which the internally generated data in the left-hand column may be used for his purposes. The point is that the data exists—is he justified in ignoring it simply because it does not form a part of the company's "normal" accounting records? The statutes give the auditor the right to receive *all* information and explanations which he considers necessary for his purposes, as well as the right to examine *all* records, documents and vouchers. There is therefore no restriction other than that which he imposes upon himself!

Nevertheless, in practice, far too few auditors take the trouble to examine the management and costing records when forming or corroborating their opinion on the reliability of the financial and accounting records, and hence the draft published accounts. If, for example, divisional profit figures are produced internally each month it is unlikely that they will agree with the figures in the published accounts—but some form of reconciliation, possibly within predictable margins, should certainly be possible.

Note:

The above material refers to only one aspect of the use by auditors of statistics. Other aspects are dealt with in Chapter 9.

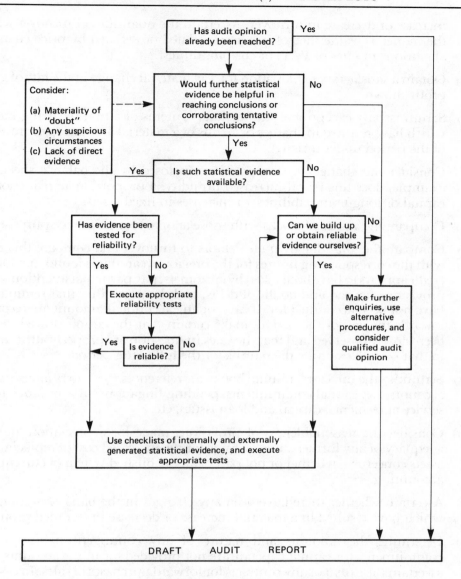

Fig. 11. *Flow-chart—review of final accounts.*

7.0 ADDITIONAL ANALYTICAL TESTS

The table in section 6.0 above provides only a handful of examples of the use of statistical evidence in the context of the analytical review. The full review of the final accounts would, so far as the auditor's own comparisons etc. are concerned, include the following additional tests and examinations:

    (a) Consider whether increases or decreases in charges for wages, materials consumed and other variable expenses appear to be proportionate to the increase or decrease in turnover. Ascertain the quantities of turnover where the monetary value thereof has been inflated or deflated by price changes, alterations in rates of VAT, or customs duties.

(b) Obtain a satisfactory explanation for any material change in the rate of gross profit shown.

(c) Scrutinise any exceptional transactions or items of a non-recurring nature which have resulted in charges or credits of a material amount to the revenue of the period under review.

(d) Consider the changes in the position disclosed by the balance sheet; for example, does this reveal increased liquidity, a proportionate reduction in capital or long-term liabilities, or increases in fixed assets?

(e) Compare the values of stocks with those adopted for insurance purposes.

(f) Compare the total due by trade debtors to turnover and compare this ratio with the corresponding figures for the previous year. If it is found that longer credit appears to have been taken by customers, pay particular attention to the provisions for bad and doubtful debts, and the possibility that remittances have not been accounted for. If sales of an exceptional amount are recorded towards the end of the period, make certain that the cut-off procedure has been closely observed and that the sales in question are properly attributable to that period; examine the returns for the following period.

(g) Scrutinise the directors' minute books for references to matters affecting the accounts, e.g. capital commitments, pending litigation, sums payable under service agreements, capital and loan issues, etc.

(h) Consider the reasonableness of provisions made for depreciation and the adequacy of any further sums set aside for the increased cost of replacing the assets concerned, whether or not part of an established system of current cost accounting.

(i) Ascertain whether there have been any changes in the basis of accounting which have resulted in a material increase or decrease in recorded profit.

(j) Determine the amounts and nature of any contingent liabilities and commitments for capital expenditure not provided for in the accounts, and ascertain the extent of any contracts for forward purchases of sales. In cases of forward contracts, consider whether any provision for anticipated losses is required at the balance sheet date.

8.0   VERIFICATION OF TRADE DEBTORS AND CREDITORS

8.1   General

Reference has already been made to the independent verification of certain assets and liabilities by means of externally derived confirmations. This method has the obvious advantage of minimising the risk of collusion between third parties and the company's staff with a view to deceiving the auditor. As a general rule we may regard any form of independent documentary evidence as superior, in terms of usefulness to the auditor, to documentary evidence compiled by members of the company's staff, irrespective of their level of authority.

It is common practice for auditors to circularise a carefully selected sample of the company's debtors and creditors respectively, as a means of

(a) ensuring the accuracy of book entries in the sales and bought ledgers, and the resulting balances;

(b) ensuring the proper functioning of the system of credit control as laid down by the directors;

(c) identifying accounts in dispute; and

(d) ensuring that the records concerned are completely up-to-date.

8.2 Creditors

Where suppliers are circularised, the independent confirmations received will support not only the creditors' ledger balances, but also the monthly statements which most suppliers send their customers anyway. We may therefore regard supplier circularisation as a secondary test, to be performed on a rotational basis—perhaps during every second or third audit cycle.

8.3 Circularisation of debtors

Before reading further, reference should be made to the example in section 6.0 of Chapter 9. This demonstrates the usefulness of statistical techniques when verifying a large number of debtor accounts by means of external circularisation.

Many audit firms use external confirmations so extensively that they have developed standardised formats for the purpose. The circularisation (with the client's permission) of a sample of debtors, requesting them to confirm the amounts outstanding, is an obvious example, and is the subject of ICAEW Guidance Statement U7. Despite the low response rate (mainly due to computerisation of records) this is still a common practice, and takes two forms:

(a) the *negative* circular, which requires a reply only if the debtor disputes the balance shown on the form; and

(b) the *positive* circular, which requests in every case confirmation of details of sums shown as outstanding in the records of the debtor.

Although the negative method is simpler and requires no follow up, it should be used only:

(a) where the auditor already has a good deal of faith in the internal control governing sales and debtors;

(b) where other verification work on the records of sales and debtors has already been executed; and

(c) in conjunction with a large and carefully selected sample—otherwise the value of the test may be negated by the number of debtors who simply throw such requests into the wastepaper basket.

The usefulness of the positive method, by contrast, depends largely upon the auditor's tenacity in following up the non-replies, by telephone or even personal call if necessary. It is essential that replies be sent to the auditor directly at his own office, otherwise there is a risk of tampering or suppression by client staff. (In this context one calls to mind once again the lessons of the *Equity Funding* case, where the auditors on occasion attempted to verify with branch managers by telephone the amount of life insurance business undertaken at each branch. The calls were dialled in the Equity Funding offices, but the switchboard, acting under instructions from one of the senior "conspirators", transferred all calls to the làtter's office. He then proceeded to confirm every figure given by the auditors, call after call, even remembering to fake the accent appropriate to the location in question!)

Skill is also needed, of course, in *selecting* the debtor accounts for circularisation. But it is important for the auditor first to scrutinise the accounts individually to ensure that the sample includes the "special cases" of accounts which may be significant, such as:

(a) accounts which show negative balances;

(b) accounts which have been written off as bad, or against which specific provision for loss has been made;

(c) accounts in which debits and credits do not appear to relate, e.g. round sums "on account" are constantly received—especially where this process results in an ever-enlarging balance;

(d) nil balances on active accounts;

(e) accounts which remain unpaid beyond the normal terms of credit;

(f) accounts showing balances which habitually exceed the designated credit limit;

(g) accounts showing balances which are materially smaller at the balance sheet than the usual amount outstanding, i.e. where it appears that the balance has been specially reduced at the year end to escape the auditor's attention;

(h) accounts of debtors known to have connection with the client company or its officers (i.e. accounts of "related parties");

(i) accounts which reveal unusually favourable (to the debtor) "terms of trade" in terms of discounts, credit period and credit limits allowed; and

(j) accounts which, when in arrear, do not appear (for any obvious reason) to be followed up by normal credit control procedures as rigorously as would be expected.

8.4 Routine audit tests

The following tests would normally be carried out by auditors on a correctly selected sample:

(a) compliance tests confirming segregation of duties as laid down in the procedures manual of the company;

(b) check despatch documents against invoices to ensure that each despatch results in a charge;

(c) check goods inwards documents to ensure that all returns result in credit notes, after authorisation;

(d) check the sequence of invoices and credit notes to ensure that these are *completely* reflected in the appropriate ledger accounts;

(e) check the calculation and extension of prices and authorisations on invoices and credit notes, and ensure that these are correctly entered in the appropriate day book;

(f) perform exhaustive tests to ensure that all bad debts written off represent genuine losses, having been authorised at the appropriate level;

(g) prepare independently a debtors' ledger control account, and agree with the schedule of debtors extracted from the ledger.

8.5 Provision for bad and doubtful debts

The circularisation of debtors provides only a portion of verification of value of debtors. To verify the value of debtors and to ensure that adequate provision for bad debts is provided the auditor should:

(a) examine the client's procedure for reviewing the ledger accounts, particularly in respect of all those balances which are outstanding longer than the normal credit period;

(b) discover what action has been taken in respect of debts which he discovered in his examination to be overdue;

(c) refer to remittances received and other events occurring subsequent to balance sheet date to see whether overdue accounts have since been paid or whether the lack of any payment indicates the existence of a possible bad debt;

(d) where books of account show that debtors have paid amounts shown as outstanding on balance sheet date, test the correctness of at least a portion of the entries, from the cash received back to the individual bank deposit slip.

Where provisions for doubtful debts or bad debts are excessive the amounts involved are *reserves* rather than provisions, and should be shown as such in the balance sheet.

The stipulation that the amount by which any provision is surplus to requirements should be treated as a reserve is included in the Companies Act 1985. It is worth noting that a good deal of controversy currently surrounds the treatment of provisions in the balance sheets of banks. Regulatory bodies in the City of London, reporting during 1979 on steps which should be taken by the Bank of England to prevent a repeat of the 1974/75 crisis, have drawn attention to the tendency for banks (a) to create secret reserves, and (b) to hide movements on such reserves, by manipulating provisions allegedly required for bad and doubtful debts. The potential for such manipulation is prodigious, and this would easily be concealed in a balance sheet since provisions are simply "netted off" against the overall figures for overdrafts and other debtors.

9.0 CONTINGENT LIABILITIES

The Companies Acts require contingent liabilities to be disclosed by way of note, if material. The auditor should bear in mind that directors may be tempted to show real liabilities as contingent, to avoid having any effect on the published accounts. In this context it is vital that the Subsequent Events Programme (see Chapter 6, section 2.0) should pay particular attention to the possibility of contingent liabilities having crystallised after the accounting reference date.

Three of the most frequently encountered contingent liabilities, which may therefore be safely cited as examples in examinations, are:

(a) pending litigation (see Chapter 6, section 5.0);

(b) guarantees provided by the client company, covering the debts of others (e.g. individual directors; holding, subsidiary or associated companies); and

(c) bills receivable discounted with the company's bankers prior to the accounting reference date, due to be met at some later date. Should the acceptor of such a bill fail to meet it on the due date, the bank will have recourse to the client company.

10.0 PROVISIONS AND RESERVES

A certain amount of confusion surrounds the correct use of the terms "provision" and "reserve". It is important to realise that the Companies Act provides comprehensive definitions, which may be broadly paraphrased as follows. A provision is any amount set aside to provide for:

(a) depreciation (see section 13.0 below);

(b) renewals;

(c) diminution in value of assets; and

(d) a known liability, the amount of which cannot be determined with substantial accuracy.

The Companies Act 1985 also states that sums set aside for the purpose of equalising tax charges (deferred taxation) shall not be considered to be provisions.

The definition of "reserve" is simple: any amount set aside which is not a provision is automatically a reserve. "Capital reserves" may be regarded as those which:

(a) have been created by the directors, at their discretion, for any specific purpose, thus ensuring that they will not be distributed by way of dividend; or

(b) the law has established for the purpose of maintaining a company's capital, and which cannot therefore be distributed by way of dividend.

Share premium account and capital redemption reserve are the two such reserves identified by law. Should current cost accounting be embodied in company law, the current cost reserve (or capital maintenance reserve) will undoubtedly feature as a statutory requirement. The law on capital maintenance and divisible profits has been affected by the Companies Act 1985, dealt with in Chapter 7.

In anticipation of regularised current cost accounting, many companies (in some cases for the past thirty to forty years—e.g. Philips, Unilever, ICI and Pilkingtons) have adopted the practice of setting aside out of profits otherwise available for distribution, sums required to meet the increased cost of replacing their major fixed assets. It is important to realise that these sums are reserves and not provisions: *the replacement of an asset with another asset* should never be confused with expenditure on the repair or renewal of an existing asset designed to restore it, as closely as possible, to its original condition. The latter type of expenditure, if provided for, would feature under item (b) of the definition of "provision" given above.

11.0   VERIFICATION OF FIXED ASSETS

11.1   Internal control

As the first step in any verification programme, the auditor will pay attention to the company's system of internal control, and in this context reference should be made to Chapter 2, section 6.0. Considerations relating to valuation, existence and ownership, the distinction between capital and revenue expenditure, and the importance of authorisation, have already been dealt with in this chapter.

11.2   Asset registers

An asset register will normally contain the following information for each asset:

   (a)   supplier's name;

   (b)   date of purchase;

   (c)   original cost;

   (d)   estimated useful life;

   (e)   estimated residual value;

   (f)   summary of expenditure on repairs to date;

   (g)   estimated replacement cost entered at annual intervals;

   (h)   details of eventual disposal.

The sections which follow deal with specific assets, depreciation and the importance of physical inspection.

12.0   PARTICULAR ASSETS

In addition to the matters already covered, the following special points may provide a brief but useful summary of documents to be examined and procedures to be observed in relation to particular assets:

   (a)   Freehold property:

      (i) title deeds or Land Registry certificates;

      (ii) architects' certificates for partly completed work;

      (iii) insurance cover—adequacy.

(b) Leasehold property:

      (i) lease or Land Registry certificates;

      (ii) provisions for dilapidations;

      (iii) compliance with covenants;

      (iv) insurance cover—adequacy.

(c) Plant and machinery, furniture, fixtures and fittings:

      (i) distinction between capital and revenue expenditure;

      (ii) asset registers.

(d) Motor vehicles: as (c) above; check registration documents.

(e) Loose tools:

      (i) accounting and control procedures;

      (ii) method of valuation or depreciation.

(f) Patents:

      (i) examine patent and assignment, which can be granted only to an individual (perhaps employee), who will assign to company;

      (ii) payment of renewal fees;

      (iii) life sixteen years from grant of patent;

      (iv) accounting for royalties receivable.

(g) Copyright:

      (i) document of title;

      (ii) assignment, if purchased;

      (iii) life is author's life plus fifty years.

(h) Trade marks:

      (i) certificate issued by Patent Office;

      (ii) assignment, if purchased;

      (iii) reasonableness of design costs capitalised;

      (iv) payment of renewal fees.

(i) Goodwill:

      (i) in a company situation, will arise on purchase of a business;

      (ii) examine contract and allocation of purchase price to assets;

(iii) normally remains in accounts at cost (but write off now prescribed under Companies Act 1985; see Chapter 7).

(j) Trade investments:

(i) share certificate;

(ii) basis of valuation;

(iii) if quoted, show at cost with market value shown by note;

(iv) if unquoted, cost with directors' valuation by note.

13.0 DEPRECIATION

13.1 Assessment and periodic revision

(a) Assessment of depreciation involves four factors:

(i) historical cost of asset;

(ii) probable value realisable on ultimate disposal;

(iii) anticipated useful commercial life to the undertaking;

(iv) current and probable (eventual) replacement cost.

(b) Periodic revision of depreciation is required for:

(i) prolongation of useful life due to exceptional maintenance expenditure;

(ii) curtailment due to excessive use;

(iii) obsolescence not allowed for in the original estimate of the commercially useful life of the asset.

13.2 Methods of providing depreciation

There are several methods of apportioning depreciation between the financial periods which constitute the anticipated useful life of the asset:

(a) The *straight-line method* (computed by providing each year a fixed proportion of the cost of the asset) spreads the provision equally over the period of anticipated use.

(b) The *reducing balance method* spreads the provision by annual instalments of diminishing amount, computed by taking a fixed percentage of the book value of the assets as reduced by previous provisions. It involves heavier charges in the earlier years and relatively light charges in the later years.

(c) A third method, known as the *sinking fund method*, by which fixed instalments are provided and invested which, with compound interest, will accumulate to the cost of the asset by the end of its useful life.

(d) A fourth method, is the *renewals reserve method*. Round sums, not necessarily computed by reference to the useful lives of the assets, and sometimes determined largely by the results of the year's trading, are provided and set aside as general provisions towards meeting the cost of future renewals. This method does not accord with a strict view of depreciation and may distort the annual charges to revenue.

Whatever method is adopted must be applied consistently from year to year.

13.3   Classes of asset

Provisions should be computed on the basis mentioned below as being appropriate to the particular class of asset concerned:

(a) Freehold land: depreciation does not normally arise through use in the company's business.

(b) Buildings, plant and machinery, tools and equipment, and vehicles: use the straight-line method. If life is very short (e.g. loose tools) then revaluation is more appropriate.

(c) Leaseholds, patents, etc.: use the straight-line basis, with provision for dilapidations in case of leaseholds.

(d) Mines, oil wells, quarries; provision for depletion should be made on the basis of estimated exhaustion. If the practice is to make no provision, accounts to shareholders should say so.

Although the above notes are of a general nature, they conform with the requirements of SSAP 12 on accounting for depreciation, which should be separately studied.

14.0   PHYSICAL INSPECTION—SOME MAJOR FRAUDS

No matter how sophisticated auditing techniques become, there can never be any effective substitute for verification by means of *direct inspection*, and it is worth noting that many notorious frauds might have come to light much earlier had the auditors concerned paid more attention to this rather obvious point.

14.1   McKesson and Robbins Inc

The famous McKesson and Robbins swindle in the United States during the 1930s arose from a conspiracy between the four brothers who headed this large pharmaceutical company, to make the company appear to be far more profitable and financially more substantial than it really was. This was achieved by fabricating documentation which purported to reflect transactions that had, in fact, never taken place. The illusion was therefore created of a vast amount of trading activity which was entirely fictitious. While the auditors meticulously authenticated the transactions via the forged documentation, they were regarded by the SEC as negligent in the execution of their duties in view of their failure (a) to confirm the stock levels by direct inspection, and (b) to confirm the level of debtors by direct circularisation. These assets were overstated by no less than $25 million. These two vital procedures became mandatory for auditors of listed companies in the United States immediately following this celebrated case.

14.2   Allied Crude Vegetable Oil Refining Corporation of America

The "Great Salad Oil Swindle", exposed in 1963, provides another transatlantic example of a mammoth fraud which rested on the fabrication of paper appearances, devoid of any substance. These losses exceeded $200 million, spread over some fifty banking and other financial institutions in the United States and several European countries. The documents which purported to represent genuine stocks of vegetable oils were essentially the "warehouse certificates" issued by the American Express Corporation, who established a "field warehouse" (see section 5.0 above for an explanation of this practice) over the tank farm operated by the salad oil company. Stocktaking procedures were so haphazard, and opportunities so rife for transferring oil from one tank to another without any of the American Express officials knowing, that there was very little effective control over, nor the means of determining, actual quantities. Despite this the American Express auditors had given a clean bill of health to the system operated—they too being completely taken in by the massive charade.

The value of the warehouse certificates, of course, lay in their negotiability—for which purposes they were used by the conspirators to raise vast sums of money, with the illusory vegetable oil as security. When the fraud was eventually discovered, the book stocks of vegetable oil showed volumes considerably in excess of the total amount of such oil in the entire United States of America.

14.3   Equity Funding Corporation of America

Although in an entirely different context, the infamous case of Equity Funding demonstrates exactly the same principle. Life insurance policies were fabricated by the conspirators and sold at commercial rates to reinsurance companies, who were also frequently required to pay out capital sums on the death of fictitious persons. As the fraud continued, the volume of "phoney business" escalated, a computerised projection revealing in 1972 that by 1978 the number of insurance policies would exceed the population of the United States. Although the conspirators attempted to "dilute the fraud" by exchanging the company's shares with the shares of other, genuinely valuable, companies, one of their number "blew the whistle", and the mammoth proportions of the fraud were brought to light.

Losses were estimated at between $200 million and $300 million and damages against the auditors, spread over two or three firms, amounted to some $61 million. Although the auditors had attempted, in a half-hearted way, to obtain the independent verification which they clearly needed, their negligence was clearly established in the proceedings which followed. Confirmation letters were unwittingly circularised to "trusted" employees who had been previously forewarned by the conspirators. Share certificates were forged on a mammoth scale, and the auditors failed to confirm with the companies concerned that Equity Funding was the registered holder of the shares in question.

The full details of the Equity Funding and "salad oil" cases are included in the author's book *Auditing Today* (Prentice-Hall), on which this text is based.

14.4   Giant Stores Corporation

The fourth United States fraud which is worth recounting in emphasising the importance of independent confirmation is more recent. It relates to the Giant Stores Corporation, and the following information is taken from the October 1979 issue of the *Auditing and Accounting Newsletter* of Deloitte, Haskins and Sells:

Background
The Giant Stores Corporation went public in 1969. Between 1969 and 1973, the corporation expanded the number of its outlets from 6 to 43. To finance this expansion, it made three public stock offerings and took up substantial loans. In order to obtain finance for further expansion, management considered it imperative that Giant's results for the year ended 29th January 1972 met market expectations. The management of the corporation suppressed an anticipated loss for the year of $2.5 million and the corporation published a profit of $1.2 million on a turnover of $64 million. The major part of the loss was concealed by creating false credits from suppliers totalling $1 million (which were deducted from trade creditors), and by suppressing $1.4 million of suppliers' invoices at the end of the year.

The deficiencies in the audit procedures
The deficiencies in the audit procedures which were identified in the SEC report are summarised below:

INADEQUATE THIRD-PARTY CONFIRMATION PROCEDURES
The majority of the false credits arose in respect of a few major suppliers and were supported only by the internal documentation of the client. The explanations offered by the client's management were often incomplete and were the subject of frequent change. In one instance, three different contradictory explanations were offered to support an amount of $257,000.

The auditors did not insist on sending written confirmations to third parties but, with the permission of the client, agreed a number of balances by telephone.

In each instance, the client telephoned the supplier and passed the telephone to the auditor. In at least one case, it subsequently became apparent that the person with whom the balance was "confirmed" was an imposter.

ACCEPTANCE OF UNRELIABLE REPRESENTATIONS FROM MANAGEMENT
The audit was conducted under considerable duress. Giant asked for the removal of the partner, and senior management physically and orally threatened the audit staff. Management offered inconsistent explanations of major adjusting items. Despite these circumstances, considerable audit reliance was placed on management representations in preference to, and almost to the exclusion of, third party confirmations.

FAILURE TO RECOGNISE AN ACCUMULATION OF IRREGULARITIES
The auditors accepted inconclusive audit evidence for a series of accounting adjustments. Several of the adjustments were material to the appreciation of the

financial statements, and others were material in total. The auditors failed to appreciate the cumulative significance of the contentious items, and consequently they applied neither sufficient nor adequate verification procedures to ensure that no material mis-statement was present in the financial statements.

INADEQUATE ADJUSTMENT OF ERRORS

The work conducted on accruals by the auditors indicated a substantial understatement of trade liabilities at the year end. The test on suppliers' statements at the year end produced an estimated understatement of liability of $290,000, and an examination of invoices received after the year end indicated an understatement of liability of $500,000. Both these amounts were recorded in the working papers. The adjustment subsequently agreed with the client was $260,000. The auditors considered this figure was adequate because, in their opinion, the client had valued stock conservatively, and thus the "net effect" was acceptable.

The SEC heavily criticised the practice of "trading off" adjustments to the financial statements. The report stated that each accounting area must be considered in isolation and stated in the financial statements at a figure consistent with that indicated by the audit evidence obtained.

STRUCTURE OF THE AUDIT TEAM

The responsibilities of the audit team were ill-defined. The initial audit team did not have the specialised experience to test adequately all the accounting areas, primarily stock and creditors.

With the existing staff under pressure from the client, two additional partners were called in to provide specialised assistance, but this caused conflict and confusion. Eventually, when the client pressed strongly for the finalisation of the financial statements, a supervising partner was brought in. He was not fully informed of the facts of the situation by his colleagues, notably the serious doubts over the attitude and the integrity of the management. The report stated that, at a final meeting with the client, he acted more as an arbitrator than an auditor, and he expected and obtained compromises on various contentious adjustments.

Conclusions

In the light of the above, auditors should pay particular attention to the following matters:

(a) the provision of personnel of sufficient seniority and experience to staff adequately the engagement;

(b) the identification of contentious areas and adjustments that may interact to produce material mis-statements in the financial statements, and the adequate verification of the adjusting items;

(c) the requirements to obtain reliable audit evidence in each accounting area. Auditors should consider carefully the reliance that they are able to place on management representations to provide audit evidence. Where they have reason to doubt the integrity of management they must obtain increased assurance from alternative audit procedures, and these should incorporate independent verification. Where they apply third party confirmation procedures, they should ensure that they control the conduct of these procedures.

PROGRESS TEST 5

1. List those assets and liabilities which will normally be confirmed by reference to third parties. (5.0)

2. How may statistical evidence assist the execution of an analytical review? (6.0)

3. Summarise the procedures involved with debtor circularisation. (8.3)

4. Summarise the main features of verification procedures in relation to fixed assets. (11.0)

CHAPTER SIX

Verification of Assets and Liabilities (2) — Advanced Aspects

1.0 LETTERS OF REPRESENTATION

1.1 Why obtain the letter?

An audit entails not only an examination of books and documentary records, but the questioning of responsible officials.

There may be important matters of fact which are not ascertainable from the books and there are also a number of important questions which are essentially matters of opinion (e.g. obsolescence and wear and tear of plant). On points such as these the auditor is duty bound to confirm by whatever means are practicable the validity of the information and explanations which he obtains about the accounts on which he has to report. He will be obliged to give special weight to the representations made to him by the management. For this reason the auditor should request that such representations be made to him by means of a formal statement on behalf of the management in writing.

The accounts are the responsibility of the directors, and such a letter should serve to remind both management and directors of their responsibility for the overall completeness of the accounts, whilst not relieving the auditors of their own responsibility. Its purpose is twofold. Firstly, to put on record those matters of importance on which, because of their nature, it is incumbent on the auditors to obtain information, or an expression of opinion, from a source which carries high authority. Secondly, to ensure that on these matters there is no misunderstanding of the information and opinions given and as to the identity and authority of those by whom they are given.

The letter is an authoritative source of internal evidence and is therefore an important verification procedure.

1.2 Recommended procedure

For the reasons indicated, the statement should normally be obtained from the client's principal executive. There may be circumstances which indicate otherwise, for instance, when in a large company the executive responsibilities are divided. In such a case a single all-inclusive letter would be inappropriate, and it might be best to obtain separate statements from the members of the executive who are responsible for particular matters. It may be desirable, however, to obtain a general overriding letter covering all the relevant matters.

The statement should take the form of a letter on behalf of the management on the client's headed notepaper, and should be addressed to the auditors and should be signed and handed to them as close as possible to the date on which financial statements are approved. The relevant representations may either be incorporated in full in the text of the letter itself or set out in a memorandum annexed to the letter. In certain circumstances it may be desirable that any opinions should be formally recorded in the minutes of the directors.

1.3   Form of letter

(a) On the first occasion on which a representation letter is requested special care needs to be taken in drafting it and presenting it to the client. It is to be expected that the client will ask the reasons for the request. In subsequent years the form of letter should be considered in the light of any changed circumstances.

(b) If the client is a subsidiary the holding company of which is also audited by the same firm, a form of letter may have to be settled for use throughout the group. Enquiries should be made about this before suggesting alterations to the form of the subsidiaries' letter.

(c) If a standard letter is used it should be adapted to meet the circumstances of each client and should concentrate on the matters of major impact. It is important to avoid any suggestion that the letter is a matter of form only or that it is regarded by the auditors as being a mere "routine".

1.4   APC Guideline: Representations by Management

The following is the complete text of the Guideline:

Preface
This guideline should be read in conjunction with the operational and reporting standards, their related guidelines and, where applicable, legislation relating to the disclosure of information to auditors. In this context, s. 393 of the Companies Act 1985 provides that an officer of a company will be guilty of an offence where he knowingly or recklessly makes a statement (orally or in writing) to the company's auditor which is misleading, false or deceptive in a material particular. (*Issued May 1983.*)

Introduction
1.   Para 4 of the Auditing Standard "The Auditor's Operational Standard" states that "the auditor should obtain relevant and reliable audit evidence sufficient to enable him to draw reasonable conclusions therefrom". This evidence will be

obtained from many different sources. Representations by management are one such source.

2.   Oral representations will be made throughout the audit in response to specific enquiries. Whilst representations by management constitute audit evidence, the auditor should not rely solely on the unsupported oral representations of management as being sufficient reliable evidence when they relate to matters which are material to the financial statements.

3.   In most cases, oral representations can be corroborated by checking with sources independent of the enterprise or by checking with other evidence obtained by the auditor, and therefore do not need to be confirmed in writing.

4.   However, in certain cases, such as where knowledge of the facts is confined to management or where the matter is principally one of judgment and opinion, the auditor may not be able to obtain independent corroborative evidence and could not reasonably expect it to be available. In such cases, the auditor should ensure that there is no other evidence which conflicts with the representations by management and he should obtain written confirmation of the representations.

5.   Where written representations are obtained, the auditor will still need to decide whether in the circumstances these representations, together with such other audit evidence as he has obtained, are sufficient to enable him to form an unqualified opinion on the financial statements.

6.   In circumstances where the auditor prepares the financial statements for the company, it may be appropriate for the directors to acknowledge their responsibility for the financial statements when confirming their representations in writing. This is because the directors have the ultimate responsibility for ensuring the completeness and accuracy of the enterprise's accounting records and for the view shown by the financial statements.

Procedures
7.   Where oral representations by management are uncorroborated by sufficient other audit evidence and where they relate to matters which are material to the financial statements, they should be summarised in the auditor's working papers. The auditor should ensure that these representations are either formally minuted as being approved by the board of directors or included in a signed letter, addressed to the auditor, known as a "letter of representation".

8.   Because the representations are those of management, standard letters of representation may not be appropriate. In any event, management should be encouraged to participate in drafting any letter of representation or, after review and discussion, to make appropriate amendments to the auditor's draft, provided that the value of the audit evidence obtained is not thereby diminished.

9.   A letter of representation should be signed by persons whose level of authority is appropriate to the significance of the representations made—normally by one or

more of the executive directors (for example by the chief executive and the chief financial officer), on behalf of the whole board. The signatories of the letter should be fully conversant with the matters contained in it. The auditor should request that the consideration of the letter and its approval by the board for signature be minuted. He may request that he be allowed to attend the meeting at which the board is due to approve the letter. Such attendance may also be desirable where the representations are to be formally minuted, rather than included in a letter.

10. Procedures regarding written representations should be agreed at an early stage in order to reduce the possibility of the auditor being faced with a refusal by management to co-operate in providing such representations. However, management may at the outset indicate that they are not willing to sign letters of representation or to pass minutes requested by the auditor. If they do so indicate, the auditor should inform management that he will himself prepare a statement in writing setting out his understanding of the principal representations that have been made to him during the course of the audit, and he should send this statement to management with a request for confirmation that his understanding of the representations is correct.

11. If management disagrees with the auditor's statement of representations, discussions should be held to clarify the matters in doubt and, if necessary, a revised statement prepared and agreed. Should management fail to reply, the auditor should follow the matter up to try to ensure that his understanding of the position, as set out in his statement, is correct.

12. There may, however, be circumstances where the auditor is unable to obtain the written representations which he requires. This may be because of a refusal by management to co-operate, or because management properly declines to give the representations required on the grounds of its own uncertainty regarding the particular matter. In either case, if the auditor is unable to satisfy himself, he may have to conclude that he has not received all the information and explanations that he requires, and consequently may need to consider qualifying his audit report.

Groups

13. Because the directors and auditors of holding companies have responsibilities to prepare and audit respectively group financial statements, auditors should, where appropriate, obtain written representations for those financial statements as well as for the financial statements of the holding companies themselves. The way in which the auditor of the holding company obtains these representations will depend upon the pattern of delegation of managerial control and authority which can vary both between and within different groups of companies. For instance, the auditor of a holding company may be able to obtain the written representations that he requires, regarding the group financial statements, from the directors of the holding company by virtue of their involvement in the management of the subsidiaries. Alternatively, there will be circumstances where the management structure of a group dictates that the auditor of the holding

company will wish to have sight of appropriate written representations made by the directors of subsidiary companies to the auditors of those subsidiaries.

Dating

14. The formal record of representations by management should be approved on a date as close as possible to the date of the audit report and after all other work, including the review of events after the balance sheet date, has been completed. It should never be approved after the audit report since it is part of the evidence on which the auditor's opinion, expressed in his report, is based.

15. If there is a substantial delay between the approval of the formal record of representations by management and the date of the audit report, the auditor should consider whether to obtain further representations in respect of the intervening period and also whether any additional audit procedures need to be carried out, as described in the Auditing Guideline "Events after the Balance Sheet Date".

Contents and wording

16. The precise scope of the formal record of representations should be appropriate to the circumstances of each particular audit. The representations will be necessary where there are matters which are material to the financial statements, in respect of which the auditor cannot obtain independent corroborative evidence and could not reasonably expect it to be available, as indicated in para 4 above. Set out in the appendix is an example of a letter of representation together with examples of additional paragraphs which may be appropriate for inclusion in a letter of representation or in board minutes.

Appendix: examples of representations by management

Set out below is an example of a letter of representation which relates to matters which are material to financial statements prepared by an auditor for the company, and to circumstances where the auditor cannot obtain independent corroborative evidence and could not reasonably expect it to be available (see para 4 of the guideline above). It is not intended to be a standard letter because representations by management can be expected to vary not only from one enterprise to another, but also from one year to another in the case of the same audit client.

Dear Sirs,

We confirm to the best of our knowledge and belief, and having made appropriate enquiries of other directors and officials of the company, the following representations given to you in connection with your audit of the company's financial statements for the year ended 31st December . . .

1. We acknowledge as directors our responsibility for the financial statements, which you have prepared for the company. All the accounting records have been made available to you for the purpose of your audit and all the transactions undertaken by the company have been properly reflected and recorded in the accounting records. All other records and related information, including minutes of all management and shareholders' meetings, have been made available to you.

2.   The legal claim by Mr G. H. ... has been settled out of court by the company paying him £38,000. No further amounts are expected to be paid, and no similar claims by employees or former employees have been received or are expected to be received.

3.   In connection with deferred tax not provided, the following assumptions reflect the intentions and expectations of the company:

   (a)   Capital investment of £260,000 is planned over next three years.

   (b)   There are no plans to sell revalued properties.

   (c)   We are not aware of any indications that the situation is likely to change so as to necessitate the inclusion of a provision for tax payable in the financial statements.

4.   The company has had at no time during the year any arrangement, transaction or agreement to provide credit facilities (including loans, quasi loans or credit transactions) for directors nor to guarantee or provide security for such matters, except as disclosed in note 14 to the financial statements.

5.   Other than the fire damage and related insurance claims described in note 19 to the financial statements, there have been no events since the balance sheet date which necessitate revision of the figures included in the financial statements or inclusion of a note thereto. Should further material events occur, which may necessitate revision of the figures included in the financial statements or inclusion of a note thereto, we will advise you accordingly.

Yours faithfully,

Signed on behalf of the board of directors.

   The paragraphs included in the example relate to a specific set of circumstances. Set out below are some examples of additional paragraphs which, depending on the circumstances, may be appropriate for inclusion in a letter of representation or in board minutes. It is not expected that the auditor will obtain all these written representations as a matter of routine.

   (a)   There have been no breaches of the income tax regulations regarding payments to subcontractors in the construction industry which may directly or indirectly affect the view given by the financial statements.

   (b)   Having regard to the terms and conditions of sale imposed by major suppliers of goods, trade creditors include no amounts resulting from the purchase of goods on terms which include reservation of title by suppliers, other than £96,544 due to ABC plc.

   (c)   With the exception of the penalties described in note 17, we are not aware of any circumstances which could produce losses on long-term contracts.

   (d)   DEF Ltd, an associated company, is about to launch a new product which has received excellent test results. As a result, the amount of £155,000 outstanding since 6th January ... is expected to be fully recoverable.

(e) The company has guaranteed the bank overdraft of its subsidiary A Ltd but has not entered into guarantees, warranties or other financial commitments relating to its other subsidiary or associated companies.

(f) The transaction shown in the profit and loss account as extraordinary is outside the course of the company's normal business and is not expected to recur frequently or regularly.

(g) Since the balance sheet date, the company has negotiated a continuation of its bank overdraft facilities with a limit of £200,000. There have been no other events which are likely to affect the adequacy of working capital to meet foreseeable requirements in the year following the adoption of the financial statements.

(h) The indices used in the current cost financial statements for the year ... are, in our opinion, appropriate to the business of the company and have been properly applied on a consistent basis to assets and liabilities.

2.0   POST BALANCE SHEET EVENTS

2.1   Accounting for Post Balance Sheet Events (SSAP 17)

The provisions of this Statement of Standard Accounting Practice should be read in conjunction with the Explanatory Foreword to accounting Standards and need not be applied to immaterial items. The previous apply equally to financial statements prepared under the historical cost convention and to financial statements prepared under the current cost convention.

Part 1—explanatory note
1. Events arising after the balance sheet date need to be reflected in financial statements if they provide additional evidence of conditions that existed at the balance sheet date and materially affect the amounts to be included.

2. To prevent financial statements from being misleading, disclosure needs to be made by way of notes of other material events arising after the balance sheet date which provide evidence of conditions not existing at the balance sheet date. Disclosure is required where this information is necessary for a proper understanding of the financial position.

3. A post balance sheet event for the purpose of this Standard is an event which occurs between the balance sheet date and the date on which the financial statements are approved by the board of directors. It is not intended that the preliminary consideration of a matter which may lead to a decision by the board of directors in the future should fall within the scope of this Standard.

4. Events which occur after the date on which the financial statements are approved

by the board of directors do not come within the scope of this Standard. If such events are material the directors should consider publishing the relevant information so that users of financial statements are not misled.

5.   The process involved in the approval of financial statements by the directors will vary depending on the management structure and procedures followed in preparing and finalising financial statements. However, the date of approval will normally be the date of the board meeting at which the financial statements are formally approved, or in respect of unincorporated enterprises the corresponding date. In respect of group accounts, the date of approval is the date the group accounts are formally approved by the board of directors of the holding company.

CLASSIFICATION OF POST BALANCE SHEET EVENTS

6.   Events occurring after the balance sheet date may be classified into two categories: "adjusting events" and "non-adjusting events".

7.   Adjusting events are events which provide additional evidence relating to conditions existing at the balance sheet date. They require changes in amounts to be included in financial statements. Examples of adjusting events are given in the Appendix.

8.   Some events occurring after the balance sheet date, such as a deterioration in the operating results and in the financial position may indicate a need to consider whether it is appropriate to use the going concern concept in the preparation of financial statements. Consequently these may fall to be treated as adjusting events.

9.   Non-adjusting events are events which arise after the balance sheet date and concern conditions which did not exist at that time. Consequently they do not result in changes in amounts in financial statements. They may, however, be of such materiality that their disclosure is required by way of notes to ensure that financial statements are not misleading. Examples of non-adjusting events which may require disclosure are given in the Appendix.

10. Disclosure would be required of the reversal or maturity after the year end of transactions entered into before the year end, the substance of which was primarily to alter the appearance of the company's balance sheet. Such alterations include those commonly known as "window dressing".

11. There are certain post balance sheet events which, because of statutory requirements or customary accounting practice, are reflected in financial statements and so fall to be treated as adjusting events. These include proposed dividends, amounts appropriated to reserves, the effects of changes in taxation and dividends receivable from subsidiary and associated companies.

DISCLOSURE IN FINANCIAL STATEMENTS

12. Separate disclosure of adjusting events is not normally required as they do no more than provide additional evidence in support of items in financial

statements.

13. In determining which non-adjusting events are of sufficient materiality to require disclosure, regard should be had to all matters which are necessary to enable users of financial statements to assess the financial position.

Part 2—definition of terms

14. *Financial statements* are balance sheets, profit and loss accounts, statements of source and application of funds, notes and other statements, which collectively are intended to give a true and fair view of financial position and profit or loss.

15. *Company* includes any enterprise which comes within the scope of statements of standard accounting practice.

16. *Directors* include the corresponding officers of organisations which do not have directors.

17. *The date on which the financial statements are approved by the board of directors* is the date the board of directors formally approves a set of documents as the financial statements. In respect of unincorporated enterprises, the date of approval is the corresponding date. In respect of group accounts, the date of approval is the date when the group accounts are formally approved by the board of directors of the holding company.

18. *Post balance sheet events* are those events, both favourable and unfavourable, which occur between the balance sheet date and the date on which the financial statements are approved by the board of directors.

19. *Adjusting events* are post balance sheet events which provide additional evidence of conditions existing at the balance sheet date. They include events which because of statutory or conventional requirements are reflected in financial statements.

20. *Non-adjusting events* are post balance sheet events which concern conditions which did not exist at the balance sheet date.

Part 3—standard accounting practice

21. Financial statements should be prepared on the basis of conditions existing at the balance sheet date.

22. A material post balance sheet event requires changes in the amounts to be included in financial statements where:

    (a) it is an adjusting event; or

    (b) it indicates that application of the going concern concept to the whole or a material part of the company is not appropriate.

23. A material post balance sheet event should be disclosed where:

(a) it is a non-adjusting event of such materiality that its non-disclosure would affect the ability of the users of financial statements to reach a proper understanding of the financial position; or

(b) it is the reversal or maturity after the year end of a transaction entered into before the year end, the substance of which was primarily to alter the appearance of the company's balance sheet.

24. In respect of each post balance sheet event which is required to be disclosed under para 23 above, the following information should be stated by way of notes in financial statements:

(a) the nature of the event; and

(b) an estimate of the financial effect, or a statement that it is not practicable to make such an estimate.

25. The estimate of the financial effect should be disclosed before taking account of taxation, and the taxation implications should be explained where necessary for a proper understanding of the financial position.

26. The date on which the financial statements are approved by the board of directors should be disclosed in the financial statements.

DATE FROM WHICH EFFECTIVE

27. The accounting practices set out in this statement should be adopted as soon as possible and regarded as standard in respect of financial statements relating to accounting periods beginning on or after 1st September 1980.

Part 4—compliance with international accounting standard no. 10 "Contingencies and Events occurring after the Balance Sheet Date"

28. The requirements of International Accounting Standard No. 10 "Contingencies and Events occurring after the Balance Sheet Date" concerning post balance sheet events accord very closely with the content of the UK and Irish Accounting Standard No. 17 "Accounting for Post Balance Sheet Events" and accordingly compliance with SSAP 17 will ensure compliance with IAS 10 in all material respects so far as post balance sheet events are concerned.

Appendix

This Appendix is for general guidance and does not form part of the Statement of Standard Accounting Practice. The examples are merely illustrative and the lists are not exhaustive.

The examples listed distinguish between those normally classified as adjusting events and as non-adjusting events. However, in exceptional circumstances, to accord with the prudence concept, an adverse event which would normally be classified as non-adjusting may need to be reclassified as adjusting. In such circumstances, full disclosure of the adjustment would be required.

ADJUSTING EVENTS

The following are examples of post balance sheet events which normally should be classified as adjusting events:

(a) *Fixed assets.* The subsequent determination of the purchase price or of the proceeds of sale of assets purchased or sold before the year end.

(b) *Property.* A valuation which provides evidence of a permanent diminution in value.

(c) *Investments.* The receipt of a copy of the financial statements or other information in respect of an unlisted company which provides evidence of a permanent diminution in the value of a long-term investment.

(d) *Stocks and work in progress:*

    (i) The receipt of proceeds of sales after the balance sheet date or other evidence concerning the net realisable value of stocks.

    (ii) The receipt of evidence that the previous estimate of accrued profit on a long-term contract was materially inaccurate.

(e) *Debtors.* The renegotiation of amounts owing by debtors, or the insolvency of a debtor.

(f) *Dividends receivable.* The declaration of dividends by subsidiaries and associated companies relating to periods prior to the balance sheet date of the holding company.

(g) *Taxation.* The receipt of information regarding rates of taxation.

(h) *Claims.* Amounts received or receivable in respect of insurance claims which were in the course of negotiation at the balance sheet date.

(i) *Discoveries.* The discovery of errors or frauds which show that the financial statements were incorrect.

NON-ADJUSTING EVENTS

The following are examples of post balance sheet events which normally should be classified as non-adjusting events:

(a) Mergers and acquisitions.

(b) Reconstructions and proposed reconstructions.

(c) Issues of shares and debentures.

(d) Purchases and sales of fixed assets and investments.

(e) Losses of fixed assets or stocks as a result of a catastrophe such as fire or flood.

(f) Opening new trading activities or extending existing trading activities.

(g) Closing a significant part of the trading activities if this was not anticipated at the year end.

(h) Decline in the value of property and investments held as fixed assets, if it can be demonstrated that the decline occurred after the year end.

(i) Changes in rates of foreign exchange.

    (j)   Government action, such as nationalisation.

    (k)   Strikes and other labour disputes.

    (l)   Augmentation of pension benefits.

2.2   Comment on SSAP 17 and the APC Guideline

It is surprising that so much time elapsed before the implementation of a definitive standard on what, after all, must be one of the most controversial of accounting problems. One of the most contentious aspects of SSAP 17, however, undoubtedly lies in its suggestion that "post balance sheet events", as defined, are those events which take place between the accounting date and the date on which the directors approve the accounts. This means that anything happening after the latter date would not be classified as a post balance sheet event—and this suggestion is nothing short of a misguided attempt to change the meaning of words, since *all* events following the accounting date must, by definition, be post balance sheet events. It may be that the imposition of a "backstop" date in this context represents an attempt primarily to curtail the liability of auditors.

The American SAS 1 more sensibly divides the post balance sheet period between

    (a)   the phase between the accounting date and the date on which the auditors complete their fieldwork—a period of *primary* audit responsibility, to which the usual rules of adjusting and non-adjusting accounting treatment would apply; and

    (b)   the period after the completion of audit fieldwork—a period of *secondary* audit responsibility, during which adjustments would arise only on the basis of information which reaches the auditors' attention. During this phase no active investigative duty is imposed upon them.

Should the issue ever be tested in the courts or in any other arena in which public expectation of auditors may be gauged, it is likely that auditors would be regarded as having a duty to make known to all readers of accounts the effect upon those accounts of all material subsequent events—irrespective of whether those events took place before or after the approval of the accounts by the directors.

This point has recently been clarified somewhat by the Auditing Practices Committee. Issue No. 16 of *True & Fair* reported that the APC had taken counsel's opinion on the matter, following which the following Guideline was issued:

Auditing Guideline: Events after the Balance Sheet Date

PREFACE
This guideline is intended to clarify the responsibilities of the auditor for examining and reporting on events which occur after the date of the balance sheet. It also gives guidance on the procedures for the audit of events after the balance sheet date, and on the dating of the audit report. Counsel's opinion on the dating of audit reports was obtained before the guideline was developed. Counsel has subsequently confirmed that this guideline is in accordance with the relevant statutory provisions and legal principles and that he approves it accordingly.

The guideline is supplementary to and should be read in conjunction with the auditor's operational and reporting standards and related guidelines.

INTRODUCTION AND SCOPE

1. This guideline is written in the context of the audit of limited companies. However, its principles apply to the audit of other enterprises whose financial statements are intended to give a true and fair view. In other circumstances, the auditor will be guided by the terms of his particular appointment or by relevant legislation.

2. In the absence of specific provisions to the contrary, either in legislation or in the auditor's terms of appointment, the general principle holds that the auditor's responsibility to his client extends to the date on which he signs his audit report. Further, he may retain some responsibility after that date as described in this guideline. It is for this reason that the auditor should not confine himself to those events after the balance sheet date which are defined in Statement of Standard Accounting Practice No. 17 as "post balance sheet events", i.e. those events both favourable and unfavourable which occur between the balance sheet date and the date on which the financial statements are approved by the board of directors.

DATING OF THE AUDIT REPORT

3. The auditor should always date his audit report. The date used should, generally, be that on which he signs his report on the financial statements. The auditor should plan his work so that, wherever practicable, his report is dated as close as possible to the date of approval of the financial statements by the directors. If for administrative reasons, final copies of the financial statements are not available at the date that the auditor declares, to the directors, that he is willing to sign his audit report, he may use that date, provided the delay in preparation of final copies is only of short duration. An example of such administrative reasons would be the non-availability, through illness or overseas location, of directors to sign the financial statements on behalf of the company.

4. The auditor's responsibility is to report on the financial statements as presented by the directors. Legally, such statements do not exist until they have been approved by the directors. It follows that the auditor can never date his report earlier than the date on which the complete financial statements were approved by the directors. Before signing his report, the auditor should obtain evidence that the financial statements have been approved by the directors. Statement of Standard Accounting Practice No. 17 requires disclosure of the date on which the directors approved the financial statements.

5. At the date on which the financial statements are approved by the directors, they do not have to be in the precise printed or typewritten form submitted to members. However, the auditor should satisfy himself that the approved financial statements are complete in all material respects. Accordingly, the financial statements approved by the directors should not leave unresolved any matters which require exercise of judgment or discretion (although they may omit items which merely require mechanical calculation: for example, the

provision of a dividend at a rate already agreed by the directors). As compliance with the Companies Act and Statements of Standard Accounting Practice may require the exercise of judgment or discretion, financial statements which do not take account of these matters cannot be regarded as complete in all material respects.

ACTION UP TO THE DATE OF THE AUDIT REPORT

6.   The auditor should take steps, as described in para 13, to obtain reasonable assurance in respect of all significant events up to the date of his report. He should ensure that any such significant events are, where appropriate, accounted for or disclosed in the financial statements. If not, he should consider whether to qualify his report.

ACTION AFTER THE DATE OF THE AUDIT REPORT

7.   After the date of the audit report the auditor does not have a duty to search for evidence of post balance sheet events. However, if before the general meeting at which the financial statements are laid before the members the auditor becomes aware of information, from sources either within or outside the company, which might have led him to give a different audit opinion had he possessed the information at the date of his report, he should discuss the matter with the directors. He should then consider whether the financial statements should be amended by the directors. If the directors are unwilling to take action which the auditor considers necessary to inform the members of the changed situation, the auditor should consider exercising his rights under s. 387 of the Companies Act 1985 to make a statement at the general meeting at which the financial statements are laid before the members. He should also consider taking legal advice on his position. The auditor does not have a statutory right to communicate directly in writing with the members. (Where he wishes to resign or where it is proposed to remove him, s. 390 of the Companies Act 1985 enables him to communicate in writing with the members via the company.)

8.   If the directors wish to amend the previously approved financial statements after the auditor has signed his report but before they had been sent to the members, the auditor will need to consider whether the proposed amendments affect his report. His report, revised if necessary, should not be dated before the date on which the amended financial statements are approved by the directors. The auditor should take steps, as described in para 13, to obtain reasonable assurance in respect of all significant events up to the date on his report on the amended financial statements.

9.   Where, after the financial statements have been sent to the members, the directors wish to prepare and approve an amended set of financial statements to lay before the members in general meeting, the auditor should perform the steps described in para 13 before making his report on the amended financial statements. In this latter report he should refer to the original financial statements and his report on them.

10.   If after the general meeting the auditor becomes aware of information which

suggests that the financial statements which were laid before that meeting are wrong, he should inform the directors. He should ascertain how the directors intend to deal with the situation, in particular whether they intend to communicate with the members. Where, in the auditor's opinion, the directors are not dealing correctly with the situation, he should consider taking legal advice on his position.

PROCEDURES FOR THE AUDIT OF EVENTS AFTER THE BALANCE SHEET DATE

11. Certain events and transactions occurring after the balance sheet date are examined by the auditor as part of his normal verification work on the balance sheet. For example, he may check cash received from certain debtors or the amounts realised from the sale of stock after the year end. In addition, the auditor should carry out audit procedures which are described as a "review of events after the balance sheet date".

12. The objective of the review of events after the balance sheet date is to obtain reasonable assurance that all such material events have been identified and, where appropriate, either disclosed or accounted for in the financial statements.

13. The review should consist of discussions with management relating to, and may also include consideration of:

    (a) procedures taken by management to ensure that all events after the balance sheet date have been identified, considered and properly evaluated as to their effect on the financial statements;

    (b) any management accounts and relevant accounting records;

    (c) profit forecasts and cash-flow projections, for the new period;

    (d) known "risk" areas and contingencies, whether inherent in the nature of the business or revealed by previous audit experience;

    (e) minutes of shareholders', directors' and management meetings and correspondence and memoranda relating to items included in the minutes;

    (f) relevant information which has come to his attention, from sources outside the enterprise including public knowledge, of competitors, suppliers and customers.

    This review should be updated to a date as near as practicable to that of the audit report by making enquiries of management and considering the need to carry out further tests.

CONTINGENCIES

14. As part of his review of events after the balance sheet date, the auditor should consider the existence of contingencies and their treatment in the financial statements. Statement of Standard Accounting Practice No. 18 "Accounting for Contingencies" requires accrual, or except where the possibility of loss is remote, the disclosure of material contingent losses, and the disclosure of material contingent gains only if it is probable that the gain will be realised. The auditor will need to use his judgement in determining "remoteness" and "probability"

in individual cases. He should pay particular regard to the different treatment required by the Standard, on grounds of prudence, for contingent gains on the one hand and contingent losses on the other.

WORKING PAPERS AND MANAGEMENT REPRESENTATIONS

15. The audit working papers should contain a record of the work carried out to identify events after the balance sheet date. Where discussions have taken place with the management regarding matters arising from the review of events after the balance sheet date, a note of the discussions should be retained by the auditor. The auditor may wish to obtain formal management representations about events after the balance sheet date or the fact that there have not been any. If such representations are obtained, they should be dated as close as possible to the date of the audit report.

GROUPS

16. When the review of events after the balance sheet date is made in respect of consolidated financial statements, the auditor of the holding company will need to have regard to the work carried out in this area by the auditors of subsidiaries. In normal circumstances, audited financial statements of the subsidiaries will be available to him at the time he signs his report on the consolidated financial statements, and the auditors of the subsidiaries will have carried out a review of the events up to the date of their reports. The auditor of the holding company will need to ensure that appropriate audit procedures are carried out to identify events after the balance sheet date which are of significance to the group between the dates of the reports of the auditors of subsidiaries and the date of his own report. Such audit procedures can include the performance by him of the steps, described in para 13, in the context of the group as a whole. They may also include the performance of updated reviews by the auditors of subsidiary companies.

17. The auditor of the holding company may wish to obtain management representations from its directors, not only in respect of the company but also in respect of the group. It is conceivable, for instance, that the holding company may be aware of, or have instigated, events which have not been communicated to the management of the subsidiaries.

2.3   Liabilities

Where a liability, or a contingent liability, existed on the balance sheet date, it cannot be ignored in the accounts merely because the amount was unknown or uncertain on that date. An estimate is normally needed and for this purpose guidance may be obtained from developments which have taken place since the balance sheet date.

Where there have been changes in taxation since the balance sheet date, which affect the amounts to be set aside for taxation on the basis of the profits up to that date, it will be necessary to take the new taxation position into account if significant figures are to be shown in respect of the charge for corporation tax.

2.4   Fixed assets

In general the balance sheet statement of fixed assets as on the balance sheet date will remain unaffected by events occurring after that date. The disposal or destruction of assets or the acquisition of new assets are not relevant to the position as it then existed. They are later happenings which fall to be dealt with in the next period together with their related matters, such as the receipt of sale proceeds, the collection of insurance claims, or the financing of new acquisitions.

Subsequent events may, however, be of assistance in deciding the amount to be included in the balance sheet where the amount was in doubt on the balance sheet date, for example, where an asset has been acquired and the purchase consideration had still to be ascertained at that date, although it became settled later.

2.5   Debtors

Some of the debts owing to a business on the balance sheet date may have to be estimated because the amounts thereof had not been agreed on that date. Guidance may be obtained from developments after the balance sheet date. The more usual problem in relation to debtors is that of deciding the extent to which the amounts owing by them should be regarded as realisable. Normal accounting practice is to estimate, by reference to all the available information, including that relating to events occurring after the balance sheet date, the extent to which it may be necessary to recognise that on the balance sheet date the debts had a realisable value in the ordinary course of business less than the amount at which they were carried in the books and to make provision accordingly.

2.6   Stock in trade

Stock in trade is held for realisation in the ordinary course of business and is therefore normally shown in the balance sheet at the lower of cost or net realisable value. Hence an estimate of market value is required as on the balance sheet date, in order to decide whether a deduction should be made from the cost of stock because, on the balance sheet date, it had a market value lower than cost. Normal accounting practice is to make this estimate by reference to all the available information, including changes in selling prices since the balance sheet date, so far as the information is of assistance in determining the market value of the stock in the ordinary course of business on the balance sheet date.

2.7   Investments

Investments held as current assets are normally viewed as being capable of realisation on the balance sheet date. Subsequent changes in market value are therefore not normally relevant for balance sheet purposes.

2.8   Foreign exchange

Where rates of exchange have altered after the balance sheet date the alterations would normally be disregarded unless the rates of exchange on the balance sheet date were not realistic and the amounts affected are material.

2.9   The "subsequent events" audit programme

Audit management

Current auditing examination questions often concern what we might call "audit management", a subject to which professional practices are paying increasing attention. In its fullest sense this covers a substantial range of matters, including the use of checklists, standardisation of working schedules, questionnaires, systems documentation, confirmations, letters and reports, sampling and review procedures, as well as the organised training which necessarily accompanies the above. In essence, the phrase "audit management" encapsulates the art of performing an audit

(a) *conscientiously*, without material omission, and hence with minimum risk of liability;

(b) *profitably*, and

(c) as *rapidly* as is compatible with (a) and (b) above, so as not to cause any delay in the presentation of accounts to shareholders.

Elaborating on the latter objective, although it is generally accepted that the earliest possible publication of the accounts materially enhances their value to all interested parties, there is a certain conflict which should not be overlooked: this lies in the extraordinary usefulness to the auditor of the period between the balance sheet date and the signing of the accounts. Events which take place during this period may be highly instructive as to the true position at the end of the financial period in question, and a shortening of this period may therefore be correspondingly disadvantageous from the point of view of accuracy.

Format of the programme

In order to make optimum use of the post balance sheet period it is preferable that a formal, but flexible, *written programme* be used rather than the haphazard approach of leaving matters to the intuition of the audit clerks (an attribute for which, generally, they are not famous). Such a standard programme should be divided into *four* stages, and would normally commence with the rather obvious test of *year-end cut-off arrangements*; these tests would ensure, on the evidence of

(a) subsequently recorded book entries,

(b) independently received documents (from customers and suppliers), and

(c) movements of goods in and out of stores,

that balance sheet quantities had been determined on a valid basis, consistent with that used for arriving at purchases and sales respectively.

Stage two comprises a *comparison of business activity levels* before and after the year end. Normally this comparison would focus on the monthly totals for sales, purchases, receipts and payments and, if available, would also include the results of operations. Any unexplained material discrepancies would be thoroughly investigated.

The *third stage* involves *formal discussions* with senior executives of the client company (during which full notes must be taken) on a wide range of post balance sheet matters, including:

(a) current market conditions, the effect of new products and changes in competition;

(b) changes in selling prices of company products;

(c) significant variations in production and other costs;

(d) subsequent bookings/cancellations of sales orders, and losses of major customers;

(e) capital expenditure commitments;

(f) new borrowings and share or loan issues;

(g) liabilities (e.g. guarantees) in dispute and pending lawsuits; and

(h) changes in accounting and financial policy.

Minutes of all post balance sheet board meetings would be carefully examined in the course of this stage.

The *final stage* of the programme involves a *thorough review* of findings to date, so that decisions may be reached on any necessary adjustments in the light of subsequent events, and these should be discussed in detail with the directors.

It should be stressed that the above is little more than an outline of the enquiries which may lead to adjustment of the draft accounts. Its adaptation to meet the particular situation is therefore essential.

3.0   THE CONCEPT OF MATERIALITY IN ACCOUNTS

3.1   Introduction

The use of the word "material" in relation to accounting matters is intended to give scope to a reasonably wide interpretation according to the variety of circumstances which can arise. It is not possible or desirable, therefore, to give a precise definition of such an expression. By literal definition the adjective "material" can vary in meaning from "significant" to "essential". In an accounting sense, however, a matter is material if its non-disclosure, mis-statement or omission would be likely to distort the view given by the accounts or other statement under consideration.

3.2   General accounting requirements

The principle of materiality is and has always been fundamental to the whole process of accountancy, and is not therefore confined to statutory requirements. The whole process of preparing accounts consists of the aggregation, classification and presentation of all the transactions in such a way as to give a true and fair view of the results for a period and of the position at a specified date. Each of these processes involves the application of the principle of materiality. Questions of materiality arise in simple receipts and payments accounts or detailed profit and loss accounts as they do in any other kind of accounts.

3.3 Interpretation

The interpretation of what is "material" is a matter for the exercise of professional judgment based on experience and the requirement to give a true and fair view. Some general considerations are set out below, but their application will depend upon the context in which a matter falls to be judged.

3.4 Application

The question of materiality can arise in various circumstances, including whether or not:

(a) any item should be disclosed:

    (i) by description in an omnibus item;

    (ii) separately;

    (iii) as an important reservation or a matter of deliberate emphasis in presentation (e.g. profit of the year before deducting special loss);

(b) an error or oversight needs correction;

(c) a method of computation, basis or formula properly allows for relevant factors.

The application of the term "material" to any item will include consideration of:

(a) the amount itself, in relation to:

    (i) the overall view of the accounts;

    (ii) the total of which it forms or should form a part;

    (iii) associated items (whether in the profit and loss account or in the balance sheet);

    (iv) the corresponding amounts in previous years;

(b) the description, including questions of emphasis;

(c) the presentation and context;

(d) any statutory requirements for disclosure.

Materiality can be considered only in relative terms. In a small business £500 may be material, whereas £1 million may not be material in classifying the expenditure of a very large undertaking, especially as too much elaboration could obscure the true and fair view. Those responsible for preparing and auditing accounts have to decide which, out of the many facts available to them, are the ones that have a real bearing on the true and fair view which the accounts must give. In some circumstances, a difference of about 10% might be acceptable, but in other circumstances a difference as low as 3% might be too much. While percentage comparisons can, properly used, constitute useful broad guides, it must be kept in mind that they are no more than rough rules of thumb, and should not be applied indiscriminately without regard to particular circumstances.

3.5   Context—precision v. latitude

An item may be material, in either a general or a particular context. The general context refers to the true and fair view given by the statement as a whole. The particular context relates to the total of which an item forms or should form part and any directly associated items. If an item is not material in the general context, the degree of latitude acceptable in the particular context may depend upon its nature. There is an important distinction between cases where the amount at issue is arrived at on the basis of assumption and exercise of judgment and those where it is capable of precise and objective determination.

On the one hand, there are items such as depreciation where some measure of arbitrary assessment can be inherent in determining the amount to be written off in any one year. A margin of error which is high in relation to the item itself might be acceptable, if it is acceptable when viewed in the context of the profit and of the associated balance sheet item. On the other hand, items such as directors' emoluments, audit fees and investment income may have a particular interest or importance to shareholders, so that an error which might be trivial in the general context, and indeed may not be large in relation to the item itself, might nevertheless be considered material. It is relevant to observe that these items are usually capable of precise measurement, so that any departure from the exact figure would call for some justification. Indeed, in the case of directors' emoluments, the directors' fiduciary relationship inhibits any latitude in this respect.

3.6   Miscellaneous factors

(a) *Degree of approximation.* The degree of estimation or approximation which is unavoidably inherent in arriving at the amount of any item may be a factor in deciding on materiality. Examples include contingency provisions, stock and work in progress, and taxation provisions.

(b) *Losses or low profits.* The use of the profit figure as a point of comparison tends to be vitiated when the profits are abnormally low or where there is a loss; when judging the materiality of individual items in the profit and loss account, in such cases the more normal dimensions of the business have to be considered.

(c) *Relative materiality.* The view given by accounts may sometimes be affected by the trend of profit, or turnover, and of various expense items. An inaccuracy which might not otherwise be judged to be material could have the effect of reversing a trend, or turning a profit into a loss, or creating or eliminating the margin of solvency in a balance sheet. Where an item affects such a critical point in accounts, then its materiality has to be viewed in that narrower context.

Materiality is a relative factor and each case must be looked at on its individual merits. Percentage differences are often useful guides to materiality, and the figure most often given for the point at which a difference becomes material is 5%. But if a difference of say 5% is material to the item specifically being reviewed, this does not necessarily mean that it is material within the context of the accounts as a whole; equally, the converse may be true in that a change in the valuation of the stock, which is immaterial *per se*, may dramatically affect the profit. It is necessary to consider the effect that this difference would have on:

(i)   shareholders' funds;

(ii) total assets;

(iii) net profit; and

(iv) turnover.

If the item is not material in the general context, the degree of latitude acceptable in the particular context may depend upon its nature.

It is usual to consider materiality in relation to the largest possible base, e.g. turnover or gross assets, for purposes of determining "high value" items and sampling intervals. This is examined more closely in Chapter 9.

(d) *Disproportionate significance.* An item of small amount may nevertheless be of material significance in the context of the company's particular circumstances, especially if the context would lead the reader to expect the item to be of substantial amount.

(e) *Offset and aggregation.* It frequently happens that two items, which might each be material taken separately, will be of opposite effect. Care should be taken before offsetting such items. For example, a profit arising as a result of a change in the basis of accounting should not be offset against a non-recurring loss. It may also be necessary, where there are a large number of small items, for them to be aggregated to ascertain if they are material in total. The principle of "aggregation" now required under the Companies Act 1985 precludes the setting-off of items, e.g. bank overdrafts and balances in hand.

4.0   VERIFICATION OF STOCKS AND WORK IN PROGRESS

The Council of the Institute of Chartered Accountants in England and Wales has issued two statements for the guidance of members, numbered U9 and U11. These statements relate primarily to company audits, but the considerations outlined apply equally to other audits which involve the auditor in expressing an opinion on the truth and fairness of the view given by the accountants. Statement U9 is primarily concerned with the auditors' duties in relation to the physical stocktaking, while the broader aspects of stock verification are dealt with in U11. The following extract has been modified by the Guideline issued by the APC on "Attendance at Stocktaking".

4.1   General considerations on stocktaking (Statement U9)

Although it is not the auditors' duty to take stock, they must satisfy themselves as to the validity of the amount attributed to this asset in the accounts which are the subject of the audit. In determining the nature and extent of the audit steps necessary for this purpose the auditors must examine the system of internal control in order to assess its effectiveness relative to the ascertainment and evaluation of stock and work in progress.

An important element in this system is the client's procedures for ascertainment of the quantities of stocks on hand and their condition. In most circumstances the best method by which the auditors can satisfy themselves as to the effectiveness of the application of the client's stocktaking procedures is by observation of those procedures. Normally this will be done on a test basis and it will not be necessary for the auditors to observe the application of the stocktaking procedures to the whole of the stock or to the stock at all locations. The extent of the auditors' test observation will depend on their assessment of the soundness of the system prescribed by the client.

Therefore whenever it is practicable and stock in trade and work in progress is a material factor in the business, the auditors should satisfy themselves as to the effectiveness of the application of the client's stocktaking procedures by observation on a test basis of these procedures whilst the stocktaking is in progress.

The presence of auditors at stocktaking does not relieve the management in any way of their responsibilities; in order to avoid misunderstanding the auditors should make it clear to the management that the reason for their attendance is not to take stock but to satisfy themselves as to the effectiveness of the application of the client's procedures. The auditors are neither stocktakers nor valuers, nor have they any responsibility for supervising the stocktaking. Their presence is to enable them as auditors to consider the adequacy and effectiveness of the client's procedures. They will, however, be ready to advise or make recommendations, just as they would on other matters, when they consider that the system of internal control is weak or not being properly carried out.

While it will not normally be necessary for the auditors to observe the application of the client's procedures in their entirety or at all locations, the auditors' tests should cover a representative selection of the stock and of the procedures. Where stock is held at a number of locations, the selection of the location or locations to be visited by the auditors may be planned so as to cover all significant locations over a period of years. There may be instances where it is not practicable to test the client's procedures by attendance and observation of the stocktaking, for example because the stocks are situated at locations at which the auditors cannot readily attend. Where the auditors cannot observe the stocktaking, for any reason, they should adopt some or all of the additional procedures suggested below.

4.2   Client's stocktaking procedure

The amount at which stock is stated in the accounts may be based upon a physical stocktaking at the year end or upon information taken from stock records. Stock records may in turn be substantiated by complete physical stocktakings taken earlier in the year, or upon continuous or periodical physical stocktaking, or upon combinations of these in relation to various sections of stock. Under some accounting systems it is common practice for work in progress to be based solely upon costing records. Where stock at the year end is based on a physical stocktaking earlier in the year, the client's procedures should include a review of entries in the intervening periods. Usual variations from the normal pattern should be explained. These procedures will involve comparison of the amount at the year end with previous years and with current production and sales to check that these also appear to follow a normal pattern.

Where stock is based on records substantiated by continuous or periodical physical stocktakings, the procedures should ensure that:

(a) adequate stock records are kept up to date;

(b) each category of stock is checked at least once a year and a record of checks maintained;

(c) if the checking is continuous, it is done systematically over the year, or if periodic, at suitable times such as when stocks are low or have reached a specific re-order point;

(d) all the differences are properly investigated and the records amended accordingly.

A schedule of differences, with action taken, should be maintained.

The procedures for carrying out a physical stocktaking vary in detail according to the size and circumstances of the business and the nature of its stock records. Definite instructions, preferably in writing, should be issued in all cases, however, for the guidance of those who will be engaged in the actual stocktaking. The procedures will consist essentially of:

(a) identification of the articles and their ownership;

(b) counting, weighing or measuring;

(c) reporting of stocks which are damaged or otherwise defective;

(d) recording the information.

Although considerations will differ in each case, there are certain general procedures which can be applied in most stocktakings but which may need some adaptation to meet particular circumstances, such as where the stocktaking is on a continuous basis:

(a) The stocktaking should be planned well in advance and carried out carefully and systematically by persons fully informed of the duties involved. Those taking part should include persons familiar with the various sections of stock, and where practicable supervisors and checkers drawn from departments which have no control over the usual custody or movement of stock. Where specialist knowledge is necessary to identify the nature or quality of items of stock, the client should ensure that personnel properly qualified for this purpose other than those responsible for custody of the stock are available at the stocktaking. In exceptional circumstances it may be desirable for the services of an independent expert to be utilised, e.g. for the chemical analysis of samples taken at the time of the stocktaking from bulk stocks of high value.

(b) The whole of the stocktaking area should be divided into sections for control purposes, and the movement of stock during the stocktaking should be strictly controlled.

(c) Arrangements should be made to ensure a proper "cut-off". This means that despatch documentation should have been originated for all goods despatched before stocktaking and, if still on hand, for all goods in which the property has passed to the customer. The latter must not be included as stock when the count is made. The procedures should ensure that the appropriate sales invoices are recorded in the correct financial period. Liabilities should also be set up for all goods received and included in stock, and for all goods purchased the property in which has been passed to the client. These should be included in stock even though they are not then on the company's premises. Where only certain sections of stock, such as raw materials, work in progress, finished goods, etc., are being taken physically, the arrangements would ensure a proper "cut-off" between the various sections.

(d) Arrangements should be made to identify slow moving, obsolete or damaged stock.

(e) Arrangements should be made to ensure that goods held in safe custody for others are not recorded as part of the client's stock.

(f) Arrangements should be made to confirm and record in the stock sheets details of goods held for the company by outside parties.

The client's stocktaking procedures should also call for records of the following information, which should be available to the auditors during and at the conclusion of the stocktaking:

(a) details of stock movements during the count;

(b) last numbers of goods inward and outward records;

(c) details of the numbering of stock sheets issued, of those completed and of those cancelled and unused.

4.3   Stocktaking instructions—a summary of controls and procedures

The auditor should have regard to the following being included in the stocktaking instructions:

(a) supervision of the planning and execution of the stocktake by sufficiently senior and qualified personnel drawn from various departments: at least some of the officials should not normally be involved with the custody of stocks;

(b) tidying and marking stock to facilitate counting and to minimise the risk of omission or double counting of items of stock: the whole of the stocktaking area should be divided into sections for control purposes;

(c) the serial numbering and control of the issue and return of all the rough count records, and their retention as required by the Companies Act 1985;

(d) systematic carrying out of counts to ensure coverage of the whole stock;

(e) arrangements for the count to be conducted by at least two people, with one counting and the other primarily to check the count, or alternatively for two independent counts to be carried out; and for any differences arising to be investigated and resolved;

(f) stock sheets being completed in ink and being signed by those who carried out and checked the count;

(g) information to be recorded on the count records (normally this will include the location and identity of the stock items, the unit of count, the quantity counted, the condition of the items and the stage reached in the production process);

(h) restriction and control of the production process and of stock movements during the count;

(i) identification and segregation of damaged, obsolete, slow moving and third parties' stock, returnable containers, plant items, and returned stock, so that these can be properly accounted for and recorded;

(j) recording the quantity, condition and stage of production of all the work in progress for subsequent checking with the costing and stock records;

(k) co-ordination of the count with cut-off procedures so that documentation concerned with the flow of goods can be reconciled with the financial records: for this purpose, last numbers of goods inward and outward records and of internal transfer records should be noted; and

(l) reconciliation with the stock records, if any, and identification and correction of differences.

4.4　Suggested audit procedures

The audit steps relating to observations of the stocktaking by the auditors will cover three stages: *before, during* and *after* the stocktaking. The procedures described below are intended to be a broad outline which will need adaptation to meet the circumstances of the client, for example where a client's stocktaking is based on records sustained by continuous physical stocktakings.

1. Before the stocktaking: planning
The auditor should plan his audit coverage of a stocktaking by reviewing his prior-year's working papers and by:

(a) familiarising himself with the nature and volume of the stocks, the location of high-value items, and the way stocks are accounted for;

(b) considering the location of the stock and assessing the implications of this for the controlling and recording of the stocks;

(c) reviewing the system of internal control relating to stocks, so as to identify potential areas of difficulty;

(d) considering any internal audit involvement, with a view to deciding the reliance which can be placed on this by the auditor;

(e) ensuring that he covers a representative selection of locations, stocks and procedures, giving particular attention to high-value items where these form a significant proportion of the total stock value;

(f) arranging to obtain from third parties confirmation of stocks held by them, but if he considers that such stocks are material when compared to the enterprise's stock as a whole, or the third party is not considered to be sufficiently independent or reliable, then arranging where possible to attend a stocktaking at the third party's premises;

(g) in exceptional circumstances, establishing whether the nature of the stock is so specialised that he needs expert help to verify quantities or identify the nature and condition of the stock.

The auditor should examine the way the stocktaking is organised and should review the client's stocktaking instructions and their communication to those involved in the stocktaking. If the instructions are found to be inadequate, the auditor should discuss the matter with the client before the stocktake, with a view to improving the instructions and, where appropriate, the stock-control system generally. Controls and procedures which should normally be covered in a typical set of stocktaking instructions are set out in section 4.3 above.

2. *During the stocktaking*

The auditor will need to be satisfied that the stocktaking instructions and procedures provide reasonable assurance that the stocktaking will be accurate. He should observe whether the client's staff are carrying out their instructions properly, and should record how all the points which are relevant and material to the stock being counted are dealt with. He should make test counts to satisfy himself that procedures and internal controls for the stocktaking are working properly. If the manner of carrying out the stocktaking or the results of the sample tests are not satisfactory, the auditor should immediately draw the matter to the attention of management and ultimately he may have to request a recount of part, or all of the stocks.

When carrying out test counts the auditor should particularly consider those stocks which he knows, either from the stock records or from his prior year working papers, to have a high value, whether individually or as a category of stock. He should select items both from count records and from the physical stocks and should check one against the other to gain assurance as to the accuracy of the count records.

The auditor should see that the client deals properly with all movements of stock during the count and should identify items for subsequent testing with the stock records and accounting records to satisfy himself that the cut-off has been properly made.

At the stocktake, the auditor should try to gain from his observations an overall impression of the levels of stock held and its condition, to confirm his initial planning procedures and to support, in principle, the stock figure eventually appearing in the financial statements. He should also obtain information about the stock's condition, age and movements, for example by discussion with storekeepers.

The auditor should compile working papers recording his observations, and the tests he has carried out during his attendance. The working papers should, where relevant, include:

(a) details of the sequence of stock sheets and the serial numbers of the last goods inwards and outwards notes before, and the first ones after, the stocktaking date;

(b) details of samples of stock selected by the auditor for comparison with the final stock records;

(c) photocopies of, or extracts from, rough stocksheets for comparison with the final stock records;

(d) items actually counted in the auditor's presence or by the auditor himself;

(e) details of tests carried out to ensure that proper treatment of, for example, slow moving or damaged stock, work in progress, customer stocks, stocks purchased from other group or associated companies, and containers;

(f) details of tests made to ensure that all stocks have been counted and that all queries raised by the client's staff during the count have been satisfactorily cleared;

(g) a record of attendance with details of the audit tests carried out and any audit check lists completed;

(h) details of instances where the procedures were not satisfactorily carried out (normally, the auditor should resolve such matters with the client officials before the stocktaking is completed);

(i) the conclusions reached as to whether or not the stocktaking was satisfactory, and hence provides reliable evidence supporting the stock figure in the financial statements.

3. After the stocktaking

The auditor should follow up the matters recorded on his working papers at the time of the count:

(a) by checking the cut-off using details of stock movements and the numbers of the last goods inwards and outwards notes in conjunction with records of sales and purchases;

(b) by testing that the final stock sheets are complete, by checking the numerical sequence of the stock sheets and by tracing sample items from the information recorded in the working papers;

(c) by ensuring that any continuous stock records have been adjusted or reconciled to the physical count and the differences have been investigated; and

(d) by following up all queries.

4.5   If attendance during stocktaking is not practicable

As stated above, there may be occasions when it will not be practicable for the auditors to observe the client's stocktaking. In such cases they should carry out such additional procedures (distinct from those usually followed when forming an opinion on stocks) as in their judgment, as skilled professional men, are necessary in the circumstances to satisfy themselves that:

(a) the records of the stocktaking produced to them represent a substantially correct inventory of the stocks and work in progress owned by the company on the stocktaking date, and

(b) the condition of the stocks and work in progress has been properly assessed.

The additional procedures to be followed for this purpose will depend on the circumstances which make it impracticable for the auditors to attend for the purpose of observing the stocktaking. In some instances, such as where stock is held overseas, it may be possible for the auditors to arrange for a suitably qualified agent to attend the stocktaking on their behalf and for him to report to them.

In other instances auditors who have numerous client companies, which may have a common accounting date and which take stock on that date, may find that their resources in manpower are insufficient for them to attend on every client for the purpose of observing at least some part of the stocktaking. If auditors find that they cannot attend every year, this does not relieve them of their responsibilities. They will have to consider carefully whether the alternative procedures available to them will be sufficient to discharge those responsibilities in the circumstances of each of the clients concerned. Where the client has a well-developed system of internal control and of stock recording it will usually be possible for the auditors to substantiate to their satisfaction the validity of the stocktaking records. This can be done by arranging for the test counts of selected items to be made at an earlier or later date when a representative can attend and observe.

In the case of smaller businesses, however, the systems of internal control are necessarily more elementary and in many instances the records of annual stocktaking are not supported by any continuous stock records. Sometimes it may be possible to arrange for the stocktaking to take place on a date close to the accounting date at a time when the auditors can attend and for records of movements of stocks in the intervening period to be maintained. These records must be in such a form that the auditors can satisfy themselves as to their accuracy.

If, however, the auditors are unable reasonably to satisfy themselves as to the reliability of the stocktaking and stock is a material factor in the business, they will have no alternative but to make an appropriate qualification in their report on the accounts.

4.6 The broader context (Statement U11)

Stock in trade and work in progress generally constitutes one of the largest items in the balance sheets of manufacturing firms, and relatively small errors in computing the amount at which stock is stated in the accounts can have a marked effect on reported profits.

Auditors must therefore satisfy themselves as to the validity of the amount attributed to stock. In order to reach an opinion they will have to ascertain and consider the soundness of the procedures adopted and to test the competence with which these procedures are carried out. The nature and extent of the audit tests are matters for the auditors' professional judgment. Where applicable, however, and having regard to the nature of the business, these tests will include examination "in depth".

The responsibility for properly determining the quantity and value of stock rests with the management of the business. It is therefore the directors' responsibility to ensure that:

(a) the physical quantities owned by the company are properly ascertained and recorded and that the condition is properly assessed (as already described); and

(b) the amount to be carried forward in the balance sheet has been properly determined on an appropriate basis by suitable methods.

Auditors should arrange that the client's instructions for stocktaking and for evaluation of stock are available to them for examination before they are issued, with a view to changes being made to remove any defects which may exist.

Additional audit procedures to enable auditors to satisfy themselves that stock has been properly ascertained will include such of the following as the auditors may consider appropriate:

(a) general scrutiny of the inventory or the stock records (and comparisons with the previous year), including attention to the possibility of material omissions or the inclusion of items such as loose tools which ought not to be included because they appear elsewhere in the accounts;

(b) where applicable, tests by reference to statistical information, covering matters such as yields which may be expected from given quantities and normal losses or gains by evaporation or absorption of moisture.

Where stock is defective or is obsolete or slow moving, these factors must be taken into account in determining the amount at which stock is stated in the balance sheet. Appropriate audit tests of the company's procedure for judging the physical condition will normally include:

(a) scrutiny of stock records during the tests referred to previously, to ascertain what information as to condition and slow moving stocks has been recorded and what action has been taken on that information;

(b) comparison with the stock records relating to the previous balance sheet date;

(c) examination by reference to normal experience of wastage due to rejects and deterioration;

(d) examination of the relationship between stocks and turnover including consideration of current trading conditions and any changes in sales or stockpiling policies;

(e) discussions with the management.

4.7   Amount at which stock is stated

Audit procedures will be designed to ascertain whether the amount at which stock in trade and work in progress is stated has been computed on a basis (or bases) and by methods which, consistently applied and having regard to the nature and circumstances of the business, will enable the accounts to show a true and fair view of the trading results and the financial position. The accounting principles involved are dealt with in SSAP 9.

After examining the principles adopted by the management, audit procedures to test the application of those principles will normally include:

(a) tests of stock sheets or continuous stock records with relevant documents such as invoices, costing records and other sources for the ascertainment of "cost";

(b) examination and testing of the treatment of overhead expenses;

(c) tests of "net realisable value";

(d) careful enquiry of responsible officials and examination of evidence supporting the assessment of net realisable value, with particular reference to defective, obsolete or slow moving stock, and consideration of the reasonableness of the replies from officials to the enquiries made;

(e) tests of the arithmetical accuracy of the calculations;

(f) tests of the consistency, in principle and in detail, with which the amounts have been computed;

(g) consideration of the adequacy of the description applied to stock in trade and work in progress in the accounts.

Net realisable value can be defined as the amount which it is estimated, as on the balance sheet date, will be realised from disposal of stock in the ordinary course of business, either in its existing condition or as incorporated in the product normally sold, after allowing for all expenditure to be incurred on or before disposal. In estimating this amount regard should be had to excess and obsolete stocks, the trend of the market and the prospects of disposal. It is normal to estimate net realisable value by reference to all available information, including changes in selling prices since the balance sheet date, so far as the information is of assistance in determining the realisable value of the stock at the balance sheet date. Net realisable value may, alternatively, be described as the amount at which stocks may be disposed of without creating a profit or a loss in the year of sale.

In many instances the estimation of net realisable value requires the exercise of judgment of officials of the company who are responsible for the sale or realisation of the stock or work in progress. While, therefore, the auditors' view of such estimates will include consideration of the explanations given by the responsible officials it will be necessary for the auditors to review and test supporting evidence available to them in order to form an opinion as to whether the estimates of realisable value are fair and reasonable.

4.8 Work in progress

Appropriate audit tests in relation to work in progress will include examination and testing of available records, including costing records and work tickets attached to unfinished articles and, where there are long-term contracts, examination of the relevant contracts, including any modifications thereof, and other information such as subsequent cost reports and estimates of costs to complete. Physical checking of work in progress will often not be possible by methods similar to those adopted for stocks. Reference to costing records is frequently necessary and it may not be possible to separate the question of physical quantity from the question of the amount to be attributed to the work in progress. Where it is not possible or practical to identify the work in progress with either the components which have gone into it or the products which will emerge from it, the auditors will be particularly concerned to ascertain:

(a) the costing system from which the work in progress is ascertained;

(b) whether the costing system is reliable and in particular whether it is integrated with the financial accounting;

(c) the extent to which checks are made by reference to statistical information concerning outputs of main products and of by-products (if any) which ought to be obtained from materials used;

(d) the system of inspection and reporting thereon to enable allowance to be made in the costing records for scrapping and rectification;

(e) the basis on which overheads are dealt with in the costing records;

(f) any profit element included for which adjustments are required.

4.9   Overall tests

Audit tests which may often be appropriate by way of overall assessment of the reliability of the records will include, according to circumstances:

(a) reconciliation of changes in stock quantities as between the beginning and end of the financial year with the records of purchases, production and sales;

(b) comparison of the quantities and amounts of stock in the various categories with those included at the previous balance sheet date and with current sales and purchases;

(c) consideration of the gross profit ratio shown by the accounts and its comparison with the ratio shown in previous years;

(d) consideration of the rate of turnover of stocks and its comparison with previous years;

(e) consideration of the relationship of the quantities ready for sale and in course of production with the quantities shown in operating the sales budgets;

(f) where applicable, examination of standard costing records and consideration of the variances shown thereby and their treatment in the accounts.

4.10   Independent stocktakers

In some trades it is common practice to employ firms of independent surveyors and valuers. These stocktaking firms are specialists and, provided the auditor is satisfied as to their independence and standing, it is usual to accept their stock counts as reliable. The auditors, however, normally ascertain direct with the stocktaking firm the basis of valuation used, and assure themselves that proper "cut-off" procedures were operated.

Sometimes the circumstances are such that physical count and valuation are operations where it is not practicable for the auditors to make any independent test of the basis of appraisal, so that they will have to rely on the independent stocktaker. A case in point might be an inventory of precious stones, but the situation may be met in a number of types of business. Nevertheless, the fact that auditors are obliged to rely on reports of independent stocktakers does not relieve them of their responsibility for forming an opinion on the amount at which stock is stated in the balance sheet.

4.11   Inventory letters

It is usual and desirable practice to obtain from a director or other responsible official of the company a written statement outlining in detail the method of ascertaining stock quantities and bases of valuation. This statement may take the form of a separate inventory letter or may be included in a comprehensive letter of financial representations. It in no way relieves the auditors of their responsibility for forming their opinion whether stock has been fairly reported and presented in the accounts. The significance of inventory letters is that they constitute a record of the action taken by management and a formal reminder and acknowledgment of management's responsibility, and for this reason considerable importance attaches to these representations.

4.12   Preservation of records

The need to retain records applies particularly to stock inventories, including not only the fair copies, but also the rough stock sheets made out at the time when a physical count was taken. This is a statutory requirement under the Companies Act 1985, s. 221, which includes these documents within the definition of "proper accounting records".

4.13   Auditing Guideline issued by APC in November 1983: Attendance at Stocktaking

Much of what has already been said is succinctly restated in the following guideline:

Preface
Paragraph 4 of the Auditing Standard, "The Auditor's Operational Standard" states that: "The auditor should obtain relevant and reliable audit evidence sufficient to enable him to draw reasonable conclusions therefrom." This Auditing Guideline gives guidance on how that paragraph may be applied in relation to attendance at stocktaking. It is supplementary to and should be read in conjunction with the auditor's operation and reporting standards and related guidelines.

Introduction
1.   The value of stock and work in progress ("stocks") in the financial statements of a trading enterprise will often be material to the profit and loss account and to the balance sheet and, as such, is of great importance to the financial statements. There are three main elements in the audit of stocks: existence, ownership and valuation. This guideline is primarily concerned with the first of these elements.

Responsibilities
2.   It is the responsibility of the management of an enterprise to ensure that the amount at which stocks are shown in the financial statements represents stocks physically in existence and includes all stocks owned by the enterprise. Management satisfies this responsibility by carrying out appropriate procedures

which will normally involve ensuring that all stocks are subject to a count at least once in every financial year. Further, where the auditor attends any physical count of stocks in order to obtain audit evidence, this responsibility will not be reduced.

3.   In the case of a company incorporated under the Companies Act, management also has responsibilities to maintain proper accounting records and to include all statements of stocktakings in those records.

4.   It is the responsibility of the auditor to obtain audit evidence in order to enable him to draw conclusions about the validity of the quantities upon which are based the amount of stocks shown in the financial statements. The principal sources of this evidence are stock records, stock control systems, the results of any stocktaking and test-counts made by the auditor himself. By reviewing the enterprise's stock records and stock control systems, the auditor can decide to what extent he needs to rely upon attendance at stocktaking to obtain the necessary audit evidence.

Attendance as a means of providing evidence
5.   Where stocks are material in the enterprise's financial statements, and the auditor is placing reliance upon management's stocktake in order to provide evidence of existence, then the auditor should attend the stocktaking. This is because attendance at stocktaking is normally the best way of providing evidence of the proper functioning of management's stocktaking procedures, and hence of the existence of stocks and their condition.

6.   Evidence of the existence of work in progress will frequently be obtained by a stocktake. However, the nature of the work in progress may be such that it is impracticable to determine its existence by a count. Management may place substantial reliance on internal controls designed to ensure the completeness and accuracy of records of work in progress. In such circumstances there may not be a stocktake which could be attended by the auditor. Nevertheless, inspection of the work in progress will assist the auditor to plan his audit procedures, and it may also help on such matters as the determination of the stage of completion of construction of engineering work in progress.

Types of stocktaking
7.   Physical verification of stocks may be by means of a full count (or measurement in the case of bulk stocks) of all the stocks at the year end or at a selected date before or shortly after the year end, or by means of a count of part of the stocks in which case it may be possible to extrapolate the total statistically. Alternatively, verification may be by means of the counting or measurement of stocks during the course of the year using continuous stock-checking methods. Some business enterprises use continuous stock-checking methods for certain stocks and carry out a full count of other stocks at a selected date.

8.   Paragraphs 9 and 10 set out some special considerations in circumstances where the count is carried out at a date which is not the same as that of the financial

statements or where it takes place throughout the year. The principal procedures which the auditor would normally carry out in relation to his attendance at any count of stocks are set out in paragraphs 11 to 21 of this guideline.

9. The evidence of the existence of stocks provided by the stocktake results is most effective when the stocktaking is carried out at the end of the financial year. Stocktaking carried out before or after the year end may also be acceptable for audit purposes provided records of stock movements in the intervening period are such that the movements can be examined and substantiated. The auditor should bear in mind that the greater the interval between the stocktaking and the year end, the greater will be his difficulties in substantiating the amount of stocks at the balance sheet date. Such difficulties will, however, be lessened by the existence of a well developed system of internal control and satisfactory stock records.

10. Where continuous stock-checking methods are being used, the auditor should perform tests designed to confirm that management:

(a)   maintains adequate stock records that are kept up-to-date;

(b)   has satisfactory procedures for stocktaking and test-counting, so that in normal circumstances the programme of counts will cover all stocks at least once during the year; and

(c)   investigates and corrects all material differences between the book stock records and the physical counts.

The auditor needs to do this to gain assurance that the stock-checking system as a whole is effective in maintaining accurate stock records from which the amount of stocks in the financial statements can be derived. It is unlikely that he will be able to obtain such assurance if the three matters above are not confirmed satisfactorily, in which circumstances a full count at the year end may be necessary.

Procedures
11. The following paragraphs set out the principal procedures which may be carried out by an auditor when attending a stocktake, but are not intended to provide a comprehensive list of the audit procedures which the auditor may find it necessary to perform during his attendance.

BEFORE THE STOCKTAKING: PLANNING
12. The auditor should plan his audit coverage of a stocktake by:

(a)   reviewing his working papers for the previous year, where applicable, and discussing with management any significant changes in stocks over the year;

(b)   discussing stocktaking arrangements and instructions with management;

(c)   familiarising himself with the nature and volume of the stocks, the identification of high-value items and the method of accounting for stocks;

(d)   considering the location of the stock and assessing the implications of this for stock control and recording;

(e) reviewing the systems of internal control and accounting relating to stocks, so as to identify potential areas of difficulty (for example cut-off);

(f) considering any internal audit involvement, with a view to deciding the reliance which can be placed on it;

(g) ensuring that a representative selection of locations, stocks and procedures is covered, and particular attention is given to high-value items where these form a significant proportion of the total stock value;

(h) arranging to obtain from third parties confirmation of stocks held by them, but if the auditor considers that such stocks are a material part of the enterprise's total stock, or the third party is not considered to be independent or reliable, then arranging where appropriate either for him or for the third party's auditor to attend a stocktake at the third party's premises; and

(i) establishing whether expert help needs to be obtained to substantiate quantities, or to identify the nature and condition of the stock, where they are very specialised.

13. The auditor should examine the way the stocktaking is organised and should evaluate the adequacy of the client's stocktaking instructions. Such instructions should preferably be in writing, cover all phases of the stocktaking procedures, be issued in good time and be discussed with those responsible for carrying out the stocktaking to ensure the procedures are understood and that potential difficulties are anticipated. If the instructions are found to be inadequate, the auditor should seek improvements to them.

DURING THE STOCKTAKING

14. During the stocktaking, the auditor should ascertain whether the client's staff are carrying out their instructions properly so as to provide reasonable assurance that the stocktaking will be accurate. He should make test counts to satisfy himself that procedures and internal controls relating to the stocktaking are working properly. If the manner of carrying out the stocktaking or the results of the test counts are not satisfactory, the auditor should immediately draw the matter to the attention of the management supervising the stocktaking and he may have to request a recount of part, or all of the stocks.

15. When carrying out test counts, the auditor should select items both from count records and from the physical stocks and should check one to the other to gain assurance as to the completeness and accuracy of the count records. In this context, he should give particular consideration to those stocks which he believes, for example from the stock records or from his prior year working papers, to have a high value either individually or as a category of stock. The auditor should include in his working papers items for subsequent testing, such as photocopies of (or extracts from) rough stocksheets and details of the sequence of stocksheets.

16. The auditor should determine whether the procedures for identifying damaged,

obsolete and slow moving stock operate properly. He should obtain (from his observations and by discussion, e.g. with storekeepers) information about the stocks' condition, age, usage and, in the case of work in progress, its stage of completion. Further, he should ascertain that stock held on behalf of third parties is separately identified and accounted for.

17. The auditor should consider whether management has instituted adequate cut-off procedures, i.e. procedures intended to ensure that movements into, within and out of stocks are properly identified and reflected in the accounting records. The auditor's procedures during the stocktaking will depend on the manner in which the year-end stock value is to be determined. For example, where stocks are determined by a full count and evaluation at the year end the auditor should test the arrangements made to segregate stocks owned by third parties and he should identify goods movement documents for reconciliation with financial records of purchases and sales. Alternatively, where the full count and evaluation is at an interim date and year-end stocks are determined by updating such valuation by the cost of purchases and sales, the auditor should perform those procedures during his attendance at the stocktaking and in addition should test the financial cut-off (involving the matching of costs with revenues) at the year end.

18. In addition, the auditor should:

(a)   conclude whether the stocktaking has been properly carried out and is sufficiently reliable as a basis for determining the existence of stocks;

(b)   consider whether any amendment is necessary to his subsequent audit procedures; and

(c)   try to gain from his observations an overall impression of the levels and values of stocks held so that he may, in due course, judge whether the figure for stocks appearing in the financial statements is reasonable.

19. The auditor's working papers should include details of his observations and tests, the manner in which points that are relevant and material to the stocks being counted or measured have been dealt with by the client, instances where the client's procedures have not been satisfactorily carried out, and the auditor's conclusions.

AFTER THE STOCKTAKING

20. After the stocktaking, the matters recorded in the auditor's working papers at the time of the count or measurement should be followed up. For example, details of the last serial numbers of goods inwards and outwards notes and of movements during the stocktaking should be used in order to check cut-off. Further, photocopies of (or extracts from) rough stocksheets and details of test counts may be used to check that the final stocksheets are accurate and complete.

21. The auditor should ensure that continuous stock records have been adjusted to the amounts physically counted or measured and that differences have been investigated. Where appropriate, he should ensure also that management has

instituted proper procedures to deal with transactions between stocktaking and the year end, and also test those procedures. In addition, he should check replies from third parties about stocks held by or for them, follow up all queries and notify senior management of serious problems encountered during the stock-taking.

5.0 CONTINGENT LIABILITIES FOR PENDING LEGAL MATTERS— U16

The Council of the Institute of Chartered Accountants in England and Wales have issued the following statement for the guidance of members. It has been prepared after discussions with the Council of the Law Society.

It is the duty of directors to ensure that proper account is taken of all liabilities including contingent liabilities, in the preparation of company financial statements. From the audit viewpoint, pending lawsuits and other actions against the company may present problems both of ascertainment and appraisal.

5.1 Audit procedures

The following audit procedures are suggested for the verification of the existence of such claims, though they will not necessarily provide the auditor with adequate information of the likely amounts for which the company may ultimately be responsible:

(a) reviewing the client's system of recording claims and the procedure for bringing these to the attention of the management or board;

(b) discussing the arrangements for instructing solicitors with the official(s) responsible for legal matters (for example the head of the legal department, if any, or the company secretary);

(c) examining the minutes of the board of directors and/or executive or other relevant committee for references to, or indication of, possible claims;

(d) examining bills rendered by solicitors and correspondence with them, in which connection the solicitors should be requested to furnish bills or estimates of charges to date, or to confirm that they have no unbilled charges;

(e) obtaining a list of matters referred to solicitors from the appropriate director or official with estimates of the possible ultimate liabilities;

(f) obtaining a written assurance from the appropriate director or official that he is not aware of any matters referred to solicitors other than those disclosed.

In appropriate circumstances, auditors may decide to obtain written confirmation from third parties of certain representations made by directors; for example, the identification and appraisal of contingent liabilities. In the field of legal actions the normal and proper source of such confirmation is the company's legal advisers.

Requests for such confirmations should be kept within the solicitor–client relationship and should thus be issued by the client with a request that a copy of the reply should be sent direct to the auditors.

5.2   Confirmation from solicitors

In order to ascertain whether the information provided by the directors is complete, auditors (especially in certain overseas countries) may decide to arrange for solicitors to be requested to advise whether they have matters in hand which are not listed in the letter of request, and to provide information as to the likely amounts involved. When considering such a non-specific enquiry, auditors should note that the Council of the Law Society has advised solicitors that it is unable to recommend them to comply with requests for information which are more widely drawn than the specimen form of wording set out.

5.3   Specimen form of request

In these circumstances, the enquiry should normally list matters identified as having been referred to the company's legal advisers in accordance with paragraph (e) in section 5.1 above. The following form of wording, appropriate to specific enquiries, has been agreed between the Councils of the Law Society and the Institute of Chartered Accountants in England and Wales as one which may be properly addressed to, and answered by, solicitors:

> "In connection with the preparation and audit of our accounts for the year ended ... the directors have made estimates of the amounts of the ultimate liabilities (including costs) which might be incurred, and are regarded as material, in relation to the following matters on which you have been consulted. We should be obliged if you would confirm that in your opinion these estimates are reasonable.

> *Matter*   *Estimated liability including costs"*

The Council of the Institute of Chartered Accountants in England and Wales understands the reason for the view of the Council of the Law Society regarding non-specific enquiries, but nevertheless believes that there may be circumstances in which it is necessary as an audit procedure for an enquiry of a general nature to be addressed to the solicitors in order to confirm that the information provided by the directors is complete in all material particulars.

If the outcome of the enquiries set out above appears satisfactory, auditors would not normally regard the absence of a corroboration of the completeness of a list of legal matters as a reason in itself for qualifying their report. If the enquiries lead to the discovery of significant matters not previously identified, the auditors will wish to extend their enquiries and to request their clients to address further enquiries to, or arrange a meeting with, the solicitors, at which the auditors will wish to be present. If, however, having regard to all the circumstances, the auditors are unable to satisfy themselves that they have received all the information they require for the purpose of their audit, they must qualify their report.

6.0   CONFIRMATION FROM BANKS

The following is the Guideline issued by the APC in 1982:

6.1   Auditing Guideline: bank reports for audit purposes

Introduction

1.   Paragraph 4 of the Auditor's Operational Standard states that the auditor should obtain relevant and reliable audit evidence. This guideline is designed to assist auditors in complying with this standard with respect to amounts due to and from banks, and assets held by them.

2.   The practice of obtaining independent certificates or reports from banks is an important feature in the proper discharge of auditors' responsibilities. Bank reports assist auditors to ascertain the existence and the amount of liabilities and the existence, amount, ownership and proper custody of assets; they also provide other information relevant to the audit of financial statements.

3.   The standard audit request letter in the appendix to this guideline has been prepared following discussions with the Committee of London Clearing Banks, and the Committee of Scottish Clearing Banks. The standard letter has been prepared primarily for the purpose of obtaining information from the clearing banks. Many companies, however, also have dealings with other banks or licensed deposit-taking institutions, and auditors will normally need reports from them. The British Bankers' Association has indicated that the standard letter may not always be appropriate for requests to such organisations, particularly where specialised or limited services are offered, and that consequently no undertaking can be given by their members to answer every question on every occasion.

Background

4.   The information which auditors regularly need from banks is substantially the same for most audits, and can be obtained in a standard letter of request. The use of such a letter, designed to cover all normal banking activity and to facilitate the extraction of information from banking records, should smooth the processing of these audit requests. The answers received should assist in highlighting areas which require particular audit attention.

5.   As the clearing banks keep their customer records in a more or less similar manner, the use of a standard letter should facilitate the efficient preparation of their replies. The banks accept the need for their assistance in these matters, and a standard letter gives them a clearer understanding of auditors' requirements.

6.   Auditors should therefore request information from banks in the form of the standard letter set out in the appendix and in accordance with the procedures in paragraphs 11 to 13 below. It is intended that this standard letter should be primarily for audit purposes, but if it is used when members are only concerned with the preparation of accounts and not with the audit of, for instance, sole traders, partnerships or other non-statutory organisations, then any reference in it to an audit should be deleted. For certain purposes other than verification at the year-end (for example for work of an accounting nature, interim audits and accountants' reports on solicitors' accounts), it may be necessary to seek

confirmation only of selected items from the standard request. In such cases the letter should not be headed "standard request for bank report".

7.   The attached standard letter is a revision of the one set out in the Statement issued in 1976, following experience gained in the use of the earlier version. It now includes enough space for the banks to enter their replies on a copy of the letter, which should be sent at the same time as the main audit request.

8.   As indicated in paragraph 3 above, in the case of institutions other than clearing banks it may often be more appropriate for the auditor to make a specific request for the information he requires rather than to use the standard letter. If he is unable to obtain any of the information he requires, he must consider the effect of this on his audit opinion.

Authority to disclose

9.   Banks will require the explicit authority of their customers to disclose the requested information. They will always require such authority in writing, and this may be obtained either on each occasion a bank report is requested, or as an authority which continues until further notice. In the former case it is recommended that the authority should be evidenced by the customer's counter-signature to the letter of request; in the latter case the letter of request should refer to the customer's written authority given on a specified earlier date. In the case of a joint account, the authority should be given by all parties to the account.

Disclaimers

10.   The introduction to the letter states that there is no contractual relationship between banker and auditor. In addition, the banks may add a disclaimer at the end of their reply, the text of which may be as follows: "This reply is given solely for the purpose of your audit without any responsibility to you on the part of the bank, its employees or agents, but it is not to relieve you from any other enquiry or from the performance of any other duty."

Counsel has given the opinion that the inclusion of the introductory statement and of a disclaimer of this nature does not significantly impair the value of the information given as audit evidence. The information given by a reputable bank should not be regarded as inaccurate or likely to be inaccurate simply because the giving of it is not actionable. Accordingly, an auditor can reasonably rely upon information given by a banker, provided it is not clearly wrong, suspicious or inconsistent in itself, ambiguous or in conflict with other evidence gathered in the course of an audit.

Procedures

11.   Auditors should, where appropriate, adopt the following procedures in connection with requests to banks for audit purposes:

(a)   The standard letter set out in the appendix to this guideline should be sent in duplicate on each occasion by the auditor on his own notepaper to each bank branch with which it is known that the client holds an account or has had dealings since the end of the previous accounting reference period.

(b)   Auditors should ensure that the bank receives the client's authority to permit disclosure. This authority must be evidenced by:

   (i)   the client's countersignature to the standard letter; or

   (ii) a specific authority contained in an accompanying letter; or

   (iii) a reference in the standard letter to the client's specific written authority, given on a specified earlier date, which remains in force.

(c)   The letter should reach the branch at least two weeks in advance of the date of the client's financial year-end. This should enable the banks to provide the information within a reasonable time after the year-end. It should be borne in mind, however, that many requests arise at the same time and at a period of peak activity for the banks. Special arrangements should therefore be made with the banks in those cases where, because of time constraints on the audit, a reply is required within a few days of the company's year-end.

(d)   The dates to be entered on the standard letter are normally the closing dates of:

   (i)   the client's accounting reference period for which the report is requested; and

   (ii) the client's previous accounting reference period for which a full bank report was compiled. If, exceptionally, audited accounts are produced other than for an accounting reference period, alternative dates should be substituted.

(e)   In reviewing the bank's reply, it is important for auditors to check that the bank has answered all questions in full.

(f)   Auditors will need to check the authenticity of any letters not received directly from the bank branch concerned. If an auditor receives a bank report without having made a previous request, he should check with the branch concerned that the report has been prepared in compliance with the terms of the standard letter.

12.   The standard letter should be used in its complete form for all audit requests in respect of year-end financial statements and should not normally be altered or extended. In certain circumstances supplementary requests for additional information may be required for audit purposes. For administrative reasons the letter containing these supplementary requests should be submitted where possible at the same time as the standard letter. Where supplementary information is requested the banks will, as indicated above, require authority to disclose this. If the wording of the authority is not sufficiently comprehensive, additional authority may be required. For some information such as security lodged by a third party, authority from someone other than the customer may be required.

13.   The banks may choose not to reply on the copy standard letter itself, but instead on their own notepaper. If this is the case, the auditor should check that the list of replies corresponds with the questions on the standard letter and that there

have been no omissions.

6.2   Appendix: standard letter of request for bank report for audit purposes

(a)   The form of the letter is not to be amended by the auditor.

(b)   Sufficient space should be left for the bank's replies (two-thirds of each page is recommended).

The Manager,

.... (*bank*)

.... (*branch*)

Dear Sir,

.... (*Name of customer*)

Standard request for bank report for audit purposes for the year ended

....

in accordance with your above-named customer's instructions given
   (1) hereon
   (2) in the attached authority   (*delete as*
   (3) in the authority dated .... already held by you   *appropriate*)

please send to us, as auditors of your customer for the purpose of our business, without entering into any contractual relationship with us, the following information relating to their affairs at your branch as at the close of business on .... and, in the case of items 2, 4 and 10, during the period since .... For each item, please state any factors which may limit the completeness of your reply; if there is nothing to report, state 'none'.

   We enclose an additional copy of this letter, and it would be particularly helpful if your reply could be given on the copy letter in the space provided (supported by an additional schedule stamped and signed by the bank where space is insufficient). If you find it necessary to provide the information in another form, please return the copy letter with your reply.

   It is understood that any replies given are in strict confidence.

Information requested

BANK ACCOUNTS
1.   Please give full titles of all accounts whether in sterling or in any other currency together with the account numbers and balances thereon, including nil balances:

   (a) where your customer's name is the sole name in the title;

   (b) where your customer's name is joined with that of other parties;

(c) where the account is in a trade name.

Notes

(i) Where the account is subject to any restriction (e.g. a garnishee order or arrestment), this information should be stated.

(ii) Where the authority upon which you are providing this information does not cover any accounts held jointly with other parties, please refer to your customer in order to obtain the requisite authority of the other parties. If this authority is not forthcoming please indicate.

2. Full titles and dates of closure of all accounts closed during the period.

3. The separate amounts accrued but not charged or credited at the above date, of:

(a) provisional charges (including commitment fees); and

(b) interest

4. The amount of interest charged during the period if not specified separately in the bank statement.

5. Particulars (i.e. date, type of document and accounts covered) of any written acknowledgment of set-off, either by specific letter of set-off, or incorporated in some other document or security.

6. Details of:

(a) overdrafts and loans repayable on demand, specifying dates of review and agreed facilities;

(b) other loans specifying dates of review and repayment;

(c) other facilities.

CUSTOMER'S ASSETS HELD AS SECURITY

7. Please give details of any such assets whether or not formally charged to the bank.

If formally charged, give details of the security including the date and type of charge. If a security is limited in amount or to a specific borrowing, or if there is to your knowledge a prior, equal or subordinate charge, please indicate.

If informally charged, indicate nature of security interest therein claimed by the bank.

Whether or not a formal charge has been taken, give particulars of any undertaking given to the bank relating to any assets.

CUSTOMER'S OTHER ASSETS HELD

8. Please give full details of the customer's other assets held, including share certificates, documents of title, deed boxes and any other items listed in your registers maintained for the purpose of recording assets held.

CONTINGENT LIABILITIES

9. All contingent liabilities, viz.:

(a) total of bills discounted for your customer, with recourse;

(b) date, name of beneficiary, amount and brief description of any guarantees, bonds or indemnities given to you by the customer for the benefit
of third parties;

(c) date, name of beneficiary, amount and brief description of any guarantees, bonds or indemnities given by you, on your customer's behalf,
stating where there is recourse to your customer and/or to its parent or
any other company within the group;

(d) total of acceptances;

(e) total sterling equivalents of outstanding forward foreign exchange
contracts;

(f) total of outstanding liabilities under documentary credits;

(g) others—please give details.

OTHER INFORMATION
10. A list of other banks, or branches of your bank, or associated companies
where you are aware that a relationship has been established during the
period.

Yours faithfully

....
(*official stamp of bank*)

....
(*authorised signatory*)

....
(*position*)

*Reply: Sufficient space should be left for the bank's replies (two-thirds of each
page is recommended).*

6.3 Notes to the standard letter

(REFERENCES ARE TO ITEM NUMBERS IN THE STANDARD LETTER)

1. Bank accounts: The phrase "all accounts" includes details of all current, deposit,
loan and foreign currency accounts and other advances or facilities, money held
on deposit receipt. The reply should indicate whether the balance is in favour of
the bank or customer, and account numbers. Where a number of deposits have
been made or uplifted during the year, it is not necessary to give details of each
separate deposit transaction as would be required in the case of the opening and
closing of accounts.

3. Accrued charges: These can be quoted only on a provisional basis; the rate for

notional allowances will not be fixed until near the end of the charging period.

4.   Analysis of charges: For the purposes of profit and loss disclosure requirements it is only necessary to ask for details of interest charged. (But see note (6)(b) below in respect of balance sheet disclosure requirements.) The details of the rate of interest applicable to any interest-bearing accounts, or the appropriate formula by which interest is calculated, should only be required exceptionally.

5.   Set-off: Auditors will need to have an understanding of the principles governing set-off, but it should not normally be necessary to make enquiries beyond the question as put in the standard letter. Details should be available from the relevant documents. A right of set-off may exist even when there are no written arrangements.

6.   Loans and other facilities: The following details are not normally required:

(a)   the date term loans were granted if new or renewed during the period;

(b)   rate of interest charged or similar form of compensation (which information is only required by the Companies Act to be disclosed for facilities which are wholly or partly repayable in more than five years' time);

(c)   the purpose of the facility;

(d)   loan repayment arrangements, where these are included in a written agreement which is available for inspection by the auditor.

7. and 8.   Customer's assets:

(a)   *Security* includes details of charge, mortgage or other claims or security registered (e.g. debenture, memorandum of deposit), assets charged and, where appropriate, cross reference to facility specifically secured.

(b)   *Assets* include bonds, stock and share certificates, investments, bearer or other securities; title deeds relating to freehold, leasehold or other property; certificates of tax deposit, bills of exchange or other negotiable instruments receivable (other than cheques); shipping and other commercial documents; deposit receipts (as distinct from any account represented by the deposit receipt). The names of persons who are able to obtain release of the assets should be ascertained from the customer and are usually covered by the bank mandate.

(c)   *Lien:* auditors should be aware that any assets held by the bank for safe custody may be subject to some form of banker's lien, although this may only operate under particular conditions. It should be necessary to enquire only in exceptional circumstances.

(d)   *Bearer securities:* detailed enquiries on bearer securities should be made of the bank only when evidence cannot be obtained from the customer or his banking records.

9.   Contingent liabilities: The liabilities under indemnities given in respect of

missing bills of lading do not have an expiry date. From time to time the banks take a view on old liabilities and remove some of them from their records. Certain of these old liabilities may not therefore be shown in the figure quoted by the bank, but it cannot be guaranteed that no claim will be incurred subsequently.

10. Other information: Banks are often asked for introductions to other branches or banks for the purpose of establishing new sources of finance. The provision of any available information relating to introductions or new accounts will assist auditors to satisfy themselves that they have information about all of their client's banking relationships.

6.4 Notes on matters excluded from the standard letter

Supplementary requests

The standard letter contains all items found to be regularly required for audit purposes. In case of doubt, or specific requirement, auditors may wish to make supplementary requests regarding other items which are not regularly required. These may include the following:

(a) copies of bank statements;

(b) copies of paying-in slips for specified lodgment on specified dates;

(c) details showing make-up of those lodgments;

(d) any list of securities or other documents of title which have been lodged by a bank with its customer as security for deposit with that bank (this particular matter would probably apply only between banking organisations);

(e) interest on any account paid to or by third parties, and the names of those third parties;

(f) receipts for fire and other insurances, and similar documents in the bank's possession;

(g) returned paid cheques;

(h) stopped cheques—these are normally presented through the banking system within the audit period, and therefore there should be no need to seek specific details;

(i) details of third party security, including directors' guarantees: if this information is required, the request must be accompanied by a specific authority from the appropriate third parties;

(j) details of outstanding forward foreign exchange contracts, including the particulars of each contract, the dates of maturity and the currencies concerned.

Notes

(a) *The cost of providing audit information falls on the customer and supplementary requests should be kept to a reasonable minimum.*

(b) *Depending on the terms of the authority which has been given, it may be necessary to seek specific authorisation for the disclosure of supplementary information.*

Bank mandates

Auditors may require supplementary information about bank mandates as independent verification that board resolutions concerning a company's banking affairs have been duly communicated to the bank so that they may ensure that only authorised persons are acting on behalf of the company. Auditors should ensure that they receive copies of all such resolutions from their clients.

7.0 LOANS TO DIRECTORS

As a result of recent accounting *causes célèbres* there has been further press comment about the undisclosed existence of loans to directors made by banking and quasi-banking companies. It is clear that opinion has changed over the years, and what was acceptable practice ten, or even five years ago, may not be acceptable now. It is common practice for companies, all or part of whose business is the lending of money, to make loans to their directors. Often, these companies do this to attract the right calibre of person in a highly competitive market. Most frequently, they make these loans on terms similar to those which they make available to members of their staff.

Lawyers have been unable to agree on how the words "in the ordinary course of business" (in section 330 of the Companies Act 1985) should be interpreted. However, in the current climate of opinion, this should be interpreted in the following way:

(a) The amount of the loan should not exceed the amount of a loan typically made to unconnected individuals. Also, if a bank's policy is to lend money only to corporate customers, a loan to a director could hardly be said to be in the ordinary course of its business.

(b) The security required should be similar to that required for similar loans made to unconnected individuals.

(c) The interest charged should be at least the lowest rate offered on loans made to unconnected individuals, and should not be "rolled up" unless it is the company's practice to do so with similar loans.

The above guidelines are supported by section 338 of the 1985 Act, which lists the exemptions from the general prohibition. This subject is dealt with further in Chapter 7.

7.1 Procedures

(a) In practice a number of clients whose business includes the lending of money may make loans to directors which fail to measure up to one or more of the above requirements. Frequently these loans are housing loans which are secured by first or second mortgages, but carry concessionary rates of interest. Where it is known that a client has made loans to directors, the partner responsible for the audit should discuss the situation with the client as a *matter of urgency.*

(b) The partner should advise the client that this does not fall within the firm's interpretation of "in the ordinary course of business", and of the legal requirement to make disclosures in the accounts of the loans which at the balance sheet date do not fall within the restricted definition (specified above). Clients should be strongly urged either to correct the terms of the loans to bring them within this interpretation, or to make the necessary disclosure.

7.2 Disclosure

To comply with section 233 of the Companies Act 1985, disclosure in the notes to the accounts might take the following form in the case of a recognised bank:

"Loans to directors

At the end of the year	1985	1986
Number	4	5
Total	£50,000	£70,000

During the year one loan of £20,000 was repaid and loans of £30,000 and £10,000 were made to two other directors, one of whom was appointed during the year. Loans are made to assist directors with house purchase, secured by mortgage, and bear interest at the rate of 4% per annum. Loans are made to selected members of staff on similar terms."

7.3 Audit report

If the client is unwilling to make these disclosures, section 237 of the Companies Act 1985 requires the auditor to give the information in the audit report. Provided the auditors are satisfied concerning the recoverability of the loans, the report might include the following:

"The company has made loans to directors which are on terms more favourable than those available to other customers. In our opinion, such loans have not been made in the ordinary course of the company's business and therefore contravene the Companies Act 1985. It is a requirement of that Act that details of such loans must be shown in the accounts as follows:

"Loans to directors

At the end of the year	1985	1986
Number	4	5
Total	£50,000	£70,000

During the year one loan of £20,000 was repaid and loans of £30,000 and £10,000 were made to two other directors, one of whom was appointed during the year.

With this exception, in our opinion, the accounts comply with the Companies Act 1985."

N.B. Auditors should draw to the attention of any listed client the requirement in the

Stock Exchange Yellow Book that loans over £100,000 should be individually disclosed.

8.0 "QUESTIONABLE" PAYMENTS BY CLIENTS

8.1 General

A good deal of publicity has been given recently to what have been termed "illegal acts", i.e. usually questionable payments or commissions (bribes?) made to individuals in order to secure contracts. Such payments are usually discovered during detailed testing procedures by the senior in charge of an audit or his assistants. When audit procedures bring any such payments to light, they should immediately be brought to the attention of both the manager and the partner responsible for the client organisation.

8.2 Audit procedures

Where such payments have been made by a subsidiary company, its auditors should immediately inform the holding company auditors, who should, in turn, inform the directors of the holding company. The auditors should also ensure that the directors of the subsidiary have informed the directors of the holding company of the existence of the payments.

It should be recognised that, in many countries, such payments are part of normal business practices and, accordingly, when such payments arise, the auditors' policy should be:

(a) to ensure that the payments were actually received by the individuals specified;

(b) to ensure that they were made wholly in connection with the furtherance of the client's business operations; and

(c) to ensure that they have been approved by each director of the company and, where appropriate, of the holding company.

8.3 Director's representations

A suitable form of representation might be: "We confirm that the payment of £x made on 15th October 1982 to Simon Palm was made wholly in connection with the company's business operations in xxx land.

Signed (*each director of the holding company*)."

8.4 Disclosure

Where the conditions outlined above are satisfied, and a suitable representation has been received, disclosure in the published accounts would not normally be required.

Where payments have been made by a subsidiary and the holding company is audited by *another* firm the subsidiary auditors should ask the directors of the subsidiary to inform the directors of the holding company of the existence of the payments.

9.0 RELATED PARTY TRANSACTIONS

9.1 Introduction

"Related party" transactions require special attention and scrutiny by the auditor since the terms and conditions of these transactions may be unduly favourable to one of the parties.

Depending upon the circumstances and materiality of the transactions concerned, the auditor may wish to consider the adequacy of the disclosure of these transactions in the accounts. For example, the Companies Act 1985 requires disclosure of significant contracts in which directors have a material interest, but apart from such statutory provisions the auditor may take the view that the disclosure of related party transactions is required to enable the accounts to show a true and fair view.

9.2 Who are related parties?

The following might be included within a definition of related parties:

(a) organisations under common control with the client company (regarding "control" as the power to direct management and policy through ownership, contract or otherwise);

(b) shareholders with substantial holdings of voting shares (exceeding, say, 10%);

(c) the executive directors and their immediate families;

(d) associated companies;

(e) any other party which has the ability to prevent the company from pursuing its own interests independently.

9.3 Indications

The following types of transaction may indicate to an auditor the existence of related parties:

(a) borrowing/lending at rates of interest substantially higher/lower than current market rates;

(b) sales/purchases of assets at prices substantially different from those currently ruling;

(c) straightforward exchanges of assets in a manner which masks the underlying value of the assets exchanged;

(d) granting of loans with no scheduled repayment terms.

9.4 Identification of related parties

The auditor should:

(a) evaluate the company's own procedures, if any, for identifying and properly accounting for related party transactions;

(b) enquire of appropriate management personnel for the names of all related parties and details of any transactions with these parties during the period;

(c) review the annual return to ascertain in which other companies directors hold directorships;

(d) find out the names of all pension funds connected with the company and the managers thereof;

(e) review the register of substantial shareholders to identify shareholders with more than 10% of the voting shares;

(f) review material investment transactions during the period to determine whether the nature and extent of investments created related parties.

9.5   Audit procedures

All audit staff members should be supplied with the names of the related parties so that they may become aware of transactions with the parties during their examination.
    The following additional steps should also be carried out:

(a) the minutes of meetings of the board of directors and executive or operating committees should be examined to find out material transactions authorised or discussed;

(b) consideration should be given to whether free accounting, management or other services are provided or received or a major shareholder absorbs company expenses;

(c) bills from solicitors or counsel who have performed regular or special services for the company should be reviewed for indications of related party transactions;

(d) confirmations of loans receivable and payable should be examined for indications of guarantees: when such guarantees are found the relationship of the guarantors to the company should be established;

(e) obtain an understanding of the real purpose of the transactions and the substance of the transactions rather than their legal form;

(f) confirm transaction amounts and items, including guarantees and other significant data with the other party or parties to the transaction, where appropriate;

(g) confirm significant information with intermediaries such as banks, guarantors, agents or solicitors to obtain a better understanding of the transaction;

(h) refer to financial publications, trade journals, credit agencies and other information sources if there is reason to believe that customers, suppliers or other organisations with which material amounts of business have been transacted may lack substance;

(i) obtain in respect of material uncollected balances, guarantees and other obligations, information as to the financial standing of the other party or parties: such information may be obtained from audited accounts, management accounts, financial publications and credit agencies.

9.6 Disclosure

The Companies Act 1985 requires the disclosure of significant contracts in which directors have a material interest. It should be remembered that a "director" is deemed to include any person in accordance with whose directions or instructions the directors of the company are accustomed to act. In some circumstances it may therefore be necessary to disclose material related party transactions in the accounts, so as to show a true and fair view.

9.7 Typical examination questions

Most advanced auditing examination papers now include one or more questions of a "mini-case study" type, clearly involving related parties, and students are expected to annotate the further enquiries which an auditor should make in the circumstances, as well as the audit evidence he would seek. It should be remembered that related party transactions are not illegal—the questions which arise relate purely to disclosure in the accounts and/or the directors' report. Many related party situations result in one or more companies within a group incurring expenditure at a level which exceeds what would be incurred if they were dealing with outsiders on an arm's length basis. In such situations it is of paramount importance for the auditor to ensure:

(a) that all directors of the companies adversely affected are fully aware of the situation and that the amounts have been quantified so far as possible; and

(b) that the position of minority interests has been considered.

Where an auditor is responsible for the accounts of a subsidiary thus adversely affected, he has a primary duty to ensure that minority interests in that subsidiary are made aware of the position in the notes to the accounts or, if necessary, in the auditor's report.

Accounts which do no more than reflect the trading results in terms of accurate monetary amounts cannot be said to give a *fair* as well as a *true* view, since they give no indication of profitability/net asset levels attainable in circumstances in which all transactions with outsiders are conducted at arm's length.

10.0 TRANSACTIONS INVOLVING RESERVATION OF TITLE

10.1 Introduction

The *Romalpa* case (*Aluminium Industrie Vaassen BV* v. *Romalpa Aluminium Ltd*) decided in the Court of Appeal on 16th January 1976 has many implications for auditors whose clients purchase goods or sell them subject to reservation of title. While the terms of sale of such transactions may vary from case to case, the general effect is that the seller retains title over the goods sold until paid for, and may even have rights over other goods produced from them, and the ultimate sale proceeds.

Banks and others who lend money secured by a floating charge are vitally concerned with the strength of the borrower's balance sheet, and the inclusion in stock of an unrecognised value of goods purchased under Romalpa-type contracts could seriously undermine their security. Where both the company and its auditors fail to detect and indicate the value of stock so purchased they could be laying themselves open to serious consequences if the company fails, and its suppliers exercise their rights.

Clearly, therefore, the auditor has a responsibility to enquire whether the client purchases goods from suppliers on terms which include reservation of title by the suppliers and, if the answer is in the affirmative, to review the client's procedures for determining the value of the goods.

The Institute has issued a guidance statement which points out the need to decide at what stage such goods should be treated as sold by the supplier, and as purchased by the purchasing company. *In reaching this decision, it is considered that the commercial substance of the transaction should take precedence over its legal form.* If the circumstances indicate that the reservation of title is regarded by the client company as having no practical relevance (except in the event of the insolvency of the purchasing company) then it is recommended that, to give a true and fair view, goods should be treated as *purchases in the accounts of the purchasing company, and as sales in the accounts of the supplier* (i.e. a *commercial basis*).

Note that if the financial position of the purchasing company throws doubt on the going concern concept, the accounting treatment of goods supplied on such terms will need particular consideration. In the rare circumstances that the accounts have been drawn up on some basis other than the going concern basis, it would be necessary to have regard to the strict legal position in relation to the transactions.

10.2   Disclosure

There are *two* matters that may require to be disclosed in the accounts:

(a) *Accounting policy:* if the accounts are materially affected by the accounting treatment adopted in relation to sales or purchases subject to reservation of title, the policy adopted should be disclosed.

(b) *Secured liability:* where, as would normally be the case, the commercial basis has been adopted, the accounts of the purchasing company should disclose that liabilities, subject to the reservation of title, are secured. The secured liability should be quantified in the accounts.

10.3   Taxation implications

The Inland Revenue has stated that, as long as both parties adopt the commercial basis recommended in the English Institute's statement, they will accept this basis for taxation purposes. If, however, either party draws up its tax computation or accounts on the legal basis, the Revenue reserves the right to insist on the legal basis being adopted by both parties.

10.4   Audit implications

Auditors of the *purchasing company* should adopt the following procedures:

(a) Ascertain from the directors, and from those responsible for purchasing, what steps they have taken to identify suppliers selling on terms subject to reservation of title.

(b) Review the steps taken to quantify the secured liability to suppliers at the balance sheet date, including goods not yet invoiced at that date.

(c) Examine the conditions of sale laid down by suppliers selected for testing. Where these tests identify creditors who have supplied goods subject to reservation of title, check that the disclosed year-end secured liability to these creditors is correctly stated.

(d) Where there are material secured liabilities to suppliers:

   (i) ensure that these liabilities are stated as being secured in the accounts;

   (ii) ensure that the relevant accounting policy has been disclosed in the accounts.

(e) Obtain formal written representations, in the letter of representation, from the directors either that there are no material liabilities of this nature to be disclosed, or that the amount is fully disclosed in the accounts.

To auditors of the *supplying* company, reservation of title will be relevant only in considering the valuation of the debt. Where a provision for bad or doubtful debts is contemplated, the ability to recover the goods may have some bearing on the value of the debt.

In view of the increase in the number of contracts which include Romalpa-type clauses, audit sampling procedures should now especially be designed to discover their presence, and to ascertain whether the client was aware of their existence and contractual implications. In certain cases the client will have attempted to revoke such clauses, and if the auditor is in any doubt as to the exact legal position he should consider the need to seek legal opinion for clarification purposes.

10.5 Recent developments

Two subsequent cases have significantly altered the ability of the supplier to enforce retention clauses. In the action brought by Monsanto Ltd against the joint receivers of Bond Worth Ltd, Monsanto attempted to claim not that they retained legal title to the goods, but that they retained equitable and beneficial ownership and, as such, had the benefit of a trust over the goods. The court concluded that the clause in the contract was intended to be a charge over property and accordingly had to be registered at Companies House in accordance with section 395 of the Companies Act 1985. Because the charge had not been registered it was void against the creditor.

The second case was an action brought by Borden (UK) Ltd against the receiver of Scottish Timber Products Ltd. Borden, the supplier, claimed title over not only its unprocessed goods that were still held by the purchaser, but also over new goods manufactured by the purchaser which contained the supplier's goods. The supplier also claimed the right to trace the proceeds from the sales of any of the purchaser's products which contained its goods. The three judges in the Court of Appeal decided unanimously that a supplier's retention of title applied only to the goods that still existed. The Court of Appeal said that it was indefensible to claim to retain title to something that no longer existed. These cases are considered in more detail below.

The present position regarding retention of ownership clauses can be summarised as follows:

(a) A clause that reserves the legal and equitable title in the goods supplied until payment is made is likely to be effective to preserve the seller's rights to recover the goods intact if the sale contract is breached, provided that the goods have not been mixed with other goods from which they cannot be separated, and provided that the purchaser was both notified of, and accepted, the terms of trade.

(b) A simple clause that reserves property is not sufficient either to give a seller any rights to the ownership of, or to trace the proceeds of the sale from, any goods into which its goods have been mixed, and from which they cannot be separated. In order to achieve reservation of title in such circumstances a specific provision in the selling terms must be included to give the seller specific rights over the new goods and the proceeds.

(c) If the contract does provide specific provisions to give the seller rights over either new goods, or the proceeds of their sale, the provisions may be void unless they are registered as a charge under section 395 of the Companies Act 1985. These points have not yet been expressly decided by the courts.

There is a general feeling amongst lawyers that seems to indicate that retention of ownership will, in practice, be effectively restricted to those goods of the supplier which remain in the customer's stock, which are identifiable, and which have not undergone part of any manufacturing process. Therefore, if a company wants to include a retention of ownership clause in the terms of sale, it should consult its solicitors.

10.6   Legal background

There is in fact nothing new about retention of title. The Sale of Goods Act 1979 specifically provides for it and in some trade sectors these clauses have been common. In Europe sellers take active steps to impose terms of this kind, and with an increase in inter-EEC trade, UK traders must understand the consequence of agreeing to a contract term of this kind.

Put at its simplest, the seller says, "I will supply you with these goods for you to sell but I will retain legal ownership of them until you have paid me in full for *everything* supplied". Thus the purchaser has no legal ownership at any time even if the goods are received and re-sold, until he pays for them. The ultimate buyer *does* get good title, however, unless he is aware of the retention of title clause. For a retailer not to own the goods means that he cannot use them as security for an overdraft or floating charges; nor can his creditors seize the goods. So credit may be difficult to obtain, and a receiver's job becomes a nightmare.

However, it is essential that the clause is drafted in crystal clear terms, particularly where the goods being sold are not finished goods to be re-sold as they stand, but raw materials to be incorporated in the manufacture of a product. In each of the important recent cases the seller sought to protect itself in case the buyer defaulted on the payment of goods sold, and the goods were to be added by the purchaser to other goods in a process of manufacture, thus losing their original identity.

In the *Romalpa* case, the Dutch seller had retained legal title to aluminium foil by express reservation until it was paid all money due to it from the buyer. The seller was entitled to recover all unused or unsold foil if the buyer defaulted and, as the clause had imposed on the buyer a duty to account to the seller for the proceeds of sale of all unmixed foil, it was held that the buyer was fully accountable to the seller who had priority over all other creditors. Although the *Romalpa* clause was worded tortuously (and was not improved by translation), it was extremely effective because the buyer was treated as the agent for the seller until such time as he had paid for all aluminium foil with which he had been supplied.

In *Borden (UK) Ltd* v. *Scottish Timber Products Ltd* another retention of title clause was scrutinised on an appeal against a decision upholding its validity. Borden sold resin to the defendants who used it with other products to make chipboard. The clause said that the property in the resin being sold would pass only when the goods comprised in the contract had been paid for in full. The lower court implied a licence on the part of the buyer to use the resin to make chipboard and held that the seller had no title to the chipboard in which the resin had been incorporated. What the seller did have, said the judge, was an equitable right to trace the proceeds of sale of the resin and chipboard mixture. The Court of Appeal gave short shrift to this argument. Once used, the resin was completely changed in character and it was quite impossible to recover it. The resin no longer existed, and the court said that it was untenable to claim to retain title to something which no longer existed.

In *Re Bond Worth Ltd*, known as the *Monsanto* case, the seller had attempted to impose a condition in its contract retaining "equitable and beneficial" ownership of acrilan which it had sold for use in the process of making man-made fibre. Monsanto, the seller, lost the case because the judge held that the clause did not give it any legal ownership—which, he said, had passed on delivery of the acrilan. He said Monsanto had an equitable interest capable of being registered at Companies House under Companies Act 1985, s. 395 but, as it had not been so registered, he held that Monsanto had no priority over creditors and was totally unsecured.

The lessons to be learned from these major cases are varied. To be effective, a retention of title clause must specifically retain legal ownership. Sellers seeking to protect themselves will run into substantial difficulties where what is being sold is to be used in a manufacturing process, rather than re-sold in the same (or similar) form. Buyers seeking credit of whatever kind from external sources must be prepared to disclose their contracts to potential lenders who will need to be satisfied that the debtor does in fact own what it is offering as security. Above all, traders must understand the wording and effect of the contracts which they make. In both the *Borden* and *Monsanto* cases the clauses were held to be ineffective. Simply because a contract contains certain terms they are not necessarily effective, binding or sacrosanct.

Consideration must also be given to the question of insurance, which is primarily concerned with risk rather than ownership. In two of the above cases risk was expressed to pass on delivery, which is the normal rule under the Sale of Goods Act 1979, and so the buyer, though not owning the goods, had an insurable interest. In the event of a company failing, or a receiver being appointed, loss or damage to goods subject to a valid retention of title clause could constitute a double burden in the absence of adequate insurance.

In the opinion of *True & Fair*, the statement on auditing "Guidance for auditors on the implications of goods sold subject to reservation of title" is still relevant. However, clients should review the type of clauses incorporated in their conditions of sale in the light of the *Monsanto* and *Scottish Timber* decisions. From an audit point of view, every reservation clause should be subject to critical examination.

11.0   VERIFICATION OF DEFERRED TAXATION

11.1   Introduction

When SSAP 11 was passed as a standard, it appears that the full impact on amounts set aside for deferred taxation was not fully appreciated. The causes of the problem lay in:

(a) the effect of substantial price increases on the amount of balancing charges arising on asset replacement;

(b) stock relief for corporation tax purposes;

(c) capital gains rolling-over provisions resulting in the deferment of corporation tax while the business or division involved remained a going concern.

As a result of the above very large amounts of deferred taxation were set aside—not to be included as part of shareholders' funds—but which, at the same time, were extremely unlikely ever to result in the actual payment to the Revenue of a taxation liability.

Due to the resistance and resentment generated by this situation, SSAP 11 was withdrawn by the ASC in 1976, and SSAP 15, "Accounting for Deferred Taxation", replaced it in October 1978, to take effect for accounting periods beginning on or after 1st January 1979. In May 1985 a revised SSAP 15 was published.

11.2   Audit implications

SSAP 15 (revised) introduces new areas of judgment and assessment of probability for the auditor. Its main proposals are:

(a) deferred tax should be accounted for on the liability method in respect of the tax reduction arising from all originating timing differences of material amount;

(b) if a company is a going concern and can *demonstrate* with *reasonable probability* that any tax reduction will continue for the *foreseeable future*, deferred taxation need not be provided for within the profit and loss account;

(c) the potential amount of deferred tax on all timing differences should be disclosed by way of notes to the accounts;

(d) deferred tax should not be shown as part of shareholders' funds.

11.3   Critical audit factor

It follows from the previous section that the critical problem for the auditor is to determine whether the directors' decision whether or not to provide for deferred taxation is soundly based on reasonable evidence of future intentions. If there is doubt as to whether tax will or will not be payable, provision for deferred tax should be made.

The existence of material unutilised capital allowances at the balance sheet date will usually mean that the company does not have to demonstrate to the auditor as much in the way of future expenditure intentions and availability of finance, as will be the case where no backlog of unutilised allowances exists.

11.4   The need to examine budgets

In other instances, the pattern of past capital expenditure and stock investment may mean that the auditor will not need to rely solely on future projections. Differing circumstances, therefore, will probably require companies to provide differing degrees of supporting documentation for auditors. However, it may be necessary (particularly where no backlog of unutilised allowances exists, or where no consistent pattern of expenditure can be shown from past experience) for a *company* to prepare, and for the *auditor* to examine, a series of budgets in respect of:

(a) the trading position showing estimated profit and the depreciation charge;

(b) a cash flow budget;

(c) a capital expenditure and disposals budget;

(d) a forecast of stock values.

A company which does not provide these statements may well find it difficult to convince its auditor that a deferred tax provision is not required.

11.5   "Reasonable probability"

After examining all available evidence (including directors' minutes and the company's past level of success in forecasting) the auditor must decide whether a deferred tax provision is necessary or not. A 50:50 chance of success, on the one hand, would be too low, and absolute certainty, on the other, impossible to achieve. Auditors will therefore need to judge which types of timing difference in a company are likely to be most susceptible to variation from the forecast level. For example, in some cases the degree of probability of obtaining stock relief may, given the risk of supply shortages, be less than that of being able to incur the requisite level of capital expenditure. The degree of certainty required will then depend upon the materiality of the amounts involved in the context of all other factors affecting a company's future.

11.6   Land and buildings

Deferred taxation on revaluation surpluses on land and buildings will generally no longer be necessary, but as soon as the directors have taken a decision to dispose of the property and not to re-invest the proceeds to obtain roll-over relief, a provision should be made.

11.7   Conclusion

In order that auditors can form a view as to the general acceptability of the provisions of SSAP 15 (revised), they need to consider, in the light of their everyday experience, the following questions:

(a) How far ahead in time should forecasts extend, be they documented or not?

(b) To the extent that forecasts do need to be documented, what degree of supporting evidence will be needed, and is such information likely to be available?

(c) What, in practical terms, constitutes "reasonable probability"?

11.8   General comment

It is of some interest to note that attempts over the past few years to establish a standard accounting treatment on deferred taxation appear to have reflected inversely the country's economic situation. The first standard on this subject, SSAP 11, was drafted during the aftermath of the recession of the early/mid-1970s, and was regarded as suitably restrictive in its import. During the latter years of the decade, with the improvement in corporate profitability, it was felt that substantial sums of what were, in effect, shareholders' funds, were being locked in the deferred taxation provision despite the fact that these sums were unlikely ever to result in payment to the Revenue of a corporation tax liability. For this reason, SSAP 11 was withdrawn and replaced by the more liberally drafted SSAP 15. These provisions are still included in SSAP 15 (revised).

This standard incorporates phraseology of extraordinary vagueness—"foreseeable future" and "reasonable probability", in particular. The recent economic recession saw the level of corporate bankruptcy rising sharply; foreign competition and the fluctuating value of the pound were undermining industrial performance; and the unemployment figures were the highest they had been since the 1930s. In such circumstances a realistic application of SSAP 15 (revised) terminology was virtually impossible and many auditors must have acknowledged that SSAP 11 might have been a more appropriate standard at that time, for all its restrictiveness.

12.0   GOING CONCERN PROBLEMS

12.1   Introduction

One of the concepts described in SSAP 2 is that which assesses the client company as a "going concern". If this assumption is not justified the valuations used for financial reporting purposes may be dramatically affected. The auditor should therefore take all possible steps to diagnose the client's financial strength.

12.2   The symptoms

The diagnosis should begin by considering whether the client displays any of the following symptoms:

(a) loan repayments are falling due in the near future;

(b) high or increasing debt to equity ratios existing (high gearing);

(c) companies are heavily or increasingly dependent upon short-term finance;

(d) there is inability to take advantage of discounts, necessity to pay on cash terms, or the time taken to pay creditors is increasing;

(e) substantial losses are occurring, or the rate of profitability is declining;

(f) purchases are being deferred, thereby reducing stocks to dangerously low levels;

(g) capital expenditure is being switched to leasing agreements;

(h) a company is in an exposed position in relation to future commitments, such as long-term assets financed by short- or medium-term borrowings;

(i) a company has a net deficiency of assets, or its ratio of current assets to current liabilities is declining;

(j) a company is near to its present borrowing limits, with no sign of a reduction in requirements;

(k) collection from debtors is slowing down;

(l) rapid development of business creates a dangerous overtrading situation;

(m) there is substantial investment in new products, ventures or research which are not yet successful;

(n) there is reliance on a limited number of products, customers or suppliers;

(o) there is evidence of reductions or cancellations of capital projects;

(p) there is heavy dependence on an overseas holding company (for finance or trade).

12.3 Further audit steps

If the presence of *any* of the above factors is evident, further steps must be taken to confirm that the client is a going concern—and not on the way out. At the very least the auditor must:

(a) compare the client's cash flow forecast with the overdraft or other loan facilities available for up to twelve months from the accounting date;

(b) obtain written confirmation from the holding company that it intends its subsidiary to continue in business and will not withdraw loan facilities;

(c) enquire into or obtain written evidence of any steps the client is taking to correct its decline in fortunes.

If the auditor cannot satisfy himself that the client will remain in business in the foreseeable future, then he must reconsider the going concern basis.

12.4   Small companies

Particular care should be taken in reviewing small or proprietor-controlled companies, especially where there are substantial "loans" from directors.

Such loans are often regarded as forming part of the long-term capital of the company. For the purposes of the going concern assessment, they should be so treated only if they are legally subordinated to all other creditors. There should be adequate disclosure of the position.

Where directors' loans rank *pari passu* with other unsecured creditors, they should be treated as ordinary current liabilities. This will help to emphasise any deficiency of assets as regards unsecured creditors unless other financial support has been arranged, and will indicate that the going concern basis of valuation of assets may not be applicable.

12.5   Auditing Guideline (August 1985): The Auditor's Considerations in Respect of Going Concern

Preface

This guideline gives guidance on the auditor's considerations as to whether or not it is appropriate for an enterprise to prepare financial statements on a going concern basis, i.e. on a basis which assumes that the enterprise is able to continue in operational existence for the foreseeable future. It is supplementary to, and should be read in conjunction with, the auditor's operational and reporting standards and related guidelines.

This guideline is written in the context of the audit of companies incorporated under the Companies Acts. However, in the absence of specific provisions to the contrary, the principles embodied in this guideline apply also to the audit of other enterprises.

Introduction

1.   The directors of a company have a statutory responsibility to prepare financial statements which give a true and fair view and comply with the Companies Acts. This means that the directors are responsible for the appropriateness of the basic assumptions underlying the financial statements.

2.   Schedule 4 of the Companies Act 1985 provides that items shown in the financial statements of a company should be determined in accordance with the principle that it is presumed to be carrying on business as a going concern. Departures from this principle may be made if it appears to the directors that there are special reasons for doing so. Disclosures of the departure, the reasons for it and its effect are required to be made in the financial statements.

3.   Statement of Standard Accounting Practice No. 2 identifies going concern as one of the fundamental accounting concepts and provides that if financial statements are prepared on the basis of assumptions which differ materially from that concept the facts should be explained in the financial statements.

4.   The going concern concept identified in Statement of Standard Accounting Practice No. 2 is "that the enterprise will continue in operational existence for the

foreseeable future. This means in particular that the profit and loss account and the balance sheet assume no intention or necessity to liquidate or curtail significantly the scale of operation.''

5.   Where the going concern basis is no longer appropriate, adjustments may have to be made to the values at which balance sheet assets and liabilities are recorded, to the headings under which they are classified and for possible new liabilities.

6.   The auditor of a company has a statutory responsibility to express an opinion as to whether the financial statements give a true and fair view and comply with the Companies Acts. When forming his opinion, the auditor needs to consider whether there are reasonable grounds for accepting that the financial statements should have been prepared on a going concern basis. The auditor should therefore be satisfied when planning, performing and evaluating the results of his audit procedures that the going concern basis is appropriate. If, during the course of his audit, the auditor becomes aware of any indications that the going concern basis may no longer be valid, he should carry out the additional procedures outlined in this guideline. If the auditor's procedures reveal no such indications, it will be reasonable for him to accept that the going concern assumption is appropriate.

7.   It is implicit in assessing the foreseeable future that a judgment must be made about uncertain future events. No certainty exists nor can any guarantee be given that any enterprise will continue as a going concern. Hence the auditor's judgment will always involve an assessment, made at the time that the audit report is signed, of the risk that liquidation or enforced substantial curtailment of the scale of operations will occur.

8.   While the foreseeable future must be judged in relation to specific circumstances, it should normally extend to a minimum of six months following the date of the audit report or one year after the balance sheet date whichever period ends on the later date. It will also be necessary to take account of significant events which will or are likely to occur later.

Background

9.   A company rarely ceases to carry on business without any prior indications, either of inability to meet debts as they fall due or of other problems that raise questions about the continuation of business. The indications may vary in importance depending upon specific circumstances. They may be interdependent and some may only have significance as audit evidence when viewed in conjunction with others. Further, their significance may diminish because they are mitigated by other audit evidence. Paras 10 and 11 below list examples of such indications and paras 12 and 13 list examples of mitigating evidence. The lists are not intended to be exhaustive.

10.   Indications that a company may be unable to meet its debts as they fall due include recurring operating losses, financing to a considerable extent out of overdue suppliers and other creditors (for example, VAT, PAYE, National

Insurance), heavy dependence on short-term finance for long-term needs, working capital deficiencies, low liquidity ratios, over-gearing in the form of high or increasing debt to equity ratios, and under-capitalisation, particularly if there is a deficiency of share capital and reserves. Other matters that could indicate difficulty would include borrowings in excess of limits imposed by debenture trust deeds, default on loan or similar agreements, dividends in arrears, restrictions placed on usual trade terms, excessive or obsolete stock, long overdue debtors, non-compliance with statutory capital requirements, deterioration of relationship with bankers, necessity of seeking new sources or methods of obtaining finance, the continuing used of old fixed assets because there are no funds available to replace them, the size and content of the order book and potential losses on long-term contracts.

11. Indications of problems that raise questions about the continuation of a business and which might lead to an inability to meet its debts might include internal matters, for example loss of key management or staff, significantly increasing stock levels, work stoppages or other labour difficulties, substantial dependence on the success of a particular project or on a particular asset, excessive reliance on the success of a new product and uneconomic long-term commitments. Alternatively, indications may relate to external matters, for example legal proceedings or similar matters that may jeopardise a company's ability to continue in business, loss of a key franchise or patent, loss of a principal supplier or customer, the undue influence of a market dominant competitor, political risks, technical developments which render a key product obsolete, and frequent financial failures of enterprises in the same industry.

12. Indications that the company may be unable to meet its debts might be mitigated by factors relating to alternative means for maintaining adequate cash flows. Such factors include, for example, the ability to dispose of assets or to postpone the replacement of assets without adversely affecting operations, to lease assets rather than purchase them outright, to obtain new sources of finance, to renew or extend loans, to restructure debts, to raise additional share capital, and to obtain financial support from other group companies.

13. Similarly, indications of problems that raise questions about the continuation of business might be mitigated by factors relating to the company's capacity to adopt alternative courses of action, for example the availability of suitable persons to fill key positions, the likelihood of finding alternative sales markets when a principal customer is lost, the ability to replace assets which have been destroyed and the possibility of continuing the business by making limited reductions in the level of operations or by making use of alternative resources.

Audit procedures and reports

PROCEDURES

14. In performing the preparatory procedures identified in the Auditing Guideline "Planning, Controlling and Recording", the auditor should consider whether any of the indications of the nature described in paras 10 and 11 above are present.

15.   Such procedures would not generally encompass any specific additional procedures, since the matters identified above would normally be known to the auditor as a result of his other audit procedures. However, in this context the auditor will be particularly concerned with interim accounts or management information, and consulting with the directors and staff of the company. Such consultations should address not only the current situation but also the future. Where formal forecast and budget systems exist, they should be considered. Where they are not formalised, discussions should be directed to the directors' outline plans, including a comparison of anticipated needs with borrowing facilities and limits.

16.   The auditor should continue this consideration to the date of the audit report, although early identification of evidence that the company may be unable to continue in business will give the directors more time to consider their response and to obtain suitable professional advice.

17.   Where as a result of these procedures, evidence comes to the auditor's attention that suggests that the company may be unable to continue in business, he should review any factors that may counterbalance that evidence. The review should include further discussions with the directors and may also embrace other work as described in the following four paragraphs. These paragraphs are only indicative of the matters to be considered and are not intended to be exhaustive.

18.   Where the directors have developed plans to overcome the company's problems, the auditor should consider the bases on which they have been prepared, consider whether they conform with facts already known to him and compare them with such independent evidence as is available. If such plans are to have value for audit purposes, they should be specific rather than general and above all be feasible courses of action. The auditor should be aware that the relevance of such plans generally decreases as the time period for planned actions and anticipated events increases. A company which does not provide adequate forecasts and budgets as a matter of course will need to develop such information if it is facing difficulties, although small companies need not be expected to provide the same amount and quality of evidence as large companies.

19.   In certain circumstances (for example, where finance is to be provided by third parties or where there are detailed plans to dispose of assets, borrow, restructure debt or increase share capital) the auditor may need to obtain written confirmations from banks or other third parties in order to be able to assess the degree of their commitment.

20.   The auditor should consider any professional advice obtained by the directors as to the extent of the company's difficulties and the practicalities of overcoming them. The directors are responsible for obtaining such professional advice and, in addition to advice which the auditor himself may be able to provide, may need to consult others such as bankers, insolvency practitioners and solicitors. In particular, it may be necessary for the directors to obtain legal advice on the consequences of the company continuing to trade while it is known by the directors to be insolvent.

21.   Where the company is a member of a group, the auditor should consider the implications of any obligations, undertakings or guarantees which exist between the company and other group members. Consideration should be given both to undertakings or guarantees given by the company and to those received by it. There are many different ways of providing support within a group and a proper understanding of complex agreements may not be possible without legal advice. When considering whether to place reliance on such agreements the auditor has to judge the probability that, in the event that support becomes necessary, it will be forthcoming. He should consider whether the agreements are prima facie legally binding or merely expressions of intent, whether they have been formally approved and minuted, and whether the supporting company is in a position to provide support. He may need to examine the financial statements of other group companies, consult with the management of such companies and, where appropriate, liaise with their auditors. Similar considerations arise where a company is dependent upon the support of another entity, even if no group relationship exists.

22.   Having carried out the procedures and review referred to in paras 14 to 21, the auditor can then consider whether he has sufficient evidence on which to reach a decision as to whether it is appropriate that the financial statements should have been prepared on a going concern basis.

UNQUALIFIED AUDIT REPORTS

23.   Where the auditor is satisfied that it is proper that the financial statements have been prepared on a going concern basis, no mention of any matters relating to the application of that basis will normally be required in the audit report.

24.   There may, however, be circumstances where the reader will obtain a better understanding of the financial statements, and of the appropriateness of the basis on which they are prepared, if his attention is drawn to important matters. Examples might include events or conditions, such as operating trends, borrowing facilities or financing arrangements, awareness of which is fundamental to an understanding of the financial statements. In such circumstances, the auditor may decide to refer to these matters in his report as an emphasis of matter in accordance with the Auditing Standard "The Audit Report".

QUALIFIED AUDIT REPORTS

25.   Where there is uncertainty about the appropriateness of the going concern basis, the auditor should consider the effect of that uncertainty upon the view given by the financial statements. In doing so, he should consider both the adequacy of the disclosure of the uncertainty in the financial statements and the extent of the adjustments that might need to be made to the financial statements in the event that they were not to be prepared on a going concern basis.

26.   In particular, the auditor should consider the recoverability and classification of assets, the classification of liabilities and the possibility of new liabilities were the company to cease to be a going concern. For example, there may be a need for provisions or amounts to be written off in respect of stocks and debtors,

reclassification of long-term liabilities which become due immediately, provisions in respect of redundancy payments and revaluations of assets at their market values. While it will not normally be practicable to quantify precisely the extent of the adjustments that would be necessary were the financial statements not to be prepared on a going concern basis, the auditor should form an opinion as to their likely impact on the financial statements.

27. Where the auditor considers that the uncertainty as to the appropriateness of the going concern assumption materially affects the view given by the financial statements, he should qualify his audit report giving a "subject to" opinion. Materiality should be judged in terms of the extent of the adjustments that would need to be made to the financial statements in the event that they were not to be prepared on a going concern basis. The audit report should refer to the going concern assumption upon which the financial statements have been based, the nature of the related uncertainty and the nature of the adjustments that may have to be made to the financial statements.

28. Set out below is an example of a qualified audit report which would be appropriate when uncertainty about the appropriateness of the going concern assumption materially affected the view given by the financial statements.

The example illustrates a form of wording which might be appropriate when the circumstances giving rise to the uncertainty were that the company was loss-making, current liabilities exceeded current assets, negotiations about vital financing arrangements had not been successfully completed at the date of the audit report, adequate disclosure of these facts had been made in the notes to the accounts, and adjustments would be needed to the financial statements were they not to be prepared on a going concern basis. In practice, the circumstances necessitating a qualified report may be different from those of the example, and the form of wording will need to be amended to fit the particular circumstances.

"Auditors' report to the members of ...

We have audited the financial statements on pages ... to ... in accordance with approved Auditing Standards.

The financial statements have been prepared on a going concern basis. This basis may not be appropriate because the company incurred a loss after taxation of £ ... during the year ended 31st December 19 ... and at that date its current liabilities exceeded its current assets by £ ... Further, the company is currently negotiating for long term facilities to replace the loan of £ ... which is repayable on ... These factors, which are explained in note ..., indicate that the company may be unable to continue trading.

Should the company be unable to continue trading, adjustments would have to be made to reduce the value of assets to their recoverable amount, to provide for any further liabilities which might arise, and to reclassify fixed assets and long-term liabilities as current assets and liabilities.

Subject to the company being able to continue trading, in our opinion the financial statements, which have been prepared under the historical cost convention, give a true and fair view of the state of affairs of the company at 31st December 19 ... and of its loss and source and application of funds for the year then ended and comply with the Companies Act 1985."

29. Where the uncertainty about the appropriateness of the going concern assumption is so fundamental as to prevent the auditor from forming an opinion on the financial statements, he will need to disclaim an opinion.

30. In rare cases, the auditor may conclude that the evidence indicating that the company is unable to continue in business is so overwhelming that he will wish to qualify on grounds of disagreement. In such cases, he should give an "except for" or "adverse" opinion depending on the extent of the adjustments that would be necessary were the financial statements not to be prepared on a going concern basis.

31. As discussed in paras 2 and 3, there is a presumption in both law and accounting standards that the financial statements are prepared on a going concern basis. Where there is significant uncertainty about the enterprise's ability to continue in business, this fact should be stated in the financial statements even when there is no likely impact on the carrying value and classification of assets and liabilities. Where this is not stated in the financial statements, the auditor should refer to it in his report.

32. The auditor should not refrain from qualifying his report if it is otherwise appropriate, merely on the grounds that it may lead to the appointment of a receiver or liquidator.

Appendix

LEGISLATION IN IRELAND EQUIVALENT TO SCHED. 4 OF THE COMPANIES ACT 1985

The equivalent legislation for Northern Ireland is contained in Sched. 6 of the Companies Act (Northern Ireland) 1960 [as amended by Sched. 1 of the Companies (Northern Ireland) Order 1982].

The Companies (Amendment) Bill 1985 when enacted will impose similar legislative requirements in the Republic of Ireland.

12.6   Commentary on guideline

The draft guideline issued in November 1983 has been replaced by the 1985 guideline above; however, in view of the controversial nature of the suggestions in the 1983 draft guideline, the author's response, published in the November 1983 issue of "Accountancy", is reproduced below in full.

The persistent difficulties which befell the economy in the 1970s have forced auditors to face up to one of the most enigmatic puzzles of the accounting framework: the effect on financial statements of the failure of the going concern concept to apply. Although included some thirteen years ago in SSAP 2 as one of the four fundamental concepts on which all accounting, as we know it, rests, its essential distinction from the other three concepts was never fully appreciated until we were first confronted by an appalling increase in the rate of business failure (averaging between 600 and 900 liquidations/bankruptcies per week throughout the recession). Almost all of these businesses will have produced their swansong financial statements on the assumption, in every case shown subsequently to be unfounded, that they were going concerns.

If financial statements are found to be in breach of the concepts of consistency, prudence or accruals (indeed both SSAP 2 and the Companies Act 1985 allows for such a possibility), the effect is usually capable of being quantified, explained, justified (hopefully) and, if necessary, referred to in the auditor's report.

In some cases it is even necessary to depart from these concepts to *avoid* a qualified audit report—such as where a company changes an accounting policy to comply with a new accounting standard—which is clear (but legitimate) breach of the consistency concept.

Fundamental difference

But the going concern concept is quite different. A set of financial statements drafted on any other basis would not be financial statements as we know them—and would indeed require a different title, e.g. liquidator's accounts. In the case of the other fundamental concepts, it is a *departure* that has to be justified; but when a company's financial position is such that its ongoing viability is subject to doubt, it is the validity of (and hence *adherence* to) the going concern assumption which requires, if possible, to be justified.

Further, the other concepts are all quite capable of being breached in relation to a *part* of the financial statements; for example, the inconsistent treatment of one type of transaction compared with its treatment in earlier periods; or the (imprudent) failure to provide for a debt which is clearly doubtful; or the inclusion of income which has not yet been earned. But the going concern concept not only relates to the entity *as a whole*; it also cannot ever be breached—not realistically, anyway. For curiously enough, no-one (to my knowledge) has ever seen a set of published financial statements drafted on a basis *other* than that of the going concern.

Doubts there may be, and these should always be expressed—in the auditor's report if nowhere else—but the basis used is inevitably that of the going concern, for one single reason: there is no valid or reliable alternative.

Should directors ever attempt to include assets at a value other than that based on their expected useful life, they would have to speculate on their immediate realisable value in the context of a forced sale—and such speculation would of itself be regarded by one and all (including the auditors) as an admission that their business was now a "gone" concern, and would invoke all due processes of liquidation upon the instant.

If the auditors, of their own volition, tried to quantify the difference in the value of assets on a "realisable" as opposed to a going concern basis, they would find that they are totally lacking in the expertise required for such an exercise (and indeed the necessary equipment, i.e. a crystal ball!). An extended investigation performed to this end would, moreover, incur heavy fees which their beleaguered client can clearly ill afford, and which they would in any case be unlikely to receive.

From what has been said it should be clear that the going concern concept is so radically different from the others that it may be misleading to lump them all together, as they are in SSAP 2 and the Companies Act 1985, in which they are now enshrined as "accounting principles". The going concern concept is of a different order of "fundamentality"—being no less fundamental than, say, insistence that financial statements should be written rather than verbal; or that the balance sheet should balance. Since these requirements are so obvious as not to need any supporting legal stipulation, it may be preferable on practical grounds that references to the going concern assumption should be expunged from the accounting regulations. What, after all, is the point in insisting that a basis should be used when no alternative exists (other than as a theoretical proposition), and has certainly never been attempted outside of a winding-up?

Let me hasten to add that I am not suggesting that we, in our auditing capacity, should relax our concern (or the procedures which underlie that concern) regarding the viability of client businesses in the foreseeable future: indeed, if our doubts in this regard are significant when the time comes to sign the audit report, normal standards of professional competence dictate that these should be fully expressed in terms which make their import abundantly clear to all who will read that report. The point is rather that for all our skills, we are simply not endowed with the prophetic insight needed to predict and quantify the financial consequences for all who might be affected should the company fail. There is therefore no point in attempting the impossible, and much point in *not* attempting it.

The new guideline

The effect of going concern considerations on auditing work has been exercising the energies of the APC, and their draft Guideline is reproduced above (see 12.5) from the November 1983 issue of *Accountancy*. It will be seen that the APC's approach hardly reflects the above obversations which, by and large, suggest that a passive attitude is appropriate, in line with that of SAS 34 operative in the US. On the other hand the APC may, with some justification, feel that North American attitudes to audit practice and procedures are no more than partly applicable to circumstances in the UK, since only listed companies in the US are subject to the Securities and Exchange Commission's mandatory audit requirements.

This distinction is of particular relevance in relation to going concern problems, which tend to affect auditors of small companies far more acutely than those of public companies. When large companies are in trouble, information on their difficulties tends to be widespread at an early date, and any reference thereto in the eventual audit report is likely to do no more than confirm what is fairly generally known. The institutional investors whose proportion of all quoted securities has been rising inexorably over the past twenty years, and now exceeds 60% of the total, have developed a sophisticated and reliable network of up-to-date information sources relating to both individual companies and the sectors in which they operate, and are hardly likely to be caught unawares by anything the auditors have to say in a report issued several months after the balance sheet date.

Small company auditors, like it or not, are often the only providers of impartial information to a wide range of interested groups, including banks and other providers of capital, potential investors and purchasers, outside shareholders, trade creditors, employees and trade unions, Revenue and VAT authorities, etc. An absence of going concern warnings when their inclusion is required by the circumstances is a virtual invitation to litigation. Yet despite these potential dangers, great caution has to be exercised in the formulation of the reports which issue such warnings.

In the light of these factors, APC had to decide first of all which of two basic approaches the Guideline should adopt:

(a) *the passive approach:* this allows auditors to *assume* financial viability unless they encounter clear indications that such an assumption is not justified, in which case a secondary series of enquiries would be triggered into action; or

(b) *the active approach:* this requires auditors to pursue a specific line of enquiry invoking vigorous testing of the going concern assumption, irrespective of whether any of the indications referred to in (a) above manifested.

It is my own view that there is no feasible mid-way point between these two approaches, and the eventual Guideline will have to identify which it has adopted as its premise. The advantages in favour of each approach are:

PASSIVE

(a) This will involve less audit time, and hence give rise to lower fee levels—an important factor for small clients (with the subsidiary advantage that the audit fee is less likely to be the final straw that actually pushes the company into insolvency—and hence that the auditor, as an unsecured creditor, will not be paid!).

(b) The recession, we are told, is moving to its close, and with it a reduction in the statistical probability that this particular client (i.e. the one being audited) is about to "go under".

(c) The positive enquiries pursued under the active approach will be regarded by many clients as unwarranted (which, it is to be hoped, will be true for the majority of them). Thus the active approach can be resented by clients.

ACTIVE

(a) Reliance on mere "indications" that viability is in doubt would be far too subjective to be workable. After all, different auditors possess varying degrees of talent for spotting such indications—what one might regard as a danger sign; (such as factoring book debts) may well be seen by another as an example of sound financial management!

(b) Many of the procedures in the active approach should in any case be performed in the context of a normal balance sheet verification programme, with particular reference to determining adequacy of provisions; asset lives and valuations; write-off periods; justification and basis for capitalisation of costs etc. as well as the usual analytical reviews.

In practice the active approach should not therefore involve a vast amount of incremental effort. The most important features which the active approach would include are:

(a) review of cash flow and profit forecasts;

(b) review of margins and profitability of main activities;

(c) review of new projects and developments and their conversion into profitable activities;

(d) review of trading and economic conditions for the industry;

(e) heavy dependence on a small number of key *contracts, customers, products, suppliers,* and *technical staff;*

(f) review of pricing and marketing policies, and the threat of competition.

Need for forecasting

The approach selected will, of course, determine to a large extent the nature of the guidance which follows, but there are certain issues which will in any case have to be dealt with, such as measuring the "foreseeable future" to be covered by the auditor's projected review of the post balance sheet period. This period is naturally subdivided between (i) the past (ending on the date on which the audit report is signed) and (ii) the future. The first part is not due for consideration here, since it is already covered in the Guideline on post balance sheet events. The remaining question therefore relates to (ii), the future. How far ahead should the auditor be looking? This is a matter on which it would be dangerous to be dogmatic, but a Guideline must, by definition, provide some sort of indication as a reference point.

To take a fixed measure of, say, six months from the date of the audit report would be quite unsatisfactory, since this would in practice give no consistency, and the length of the foreseeable future would vary from year to year and from company to company, depending on the promptness with which the financial statements are finalised and signed. Consistency can therefore be achieved only by reference to a fixed point, such as the balance sheet date.

It would therefore seem to be preferable to prescribe a *minimum* period of, say, twelve months from the balance sheet date, certain events of known significance beyond that period also being given due consideration, such as a loan stock redemption date, when a significant measure of refinancing will have to be negotiated.

Use of checklists

Although most firms have checklists of circumstances which either individually or collectively suggest going concern problems, it might be useful for such indications to be included within the Guideline, provided it is made abundantly clear that no checklist can ever be claimed to be exhaustive. Such indications should be scheduled with care, so as to include items which reflect the experience gathered over the past few years.

This experience has shown that providers of finance, banks in particular, are flexible in their approach to companies in difficulty, and do not generally foreclose if there is a reasonable expectation of recovery, provided that such expectation is supported by a realistic and fully documented management plan. The Revenue and VAT authorities, on the other hand, are sometimes far less understanding. All in all, following the experience of the past ten difficult years, the auditing profession is now ideally placed for assessing going concern risks efficiently and realistically, which means being able to discern those symptoms which, if present, are most likely to lead to a swift (as opposed to a gradual) decline.

It is, for example, not unknown for companies to publish balance sheets which present a picture of impending doom by any conventional criteria; and yet the same gloomy outlook is revealed year after year. Some other factor, such as the ability to generate a prodigious cash-flow at critical moments, keeps them going against all apparent odds. It may be that the cash is masking an inherent lack of profitability— but it is survival that ultimately counts.

The auditors of such a company must exercise great caution, for their own sakes as much as anyone's—for it can hardly be appropriate to issue a going concern qualification on the same company's accounts for ten years running! The company is clearly a hardy specimen and, on probabilities projected from its own track record (due to factors clearly not divined by its auditors), is likely to outlast many of us (apparently) more robust competitors.

The converse situation was described by Professor Tom Lee in his article in *Accountancy*, June 1982, on Laker Airways, whose published high profits for several successive years masked an immense deficiency in cash-flow generated from operations, as a result of which the end, when it came, was swift, relentless and devastating. The company's published accounts revealed trading profits in all of its last five years, although the "quality" of those profits was sometimes dubious—arising, for example, from currency translation rather than running an airline.

It is hoped that by now auditors are in a position to *refine* their checklists in such a way as to identify far more than the conventional risk indicators, and are able also to allocate individual indicators to particular "risk groups", to be used on a selective basis, depending on the particular circumstances of the client under review.

The relevant consideration would therefore be not simply the presence of a few indications included on the bland, generalised, multi-purpose checklists which now abound (in which it is often impossible to distinguish between symptoms and remedies!), but rather the presence of a particular *combination* of symptoms which, for the company displaying them, justify genuine concern and the need for urgent remedies to be applied.

Legal risks

The full Guideline should suggest that auditors of a company in such straits inform its directors of the statutory and common law consequences of trading while insolvent, suggesting that they should take their own independent legal advice on the matter. By no means all directors are aware, for example, of the personal financial liability which may attach to them in respect of national insurance which is unpaid in respect of the six months prior to the appointment of a liquidator.

By the same token, not all auditors are aware of the fact that the civil and criminal penalties imposed on "officers" of companies in the course of winding-up apply equally to their auditors in respect of offences committed (often inadvertently rather than knowingly) within the preceding two years. Still fewer auditors have realised that the criminal penalties on fraudulent trading now apply irrespective of whether the company is being wound up, this extension having been effected by s. 458 of the Companies Act 1985.

There is another factor which has considerable practical relevance: the question of whether the auditor is likely to be paid for the additional work involved in assessing the company's liability as a going concern. After all, it is usually suggested that auditors who doubt a client's viability should, *inter alia*, examine forecasts and budgets and perform a series of special going concern review tests; and that where, in the case of small companies, the management information required for the tests is not available, it should be produced by the auditor. While this is eminently sensible in theory, the outlook revealed by the tests may be negative, and auditors should therefore be particularly careful to reduce the time spent on such tests and procedures to the very minimum necessary.

There will be many marginal cases in which the company's circumstances give cause for concern, but do not merit a qualified audit report. None the less, the auditors may believe that to give a true and fair view the accounts should (just in case) distinguish preferred, secured and unsecured liabilities respectively, if necessary in more detail than the Companies Act requires. Although the audit report is unqualified, it may be advisable to draw attention to this additional information in the form of an emphasis of matter.

Communicating the problem

Another practical consideration relates to the possibility that the auditor's report, qualified on the grounds that the going concern assumption is of dubious validity, may itself prove to be the instrument of ultimate fatality, leading to the appointment of a receiver or liquidator. This is a matter of great importance to the auditor since, on the one hand, it is clearly not part of the auditor's function to push a client into liquidation if there is even a remote possibility of survival as a going concern (with or without the direct co-operation of creditors, banks or other group companies); but, by contrast, there may well be severe legal consequences for the auditor's own liability if he refrains from sounding the appropriate alarm bells which subsequent events show (with all the benefits of hindsight) to have been warranted.

In such circumstances the action against the auditor would in all probability be brought by the liquidator, on the grounds that:

(a) the auditor's clean report was issued negligently; and

(b) this negligence allowed the company to continue to trade beyond the point at which it had any reasonable expectation of being able to meet the liabilities accruing as a result of that further trading activity.

There is also the risk of a supplementary action against the auditors by the directors in respect of any liabilities which they are forced to bear personally, on the grounds that they allowed the company to continue to trade only on the strength of the clean audit opinion; and, finally, the risk already mentioned above under the winding-up provision of the Companies Act, the auditors (as officers) being party, albeit passively, to the company's continued trading while insolvent.

Not, all in all, a particularly delectable situation; and it is for this reason that the full Guideline should state, as explicitly as possible, that auditors have a public duty (i.e. far wider than a duty to the shareholders) to express their reservations about the client company's survival prospects, irrespective of the possible consequences of so doing.

Having said this, it is obviously advisable, if there is a choice, to allow events to take their own course as far as possible *before* issuing the audit report; with luck (one cannot say whose) it may never become necessary to draft it. In other words, if the client company is manifestly in trouble, it may be best for all concerned if the auditors keep well away. This has the double advantage for the auditor of:

(a) avoiding the expenditure of chargeable time which is not going to be paid for; and

(b) avoiding the problems referred to above concerning the drafting of the audit report (or, *how to impart the bad news without becoming a part of it!*).

The other advantage of adopting this policy of masterly inactivity is that in the auditor's absence the client's business may not only revive but thrive and, once again, the problem will have conveniently disappeared. (We shall, of course, leave aside the question of whether the company's new-found prosperity is in any way connected with the cessation of advice from its auditors.)

Conclusion

Let me conclude these thoughts by expressing the hope that the APC will *abandon* its recommendations that the auditor should assess the nature and extent of the adjustments to the financial statements which would be needed if the company proves not, in fact, to be a going concern. Such adjustments (which, I repeat, we should *not* attempt to calculate) would relate to:

(a) a revised classification of liabilities, those which are deferred in the accounts becoming immediately repayable;

(b) the possibility of new liabilities arising in the form of professional fees and redundancy payments; and

(c) a revised assessment of recoverable asset values (and a corresponding increase in the amount of provisions).

The reasons why such an exercise should not be attempted are, as already stated, quite simply that we are not (and could not ever be expected to be) clever enough, and would inevitably get it wrong; and, secondly, public expression of its results would become the immediate and efficient cause of the disaster it envisages—in effect, a self-fulfilling prophecy.

The draft Guideline recommends changes in the existing example (No. 7) of the audit report describing going concern uncertainty. I hope, in the light of the foregoing observations, that the APC will reconsider the need for any such changes. Example 7 adequately describes the matter (the need to refinance a substantial and imminent loan repayment) which is the immediate cause of the going concern doubts; it states what steps are being taken to solve the problem; it states that the company's viability is dependent on such a solution being found; and finally it states that the validity of the audit opinion on the truth and fairness of the financial statements is itself "subject to" the achievement of a satisfactory outcome.

That, in my view, makes the company's precipitous and unresolved state as clear to intelligent readers as the circumstances allow, and is therefore as far as any auditor can reasonably be expected to go.

13.0   AUDIT IMPLICATIONS OF GROUP VAT RELIEF

13.1   Legal background

Section 21 of the Finance Act 1972 allows a group of companies to elect to be treated as one company for VAT purposes. One company needs to be selected as the "representative member" within the group that is actually registered for tax purposes. As a result, any supply of goods or services by a member of the group to another member can then be disregarded for VAT purposes, and any other supply of goods or services by or to any member of the group is treated as a supply by or to the representative member.

In the circumstances when a group elects to be treated in this way for VAT purposes, all members of the group become liable jointly and severally for any tax due from the representative member. To this end, all companies within the group are required to sign a form which states that they "understand that all members of the group be jointly and severally liable for the VAT due from the representative member".

Several cases have arisen where such cross guarantees have caused audit problems, because the implication of the guarantee has not been considered. As a result, it is suggested that on all audits of group companies and on all audits of any company that is either a holding company or a subsidiary company within a group, auditors should ask the question "Has the group elected to be treated as one entity for VAT purposes under section 21 of the Finance Act 1972?"

13.2   Audit procedures

If the answer to this question is in the affirmative auditors should carry out the following additional procedures:

(a)   identify the company within the group that is the representative member;

(b)   enquire into the rights and duties of the members of the group against and towards each other as a result of the grouping treatment, and ensure that such arrangements are *intra vires*;

(c)   obtain confirmation from the management of the holding company that the group's VAT position is up to date and not in arrears;

(d)   consider whether the total VAT liability to the balance sheet is sufficiently material to be disclosed as a contingent liability in the individual accounts of the subsidiary companies.

Where the auditors are unable to obtain satisfactory evidence that the VAT position is both current and accurately stated, they should consider the effect this has on the overall going concern situation within the group and, if applicable, within individual subsidiaries.

It may be of interest that in the same way that the various members of the group may find it more convenient to be treated as if they were a single person, a single body corporate that is carrying on a business in several divisions may prefer to have those divisions treated as separate entities for VAT purposes. It is therefore provided that, if that body so requests and the Commissioners see fit, the registration may be in the names of those divisions. The auditors may need to take this into account when considering audit procedures within a company that has a divisional structure.

PROGRESS TEST 6

1.   What are the main purposes of obtaining a letter of representation? (1.1)

2.   Distinguish between adjusting and non-adjusting post balance sheet events. (2.0)

3.   Summarise the main features of stock verification with regard to:

(a)   physical verification; and

(b)   valuation in the balance sheet. (4.0)

4.   List the main contents of the standard bank confirmation letter. (6.0)

5.   What do you understand by "reservation of title"? (10.0)

CHAPTER SEVEN

The Auditor and the Companies Act 1985

GENERAL NOTE

The Companies Act 1985 was introduced to consolidate the requirements of the earlier Companies Acts (1948, 1967, 1976, 1980 and 1981). The ensuing pages have been set out to provide auditing students with a detailed summary of all companies' legislation which has a direct effect on auditors acting in a statutory capacity.

1.0 APPOINTMENT

COMPANIES ACT 1985, s.384

1.1 Basic rule

Every company shall at *each* AGM appoint an auditor (or auditors) to hold office until the conclusion of the next AGM.

1.2 Exceptions

    (a) The directors may appoint:

        (i) the first auditors, to hold office until the conclusion of the first AGM;

        (ii) auditors to fill a casual vacancy.

    (b) The Secretary of State for Trade and Industry may appoint auditors if neither members nor directors have done so. The company has a duty to inform the Secretary within one week of this power becoming exercisable.

2.0   REMOVAL

COMPANIES ACT 1985, ss. 386 and 388

A company may by ordinary resolution remove an auditor before the expiry of his term of office. Where such a resolution is passed the company shall notify the Registrar of Companies within fourteen days.

Note the resolutions at a general meeting for which *special notice* (twenty-eight days) is required:

(a) appointing an auditor *other* than the retiring auditor;

(b) filling a casual vacancy;

(c) reappointing a retiring auditor originally appointed by directors to fill a casual vacancy;

(d) removing the auditor before expiry of his term of office.

Note the steps designed to protect the auditor from unwarranted removal:

(a) On receipt of such notice the company shall send a copy to the existing auditor.

(b) The auditor has the right to make representations in writing, not exceeding a reasonable length, and may request that these shall be notified to the members.

(c) Upon receipt of such representations the company has a duty:

(i) in any notice of resolutions given to members of the company, to state the fact of the representations having been made; and

(ii) to circularise copies of the representations to every person entitled to receive notice of the meeting.

(d) If the representations are not circularised as prescribed (either because received too late or due to the company's default), the auditor may have them read out at the meeting, quite apart from his right to be heard orally on any matter which affects him as auditor.

(e) The representations need not be circularised, nor will the auditor possess the right to have them read out at the meeting, if, on the application of any person who claims to be aggrieved by the contents thereof, the court is satisfied that the auditor is abusing his rights in order to obtain needless publicity for defamatory matter. The court may order the costs of such an application to be borne (wholly or in part) by the auditor.

3.0   RIGHTS OF EX-AUDITOR

COMPANIES ACT 1985, s. 387

An auditor who has been *removed* may:

(a) attend the general meeting at which his term of office would have expired; and

(b) attend any general meeting at which it is proposed to fill the vacancy caused by his removal; and

(c) be heard at any such meeting on any business which concerns him as former auditor.

4.0   REMUNERATION

COMPANIES ACT 1985, s. 385
The auditor's remuneration shall be fixed by whomever makes the appointment. In practice this is not necessarily fixed in advance, the auditor simply making clear (in the letter of engagement) the basis of arriving at the audit fee. The audit fee, together with expenses incurred in connection with the audit, must be disclosed in the company's published accounts regardless of how the fees are determined.

5.0   QUALIFICATION

COMPANIES ACT 1985, s. 389
The following shall *not* be qualified to act as auditor of a limited company:

(a) a body corporate;

(b) a person who is *not* a member of one of the following:

(i)   the Institute of Chartered Accountants (ICA) in England and Wales;

(ii) the ICA in Scotland;

(iii) the ICA in Ireland;

(iv) the Chartered Association of Certified Accountants;

(c) an officer or servant of the company;

(d) a partner or employee of an officer or servant of the company.

5.1   Explanatory notes

Body corporate
A body corporate is a legal "person", whose liability is usually limited in some way. The audit is in the nature of a personal service, and this is incompatible with the idea of limited liability. The auditor is to be regarded as personally responsible for the quality of his work and that of any persons to whom he may delegate it.

It is of interest to note, however, that the professional bodies have sought to obtain some form of limited liability, especially due to the increased range of potential liability that has become apparent in recent years, and the difficulty in obtaining adequate insurance cover for professional negligence risks. It is suggested that liability should be restricted in proportion to the audit fee (e.g. ten times the fee), with a specified maximum upper limit. Presumably, the "price" of such a limitation would be:

(a) a suitable form of disclosure of the firm's accounts; and

(b) a requirement to guarantee professional indemnity insurance cover up to the amount of maximum liability.

Professional qualification

(a) Apart from what is specified above, the Secretary of State will grant similar status to the holder of an equivalent qualification obtained abroad, provided reciprocal arrangements exist in the country concerned for holders of UK qualifications.

(b) Any person without a professional qualification, but holding Department of Trade and Industry authority as having had equivalent experience in practice prior to 6th August 1946 (the date on which the 1948 Act was introduced as a Bill), *may accept appointment without restriction.*

(c) Any person without a professional qualification, but who:

    (i) has had sufficient experience as an accountant and auditor in practice throughout the twelve months to 3rd November 1966 (the date on which the 1967 Act was introduced as a Bill); and

    (ii) was on that date the duly appointed auditor of at least one company classed as an "exempt private company"; may continue to act as auditor of limited company clients and may accept further such appointments, *provided* that no shares or debentures of the company in question have been quoted publicly.

But note that authority from the Secretary of State was necessary before exemption on these grounds was possible, and *no further such authorities are now being issued.*

Officer or servant

Any member of staff on the full-time payroll establishment may be regarded as a servant for this purpose. "Officer" is defined in section 744 of the Act—the "definitions" section—as including a director, secretary or manager. See appendix to this chapter.

Partner or employee of officer or servant

If, for example, A, B and C are partners in the firm of ABC & Co, chartered or certified accountants, and A is also a director of XYZ Ltd:

(a) A obviously cannot act as auditor of XYZ Ltd, since he is an officer;

(b) neither B nor C can act as auditors of XYZ Ltd since they are *partners* of an officer (A) of the company: similarly, the firm ABC & Co, cannot be appointed auditors;

(c) the managing clerk, L, of ABC & Co, cannot act as auditor of XYZ Ltd, even though he may have the necessary professional qualifications, since he is an *employee* of an officer (A) of the company.

But note that if L were a director of a family company LMN Ltd, there would be no legal objection (except in the unlikely event of LMN Ltd being a building society—see the Building Societies Act 1962) to ABC & Co, acting as auditors of LMN Ltd, since A, B and C would be *employers* of an officer of the company. From the independence point of view this is clearly undesirable, but there is no legal objection.

6.0 STATUS

The question of the auditor's precise status has been raised from time to time. It is fairly safe to regard him as agent for the members to whom he is responsible (*Spackman* v. *Evans*). In this House of Lords case Lord Cranworth said "the auditors may be agents of the shareholders as far as relates to the audit of the accounts. For the purposes of the audit, the auditors will bind the shareholders."

The question of whether the auditor is an *officer* of the company is more problematic. As has already been pointed out, the term "officer" does not, as defined in the Act, include the auditor. Yet for the following two reasons it is possible that, for certain purposes anyway, the auditor is to be regarded as an officer:

(a) section 384 of the Act described above speaks of the auditors as holding "*office*"; and

(b) section 389 of the Act itself states (rather obviously) that for the purposes of the provision that an officer is disqualified from acting as auditor, the references to "officer" are *not* to be construed as including the auditor! This nevertheless suggests that the term officer may include the auditor in some other context.

As a result of this statutory confusion the courts have from time to time been called upon to decide whether, for a particular purpose, the auditor should be regarded as an officer of the company. This is fully explained in the Appendix to this chapter.

7.0 RIGHTS (OR POWERS)

COMPANIES ACT 1985, ss. 387, 392 and 237

The following constitute the counterpart to the auditors' duties. Duties without the corresponding rights needed to make them effective would clearly be unacceptable:

(a) the right to receive notice of all general meetings of the company, *and* to attend such meetings;

(b) the right to be heard at all general meetings of the company on any matter which concerns him in his capacity as auditor;

(c) the rights associated with a proposal to replace him or remove him from office (see sections 2.0 and 3.0 above);

(d) the right of access at all times to all books, documents and vouchers of the company;

(e) the right to require from the officers of the company such information and explanations as he considers necessary for the purposes of his audit;

(f) the right to require subsidiaries and their auditors to provide such information and explanations as may be needed in the course of their duties.

8.0   DUTIES

8.1   The report to members

The most important duty of the statutory auditor is *to report* to the members as required under section 236 of the Act. *Every* auditor's report on the accounts of a limited company must state, at the very least, whether in the auditor's opinion:

(a) the balance sheet gives a true and fair view of the state of the company's affairs at the balance sheet date;

(b) the profit and loss account gives a true and fair view of the profit (or loss) for the period ended on that date; and

(c) the accounts have been properly prepared in accordance with the provisions of the Companies Act 1985. (In the case of group accounts submitted by the holding company, the auditor's opinion must deal with the state of affairs and profit or loss of the company and its subsidiaries dealt with thereby, so far as concerns members of the holding company.)

But note that the principle of "exception reporting" applies to certain *other* matters specified in section 237 of the Act. The Jenkins Committee Report (1962) on company law reform expressed the view that the auditor's statutory report was too long, as required under the 9th Schedule (since repealed) to the 1948 Act. Hence the requirement to report on these matters *only* where the auditor's opinion is adverse. Where the report is silent on them it will obviously be assumed that the auditor was satisfied. The specific matters arising in this context are:

(a) Whether, in the auditor's opinion, proper accounting records have been kept by the company, as defined in section 221 of the Act. These records must contain a complete record of:

   (i) purchases and sales of goods, identifying buyers and sellers (except in case of normal retail sales);

   (ii) receipts and payments of cash;

   (iii) assets and liabilities, at all times, which must include a statement of stock held at the end of the financial year, together with compilations from any detailed stocktaking conducted.

   (Note also that section 722 of the Act specifies that where the records are not kept in the form of bound books, adequate precautions shall be taken for guarding against falsification and for facilitating its discovery.)

(b) Whether proper returns, adequate for audit purposes, have been received from branches not visited by them.

(c) Whether the balance sheet and profit and loss account are in agreement with the records.

(d) Whether he has received all information and explanations which he required for the purposes of his audit.

(e) Whether the contents of the directors' report are *consistent* with the financial statements.

8.2 Inclusion of further information (Schedule 5 and s. 231)

The following five requirements on *disclosure* of information in published accounts are all supported by a stipulation which requires the information specified to be given in the auditor's report, if not given as required in the accounts themselves, or the notes thereto:

(a) directors' emoluments;

(b) emoluments of the chairman, highest paid director, and the number of directors whose total UK emoluments fall within each of the specified bands;

(c) total directors' emoluments waived;

(d) the number of employees whose total UK emoluments fall within each of the specified bands;

(e) loans and quasi-loans to officers, credit transactions and directors' interests in contracts (see section 12.0 below).

8.3 Reports in prospectuses (Schedule 3, Part II)

If a company makes an issue of shares or debentures to the public a report must be placed in the prospectus by the company's auditors, giving details of:

(a) profits and losses arising in each of the previous five years;

(b) rates of dividend declared in each of the previous five years in respect of each class of shares for the time being paid up;

(c) assets and liabilities as at the latest balance sheet date.

More detailed information on prospectus reports is given in Chapter 13, section 5.5.

Notes

(a) If the company seeks a Stock Exchange quotation for its shares it will be necessary to comply with the requirements of the Quotations Department of the Council of the Stock Exchange, as set out in the "yellow book" entitled "The Admission of Securities to Quotation". These requirements are far more extensive than those of the 1985 Act, Sched. 3, Part II.

(b) The amounts of past profits and losses disclosed should be adjusted by the reporting auditors as they consider necessary, bearing in mind the purposes of the report.

Other duties originally arising under the Acts of 1980 and 1981 are dealt with in sections 12.0 to 15.0 below.

9.0   RESIGNATION

COMPANIES ACT 1985, ss. 390 and 391

These sections provide for the auditor's resignation during office. A resignation notice will be effective, however, only if it contains either:

(a) a statement to the effect that there are no circumstances connected with the resignation which the auditor considers should be brought to the notice of members *or creditors*; or

(b) a statement of such circumstances.

Where (b) is appropriate, the auditor may also requisition the directors *to call an extraordinary general meeting* for the purpose of considering the resignation circumstances.

It is regrettable that these powers may be exercised by auditors only in the context of their own resignation. It should, incidentally, be noted that this is the only instance in UK company law that a responsibility towards creditors is conceded.

10.0   FALSE STATEMENTS TO AUDITORS

COMPANIES ACT 1985, s. 393

Finally, largely as a consequence of the unwholesome disclosures in the Department of Trade Inspector's report on London and County Securities, it is now an offence for any officer of a company to make a materially false statement (either orally or in writing) to the auditor, whether knowingly or recklessly. Penalties of imprisonment and/or fines are specified. This is a substantial advance on the 1948 Act, s. 438, under which the false statement had to fall within the context of a document listed in the Sched. 15; nor did it allow the possibility of the statement being made "recklessly": there is therefore no need now to establish a "state of moral turpitude" in order to secure a successful prosecution.

11.0   ACCOUNTING DATES AND FILING RULES

11.1   Accounting reference period

This is the technical term for the financial year, and it terminates on the *accounting reference date*. Unless companies notify the Registrar otherwise, this date will be deemed to be 31st March in each year, although there are provisions for subsequent change. Directors may alter an accounting reference date by up to seven days (usually to ensure a fifty-two week period for comparison purposes).

11.2   Filing

Audited accounts of public companies must be filed with the Registrar no later than seven months after the accounting reference date (ten months for private companies).

11.3 Penalties for late filing

These are realistic at £400 plus £40 per day for *each* director in office on the expiry of the deadline; the company is also liable for heavy default fines, and a notice demanding compliance with filing regulations may be served on directors by the Registrar, a member or a creditor.

11.4 Retention period

Accounting records of public companies must be preserved for six years; for private companies the period is three years. There are heavy penalties, including imprisonment, for failure to comply with any of the requirements relating to accounting records.

12.0 PROVISIONS ORIGINALLY INTRODUCED BY THE COMPANIES ACT 1980

12.1 Introduction

The contents of the Companies Act 1980 could be divided into the following main provisions:

(a) classification of companies (implementation of the EEC Second Directive);

(b) the allotment and maintenance of share capital (also concerned with Second Directive implementation);

(c) insider dealing;

(d) the duties of directors; and

(e) the distribution of dividends (implementation of the Second Directive).

Only items (b), (d) and (e) involve specific audit duties.

All these provisions have now been included in the Companies Act 1985, apart from those concerning insider dealing which have been incorporated into the Company Securities (Insider Dealing) Act 1985.

12.2 Loans and quasi-loans to directors

(SEE ALSO CHAPTER 6, SECTION 7.0)

The new provisions on directors' loans are designed to overcome the abuses revealed in successive Department of Trade Reports throughout the 1970s, in which major companies adopted "banking articles", as a result of which loans were made to directors, ostensibly "within the ordinary course of the company's business". By this means, the company exploited the exemptions previously included in section 190 of the Companies Act 1948 (now repealed), a practice to which auditors appeared rarely to take exception. It is worth noting that most auditors will now apply more rigorous criteria to this question, as follows:

(a) The amount of the loan should not exceed the amount of a loan typically made to unconnected individuals. Also, if a bank's policy is to lend money only to corporate customers, a loan to a director could hardly be said to be in the ordinary course of its business.

(b) The security required should be equivalent to that required for similar loans made to unconnected individuals.

(c) The interest charged should be at least the lowest rate offered on loans made to unconnected individuals, and should not be "rolled up" unless it is the company's practice to do so with similar loans.

In practice, clients whose business includes the lending of money may be found making loans to directors which fail to measure up to one or more of the above requirements. Frequently these loans are housing loans which are secured by first or second mortgages, but carry concessionary rates of interest. Where it is known that a client has made loans to directors, the partner responsible for the audit should discuss the situation with the client as a *matter of urgency*.

In view of the complexity of the regulations concerning loans and other transactions affecting directors, Tables 6 and 7 are provided in order to clarify the situation so far as possible. They are included in the text with the kind permission of their compilers, Messrs Richard Wyld and Ian Lawson, members of the research team of Touche Ross & Co.

NB: Many transactions which are permitted are nevertheless subject to disclosure requirements.

Transactions, agreements, arrangements and guarantees between a company (or its subsidiary) and a director of the company (or a person connected with the director) in relation to loans, quasi-loans and credit transactions are generally prohibited, except as noted below. Other transactions, etc., are generally permitted, except that special rules apply to directors' service contracts and substantial transfers of non-cash assets between companies and directors.

Loans, quasi-loans and credit transactions which are permitted are given below in Table 6.

Table 6. Permitted transactions concerning directors under the provisions of the Companies Act 1985

	Loans	Quasi-loans	Credit transactions
Permitted for:			
1. Any company	A company may provide a director with funds (up to £10,000 in the case of a public company or the subsidiary of a public company) to meet expenditure for the purposes of the company or to enable him to perform his duties. Approval of the company in general meeting is required, failing which the loan etc. must be repayable within six months.		

Table 6 —*cont.*

	Loans	Quasi-loans	Credit transactions
2. Public company or subsidiary of a public company	Allowed up to £2,500. Otherwise prohibited to directors and other associated people.	Only if reimbursible within two months, and the total for the director does not exceed £1,000.	Either (i) where transaction is under normal commercial terms, or (ii) where the total for the director does not exceed £5,000.
3. Private company not the subsidiary of a public company	Allowed up to £2,500. Otherwise permitted to connected persons, but not to directors.	Permitted	Permitted
4. Moneylending company	Either (i) where loan etc. is under normal commercial terms, with upper limit of £50,000 per director (no upper limit for a recognised bank or for a private company not the subsidiary of a public company), or (ii) where loan etc. is on terms available to other employees and is in connection with the purchase or improvement of the director's main residence, with an upper limit of £50,000 per director.		No special rules.

The particulars indicated in Table 7 should be disclosed in relation to each transaction, agreement, arrangement or guarantee, whether permitted or not, between a company (or its subsidiary) and a director of the company (or a person connected with the director) in respect of loans, quasi-loans, credit transactions, and other transactions.

Table 7. Disclosure of transactions concerning directors under the provision of the Companies Act 1985

Particulars to be disclosed	Loans	Quasi-loans	Credit transactions	Other transactions
1. A statement that the transaction etc. was made or subsisted during the year.	Yes	Yes	Yes—except where the aggregate outstanding sum for a director did not exceed £5,000 during the financial year	Only where the director's interest is material in the opinion of the majority of the other directors. Excludes service contracts.
2. The name of the director (and, where applicable, the connected person).				
3. The principal terms of the transaction etc.				

Particulars to be disclosed	Loans	Quasi-loans	Credit transactions	Other transactions
4. The amount due (including interest) at the beginning and end of the financial year.				
5. The maximum amount due during the financial year.	Yes	No	No	No
6. The amount of unpaid interest.				
7. The amount of any provision.				
8. The amounts guaranteed at the beginning and end of the financial year.				
9. The maximum liability guaranteed.	Yes	Yes	Yes—except as above	No
10. Any amounts paid or incurred since the inception of the guarantee				
11. The value of the transaction etc.	No	Yes	Yes—except as above	No
12. The name of any director with direct or indirect material interest in a transaction (other than a service contract) and the nature of his interest. If no such transaction exists a statement of that fact should be disclosed in the directors' report (listed companies only).	No	No	No	Yes—except where the aggregate interest for a director did not exceed either (i) the lower of £5,000 and 1% of net asset value or (ii) £1,000, during the financial year.

If the accounts do not give this information, the auditors must give it in their report.

A further abuse commonly found in the past relates to loans made by companies to apparently unconnected outside parties who, in the event, simply recycled the loan to a director otherwise precluded from borrowing in this way. These loans are now included within the definition of "quasi-loan", as given in section 330. Further abuses, whereby loans were made to members of directors' families, are also covered by the new provisions.

12.3   Transactions with directors

Under the 1985 Act, s. 335, a transaction with a director is permitted (unless otherwise forbidden specifically), provided its value "is not greater, and the terms on which it is entered into are no more favourable ... than that or those on which it is reasonable to expect the company to have offered to ... a person of the same financial standing but unconnected with the company".

12.4   Distribution of dividends

(SEE ALSO SECTIONS 15.7 AND 15.8 BELOW)

Section 263 of the Act provides that a company shall not make a distribution except out of profits available for the purpose, and defines these profits as:

    (a)   its accumulated, realised profits, so far as not previously utilised whether by distribution or capitalisation; *less*

(b) its accumulated, realised losses, so far as not previously written off in reduction or reorganisation of capital duly made.

Various provisions are made regarding the application of unrealised profits, the measuring of a provision, depreciation of revalued fixed assets, original costs of assets and inability to distinguish whether profits/losses are realised or unrealised.

Provisions and capitalised development expenditure are both to be treated as realised losses for dividend purposes, and additional depreciation on an unrealised revaluation surplus may be treated as part of realised profits. This is logical, since the revaluation surplus is not distributable. (See section 14.0 below.)

Section 264 of the Act permits a public company to make a distribution only when its net assets are not less than the aggregate of its called-up share capital and undistributable reserves, and to the extent that the distribution does not reduce the amount of those assets to less than that aggregate. Undistributable reserves are defined as:

(a) share premium account;

(b) capital redemption reserve;

(c) accumulated unrealised profits, less accumulated unrealised losses (in both cases in so far as not previously used);

(d) any reserve prohibited from distribution by law or the company's memorandum or articles.

Section 265 of the Act, applicable to investment companies, stipulates that the effect of a dividend must *not* be to reduce its gross assets to less than one-and-a-half times its liabilities.

Section 270 of the Act provides that the right of a company to make a distribution, and the amount of any distribution, is to be determined by reference to accounts complying with specific requirements. The accounts are *the most recent audited accounts*, made up as at the company's accounting reference date, or, if the distribution would not be permitted by reference to these accounts, more recent interim accounts. The accounts must carry an *unqualified audit report* or *a statement in writing*.

This means broadly that either a "clean" opinion is given for the balance sheet being audited or, in the case of a qualified report, *a written statement* (laid before the members in general meeting) that the qualification is not material in determining the propriety of the company's proposed distribution. (See section 13.0 below.)

12.5 The effect on case law

It is worth noting that section 263 of the Act effectively repeals the decision in the case of *Ammonia Soda Co* v. *Chamberlain*, in which it was held that a company may pay a dividend out of profits earned in the current period, despite the fact that past losses have not been made good.

Reporting in 1962, the Jenkins Committee on Company Law Reform observed that a company's life is divided into accounting periods for convenience of reporting, and not for determining whether distributable profits have been earned. It is necessary to consider the availability of distributable reserves over the entire life of a company, from its incorporation to the proposed date of payment of a dividend.

Section 263 also nullifies the effect of the infamous dicta in *Dimbula Valley (Ceylon) Tea Co* v. *Laurie* (1962), in which Buckley J permitted the distribution by way of dividend of unrealised revaluation surpluses on the grounds that such sums would be available for distribution to members as bonus shares. The Jenkins Committee recommended that there should be a statutory requirement that capital profits should be realised prior to their distribution, and this has now been implemented under section 263 of the Act. Section 263 also contains a convoluted clause which deals with the extra depreciation charge which may arise on the revaluation of a fixed asset, from which it appears that additional (CCA) depreciation, arising on a revaluation surplus, may be treated as part of a company's realised profit for dividend purposes.

Section 264 of the Act has the effect of classifying a company's balance sheet so as to distinguish:

(a) share capital and undistributable reserves;

(b) free reserves; and

(c) assets less liabilities (net assets).

The section requires that public companies may make a distribution only while there is a positive balance under (b) above, and provided that the effect of the distribution will not create a negative balance under this heading.

12.6 Registration as a public company

If a private company re-registers as a public company, section 43 of the Act will apply. This details the procedures to be followed which include delivering to the registrar a *written statement by the auditors,* and a copy of the relevant balance sheet with *an unqualified audit report.* The "written statement" must report on the company's net assets being not less than the aggregate of its called-up share capital and undistributable reserves. The term "unqualified audit report" has a similar meaning to that of section 270 of the Act mentioned above, but in the case of a qualified report a written statement must comment on the net assets rather than the proposed distribution of the company.

12.7 Non-cash consideration for share capital

If a public company issues shares for a non-cash consideration, it will require an independent accountant's report on the value of the non-cash assets used for payment of the shares. The independent accountant is anyone qualified to be auditor of the company and he must value the non-cash assets himself unless it appears reasonable to accept a valuation made by some other person. The report to the company must:

(a) describe the assets to be transferred to the company and the payment to be made by the company, specifying any amounts to be given in cash;

(b) state the method and date of valuation of the asset;

(c) state that, on the basis of the valuation used, the value of the asset to be received by the company is not less than the value of the payment to be made by it;

(c) state that, or be accompanied by a note stating that:

  (i) the method of valuation was reasonable in all the circumstances;

  (ii) (if the valuation has been delegated to another person) it appeared to the independent accountant to be reasonable to delegate the valuation.

12.8 Prohibition of "insider" deals

The prohibition of insider trading was introduced by sections of the Companies Act 1980 amid much speculation as to whether their bark will prove to be worse than their bite. These provisions seek to outlaw the use of price-sensitive information which is not generally available to outside shareholders, and add an effective edge to the Stock Exchange's own disciplinary powers. Dealers appreciate that direct share dealing is covered by the new rules, but the Department of Trade and Industry has made it clear that the law now extends to dealings in "any right to subscribe for, call for, or make delivery of a share of debenture"—which includes all dealings in the highly volatile options market.

Ironically, only days before the starting date of the new laws, certain unnamed dealers in one of the largest UK property companies appeared to use inside information to produce an overnight profit of around £60,000 on "option" contracts. On average there are no more than ten to fifteen option contracts in this particular company's shares each day. But during the three days prior to the announcement of this giant group's £108 million rights issue (the largest cash call to hit the market in four years), no fewer than 609 option contracts were written!

Although the Stock Exchange announced no enquiry into the matter, a pre-rights dealing surge on this scale, if now staged, would almost certainly spark a full-scale Department of Trade and Industry investigation, possibly leading to the deposition of criminal charges. It is to be expected that even relatively minor market raids (in relation to the size of the issue) of this sort will become increasingly risky. To quote *Financial Weekly*, "What was last week's profitable trade, could easily become next month's trip to the courts!"

Auditors' ethics rules have for some years precluded dealing in the shares of client companies, and although auditors are obviously insiders, it is not thought likely that they will be affected by this legislation in any new regard.

These provisions are no longer part of a Companies Act, but are included in the Company Securities (Insider Dealing) Act 1985.

13.0 QUALIFIED AUDIT REPORTS AND DISTRIBUTIONS

As already stated, section 270 of the Act requires the auditors, if they have qualified their opinion on the financial statements, to state in writing whether the subject matter of their qualification is material in determining the legality of the proposed distribution. Consequently, where auditors qualify their report on the financial statements of a company that is proposing to pay a dividend, they will need to make an additional statement to the members of the company.

Set out below are some of the matters to be considered when determining the format of the additional statement to the members, as adapted from the Deloitte Haskins &

Sells *Auditing and Accounting Newsletter.*

13.1 Where the audit report qualification arises from a disagreement

Where an audit report qualification arises from a disagreement between auditors and directors as to the amount at which an item should appear in the financial statements, generally it will be fairly easy to decide whether the qualification is material in determining the legality of the proposed distribution.

Example 13 in the Auditing Guideline on "Audit Report Examples" illustrates this point. The following is an extract from Example 13:

> "No provision has been made against an amount of £ ... owing by a company which has been placed in liquidation since the year end. The liquidator has indicated that unsecured creditors are unlikely to receive any payment and in our opinion full provision should be made.
>
> Except for the failure to provide the amount described above, in our opinion the financial statements, which have been prepared under the historical cost convention, give a true and fair view of ..."

In these circumstances, the proposed distribution would be legal if, by deducting from distributable reserves the amount of the required provision against the debt, the net figure is adequate for the purposes of the distribution.

13.2 Where the audit report qualification results in a "subject to" opinion

Where an audit report qualification arises from an uncertainty as to the amount at which an item appears in the financial statements, it will be possible to decide whether the qualification is material in determining the legality of the proposed distribution only if the auditors can place an upper limit on the liabilities affected, and a lower limit on the assets affected.

Example 5 in the Auditing Guidelines on "Audit Report Examples" illustrates this point. The following is an extract from Example 5:

> "One branch of the company did not carry out a physical count of stock at 31st December 19 ... and there was no practicable alternative auditing procedure that we could apply to obtain all the information and explanations considered necessary to satisfy ourselves as to the existence of stock valued at £ ... at 31st December 19 ... which is included as part of the total stocks of £ ... in the balance sheet. In our opinion, in the case of the stocks referred to above, proper accounting records have not been kept as required by section 221 of the Companies Act 1985.
>
> Subject to the effects of any adjustments which might have been shown to be necessary had a physical count of branch stock been carried out, in our opinion the financial statements, which had been prepared under the historical cost convention, give a true and fair view of ..."

In these circumstances, the proposed distribution would be legal, if, by deducting from distributable reserves the amount of the stock affected (for example, by valuing that stock either at nil or at a reduced amount that depends on the nature of the qualification), the net figure is adequate for the purposes of the distribution.

If they cannot quantify the financial effect of an uncertainty, auditors should regard the effect as infinite in respect of a possible understatement of liabilities. In respect of a possible overstatement of assets, auditors will obviously regard the effect as being limited to the amount at which the asset is stated.

13.3   Where the audit report qualification results in a disclaimer of opinion

In circumstances where auditors disclaim an opinion on the financial statements as a whole, they will not be in a position to confirm the amount at which the company's net assets are stated. Accordingly, they will not be able to state that the qualification is "not material" in determining the legality of the proposed distribution.

13.4   The wording of the additional statement

Where the audit qualification is not material (or is material but favourable) in determining the legality of the proposed distribution, the following paragraph, added as the final paragraph to the audit report, is suggested:

> "In our opinion the qualification is not material for the purpose of determining, by reference to these financial statements, whether the final dividend for the year ended 31st March 1985 proposed by the company is permitted under the Companies Act 1985."

Where the audit qualification *is* material in determining the legality of the proposed distribution, the word "not" before the word "material" should be deleted. In addition, the auditors should, if practicable, add a brief explanation of the effect of the qualification on the company's ability to make the distribution.

14.0   SURPLUSES ON REVALUATION OF FIXED ASSETS AND THE DISCLOSURE OF NON-DISTRIBUTABLE RESERVES

14.1   Introduction

All major changes in the realm of accounting and law are of direct concern to auditors, and this is especially true in respect of the 1985 legislation on divisible profits.

The requirement of the Companies Act 1985 to separate realised profits from unrealised profits in order to determine the amount of profits that are legally distributable has reopened the debate on the appropriate accounting treatment of surpluses that arise on the revaluation of fixed assets. It has also reinforced the need to keep "realised reserves" separate from "unrealised reserves", and to distinguish them in that way. The recommendations set out in this section are based on those issued in the Deloitte Haskins & Sells *Auditing and Accounting Newsletter*.

14.2   Background

Although the Companies Act 1967 abolished the categories "capital" reserve and "revenue" reserve, many companies have continued to use these descriptions. Capital reserves traditionally comprise both realised and unrealised surpluses on capital assets (such as property) as well as statutory reserves, such as share premium account. Revenue reserves traditionally comprise (principally) undistributed profits.

14.3 The treatment of surpluses on the revaluation of fixed assets

Where a depreciable asset, such as a building, is revalued, the surplus comprises *two* elements. The first is the depreciation that the company provided on the building in past years (assuming it has done so, in accordance with SSAP 12). The second is the difference between the revaluation amount and the original cost (or the previous valuation of the building). When reserves were divided between "capital" and "revenue" (as opposed to " realised" and "unrealised") one method of accounting was to take the total of these two elements to capital reserve, because the revalued building was regarded as being stated at "new cost" (which was its current purchase value). The other method was to take the first element to "revenue" reserves and the second to "capital" reserves.

In the absence of an accounting standard on the treatment of revaluation surpluses, it is considered that the most appropriate accounting treatment is to follow the latter alternative and split the revaluation surplus into the above two elements, and to deal with these elements by:

(a) taking directly to *realised* reserves (in the balance sheet) the element that relates to the depreciation the company has previously provided on the asset;

(b) taking directly to *unrealised* reserve (in accordance with SSAP 6) the other element, which is the difference between the new valuation and the original cost (or the previous valuation).

14.4 The treatment of depreciation on revalued fixed assets

A revalued fixed asset will be subject to an annual depreciation charge based on the new and, usually, higher figure. This new annual charge (the whole of which is debited to profit and loss account) can notionally be divided between the part that relates to original cost, and the part that relates to the uplift on revaluation. The latter is, in effect, a reversal over a long period of time of the surplus taken to unrealised reserves. Accordingly, as we have seen, the Companies Act 1985, s. 263, allows a company which has revalued a depreciable fixed asset to treat, as a realised profit, the depreciation charged on the "uplift". Each year, therefore, the unrealised reserves will be reduced by, and the realised reserves will be increased by, an amount equivalent to the additional depreciation charge which results from the revaluation.

If the two reserves are shown separately in the balance sheet, it will be necessary to show this transfer in the notes to the accounts.

14.5 The treatment of surpluses on the disposal of revalued fixed assets

In the year in which a company sells a revalued fixed asset, the surplus it realises on the sale can be calculated in one of the following two ways:

    (a) the difference between the sale proceeds and the net book value at the date of the sale; or

    (b) the difference between the sale proceeds and the net book value at the date of the sale, *together with the previously unrealised surplus on revaluation.* This unrealised surplus will be the original surplus on revaluation, less the amount subsequently transferred to realised reserves when the asset is depreciated.

Again, there is no accounting standard on the subject and, accordingly, these alternative methods of accounting for the surplus are available. If, however, companies adopt the approach in (b) above, and this amount is credited to the profit and loss account, shareholders may be led to believe that the *whole* surplus arose in the current year. This is not so. (As a result of the revaluation, the balance sheet already reflects the credit for part of this surplus.)

    Accordingly, it is necessary for the company to disclose the realised surplus in the profit and loss account in one of the two following ways:

		£
(1)	Realised surplus on the sale of the property	X
	Less: Amount included in unrealised reserves in previous years	X
		X

or

(2)	Realised surplus on the sale of the property (including £X in respect of amount included in unrealised reserves in previous year)	X

(If the company uses method (a) it will need to transfer the amount that relates to the realisation of a prior-year revaluation surplus from unrealised reserves to realised reserves.)

14.6   Disclosure of non-distributable reserves in the financial statement of companies

Although the Companies Act 1985 does not require companies to disclose separately realised and unrealised reserves, it is preferable to disclose in a note the amount of the reserves that is not legally distributable. This is because the amount of the total reserves that cannot by law be paid to shareholders by way of dividend could be an important factor to some users of the financial statements. The wording of the note should *not* suggest, however, that the balance *is* distributable, since there may well be other restrictions, such as cash limitations. A suggested wording is as follows: "The amount of the above reserves that may not be legally distributed under section ... of the Companies Act 1985 is £X (1984—£Y)."

15.0 PROVISIONS ORIGINALLY INTRODUCED BY THE COMPANIES ACT 1981

15.1 Introduction

The Companies Act 1981 made profound changes to the disclosure requirements for company accounts and to this extent was obviously relevant for auditing. The purpose of this section is to detail the further requirements of the Act which have a bearing upon the auditor's work. All these provisions have now been included in the Companies Act 1985.

References to sections are to those of the Companies Act 1985 unless otherwise stated.

15.2 Auditors' report

Small and medium-sized companies (Schedule 8)
Small and medium-sized companies (as defined by the Act) are allowed to submit modified accounts to the Registrar. In this connection the auditors must:

(a) provide a report *to the directors* stating whether in their opinion the accounts qualify for the exemption;

(b) provide a special report to accompany the accounts lodged with the Registrar stating that in their opinion the exemption requirements are satisfied, and reproducing the full text of the report sent to the members: if the auditors do not confirm that the exemption requirements are satisfied, full statements must be filed.

A company qualifies as a small company if it satisfied (for both the financial year in question and the preceding year) any two of the following three conditions:

(a) the amount of its turnover did not exceed £1,400,000;

(b) the balance sheet total (basically, fixed assets plus investments plus current assets) did not exceed £700,000;

(c) the average number of employees employed by the company did not exceed fifty (s. 248).

A medium-sized company, if it fails to satisfy the criteria for a small company, must satisfy for both the year in question and the preceding year, any two of the following three conditions:

(a) the amount of its turnover did not exceed £5,750,000;

(b) the balance sheet total did not exceed £2,800,000;

(c) the average number of employees employed by the company in the financial year did not exceed 250 (s. 248).

Publication of accounts (s. 254)
All companies except unlimited companies are required to provide full accounts for their members, and "small" or "medium-sized" companies may file modified accounts with the Registrar.

Section 254 is designed to prevent anyone being misled by accounts published in any other way. Its provisions are:

(a) Any accounts, full or modified, which are published must be accompanied by the "relevant" auditors' report. This means that published full accounts must be accompanied by the full auditors' report and that published modified accounts must be accompanied by the special auditors' report required by Schedule 8 of the 1985 Act.

(b) If a company required to produce group accounts publishes its own accounts it must also publish the group accounts, which may be in modified form if the company is small or medium-sized.

(c) Any company publishing an abridged form of its accounts must include a statement that they are not full accounts, indicating also whether full accounts have been delivered to the Registrar and whether the auditors' report on those accounts was qualified. The auditors' report itself must *not* be published with abridged accounts.

Although it is obviously the directors' responsibility to comply with these requirements, auditors should be alert to ensure that their clients do not infringe them. See section 15.9(i) below.

MODIFIED BALANCE SHEET—SMALL COMPANY

	£	£
Fixed assets		
Intangible assets		x
Tangible assets		x
Investments		x
Current assets		
Stocks	x	
Debtors	x	
Investments	x	
Cash	x	
	x	
Creditors due within one year	x	
Net current assets		x
Total assets less current liabilities		x
Creditors (due after more than 1 year)		(x)
Provision for liabilities and charges		(x)
Net assets		x
Capital and reserves		
Share capital		x
Reserves		x
Profit and loss account		x
		X

Application of auditors' report to directors' report (s. 237)

It has always been good auditing practice for the auditor to confirm that the directors' report is consistent with the accounts on which the auditor is reporting. This is now a statutory requirement under section 237—the auditors must qualify their report if they are of the opinion that the information given in the directors' report is not consistent with the company's accounts.

Until the 1985 Act there was considerable confusion about the directors' report. The 1967 Act required information, such as number of employees and total wages and salaries costs, to be included in the directors' report and not the accounts. There was no requirement, however, for the directors' report to be audited. The 1985 Act states: "It shall be the duty of the auditors . . . to consider whether the information given in the directors' report relating to the financial year in question is consistent with those accounts. If the auditors are of the opinion that the information given in the directors' report is not consistent with the company's accounts for the financial year, they shall state that fact in their report."

The previous Acts allowed information to appear in the directors' report instead of the accounts and this discretion is now withdrawn. The Act therefore reduced the importance of the directors' report. Many items which were required to be shown previously in the directors' report must now be disclosed in the notes to the financial statements.

Reference should be made to appendix 2 to this chapter.

15.3   Dormant companies (s. 252)

Section 252 exempts dormant companies from the obligation to appoint auditors. A company qualifies as dormant for this purpose if it is a "small" company as defined in s. 248, is not a holding company and has had no "significant accounting transactions" since the end of the previous financial year.

The procedure is for the company to pass a special resolution that auditors are not to be appointed.

The company is still required to lodge accounts with the Registrar, but instead of an auditors' report a statement from the directors that the company was dormant must be filed.

15.4   Redemption of redeemable shares—private companies

If a private company redeems shares out of capital, as they are allowed to do by sections 171 to 177, subject to certain safeguards, the directors must make a statutory declaration of the solvency of the company, accompanied by a report addressed to the directors by the auditors stating that:

(a) they have enquired into the company's state of affairs;

(b) the amount to be paid out of capital has been properly determined; and

(c) the opinion expressed by the directors is reasonable.

The statutory declaration and the auditors' report on it must be open for inspection by the members at the meeting to pass the special resolution approving the payment. Under this onerous requirement the auditors are virtually being asked to ensure that the company is solvent.

15.5 Private company purchasing its own shares

An auditors' report identical with that described in section 15.4 above is required to accompany the directors' declaration when a private company purchases its own shares out of capital.

15.6 Private company providing financial assistance for the purchase of its own shares

Before such assistance can legally be provided the directors must file a statutory declaration of solvency which must again be accompanied by auditors' report to the directors similar to that indicated in section 15.4 (a) to (c) above.

15.7 Profits available for distribution—treatment of capitalised development costs (s. 269)

This provides that any capitalised development cost is to be treated as a realised loss for the purpose of determining distributable profit under the Company Act 1985, s. 263, unless the directors are of the opinion that there are special circumstances making it reasonable not to treat that development cost as a realised loss. If the directors are of this opinion they must state so in the note to the accounts required by para 20 of Schedule 4.

The provision applies also for the purpose of s. 265 in determining the distributable profit of an investment company.

15.8 Distribution in kind (s. 276)

This provides that where a company makes a distribution in kind and the value of the asset distributed includes an unrealised profit, that profit is to be treated as a realised profit for the purpose of determining the legality of the distribution.

15.9 Other matters of importance to auditors

Formats
The 1985 Act sets out, in Schedule 4, *two* alternative formats for the balance sheet, and *four* alternative formats for the profit and loss account. The directors may select which formats to use, but if they are subsequently changed (with good reason) the notes to financial statements must disclose this fact, with the directors' reasons for the change. The auditor must ensure that the formats are correct, and that prescribed information disclosing and explaining a change is given.

Capitalised expenditure
Certain items are no longer permitted to be carried forward in this way, and must now be written off (including existing balances). These are:

(a) preliminary expenses;

(b) expenses and commission on issue of shares or debentures;

(c) research expenditure.

For treatment of *development expenditure,* see section 15.7 above. If capitalised, the auditor must ensure that he is satisfied with the reasons for so doing.

Other balance sheet items

    (a) Concessions, patents, licences, trade marks, etc., may only be included in the balance sheet when either of the following conditions is satisfied:

        (i) they were acquired for valuable consideration in circumstances that do not qualify them to be shown as goodwill;

        (ii) they were created by the company itself.

    (b) Goodwill may be shown as an asset only if it was acquired for valuable consideration. A company may therefore not record internally generated goodwill as an asset.

    (c) Debtors must be split between those receivable within one year and those receivable later than that.

    (d) Paid-up capital (as well as authorised and issued capital) must be shown.

    (e) Creditors payable within one year and creditors payable in more than one year, and their aggregates, must be shown separately.

    (f) Creditors in respect of taxation and social security must be shown separately from other creditors.

    (g) Payments received on account of orders must be shown under creditors, unless they are shown as a deduction from stocks.

Accounting principles

Schedule 4 to the Companies Act 1985 includes as "accounting principles" the four fundamental accounting concepts explained in SSAP 2 ("disclosure of accounting policies"). It adds a fifth principle (the "aggregation" principle) which states that the amount of each individual asset or liability within the aggregate amount shall be determined separately: the Act does not permit assets or liabilities to be "set off" against each other.

    The following summarises and explains the four familiar accounting principles (concepts) as included in the 1985 Act:

GOING CONCERN

The company shall be presumed to be a going concern. This means that at the date on which the audit report to the members is signed it is believed that the company will continue to be financially viable for the foreseeable future. Such belief therefore justifies, for example, the carry forward of the value of assets not yet written off.

CONSISTENCY

The company's accounting policies shall be applied consistently from one financial period to the next. This ensures that the financial statements of successive periods may be used for the purpose of making valid comparisons. An unwarranted change of accounting policy, or a change whose effect is not adequately disclosed, will render such comparison misleading.

PRUDENCE

Items included in financial statements shall be determined on a prudent basis. In particular:

(a) only profits realised at the balance sheet date shall be included in the profit and loss account;

(b) all liabilities and losses which have arisen or are likely to arise in respect of the period reported on shall be reflected in the financial statements, including those which become apparent after the balance sheet date but before the financial statements are approved.

ACCRUALS

All income and charges which relate to the financial period in question shall be reflected in the financial statements without regard to the time of receipt or payment.

Without this concept financial statements would be prepared on a receipts and payments basis, which would be misleading since accrued income and accrued charges, due for settlement after the balance sheet date, would consequently be disregarded.

REALISED PROFITS

It should be noted that the "prudence" principle refers to "realised profits". To explain what is meant by "realised profits" the Act states, "in relation to a company's accounts realised profits are references to such profits of the company as fall to be treated as realised profits, for the purposes of those accounts, in accordance with principles generally accepted with respect to the determination for accounting purposes of realised profits at the time when these accounts are prepared".

This means that, in general, we may assume that profits which have been determined in accordance with Statements of Standard Accounting Practice may be assumed to be realised profits for this purpose. Even attributable profits arising during the progress of a long-term contract, provided the rules of SSAP 9 are observed, may thus be regarded as realised profits.

True and fair

The Act does not define this requirement, but it is clear from the above that SSAPs should be taken into account by the auditor in reaching a decision on whether financial statements give a true and fair view.

The Act states that if the directors of a company depart from the five basic accounting principles they must give the particulars of the departure, the reason for it and its effect, in a note to the accounts. Again, the auditor will have to ensure that if there is such a departure from the basic principles, he is satisfied with such a departure and that the note to the accounts is satisfactory.

HC and CC conventions

Rules are given for historical cost accounting which largely implement many of the SSAPs. Rules are given for the treatment of fixed assets which largely follow SSAP 12, "Accounting for Depreciation". Goodwill must be written off by the directors over its useful economic life. The period the directors use and the reason for choosing that particular period must be disclosed in the notes in the financial statements. In general, current assets must be shown at the lower of purchase price or production cost and net realisable value. The Act allows stock to be valued under the LIFO (last in first out) method, which is not allowed by SSAP 9; otherwise the method of stock valuation is the same as required by SSAP 9.

For the first time a Companies Act takes account of inflation accounting. Intangible assets except goodwill may be valued at their *current cost*. Tangible fixed assets may be stated either at their market value on the date when they were last valued, or at their current cost. Stocks may be stated at their current cost. The effect of these provisions is to permit financial statements to be prepared in any of the following ways:

(a) according to the historical cost convention;

(b) according to the historical cost convention modified to take account of selective revaluations;

(c) according to current cost principles.

Notes to financial statements—a checklist
The following must be disclosed:

(a) The accounting policies adopted.

(b) The amount of a company's authorised share capital together with details of share capital allotted and information about redeemable shares. Where shares are allotted during the year, the reason for shares being allotted must be given. (The reason for issuing shares previously had to be shown in the directors' report.)

(c) Similarly, details must be disclosed of debentures.

(d) Details of reserves and provisions, including amounts at the beginning of the year, transfers in or out, and amounts at the end of each year.

(e) The information about fixed assets is increased by requiring depreciation to be shown, both at the beginning and the end of the financial year, together with the provision during the year.

(f) Additional information is to be given where shares in another company exceed 10% of the total allotted share capital of a company, and also if the share holding exceeds 20%.

(g) Further information must be given about creditors payable in more than one year.

(h) Details of contingent liabilities must be given in line with SSAP 18, "Accounting for Contingencies".

(i) As in previous Acts, details of capital expenditure authorised must be given split between that contracted for and that which is not contracted for.

(j) Information on pensions must disclose separately pension commitments that have been provided for and pension commitments that have not been provided for.

(k) Information about turnover and profits of different classes of business (previously in the directors' report).

(l) Numbers of employees and their aggregate remuneration (also previously in the directors' report).

(m) Details of taxation.

(n) Other details from the Fourth Schedule such as details of interest, details of amounts set aside for redemption of share capital and loans, amounts charged in respect of the hire of plant and machinery, auditors' remuneration and exceptional items.

(o) Remuneration of directors and information about remuneration of highest paid employees.

Contents of directors' report

(SEE ALSO SECTION 15.2 (c) ABOVE)
Information still required in the directors' report is as follows:

(a) a fair review of the development of the business of the company and its subsidiaries during that year and of their position at the end of it;

(b) any important post balance sheet events;

(c) the company's or group's future developments;

(d) the company's acquisition of its own shares;

(e) an indication of the activities (if any) of the company and its subsidiaries in the field of research and development.

Modified accounts

(See also section 15.2 (b) above.)

SMALL COMPANIES—EXEMPTIONS
A small company need only deliver a modified balance sheet and notes to the Registrar of Companies. The directors of a small company need not deliver a profit and loss account, a directors' report, or any information relating to emoluments of directors or higher paid employees.

Only the following notes to the financial statements are required:

(a) accounting policies;

(b) share capital;

(c) particulars of allotments of shares;

(d) particulars of creditors payable in over five years, and particulars of security given;

(e) the basis used in translating foreign currency amounts into sterling.

Comparative amounts for the previous year must also be given in respect of each of the above items.

MEDIUM-SIZED COMPANIES

In respect of medium-sized companies the main relaxations apply to the profit and loss account.

The following items may be combined and shown as one item under the heading of "gross profit and loss":

(a) in the formats where the expenses are classified by function: turnover; cost of sales; gross profit or loss and other operating income;

(b) in the formats where expenses are classified by type: turnover; changes in stocks of finished goods and work in progress; own work capitalised; other operating income; raw materials and consumables; other external charges.

The notes need not disclose the turnover and profits of different classes of business.

Note: Other sections of the 1985 Act concerning investigations are dealt with in Chapter 13.

APPENDIX 1: THE AUDITOR AS AN OFFICER

Introduction

This question is of particular concern in connection with the winding-up penalty provisions in sections 624 to 631 of the Companies Act 1985. The last of these concerns civil offences, but all the others involve criminal offences. All the sections, however, refer to "any *officer* of a company".

Civil offences

COMPANIES ACT 1985, s. 631

This section is part of the general winding-up provisions under the Companies Act.

Section 631 is concerned with the civil offences entitled "misfeasance" and "breach of trust". Broadly speaking, these terms relate to the misuse of a position of authority with the object of personal gain. For example, the directors of a company may bind the company in a contract with an outside party with whom they have an existing financial relationship, i.e. a transaction which is not at arm's length. If a similar contract could have been entered into by the company on more favourable terms, it could be argued that the directors have abused their power and position in order to achieve a personal benefit, at the expense of the company for whom they are acting as stewards. In the event of such an offence being proved, the appropriate remedy would be financial damages, making up the loss.

It was decided in the two famous legal cases of *Kingston Cotton Mill* and *London and General Bank* at the end of the last century that for the purposes of the above provisions, *the auditor is to be regarded as an officer of the company.*

Criminal offences

COMPANIES ACT 1985, ss. 624 to 630

The other winding-up sections referred to above all involve criminal offences, and in each case reference is made to "officers" of the company. The question has therefore arisen as to how far, if at all, the auditor may be regarded as being an officer of the company for the purposes of these sections, bearing in mind that the two cases referred to in the previous paragraph related *only* to civil liability.

It was held in the case of *R.* v. *Shacter* (1960) that the term "officer" must be taken to include the auditor. In 1953 the appellant was appointed auditor of a company and his appointment was continued from year to year thereafter. He was convicted as "an officer" of the company, of making false entries, fraud and defaults contrary to sections 328(1)(*j*), 330 and 331 (now repealed) of the Companies Act 1948, now incorporated into ss. 624 and 625 of the Companies Act 1985.

APPENDIX 2: DRAFT AUDITING GUIDELINE—FINANCIAL INFORMATION ISSUED WITH AUDITED FINANCIAL STATEMENTS

Preface

This guideline is intended to clarify the responsibilities of the auditor in connection with the directors' report and to explain his role with regard to other financial information issued with audited financial statements. Counsel has confirmed that this guideline is in accordance with the relevant statutory provisions and legal principles and that he approves it accordingly. The guideline is supplementary to and should be read in conjunction with the auditor's operational and reporting standards and related guidelines.

Introduction and scope

1. This guideline is written in the context of the audit of companies incorporated under the Companies Act. The auditor of an enterprise other than such a company will be guided by the terms of his particular appointment or by relevant legislation or other requirements. However, in the absence of specific provisions to the contrary, the general principles embodied in this guideline should be followed.

2. Financial information contained in annual reports is not confined to the statements encompassed by the auditor's report. Other financial information may be included in the directors' report or in other unaudited statements such as a chairman's statement, a report on operations, a value added statement or a summary of past results.

Directors' reports

3. The auditors' statutory responsibilities, prior to the passing of the Companies

Act 1985, were limited to the financial statements identified in their audit reports. Section 237 of the Companies Act 1985 has extended the statutory responsibilities of auditors of most companies as follows:

"It shall be the duty of the auditors of the company, in preparing their report under section 236 of this Act on the company's accounts, to consider whether the information given in the directors' report relating to the financial year in question is consistent with those accounts.

If the auditors are of the opinion that the information given in the directors' report is not consistent with the company's accounts for the financial year, they shall state that fact in their report under section 236."

It should be noted, however, that auditors of companies (e.g. banks, insurance and shipping companies) which have availed themselves of the right to prepare accounts under Schedule 9 to the Companies Act 1985 are not required to follow s. 237 of the Companies Act 1985. As a result, such auditors should regard directors' reports as being on the same footing as other financial information issued with audited financial statements, and they should where appropriate follow the procedures described in paras 11 to 14 below.

4.   While the statutory responsibilities of an auditor have been extended by the Companies Act 1985, they have not been extended so as to require him to form an opinion on the directors' report itself. As a result, under normal circumstances, the auditor should confine his work to satisfying himself whether or not the directors' report contains any matters which are inconsistent with the audited financial statements.

5.   Matters which may give rise to an inconsistency include the following:

(a)   an inconsistency between actual figures appearing in, respectively, the audited financial statements and the directors' report;

(b)   an inconsistency between the bases of preparation of related items appearing in the audited financial statements and the directors' report, where the figures themselves are not directly comparable;

(c)   an inconsistency between figures contained in the audited financial statements and a narrative interpretation of the effect of those figures in the directors' report.

6.   The auditor should consider the implications of any inconsistency and should hold discussions with directors of the company, or other senior members of management, in order to achieve its elimination.

7.   Where, after holding such discussions, the auditor is of the opinion that an inconsistency still exists, his course of action will depend on whether he believes that an amendment is required to the audited financial statements or to the directors' report.

8.   If, in the auditor's opinion, it is the audited financial statements which require amendment, he should consider qualifying his report on those financial

statements. In these circumstances, the auditor should make use of the Auditing Standard "Qualifications in Audit Reports" and the Auditing Guideline "Audit Report Examples".

9.   If, in his opinion, it is the directors' report which requires amendment, the auditor should refer in his report to the inconsistency in order to comply with s. 237 of the Companies Act 1985. An example of such a report is set out in the appendix.

10.   The auditor does not have a responsibility to search the directors' report for items which, while not inconsistent with the audited financial statements, are misleading in some other respect. Furthermore, counsel has advised that it is doubtful that he has a right to comment on misleading as opposed to inconsistent items in his report on the audited financial statements. However, should the auditor become aware of such items, he should respond where appropriate by taking one or both of the following courses of action:

      (a)   After consulting his legal advisors, make use of his right under s. 236 of the Companies Act 1985 to be heard at any general meeting of the members on any business of the meeting which concerns him as auditor. This would include the right to draw attention to an item in the directors' report which, while not inconsistent with the audited financial statements, is misleading in some other respect.

      (b)   Seek legal advice on what further action may be appropriate in the circumstances.

Other financial information

11.   The auditor has no statutory responsibilities in respect of other financial information issued with audited financial statements. Nevertheless it should be reviewed by the auditor as, where there is a material inconsistency with the audited financial statements or an item which is misleading in some other respect, the credibility of the audited financial statements may be undermined.

12.   Where the auditor considers that a material inconsistency or an item which is misleading in some other respect exists, he should consider its implications and hold discussions with directors, or other senior members of management, and may also make his views known in writing to all the directors in order to achieve its elimination. Where communication with directors and their representatives does not result in the elimination of the problem, he should consider whether an amendment is required to the audited financial statements or the other financial information.

13.   If, in the auditor's opinion, it is the audited financial statements which require amendment, he should follow the guidance given in para 8 above.

14.   Counsel has advised that it is doubtful whether the auditor has a right to comment on other financial information in his report on the audited financial statements. Therefore, if in his opinion it is the other financial information

which requires amendment, the auditor should take one or both of the courses of action described in para 10. The auditor has a right to draw the members' attention, at a general meeting, to financial information issued with the audited financial statements which is inconsistent with those financial statements or which is misleading in some other respect.

15.   Where a summary of past results is issued with audited financial statements and it incorporates figures which have been prepared using bases that have not remained consistent but a note to this effect is included, the auditor need not concern himself.

Other considerations

16.   The directors' report and the other financial information contained in the annual report do not normally form part of the audited financial statements on which the auditor is reporting. Therefore, the pages of the annual report, to which the audit report refers, should not include the directors' report and the other financial information unless the audit report is specifically intended to extend to that information.

17.   The auditor should urge the company not to publish its annual report until after he has completed his review of the financial information issued with the audited financial statements. In this regard, it may assist the auditor if this procedure is dealt with in the audit engagement letter. Where, notwithstanding this, the auditor is not given an opportunity to complete his review before the date of issue, he should complete it before the general meeting at which the financial statements are laid before the members. In the event that there is something with which he disagrees, the auditor can then take one or both of the courses of action set out in para 10.

Appendix

Qualified Audit Report in respect of a company which has not availed itself of the right to prepare accounts under Schedule 9 to the Companies Act 1985.

Inconsistency between the directors' report and the audited financial statements
Auditors report to the members of ...

We have audited the financial statements on pages ... to ... in accordance with approved Auditing Standards.

In our opinion the financial statements, which have been prepared under the historical cost convention, give a true and fair view of the state of the company's affairs at 31st December 19.. and of its results and source and application of funds for the year then ended and comply with the Companies Act 1985.

In our opinion, the information given in the directors' report is not consistent with the company's financial statements for the financial year. Paragraph 7 of the directors' report states without amplification that the company's trading resulted in a profit before tax of £X. The profit and loss account, however, states that the company incurred a loss before tax for the year of £Y and, as an extraordinary item, a profit from the sale of land £Z.

APPENDIX 3: SPECIAL AUDIT REPORTS UNDER THE COMPANIES ACT 1985

The Companies Act 1985 has created a variety of situations in which the auditor is required to report to shareholders, directors or the registrar of companies. The auditor must be able to recognise a situation where a statutory report is required. Once alerted, he is then able to plan his work and prepare his report.

This *aide memoire* sets out the circumstances in which a report may be required and provides references to the Act, to enable detailed consideration where necessary.

1. Re-registration of a private company as a public company

Written statement expressing opinion that, at balance sheet date within seven months before application for re-registration, the company's net assets exceed the aggregate of called-up share capital and undistributable reserves (as defined in CA 1985, s. 264).

s. 43(3)(*b*) Auditors' statement to Registrar of Companies

—audit report at balance sheet date must be unqualified (s. 43(3)(*c*)) or without material qualification (s. 46).

2. Allotment of shares by a public company otherwise than for cash

Report on value of consideration for allotment:

s. 108(1)–(7) Independent accountants' report

(a)　required within six months before allotment.

(b)　not applicable in respect of bonus issues, mergers or certain share exchanges.

3. Transfer of non-cash assets to a public company by a shareholder

Report on assets transferred and value of consideration:

s. 109(1)–(3) Independent accountants' report

(a)　required where, within two years of registration (or re-registration, if previously a private company), a public company receives from a member a non-cash asset worth more than 10% of the nominal value of the company's issued share capital.

(b)　required within six months before transfer.

(c)　not required where transaction carried out under supervision of the court or in the course of ordinary business.

4. *Profits available for distribution*

Profits available for distribution are defined in CA 1985, s. 263 and additionally for public companies, s. 264:

(a)   Distribution proposed in circumstances of qualified audit report:

   Statement to members in general meeting expressing opinion whether qualification is material in determining whether proposed distribution is permissible under CA 1985.

s. 271(3)
Auditors'
statement to
members

(b)   Proposed distribution supported by interim accounts where preceding annual accounts disclose insufficient distributable reserves (s. 270(4)):

   No audit report required.

   —but, for public company, such interim accounts must have been "properly prepared" (s. 272(2)).

(c)   Distribution during first period of trading:

   Report (public companies only) on "initial accounts" (s. 273(4)) expressing opinion that accounts have been "properly prepared".

   —true and fair view audit required.

s. 273(4)
Auditors'
report to
Registrar of
Companies

5. *Banks: transactions involving directors*

Report on statement of transactions with directors.

s. 343(6)
Auditors'
report to
members

6. *Transactions involving directors and connected persons (ss. 232–234)*

Where disclosure requirements of CA 1985, ss. 232 to 234, not complied with, it is duty of auditors to include in their report on annual accounts a statement giving the required particulars, so far as they are reasonably able to do so.

s. 237

7. *Special auditors' report on modified accounts of small or medium-sized companies*

Report required to:

Schedule 8
Auditors'
report to
directors

(a)   express opinion that:

   (i)   requirements for exemptions have been satisfied;

   (ii)   modified accounts have been properly prepared;

(b)   include full text of auditors' report on the full accounts prepared for shareholders.

A true and fair view audit opinion cannot—and should not—be given on modified accounts.

8. Financial assistance for acquisition of shares

Report in connection with private company giving financial assistance for the purchase of its shares or those of its holding company—where permitted by CA 1985, ss. 151–155.

s. 156(4)
Auditors' report to directors

The directors are required to make a statutory declaration concerning the company's ability to pay its debts. The audit report must state that the auditors:

(a)   have enquired into the state of affairs of the company, and

(b)   are not aware of anything to indicate that the opinions expressed in the directors' statutory declaration are unreasonable in all the circumstances.

9. Redemption or purchase by a private company of its own shares out of capital

A private company limited by shares or limited by guarantee and having a share capital may, subject to authorisation in the articles of association, make a payment in respect of the redemption or purchase of any of its own shares otherwise than out of distributable profits or the proceeds of a fresh issue of shares.

s. 173(5)
Auditors' report to directors

The directors are required to make a statutory declaration specifying the amount of the "permissible capital payment" (as defined in s. 171(3)) and concerning the company's ability to pay its debts. The audit report must:

(a)   state that the auditors have enquired into the state of affairs of the company, and

(b)   express the opinion that the amount of the permissible capital payment stated in the declaration has been properly determined in accordance with s. 171, and

(c)   state that the auditors are not aware of anything to indicate that the opinions expressed in the directors' statutory declaration are unreasonable in all the circumstances.

10. Dormant companies

A dormant company which is not obliged to prepare group accounts and which is "small" (or would have been "small" if not a member of an "ineligible" (basically public) group) may agree by special resolution not to appoint an auditor.

s. 252

11. Directors' reports   s. 237
The auditors of a company preparing accounts under CA
1985, Schedule 4, have to consider whether information
given in the directors' report is consistent with the
accounts. If such information is *not* consistent, the fact
must be stated in the auditor's report.

12. Auditors' reports CA 1985, s. 236
All audit reports dated on or after 1st July 1985
(other than for banking, insurance and shipping
companies, that are exempt in certain circumstances)
should include the phrase: "... the Companies Act
1985".

PROGRESS TEST 7

1.   Summarise the principal legal matters concerning:

     (a)   the auditor's appointment; (1.0)

     (b)   removal; (2.0)

     (c)   qualification; (5.0)

     (d)   rights; (7.0)

     (e)   duties. (8.0)

2.   List the matters of particular concern to auditors under the original provisions of
     the Companies Act 1980. (12.0)

3.   (a)   How will the issue of a qualified audit report affect a company's ability to
           pay dividends under the Companies Act 1985? (13.0)

     (b)   When may a private/public company pay a dividend? (15.0)

CHAPTER EIGHT

Considerations affecting Audit Reports

1.0 THE STANDARDS GOVERNING AUDIT REPORTS

The full text of the Auditor's Operational Standard and its accompanying Guidelines is given in section 17.0 of Chapter 1.

1.1 The audit report

Part 1: statement of auditing standard

1. This Auditing Standard applies to all reports in which the auditor expresses an opinion on financial statements intended to give a true and fair view of the state of affairs, profit or loss and, where applicable, source and application of funds. The Standard is not intended to override the statutory exemptions granted in respect of certain types of enterprise but is intended to apply to the audit reports relating to such enterprises in other respects.

2. The audit report should identify those to whom it is addressed and the financial statements to which it relates.

3. The auditor should refer expressly in his report to the following:

   (a) whether the financial statements have been audited in accordance with approved Auditing Standards;

   (b) whether in the auditor's opinion the financial statements give a true and fair view of the state of affairs, profit or loss and, where applicable, source and application of funds; and

   (c) any matters prescribed by relevant legislation or other requirements.

Part 2: explanatory note

COMPLIANCE WITH APPROVED AUDITING STANDARDS

5. The auditor should comply with approved Auditing Standards and it is

appropriate that his report should refer to this fact in arriving at his opinion. Approved Auditing Standards are defined as those Statements of Auditing Standards which are approved for issue by the councils of the accountancy bodies listed in the explanatory foreword and which are effective for the period covered by the financial statements on which the auditor is reporting.

TRUE AND FAIR

6.   The majority of audit reports are issued under the Companies Act which normally requires the use of the words "true and fair view". For the purpose of this standard, therefore, the phrase "true and fair view" has been retained. When expressing an opinion that financial statements give a true and fair view the auditor should be satisfied, *inter alia*, that:

(a)   all relevant Statements of Standard Accounting Practice have been complied with, except in situations in which for justifiable reasons they are not strictly applicable because they are impracticable, or exceptionally, having regard to the circumstances, would be inappropriate or give a misleading view; and

(b)   any significant accounting policies which are not the subject of Statements of Standard Accounting Practice are appropriate to the circumstances of the business.

REFERENCE TO ACCOUNTING CONVENTION

7.   The auditor should refer in his report to the particular convention used in preparing the financial statements if he considers it necessary in order to avoid misunderstanding.

EMPHASIS OF MATTER

8.   As a general principle the auditor issuing an unqualified opinion should not make reference to specific aspects of the financial statements in the body of his report as such reference may be misconstrued as being a qualification. In rare circumstances, however, the reader will obtain a better understanding of the financial statements if his attention is drawn to important matters. Examples might include an unusual event, accounting policy or condition, awareness of which is fundamental to an understanding of the financial statements.

9.   In order to avoid giving the impression that a qualification is intended, references which are intended as emphasis of matter should be contained in a separate paragraph and introduced with a phrase such as "We draw attention to ..." and should not be referred to in the opinion paragraph. Emphasis of matter should not be used to rectify a lack of appropriate disclosure in the financial statements, nor should it be regarded as a substitute for a qualification.

COMPLIANCE WITH RELEVANT LEGISLATION OR OTHER REQUIREMENTS

10.   The auditor should comply with any reporting requirements imposed by legislation and any other reporting requirements relevant to the financial statements. It should be noted that the Companies Acts of Great Britain,

Northern Ireland and the Republic of Ireland contain different reporting requirements.

11. Set out below is a form of audit report appropriate to a company incorporated in Great Britain which meets the requirements of this standard where the auditor is able to report affirmatively on all the matters contained in paragraph 3 above.

"Auditor's report to the members of ....
We have audited the financial statements on pages ..... to ... in accordance with approved Auditing Standards.
In our opinion the financial statements [which have been prepared under the historical cost convention as modified by the revaluation of land and buildings] give a true and fair view of the state of the company's affairs at 31st December 19 .. and of its profit and source and application of funds for the year then ended and comply with the Companies Act 1985."

1.2 Qualifications in Audit Reports

Part 1: statement of auditing standard

1. When the auditor is unable to report affirmatively on the matters contained in paragraph 3 of the Auditing Standard "The Audit Report" he should qualify his report by referring to all material matters about which he has reservations. All reasons for the qualification should be given, together with a quantification of its effect on the financial statements if this is both relevant and practicable. Additionally, reference may need to be made to non-compliance with relevant legislation and other requirements.

2. A qualified audit report should leave the reader in no doubt as to its meaning and its implications for an understanding of the financial statements. To promote a more consistent understanding of qualified reports the forms of qualification described in this standard should be used unless, in the auditor's opinion, to do so would fail to convey clearly the intended meaning.

3. The nature of the circumstances giving rise to a qualification of opinion will generally fall into one of two categories:

    (a) where there is an uncertainty which prevents the auditor from forming an opinion on a matter (uncertainty); or

    (b) where the auditor is able to form an opinion on a matter but this conflicts with the view given by the financial statements (disagreement).

    Each of these categories gives rise to alternative forms of qualifications depending upon whether the subject matter of the uncertainty or disagreement is considered to be fundamental so as to undermine the view given by the financial statements taken as a whole.

4.   The forms of qualification which should be used in different circumstances are shown below.

Nature of circumstances	Material but not fundamental	Fundamental
Uncertainty	"Subject to" opinion	Disclaimer of opinion
Disagreement	"Except" opinion	Adverse opinion

(a)   In a disclaimer of opinion the auditor states that he is unable to form an opinion as to whether the financial statements give a true and fair view.

(b)   In an adverse opinion the auditor states that in his opinion the financial statements do not give a true and fair view.

(c)   In a "subject to" opinion the auditor effectively disclaims an opinion on a particular matter which is not considered fundamental.

(d)   In an "except" opinion the auditor expresses an adverse opinion on a particular matter which is not considered fundamental.

Part 2: explanatory note

INTRODUCTION

5.   There are occasions when, in order to convey clearly the results of his audit, the auditor needs to depart from the form of wording normally used for unqualified audit reports. Such departures are generally referred to as qualifications. The principles set out in this Standard are intended to make qualified audit reports more understandable by developing a consistent use of language to distinguish the types of qualification appropriate to different circumstances.

REASONS FOR QUALIFICATION

6.   As indicated in Part 1, circumstances which give rise to a qualification of opinion in an audit report may be in the nature of uncertainty or disagreement.

7.   Circumstances giving rise to uncertainties include the following:

(a)   *Limitations in the scope of the audit.* Scope limitations arise if the auditor is unable for any reason to obtain all the information and explanations which he considers necessary for the purpose of his audit; for example, inability to carry out an audit procedure considered necessary, or the absence of proper accounting records.

(b)   *Inherent uncertainties.* Inherent uncertainties result from circumstances in which it is not possible to reach an objective conclusion as to the outcome of a situation due to the circumstances themselves rather than to any limitation of the scope of audit procedures. This type of uncertainty may relate to major litigation, the outcome of long-term contracts or doubts about the ability of the enterprise to continue as a going concern. Inherent uncertainties will not normally include instances where the auditor is able to obtain adequate evidence to support estimates and use his experience to reach an opinion as to their reasonableness, for example as regards collectability of debts or realisability of stock.

8. The wording in expressing the audit opinion describes the effect of uncertainties on that opinion and does not distinguish those arising from a limitation of scope from those which are inherent. The cause of uncertainty will be described elsewhere in the audit report.

9. Circumstances giving rise to disagreement include the following:

(a) departures from acceptable accounting practices where:

(i) there has been failure to comply with a relevant Statement of Standard Accounting Practice (SSAP) and the auditor does not concur;

(ii) an accounting policy not the subject of an SSAP is adopted which in the opinion of the auditor is not appropriate to the circumstances of business;

(iii) exceptionally, an SSAP has been followed with the result that the financial statements do not present a true and fair view;

(b) disagreement as to the facts or amounts included in the financial statements;

(c) disagreement as to the manner or extent of disclosure of facts or amounts in the financial statements:

(d) failure to comply with relevant legislation or other requirements.

SMALL ENTERPRISES

10. The auditor needs to obtain the same degree of assurance in order to give an unqualified opinion on the financial statements of both small and large enterprises. However, the operating procedures and methods of recording and processing transactions used by small enterprises often differ significantly from those of large enterprises. Indeed, many of the controls which would be relevant to the large enterprise are not practical, appropriate or necessary in the small enterprise. The most effective form of internal control for small enterprises is generally the close involvement of the directors or proprietors. This involvement will, however, enable them to override controls and purposely to exclude transactions from the records. This possibility can give rise to difficulties for the auditor not because there is a lack of controls but because of insufficient evidence as to their operation and the completeness of the records.

11. In many situations it may be possible to reach a conclusion that will support an unqualified opinion on the financial statements by combining the evidence obtained from extensive substantive testing of transactions with a careful review of costs and margins. However, in some businesses such as those where most

transactions are for cash and there is no regular pattern of cost and margins, the available evidence may be inadequate to support an opinion on the financial statements.

12.   There will be other situations where the evidence available to the auditor is insufficient to give him the confidence necessary for him to express an unqualified opinion but this uncertainty is not so great as to justify a total disclaimer of opinion. In such situations the most helpful form of report may be one which indicates the need to accept the assurances of management as to the completeness or accuracy of the accounting records. Such a report should contain a "subject to . . ." opinion. It would be appropriate to use this form of report only if the auditor has taken steps to obtain all the evidence which can reasonably be obtained and is satisfied that:

(a)   the system of accounting and control is reasonable having regard to the size and type of the enterprise's operations; and is sufficient to enable management to give the auditor the assurances which he requires;

(b)   there is no evidence to suggest that the assurances may be inaccurate.

DISCLOSURE OF REASONS FOR QUALIFICATIONS

13.   The audit report should include a brief recital of the reasons for qualification and should quantify the effects on the financial statements if this is relevant and practicable. Whilst reference may be made to relevant notes in the financial statements such reference should not be used as a substitute for a description of the basic circumstances in the audit report.

14.   The auditor should refer in his report to all material matters about which he has reservations. Thus, a qualification on one matter should not be regarded as a reason for omitting other unrelated qualifications which otherwise would have been reported.

15.   The manner in which the reasons for qualifying are disclosed is for the auditor to decide in the particular circumstances of each case, but the overall objective should be clarity. The inclusion of a separate "explanatory" paragraph before the paragraph in which the auditor gives his opinion is likely to be the clearest method of outlining the facts giving rise to the qualifications.

STATUTORY REQUIREMENTS

16.   The auditor will also need to consider whether the circumstances which give rise to his qualification impinge on his statutory duties to report. For instance, shortcomings in the sales records which give rise to a qualified opinion on the financial statements will generally mean that proper account records (*described in some legislation as "proper books of account"*) have not been maintained. Similarly, limitations in scope may mean that the auditor has not obtained all the information and explanations he considers necessary.

OMISSION OF STATEMENTS OF SOURCE AND APPLICATION OF FUNDS

17.   SSAP 10 requires, with certain specified exceptions, that financial statements

should include a statement of source and application of funds. Omission of such a statement from financial statements to which SSAP 10 applies presents a particular problem to the auditor in that the omission of a funds statement does not justify, on this ground alone, a qualified report on the profit and loss account and balance sheet.

18. It is considered that the standards set out in this statement will be met if the auditor reports the omission of a funds statement by adding a separate paragraph which follows his opinion. An example of the manner in which this matter could be reported is: "The financial statements do not specify the manner in which the operations of the company (group) have been financed or in which its financial resources have been used during the year as required by Statement of Standard Accounting Practice No. 10".

MATERIALITY

19. In deciding whether to qualify his audit opinion, the auditor should have regard to the materiality of the matter in the context of the financial statements on which he is proposing to report. In general terms a matter should be judged to be material if knowledge of the matter would be likely to influence the user of the financial statements. Materiality may be considered in the context of the financial statements as a whole, the balance sheet, the profit and loss account, or individual items within the financial statements. In addition, depending upon the nature of the matter, materiality may be considered in relative or absolute terms.

20. If the auditor concludes that, judged against the criteria he believes to be most appropriate in the circumstances, the matter does not materially affect the view given by the financial statements, he should not qualify his opinion.

21. Where the auditor has decided that a matter is sufficiently material to warrant a qualification in his audit report, a further decision is required as to whether or not the matter is fundamental, so as to require either an adverse opinion or a disclaimer of opinion on the financial statements as a whole. An uncertainty becomes fundamental when its impact on the financial statements is so great as to render the financial statements as a whole meaningless. A disagreement becomes fundamental when its impact on the financial statements is so great as to render them totally misleading. The combined effect of all uncertainties and disagreements must be considered.

22. It is emphasised that the adverse opinion and the disclaimer of opinion are the extreme forms of the two main categories of qualification of opinion arising from disagreement and uncertainty. In most situations the "except" or "subject to" form of opinion will be the appropriate form to use; the adverse opinion and the disclaimer should be regarded as measures of last resort.

1.3 Audit report examples

Notes

(a) *All reports commence with the heading "Auditors' report to the members of... Ltd."*

(b)   All reports should be signed and dated.

Example 1: unqualified audit report

COMPANIES WITHOUT SUBSIDIARIES—GREAT BRITAIN

We have audited the financial statements on pages ... to ... in accordance with approved Auditing Standards.

In our opinion the financial statements, which have been prepared under the historical cost convention as modified by the revaluation of land and buildings, give a true and fair view of the state of the company's affairs at 31st December 19 .. and of its profit and source and application of funds for the year then ended and comply with the Companies Act 1985.

Example 2: unqualified audit report

COMPANIES SUBMITTING GROUP ACCOUNTS—GREAT BRITAIN

We have audited the financial statements on pages ... to ... in accordance with approved Auditing Standards.

In our opinion the financial statements, which have been prepared under the historical cost convention as modified by the revaluation of land and buildings, give a true and fair view of the state of affairs of the company and the group at 31st December 19 .. and of the profit and source and application of funds of the group for the year then ended and comply with the Companies Act 1985.

Example 3: unqualified audit report

EMPHASIS OF MATTER: TRANSACTIONS WITH A GROUP COMPANY

We have audited the financial statements on pages ... to ... in accordance with approved Auditing Standards.

We draw attention to note ... which outlines a number of transactions with the parent company during the year without which the company would have incurred a loss.

In our opinion the financial statements, which have been prepared under the historical cost convention, give a true and fair view of the state of the company's affairs at 31st December 19 .. and of its profit and source and application of funds for the year then ended and comply with the Companies Act 1985.

Example 4: qualified audit report

UNCERTAINTY—SUBJECT TO: NO STOCK COUNT AT A BRANCH

We have audited the financial statements on pages ... to ... Our audit was conducted in accordance with approved Auditing Standards except that the scope of our work was limited by the matter referred to below.

One branch of the company did not carry out a physical count of stock at 31st December 19 .. and there were no practical alternative auditing procedures that we could apply to confirm quantities. Accordingly, we have been unable to obtain all the information and explanations considered necessary to satisfy ourselves as to the existence of stock valued at £ ... at 31st December 19 .. which is included as part of the total stock £ ... in the balance sheet. In our opinion, in the case of the stocks referred to above, proper accounting records have not been kept as required by section 221 of the Companies Act 1985.

Subject to the effects of any adjustments which might have been shown to be necessary had a physical count of the branch stock been carried out, in our opinion the financial statements, which had been prepared under the historical cost convention, give a true and fair view of the state of the company's affairs at 31st December 19 .. and of its profit and source and application of funds for the year then ended and comply with the Companies Act 1985.

Example 5: qualified audit report

UNCERTAINTY—SUBJECT TO: ACCEPTANCE OF MANAGEMENT ASSURANCES (SMALL BUSINESS)

We have audited the financial statements on pages ... to ... Our audit was conducted in accordance with approved Auditing Standards having regard to the matters referred to in the following paragraph.

In common with many businesses of similar size and organisation the company's system of control is dependent upon the close involvement of the directors/managing director [who are major shareholders]. Where independent confirmation of the completeness of the account records was therefore not available we have accepted assurances from the directors/managing director that all the company's transactions have been reflected in the records.

Subject to the foregoing, in our opinion the financial statements, which have been prepared under the historical cost convention, give a true and fair view of the state of the company's affairs at 31st December 19 .. and of its profit and source and application of funds for the year then ended and comply with the Companies Act 1985.

Example 6: qualified audit report

UNCERTAINTY—SUBJECT TO: GOING CONCERN

We have audited the financial statements on pages ... to ... in accordance with approved Auditing Standards.

As stated in note ... the company is currently negotiating for long-term facilities to replace the loan of £ ... which becomes repayable on [a date early in the next financial year]; continuation of the company's activities is dependent upon a successful outcome of these negotiations. The financial statements have been drawn up on a going concern basis which assumes that adequate facilities will be obtained.

Subject to a satisfactory outcome of the negotiations referred to above, in our opinion the financial statements, which have been prepared under the historical cost convention, give a true and fair view of the state of affairs of the company and the group at 31st December 19 .. and of the profit and source and application of funds of the group for the year then ended and comply with the Companies Act 1985.

Example 7: qualified audit report

UNCERTAINTY—SUBJECT TO: MAJOR LITIGATION

We have audited the financial statements on pages ... to ... in accordance with approved Auditing Standards.

As more fully explained in note ... to the financial statements a claim has been lodged against a subsidiary company in respect of one of its major contracts. The claim calls for rectification and for substantial compensation for alleged damage to the customer's business. The directors have made provision for the estimated cost of rectification but no provision for compensation as that part of the claim is being strongly resisted. At this time it is not possible to determine with reasonable accuracy the ultimate cost of rectification and compensation, if any, which may become payable.

Subject to the adjustment, if any, that may be required when the claim referred to above is determined, in our opinion the financial statements, which have been prepared under the historical cost convention, give a true and fair view of the state of affairs of the company and the group at 31st December 19.. and of the profit and source and application of funds of the group for the year then ended and comply with the Companies Act 1985.

Example 8: qualified audit report

UNCERTAINTY—DISCLAIMER: ACCOUNTING BREAKDOWN

We have audited the financial statements on pages ... to ... Our audit was conducted in accordance with approved Auditing Standards except that the scope of our work was limited by the matter referred to below.

As stated in note ..., a fire at the company's computer centre destroyed many of the accounting records. The financial statements consequently include significant amounts based on estimates. In these circumstances we were unable to carry out all the auditing procedures, or to obtain all the information and explanations we considered necessary.

Because of the significance of the matter referred to in the preceding paragraph, we are unable to form an opinion as to

(a) whether the financial statements give a true and fair view of the state of the company's affairs as at 31st December 19 .. and of its profit and source and application of funds for the year then ended;

(b) whether proper accounting records have been kept or;

(c) whether the financial statements comply in all respects with the Companies Act 1985.

Example 9: qualified audit report

UNCERTAINTY—DISCLAIMER: INABILITY TO SUBSTANTIATE CASH TRANSACTIONS

We have audited the financial statements on pages ... to ... Our audit was conducted in accordance with approved Auditing Standards except that the scope of our work was limited by the matter referred to below.

A major part of the company's income comprises cash sales. There was no system of control over such sales upon which we could rely for the purpose of our audit and there were no satisfactory procedures which we could adopt to verify the completeness of the income. We were therefore unable to obtain all the information and explanations we considered necessary. Consequently, we were unable to satisfy ourselves as to the completeness and accuracy of the accounting records.

Because of the significance of the matter referred to in the preceding paragraph, we are unable to form an opinion as to

(a) whether the financial statements give a true and fair view of the state of the company's affairs at 31st December 19 .. and of its profit and source and application of funds for the year then ended;

(b) whether proper accounting records have been kept; or

(c) whether the financial statements comply in all respects with the Companies Act 1985.

Example 10: qualified audit report

UNCERTAINTY—DISCLAIMER: VALUATION OF LONG-TERM CONSTRUCTION CONTRACTS

We have audited the financial statements on pages ... to ... in accordance with approved Auditing Standards.

As indicated in note ... the estimates of losses to completion of long-term construction contracts depend on a number of assumptions including those relating to substantially increased production and productivity which have yet to be achieved. In view of these uncertainties we are unable to confirm that the provision of £ ... is adequate.

Because of the significance of this matter, we are unable to form an opinion as to whether the financial statements give a true and fair view of the state of the company's affairs at 31st December 19 .. and of its profit and source and application of funds for the year then ended.

In other respects the financial statements in our opinion comply with the Companies Act 1985.

Example 11: qualified audit report

DISAGREEMENT—EXCEPT: FAILURE TO APPLY SSAP 4

We have audited the financial statements on pages ... to ... in accordance with approved Auditing Standards.

As explained in note ... Regional Development Grants have been credited in full to profits instead of being spread over the lives of the relevant assets as required by Statement of Standard Accounting Practice No. 4; the effect of so doing has been to increase group profits before and after taxation for the year by £ ... (19 .. £ ...).

Except for the effects of accounting for Regional Development Grants in the manner described in the preceding paragraph, in our opinion the financial statements, which have been prepared under the historical cost convention, give a true and fair view of the state of affairs of the company and the group at 31st December 19 .. and of the profit and source and application of funds of the group for the year then ended and comply with the Companies Act 1985.

Example 12: qualified audit report

DISAGREEMENT—EXCEPT: NO PROVISION FOR DOUBTFUL DEBT

We have audited the financial statements on pages ... to ... in accordance with approved Auditing Standards.

No provision has been made against an amount of £ ... owing by a company which has been placed in liquidation since the year end. The liquidator has indicated that unsecured creditors are unlikely to receive any payment and in our opinion full provision should be made.

Except for the failure to provide for the amount described above, in our opinion the financial statements, which have been prepared under the historical cost convention, give a true and fair view of the state of the company's affairs at 31st December 19 .. and of its profit and source and application of funds for the year then ended and comply with the Companies Act 1985.

Example 13: qualified audit report

DISAGREEMENT—EXCEPT: INFORMATION NOT DISCLOSED

We have audited the financial statements on pages ... to ... in accordance with approved Auditing Standards.

As explained in note ... the information concerning overseas investments acquired during the year has not been disclosed in accordance with section 231 of the Companies Act 1985.

In our opinion the financial statements, which have been prepared under the historical cost convention, give a true and fair view of the state of the affairs of the company and the group at 31st December 19 .. and of the profit and source and application of funds of the group for the year then ended and except for the omission of the disclosure concerning overseas investments referred to above comply with the Companies Act 1985.

Example 14: qualified audit report

DISAGREEMENT—ADVERSE OPINION: CONTRACT LOSSES NOT PROVIDED FOR IN ACCORDANCE WITH SSAP 9

We have audited the financial statements on pages ... to ... in accordance with approved Auditing Standards.

As more fully explained in note ... no provision has been made for losses expected to arise on certain long-term contracts currently in progress because the directors consider that such losses should be offset against expected and unearned future profits on other long-term contracts. In our opinion provision should be made for foreseeable losses on individual contracts as required by Statement of Standard Accounting Practice No. 9. If losses had been so recognised the effect would have been to reduce the profit before and after tax for the year and the contract work in progress at 31st December 19 .. by £ ...

In view of the significant effect of the failure to provide for the losses referred to above, in our opinion the financial statements do not give a true and fair view of the state of the company's affairs at 31st December 19 .. and of its profit and source and application of funds for the year then ended.

In other respects the financial statements in our opinion comply with the Companies Act 1985.

Example 15: qualified audit report

DISAGREEMENT—ADVERSE OPINION: GOODWILL

We have audited the financial statements on pages ... to ... in accordance with approved Auditing Standards.

Goodwill included in the consolidated balance sheet at £ ... relates to a subsidiary which has incurred material losses during the year. In our opinion there are insufficient grounds to support the directors' contention that the subsidiary can be expected to become profitable in the foreseeable future. Accordingly we consider that goodwill should be written off in the consolidated financial statements and the investment in the subsidiary should be written down by a similar amount in the holding company's financial statements.

Because of the significance of the foregoing matter, in our opinion the financial statements do not give a true and fair view of the state of affairs of the company and the group at 31st December 19 .. and of the profit of the group for the year then ended.

In our opinion, the financial statements give a true and fair view of the source and application of funds of the group for the year ended 31st December 19 .. and, except for the matter set out above, comply with the Companies Act 1985.

Example 16: qualified audit report

MULTIPLE QUALIFICATION—BASED ON EXAMPLES 5 AND 13

We have audited the financial statements on pages ... to ... Our audit was conducted in accordance with approved Auditing Standards except that the scope of our work was limited by the matter referred to below.

One branch of the company did not carry out a physical count of stock at 31st December 19 .. and there were no practicable alternative auditing procedures that we could apply to confirm quantities. Accordingly, we have been unable to obtain all the information and explanations considered necessary to satisfy ourselves as to the existence of the stock quantities valued at £ ... at 31st December 19 .. and included as part of the total stock of £ ... in the balance sheet. In our opinion in the case of the stocks referred to above proper accounting records have not been kept as required by section 221 of the Companies Act 1985.

No provision has been made against an amount of £ ... owing by a company which has been placed in liquidation since the year end. The liquidator has indicated that unsecured creditors are unlikely to receive any payment and in our opinion full provision should be made.

Subject to the effects of any adjustments which might have been shown to be necessary had a physical count of the branch stock occurred and except for the failure to make provision against an amount receivable, in our opinion the financial statements, which have been prepared under the historical cost convention, give a true and fair view of the state of the company's affairs at 31st December 19 .. and of its profits and source and application of funds for the year then ended and comply with the Companies Act 1985.

2.0 GROUP ACCOUNTS—RELIANCE ON OTHER AUDITORS (U21)

2.1 Introduction

The question of how far the parent company auditors are responsible for the truth and fairness of the view presented by the accounts of subsidiaries has long been a matter of grave concern to the profession. Legal cases such as *Reid Murray (Holdings), Pacific Acceptance Corporation*, and *Atlantic Acceptance Corporation* have each highlighted the risks to which the parent company auditors are subject in such circumstances, and although detailed questionnaires are usually sent out to subsidiary auditors and detailed enquiries are made, such measures are not effective substitutes for an adequate legal safeguard.

The Companies Act 1985 attempted to go some way towards resolving this problem by giving parent company auditors a right which has never previously existed in company law, i.e. the right to receive whatever *information and explanations* they consider necessary (for the execution of their statutory duties) *from the subsidiary directors and auditors*. Although this does not solve the problem entirely, it is a step in the right direction. Sections 2.2 to 2.19 which follow, and which deal with this problem, have been issued by the CCAB Bodies.

2.2   Subsidiary companies

Sections 229 and 230 of the Companies Act 1985 provide that where at the end of its financial year a company has subsidiaries, group or consolidated accounts shall be laid before the company in a general meeting, and that such group accounts shall give a true and fair view of the state of affairs and profit or loss of the company and its subsidiaries dealt with thereby as a whole, so far as concerns members of the company.

2.3   Associated companies

Statement of Standard Accounting Practice No. 1 "Accounting for the Results of Associated Companies" requires the investing group or company, except in certain circumstances, to incorporate in its accounts its share of the profits less losses of its associated companies.

2.4   Company partnerships and joint ventures

Where a company acts as a member of a partnership or joint venture the relevant figures of its interests in such consortium activities will normally be included in the accounts of the company itself.

2.5   Duties of directors

The directors of a primary company have a duty to produce group accounts which show a true and fair view, and consequently they need to satisfy themselves that amounts taken from the accounts of other group companies and interests are sufficiently reliable to be properly incorporated into the group accounts.

2.6   Duties of auditors

The Companies Act 1985 provides that in the case of a holding company submitting group accounts its auditors ("the primary auditors") shall expressly state whether, in their opinion, the group accounts have been properly prepared in accordance with the provisions of the Companies Act 1985 and whether they give a true and fair view of the state of affairs and profit or loss of the company and its subsidiaries dealt with thereby, so far as concerns members of the company. This opinion is wholly their responsibility. They are not relieved of this responsibility where group accounts contain amounts, which may be material, relating to other companies of which they are not the auditors, nor is the responsibility discharged by an uninformed acceptance of the accounts of those other companies, even if they have been independently audited. Whilst they are entitled to take account of the extent of the work and the report of other auditors, nevertheless they should conduct such further enquiries as they consider necessary in order to satisfy themselves that, with the inclusion of figures which they themselves have not audited, the group accounts disclose a true and fair view.

The principles set out above apply whether the results to be incorporated are those of subsidiary, associated or consortium companies.

2.7 The primary auditors' responsibilities

As the primary auditors have the sole responsibility for the opinion expressed in the auditors' report on the group accounts, amongst the principal matters which they need to examine before relying on accounts not audited by them are:

(a) accounting policies;

(b) availability of information;

(c) scope of work of the secondary auditors;

(d) the materiality of the amounts involved.

These matters are discussed in the following paragraphs.

2.8 Accounting policies

The primary auditors should discuss with the primary company's directors, or other responsible officials, the accounting policies and arrangements in force throughout the group in order to ensure that these are in their opinion appropriate to and consistent with the proper preparation of the group accounts. In many cases the directors will have adopted accounting policies on a uniform basis throughout the group. This will help the primary auditors in assessing whether the accounts present a true and fair view of the group as a whole.

In certain exceptional cases it may not be possible or desirable for the directors of a primary company to require their accounting policies to be adopted in the accounts of other group companies as these are normally the responsibility of their directors, who in many cases will have to consider the interests of minority shareholders. Moreover, local legislation may require the adoption of accounting policies different from those of the primary company. In such circumstances the primary auditors should check that the directors of the primary company have obtained from the other group companies such information as is necessary to enable them to make the appropriate adjustments. Where it is necessary to incorporate in the group accounts figures based on different accounting policies for a material section of the group, the primary auditors should ensure that those policies are fully explained in the group accounts.

2.9 Availability of information

The directors of a holding company should be able to exercise sufficient control over, and to secure sufficient information from its subsidiaries to satisfy themselves that the group accounts give a true and fair view and disclose all the information required by statute and other appropriate regulations.

In the case of associated companies, the control by the directors of the investing company may be less complete than in the case of subsidiaries; nevertheless it follows from the definition of "associated company" that the directors of the investing company will normally be in a position to ensure that the necessary financial and accounting information is made available to the primary auditors. In the case of associated companies which are listed on a recognised stock exchange, only published financial information should be used for incorporation in the accounts of the investing company (see SSAP 1, "Accounting for the Results of Associated Companies").

The primary auditors have the responsibility for verifying that the directors of the primary company have taken the necessary steps to provide the information discussed in (a) and (b) of section 2.7 above. If the primary auditors find that the directors of the primary company lack information about the accounting policies, items for disclosure, or consolidation adjustments relating to accounts of other group companies, they must ask for the omission to be made good. It may also be necessary to seek permission to obtain the additional information direct from the other companies or from their auditors. It is important for the primary auditors to discuss these requirements at an early date with the directors of the primary company.

2.10   Scope of the work of the secondary auditors

Before the primary auditors form their opinion on the group accounts, they need to determine whether in their opinion the underlying accounts are acceptable for the purpose of incorporation in the group accounts. In arriving at their opinion, the primary auditors will need to consider at least the following matters:

(a) Have all the material aspects of the underlying accounts been subject to an audit examination? If so:

(b) Are they, as primary auditors, aware of any reasons why they should not rely on the work and reports of the secondary auditors?

(c) The answer to these questions will depend on:

  (i) What is the primary auditors' knowledge of the standard of work of the secondary auditors?

  (ii) What auditing "standards" govern the work of the secondary auditors?

  (iii) What are the auditing requirements in the country in which the secondary auditors work?

  (iv) Who appointed the secondary auditors and to whom do they report?

  (v) Has any limitation been placed on the work of the secondary auditors, or are they free to decide the scope and levels of their audit tests?

  (vi) Are the secondary auditors independent in all respects?

  (vii) Is the nature and extent of the secondary auditors' examination adequate and reasonable *in the judgment of the primary auditors* to provide a sound basis on which the primary auditors can form their opinion?

Before drafting their report, the primary auditors will also need to consider:

(a) whether the secondary auditors' reports contain any qualifications which should be incorporated in the primary auditors' report; and

(b) whether any answers to the above questions require the primary auditors to qualify their report.

It follows from the considerations set out above, that in all cases the secondary auditors should appreciate that the accounts of the company which they are auditing will ultimately be an ingredient of the group accounts and that they should therefore be prepared to co-operate with the primary auditors and make available to them such information as they may require in order properly to discharge their duties as auditors of the group accounts.

2.11   Materiality

In deciding how extensive their enquiries ought to be, and therefore in selecting the type of audit procedures required, the primary auditors will need to consider the materiality of the amounts involved in so far as concerns the members of the primary company. The primary auditors may need to review in detail each year only those secondary companies which are judged to be material.

2.12   Consultations with other auditors

In all material cases the primary auditors will need to consult the auditors of other group companies so that they may be familiar with the auditing procedures and standards applied by the auditors of the other subsidiary and associated companies (the secondary auditors). However, they should not contact the secondary auditors until they have received proper authority by means of arrangements made through the respective boards. In conducting these consultations the primary auditors would normally use one or more of the following procedures:

(a) requests for written explanations of the secondary auditors' procedures and findings, and the secondary company's accounting policies, supplemented as necessary by

(b) oral explanations;

(c) examination of audit files, working papers and any relevant management letters.

In practice it is often found convenient to use audit questionnaires for completion by the secondary auditors. Care should be exercised in using such questionnaires, which may not be particularly helpful unless they are:

(a) suitably compiled with the specific circumstances of the group in mind (including the degree of control exercised over the subsidiary and associated companies);

(b) discussed in advance with the secondary auditors;

(c) properly completed.

If the primary auditors are not satisfied as a result of the above review, or if they need to obtain independent confirmation of additional accounting information required specifically for the group accounts, they should arrange for additional audit tests to be conducted, either directly by the secondary auditors on their behalf, or conjointly with them. Only in exceptional circumstances are primary auditors likely to need to conduct their own tests independently of the secondary auditors. It should be borne in mind that the secondary auditors are fully responsible for the standard of their own work and reports on the subsidiary or associated companies' accounts, and that the additional tests discussed above are those required solely for the audit of the group accounts.

It follows from the above considerations that it is important, in order that the secondary auditors may be aware in advance of the primary auditors' requirements, to arrange for consultations to take place when the secondary auditors are planning their audits and not to defer such consultations until the audits have been completed. Such a procedure is especially necessary where overseas firms of auditors are involved. Among the benefits which may arise from such advance consultations are:

(a) that the secondary auditors may be advised of the standard of audit required to enable their work to be relied on in the preparation and audit of the group accounts; and

(b) that the secondary auditors will be encouraged to discuss any proposed qualifications in their own reports with the primary auditors.

2.13 Reference to other auditors

The primary auditors are fully responsible for their opinion on the group accounts and need not for this reason refer in their report to the fact that the accounts of some subsidiary or associated companies have been audited by other firms. Such a reference may be misleading as it may be taken to imply a limitation of the scope of the primary auditors' opinion. This in no way takes away from the secondary auditors their responsibility for the audit of their client companies' accounts.

It is considered, however, that the shareholders of the primary company are entitled to know that the accounts of some of the companies in the group have been audited by other auditors and the materiality of those companies to the group, and accordingly that appropriate information should be disclosed. A suitable way in which this information may be included is to state in the schedule of principal, subsidiary and associated companies (or in the directors' report or in the notes to the accounts), which of those companies have been audited by the other auditors. It is desirable to indicate the significance to the group of the companies that have been so audited by reference to the amount of their assets, sales or profits or losses before tax.

2.14 The absence of an audit

The fact that the accounts of a subsidiary or associated company are not subject to regular audit, for example, because it is situated in a country in which there are no requirements for audit, does not alter the duty of the directors of the primary company to prepare accounts which disclose a true and fair view. If the amounts involved are material the primary auditors should request the directors of the primary company to arrange for an audit to be carried out, otherwise it may be impossible for them to report that the group accounts disclose a true and fair view.

2.15   Branches

In the case of branches, it may be necessary for the primary auditors to arrange for audit work to be carried out by local auditors. Such auditors act on behalf of the primary auditors, who must take full responsibility for the work of the local auditors. The primary auditors should ensure that the specified procedures have been properly carried out by the local auditors.

2.16   Auditors' reports where satisfactory information has been obtained

If having carried out with due care the procedures as above, the primary auditors are satisfied with the reliability of the financial information about the secondary company for the purpose of incorporating it in the group accounts, they will be able to express an unqualified opinion.

2.17   Auditors' report where satisfactory information is not available

Where the primary auditors have not been able to satisfy themselves in relation to secondary companies which they themselves have not audited, they should qualify their report, clearly indicating their reasons and identifying the material items affected.

2.18   Auditors' reports where material unaudited amounts are incorporated in group accounts

Where material accounts are incorporated from unaudited accounts, the primary auditors should express a reservation in their report, even though no information has come into their possession that those accounts are not reliable. The primary auditors cannot be as satisfied as to the true and fair view presented by the unaudited accounts as if they had been audited.

2.19   Information about companies audited by other auditors

Where material information recommended in section 2.13 is not disclosed about material group companies that have been audited by other auditors, the primary auditors should consider whether to refer to this fact in their report. It is important, however, to ensure that the additional information is not placed so as to mislead the reader into thinking that the scope of the audit opinion is thereby limited.

This concludes the CCAB Guidance statement.

2.20   Requests for "comfort" from parent and subsidiary company auditors

A recent issue of the technical and training newsletter of one of the major international firms draws attention to this particular problem area. It arises when auditors of a holding company, other than the firm in question, have written requesting general statements about the accounts of a subsidiary which the firm have been auditing. It appears that these statements are intended to give the auditors of the holding company "comfort" before they sign their report on the group. An example of the type of statement they have asked subsidiary auditors to make is as follows:

> "We know of no reason why the enclosed statements of our report cannot be used by you in forming an opinion on the consolidated financial statements of XYZ Ltd and we know of no inter-company transactions or other information, not fully disclosed in the financial statements, which should be considered by you in relation to such purposes except as set forth below:"

It is believed to be unwise to make such a statement. It is not generally possible for auditors of a subsidiary company to know whether information which, for instance, auditors of the subsidiary do not consider relevant for their purposes might be relevant to the auditors of the holding company. It is considered that the request for such a representation should be put to the management of the holding company and to the management of the subsidiary and not to the auditors.

Advice to those offices who have already received such letters has been that a reply along the following lines should be made:

> "We refer to your request dated ... asking for certain general confirmations.
>
> We regret that it is not our practice to make such general statements on financial statements audited by us as we are not aware what matters you should consider when forming your opinion, and we believe such information should be supplied to you by your client.
>
> Should you have any specific query which you would like us to consider please do not hesitate to let us know."

Similarly, requests are received from auditors of subsidiaries and submitted to auditors of the parent company. This is a complementary situation to that described above. It is believed, here again, that a general statement of "comfort" should not be made. Auditors of the parent company do not necessarily know whether information which (for instance) they as parent company auditors are aware of, is relevant to the auditors of, or some of, the subsidiaries. It is considered that the request for such a general statement should be made to the management of a subsidiary company for them to transmit it to the management of the parent company. It is not considered that the request should be made to parent company auditors.

It is suggested that offices should reply to any such requests along the following lines:

> "We refer to your request dated ... which requested certain information from us in connection with your audit of the above subsidiary companies of the XYZ Group for the year ended 31st December 1984.
>
> We regret that it is not our practice to make such general statements in respect of matters which might affect the audit of subsidiary companies not audited by us, because we are not necessarily aware what matters you should consider when forming your opinion. We believe such information should be supplied to you by your client.

Should you have any specific query which you would like us to consider, please do not hesitate to let us know."

2.21   Draft Auditing Guideline: Group Financial Statements— Reliance on the Work of Other Auditors

In August 1985 the APC issued a draft Guideline on the reliance on the work of other auditors. The text is reproduced below.

Preface

This guideline is intended to clarify the duties, responsibilities and practices of the auditor when reporting on group financial statements that include amounts derived from the accounts of subsidiaries or of associated companies which have been audited by other auditors. It should be of use to auditors who act as either primary or secondary auditors.

For the purposes of this guideline, the term "primary auditor" refers to an auditor who is responsible for the audit opinion on group financial statements. A "secondary auditor" is an auditor of a subsidiary or associated company who is not the primary auditor and is responsible for his own audit opinion on the secondary company's financial statements. All other definitions of terms used in the guideline are included in the appendix.

The relationship between primary and secondary auditors is not the same as that between the auditors involved:

(a)   in a joint audit; or

(b)   where a company has operations based at several locations or branches, and local auditors acting as agents work on behalf of the primary auditor.

Accordingly, neither of these situations is covered by this guideline.

Introduction

1.   This guideline is written in the context of companies and company legislation, which imposes on the directors of a holding company the responsibility to prepare accounts which give a true and fair view so far as concerns the members of the holding company. The auditor of any other form of enterprise is guided by the terms of his particular appointment and by the relevant legislation, but in the absence of specific provisions to the contrary, the general principles embodied in this guideline should be followed.

2.   The primary auditor is required to express an opinion on the group financial statements and has sole responsibility for this opinion even where those group financial statements include amounts derived from accounts which have not been audited by him. As a result, he cannot discharge his responsibility to report on the group financial statements by an uninformed acceptance of secondary companies' financial statements, whether audited or not.

3.   As explained below, however, the primary auditor can take account of the extent of work and the report of other (secondary) auditors through carrying out certain

procedures. The extent of these procedures will be determined by the materiality of the amounts derived from the financial statements of secondary companies, and the level of risk that the auditor is willing to accept that such statements contain material errors.

The relationship between the primary and the secondary auditor

4.   The relationship between a primary and a secondary auditor is not that between a principal and an agent. If, however, the secondary company is a subsidiary, and both the primary company and the secondary company are incorporated in Great Britain, the secondary company and its auditor have a statutory duty under s. 392(1)(a), Companies Act 1985, to give to the primary auditor such information and explanations as that auditor may reasonably require for the purposes of his duties as auditor of the primary company. Similarly, legislation in Northern Ireland (contained in article 31(1)(a) of the Companies (Northern Ireland) Order 1978) imposes this obligation on a subsidiary company and its auditor, when both the holding and subsidiary companies are incorporated in Northern Ireland. (There is no equivalent legislation in the Republic of Ireland.)

5.   Where the statutory duty described in the previous paragraph does not exist, the primary company has a statutory duty under s. 392(1)(b), Companies Act 1985 (with reference to Northern Ireland contained in article 31(1)(b) of the Companies (Northern Ireland) Order 1978), to take all steps reasonably open to it to obtain from the subsidiary such information and explanations as the primary auditor may reasonably require for the purposes of his duties as auditor of the primary company.

6.   Even where his responsibilities in this regard are not set down by statute, the secondary auditor should appreciate that the secondary company's financial statements will ultimately form a part of the group financial statements. In principle, the secondary auditor should therefore be prepared to co-operate with the primary auditor and make available such information as the primary auditor may require in order to discharge his duties as auditor of the group financial statements.

7.   The primary auditor should as a matter of courtesy inform the directors of the primary company of his intention to communicate with the secondary auditor. The nature of the instructions which are to be given to the secondary auditor, and the information required from him, should be discussed by the primary auditor with the directors of the primary company at the planning stage. Where the primary auditor has not statutory right to approach the secondary auditor, he should arrange for the secondary auditor to be instructed to co-operate by the directors of the secondary company, in order to ensure that the duty of confidentiality owed by the secondary auditor to his client is maintained. This may not be possible where the secondary company is an associated company, as the directors of the primary company may have less control than in the case of a subsidiary company.

8.   The primary auditor should inform the secondary auditor in advance of the

standard and scope of work required and any reporting deadlines that are to be met. For effective co-operation to take place, the primary and secondary auditors should communicate with each other as early as possible in the planning stage of the audit. The secondary auditor should discuss problems that may lead to delay in reporting or qualification of his opinion as soon as they arise.

Operational procedures

MATERIALITY

9. In deciding what audit procedures are necessary, the primary auditor should consider the audit risk involved and the materiality of the amounts in the context of the group financial statements. This will involve an evaluation of the significance of each secondary company and also of each account area or item of disclosure, as it is possible that a particular area (e.g. stock or fixed assets) will be considered material in the context of the group as a whole.

10. A secondary company which is not itself material in the context of the group financial statements may, when taken together with other non-material secondary companies, result in a combination which is material. When this occurs, the primary auditor should proceed as if those secondary companies were material when considered individually.

11. Any decisions taken regarding materiality should be reassessed each year.

GENERAL PROCEDURES

12. The scope and nature of the primary auditor's procedures will vary depending on the particular circumstances of each case. Judgments will need to be made in the light of factors such as the scope of work of the secondary auditor, specific audit problems encountered in the past, and the likely degree of change in the secondary company's results and state of affairs. At the planning stage the primary auditor should assess the risk inherent in the assignment and the related likelihood of audit problems. The information relevant to this preliminary assessment will include the financial statements for earlier periods for both the group and the secondary company.

13. The primary auditor should obtain and read the financial statements of the secondary company for the period under consideration at the earliest opportunity. This, when taken in conjunction with other information which the primary auditor has, may enable him to determine that the secondary company is immaterial in the context of the group financial statements. In all other cases the primary auditor should then, as a minimum, consider and be satisfied about the general scope of the work of the secondary auditor and in particular:

   (a) the terms of the secondary auditor's engagement and any limitation placed on his work;

   (b) the standard of work of the secondary auditor and the nature and extent of his audit examination;

(c)   any differences between the auditing, accounting and other professional standards governing the secondary auditor's work and those applicable in the UK and Ireland, and any steps taken by the secondary auditor to conform to UK and Irish standards; and

(d)   the independence of the secondary auditor.

14.   These matters may be dealt with by means of a questionnaire. The completed questionnaire should be reviewed by the primary auditor who should evaluate the reasonableness of the information provided in the light of his knowledge of the business and follow up any matters which require further explanation.

15.   Frequently the secondary company will be of such significance that the primary auditor will supplement the above procedures by a review of the secondary auditor's working papers.

16.   The principal objective of such a review is to ensure that it is reasonable for the primary auditor to rely on the work of the secondary auditor when expressing an opinion on the group financial statements. He is not expressing his own opinion on the financial statements of the secondary company, and he is not required to re-perform the secondary auditor's work or re-evaluate the audit evidence examined by the secondary auditor. The primary auditor should instead satisfy himself that the audit has been carried out in accordance with approved Auditing Standards and that the conclusions reached by the secondary auditor are both reasonable and reliable.

17.   In the circumstances described in para 10, the review of the secondary auditors' working papers may be carried out on a periodic basis.

18.   In addition, any qualification in the secondary auditor's report should be considered by the primary auditor to ascertain whether it affects his report on the group financial statements.

ADDITIONAL PROCEDURES
19.   If as a result of the above procedures the primary auditor is not satisfied for the purpose of reporting on the group financial statements, he should discuss the problem with his client. If necessary, he should arrange for the secondary auditor to conduct additional audit tests (either alone or jointly with the primary auditor). In exceptional circumstances only, the primary auditor may need to conduct his own tests independently of the secondary auditor. The secondary auditor is fully responsible for the standard of his own work and for his report on the secondary company's financial statements. Therefore any additional tests are those required solely for the audit of the group financial statements.

Further considerations

AVAILABILITY OF INFORMATION
20.   Primary company directors need to secure sufficient information to satisfy

themselves that the group financial statements give a true and fair view, and disclose all the information required by statute and other appropriate regulations. Problems due to the lack of necessary information are likely to arise in two specific situations: where the primary and secondary companies are incorporated in different countries, and are not subject to the same legislation, or where secondary companies' year ends differ from that of the primary company.

21. If the primary auditor finds that the directors of the primary company lack information about the accounting policies, items for disclosure, or consolidation adjustments relating to the financial statements of secondary companies, he should ask for the omission to be made good. Occasionally it may be necessary for the primary auditor, after obtaining permission, to obtain the additional information directly from the secondary companies concerned or from their auditors. The primary auditor may need to arrange for such additional information to be audited by the secondary auditor.

ACCOUNTING POLICIES

22. The primary auditor should discuss with the primary company's directors, or other responsible officials, the accounting policies in force throughout the group in order to ensure that these are, in his opinion, appropriate to and consistent with the proper preparation of the group financial statements.

23. Consistent accounting policies will normally be adopted throughout the group. However, in certain exceptional cases this may not be possible because financial statements of secondary companies are the responsibility of their directors who will have to consider the interests of minority shareholders and comply with local legislation or practice. Where the use of differing accounting policies results in adjustments being necessary to arrive at consolidated figures, the primary auditor should both ensure that the primary company's directors have obtained all the information necessary to make these adjustments, and satisfy himself that any adjustments are appropriate.

24. Where adjustments are impracticable and material figures based on different accounting policies are included in the group financial statements, the primary auditor should ensure that the policies adopted are fully explained and, where possible, the effects of the different policies are quantified.

EVENTS AFTER THE BALANCE SHEET DATE

25. The Auditing Guideline "Events after the Balance Sheet Date" requires the primary auditor to ensure that appropriate audit procedures are carried out to identify events after the balance sheet date which are of significance to the group between the dates of the reports of the secondary auditor and the date of his own report. These audit procedures may include the performance of updated reviews by secondary auditors. The primary auditor should contact the secondary auditor to ensure that all necessary further work has been performed.

Reporting

26. Where there are material subsidiary or associated companies not audited by the

primary auditor, the primary company may find it helpful to indicate this in the notes to the group financial statements. However, whether or not this information is given, the primary auditor should not ordinarily refer in his report to the name of any secondary auditor, or to the fact that secondary companies have been audited by other auditors. This is because the primary auditor cannot delegate the responsibility for his opinion and any such reference might mislead the reader into believing otherwise.

27.   In the event of any restriction in the scope of his audit of the group financial statements the primary auditor should consider qualifying his report.

Appendix

DEFINITION OF TERMS

Associated company: a company as defined by SSAP 1, para 13.

    Holding company: a company having interests in one or more subsidiary companies as defined by the Companies Act.

    Primary company: a company which is required to produce group (normally consolidated) financial statements which may incorporate amounts taken from the financial statements of subsidiary or associated companies.

    Secondary company: a subsidiary or associated company which is audited by a secondary auditor.

    Subsidiary company: a company as defined by the Companies Act.

3.0   CURRENT COST ACCOUNTING AND THE AUDITOR

The publicity attending the publication of the report of the Sandilands Committee, the work of the Inflation Accounting Steering Group and the subsequent publication of SSAP 16, "Current Cost Accounting", have created in some quarters the fear that the introduction of current cost accounting will change overnight all the procedures familiar to an auditor in the course of his work. This is not true. The bulk of the work carried out by an auditor is unaffected by the introduction of current cost accounting. Clients' staff will still be occupied in buying goods, paying wages and invoicing sales and all of these will require auditing as in the past.

    Similarly, in auditing the balance sheet, the auditor will still be examining assets from the point of view of the authority for the purchase, evidence of their existence and of their ownership; the aspect of assets which will change on the introduction of current cost accounting will be the examination of the value at which they are stated.

    The essence of the CCA convention is extremely simple, namely to adjust income, in arriving at the CCA profit for the year, for:

(a)   the value to the business, at the date of the consumption rather than at the date of purchase, of stocks consumed;

(b)   depreciation equal to that proportion of the fixed assets' value to the business (as opposed to historical cost) which is being consumed during the year; and

(c)   the extent to which (a) and (b) are affected by the presence of net monetary assets/liabilities and working capital.

Since balance sheets have in recent years often reflected the revaluation of certain assets, the significance of CCA for users of published accounts and thus for the auditor will be reflected more in the profit and loss account than in the balance sheet.

Some of the principal areas in which they will need to take account of changes in accounting principles are set out below.

(a) *Fixed assets.* With the introduction of a new basis for the valuation of fixed assets in the balance sheet the auditor needs a deeper knowledge of the basic decision-making process of management as to the use, suitability and expected life-span of major items of plant and machinery. Such study will be essential if the auditor is going to be able to assess adequately whether or not the basis of valuation, as proposed by management, is supported by acceptable opinions and evidence and is in accordance with the principles laid down in the Standard.

(b) *Deferred taxation.* In determining the amount to be provided for the deferred tax liability the Standard introduces the consideration, as yet undefined, of "reasonable probability" and "foreseeable future", in assessing the amount to be provided for the deferred tax liability.

(c) *Transfer to reserves.* The directors will determine, from the CCA supplementary statement the extent to which the company's current cost reserves require to be adjusted each year, and will explain the basis of their calculations and their reasons either in the directors' report or in the notes to the accounts.

(d) *Distributable profits.* Much of the law on distributable profits originates from cases in the early part of this century and is neither codified nor precise. Updated legislation in this area has been urgently required, and the advent of CCA makes it even more important. Major changes on this front have already been introduced in sections 263 to 270 of the Companies Act 1985.

A familiarity with CCA principles as implemented under SSAP 16 is of considerable importance to auditors.

In October 1980, the Auditing Practices Committee issued a Guideline on the audit of inflation accounts, and this is reproduced below:

3.1 Auditors' reports and SSAP No. 16, "Current cost accounting"

Introduction

1. This auditing Guideline is intended to assist auditors when reporting on statements produced by enterprises in accordance with Statement of Standard Accounting Practice No. 16 "Current Cost Accounting" (SSAP 16). It should be read in conjunction with the Explanatory Foreword to Auditing Standards and Guidelines (including the glossary of terms) and the Auditing Standards "The Audit Report" and "Qualifications in Audit Reports".

Background

2. An enterprise will, when complying with SSAP 16, provide current cost

accounting (CCA) information in one of the following forms:

(a) the presentation of historical cost accounts as the main accounts with supplementary current cost accounts which are prominently displayed;

(b) the presentation of current cost accounts as the main accounts with supplementary historical cost accounts; or

(c) the presentation of current cost accounts as the only accounts accompanied by adequate historical cost information.

3.   Annual financial statements of enterprises coming within the scope of SSAP 16 are required to include current cost accounts. Therefore, when reporting on such financial statements the auditor should report on the current cost accounts included therein.

4.   The objective of the management of an enterprise preparing current cost accounts should be that they give a true and fair view under the current cost principles described in SSAP 16. Equally, the objective of the auditor should be to give his opinion in true and fair terms. However, in the early years of CCA it is expected that many enterprises will continue to present historical cost accounts as the main accounts. In such cases the current cost accounts will be supplementary to the historical cost accounts on which the auditor reports in accordance with any statutory obligation.

Supplementary current cost accounts

5.   The supplementary current cost accounts may in practice take the form of either unabridged or abridged accounts. An unabridged set of supplementary current cost accounts is for the purpose of this guideline deemed to be a set of accounts, which together with notes, give all the information required for accounts intended to give a true and fair view under current cost principles of the state of affairs and results for the year. Such a set of accounts goes beyond the minimum requirements of SSAP 16. Other forms of accounts, including those drawn up in a form similar to that shown in the appendix to SSAP 16, are for the purpose of this guideline, abridged accounts.

6.   Enterprises which consider that they have developed an appreciation for CCA as a whole and its application in their particular circumstances, will be in a position to go beyond presenting the minimum information required by SSAP 16 and prepare an unabridged set of current cost accounts and notes which together are intended to show a true and fair view. Where such unabridged accounts are supplementary to the main accounts, the auditor should report in true and fair terms, referring to the accounting policies and methods used, in an additional paragraph to the report on the historical cost accounts. A suitable form of wording is as follows:

"In our opinion the supplementary current cost accounts set out on pages x to x have been prepared in accordance with the accounting policies and methods described in notes x to x and give, under the current cost principles described in SSAP 16, a true and fair view of the state of the company's affairs at 31st December

19 .. and of its results for the year then ended.''

7.   However, in the case of many enterprises the objectives of the management, set out in para 4 above, will not be achievable because they have not yet developed the necessary appreciation and experience. The preparers of the current cost accounts of these enterprises will not therefore be in a position to claim that their supplementary accounts do give a true and fair view. Where the supplementary accounts are abridged, or where the supplementary accounts are unabridged but their experimental nature is made clear in the accounts, it will not be appropriate for the auditor to report on such supplementary current cost accounts in true and fair terms. Nevertheless, in these cases, it will be helpful to the user of the current cost accounts to know whether in the opinion of the auditor, the accounting policies and procedures adopted comply with the provisions of SSAP 16. Therefore, it is recommended that in these cases the auditor's report be expressed in terms which confirm "compliance" and be set out in an additional paragraph to his report on the historical cost statements.

8.   A form of wording which will be suitable for "compliance" reports on abridged accounts is:
      "In our opinion the abridged supplementary current cost accounts set out on pages x to x have been properly prepared, in accordance with the policies and methods described in notes x to x, to give the information required by Statement of Standard Accounting Practice No. 16."

9.   If the auditor concludes that it is necessary to qualify his opinion on the supplementary current cost accounts, the qualification should be framed in accordance with the Auditing Standard "Qualifications in Audit Reports".

Main current cost accounts
10.   Where an enterprise chooses to present current cost accounts as the main or only accounts, the auditor will usually have a statutory obligation to report in "true and fair" terms.

11.   In these cases the provisions of the Auditing Standards "The Audit Report" and "Qualifications in Audit Reports" apply directly. All such reports should refer specifically to the current cost principles as described in the relevant notes setting out the particular accounting policies and methods adopted to comply with SSAP 16.

12.   When reporting on current cost accounts which are the main or only accounts, it will not normally be necessary to make separate reference to the historical cost information presented either in the form of supplementary statements or in the form of additional notes. Nevertheless, the scope paragraph of the audit report should make clear that such information has been subjected to examination by the auditor.

Failure to present current cost accounts
13.   Where an enterprise to which SSAP 16 applies does not present current cost

accounts, it is not appropriate merely because of this omission for the auditor to qualify his opinion on the historical cost accounts. However, he should refer to the omission using wording on the following lines for an additional final paragraph to his report—"The financial statements do not contain the current cost accounts required by Statement of Standard Accounting Practice No. 16".

4.0   REPORTS ON ACCOUNTS OF SOLE TRADERS AND PARTNERSHIPS

(STATEMENT S 19)
4.1   Introduction

When members of professional bodies undertake accountancy and audit work for sole traders and partnerships, as distinct from corporate bodies, their responsibility is governed not by statute but by any instructions of each particular client defining the scope of the work to be done and by the nature and extent of the records to be made available.

It is important to avoid any misunderstanding of the responsibility accepted by members for accounts prepared or audited for sole traders and partnerships. The possibility of misunderstanding will be lessened if there is uniformity among members in the way in which they associate their names with such accounts.

4.2   Need for a report

Members should ensure that a report is always appended to the accounts which they have prepared or audited. Such report should make clear the extent of the responsibilities which members accept for accounts which they have prepared and should give an opinion only on accounts which they have audited.

4.3   Accountants' reports

Where members have been instructed to prepare accounts but not to audit them, their report should be headed "Accountants' report" and should be worded so that the association of their name with the accounts cannot be misunderstood. A suitable form of report would be:

"ACCOUNTANTS' REPORT
In accordance with instructions given to us we have prepared, without carrying out an audit, the annexed accounts [the accounts set out on pages ...] from the accounting records of ... and from information and explanations supplied to us."

Without carrying out the work necessary for an audit, members cannot properly form an opinion whether the accounts give a true and fair view. Reports on accounts prepared without audit should not therefore be extended to include expressions of opinion or to disclaim responsibility for particular items. However, where in exceptional circumstances members are instructed to carry out specific checks without undertaking an audit, it may be necessary for them to refer in their report to the specific checks carefully avoiding any suggestion that they are expressing an opinion on the accounts as a whole.

4.4   Accepted accounting principles and estimates

As far as is practicable in the absence of an audit, members should ensure that the accounts which they prepare conform to accepted accounting principles. Where they do not do so or where accounting policies adopted are not immediately apparent, this should be made clear in the accounts.

It may be necessary, because of the nature of the records, for certain items in the accounts to be based on estimates by the client; such estimated items should be so described where material. Members should not allow their names to be associated with accounts, even though unaudited, which they believe give a misleading view.

N.B. Where an audit has not been carried out, care should be taken that any reference to the accountants' fees, for instance in the accounts, fee notes or correspondence, does not describe them as audit fees.

4.5   Client's declaration

Accounts, prepared with or without audit, should be approved by the client before the report is signed. The client's and accountant's responsibility should be clearly explained to the client at that time and he should be asked to sign a declaration on the face of a copy of the accounts retained by the accountant. A suitable declaration would be: "I approve these accounts and confirm that I have made available all records and information relevant for their preparation."

In the case of partnerships, the declaration should be signed by all partners or by the partner(s) duly authorised to sign on behalf of the partners.

(Although this Statement is concerned with the accounts of sole traders and partnerships, many of the considerations will apply to other financial statements and accounts not subject to statutory provisions or other regulations.)

5.0   THE AUDIT OF THE FUNDS STATEMENT

Certain Accounting Standards have a particular effect on audit reports. SSAP 10 "Statements of Source and Application of Funds" is an example. This has relevance for all companies whose turnover exceeds £25,000, and specifies that the funds statement is to be treated as part of the financial statements subject to audit.

According to the 1980 Auditing Standards, the omission of the funds statement presents a particular problem to the auditor in that the omission of funds statement does not justify, on this ground alone, a qualified report on the profit and loss account and balance sheet.

The APC considers that the Auditing Standards will be met if the auditor reports the omission of a funds statement by adding a separate paragraph which follows his opinion. An example of the manner in which this matter could be reported is: "The financial statements do not specify the manner in which the operations of the company (group) have been financed or in which its financial resources have been used during the year as required by Statement of Standard Accounting Practice No. 10."

In their *Auditing Newsletter*, Deloitte, Haskins and Sells have set out the audit work required in relation to the funds statement, summarised as follows:

Audit work on the funds statement

1. Obtain from the client, or prepare, working papers that both support every item in the funds statement and reconcile every item with the movements of funds between the opening and the closing balance sheets.

2. Check that the opening balance sheet used to prepare the funds statement agrees with the signed financial statements for that year.

3. Check that the closing balance sheet used to prepare the funds statement is either the final agreed balance sheet or the latest available draft balance sheet.

4. Test-check the casts and the calculations on the supporting working papers.

5. Scrutinise the adjusting entries the client has made in arriving at both the sources and the application of funds. In particular, ensure that all the necessary adjustments have been made and that all the adjustments are both reasonable and necessary.

6. Check, where it is possible to do so, each source and each application of funds with the other information that is either disclosed in the financial statements or contained elsewhere within the working papers.

7. Scrutinise the proposed funds statement to ensure both that it discloses the specific items required by SSAP 10 and that it presents the information fairly.

8. Check the casts of the proposed funds statement, and cross-reference it to the working papers.

Auditors should record sufficient details of their work in their working papers. They should, therefore, support each funds statement not only by a schedule that records the necessary reconciliation of monetary amounts, but also by details of the audit work performed. In addition, working papers should include a conclusion by the member of staff who has performed the audit work. This conclusion should comment on the following matters:

(a) compliance with the requirements of SSAP 10;

(b) agreement of the amounts with the other financial statements and, hence, with the company's/group's accounting records;

(c) consistency of calculation and presentation of the amounts disclosed.

It is important that working papers include adequate details of the audit work performed on the funds statement. Without working papers and adequate details of the audit work performed on this area, auditors would have no evidence to support the audit report on the funds statement.

6.0 AMOUNTS DERIVED FROM PRECEDING FINANCIAL STATEMENTS

6.1 Introduction

In contrast with US reporting practice, UK auditors express an opinion on the results for only the later of the two years' figures required by law to be published in financial statements, and on the company's position as at only the latest accounting date. Auditors' reports in the US, however, refer specifically to *both* periods and dates. To illustrate the point, here is an abbreviated extract from the audit report on the 1981 accounts of Citicorp:

"In our opinion, the aforementioned financial statements present fairly the consolidated financial position of Citicorp subsidiaries at 31st December 1980 and 1979, and the results of their operations and changes in their financial position for the years then ended, in conformity with generally accepted accounting principles applied on a consistent basis."

Although the prior period comparative figures (whose disclosure is not essential to a true and fair view being given by the accounts for the *later* period) are included within the scope of UK reports, as clearly indicated by the page number reference with which our reports commence, the audit opinion appears to ignore them entirely. This practice is unsatisfactory and raises particular doubts when a new audit is undertaken for the first time. Do auditors take *full/limited/no* responsibility for the view presented by the prior period figures, audited by another firm?

To what extent does the audit of *this* year's results and position require the re-audit of prior period records? After all, every transaction is automatically reflected, materially or otherwise, in the accounts of all subsequent periods, and if auditors take less than *complete* responsibility for the truth and fairness of amounts brought forward (or last year's results re-stated this year), their reports should declare this explicitly.

6.2 APC Guideline

In the light of this anomaly, the APC has issued a Guideline which provides useful advice on how auditors should deal with certain specific issues arising therefrom. Extracts from this Guideline are reproduced below:

Auditing Guideline: amounts derived from the preceding financial statements

INTRODUCTION

1.   Consideration of the financial statements of the preceding period is necessary in the audit of the current period's financial statements in relation to the following three aspects, namely:

(a)   the opening position: obtaining satisfaction that those amounts which have a direct effect on the current period's results or closing position have been properly brought forward;

(b)   accounting policies: determining whether the accounting policies adopted for the current period are consistent with those of the previous period; and

(c) corresponding amounts: determining that the corresponding amounts, which are commonly known as comparative figures, are properly shown in the current period's financial statements.

2. Financial statements of companies incorporated under the provisions of the Companies Act are required to disclose corresponding amounts for all items in a company's balance sheet and profit and loss account. In other cases, financial statements usually contain corresponding amounts as a matter of law, regulation or good practice. Their purpose, unless stated otherwise, is to complement the amounts relating to the current period, and to re-present the complete financial statements for the preceding period.

3. The auditor is not required to express an opinion on the corresponding amounts as such. His responsibility is to ensure that they are the amounts which appeared in the preceding period's financial statements or, where appropriate, have either been properly restated to achieve consistency and comparability with the current period's amounts, or have been restated due to a change of accounting policy or a correction of a fundamental error as required by SSAP 6.

AUDITOR'S PROCEDURES

4. If the auditor has issued an unqualified report on the preceding period's financial statements and his audit of the current period has not revealed any matters which cast doubt on those financial statements, he should not need to extend his audit procedures beyond:

(a) satisfying himself that balances have been correctly brought forward and incorporated in the accounting records of the current period; and

(b) ensuring that the amounts from the preceding period's financial statements are consistently classified and properly disclosed as corresponding amounts.

If he is satisfied with the results of these procedures, it should not be necessary for him to make any reference to amounts taken from the preceding period's financial statements in his report on the current period's financial statements.

5. Additional considerations may apply in the following circumstances:

(a) the opening position and corresponding amounts are derived from financial statements which have not been audited by the present auditor; or

(b) the audit report on the financial statements of the preceding period was qualified.

PRECEDING PERIOD NOT AUDITED BY THE PRESENT AUDITOR

6. The new auditor will have to satisfy himself as to the opening position as disclosed by the preceding period's balance sheet in order to express an opinion on the current period's profit or loss and source and application of funds. He will need also to ensure that there is consistency in accounting policies and classification of balances. His lack of prior knowledge of the preceding period's financial statements will require him to apply additional procedures to them in

order to obtain the necessary assurance on these matters.

7. The additional procedures that should be performed by the auditor may include any of the following:

    (a)   consultations with the client's management;

    (b)   review of the client's records, working papers and accounting and control procedures for the preceding period, particularly in so far as they affect the opening position;

    (c)   audit work on the current period, which will usually provide some evidence regarding opening balances; and

    (d)   in exceptional circumstances, substantive testing of the opening balances, if he does not consider the results of procedures (a) to (c) to be satisfactory.

8. In addition, the auditor may be able to hold consultations with the previous auditor. Whilst outgoing auditors can normally be expected to afford reasonable co-operation to their successors, neither ethical statements nor the law place them under a specific obligation to make working papers or other information available to these successors. Consultations would normally be limited to seeking information concerning the previous auditor's examination of particular areas which are important to his successor, and to obtaining clarification of any significant accounting matters which are not adequately dealt with in the client's records. If, however, such consultations are not possible or, alternatively, if the preceding period's financial statements are unaudited, the only evidence about the opening position available to the auditor will be that generated by procedures such as those set out in para 7 above.

9. Under normal circumstances the auditor will be able to satisfy himself as to the opening position by performing the work set out in paras 7 and 8. If he is not able to satisfy himself in any material respect he will need to qualify his report for the possible effect on the financial statements. A form of report is set out below which might be suitable where the area of difficulty was material but not fundamental.

Auditors' report to the members of ....

We have audited the financial statements on pages ... to ..., which have been prepared under the historical cost convention. Our audit was conducted in accordance with approved Auditing Standards, except that the scope of our work was limited by the matter referred to below.

We were not appointed auditors of the company until ...... and in consequence did not report on the financial statements for the year ended ...... It was not possible for us to carry out the auditing procedures necessary to obtain our own assurance as regards certain stock and work in progress, appearing in the preceding period's financial statements at £ ..... Any adjustment to this figure would have a consequential effect on the profit for the year ended 31st December 19...

In our opinion the balance sheet gives a true and fair view of the state of the company's affairs at 31st December 19 .... and, subject to the effect of any adjustment which might have been necessary in respect of the foregoing, the financial statements give a true and fair view of its profit and source and application of funds for the year then ended, and comply with the Companies Act 1985.

If the area of difficulty was fundamental then the auditor would need to consider whether to disclaim an opinion on the profit and source and application of funds.

PRECEDING PERIOD'S QUALIFICATIONS

10. If the audit report on the preceding period's financial statements was qualified, but the matter giving rise to the qualification has been resolved and properly dealt with in the financial statements, then normally no reference need be made to the previous qualification in the current period's audit report. If, however, the matter which gave rise to the qualification remains unresolved and is material in relation to the current period's financial statements, the audit report should be qualified. In such a case, the notes to the financial statements should adequately disclose the circumstances surrounding the qualification. The auditor may consider it advisable to refer to the previous qualification so as to make it clear that the matter giving rise to the qualification did not arise in the current period.

   One possible form of report which includes a reference to a previous qualification is set out below:

   Auditors' report to the members of . . . .
   We have audited the financial statements on pages . . . to . . . in accordance with approved Auditing Standards.
   As indicated in note . . . . . . to the financial statements debtors include an amount of £ . . . . . which is the subject of litigation but against which no provision has been made. We have not been able to satisfy ourselves that this amount will be recoverable in full. We qualified our audit report on the financial statements at 31st December 19 . . . . . [date of preceding financial statements] with regard to this same uncertainty.
   Subject to the adjustment, if any, that may be required when the litigation is resolved in our opinion the financial statements, which have been prepared under the historical cost convention, give a true and fair view of the state of the company's affairs at 31st December 19 . . . . . and of its profit and source and application of funds for the year then ended and comply with the Companies Act 1985.

MIS-STATED CORRESPONDING AMOUNTS

11. The auditor should refer in his audit report to an actual or possible material mis-statement in the corresponding amounts even though the mis-statement does not directly affect the current period's figures. Such a mis-statement may result from:

   (a)   uncertainty affecting the preceding period's profit and loss account, but not the balance sheet;

   (b)   misclassification of amounts in the preceding period's financial statement; or

   (c)   restatement of the preceding period's figures where the auditor does not concur with restatement, or if in his opinion a restatement is necessary but has not been made.

If corresponding amounts are required by law or by regulations the reference in the audit report should be in the form of a qualification on the grounds of non-compliance with that requirement. If corresponding amounts are presented solely as good practice, the audit report reference should be made as an "emphasis of matter".

12. The following is an example of an audit report on the financial statements, which has been qualified on these grounds:

Auditors' report to the members of ....
We have audited the financial statements on pages ... to ... in accordance with approved Auditing Standards.

The corresponding amounts in the current period's financial statements are derived from the financial statements for the year ended 31st December 19 ..... In our report on those financial statements we stated that we were unable to express an opinion on the profit and source and application of funds for the year ended on that date because we were unable to substantiate the amount of stock at 1st January 19 ..... [preceding year]. Accordingly the corresponding amounts shown for the profit and source and application of funds may not be comparable with the figures for the current period.

In our opinion the financial statements, which have been prepared under the historical cost convention, give a true and fair view of the state of the company's affairs at 31st December 19 ..... and of its profit and source and application of funds for the year then ended and, subject to any effects of the matter set out above, comply with the Companies Act 1985.

PROGRESS TEST 8

1. Summarise the forms of qualification which should be used to distinguish between:

    (a) material and fundamental uncertainty;

    (b) material and fundamental disagreement. (1.3)

2. Provide a specimen audit report where the auditor has reservations regarding the company's going concern status. (1.3, Example 7)

3. What considerations arise before an auditor may rely on the work of other auditors? (2.0)

CHAPTER NINE

Statistical Sampling in Auditing

1.0   INTRODUCTION

This is a method of audit testing which is more scientific than testing based entirely on the auditor's own judgment, since it utilises the mathematical laws of probability in determining the appropriate sample size in varying circumstances. The theory of any form of sampling rests on the statistical principle that the objective examination of an unbiased selection of items from a larger "population" enables the observer to draw mathematically valid conclusions about the population as a whole from the items supplied.

It is obviously essential, therefore, that:

(a) the population should be homogeneous (i.e. uniform in every material detail); and

(b) the individual items examined should be selected on a completely random basis.

It is unnecessary for the auditor to gain a detailed knowledge of statistics before making use of statistical sampling in the execution of the audit programme, since sets of statistical tables have been published which indicate the sample sizes, based on pre-determined criteria. Modern, or "risk-based", auditing now incorporates sampling methods which do not require the use of statistical tables. This approach will be dealt with later in this chapter.

The use of sampling in this way does not relieve the auditor of the responsibility to exercise care, skill and judgment in testing the client company's records. Although the sampling tables reveal the size of sample required, it is still necessary for certain criteria to be determined by the auditor in advance.

2.0   CRITERIA FOR "ACCEPTANCE" SAMPLING

In essence, before the tables can be used, the following data is needed:

(a)   The approximate *population* size.

(b)   The *confidence level* required by the auditor. *Confidence level is complementary to risk.* Another way of expressing this criterion would therefore be the risk which the auditor is prepared to accept that the sample size is unrepresentative of the whole population under review. (There is always some degree of risk in sampling—total elimination of this risk would entail examination of 100% of the population, and clearly this would have little to do with statistical sampling.) If the confidence level required is 80%, this therefore means that the auditor is prepared to accept a risk of one chance in five (20%) that the sample is unrepresentative.

(c)   The *precision limits.* This represents the degree of precision which the auditor requires from the sample, and is decided at the same time as the confidence level. The precision is a range (ordinarily expressed as plus/minus a given number of percentage points, e.g. plus/minus 2%) within which the true answer concerning the characteristic under study (*errors*, in the case of auditing) should fall, at the particular confidence level selected.

(d)   *Anticipated error rate.* This is based upon the auditor's previous experience of examining the records for errors, as well as his assessment of the efficiency with which the system of internal control operates in practice. At the same time as gauging the anticipated error rate, normally expressed as a percentage, the auditor must consider the rate of errors which he will regard as acceptable. (If he anticipates, as a result of discovering material weaknesses in the system, an error rate which he regards as unacceptable, he will probably avoid statistical sampling altogether, since a considerable quantity of checking will be necessary before he is in a position to form an opinion on reliability of the records. In such a situation the haphazard nature of the system will render the dependence on a small sample correspondingly hazardous.)

When sampling for "attributes", e.g. errors, the maximum acceptable error rate will be the anticipated error rate plus the precision margin.

The above requirements may be more clearly understood in the context of the following illustration.

Illustration

A company's inventory of stock in trade comprises 10,400 items which may be broadly stratified into two distinct groups, viz. relatively large items, totalling 1,900 (Group I) and the balance of 8,500 items, all relatively small (Group II). It is anticipated that the rate of errors as defined in advance (valuation errors, clerical errors etc.) will not exceed 2% and 5% in Groups I and II respectively, and the auditor is prepared to accept a precision margin of plus/minus 1.75% in the case of Group I and plus/minus 2.5% in the case of Group II at a level of confidence of 95% for both groups.

Reference to the tables shows that the appropriate sample size for Group I is 217 items, and that for Group II is 282 items, i.e. total of 499 items to be checked out of the total of 10,400. Provided the proportion of errors possible in the Group I sample does not exceed 3.75 (2±1.75)%, and that in the Group II sample does not exceed 7.5 (5±2.5)%, the inventory may be passed by the auditor.

It should be noted that in determining confidence level and precision limits, the auditor should carefully assess:

(a) his own previous experience of the particular area under examination;

(b) the results of his earlier enquiry into the functioning of the system in theory and in practice—as evidenced in the replies to his questionnaires, evaluation summaries, etc., and in carrying out procedural tests;

(c) the materiality of the items concerned.

Confidence level and precision directly affect the sample size whereas the latter is hardly affected by the population size.

3.0 PRACTICAL STEPS

In practice, the following steps would have to be taken in order to test a population of entries, vouchers, etc. for errors:

(a) *The population category and the population unit should be clearly defined.* All units within a total population must be the same type (e.g. cheques returned from the bank), and the population must be *complete*. Where there have been changes in the system operated during the period under review, *separate* populations exist on either side of the date of change, and separate tests must be devised.

(b) *The population size must be determined.* This is simplified if all documents within the population are pre-numbered, but in other circumstances it may be difficult to estimate, in which event the largest estimate should be adopted (bearing in mind that the effect of the population on the sample size is minimal).

(c) *Examine the way in which the population is constituted and consider whether stratification is necessary.* This step is usually taken where the population is made up of both large and small items; it is then suitably stratified and separate sampling tests are carried out on each stratum.

(d) *Define an "error"* so that there is no confusion as to this once testing has begun. The anticipated error rate in the population should then be estimated.

(e) *The precision limits and the level of confidence required for the particular population being sampled should be determined.* The precision margin is added to anticipated error rate in order to arrive at the maximum acceptable error rate.

(f) *Refer the data thus determined to specially prepared tables* in order to discover the appropriate sample size, and random-number tables should then be used for selecting the individual items in the sample.

(g) *The test should now be evaluated,* comparing the number of errors discovered in the sample with the predetermined level regarded as acceptable, in order to discover whether or not the result is satisfactory from the audit viewpoint.

(h) *Ensure that the final expression of the conclusion of the test is valid,* and if the result has been unsatisfactory the next course of action must be positively decided. This will normally involve extended audit work

  (i) to ensure the sample result was not a "freak", and

  (ii) to assess the effect of the errors and weaknesses on the accounts as a whole.

A number of professional firms have found simplified versions of the above to be satisfactory. For example, the quality of internal control in a particular area would be given a "quality designation" of which the sample size would be constant. Only when the errors discovered exceed an acceptable level (predetermined) would the sample size be increased.

4.0   "ESTIMATION" SAMPLING

Apart from sampling for attributes, statistical sampling can also be used for estimating variables, such as inventories. This involves examining and evaluating a proportion of inventory items (at random, of course) and using extrapolation techniques to project the result onto the entire inventory. A typical result of such a test might be expressed as follows: "The total value of the population (inventory) is £4,500,000 plus/minus £240,000 at a confidence level of 90%." In plain language this may be restated: "We are nine-tenths sure that the true value of the inventory lies between £4,260,000 and £4,740,000."

(It should be clear that the auditor would be precluded from complaining subsequently that the full (±) precision range is too material—after all, he selected the precision in the first place!)

5.0   THE USE OF TABLES

Students are often surprised at the apparently paradoxical statement that sample size is largely independent of population size. But at the same time it will be clear that once a population has been randomly tested on the basis of a sample size of, say, 100, the examination of further (and equally typical) items is hardly likely, statistically speaking, to produce a very different picture. This fact is demonstrated in the extract from statistical tables given in the appendix to this chapter.

The following illustration uses these tables in a typical auditing context:

Illustration

OBJECT

To test objectively the error attributes arising from the application of internal control procedures to the recording of a population of 20,000 copy sales invoices.

PROCEDURE

Past experience and internal control assessment suggest a likely error rate of 2% ("errors" in this context have been carefully defined prior to testing). The auditor wishes to be 90% confident that the error rate does not exceed 3.5% (i.e. 2% plus/minus 1.5%).

Refer to the appropriate table. It can be seen that in the situation described it is necessary for the auditor to examine a sample of 232 items.

The 232 sales invoices are now randomly selected and checked against the company's records.

EVALUATION

If the error rate discovered in the sample of 232 sales invoices is not greater than the 2% anticipated, the auditor will be satisfied that the actual percentage of errors in the whole population is not greater than the 3.5% (2.0%±precision 1.5%) which he is prepared to accept.

However, if the actual error rate discovered is, say, 3% it would then be necessary for him to refer back to the table for a 3% error rate, also shown above. The table shows that a simple examination of 343 invoices is now needed to satisfy confidence level and precision as before.

If, after checking the additional 111 invoices (343 less 232 already examined), also on a completely random basis, the actual error rate is still seen to be 3%, the auditor will express the following conclusion, which will be mathematically valid provided:

(a) a randomness of selection has been rigorously observed; and

(b) the audit work itself has been reliably executed:

"The error rate in the recording of sales invoices is 3% plus/minus 1.5% (i.e. the error rate lies between 1.5% and 4.5%) at a confidence level of 90%." Putting it more simply, he is nine-tenths sure that the actual error rate in the population falls within that rate.

Of course, the auditor must decide on the implications for the accounts as a whole, and hence for his audit report, of the possibility that a 4.5% rate exists in the recording of sales.

6.0 STRATIFICATION

The debtor's ledger, for example, may in many instances contain a large number of balances each of which amounts to relatively little, while also containing a few "high value" accounts. Clearly, on grounds of materiality alone, it would be incorrect to treat all debtors' accounts as belonging to the same population for sampling purposes.

Illustration
Debtor circularisation

Total number of accounts   1,130
Total value of ledger   £415,756
Analysis of account balances:

	Number	Value £
Over £5,000	14	192,612
£2,501–£5,000	28	47,778
£1,001–£2,500	43	60,892
£501–£1,000	262	88,861
£0–£500	783	25,613
	1,130	415,756

This population may be stratified so that all debtors whose balances exceed £2,500, and a random sample of the remainder, are circularised. By this means over 55% of debtors *by value* are verified by means of 42 circularisation letters; the remaining 1,088 balances can be sampled by reference to the tables, making the following necessary assumptions, say:

Anticipated error rate	3%
Precision limit	plus/minus 3%
Confidence level	90%

Reference to tables (not reproduced in this section) shows that a sample size of 81 accounts will have to be circularised to satisfy the above requirements. This represents a sample of 1 in 14 (approximately). *Systematic sampling* could be used for selection in these circumstances.

By reference to *random number tables* a starting point between 1 and 14 would be fixed. The 81 balances would then be selected from the schedule of debtors by taking the balance corresponding with the random starting point, and every 14th balance thereafter. If any balance coincides with one already selected (in the 100% check of balances over £2,500) the next following balance would be taken in its place.

7.0   SELECTION TECHNIQUES

Throughout this chapter it has been stressed that failure to observe the need for unbiased selection may invalidate the sample result.

There are a number of different techniques for selecting the individual items in a sample. Each of these techniques is designed for use in particular types of situation. The more common methods for selecting the items in the sample are:

(a) *Interval sampling*, also known as *systematic sampling*, which involves selecting a random starting point and thereafter making selections so that there is a fixed interval between the items selected. If the size of sample requires that every sixtieth item needs to be selected then the starting point could be selected quite simply by the auditor glancing at the second hand of his watch. If the number selected is forty-seven the first item to be tested could be the forty-seventh, and the examination would thereafter be concentrated on the 107th, 167th item and so on.

(b) *Random sampling*, the auditor taking the numbers to be selected from random number tables, which are constructed to identify the items to be examined in a random test, provided the items in the population are suitably numbered sequentially.

(c) *Stratified sampling* involves the division of the population under examination into layers or strata, each stratum being the subject of a separate test which could be conducted by interval or random sampling methods. This type of selection technique is appropriate where the population consists of a wide range of values among the items under examination. Under such circumstances the entire population being tested would be split into a number of layers, each covering a specific range of values or prices, and each layer would then be the subject to a separate test.

(d) *Cluster sampling,* which is suitable when the data to be examined are stored in such a manner, e.g. in filing cabinet drawers, that the selection of a group or cluster would be an appropriate test. In these circumstances each drawer could be allocated a number, the particular drawer to be tested being selected by the use of random tables. The contents of the drawer selected could in turn be tested completely or by random number, or interval sampling.

7.1   Selection with the aid of a computer

The auditor may use a computer to render considerable assistance in the performance of statistical sampling tests, employing the following methods:

(a) *Interval sampling:* the computer is programmed to select every nth item stored on magnetic tape, and the items so selected can be copied on to a separate tape and printed out in the form required by the auditor (assuming "n" to be the sampling interval).

(b) *Random number selection:* the technique of random number selection can be used, the random numbers being stored on tape or created separately for each application.

(c) *Random interval selection:* the dangers of selecting a biased example by the use of a uniform interval can be avoided through the use of a random variation of the interval between successive items. Random intervals are selected from random number tables maintained on magnetic tape or produced by means of a random number generator program.

8.0   SAMPLING IN PRACTICE AND RELIABILITY FACTORS

Paragraph 8.1 below features a table, the purpose of which is to translate the required level of confidence into a "reliability factor", which is used in turn for determining the appropriate sample size. This method, developed by Deloitte, Haskins & Sells, plays an important part in the sampling methods used by that firm, on which a little more elaboration may prove useful. Essentially, the sampling plan covers two types of sampling:

(a) monetary sampling—to be used when the auditor wishes to obtain conclusions expressed in monetary terms; and

(b) numerical sampling—for use when the auditor wishes to obtain conclusions about the incidence of specified occurrences (e.g. mispostings, unauthorised despatches, etc.).

In its instructions issued to audit staff, the firm stresses the importance of deciding the purpose of each test prior to its execution, so that the most suitable population can be selected. For example, if a sample is to be selected from a list of debtors, the conclusions reached cannot be said validly to apply to any debtor balance omitted from this list. The list must therefore first be tested for completeness, which in turn entails the examination of an independent but related (or reciprocal) population. In this example, a possible approach would be to undertake tests which compare sales records with detailed ledger entries, in order to detect sales to customers which, for one reason or another, might have been omitted from the ledger balance. This approach has come to be known as "directional testing", the purpose of which is to test assets for overstatement and liabilities for understatement by ensuring the completeness of reciprocal populations (i.e. for every debit there must be a corresponding credit!).

We have already seen from the earlier sections of this chapter that statistical assurance is a combination of reliability (i.e. confidence) and precision, and that these two factors are inseparably interrelated. If, when testing for understatement of sales, a sample of despatch notes is examined, the sample evaluation might indicate 95% reliability that not more than 1% of the despatch notes have been incorrectly recorded. If a precision narrower than 1% is required, but without an increase in the sample size, a lower level of reliability would have to be accepted. Thus, the same sample size might achieve only 78% reliability at a precision level of 0.5%. Conversely, the same sample might give us 99% reliability at a potential error rate of 1.5%. Thus we see that it is totally misleading to cite the precision of a sample without at the same time, citing the reliability level.

8.1 Practical illustration of "monetary unit sampling"

This practical illustration demonstrates, among other things, the use of the "reliability factor" or "R factor", a concept developed by Deloittes in their monetary precision plan.

Table 8 shows how R-factors are related to the six confidence levels which the firm normally uses.

Table 8. R-factors

Required confidence level	R-factor
39%	0.5
63%	1.0
78%	1.5
86%	2.0
95%	3.0
97%	3.5

The aim of the Deloitte monetary precision (MP) plan is to enable the auditor to achieve a measurable level of precision and reliability for the financial statements as a whole, by predetermining the MP required in forming an opinion on the financial statements, and then using this MP in sampling all audit areas. This has the advantage of causing the volume of audit tests to vary according to the monetary totals (and hence materiality) of each area, thus achieving a "built-in" stratification plan. The MP is based on the auditor's judgment of the *maximum amount of monetary error considered to be not material in relation to the financial statements as a whole.* The following example, included in the firm's sampling manual, demonstrates the numbers involved.

Example

If we use an MP of £10,000 throughout our audit of assets, and if we find no errors in our samples, we conclude (with the predetermined level of reliability) that the errors in those assets do not total more than £10,000. However, if we find errors, they have a cumulative effect on our overall MP. Suppose that, in auditing the assets of a company, we have used an MP of £10,000, and have found errors in the two areas of stocks and debtors. The statistical evaluation of these errors will lead us to revise our MP in each area.

The table below shows the effect those errors have on the MP.

	Stocks £	*Debtors* £	*MP for the assets as a whole* £
Errors (of overstatement) in the sample	100	180	
Original MP	10,000	10,000	
Revised MP	(say) 10,700	(say) 11,100	10,000
Increases in the estimated maximum probable errors	700	1,100	1,800
Revised MP for the assets as a whole			£11,800

To allow for the possibility of finding errors, we normally set the MP at a slightly lower figure than the maximum amount of error that we would consider is not material. Suppose that, in the example given, we consider the maximum acceptable error to be £12,000. By setting the MP conservatively at £10,000 we are able (despite the errors we have found) to arrive at a revised MP (£11,800) which we can accept.

In practice, once MP and reliability (R) factors have been determined, the sampling

interval is arrived at by the fraction $\dfrac{\text{MP}}{\text{R-factor}}$. If the population is then divided by the

sampling interval, the sample size results. For example, let us suppose that the maximum monetary error which the auditor is prepared to accept is £3,000 out of a total population (for, say, work in progress) of £100,000, and a confidence level of 95% is required. Reference to the table shows that the latter level of confidence indicates an R-factor of 3.0. Thus, $\frac{£3,000}{3.0}$ gives the sampling interval of £1,000. By

dividing the population of £100,000 by the sampling interval of £1,000 we arrive at the appropriate sample size of 100.

The R-factor is simply the negative natural log of the risk percentage associated with each of the six confidence levels used in the table. This facilitates calculation, without which a hyper-geometric progression would be needed in order to determine sample sizes.

The Deloitte system is thus to be commended for its simplicity (while not in any way compromising the underlying precepts of probability theory, from which the validity of all sampling schemes is derived), and hence the ease with which, in appropriate circumstances, it may be implemented.

This simplicity and ease of application, is of course due to the ready translation of confidence levels into reliability factors, as demonstrated in the table earlier in this section. In the use of this table only six discrete confidence levels (from 39% through to 97%) are available, but this limitation hardly matters—especially since in practice the auditor will ensure that any "rounding up" to the nearest available confidence level will increase, rather than decrease, the sample size. The use of this method similarly obviates the need to refer to voluminous pages of statistical tables.

9.0 PRACTICAL SIMPLIFICATION FOR AUDITS OF ALL SIZES

9.1 Introduction

Whereas the major developments in sampling for auditors have arisen from the researches and field-tests of the largest international firms over the past twenty years, it is now possible to apply the lessons and discoveries to date for the benefit of audit practices of all sizes. This development has arisen chiefly from the *monetary unit sampling* procedures described in the previous section, in turn based on the laws of probability as applied to attributes' sampling.

9.2 The pressures

The timing of this development is fortunate, since in recent years the pressures on audit firms of all sizes have been immense, arising specifically from:

(a) major changes in companies legislation;

(b) substantial increase in the number of new Accounting Standards;

(c) more demanding Auditing Standards; and

(d) a widening of the potential liability of auditors as a result of recent case decisions (see Chapter 10).

At the same time the majority of audit clients are themselves feeling the pressures of the difficult economic climate, and are therefore in no position to pay increased audit fees arising from items (a) to (d) above.

9.3   Risk-based auditing

The modern approach to "risk-based auditing" is therefore a most welcome development, since its intelligent application will ensure full fee recovery on the majority of audit assignments without incurring any increase in potential liability risks. In essence, the method is designed to avoid over-auditing in low-risk areas, and under-auditing in high-risk areas.

Low-risk areas are those which require the application of routine "nuts and bolts" audit procedures in the ordinary course of vouching, casting, checking, etc., at both compliance and substantive stages, usually occupying up to 80% of all audit effort. *High-risk areas* are those which should be the primary concern of partners and senior managers, and will include such matters as:

(a)   adequacy of provisions;

(b)   full disclosure of liabilities, including contingent liabilities;

(c)   interpretation of SSAPs and new companies legislation;

(d)   post balance sheet review of subsequent events;

(e)   analytical reviews on draft financial statements;

(f)   implications of tax legislation;

(g)   detecting overstatement of assets, e.g. by capitalising expenditure;

(h)   identifying high-value items and "error-prone" conditions, and

(i)   drafting the audit report itself.

Full fee-recovery on an audit assignment which is completed to a high standard overall will therefore have the best chance of being achieved if routine work (low risk) is performed efficiently, intelligently and economically by junior staff in accordance with sampling criteria which are validly related to the associated level of risk.

For this reason it is essential that all *high-value items* and *error-prone conditions* within the population to be sampled are identified as risk-prone, and individually verified or covered by a specific provision, as necessary. Sampling procedures will then be applied to the remaining items in the population.

9.4   Setting materiality limits

To meet the above objectives it is clearly essential that a "materiality limit" is set (referred to in section 8.0 above as "monetary precision"), and this is unavoidably a matter for the audit partner's judgment, based on previous knowledge and assessment of the client's business and organisational structure. Materiality is a relative factor, and any decision on materiality will require a "base" to be selected, such as total revenue (in the case of companies with a turnover) or total assets (in the case of financial institutions such as banks, building societies, pension funds, investment trusts or insurance companies).

Some firms make use of a table of bases, to which a scale of materiality percentages may be applied—although it would clearly be highly dangerous to apply this mechanically, without appropriate exercise of judgment. (Table 9 is taken from the standard file of Team Auditing Systems, to whom the copyright belongs.)

Table 9. Materiality limit ranges

Range of chosen base (£)		%	Materiality limit range (£)
0 to	25,000	5.00	0– 1,250
25,000 to	50,000	4.00	1,250– 2,000
50,000 to	100,000	3.00	2,000– 3,000
100,000 to	500,000	2.00	3,000–10,000
500,000 to	2,000,000	1.50	10,000–30,000
2,000,000 to	5,000,000	1.00	30,000–50,000
5,000,000 to	10,000,000	0.75	50,000–75,000
Over 10,000,000		0.50	75,000 and over

Thus we see that the auditor of a company whose turnover is £200,000 may select 2%, or £4,000, as the materiality limit. This means, of course, that all sales transactions in excess of £4,000 will be individually vouched as high-value items.

9.5 Obtaining audit assurance

Once high-value and error-prone items have been identified in this way, the remaining items of population will be sample-tested. The sample sizes will, of course, depend on the confidence level required from our audit tests and the selected confidence level will in turn depend upon the level of assurance obtained from:

(a) our assessment of *internal controls*, following our compliance testing; and

(b) the *reasonableness* of the draft financial statements, following our analytical review.

In risk-based auditing it is assumed that *each* of the above two elements provides us with no more than one-third of the total assurance regarded as acceptable, the remaining third being obtained from our own substantive tests of transactions and balances. Assuming that we require overall assurance of, say, 95% (100% being unrealistic in requiring *all* transactions, etc., to be checked individually), we can compute our risks as follows:

(a) acceptable level of risk=5% (risk being the complement of confidence);

(b) reliance on internal control only, entails a risk of *37%*;

(c) reliance on overall reasonableness of financial statements entails a risk of *37%*;

(d) reliance on our own audit tests entails a risk of *37%*.

Thus we find, by multiplying the risk elements, that our objective of incurring no more than a 5% overall risk is satisfied: $0.37 \times 0.37 \times 0.37 = 0.05$. From this we see that if maximum assurance is already available from internal control and overall reasonableness, our further substantive tests on transactions and balances can be carried out to a confidence level of 63% (the complement of 37% risk).

The possible permutations in the risk matrix are therefore dependent upon our assessment of internal control and overall reasonableness. In the majority of small audits, assessment of internal control will not be cost-effective, and no assurance can therefore be given under this heading. Similarly, in situations in which draft accounts have not yet been prepared we can take no assurance from overall reasonableness. The "risk matrix" in Table 10 sets out the possible conditions which may be found in practice.

Table 10. Risk matrix

		Condition (1)	Condition (2)		Condition (3)
		Internal control and analytical review satisfactory	Internal control satisfactory	Analytical review satisfactory	Neither internal control nor analytical review satisfactory
		(% risk*)	(% risk)	(% risk)	(% risk)
Assessing internal control	A	37	37	100	100
Assessing overall reasonableness	B	37	100	37	100
Substantively testing balance of remaining items	C	37	14	14	5
Audit risk ($A \times B \times C$)	D	5	5	5	5
Audit assurance: ($100 - D\%$)		(95)	(95)	(95)	(95)

*NB The risk referred to is that our audit procedures fail to detect error(s) which remain undetected and result in a material misstatement in the financial statements.

© Team Auditing Systems

All three "conditions" allow for an overall confidence level of 95%, the variable factor making up the required assurance being the auditor's own substantive testing.

Figure 12 shows that as we move from condition 1 to condition 3 the required sample sizes increase in proportion to the increase in audit assurance required from our own substantive testing.

It will also be observed that, as we move from condition 1 through condition 2 to condition 3, the number of "high-value items" in the population doubles (at condition 2) and trebles (at condition 3). This is due to the fact that the materiality limit (see section 9.4 above) set for condition 1 is divided by the risk-factor (R-factor) appropriate to risk associated with conditions 2 and 3 respectively (see section 8.1 above). Thus, if we assume the materiality limit of £4,000 computed in section 9.4 above, this is divided by the appropriate R-factor, as follows:

Condition 1: $\dfrac{4,000}{1}$ = revised materiality limit of 4,000

Condition 2: $\dfrac{4,000}{2}$ = revised materiality limit of 2,000

Condition 3: $\dfrac{4,000}{3}$ = revised materiality limit of 1,333

It is for this reason that the number of high-value items under condition 3 (i.e. those transactions or balances which exceed £1,333) is three times as great as the number of high value items had the client company been given the classification of condition 1 (i.e. only transactions or balances in excess of £4,000 are classified as "high value").

It will now be obvious from the risk matrix set out in Table 10 that our substantive testing under each of the three conditions will be based on the sample sizes appropriate to the following confidence levels:

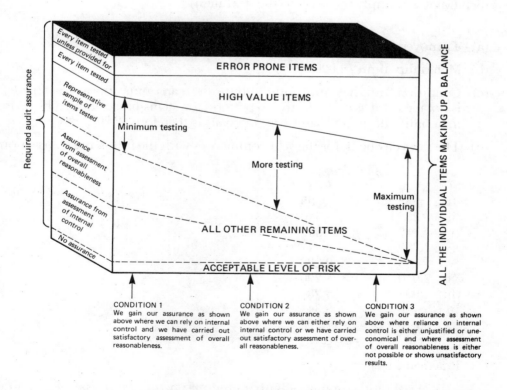

CONDITION 1
We gain our assurance as shown above where we can rely on internal control and we have carried out satisfactory assessment of overall reasonableness.

CONDITION 2
We gain our assurance as shown above where we can either rely on internal control or we have carried out satisfactory assessment of over-all reasonableness.

CONDITION 3
We gain our assurance as shown above where reliance on internal control is either unjustified or une-conomical and where assessment of overall reasonableness is either not possible or shows unsatisfactory results.

Fig. 12. *Audit assurance—sample sizes.*

Condition	Risk (%)	Confidence level (%)	R-factor
1	37	63	1
2	14	86	2
3	5	95	3

This will be seen to accord with the Deloitte table (Table 8), but without the rarely required intermediate R-factors and confidence levels.

As has already been pointed out (in section 8.1 above) the R-factor is the negative natural logarithm of the risk percentages used in the table, and facilitates the calculation of sample sizes.

9.6   Determination of sample sizes and sample selection

The determination of sample sizes under the principles of monetary unit sampling is simplicity itself. This is due to the fact that the computed materiality limit also provides us with the "sampling interval". Reference to Table 9 in section 9.4 therefore shows that a materiality limit of £4,000 (based on a turnover population of 200,000 units of £1 each) gives us a sample size of $\frac{200,000}{4,000}$ =50 items. In practice we shall therefore examine the 50 sales transactions of which the selected 50 units of £1 each form a part (unless we have *already* examined them as high-value or error-prone items, in which event we simply move on to the next item).

Example

(a)   Turnover £200,000.

(b)   Materiality limit £4,000.

(c)   Condition 2 applies since, although the draft accounts appear reasonable, it is not regarded as cost-effective to perform a systems-based audit. The revised materiality limit (and sampling interval) is therefore £2,000.

(d)   The sales day book for the year commences with the following transactions:

	£	Cumulative total (£)
(i)	20	20
(ii)	35	55
(iii)	285	340
(iv)	12	352
(v)	1,890	2,242
(vi)	38	2,280
(vii)	2,010	4,290
(viii)	994	5,284
(ix)	60	5,344
(x)	6,216	11,560
	(etc.)	(etc.)

(e)   Practical steps:

(i)   We should commence with a *random starting point* (say 58) obtained from random number tables, and then examine the 58th £ in the population. This falls into transaction (iii), as we see from the above list.

   (ii) We then add the sampling interval of 2,000 to 58 (2058th £) to identify the second transaction for our examination. This falls into transaction (v).

 (iii) The next transaction in our sample series is that into which the 4058th £ falls, i.e. transaction (vii), but we do not need to examine this transaction because we already have: since it exceeds £2,000 we examined it as a high-value item.

 (iv) The next transactions will be those into which the 6058th, 8058th, and 10058th £s respectively fall, and we see that transaction (x) includes them all. It has, however, already been tested as a high-value item.

  (v) We proceed in this way through the entire population; it is obvious that the actual sample of transactions to be tested will be less than 100 (i.e. 200,000÷2,000), since the error-prone and high-value items will already have been examined.

9.7   Monetary unit sampling—a simple proof of the method

 (a) Sampling method: attributes, based on probabilities.

 (b) Warning:

    (i) This method *assumes a* complete population.

   (ii) It cannot be used for *variables sampling* (e.g. extrapolating monetary values of a sample for application to the full population).

  (iii) All error-prone and high-value items must first be eliminated.

 (c) Given:

    (i) value of debtors £59,220;

   (ii) precision required (materiality limit) £8,000.

 (d) Required: ascertain how many items must be tested to ensure that we limit our *risks* of not finding evidence of errors to:

NNL of risk

    (i) 37% (CL 63%)   1
   (ii) 14% (CL 86%)   2
  (iii)   5% (CL 95%)   3

Probability method (using hyper-geometric progression)

Sample size			*Risk %*	*Confidence %*

1st   Draw: $\dfrac{59{,}220 - 8{,}000}{59{,}220} \times 100 = 86$ 14

2nd	Draw:	$\dfrac{51,220}{59,220} \times \dfrac{51,219}{59,219} \times 100 = 75$	25
3rd	Draw:	$(.865)^3 \qquad\qquad \times 100 = 65$	35
7th	Draw:	$(.865)^7 \qquad\qquad \times 100 = 37$	63
14th	Draw:	$(.865)^{14} \qquad\quad \times 100 = 14$	86
22nd	Draw:	$(.865)^{22} \qquad\quad \times 100 = 5$	95

ANSWER
7, 14, and 22 items, respectively, must be tested.

The simple method (using logarithms)

    (a) Risk of 37% (NNL=1) Precision of 8,000÷1=8,000

$$\therefore \text{Sample size} = \frac{59,220}{8,000} = 7 \text{ draws}$$

    (b) Risk of 14% (NNL=2) Precision of 8000 ÷ 2 = 4,000

$$\therefore \text{Sample size} = \frac{59,220}{4,000} = 14 \text{ draws}$$

    (c) Risk of 5% = R-factor of 3 = Precision of 8000 ÷ 3 = 2,667

$$\therefore \text{Sample size} = \frac{59,220}{2,667} = 22 \text{ draws}$$

Note: The R-factor is the negative logarithm of the risk percentage.

PROGRESS TEST 9

1.   What do you understand by sampling for attributes? (2.0)

2.   What do you understand by sampling for variables? (4.0)

3.   Summarise the importance of stratification. (6.0)

4.   Distinguish between confidence level and precision limits. (9.0)

5.   What do you understand by risk-based auditing? (9.3)

6.   (a) How should materiality limits be determined? (9.5)

       (b) How does materiality relate to sample sizes? (9.6)

APPENDIX: SAMPLE SIZES FOR ATTRIBUTES SAMPLING

Expected error rate not over 2%; Confidence level 90%

Population size	Sample size for precision percentage of plus or minus						
	0.50	0.75	1.00	1.25	1.50	1.75	2.00
10000	1750	861	503	328	230	170	130
11000	1778	868	505	329	230	170	131
12000	1802	874	507	330	231	170	131
13000	1823	879	509	330	231	170	131
14000	1842	883	511	331	231	171	131
15000	1858	887	512	331	232	171	131
16000	1873	890	513	332	232	171	131
17000	1886	893	514	332	232	171	131
18000	1897	895	515	333	232	171	131
19000	1908	898	515	333	232	171	131
20000	1918	900	516	333	232	171	131
22500	1938	904	518	334	233	171	131
25000	1955	908	519	334	233	171	131
27500	1969	911	520	335	233	172	131
30500	1981	914	521	335	233	172	132
32500	1991	916	521	335	234	172	132
35000	2000	918	522	336	234	172	132
37500	2007	919	522	336	234	172	132
40000	2014	921	523	336	234	172	132
42500	2020	922	523	336	234	172	132
45000	2026	923	524	336	234	172	132
47500	2030	924	524	337	234	172	132
50000	2035	925	524	337	234	172	132
55000	2042	927	525	337	234	172	132
60000	2049	928	525	337	234	172	132
65000	2054	929	526	337	234	172	132
70000	2059	930	526	337	234	172	132
75000	2063	931	526	337	234	172	132
80000	2066	931	526	338	235	172	132
85000	2069	932	527	338	235	172	132
90000	2072	933	527	338	235	172	132
95000	2075	933	527	338	235	172	132
100000	2077	934	527	338	235	172	132
110000	2081	923	527	338	235	172	132
120000	2084	935	528	338	235	172	132
130000	2087	936	528	338	235	172	132
140000	2089	936	528	338	235	172	132
150000	2091	937	528	338	235	172	132
160000	2093	937	528	338	235	172	132

Population size	Sample size for precision percentage of plus or minus						
	0.50	0.75	1.00	1.25	1.50	1.75	2.00
170000	2095	937	528	338	235	172	132
180000	2096	937	528	338	235	172	132
190000	2098	938	528	338	235	172	132
200000	2099	938	528	338	235	172	132
250000	2103	939	529	338	235	172	132
300000	2106	939	529	339	235	172	132
350000	2108	940	529	339	235	172	132
400000	2110	940	529	339	235	172	132
450000	2111	940	529	339	235	172	132
500000	2112	941	529	339	235	172	132

Expected error rate not over 3%; Confidence level 90%

Population size	Sample size for precision percentage of plus or minus						
	0.50	1.00	1.50	2.00	2.50	2.75	3.00
10000	2395	729	338	193	124	103	86
11000	2448	734	339	193	124	103	86
12000	2494	738	340	193	124	103	86
13000	2535	742	340	193	124	103	86
14000	2571	745	341	194	124	103	86
15000	2603	748	341	194	124	103	86
16000	2631	750	342	194	125	103	87
17000	2657	752	342	194	125	103	87
18000	2680	754	343	194	125	103	87
19000	2701	756	343	194	125	103	87
20000	2721	757	343	194	125	103	87
22500	2763	760	344	195	125	103	87
25000	2797	763	345	195	125	103	87
27500	2826	765	345	195	125	103	87
30000	2850	767	345	195	125	103	87
32500	2871	768	346	195	125	103	87
35000	2889	770	346	195	125	103	87
37500	2905	771	346	195	125	103	87
40000	2919	772	346	195	125	103	87
42500	2932	773	347	195	125	103	87
45000	2943	773	347	196	125	103	87
47500	2953	774	347	196	125	103	87
50000	2963	775	347	196	125	103	87
55000	2979	776	347	196	125	103	87
60000	2992	777	347	196	125	103	87
65000	3004	778	348	196	125	103	87
70000	3014	778	348	196	125	103	87
75000	3022	779	348	196	125	103	87

Population size	Sample size for precision percentage of plus or minus						
	0.50	1.00	1.50	2.00	2.50	2.75	3.00
80000	3030	779	348	196	125	103	87
85000	3037	780	348	196	125	103	87
90000	3043	780	348	196	125	104	87
95000	3048	780	348	196	125	104	87
100000	3053	781	348	196	125	104	87
110000	3062	781	348	196	125	104	87
120000	3069	782	348	196	125	104	87
130000	3075	782	349	196	125	104	87
140000	3080	783	349	196	125	104	87
150000	3085	783	349	196	125	104	87
160000	3089	783	349	196	125	104	87
170000	3092	783	349	196	125	104	87
180000	3095	784	349	196	125	104	87
190000	3098	784	349	196	125	104	87
200000	3100	784	349	196	125	104	87
250000	3110	784	349	196	125	104	87
300000	3117	785	349	196	125	104	87
350000	3121	785	349	196	125	104	87
400000	3125	785	349	196	125	104	87
450000	3127	786	349	196	125	104	87
500000	3130	786	349	196	125	104	87

CHAPTER TEN

The Liability of Auditors

1.0   INTRODUCTION

The liability of auditors may be divided into the following broad areas:

    (a) liability for negligence under the *common law*;

    (b) *statutory* liability:

        (i) *civil*—under the Companies Act 1985;

       (ii) *criminal*—under the Companies Act 1985, Theft Act 1968, and Prevention of Fraud (Investments) Act 1958.

It should be borne in mind that legal cases play an important role in creating a body of law with regard to matters governed by both the common law and statute. In the latter case, the courts will decide how a particular statutory provision is to be interpreted in the circumstances in question. Nevertheless, despite the importance of precedent, students should never adopt a dogmatic attitude on questions relating to liability, since the weight of contemporary evidence will often be regarded as more significant than a legal decision arrived at many years earlier.

2.0   NEGLIGENCE UNDER THE COMMON LAW

2.1   General liability

This liability springs from the general principle of law that where a person is under a legal duty to take care, whether imposed by specific contract or otherwise, the failure to exercise a *reasonable standard* of care will make that person responsible for any resultant damage or loss to those to whom the duty is owed. What conduct satisfies the standard of care required will, in any particular case, depend entirely upon the circumstances. The general degree of skill and diligence demanded of, and attained by, auditors today is unprecedented, and the question as to whether an auditor is or is not guilty of negligence in any particular case is largely determined by reference to the standard to which contemporary members of the profession conform.

It will readily be appreciated that contemporary standards provide an ever-shifting criterion, and this has never been more true than at the present time, when judges are likely to place far less reliance than in previous years upon legal decisions reached when the professional standards and skills demanded of an auditor were, from both a statutory and conventional viewpoint, far less exacting.

2.2 Liability to third parties

Physical injury

Liability to third parties in respect of physical injury has a long and well-established legal history. Most students will be aware of the case of *Donoghue* v. *Stevenson* (1932) in which damages were awarded in favour of the young lady who consumed the contents of a gingerbeer bottle in a seaside cafe only to be made aware, too late, that such contents included the decomposed remains of a snail! Although the contractual relationship was between her and the vendor of the bottle, damages were awarded against the manufacturers, with whom there was no privity of contract.

Similarly, in *Grant* v. *Australian Knitting Mills*, the plaintiff was awarded damages in respect of skin irritation suffered due to a defect in the underwear which he had acquired from a retailer; the damages were awarded against the manufacturer and not the retailer.

Financial injury

Legal cases relating to third party liability for *financial* (as opposed to physical) injury are by no means as consistent.

In the House of Lords case in 1954 of *Candler* v. *Crane Christmas & Co*, the majority verdict of their lordships (Lord Denning dissenting) decided that there could be no liability in the absence of a contractual relationship. This decision was reached despite the fact that Mr Candler had been induced to invest sums in a company on the strength of a set of draft accounts negligently prepared by the company's auditors. The auditors knew that this was the purpose of the accounts which they had been asked to prepare (in their capacity as accountants) and did not deny that they had been negligent in executing this assignment.

The House of Lords took a totally different view in the 1963 case of *Hedley Byrne & Co Ltd* v. *Heller & Partners Ltd*, in which they held that the *Candler* case had been wrongly decided. In the 1963 case, a certificate of creditworthiness had been negligently issued by a firm of merchant bankers in response to a request from an outside company; the certificate related to the financial standing of one of the bank's customers.

The House of Lords decided that since it was quite clear that such a certificate issued in a professional capacity would be relied upon by the party to whom it was issued, the absence of privity did not constitute a valid defence in a negligence claim. Heller & Partners Ltd nevertheless escaped without having to pay any damages, but purely on the grounds that they had included a clause with the certificate specifically disclaiming responsibility for the consequences of relying upon such statement. It is therefore clear that they escaped liability by virtue of this disclaimer, rather than the absence of contractual relationship. Nor did they make a charge for providing the certificate.

Counsel's opinion

The Institute of Chartered Accountants in England and Wales in 1967, following the *Hedley Byrne* decision, sought counsel's opinion as to how far such liability might extend, and in reaching an opinion counsel paid particular attention to other cases decided abroad, notably *Ultramares Corporation* v. *Touche & Co* (New York, 1932). In this case, the judge decreed that it would be quite wrong for the auditor to be liable for an indeterminate amount, to an indeterminate class of people, for an indeterminate period of time, and that it was therefore essential that some limitation be placed upon potential liability in the absence of contract.

Counsel's opinion may be summarised in the following way. Liability to a third party in respect of a document or statement would arise only if the following criteria are fulfilled:

(a) there is clear case of negligence;

(b) financial loss has resulted;

(c) it is clear that the financial loss is attributable to reliance upon the negligently prepared document etc., and to no other cause;

(d) the party issuing the document etc. knew the purpose for which it was being prepared, and knew that it was to be relied upon *in the particular context in which it was issued* by the plaintiff.

As a consequence, counsel put forward the view that liability to shareholders would *not* extend to the consequences of their reliance upon the audit report etc. *in the context of an investment decision*, since it is not the purpose of accounts prepared under statute (or the auditor's report attached thereto) to assist existing or potential shareholders in exercising an investment decision. Such accounts are prepared for *stewardship* purposes only, within the confines of companies legislation, and these accounts, together with the auditor's report, are therefore addressed to existing shareholders.

It is extremely dubious as to whether this view expressed by counsel is of any validity today since it is difficult to see what a potential investor (or an existing shareholder contemplating disinvestment) would rely upon to assist such a decision, if not the published accounts and auditor's report. Until "The Corporate Report" becomes a reality and separate accounts are prepared specifically for investment purposes in the ordinary course of events, the statutory published accounts have to fulfil a wide variety of functions, to many of which they are ill-suited.

Counsel stated, equally questionably, that liability to the Inland Revenue would be difficult to prove in a third party context since any tax loss is always recoverable, and any permanent loss would therefore be attributable to the death or decamping of the taxpayer.

Hedley Byrne *followed*

The *Hedley Byrne* decision has been followed in a number of cases in recent years. In the Canadian case of *Myers* v. *Thompson & London Life Insurance Co* (1967), an insurance agent failed to see that his insurance company carried out the instructions of the plaintiff's solicitor for surrender of the plaintiff's term policy and issue a new one to his wife. Thus, when the plaintiff died shortly after, a part of the insurance proceeds was taxed in his estate. Following *Hedley Byrne*, the agent was held personally responsible, for he knew that reliance was being placed on him and his negligence caused the loss to the estate through his failure to exercise the implied duty of care.

In Australia, in *Evatt* v. *Citizens and Mutual Life Assurance Co Ltd*, the *Hedley Byrne* decision was restricted to situations in which the issue of the negligent opinion etc. arises *in the ordinary course of the issuing party's business*. In the *Evatt* case, the parent company of an insurance group negligently gave Mr Evatt an opinion on the financial standing of one of its subsidiaries, and Mr Evatt lost heavily as a result of such reliance. The Privy Council of the House of Lords held, on appeal, that the opinion had been issued honestly, the company believing it to be true, and, since there was no contractual relationship between the litigating parties, there was no cause for action as the statement was made outside of the ordinary course of the parent company's business.

Auditors as share valuers

Late in 1975, the House of Lords held, in *Arenson* v. *Casson, Beckman, Rutley & Co*, that an accountant or auditor of a private company who, on request, values shares in the company in the knowledge that his valuation is to determine the price to be paid for them under a contract for their sale, may be liable to be sued if he makes his valuation negligently.

In April 1970, Mr Arenson's employment in his uncle's company was terminated. He and his uncle asked the company's auditors, Cassons, to determine the "fair value" of his shares in the company as at 4th April. The value given was £4,916. On 11th June, Mr Arenson, relying on that valuation, transferred his shares to his uncle at £4,916.

In September 1970, a holding company, A. Arenson (Holdings) Ltd, was incorporated to acquire the company's issued share capital; and in 1971 the shares of the holding company were offered to the public on the basis of a valuation jointly prepared by Cassons and another firm of accountants which, if applied pro rata, would allegedly have given Mr Arenson's shares a value *six* times what he had received for them.

He issued a writ claiming among other things that Cassons' valuation was not binding on him; that a fresh valuation should be made; and that his uncle should pay him the true worth of the shares; and alternatively that Cassons were "negligent in making the valuation".

This case was of particular importance since it dealt with an unusual aspect of third party liability, i.e. where the defendant has acted in the capacity of a *valuer*, holding the scales of equity between two disputing parties (who had failed to agree on a valuation on their own). The House of Lords decided that although Cassons appeared to have acted in a quasi-judicial capacity (and might thus expect to be entitled to a "qualified privilege" or immunity from action) they were fully answerable to the plaintiff for the valuation originally determined by them. As a consequence, the case was returned to the lower court for the purpose of determining whether or not negligence had taken place, and if so the extent of the appropriate damages.

An important side-effect of this decision for auditors is the need for them to maintain total secrecy as to their method of arriving at share valuations, and of the computations supporting the valuation; only the final figure (or range) should actually be supplied. In this way it would be difficult for any party validly to contest the valuation of shares.

Once a valuation basis and supporting computation is supplied, however, it is always possible for another "expert" to provide evidence as to why such a valuation is negligent.

Class actions

While on the question of auditors' liability, it should be noted that the majority of such instances are now settled out of court, leaving the amounts involved to the insurance companies to provide, under increasingly expensive professional indemnity policies. The unfortunate effect of this situation is that there is now very little developing case law on this subject, and it is highly probable that in thus seeking blanket cover against all professional risks, firms are insuring to an unreasonable degree—i.e. against a level of liability which, in all likelihood, the English courts would regard as unwarranted.

Although neither the case of *Wallersteiner* v. *Moir* nor that of *Prudential Assurance Co* v. *Newman Industries and others* (see below) specifically involved auditors, the introduction of "class actions" (or "representative actions") as a means of litigation in the UK clearly suggests that it might no longer be necessary for aggrieved shareholders (and others?) to bring *individual* actions against auditors. This form of lawsuit permits aggrieved parties to combine in bringing a collective action, and as such represents a new and potent threat.

The concept of a class action is perfectly sound in principle: it enables any class of persons who have suffered loss or damage attributable to one general cause, to combine for the purpose of bringing a joint action for their mutual benefit—usually involving the appointment of a "class trustee" to act on their behalf.

Instances of its successful application are numerous: compensation following airline disasters attributable to a manufacturing or service defect is an oft-quoted example; the damages payable to the victims of the massive Equity Funding fraud in 1973 were similarly settled by class action. Despite its obvious advantage of administrative efficiency and promptness of settlement, we have no equivalent principle in this country: witness, for example, the delay of a dozen or more years in achieving settlements of cases brought by victims of the thalidomide drug.

Perhaps the closest we have come to the idea of a class action was the judgment of Lord Denning in the *Hartley Baird* case (*Wallersteiner* v. *Moir*) a few years ago, in permitting the considerable costs incurred by Mr Moir in bringing this successful action to be reimbursed out of corporate resources—on the ground that the shareholders, as a class, had benefited from his endeavours.

In February 1980, in what appears to be an even more explicit example of a UK class action (*Prudential Assurance Co* v. *Newman Industries and others*) the Prudential Assurance Company succeeded, as representative of all shareholders in Newman Industries, in winning heavy damages against two of the latter company's directors for circularising information which was held to be "tricky and misleading". Even though the decision was reversed on appeal, the important factor is that this *form* of action was admitted. The full implications of the decision for UK case law have still to be analysed.

The practice of charging fees on a "contingency" basis, however, is wholly unprofessional and is understandably prohibited by the Law Society in this country. Legal fees in the UK, like the fees of most professionals, are based on the time, skill and level of responsibility required for the task undertaken; whereas in the US it is permitted to charge a straight percentage of the damages awarded in cases of civil litigation.

Comparison with USA

The potential consequences of this degree of licence are as obvious as they are horrendous. A US lawyer bringing an action on behalf of a client has nothing to lose (and everything to gain) by pitching the claim as high as his mercenary imagination will stretch, for the sky is truly the limit. The vicious combination of class actions and contingency fees thus transforms every situation of corporate malpractice, even mismanagement, into a potential legal scenario:

(a) A skilled legal practitioner acquires a few shares in a company whose poor performance has produced a degree of restlessness amongst its members.

(b) He abuses his rights as a member to enquire into various aspects of corporate decision-making over the past few years, perhaps resorting to payment of a few legitimate "commissions" *en route* in return for exploitable information.

(c) He "concludes" that:

    (i) the officers have been grossly negligent in the performance of certain of their duties;

    (ii) the accounts which they and the audit committee have passed for presentation to members have been materially misleading;

    (iii) the auditors have failed in their reporting duties to draw attention to the foregoing matters in their report; and

    (iv) a *prima facie* case therefore exists against all those previously cited.

(d) He invites the shareholders to form themselves into an aggrieved class, and to appoint him as the class trustee for the purpose of the action. They, like he, have little to lose, since the game is played according to the rules of "no victory, no fee"!

Faced with vindictive damages it is not surprising that US accounting firms are so often forced, for economic reasons, to defend themselves in court. What *is* surprising, however, is the number of occasions on which extravagant charges actually result in awards of damages of comparable amount.

Third party liability—through the post

A recent issue of *True and Fair* puts a spotlight on a highly unwelcome development in the realm of potential liability. A number of auditors have recently received letters from potential investors who are about to acquire substantial interests in companies whose accounts have been audited by those to whom the letters are addressed. These letters usually contain statements along the following lines:

(a) We are writing to advise you that we are contemplating making a substantial investment in XYZ Ltd, of which we understand you are the auditor.

(b) We have not commissioned an independent report relating to the financial position of XYZ Ltd.

(c) We shall place material reliance upon the audited accounts of XYZ Ltd when making a decision as to whether or not to proceed with such an investment.

The import of such letters obviously suggests a wider accountability on the part of the auditor than is presently envisaged under the statutes, and is designed to exploit the uncertain nature of the common law in the direction of third party liability. The APC suggests that a formal reply to such letters should be made, in which it is clearly pointed out that accounts prepared and audited under the Companies Act are not designed for use in an investment context, and that while they will undoubtedly contain useful information for such a purpose, they are no effective substitute for a specially commissioned acquisition or investigation report. Reference should also be made to the fact that published accounts do not convey the company's *current* financial situation, and they will, in any case, have incorporated management estimates acceptable to the auditor in the context of the company's overall financial position, but which may turn out subsequently to be significantly different.

Whether or not such a rebuttal of the validity of stewardship accounts being used for purposes of making investment decisions will be effective, is a matter which only the courts can decide (see the *Jeb Fasteners* case below). Counsel's opinion (1966) following the famous *Hedley Byrne* decision (1963) maintained that no third party liability would attach to auditors if the accounts they have audited under the Companies Act are used, without their knowledge or consent, by outsiders in an investment context. But this opinion was given prior to the Companies Act 1967 requirement that *all* companies should publish their accounts as a matter of public record, thereby effectively putting auditors on notice that the accounts could be examined by anyone, and for any purpose—investment decisions not excluded.

Nevertheless, it is likely that the reply suggested by the APC will prove legally effective, simply because it would clearly be unwise, and grossly incautious, for anyone to rely upon conventional audited accounts *exclusively* in reaching an investment decision. What is always risky, of course, is the possibility that any reliance on the audited statements may be regarded as *reasonable*, such reliance having featured *within the context of a wider investigation*, oriented towards investment. In such a case any loss traceable to the negligence of the auditor could not easily be defended on the grounds suggested by counsel. Even the APC freely admits that "statutory accounts contain much information of use to a potential investor"—to quote *True & Fair*.

The Jeb Fasteners Case

Since the APC published the warning reproduced above concerning "open-ended" liability to outside parties, the very risk envisaged has crystallised in the case of *Jeb Fasteners Ltd* v. *Marks Bloom & Co* (QBD of High Court, December 1980).

As has already been clearly indicated, the general view of potential liability to outside parties depends upon certain key circumstances being present, including the fundamental requirement that the defendant ought reasonably to have known that the negligently prepared statement etc. was to be relied upon by the plaintiff in the context in which the statement was prepared. The absence of this crucial ingredient in the above case did not, however, deter the judge in his decision concerning the liability of the defendant accountants.

In this case, the plaintiff acquired the entire share capital of a company called B.G. Fasteners in June 1975. In so doing, he claimed to have relied on the audited accounts of that company for the year ended 31st October 1974, prepared by the defendant auditors, a firm of chartered accountants. The plaintiff alleged that such accounts, on which an unqualified report had been given by the defendants, did not give a true and fair view of the state of the company, and consequently the plaintiff had suffered substantial loss and damage as a result of the purchase of the company.

The court accepted as a fact—indeed it was common ground between the parties—that at the time the accounts were audited, the defendants did not know of the plaintiff, or his purpose, or that a takeover of the company from any source was contemplated. At the outside of his judgment Mr Justice Woolf acknowledged that there was no direct English authority on the question whether a defendant can owe a duty of care to a plaintiff in these circumstances. It was nevertheless held that:

(a) a duty of care was owed by the defendant auditors to the plaintiff;

(b) the plaintiff, in reaching his decision as to the takeover, had relied on the financial statements and unqualified report of the defendants;

(c) these accounts did not show a true and fair view of the company, and were negligently prepared in that some sales and purchases had been omitted; there had been a failure to make provision for interest due on the company's overdrawn account; and there was a valuation of stock at a figure in excess of cost of approximately £13,500: consequently, whereas the audited trading and profit and loss account had shown a net profit of £11, the reality was a loss in excess of £13,000;

(d) judgment would be given for the defendant auditors, but by reason *only* of the fact that on the evidence before the court the plaintiff would have acted no differently and would still have gone ahead with the takeover even had the true position of the accounts been known to him. Thus, on the facts, the defendants' negligence was not the cause of the plaintiff's loss.

From the above we see (in the last paragraph) that the auditors, Marks Bloom & Co, were not required to pay damages—but the grounds for this finding lay in the court's view that the plaintiffs would have acquired the shares in question in any event, i.e. irrespective of the content of the negligently prepared accounts. The court would not permit the plaintiffs merely to use the auditors as a scapegoat following the bad investment decision. The important point to note, however, is the finding of the existence of a legal duty of care owed by auditors to a complete stranger (at the time of the audit) who relied on the stewardship accounts for investment purposes.

In considering the liability of auditors the judge, Mr Justice Woolf, stated that the appropriate test for establishing whether a duty of care exists is whether the defendant auditors knew, or should reasonably have foreseen at the time the accounts were audited, that a *person* might rely on those accounts for the purpose of deciding whether or not to take over the company, and therefore could suffer loss if the accounts were inaccurate.

The position now seems to be that auditors' liability depends upon a qualified test of "reasonable foresight", i.e. on a principle whereby negligent accountants owe a duty of care to those who can be foreseen as likely to sustain damage if carelessness exists. Any prospective plaintiff must, however, first establish that it was reasonable in the circumstances for him to rely on the audited accounts.

The case is too recent to enable us to embark on a full analysis of its implications, but it is clear that the legal notion of "promixity" has undergone a major extension. In view of the accessibility of published accounts and audit reports to the public at large (for an unlimited number of purposes) one can but speculate on the potential liability opened up by the *Jeb Fasteners* case. Although the case went to appeal in July 1982, the verdict of Mr Justice Woolf was upheld in all particulars.

The *Jeb Fasteners* decision was further strengthened in the Scottish decision of *Twomax Ltd & Goode* v. *Dickson, McFarlane & Robinson* (1982) in a case also involving the decision to acquire shares, based on negligently audited financial statements. Lord Stewart cited and quoted with evident enthusiasm the *Jeb Fasteners* judgment, and awarded damages of some £65,000, plus costs, against the auditors.

The 1985 case of *Lloyd Cheyham* v. *Littlejohn de Paula* has set an important precedent regarding auditor's liability. In 1981, Cheyham purchased a trailer-hire company "Tree", a few days after Littlejohns had signed the accounts. Three months later Tree went into receivership. Littlejohns were sued by Cheyham on the grounds that there were three errors in the accounts that they had relied on when making their investment decision. The accounting policy for repairs and renewals was incorrect and a contingent liability should have been included. However, Woolf J ruled that the contingent liability was immaterial and the accounting policy was acceptable. Thus by following the Accounting Standards the auditors could not be found to be negligent.

2.3   Non-discovery of fraud

A recent issue of the *Accounting and Auditing Newsletter* of Deloitte, Haskins & Sells included a useful reminder of the responsibilities of auditors in the realm of fraud detection. This is reproduced as follows:

The possibility of fraud occurring is always real but, in times of economic depression when company profits are squeezed and interest rates and inflation rates are high, fraud becomes even more likely. One recent example was the fraud disclosed in the press at the end of April in which contractors employed by the CEGB falsely claimed sums totalling £250,000 for power station maintenance work that was never carried out. In that particular case, both the contractors and their employees directly benefited from the additional false claims. Fraud of this nature is increasingly likely when wages fail to keep pace with rising prices.

The two main areas of fraud that auditors should be alert for during their work are:

(a) the manipulating of the financial statements by members of management, either to meet business and financial expectations or to obtain indirect personal gain (including staying in a job);

(b) the abstracting of assets (primarily cash) by either members of management or employees for personal gain. When auditors fulfil audit and other engagements, they should consider the possibility that fraud may have been perpetrated for either or both of the reasons stated above. To help with this task, they should ask certain key questions. A list of appropriate (but not exhaustive) questions is set out below:

Manipulation of the financial statements
A "yes" answer to any of the following questions indicates an increased risk that the financial statements may have been manipulated:

(a) Have the company's operations deteriorated recently?

(b) Do present business conditions indicate potential future difficulties for the company?

(c) Is the company likely to have difficulty in meeting its financial obligations as they become due?

(d) Is there an intention either to liquidate or to curtail significantly the scale of operations?

(e) Does the company propose to raise substantial additional finance in the near future?

(f) Is there likely to be a contest for control of the company in the near future?

(g) Is there likely to be a change of control of the company in the near future?

(h) Is more than the usual significance likely to be attached to the financial statements?

Abstraction of assets

Auditors should consider the following:

(a) Are excessive discretionary powers granted either to new employees or to employees of comparatively low calibre?

(b) Are wage levels below the average for either the locality or the industry?

(c) Is there unexplained extravagance by any employees (especially those who are in key positions and have custody of assets)?

(d) Does any employee refuse to take his due holiday (which may be because he wishes to avoid having his duties subjected to the independent scrutiny of a relief employee)?

(e) Are any employees either excessively uncooperative or antagonistic towards the auditors or are they excessively co-operative?

(f) Does a single individual unaccountably dominate the activities of any department, branch or activity?

(g) Are accounting records consistently written up a long time after the transactions they record have taken place?

(h) Are filing systems such that, for no apparent reason, documents are difficult to retrieve?

A positive answer to any of these questions does not necessarily mean that fraud is taking place. However, a positive answer does indicate that auditors need to consider carrying out further audit tests to overcome the inherent risks. The decision to extend tests will depend upon the combination of various factors and will require consultation between the partner, the manager and the senior partner responsible for the engagement.

2.4   Fraud and the engagement letter

Although the standard form of engagement letter (see Chapter 1) clearly states that audit responsibility for fraud detection is limited to situations in which the effect of the fraud is material in relation to the financial statements, thereby affecting the auditor's statutory reporting duty, it should be borne in mind that:

(a) court decisions have never made any clear distinction when determining auditors' liability between responsibility for material and non-material frauds respectively;

(b) the form of disclaimer which currently features in engagement letters has been introduced relatively recently, chiefly by members of the profession of their own volition;

(c) a high proportion of out-of-court settlements involving auditors in recent years have related to the non-discovery of fraud; and

(d) the conduct of many systems-based audits betrays an almost obsessional concern with the manner in which client staff duties are delegated and sub-divided, and hence with the possibility of fraud taking place. This concern fails to distinguish adequately between those misdemeanours which may prove to be material and those which are unlikely to do so.

From the above it should be clear that merely to attempt to limit responsibility in the form of the engagement letter used will not of itself exonerate the auditor, and the matter therefore continues to cause considerable concern.

2.5   Draft Auditing Guideline: Fraud and Other Irregularities

In June 1985 the APC issued a draft auditing guideline on fraud and other irregularities. The text is given in full below.

Foreword

This exposure draft sets out the auditor's responsibilities with regard to the detection and reporting of fraud and other irregularities (as defined in para 2 of the draft). In line with existing guidelines, it presents the current position and does not seek to extend the responsibilities of the auditor. APC is aware, however, that there are current developments which could lead to amendments in due course. Two such examples are the White Paper "A new framework for investor protection" and the Insolvency Bill.

In addition, APC believes that the public expectation concerning the auditor's responsibilities in relation to fraud and other irregularities is greater than that currently recognised by the profession and that this difference in perception should not be ignored.

It is hoped that this exposure draft will stimulate discussion on this and other major issues involved. Comment is therefore invited on the general question of whether the auditor's responsibilities for the detection and reporting of fraud and other irregularities should be changed, in addition to comments on the detail of the guidance given.

To further contribute to the public debate APC is including with this draft a brief questionnaire which readers of the exposure draft are asked to answer. APC proposes that the replies to this questionnaire should be used as the basis for a further document summarising APC's findings and recommending changes in the law, commercial practice and/or auditing practice in response to such findings.

Preface

This guideline sets out the responsibilities of the auditor with regard to the detection of fraud and other irregularities and the impact this may have on the planning and design of an audit. It also gives guidance on the extent to which the auditor's findings should be reported to management, shareholders and third parties.

Whilst the responsibilities described in this guideline are consistent with the responsibilities of auditors operating in the public sector, in certain respects the duties of the auditor in the public sector with regard to irregularities are somewhat greater than those of his private sector counterpart. In any event, the auditor should have regard to any statutory, constitutional or contractual requirements in addition to his general responsibilities.

Introduction

1. The word *errors* is used to refer to unintentional mistakes in financial statements, whether of a mathematical or clerical nature, or whether in the application of accounting principles, or whether due to oversight or misinterpretation of relevant facts.

2. The word *irregularities* is used to refer to intentional distortions of financial statements, for whatever purpose, and to misappropriations of assets, whether or not accompanied by distortions of financial statements. Fraud is one type of irregularity. In this guideline the word *fraud* is used to refer to irregularities involving the use of criminal deception to obtain an unjust or illegal advantage.

Responsibilities for the prevention and detection of errors and irregularities

MANAGEMENT

3. The primary responsibility for the prevention and detection of errors and irregularities rests with management. This responsibility may be partly discharged by the institution of an adequate system of internal control including, for example, authorisation controls and controls covering segregation of duties. (See the Auditing Guideline: "Internal Controls" and paras 18–21 of this guideline.)

4. Management have particular responsibilities for ensuring that a strong system of internal control exists where assets are held in a fiduciary capacity on behalf of the public or a third party. In such circumstances, management may consider it appropriate to agree with the auditor that additional work be performed by him.

5. In addition to the contractual duty of care owed to an enterprise by those engaged to manage it, the directors of a company (or others in a similar executive position within the public sector) are regarded at law as acting in a stewardship capacity concerning the property which is under their control and consequently have a duty to take steps to ensure the safey of the enterprise's assets.

6. The auditor may therefore consider it appropriate to remind management of

their responsibility to maintain a proper system of internal control as an adequate deterrent to errors or irregularities. He can do this either in the audit engagement letter (see para 14) or by other communication during the audit. In addition, the auditor may ask management to provide details of any irregularities that have come to their attention during the period under examination.

7.   An officer of a company is guilty of an offence where he knowingly or recklessly makes a statement which is misleading, false or deceptive in a material particular (s. 393 of the Companies Act 1985). An auditor is therefore entitled to accept representations as truthful in the absence of any indication to the contrary and provided these are consistent with other audit evidence obtained. (See the Auditing Guideline "Representations by Management".)

THE NATURE OF AN AUDIT AND THE RESPONSIBILITIES OF THE AUDITOR
8.   The explanatory foreword to Auditing Standards and Guidelines defines an audit as "the independent examination of, and expression of opinion on, the financial statements of an enterprise by an appointed auditor in pursuance of that appointment and in compliance with any relevant statutory obligation". The auditor's responsibility is to fulfil that function.

9.   The auditor's responsibility towards errors and irregularities is limited to designing and evaluating his work with a view to detecting those errors or irregularities which might impair the truth and fairness of the view given by the financial statements. In certain circumstances, statutory obligations include a requirement to report on the adequacy of the system of internal control (e.g. building societies).

10.   Accordingly, in obtaining sufficient appropriate audit evidence to afford a reasonable basis of support for his report, the auditor seeks reasonable assurance, through the application of procedures that comply with Auditing Standards, that errors or irregularities which may be material to the financial statements have not occurred or that, if they have occurred, they are either corrected or properly accounted for in the financial statements.

11.   The duty of an auditor, when reporting upon financial statements, is to act with the skill and care that a reasonably competent auditor would employ in the circumstances. This duty can be expected to be determined by reference to the current standards generally applied by the accountancy profession in the proper and competent conduct of an audit.

The impact on the audit

KNOWLEDGE OF THE ENTERPRISE
12.   The nature of the business undertaken by an enterprise and its circumstances affect the auditor's approach to his work and may affect the type and extent of work performed. The auditor's appraisal of the risk that a material error or irregularity could occur should therefore take into account problems facing the enterprise and the actual operations of the enterprise itself.

13. In addition, the auditor should be aware that the internal control environment of the enterprise may facilitate errors and irregularities (see paras 18–21).

PLANNING

14. Having decided to accept an audit assignment, the auditor should normally send a letter setting out the terms of his engagement. The Auditing Guideline "Engagement Letters" recommends that this letter should contain a description of the nature of an audit, the responsibilities of management and the duties of an auditor with regard to the prevention and detection of irregularity and fraud. That guideline also recommends that the letter "should explain that the auditor will endeavour to plan his audit so that he has a reasonable expectation of detecting material mis-statements in the financial statements resulting from irregularities or fraud, but that the examination should not be relied upon to disclose irregularities and frauds which may exist. If a special examination for irregularities or fraud is required by the client, then this should be specified in the engagement letter, but not in the audit section."

15. It is not normal practice in certain parts of the public sector for an auditor to send a letter to his client setting out his terms of engagement. In such circumstances it is more usual for the terms of engagement to be laid down by, for example, statute or a code of practice. In the case of local authority audits, the terms of employment include adherence to a Code of Practice (in England and Wales) and the Standards and Guidelines (in Scotland), which have been issued respectively by the Audit Commission for Local Authorities in England and Wales and the Commission for Local Authority Accounts in Scotland. Such codes should be consulted with regard to any special guidance on the responsibilities of the auditor with regard to irregularities.

16. When planning the audit, the auditor should consider the likelihood of irregularities in the following stages:

Business environment
   - nature of the business, its services (e.g. assets held in a fiduciary capacity) and its products (e.g. assets readily susceptible to misappropriation)
   - circumstances which may exert undue influence on management (e.g. the desire to retain the confidence of depositors or creditors may encourage overstatement of results)
   - company performance (e.g. the deliberate distortion of the financial statements to meet a profit forecast, to increase profit related remuneration or to avoid the appearance of insolvency)

Control environment
   - the strength, quality and effectiveness of management
   - management's overall controls (e.g. degree of supervision)
   - general segregation of duties
   - existence and effectiveness of any internal audit function
   - information technology environment

Account areas
   - susceptibility to fraud

- significance of each account area in the context of overall materiality
- accounting methods
- related party transactions
- unusual transactions

This assessment may also assist the auditor in his preliminary determination as to whether the accounting and other records assist management in safeguarding the enterprise's assets.

17. In reaching his decision as to the areas to be tested and the number of balances and transactions to be examined, the auditor will need to consider information available from prior experience, where available, and knowledge of the client's business and accounting systems. More specifically, the procedures adopted by the auditor for the purpose of detecting material errors and irregularities in conducting an audit will depend on his judgment as to:

(a) the types of errors or irregularities that are likely to occur (or have occurred previously);
(b) the relative risk of their occurrence;
(c) the likelihood that a particular type of error or irregularity could have a material effect on the financial statements; and
(d) the relative effectiveness of different audit tests.

The auditor's planning procedures should be designed to assist him in making this judgment. (See the Auditing Guideline "Planning, Controlling and Recording".)

INTERNAL CONTROLS

18. The Auditing Guideline "Internal Controls" states that the auditor will need to "ascertain and record the internal control system in order to make a preliminary evaluation of the effectiveness of its component controls and to decide the extent of his reliance thereon". This recording might be carried out concurrently with the recording of the accounting system, as the auditor will need to assess this latter system to ensure it forms an adequate basis for the preparation of financial statements. Although an effective system of internal control is one of management's main methods of preventing errors and irregularities, the auditor does not have a specific responsibility to rely on it, and therefore to test it, except where required by specific legislation.

19. In considering the risk of irregularities, the auditor may wish, when assessing internal controls, to place additional emphasis on the following control aspects:

- segregation of duties
- authorisation (particularly of expense items and new ledger accounts)
- completeness and accuracy of accounting data
- safeguard procedures (e.g. signing cheques)
- comprehensiveness of controls (e.g. including all relevant sub-systems)

In addition, where accounting procedures are computerised, the auditor should be concerned to ensure that a lack of computer controls cannot be exploited to suppress evidence that an irregularity may exist or indeed to allow an irregularity to occur. (See the Auditing Guideline "Auditing in a Computer Environment".)

20.   Internal audit, when present and effective, is an important element of a system of internal control and should be a deterrent to irregularities. If he intends to place reliance on the internal audit function, the auditor will need to assess its effectiveness and degree of independence. This will involve reviewing reports made by the internal audit department for evidence of possible irregularities and assessing the extent to which management takes action based upon such reports. (See the Auditing Guideline "Reliance on Internal Audit".)

21.   If weaknesses in internal controls are identified, either from his preliminary evaluation or after compliance tests have been performed, the auditor should take into account the possible effect of these weaknesses when planning his substantive testing. Significant weaknesses in internal controls identified during the audit should be promptly reported to management. (A draft Auditing Guideline "Reports to Management" will, when published, give further guidance in this area.)

DESIGN OF TESTS

22.   The decisions that the auditor makes during the planning phase of the audit and, where appropriate, when evaluating the system of internal control will help him to design his tests to obtain relevant and reliable audit evidence sufficient to enable him to draw reasonable conclusions.

23.   In carrying out his procedures, the auditor may discover circumstances that could be indicative of irregularities. Examples of such circumstances include:

- missing vouchers or documents
- evidence of falsified documents
- unsatisfactory explanations
- figures, trends or results which do not accord with expectations
- unexplained items on reconciliations or suspense accounts
- evidence of disputes
- evidence of unduly lavish life styles by officers and employees
- unusual investment of funds held in a fiduciary capacity
- evidence that the system of internal control is not operating as it was believed or intended to.

The auditor's programme of work needs to be sufficiently flexible to follow up any such points arising and any irregularities or errors detected.

24.   Many substantive tests normally performed by the auditor may assist in isolating irregularities, if they are occurring. For example, tests performed on the debtors ledger may be aimed at revealing overstatement or bad debts, but the design of such tests also assists with cash understatement objectives and may reveal irregularities such as "teeming and lading".

25.   In addition to detailed substantive tests, analytical review procedures should be used, during field work and in the auditor's review of the financial statements, to

isolate account areas which merit further investigation or trends which seem unusual. For example, in some businesses, the reconciliation of purchases, sales and stock by volumes or quantities can be a useful technique. Where doubts exist about the appropriateness of an enterprise preparing its financial statements on a going concern basis, the auditor should be aware, particularly when carrying out his analytical review, that there is an increased risk of irregularities. (The Auditing Guideline "The Auditor's Considerations in Respect of Going Concern", when published, will suggest procedures to be followed where the going concern basis is under question.)

Action to be taken on the discovery of potential errors and irregularities

26.   If during the course of his work, the auditor obtains information (such as circumstances outlined in para 23) indicating the possible existence of errors or irregularities, the following action should be taken.

27.   Unless it is possible to conclude without additional testing that the circumstances encountered could not give rise to an irregularity or error having a material effect on the financial statements, the auditor should perform appropriate additional tests.

28.   If, after additional testing has been performed, it appears that an error or irregularity has occurred, the auditor should consider its nature, cause and likely effect on the financial statements, analysing and projecting the results of his tests as appropriate. Any changes necessary to ensure that the financial statements give a true and fair view should be agreed with management on a timely basis. If such changes are not made or there is an uncertainty which prevents the auditor from forming an opinion he should qualify his audit report accordingly.

29.   Where the auditor is satisfied that irregularities are not material to the financial statements, he should discuss nevertheless his concerns with an appropriate level of management, in order to determine what further action should be taken. For example, an amendment to the system of internal control may be appropriate in order to reduce or eliminate such errors or irregularities in the future.

Reporting

TO MEMBERS AND MANAGEMENT

30.   In addition to his statutory duty to report to the members of the enterprise on the truth and fairness of the financial statements, the auditor should report to the management of that enterprise if the audit has brought to light any irregularities. The auditor should ensure that management are informed promptly and that, in the case of a company, a report is made to the board of directors or, if appropriate, the audit committee. It is particularly important that the auditor reports to a suitably senior level within the enterprise if he suspects that management may be involved in or are condoning irregularities. Legal advice may be required if he believes that his report may not be acted upon or he is unsure as to whom he should report (see para 33).

31.   In his report to management, the auditor may consider it appropriate in

formulating his recommendations to mention, in addition to irregularities and material errors found, matters of good practice such as restrictive crossing of incoming cheques and the prohibition of signing cheques in blank or of opening crossed cheques for encashment.

32. If after taking account of any adjustments made, an irregularity materially affects the view given by the financial statements the auditor should qualify his opinion on those statements accordingly. However, except in certain parts of the public sector, he has no specific responsibility to report an irregularity in his audit report if the financial statements give a true and fair view despite the occurrence of the irregularity.

TO THIRD PARTIES

33. In the course of his audit the auditor may discover a fraud or other irregularity perpetrated by his client. Normally the auditor's duty of confidentiality debars him from reporting any matters to third parties without his client's permission. He should therefore have careful regard to the contents of any guidance issued by his accountancy body and obtain legal advice as to whether this duty of confidentiality should be disregarded and the information disclosed to the appropriate authorities.

34. In certain circumstances the auditor is not bound by his duty of confidentiality. For example, the auditor may be legally bound to make disclosure of the commission of a criminal offence if ordered to do so by a court or a government officer empowered to request such information.

35. Where there is a "public duty" to make disclosure, an auditor may elect to disclose information voluntarily. A public duty arises where an auditor possesses information of any intended criminal offence, or a serious criminal offence even if it has already been committed, if it is likely to cause serious harm to an individual or if it may affect a large number of people.

36. In some cases, the reporting procedures to be followed on discovery of an irregularity will be set out in statute. For example, the auditor of a local authority in Scotland who discovers a loss caused by wilful misconduct must report to the Controller of Audit who in turn has his own specific reporting responsibilities. The auditor of a local authority in England and Wales is required to certify that the loss is due from the person responsible and seek to recover the sum from him.

37. In most instances the auditor has the right of access at all times to the books and accounts and vouchers of the business and is entitled to seek such information and explanation from management as he thinks necessary to perform his duties. If the auditor is unable for any reason to obtain all necessary information and explanation then the scope of his audit has been limited and his audit opinion should be qualified accordingly. (See Auditing Standard "Qualifications in Audit Reports".)

38. If the auditor feels that he has been frustrated in the execution of his work to such

an extent that he is unable to report on the financial statements, he should resign. In these circumstances he should ensure that the reasons for his resignation are made known to shareholders under the provisions of ss. 390 and 391 of the Companies Act 1985. If a resolution to remove the auditor is proposed, he has the right to make a similar statement to shareholders under the provisions of s. 388.

Questionnaire

DETECTION

Question 1. Is it practicable and desirable, within the limitations of procedures and costs, for the auditor to accept a general responsibility to *detect* fraud and other irregularities?

Question 2. If the auditor were given a general responsibility as outlined in question 1, how would current audit techniques need to be altered to enable the auditor to fulfil this changed role and what effect would this have on audit costs?

Question 3. To what extent would the auditor's main role become confused if he undertook the additional specific task of detection of irregularities?

Question 4. What changes could be made to the auditor's role and responsibilities for detection without the law being changed?

Question 5. To what extent would it be practicable to change the auditor's responsibilities for detection without limiting his liability?

Question 6. What are the most cost effective methods of detecting and preventing irregularities?

Question 7. Has APC defined irregularities correctly (para 2 of the exposure draft); for example, should corrupt or sharp practices be included?

REPORTING

Question 8. Should the auditor be expected to *report* fraud and other irregularities discovered to (a) shareholders (b) interested third parties and (c) the general public?

Question 9. If so, should reporting encompass all irregularities or how should the definition of irregularities to be reported be restricted (for example, should the auditor's duty be limited only to the external reporting of irregularities perpetrated by management or should it also extend to defalcations by employees and should normal materiality criteria apply)?

Question 10. As management has the primary responsibility for the prevention and detection of irregularities, how could the primary duty to report externally all irregularities coming to its attention be placed on management?

Question 11. If external reporting of irregularities is to be required of auditors, to whom should their reports be sent and should these reports be confidential or on public record?

Question 12. If some form of external reporting is introduced, at what stage in his investigation of an irregularity should the auditor be expected to report his suspicions to the relevant authorities?

Question 13. In what circumstances would there be merit in introducing to the private sector the concept of "reports in the public interest"?

Question 14. If the concept of external reporting were introduced, how could the auditor's present duty of confidentiality to his client be overcome?

Question 15. Should there be the same requirement when an auditor does not seek reappointment or is dismissed, as when he resigns, regarding the making of a statement?

PREVENTION

Question 16. What should the auditor's responsibilities be with regard to an assessment of the client's system for preventing irregularities?

Question 17. Currently there is no statutory requirement for management to operate a satisfactory system of internal control, although there is to keep proper accounting records. Should this situation be altered and if so in what way?

Question 18. Should any requirement in relation to internal control be limited in any way, for example to enterprises of a certain type or size?

Question 19. Are there specific circumstances in which it might be in the public interest for management and auditors to have increased responsibilities, for example when assets are held in a fiduciary capacity for third parties?

3.0 STATUTORY LIABILITY

3.1 Civil liability—Companies Act 1985, section 631

This section is part of the general winding-up provisions under the Companies Act; these winding-up provisions describe penalties against "officers" of a company in circumstances delineated in sections 624–634 inclusive.

Section 631 is concerned with the civil offences entitled "misfeasance" and "breach of trust". Broadly speaking, these terms relate to the misuse of a position of authority with the object of personal gain. For example, the directors of a company may bind the company in a contract with an outside party with whom they have an existing financial relationship, i.e. a transaction which is not at arm's length. If a similar contract could have been entered into by the company on more favourable terms, it could be argued that the directors have abused their power and position in order to achieve a personal benefit, at the expense of the company for whom they are acting as stewards. In the event of such an offence being proved, the appropriate remedy would be financial damages, making up the loss.

It was decided in the two famous legal cases of *Kingston Cotton Mill* and *London and General Bank* at the end of the last century that, for the purposes of the above provisions, the auditor was to be regarded as an officer of the company.

There is a "safety clause" under section 727, however, that where in any proceedings for negligence, default, breach of duty, or breach of trust against an officer or an auditor, it appears to the court hearing the case:

(a) that he is or may be liable;

(b) that he has acted honestly and reasonably;

(c) that, having regard to all the circumstances of the case, including those connected with his appointment, he ought fairly to be excused for the negligence etc.,

the court may relieve him wholly or partly on such terms as it may see fit. (Section 727 applies equally to civil and criminal liability.)

3.2   Criminal liability

Companies Act 1985, sections 624–630

The other winding-up sections referred to above, i.e. sections 624–625 and 630, all involve criminal offences, and in each case reference is made to "officers" of the company. The question has therefore arisen as to how far, if at all, the auditor may be regarded as being an officer of the company for the purposes of these sections, bearing in mind that the two cases referred to in the previous section related only to civil liability.

It was held in the case of *R. v. Shacter* (1960) that the term "officer" must be taken to include the auditor. In 1953 the appellant was appointed auditor of a company and his appointment was continued from year to year thereafter. He was convicted as a "public officer" of a public company of falsifying the company's books and publishing fraudulent statements contrary to sections 83 and 84 of the Larceny Act 1861 (replaced by the Theft Act 1968—see below), and, being "an officer" of the company, of making false entries, fraud and defaults contrary to sections 328(1) (*j*), 330 and 331 (now repealed) of the Companies Act 1948 (now included in Companies Act 1985, ss. 624 and 625).

The doubt regarding this matter arises in the first place because although section 384 of the 1985 Act refers to the appointment of an auditor to hold "office", he is not included within the definition of the term "officer" in the definitions section of the 1985 Act (section 744). Furthermore, where the 1985 Act states that an officer of a company shall not be qualified to act as auditor, it also states, ironically, that for the purposes of this provision the auditor of the company is not himself to be regarded as an officer!

Theft Act 1968

This Act repealed the Larceny Acts 1861 and 1916, and Falsification of Accounts Act 1875, and re-enacted many provisions contained in earlier statutes.

Under sections 17 and 18, an *officer* of a company may be imprisoned for up to seven years if he destroys, defaces, conceals or falsifies any account, record or document required for any accounting purposes; or in furnishing information, produces or uses any account, record etc., which to his knowledge is or may be materially misleading, false or deceptive.

Section 15(1) provides: "A person who by any deception dishonestly obtains property belonging to another, with the intention of permanently depriving the other of it, shall on conviction or indictment be liable to imprisonment for term not exceeding ten years".

Section 16(1) states: "A person who by any deception dishonestly obtains for himself or another any pecuniary advantage shall on conviction or indictment be liable to imprisonment for a term not exceeding five years".

Section 13 states: Cases of pecuniary advantage arise where debts or charges are reduced, evaded or deferred; overdrafts and insurance policies are negotiated on improved terms; opportunity is given to earn greater remuneration or win money by betting (section 16).

Offences under Sections 15, 16 and 17 are extended to officers of companies and members.

Under Section 19 an officer may be imprisoned for up to seven years if shown to have published or concurred in publishing a written statement or account which to his knowledge is or may be materially misleading, false or deceptive, with intent to deceive members or creditors about the company's affairs. Section 19 is also similar to section 84 of the Larceny Act 1861 (now repealed).

It was under the latter section that Lord Kylsant was convicted in the case of *Rex* v. *Kylsant & Morland* (1931). In this case, criminal proceedings were taken against the chairman and the auditor of the Royal Mail Steam Packet Co Ltd, the allegation being that the chairman had issued false annual reports to the shareholders with intent to deceive, and that the auditor had been guilty of aiding and abetting in the issue of such false reports. Both the chairman and the auditor were acquitted of this charge, but the chairman, on a further charge, was found guilty of publishing a prospectus which he knew to be false in a material particular.

For some years the Royal Mail Steam Packet Co had incurred actual trading losses, but their published accounts revealed considerable profits available for dividend. This position was largely brought about by the utilisation of taxation and other reserves created in past years and no longer required for the purposes for which they were made.

It was alleged by the prosecution that the result of such adjustments was to cause shareholders to believe that the company was trading profitably, whereas in fact it was making losses.

The section of the Larcency Act 1861, under which this prosecution against the auditor (Mr Morland) was brought, referred to "officers", and it may be reasonably assumed that its counterpart section in the Theft Act 1968 (section 19) similarly includes auditors as officers.

Prevention of Fraud (Investments) Act 1958

Section 12 of this Act provides that "any person who, by any statement, promise or forecast which he knows to be misleading, false or deceptive, or by any dishonest concealment of material facts, *or by the reckless making of any statement, promise or forecast which is misleading, false or deceptive*, induces or attempts to induce another person to enter into, or offer to enter into, any agreement for ... acquiring, disposing of, subscribing for, or underwriting securities ..., shall be guilty of an offence and liable to penal servitude for a term not exceeding seven years."

A successful prosecution of an auditor was brought under the equivalent section of the 1939 Prevention of Fraud (Investments) Act. In the case of *R* v. *Wake & Stone* (1954) a criminal action was brought against the managing director and auditor of a company which issued a prospectus in which an inflated value was placed on the company's stocks and work in progress, as given in the auditor's report.

It was deemed in court that this figure was "false, deceptive and misleading" in that it was far too high. There had been several alterations in the inventory sheets and although the auditor asked for an explanation, he accepted, without attempting any independent corroboration, the managing director's statement that the alterations related to errors in the original valuation.

It was revealed in court that timber in the company's warehouses had been taken at a flat rate and had been measured in such a way as to include all the air as well as the timber!

The managing director pleaded guilty to the charges and was given a prison sentence. The auditor pleaded not guilty but was convicted and fined, on the grounds that he had signed his report *recklessly*.

It should be noted that, in the context of this Act, "recklessness" amounts to a criminal offence, which is not surprising in view of the long history of fraud in company law in situations where the public are invited to subscribe capital purely on the basis of information represented in a public advertisement.

4.0 RELIANCE ON INFORMATION FROM THIRD PARTIES

The leading case on this subject was *Re The City Equitable Fire Insurance Co* (1924), in which the auditors relied upon a certificate from the insurance company's stockbrokers regarding their alleged safe custody of the company's securities.

In fact, the stockbrokers had pledged the company's securities in order to make good their losses on unauthorised dealings in the investments of other clients, as a result of which the insurance company suffered severe losses.

The stockbrokers were at all material times heavily indebted to the insurance company and the action was brought against the auditors on the grounds that the certificates on which they had relied did *not* provide the *independent* evidence which they should have sought, the point being that the chairman of City Equitable was also a senior partner in the firm of stockbrokers. This fact was, of course, known to the auditors.

The important consideration in all such circumstances, therefore, is that certificates from third parties should be accepted by auditors only if such third parties are acting in a truly independent capacity. Further, the issue of the confirmation in question should take place in the ordinary course of the issuing party's business.

The interesting feature of the above case is that although the auditors were found guilty of negligence, they were indemnified by a clause in the company's articles which had the effect of relieving all officers and auditors of the company from liability consequent upon their own negligence.

PROGRESS TEST 10

1. Under what headings may the liability of auditors arise? (1.0)

2. What were the principal findings in the case of *Hedley Byrne v. Heller & Partners*? (2.2)

3. To what extent has the above judgment been affected by more recent cases? (2.2)

4. To what extent do the provisions of the Theft Act 1968 and the Protection of Fraud (Investments) Act 1958 apply to auditors? (3.2)

CHAPTER ELEVEN

The Audit Approach to Computer Systems

Note: This chapter has been prepared on the basis of the professional examination syllabus and examination questions which have been set in the past; its scope extends well beyond the Institute guidance statements U14 and U15 and reflects the 1982 APC Guideline "Auditing in a Computer Environment", consisting of:

(a) internal controls in computer-based accounting systems; and

(b) computer-assisted audit techniques.

1.0 HARDWARE

The term "electronic data processing" applies to the processing of data by means of electronic computers. Digital computers—the type used for business purposes—are controlled by a "program" of instructions, stored in the equipment, which enables them to store information, perform complete processing routines upon that information and any new data fed into the machine, and to print out final results in readable form without human intervention.

A computer operates by passing electric impulses through complicated circuits which have been constructed in such a way as to enable the computer to add, subtract, multiply, divide, move data from one position to another, and compare two or more quantities and determine which is the largest or smallest. All data must, therefore, be converted to a form readable by the machine.

2.0 SOFTWARE

The processing within the computer and the operation of subsidiary equipment, i.e. input and output devices, are controlled by means of the *program*, a detailed list of instructions to be followed in performing each step in the processing. The program may be contained on punched cards, punched tape or magnetic tape and is fed into the computer before each processing operation. "Software" is the general term used for the programs.

The program is designed and constructed by programmers skilled in the operation of the particular model of computer being used, under instruction from the systems analysts. The programmers analyse the process to be performed and construct a set of coded instructions to the computer. The program must cover every possible situation arising in the proposed routine—including errors—and also control the input and output equipment.

As programming is such a complex operation the process is first set out in the form of a flow-chart, describing the broad outlines of the procedure to be followed. Once this outline of the procedure has been agreed, a flow-chart of the detailed procedure within the computer in readable, although abbreviated, form is constructed. This chart, known as a "block diagram", details the logical steps to be followed by the computer in the execution of the program.

The programmer will then prepare a draft program in machine code which will be tested and amended until a workable program is obtained. A readable flow-chart of the revised computer procedure will then be prepared, setting out the tests and checks included in the program.

At first sight electronic data processing presents the auditor with grave difficulties, because:

(a) all information must be presented to the computer in machine-sensible form;

(b) the program of instructions is in machine-sensible form;

(c) all processing within the computer is performed electronically, and therefore there is no visible evidence of the processing for the auditor to examine.

This problem will be aggravated in the future as means of direct ("on-line") input to the computer are developed, i.e. the development of machines which enable an operator to index information on to a keyboard which will cause electronic impulses to be fed directly into the computer.

3.0 RELIANCE ON COMPUTERS

The absence of a visible audit trail does not, however, mean that a trail does not exist. Instead of checking the detail of individual transactions through the various stages of the accounting routine the auditor must examine the routine itself.

Computers have proved in practice to be extremely reliable, and if a computer failure does occur it is generally caused by a failure of a part of the circuitry. To prevent this the computer engineers will deliberately operate the computer on a very low voltage in order to reveal any weak circuits which are in need of replacement thus avoiding breakdowns during processing. Auditors can, therefore, largely rely upon their accurate functioning. If an adequate routine is laid down, the auditor may be assured that each transaction processed through it has been dealt with in accordance with that routine. It follows, therefore, that once he has proved the effectiveness of the routine the auditor has, in fact, checked the processing of every item subjected to that routine.

4.0 INTERNAL CONTROL

Clearly, internal control is extremely important in computer systems. The data processing department itself will usually be centralised and operated as a service to the other departments, which in itself serves as a measure of clerical internal control, as the custody of assets and the preparation of original documents are not within the control of the computer operators. Fraud would thus normally require the collusion of members of the programming and operating staff.

Computers, however, operate only according to the instructions and data given to them and cannot trace errors in data in the same way as a person can. If the data conforms to the instructions given in the program a computer will accept and process it. Great care, therefore, must be taken to ensure that all data fed into the computer is both accurate and complete. "Reasonableness" and other checks on input are, however, commonly incorporated in machine programs, so that certain invalid data is rejected before processing.

The internal control routines which are applied to the receipt and preparation of documents within the firm must clearly be strict. Errors may *not* be detected by the computer and, even if they are, valuable computer time will be lost as incorrect data will be referred back to its original source for correction.

The relationship between "user" departments and the "computer services" department is clearly shown by Fig. 13:

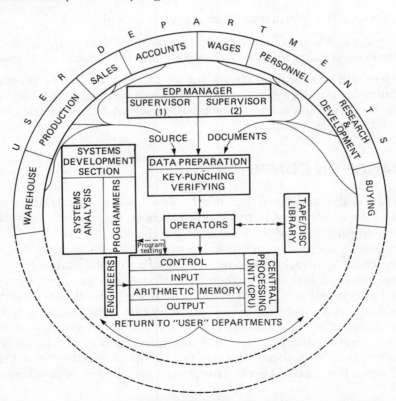

Fig. 13. *The basic EDP configuration.*

(a) "user" departments are shown on the circumference;

(b) "computer services" department occupies the central area.

4.1 APC Guideline—Auditing in a Computer Environment

The following notes summarise this Guideline regarding internal controls.

The main controls headings in computer-based systems and their relationships
The location of controls, distinguishing between those which are user-based and EDP-based respectively, is illustrated in Fig. 14.

APPLICATION CONTROLS
These are controls within a computer application which ensure the completeness and accuracy of input and processing and the validity of the resulting accounting entries. They are a combination of manual and computer-programmed procedures.

Application controls performed by computer are not controls themselves, but parts of computer programs which allow controls to be exercised. They aid the provision of controls over completeness and accuracy of input and processing and the validity of accounting entries in the same way as the manual controls. But in addition they provide control over the calculations, summarisation and categorisation carried out by the computer.

GENERAL CONTROLS
These are controls covering the environment within which such applications are developed, maintained and operated and they ensure the effective operation of programmed procedures.

The effects of the interrelationship between application controls and general controls on the balance between compliance and substantive testing
Evaluating and testing application controls is likely to be more cost-effective than evaluating and testing general controls. But where the satisfactory operation of programmed procedures is not assured by user controls, reliance will have to be placed

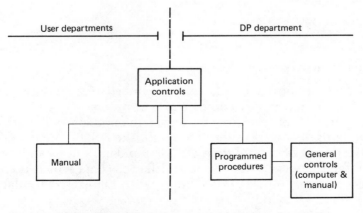

Fig. 14. *Computer-based systems—location of controls.*

on general controls, provided that they have been evaluated and tested. In practice, the assurance that the auditor may draw from general controls will be limited, particularly in small installations, and consequently the auditor will be able to limit his substantive test levels only by placing reliance on manual application controls. The bias towards substantive testing is not such a disadvantage as it might be in a manual system, since vast amounts of data can be validated using a computer audit program.

The initial stages of a computer audit

There are two initial steps in the audit procedures in relation to internal controls:

(a) initial review;

(b) evaluation of internal controls.

The purpose of the initial review is to obtain a general understanding and not a detailed knowledge of the system of internal control. The aim is to identify the existence of internal controls on which the auditor may choose to place reliance.

The evaluation of internal controls (preliminary evaluation) involves the evaluation of controls by means of internal control questionnaires. The internal control system will be more extensive than a manual accounting system due to the existence of programmed procedures and general controls in the data processing department.

The purposes and techniques of control

The guidelines are much more specific about the control techniques used to ensure completeness and accuracy of input and processing. They also specify additional techniques to ensure the validity of master files and standing data.

In designing a system of internal control for a computer application the whole system of processing must be considered, both manual and computer, from when the initial event occurs to the final output document review and follow up by the user.

Within the framework of application controls the controls are divided under the following headings (see Table 11):

(a) completeness of input;

(b) completeness of processing;

(c) accuracy of input;

(d) accuracy of processing;

(e) validity of data processed;

(f) maintenance of data on files.

In practice some of these controls may be linked (for example controls over completeness of input may ensure completeness of processing).

Some data requires a higher degree of accuracy than others and therefore it follows that higher standards of controls should be established. Standing data, for example, requires a higher degree of control than transaction data, since standing data is used in processing large numbers of transactions. Likewise data which is converted into financial terms can be of much greater importance than reference data. Of course reference data itself has varying degrees of importance.

Table 11. Application controls

| | Completeness | | Accuracy | | Master files and standing data | |
	Input	Processing	Input	Processing	Validity	Maintenance
Purpose	All transactions are recorded, input and accepted by the computer. (Control over the numbers of documents.) Each document is processed only once.	All input and accepted data updates the master file. Output reports are complete.	Control over the data fields to ensure the accuracy of data transcribed from source to input document (where applicable) and that data is accurately converted to machine-readable form.	Accurate data is carried through processing to the master file. Computer-generated data is accurate. Output reports are accurate.	Only authorised data updates the master files. No changes to the data are made after authorisation.	Data on master files cannot be changed without authority and there are no long-outstanding or unusual items on file.
Some control techniques which may be applied by the computer (programmed procedures) or by the user (manual). All rejected data must be investigated and corrected.	Control totals Matching sequence One for one	Control totals } after update Matching sequence } One for one Summary processing	Control totals Matching One for one Programmmed checks (e.g. reasonableness)	Control totals (after update) One for one Summary processing Manual reconciliation of accepted item totals with file totals	Programmed checks (e.g. authority limits) Manual authorisation and review	Manual reconciliation of file totals with manual control account Exception reports

4.2 General controls

The general controls incorporated into the data processing system will cover two major aspects:

Administrative controls
These arise chiefly from the risks implicit in:

    (a) concentration of power in the EDP department;

    (b) carrying a large number of files of important data centrally stored; and

    (c) storing data in a form which is highly inflammable, concentrated, sensitive to temperature and atmospheric conditions, and dependent for processing on machinery which is susceptible to breakdown.

Systems development controls
These are intended to ensure a valid system of processing whenever new applications are devised, meeting the requirements of management and user departments. These aims are achieved by:

    (a) the use of standard documentation;

    (b) the use of standard procedures, wherever possible;

(c) specifying rigid authorisation procedures whenever new applications are envisaged, or existing programs amended or extended;

(d) the adoption of adequate testing routines prior to implementation;

(e) instituting a comprehensive system of program and document security.

4.3   Application controls

Application controls codify the operating routines to be followed by the EDP and the user departments in their relations with each other. Application controls cover:

(a) the preparation of input, and its transfer to the computer;

(b) the processing of data within the computer;

(c) the preparation of output and its distribution;

(d) the maintenance of master files and the standing data contained therein.

5.0   GENERAL CONTROLS (1)—ADMINISTRATIVE

5.1   Division of responsibilities

The following divisions are possible:

(a) segregating the systems analysts and programmers, who design and construct the programs, from the operation of the computer and storing of the programs;

(b) segregation of input preparation and control from the operation of computers.

5.2   Use of a log

Unauthorised processing can be prevented by keeping a close check on the use of the computer by recording in a log book the programs run and the time started and finished.

5.3   Library function

The following controls, if operated, should ensure that no unauthorised alterations to programs or data are made nor any unauthorised processing of data performed:

(a) controlling the storage of the programs (and their issue to the computer operators and programmers); storage of the working files of input data; and storage of applications not being processed currently;

(b) strict control over input and output files which it is desired to retain for rebuilding of current files should they be damaged.

The computer operator is able, through the console of the computer, to monitor the processing operation, stop and start the routine and enter data manually. The importance of carefully planned division of responsibilities is therefore obvious. The auditor should ascertain that an adequate control system is enforced to ensure that no unauthorised data is processed.

5.4   File security

The security of files containing current "transaction" data and "standing" data is clearly one of the prime considerations in relation to administrative controls, from both the management and the audit viewpoint. Files may become unreadable because of some machine malfunction, physical damage, accidental or even wilful destruction etc., and certain standard security measures have been almost universally adopted.

Where information is stored *serially*, such as on magnetic tape (it being necessary to run the tape from the beginning in order to reach information stored further on), the most usual security precaution is that generally known as *grandfather/father/son*. When a new file ("father") is created by updating an existing one ("grandfather") the latter is retained until the new file has, in turn, been updated and the data transferred to a third file ("son"). Should the "son" file become mislaid, destroyed or be found to be defective in some way, it can be reconstructed by re-running the source data against the "grandfather" or "father" files which have been retained. This procedure is illustrated in Fig. 15.

It will be observed that a maximum of two tapes are on the computer at any one time, the third acting as security "back-up", normally stored in the library.

Although three file-generation is normally regarded as adequate, it is held in some quarters that yet another generation ("grandson") should be included in the arrangement.

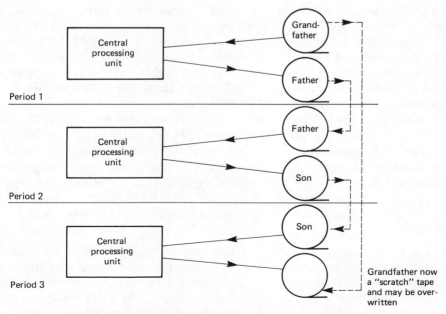

Fig. 15. *EDP file security—the "grandfather/father/son" system.*

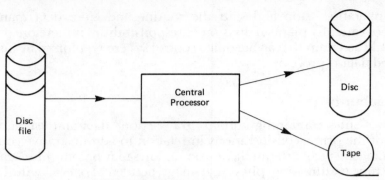

Fig. 16. *EDP file security—"dumping"*.

Where magnetic tape files are in use the above security technique may conveniently be employed, owing to the fact that new tapes are created by the updating process. On the other hand, where data is stored in a random (or direct) access organisation such as on magnetic discs, updating takes place *in situ*, no further copies being created by processing. In such cases file security is facilitated by a process known as "dumping", whereby copies of file information are made at regular intervals. These copies may consist of the whole or any part of a file, but in practice only those "addresses" which have been updated will usually require to be dumped.

Information may be dumped either on to another magnetic disc or on to magnetic tape, as illustrated in Fig. 16.

5.5   General security

The problem of general security clearly takes on mammoth proportions in the case of large computer configurations, and the multitude of aberrations, major and minor, which have arisen and been publicised from time to time are now legion. Nevertheless, this is a matter with which auditors are deeply concerned, and their duty to assess the adequacy or otherwise of EDP security is by no means the least onerous of their tasks. An article in the *Harvard Business Review* highlights the hazards to which EDP complexes are subject by quoting several actual cases where catastrophe (or near-catastrophe) was attributable to security weaknesses in the computer area.

The examples given below are drawn from these cases and give an indication of the scale on which the results of such weaknesses operate, and demonstrate the need for any organisation heavily dependent upon EDP to appoint a team of specialists in computer security who can act independently of the computer management and whose function it is to plan, implement and supervise the various control procedures which they consider necessary in all circumstances. The auditor should strongly encourage the appointment of such a group if his investigation leads him to believe in its necessity.

(a)   The EDP manager of a large airline noted that data losses were occurring in the company's procedures, and he found the answer one evening during a spur-of-the-moment visit to the computer facility. He discovered that the night operators were "speeding up" operations by by-passing an automatic safety device on the tape drives during rewind. They got away with it when they were careful but occasionally they broke tapes and consequently lost data.

(b) A programmer in a bank managed to steal large amounts of money simply by programming the computer to by-pass his account number when reporting on overdrafts. He was then free to overdraw his account by any amount he pleased.

(c) One dissatisfied EDP employee used magnets to destroy virtually every file and program that his company possessed. He accomplished this in practically no time at all, but reconstructing the data will take a very long time indeed. At last report, in fact, the auditors were not sure whether they could reconstruct enough information to keep the company in business. In this particular case the consequences of poor security in the EDP areas may have been not merely serious, but fatal.

(d) A large insurance company gave a ladies' garden club a tour of its EDP facilities. The spinning tapes and blinking lights impressed one visitor so much that she felt she had to have a souvenir of the occasion. She later said, "I hope I didn't do anything wrong. There were all those boxes of cards on the table, and I just reached into the middle of the box and took one". Perhaps this lady only caused a program to be re-run. A more serious possibility is that the card may not have been missed at all, and the centre is still trying to correct the resulting confusion.

6.0   GENERAL CONTROLS (2)—SYSTEMS DEVELOPMENT

During development, new applications and new programs pass through a number of phases, all of which must be properly authorised prior to proceeding further. An appreciation of this area of controls will be assisted by briefly considering the usual phases which have to be negotiated successfully, before a new program "goes live".

6.1   Feasibility study

The management must institute this initially, although the detailed work will normally be carried out by a committee under the head of data processing services. They will consider costs, short- and long-term economies, suitability of hardware, and other matters as relevant criteria as to whether to proceed further.

6.2   Systems analysis

This work, executed by specialists, involves the division of their attention between:

(a) those aspects of the existing system (if any) which must at all costs be preserved within the new system; and

(b) new statistics, analyses and other information which, though desirable for management to possess, has never been available under the existing system but which the proposed new system may be able to offer, such as the analysis of sales by product, geographic area, salesman etc.

The advice of the internal and external auditors, particularly under (a) will clearly be invaluable and they should play a vital role at this early planning stage.

Once the EDP manager has approved the design of the new system, depicted in flow-chart form by the systems analysts, as meeting all the essential requirements of management, he will pass the proposed system to the programmers.

6.3 Programming

This stage involves the writing of programs which will execute the proposed system precisely at all times, giving management the information required to operate the business efficiently. Provision should be made in the programs for error and exception routines, as a safeguard against incorrect or unauthorised input being passed to the computer for processing.

6.4 Program testing

The programmers will prepare "test packs" and execute "dummy runs" to ensure that the programs are performing correctly, and not until they and the head of the EDP department are satisfied will the final period of parallel running commence.

6.5 Parallel running

During this phase the existing system and the new system are operated jointly and simultaneously so that their respective results may be compared. This allows for the elimination of any "bugs" still present in the new systems programs. Once this phase has been satisfactorily completed the existing system then "goes live".

6.6 File conversion

Existing files are converted into the new computer format. Naturally, further difficulties may be encountered and further improvements, amendments and sophis-tications will subsequently be introduced into the programs. No changes of this character, however, should be introduced or effected by programmers or operators without the prior authority of the head of the EDP department.

7.0 APPLICATION CONTROLS

7.1 Input

The controls over input preparation would ensure that input is:

(a) a valid record of an actual transaction;

(b) authorised by a responsible official;

(c) correctly allocated to an account; and

(d) correctly translated into machine-sensible codes.

At present most computer input is initially on documents which are:

(a)   raised by persons authorising transactions; or

(b)   received from outside organisations.

These documents should be subjected to the same control procedures as in manual systems, batched and pre-listed for quantity, value, account codes etc. The number of transactions should also be recorded before being transferred to the input preparation section.

The input preparation section will translate the data into machine-sensible form, i.e. into punched card, punched paper tape or magnetic tape. In order to provide accurate translation the equipment will total the data as it is processed and provide totals to be agreed with the pre-list. The pre-list figures can be in the form of a "hash" total, i.e. a combined total of account numbers, quantities and values which serves no purpose other than its control function.

The number of transactions will also be counted to provide a *record count* which is used to ensure that no items are omitted during subsequent processing. Both the totals and the record count will be entered as input (see "Record counts" below).

7.2   Specific controls over input

Printed lists

Many types of input preparation equipment provide a printed list of all items which have been included in the input, thus providing the auditor with a visible record against which he can check the original documents.

Check digits

The validity of account and code numbers can be checked during input preparation by adding a check digit as an integral part of each account and code number, to make each such number comply with a simple formula. The input machinery will then subject each account code number to a simple test in order to prevent incorrect data being fed to the computer.

(Many forms of computer input are at present prepared as a by-product of a control routine, e.g. the creation of punched paper tape by cash registers. The auditors should examine the machine controls very carefully.)

Tape labelling

The input tape will include (encoded) an identifying "label" which will contain details of the application, the date the tape was made and its sequence. The computer will check each tape to ensure that it belongs to the application being processed and is the next in sequence. This prevents irrelevant data being processed and destroying other records.

Date control

In order to prevent input tapes being erroneously fitted to the output deck the label may also include a date before which the tape must not be re-used.

Mechanical checks

In addition to these controls mechanical checks may also be incorporated. If a specifically coloured disc is required to be attached to output tapes in order that they can be inserted on to the output tape deck, the fact that an input tape does not have one should serve as a control.

Record counts

A record count contained as part of each input tape should ensure that all items on the tape are, in fact, processed. The computer program will contain instructions to add the number of items processed and agree with the record count on the tape. Should any error have occurred, the computer will signify this and either stop or go into an error routine, depending on its programmed instructions. The computer may repeat this test at various control points during the processing to ascertain that all items are passing through the processing properly.

7.3 "Built in" processing controls

These consist of the following:

(a) The computer may have controls built into the circuitry to ensure correct reading of input. The reading equipment may read the data twice and compare the result, ensuring that data is transmitted to the storage section of the computer only when it has been proved accurate.

(b) The computer may also be built to operate on an odd or even *parity* code. When the input machinery is preparing data it will insert an extra "bit" (binary digit), if necessary, in order to make the number of digits for each character odd or even, as the case may be. When the computer is reading data in, it will reject any character that does not conform to the parity codes, thus signalling errors. This check is useful in ensuring that dust or atmospheric conditions have not caused a digit to be obscured.

(c) Controls built into central processing equipment include the duplication of certain circuits in order to repeat calculations separately and compare the result, thus ensuring the accuracy of the calculations. Some processors are designed so that the *complements* of the true figures are used in repeating the calculation, which is then compared with the original calculation. This method allows a different combination of machine components to be used.

(d) The computer engineer will also test the computer regularly by using a *test program* on specially prepared data. Most failures are preceded by a loss of efficiency and by running the machine at low voltage the engineer is able to locate faulty circuits and replace them before they fail. The computer will also conduct parity checks on data as it is moved from one location to another inside the computer.

(e) The computer may be designed so that, as it prints out data, punches cards or tape, the printers or punches activated cause electric impulses which are compared with those already prepared by the computer, to ensure that the output section is functioning accurately. Magnetic tape output equipment will be equipped with a reading and writing head. As the data is written on to the tape it will be read simultaneously by the reading head and compared by the computer with the data which should have been written, thus ensuring accurate output.

7.4 Programmed application controls

Such controls, which are built into the programs, are designed to ensure that:

  (a) only data relevant to the application is processed, so as to prevent tapes of other applications or old input tapes being read in as input by mistake;

  (b) magnetic input tapes cannot be inserted in the output deck by mistake, thus eliminating the risk of data being lost (new entries on tape automatically erase the old records);

  (c) tapes are not destroyed prematurely by re-use;

  (d) *all* items are processed;

  (e) all data is processed *accurately*.

7.5 Accuracy of processing

  (a) *The use of "hash" totals.* The data read into the computer will be added to make a grand total which will be checked against that encoded into the tape or cards by the input preparation equipment. This control ensures that no item has been omitted and that all descriptive figures, account numbers etc., have been correctly read into the machine.

  (b) *Check digits.* The addition of a check digit to descriptive codes such as account numbers to make them conform to a simple formula enables the computer to test the validity of the codes during processing. These checks can help to eliminate transposition and transcription errors from descriptive numbers.

  (c) *Tolerance or "reasonableness" checks.* This check is the setting of parameters for totals of calculations or data fed into the computer. The computer then checks to see that all data read in conforms to the limits and tests calculations to see that they are reasonable, e.g. if no item of data read in should exceed, say, £20 the computer will reject any item in excess of this; similarly, if the results of any particular calculation should not exceed £45, the computer will signal apparent errors in checking.

  (d) *Sequence checks.* Many small computer installations have no direct-access facilities (i.e. it is not possible to refer directly to information recorded on the middle of a reel of magnetic tape) and processing is therefore done sequentially. Input data must be sorted into sequential order either on punched card equipment outside the computer or by the computer itself before processing begins. Sequence checks are built into the program which ensure that the input data is processed in the same sequence as on the master file being updated. The magnetic disc storage devices on larger installations do, however, allow direct-access facilities by the use of "address" systems for locating a particular item of information, e.g. the number of spare machine parts in stock.

7.6   Controls over output

Third and fourth generation computers operate at electronic speeds which are faster than any method of printing out information that has yet been devised. In order to avoid delays in processing—through the computer having to wait until, say, the printer has finished one job before it can commence the next—output is first transferred to magnetic tape by the computer. Speeds of writing magnetic tape are extremely fast and thus the computer is not delayed by printing speeds.

Special printing units are then used away from the computer—"off-line"—to prepare any written reports which are required. It is important that the off-line printers are accurate, and this is ensured by a system which produces electric signals when the printer is operated. These signals are compared with the data being read into the printer and should they not agree the printer will re-read the data and, should they still disagree, will stop. The fault can then be corrected by an engineer.

Apart from the hardware controls above, the three main areas of control over output are:

(a)   distribution of output;

(b)   acting on exception reports;

(c)   verification by testing against input data.

8.0   AUDIT APPROACH AND PROCEDURES

8.1   General

The auditor should examine the data processing system in force very carefully, particularly the controls which are incorporated into the equipment or included in the programs. In new installations it is better if this examination takes place immediately before the programs are finalised. The auditor then has an opportunity to make suggestions for improving the controls and of reviewing the final system. Furthermore, he is thus able to ensure the provision of *adequate audit trials* whereby the sequence of account procedures may be traced through the system and checked. To examine the programs earlier would be wasteful as alterations would probably be made necessitating a further review, and to do so later, when the programs are already being operated, would be inconvenient and impracticable.

The clerical procedures *up to the translation of the data* into machine-sensible form are subject to the same internal control conditions as a manual system and the auditor should have little difficulty in appraising them.

The computer processing system itself can be appraised by examining the detailed flow-chart of the procedures which have been incorporated into the programs. Alterations to the programs should be strictly controlled; they should be authorised in writing by a person in authority, preferably the EDP manager, and a control book initialled when the alteration has been correctly carried out and tested by someone other than the programmer concerned.

8.2 Control file

The audit paper should include an *audit control file* containing full details of the system including:

(a) copies of all the forms which source documents might take, and details of the checks that have been carried out to ensure their accuracy;

(b) details of physical control over source documents, and any control totals of numbers, quantities or values, including the names of the persons keeping these controls;

(c) full descriptions of how the source documents are to be converted into input media, and the checking and control procedure;

(d) a detailed account of the clerical, administrative and systems development controls contained in the system, e.g. separation of programmers from operators; separation of control of assets from records relating thereto;

(e) the arrangements for retaining source documents and input media for suitable periods; this is of great importance, as they may be required for reconstructing stored files in the event of error or mishap;

(f) a detailed flow diagram of what takes place during each routine processing run;

(g) details of all tapes and discs in use, including their layout, labelling, storage and retention arrangements;

(h) copies of all the forms which output documents might take, and details of their subsequent sorting and checking;

(i) the auditor's comments on the effectiveness of the controls.

Once he has appraised the system the auditor will, as usual, decide on the amount of detailed checking to be undertaken.

8.3 The audit approach

There are two broad audit approaches—*round the machine* and *through the machine*.

Round the machine

The "round the machine" audit ignores the detailed procedures within the computer and concentrates on proving the initial input and checking its validity; that it is properly authorised and described; that it has been properly coded and correctly translated into computer input; and the finished reports.

The output from the computer will be compared exhaustively with the source documents and control totals as a check on accurate processing. This approach is familiar to auditors but, where the input information has been much changed during processing, it may be impossible to identify individual items of source data with the end product, unless unduly large samples are taken.

Again, where changes have been made in programs during the period under review, the results of the sample traced would not be applicable to all the data processed.

A reduction in the amount of "hard copy" printed out will also have the effect of making it difficult to trace a clear audit trail. As "management by exception" becomes more common, computer systems will tend to produce less and less visible trail, thus rendering the "round the machine" approach wholly impracticable.

Through the machine

The "through the machine" approach concentrates on proving the input data and includes a thorough examination of the processing procedures to:

    (a) ensure that:

        (i) all input is actually introduced into the computer;

        (ii) usual conditions in the input cannot cause misprocessing;

        (iii) the computer and operators cannot cause undetected irregularities in the final reports; and

    (b) study the effect of any alterations to programs.

This approach calls for a rather wider knowledge of data processing routines in general and of the characteristics of the particular type of equipment under audit.

Where application controls are based strongly in the user departments, the audit approach is fundamentally the same as in the case of manual systems. The detailed audit work, of necessity, must be adapted to the EDP system, chiefly because:

    (a) the volume of data involved will necessitate a considerable degree of batching, and hence greater reliance will have to be placed on total accounts;

    (b) considerable advantage is invariably taken of the facility of most computer configurations to print detailed reports covering a wide range of information, much of which is often found to be superfluous: print-outs of exception and rejection routines will, however, be of concern to the auditors;

    (c) standing data is held collectively on master files, and up-dating of this information (e.g. price catalogues, rates of pay, customer addresses, etc.) must be the subject of carefully controlled processing, unlike conventional systems, where amendments to standing data are often made manually as and when they arise.

The above features tend to have an exaggerated effect on audit procedures in cases where the EDP department participates in the implementation of internal controls, or where the major controls are included in the programs themselves, such as special exception reports and reasonableness checks.

Where the auditor is of the opinion that overall application controls are weak, greater emphasis must inevitably be placed on systems development and administrative controls. The use of specially designed questionnaires for EDP systems will in many instances be found to be invaluable. A typical example of such a questionnaire follows.

Illustration: specimen questionnaire for evaluating the system of internal control in a computer-based accounting system

Notes

(a) *This specimen deals with some of the principal questions that the auditor will wish to ask in evaluating the system of internal control in a computer-based accounting system.*

(b) *Most questionnaires include questions relating to the make, type and size of the computer and ancillary equipment. These questions do not normally affect the assessment of internal control and have been ignored in the specimen.*

(I) General controls—administrative

DIVISION OF RESPONSIBILITIES

	Tick as appropriate		
	Yes	No	Not applicable
1. Is the head of the computer department responsible to an appropriate senior official in the company?			
2. Is the following work carried out by separate sections or departments:			
(a) development;			
(b) data preparation;			
(c) computer operating;			
(d) file library;			
(e) control?			
3. Have organisation charts and job descriptions been prepared?			
4. Do the following basic restrictions apply:			
(a) access to documents containing original data is limited to the control section and data preparation staff;			
(b) computer department staff do not have access to any of the company's clerically maintained financial records;			
(c) access to the computer during production runs is limited to computer operators;			
(d) access to files and current programs is limited to computer operators and file librarian;			
(e) computer operators and programmers do not amend input data;			

	Tick as appropriate		
	Yes	No	Not applicable

    (f)   control section staff and the librarian do not have other duties within the computer department;

    (g)   computer department staff do not initiate transactions and changes to master files;

    (h)   unauthorised access to the computer room is forbidden? (*state how this is achieved*)

5.   Do the restrictions in question 4 apply at all times?

CONTROL OVER COMPUTER OPERATORS

6.   Is the work of computer operators controlled by the use of:

    (a)   administrative procedure manuals;

    (b)   work schedules;

    (c)   operating instructions for each program;

    (d)   computer usage reports (e.g. operating logs and console print-outs);

    (e)   minimum of two operators per shift;

    (f)   rotation of duties;

    (g)   any other method (*describe*)?

7.   Is all operator intervention recorded on the console print-out?

8.   Are computer usage reports, including console print-outs, reviewed by a responsible official?

FILE CONTROL: FILE STORAGE PROCEDURES

9.   Is a permanent record of files maintained (*describe*)?

10.   Are movements of files recorded (*describe*)?

11.   On what authority are files issued?

	Tick as appropriate		
	Yes	No	Not applicable

12. Are master copies of important files (e.g. programs and documentation) kept at outside locations?

FILE CONTROL: FILE IDENTIFICATION PROCEDURES

13. Are there adequate file identification procedures by use of (*describe*):

    (a) visible reference numbers;

    (b) protection rings;

    (c) header label checks on set up;

    (d) any other method (*describe*)?

FILE CONTROL: FILE RECONSTRUCTION PROCEDURES

14. Are there adequate reconstruction procedures by use of (*describe*):

    (a) the establishment of retention periods for files, input media and documents;

    (b) file generation systems;

    (c) copying of disc files at appropriate intervals;

    (d) any other method (*describe*)?

FIRE PRECAUTIONS AND STANDBY ARRANGEMENTS

15. (a) Are there adequate fire precautions (*describe*)?

    (b) Are there adequate standby arrangements for processing in case of equipment failure (*describe*)?

    (c) If so, are these arrangements regularly tested?

(II) General controls—systems development

STANDARD PROCEDURES AND DOCUMENTATION

16. Does the documentation produced for an application include the following:

    (a) narrative description of the system;

    (b) flow charts and block diagrams;

	Tick as appropriate		
	Yes	No	Not applicable

(c)   input and output data descriptions;

(d)   file record layouts;

(e)   control procedures;

(f)   program listing;

(g)   test data and results of testing;

(h)   output distribution instructions;

(i)   operating instructions;

(j)   procedure manuals?

17.   How does the system ensure that the documents in question 16 are:

(a)   properly prepared;

(b)   properly altered for system and program changes?

SYSTEMS AND PROGRAM TESTING

18.   Are programs adequately tested by means of:

(a)   desk checking;

(b)   processing with test data;

(c)   use of operating instructions without programmers being present;

(d)   any other method (*describe*)?

19.   Are systems adequately tested by means of:

(a)   processing test data;

(b)   pilot running;

(c)   parallel running;

(d)   involving the clerical and control procedures in all user departments concerned with the system;

(e)   any other method (*describe*)?

20.   Who evaluates the results of testing and what report is prepared?

	Tick as appropriate		
	Yes	No	Not applicable

FILE CONVERSION

21. Are the contents of master files checked before a system becomes operational (*describe*)?

ACCEPTANCE AND AUTHORISATION PROCEDURES

22. Is completed work reviewed and approved and further progress authorised by responsible officials in both user and computer departments at the following stages in development:

    (a) completion of outline systems report;

    (b) completion of systems specification;

    (c) completion of program and systems testing;

    (d) accepting new systems into operational use?

SYSTEMS AND PROGRAM AMENDMENTS

23. Do all changes to operational systems and programs require to be authorised?

24. Are all changes:

    (a) documented;

    (b) tested;

in the same manner as new systems and programs?

25. How does the system ensure that all changes are notified to all concerned including user departments?

(III) Application controls

A. Input controls

ESTABLISHMENT OF CONTROL

26. Is control for complete and accurate processing *first* established:

    (a) before the documents are batched by use of:

	Tick as appropriate		
	Yes	No	Not applicable

      (i) controls from prior procedures (*describe*);

      (ii) clerical sequence checks;

      (iii) retention of copies;

      (iv) any other method (*describe*)?

   (b) clerically after batching by use of:

      (i) control totals (*describe*);

      (ii) any other method (*describe*)?

   (c) by the computer by use of:

      (i) control totals (*describe*);

      (ii) sequence checks;

      (iii) any other method (*describe*)?

27.   What controls are established over data fields that contain significant reference data (e.g. check digit verification and matching with master file records)?

VERIFICATION OF CONVERSION

28.   (a) Is the conversion of data independently verified?

     (b) How does the system ensure that all errors are corrected?

AUTHORISATION OF INPUT

29.   Is all input data adequately authorised?

30.   If the documents are authorised before control is established, is the authorisation checked after control is established (i.e. to guard against the introduction of unauthorised documents)?

31.   Is the computer programmed to carry out significant authorising functions (e.g. limit and reasonableness checks)?

	Tick as appropriate		
	Yes	No	Not applicable

B. Processing controls

REJECTIONS

32.   Obtain a list of the reasons for which data can be rejected.

33.   What are the procedures for investigating, correcting and re-submitting the rejected data and recording the action taken?

34.   How does the system ensure that all rejections are promptly reprocessed (e.g. maintaining suspense control records, independent scrutiny of rejection listings)?

INTERMEDIATE PRINT-OUTS OF CONTROL DATA
DURING PROCESSING

35.   (a)   If control is established prior to processing is this control used to verify all (or some) accounting data on final output (*describe*)?

      (b)   If not, is it used to verify processing to a certain stage by checking intermediate output (e.g. input totals printed and checked on edit list) (*describe*)?

36.   If the control used to verify final output is established by the computer either on input or during processing:

      (a)   is it first printed out on intermediate output for subsequent clerical verification with final output (e.g. computer totals printed on edit list) (*describe*)?

      (b)   If so, are there adequate program controls to ensure the completeness and accuracy of the data at each stage of processing until printed out (*describe*)?

C. Output controls

GENERAL

37.   What is the print-out used for (e.g. to originate or support entries in the records for control purposes)?

	Tick as appropriate		
	Yes	No	Not applicable

38. Does the print-out contain sufficient information to:

   (a)   trace source documents to it;

   (b)   verify computer-generated calculations and totals?

OUTPUT DIRECTLY RELATED TO INPUT

39. (a)   Are the totals and details checked:

   (i) clerically with controls established prior to processing; or

   (ii) obtained from intermediate print-out?

   (b)   If not, are there adequate controls to ensure the completeness and accuracy of the data printed out (*describe*)?

OUTPUT INDIRECTLY RELATED TO INPUT

40. (a)   Are the totals and details checked clerically to external information (*describe*)?

   (b)   If not, are there adequate program controls to ensure the completeness and accuracy of the data printed out (*describe*)?

EXCEPTION REPORTS

41. Is the completeness of the report verified clerically? If so give details.

42. Are there adequate program controls to ensure the completeness (if applicable) and accuracy of the data printed out (*describe*)?

43. What are the procedures for investigating and taking action on exception report and recording the action taken?

DISTRIBUTION OF OUTPUT

44. If receipt of output is not controlled by the user department how does the system ensure it receives all print-outs intact?

	Tick as appropriate		
	Yes	No	Not applicable

D. Master file controls

AMENDMENTS TO STANDING DATA

45. (a) How are amendments authorised;

    (b) Is this authorisation adequate?

46. Are processed amendments checked in detail (*describe*)?

47. How does the system ensure that all amendments are processed:

    (a) by control totals (*describe*);

    (b) by retention of copies;

    (c) by any other method (*describe*)?

MAINTENANCE OF STANDING DATA

48. How, and how often, is standing data verified:

    (a) by print-outs of individual items for checking with external information;

    (b) by print-outs of totals for reconciliation with an independently or computer-established record of totals;

    (c) by establishment and reconciliation of totals by the computer;

    (d) by any other method (*describe*)?

MAINTENANCE OF TRANSACTION DATA

49. How, and how often, is transaction data on the file verified on a total basis:

    (a) by print-outs of totals for reconciliation with a record of independently or computer established totals;

    (b) by establishment and reconciliation of totals by the computer;

    (c) by any other method (*describe*)?

50. Are individual balances printed out and externally verified (*describe*)?

8.4   Manual recreation of data trail

Despite reluctance of management to provide the auditor with sufficient "hard copy" to create an audit trail, where he considers it necessary he should persist in his requests for this data. A certain amount of conventional detailed audit work is usually advisable, preferably on a rotation basis, simply to ensure that programmed controls are functioning correctly; detailed checking of this nature should not be avoided, even though it is occasionally met with derision on the part of the EDP staff. In any event, it may be necessary in some circumstances to recreate the audit trail manually (e.g. by casting sub-totals or checking postings) where no other method is possible.

8.5   Effect of management attitudes to EDP on the conduct of audit

The above considerations are of particular importance in the light of the shift away from the production of hard copy, towards the dominance of "management by exception" (the emphasis being on exception and rejection reporting). Inevitably, auditors are being forced to work in parallel with current processing, as opposed to "historical" auditing; apart from a dearth of visible print-out, accounting input media and source documents are retained for a limited period only after which they are either destroyed or re-sorted for an entirely different purpose.

The following brief quotation from a paper by the Chief Organising Accountant of the National Coal Board admirably assessed the position in which the auditor may find himself:

> "I suggest, however, that as EDP systems develop and fewer people become concerned with a larger volume of processing, much greater responsibility will lie on those who design the system, who determine what transactions should be recorded, and in what form, to provide the right information; they will have to decide, from the expressed needs of management, what information should be presented to permit of correct interpretation. There are obvious implications, both organisational and moral, in this concentration of planning power in the hands of a few.
>
> Clearly this is a matter of vital importance to which the auditor must apply his mind. Only when he is satisfied that the system is a true and proper one can he turn his attention to the remaining fields of least automatic operation. These are:
>
> (a)   the original recording of each transaction, with particular emphasis on standing transactions;
>
> (b)   keeping the system, and its periodic development, continually under review, to ensure that the right objectives are always being attained, and that the system is in fact operated according to the predetermined plan; and
>
> (c)   maintaining a close review over the information which the system is producing to see that it is being correctly interpreted and acted upon by management.
>
> While, therefore, there is this shift of emphasis away from concentration on the routine processing itself, there would not appear to be any particularly new problems arising for an auditor, in the sense of any new techniques to be learned.

Fundamental principles of internal check at each stage of an operation remain, whether these are automatic or carried out manually. There may, however, have to be some variation in techniques, and their particular application, to suit the new circumstances of processing. There are more possibilities for automatic control and arithmetical check within the computer program, for example.

It should also be borne in mind that a data processing centre is not, in popular terms, an 'electronic office', but is more akin to a factory. There is a planned production cycle, a flow-line of successive operations, and any ideas of these processes being interrupted or halted for audit purposes cannot be entertained. The continuous, and in some cases automatic, inspection and control processes in a factory with a production belt must be simulated by the auditor in applying his own techniques. Indeed, it may well be that the auditor, while preserving his independence, will neverthelesshave to subjugate his methods to the needs of the process, and may have to accept some disciplines in operation."

It should be pointed out, however, that there is no question of the auditor inevitably having to acquiesce in the process of eliminating visible print-out if he feels that it is in any way undermining the ability of the management itself to adequately fulfil its obligations. The auditor should therefore give consideration to the information which is regularly passed to management, in order to assess its adequacy for this purpose. A deficiency in this area represents one of the most fundamental breaches in the provisions of the Companies Act 1985, section 722, governing the requirements for accounting records and the form which they take.

8.6 Advantages of EDP systems to the auditor

The amount of detailed audit work is, as always, governed by the degree of confidence which the auditor has in the controls operated by his client, and in many ways EDP systems facilitate audit work on the final accounts through their ability to provide more immediate and effective control over company assets and liabilities.

For example, reconciliation between individual debtor and creditor account balances and total accounts may be effected monthly, weekly, or even daily, if desired and necessary. By the use of exception reporting, debts of doubtful value may be noted without delay and any necessary action taken immediately to recover the sums due.

Similar controls may be exercised over slow-moving and obsolete stocks and regular reconciliations between physical and book stocks facilitated. With many manual systems it is found that these controls and tests are applied only half-yearly, or even annually.

Computers may assist in the preparation of monthly or other interim accounts by the use of files of standing data, such as price lists and depreciation charges, allowances for taxation purposes etc. in respect of each item of plant, to be held on one such file.

8.7 Audit trails

Throughout this chapter references to "audit trails" have been made. Examples of such trails, which may easily be lost in modern EDP systems, may be observed in the (deliberately oversimplified) illustrations in Figs. 17 and 18.

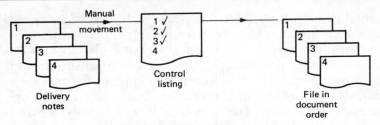

Fig. 17. *Audit trails—manual system.*

Under a system which carefully collates all input in this way, the trail may be followed through to the output stage, provided the print-out is sufficiently detailed and comprehensive, as shown in Fig. 19.

It can be seen that the computer processes the firm's official delivery notes and invoices (as well as a file copy of the order) from the source data originally batched and punched, as well as providing the day book, sales ledger entries, and a sales analysis which may be in any format desired.

Such a trail facilitates detailed checking from output back to input (or in both "directions" in the case of a depth test). Such a proliferation of print-out is not always available, however, in which event the trail may be totally lost.

8.8   Computer-assisted audit techniques (CAATs)

TEST DATA (TEST PACKS)

The auditor should consider the extent to which he can use the computer during his audit. He may devise a test set of transactions (known as an audit "test pack") covering every type of entry, including errors, which he can process through the computer, and compare the results obtained with pre-calculated answers to determine whether or not the programs contain the necessary controls.

The devised test pack input is converted into a machine-readable form, and then processed by normal means, using existing programs. Since this processing is executed by the operators, according to their standing instructions, it is necessary for the auditor (who should actually observe the processing) to be reasonably familiar with the work of the operatives. He should be capable of ascertaining whether the "edit" checks are operating as intended, and of interpreting error reports arising from the deliberate input of invalid data. After processing, the results will be compared with his solutions, already determined.

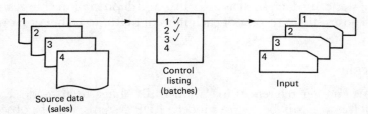

Fig. 18. *Audit trails—EDP system.*

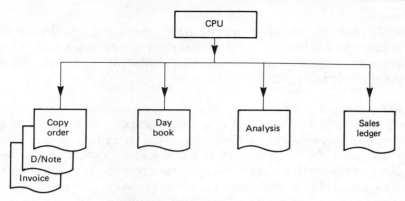

Fig. 19. *Audit trails—output stage.*

Disadvantages of test-packs

Test-packs have the disadvantage of giving an indication of correct or incorrect functioning of controls *only at the time of the test,* and results cannot be regarded by the auditor as applicable to every computer run, past and future. Notorious cases have been publicised in which operators deliberately caused the machine to by-pass certain major control routines included in the program, merely in order to save time! (Presumably, the auditors were unaware of the by-pass facility, also included in the program.) It will thus be appreciated that these audit tests must be supplemented by other tests, particularly on clerical and administrative controls. The use of a test pack is shown in Fig. 20.

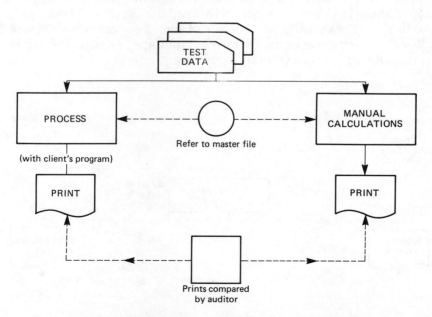

Fig. 20. *Computer-assisted auditing—use of a test pack.*

Special print-outs

The auditor may request that print-outs be made from the magnetic tape files so that he may compare detailed entries with documents or control totals. The nominal ledger, if kept on magnetic tape, should be printed out to enable the auditor to undertake detailed checking.

Computer audit software

Another way in which the auditor may use the computer is by the use of specially designed computer audit programs. Sometimes these file interrogation programs are supplied as "packages" by the manufacturers, and sometimes they are purpose written. Such programs can be used as a check on application controls by selecting individual transactions for detailed tests, and may thus be conveniently incorporated in statistical sampling schemes. Both "transaction" data and "standing" data may be tested in this way, the auditor taking full advantage of the computer's ability to read large files of data at great speed.

Exceptional items may be singled out by the auditor's program, e.g. by reading a current customer file and printing exception reports on all balances over, say, £500, and all balances outstanding for more than three months.

In view of the fact that the use of audit progams will expend valuable computer time, the auditor will not infrequently encounter a reluctance on the part of the management and the EDP department to co-operate with him in implementing them. Furthermore, the insertion of additional programs into an already "tight" schedule may cause normal processing runs to be delayed. It is therefore preferable that computer audit programs should be built into the normal programs wherever possible, preferably when the latter are being written. In any event, relatively few auditors possess the necessary skill to write their own computer programs, and they are thus dependent for this function upon the client's own programming staff, unless use is made of those packages now generally available, such as "Auditape", "Audit-thru", "Audit-find", "Ask 360", etc. One use of such a program is shown in Fig. 21.

The following description of the Deloitte's "Auditape" system explains the nature and usefulness of such computer audit programs:

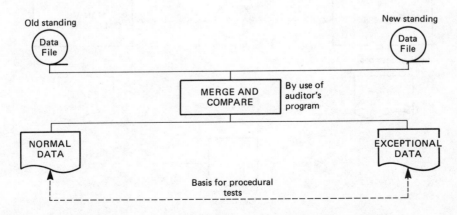

Fig. 21. *Computer-assisted auditing—use of a program package.*

ILLUSTRATION: THE AUDITAPE SYSTEM

1. The Auditape System is a set of general purpose computer programs designed primarily for professional auditors, but also useful for management or internal audit purposes.

2. Auditape can be used by persons who are not computer specialists, after a brief amount of instruction. It has been developed by practising accountants and its operation is entirely independent of client's programs and programmers.

3. Auditape comprises:

    (a) programs in machine language form on a reel of magnetic tape: no compilation is required prior to running;

    (b) a manual which describes the Auditape System in detail;

    (c) blank specification sheets by means of which the user enters the parameters for each particular application: the entering of those sheets requires no programming or specialist knowledge;

    (d) instruction sheets for computer operators which, together with messages printed out during processing, provide all instructions necessary for operating Auditape.

4. The Auditape System is being continually expanded and at present is available for the following computers:

    (a) Honeywell 200 series: ½″ tape systems;

    (b) IBM 1400 series: tape systems;

    (c) IBM S/360: tape and disc systems;

    (d) ICL 1900 series: tape and disc systems;

    (e) ICL Systems 4: tape and disc systems;

5. The programs (called routines) are continually being improved and added to and presently comprise the following:

    (a) *Edit:* Re-formats the file to be interrogated into Auditape format, establishes control totals (in certain cases this function is performed by a manufacturer's utility). All other routines then work on Auditape format files.

    (b) *Include/Exclude:* Enables selection of records with fields equal to, greater than, or less than specified identifiers. Also, if required, accumulates sub-totals on two fields for records with specified identifiers.

    (c) *Summarise:* Summarises quantitative fields of records with a common identifier (e.g. converts open-item ledger to a balance ledger). Option to select only positive or negative quantities and to check sequence of identifiers.

    (d) *Mathematical:* Performs addition, subtraction, multiplication or division of any one field against another field or a specified constant. Some versions permit performance of ten mathematical operations or logical comparisons in one pass.

(e) *Audit sample selection:* Selects a statistically based numeric or monetary random sample after stratifying the population. The sampling plan was specifically designed for use by professional auditors and is extensively used in manual as well as computer form.

(f) *Audit sample evaluation:* Evaluates the results of checks made on samples selected by the "Audit sample selection" routine.

(g) *Match/Merge:* Permits matching or merging of records from two separate files.

(h) *Insert:* Permits insertion of data from one file into specified fields of records in another file.

(i) *Print/Punch:* Produces printed output file of Auditape records with the fields in any desired order and with optional narrative column headings. Punched card output can also be obtained.

6. The output from the edit routine and the input and output of every other routine is a file of Auditape format records.

7. The cards punched from the specification sheets are validated before processing begins and printed in an expanded form. If errors are found the corrective action required is displayed on the printer.

8. Control totals of all quantitative fields and a record count are printed at the end of every routine and data assigned to one particular field is totalled in both positive and negative amounts.

9. The routines can be assembled in any order any number of times in one application. By use of this "building block" principle the Auditape System has a considerable versatility and can achieve most of the objectives that could be achieved by a specially written program.

10. Auditape has been used extensively throughout the world and among the applications for which it has been used in the UK are:

(a) arithmetical calculations, such as verifying costs and calculations of stock, debtors etc.;

(b) special analyses, such as analysis of debtors for doubtful debt provisions;

(c) selection of statistically based samples for audit tests on stock, debtors, work in progress, contract costs, purchase invoices;

(d) comparisons for audit purposes, e.g. stock usage against balances for obsolescence provisions.

9.0   THE CLIENT'S USE OF A SERVICE BUREAU

9.1   Audit approach

Concern for security is sometimes caused where the client is using the facilities of a computer service bureau in cases where many of the controls are at the bureau and therefore not under the client's direct supervision. It is most important that this consideration should be given due weight at the time the system is being designed, preferably in consultation with the internal auditor, so that the minimum reliance requires to be placed upon the controls at the bureau.

In many ways, however, audit problems are lessened when processing is executed by a bureau. Managements often wish to reduce the "gap" between the bureau and themselves by requesting more detailed print-out, and input data is frequently retained for a longer period. If the auditor is able to demonstrate to the management that the evidence required for audit purposes is necessary for the purposes of management control and general security, little difficulty will be experienced in obtaining the necessary information. Hence, in practice it is rare for bureau-oriented systems to be computer controlled.

9.2   Investigating the bureau

This problem is best understood by reference to the following past examination question:

"A client has decided to utilise the facilities available from a local computer bureau. The latter states that its own auditors satisfy themselves as to the standards maintained at the bureau so that users' auditors can thus confine their attention solely to the various controls operational in the offices of those using the service. You are asked:

(a)   to state if you consider this to be a satisfactory position, and, if not, to indicate those areas in the bureau itself to which you would pay attention as auditor to your client; and

(b)   to specify the controls that you would require to be instituted at your client's office so that you can rely on achieving a satisfactory audit 'around the computer'."

The main questions are: To what extent should the auditor of the user company transfer his attention to the bureau organisation itself? Is he entitled to enquire into its workings? What sort of reception will he get?

In fact, the examination question under discussion does not clearly state whether the critical transfer of data processing to the bureau is still being arranged, or whether the system has been operational for some time. In the former case, any points raised by the auditor are still highly relevant, and total submission to the argument set out in the opening paragraph of the question would represent a fair dereliction of his duty.

Quite apart from the auditor's natural concern with security at the bureau, the client's management would normally be equally anxious to establish that bureau employees were acting responsibly in relation to the client's data and that all purported controls are in fact operational. In practice, the bureau will take full responsibility for hiring, training and supervising the personnel who program and operate the system.

The user seldom has any voice in such matters; he is usually uninformed about the qualifications of bureau staff and has contact only with designated liaison personnel.

9.3   Bureau security

Users who are particularly sensitive about security measures are at liberty to furnish the bureau with code numbers instead of names—for say, customers or employees. Most users, however, are content to satisfy themselves as to the reliability of the bureau selected by pursuing appropriate investigations, and by ensuring its adherence to recognised codes of conduct, such as operate for all members of the CSA (Computer Services Association). If the security of the data is sufficiently critical, however, the bureau will normally appreciate the point and will co-operate, by special arrangements, allowing the user to:

(a) deliver input data in person;

(b) observe all processing;

(c) at completion, withdraw all transaction and master-file data from the bureau.

This would operate in extreme cases only. In normal situations, client and auditor would be more concerned with arrangements at the bureau for master-file reconstruction in the event of loss or destruction. The usual questions would relate to the use of fireproof vaults, off-premises storage, temperature, and controls over the other appropriate atmospheric constraints. At the same time, queries should be raised in connection with back-up facilities—especially in cases where the bureau is itself using the off-shift computer time of other organisations.

These, rather than problems of loss of trail, arise when bureaux are used, since visible; data is generally more abundant than in the case of in-house computer processing. It is, after all, the legal responsibility of the client's management (under section 722 of the Companies Act 1985) to retain adequate records of its own for reconstruction in the event of a bureau failure.

9.4   The contract with the bureau

It is worth while for the auditor to look carefully at the contract which his client is about to sign, with special reference to legal liability. If, for instance, a member of the user staff (albeit unwittingly) causes a service disruption at the bureau as a result of which other bureau users suffer loss, the contract should indemnify the first user against any claims arising. Conversely, it should be seen that the agreed upper limit of the bureau's liability to the user in respect of service or security failures will provide commensurate compensation.

Despite their independent attitude most bureaux, especially in these competitive times, will go a long way to meet user control requirements, even where the bureau regards them as mildly neurotic. In general terms, no exception could be taken to enquiries from the user on:

(a) security provisions over the client's data and files, and the effectiveness of supervision;

(b) provisions for back-up and reconstruction;

    (c) bureau procedures for handling special conditions such as:

        (i) "unmatched" transactions (i.e. no record on the master file);

        (ii) control total (or count) inconsistencies;

        (iii) error correction at bureau.

9.5 Third party reviewers

The controls at computer bureaux, in which the auditor will be interested, are likely to be those relating to the computer installation ("general controls") but may include specific controls over individual applications ("application controls") such as controls built into the computer programs (e.g. feasibility or limit checks) and controls over transactions applied by staff of the bureau (e.g. control of cheque stationery).

Where the auditor wishes to evaluate and test the controls at a bureau and permission is obtained, there appears to be two options available:

(a) a separate examination of controls by the auditors of each of the bureau's clients;

(b) an examination of controls by a third party reviewer (probably another firm of auditors) and issue of a report which can be made available to auditors of each of the bureau's clients.

The first option may meet with some opposition from the bureau since it may understandably be alarmed at the prospect of each of its client's auditors performing separate examinations of its controls.

The second option also has some problems:

(a) a particular auditor may be unwilling to place reliance on an examination of controls commissioned by the computer bureau;

(b) the interaction between the general controls exercised by the bureau and the application controls exercised by the client may be unclear;

(c) it is often the case that different users place varying degrss of reliance on certain controls and hence their auditors need to gain different levels of knowledge about these controls.

The auditor may conclude that he can rely on an examination by a third party reviewer if he is satisfied that all the procedures which he himself would have wished to perform have indeed been carried out and with the same level of expertise as he would have applied. This is likely to involve consultations with the third party reviewer, where the evidence provided by him is, in the auditor's opinion, insufficient for his particular purpose. Remember that the bureau is the client of the third party reviewer and as such must give permission before a consultation can take place.

Finally, it is important in all cases for the auditor to consider the circumstances of the use of the computer bureau's services and the extent to which the control procedures within the computer bureau and at the client are comprehensive. Where the auditor is unable to rely on an examination by a third party reviewer and is not granted permission to perform his own examination of the controls at the bureau, he may seek to rely on the application controls exercised by his client. Alternatively, he may seek to carry out additional substantive testing.

9.6 Controls at client

The establishment of major controls at the client's office, on the other hand, may best be summarised as in Table 12.

Table 12. Summary of major control procedures

No.	Control area	Example of control	Special considerations
1	Transmission of data to bureau	(a) Document count (b) Transaction count (c) Control totals, e.g. batched, sterling totals	Additional controls needed if data conversion is performed by client
2	Master-file amendments	(a) Routine print-out of all changes (b) Control count of master records (c) Control totals of all master-file contents (d) Control over pre-numbered amendment/input slips	Regular file reviews should include period print-outs of selected data. Special file analysis programs should be used
3	Error correction routines and re-submissions	(a) Planned procedures at user and bureau locations for identifying input errors (b) Programs to provide detailed error print-out, identifying all errors not detected at input (c) Client-controlled error log (d) Correction and review of re-submissions	Re-submissions should be given prior approval by liaison personnel at client's after investigation into cause
4	Output	(a) Approved distribution list (b) Surprise test packs for control purposes (c) Control over action on exception reports (d) Periodic print-outs, e.g. ledger balances or plant schedules	Controls should ensure that all exception reports are received. Auditor should be invited to participate in planning and execution of test pack, with facility to compile his own limited test data

No.	Control area	Example of control	Special considerations
5	Security and reconstruction	(a) Microfilming of source documents transmitted to bureau (b) Provision by client for file construction on basis of "worst case" loss (c) Ensure bureau capability for routine reconstruction (d) Security supervision over all client files retained at bureau	Assurances should be periodically obtained from bureau liaison personnel in connection with (c) and (d), and arranging for periodic reconstruction test checks

In connection with (1), data transmission, it should be remembered that these days data can be sent in a variety of forms—source documents, punched cards, punched paper tapes, magnetic tapes, drums, discs, or stripes. Transport may be by vehicle, by hand or by British Telecom telephone lines. The important thing is to establish controls at the very point where the bureau takes over the responsibility for the data.

Since the client has no physical control over the master files, control over amendments and security of these files is essential. As indicated under (2) all master-file amendments should be printed out and carefully checked, particularly to ensure that only those properly authorised have been processed. The importance of this will be readily appreciated in situations where the computer itself originates several major control routines within the programs—such as stock availability or credit checks.

9.7 The bureau ICQ

Although most firms who regularly undertake computer audits make full use of questionnaires specially designed for the purpose, a few of these forms have a section which is exclusively concerned with the assessment of control where a service bureau is processing the data. Such questionnaires usefully highlight the major control criteria referred to above, as demonstrated in the following questionnaire extract:

Questionnaire for assessment of controls over processing performed by an independent bureau

	Yes	No	Ref. to weakness letter re "no" answers

A—GENERAL

1. Name, address and telephone number of independent bureau:

2. Name and title of bureau personnel responsible for liaison over client's work:

	Yes	No	Ref. to weakness letter re"no" answers
3. Name and title of client personnel responsible for liaison with service bureau:			
4. Major computer equipment in use at service bureau:			
5. Details of client applications being processed at bureau:			
(a) number:			
(b) application:			
(c) frequency:			
(d) input preparation client/ bureau:			
B—REVIEW OF OPERATIONS OF SERVICE BUREAU 6. Do adequate provisions exist at the service bureau for back-up in case of equipment failure?			
7. Are client bank accounts and monthly charge accounts with suppliers inaccessible to bureau personnel?			
8. Does security over client records at service bureau appear adequate?			
9. Does service centre have adequate insurance to protect client against substantial loss (e.g. lost data, files, processing errors)?			
C—INPUT CONTROLS 10. Is the original (or a copy) of each source document transmitted to the bureau retained by client?			
11. Are controls established over all data sent for processing? (*indicate control below*)			

	Yes	No	Ref. to weakness letter re "no" answers

Sequential numbering of documents

Transaction count

Document count

Control totals (*provide list*)

Other (*specify*)

12. Do edit controls in program appear adequate to detect incorrect input data?

13. Does client reconcile his input control figures with control figures furnished by the bureau prior to processing?

14. Is there a listing of input data for purposes of identifying transactions processed by the service bureau?

D—ERROR CORRECTION AND RE-SUBMISSION CONTROLS

15. Does error print-out identify all errors?

16. Does client maintain log of all errors?

17. Does client have adequate procedures for controlling correction and re-submission?

18. Do service bureau and client error procedures appear adequate for handling:

    (a) unmatched transactions?

    (b) control total or count inconsistencies?

E—OUTPUT CONTROLS

19. Are client procedures adequate for reviewing and testing output prior to distribution?

	Yes	No	Ref. to weakness letter re"no" answers
20. Does output from bureau include details of input controls data (e.g. sterling batch totals)?			
21. Does client maintain adequate procedures for controlling distribution of output?			
F—CONTROL OVER MASTER-FILE AMENDMENTS			
22. Is a control print-out provided by the bureau detailing all master-file changes?			
23. Does bureau provide a master-file control record count to enable client to check for loss or non-processing of master-file records?			
24. Does client regularly check and reconcile this control figure?			
25. Is there provision for ledger and other major balances to be printed out at the ad hoc request of client or auditor?			
26. Does bureau have adequate provision for file reconstruction?			
27. Has client made adequate provision for "worst case" file reconstruction, e.g. if all files at service centre are destroyed?			
28. Does client have complete documentation and copy of source programs for all programs owned by him (i.e. written specifically for client for which full fee has been paid)?			

9.8 Conclusion

Two final reminders about bureau processing situations:

(a) the client will be one of many companies using the bureau, and a number of the others will be larger, and hence more important to the bureau; it could therefore prove to be a formidable task to gain maximum co-operation from the bureau staff;

(b) the client's end of the data processing system may appear straightforward enough—but it is worth remembering that operations at the bureau may be exceedingly complex.

The audit approach described above is consistent with contemporary standards of investigation, and a less conscientious attitude is fraught with risks. The scale of computer frauds today is difficult to assess objectively, since it is impossible to know whether those that are brought to light and publicised represent more or less than the very small tip of a substantial iceberg.

10.0 AUDIT PROBLEMS ARISING FROM THE USE OF REMOTE TERMINALS

10.1 Introduction

Technical innovations have increased the use of remote terminals, and these have a widespread application in a number of commercial organisations. Examples include:

(a) airline bookings terminals;

(b) bank cash-dispenser/terminals.

Many other examples abound, but in each case the chief audit problem arises from the fact that master files held in the central computer store (invariably on disc because of access speed and storage capacity) may be both read and updated by remote terminal without an adequate audit trail or, in some cases, any record, remaining. Information from branches can be keyed in on a daily or weekly basis through remote terminals. Such data may relate to current purchases, sales or stock movements.

Necessary precautions should therefore be made to ensure that these terminals can be used in a controlled way by authorised personnel only.

10.2 Security techniques

In view of the risks outlined above, a number of recognised techniques have come into general operation in order to control the use of terminals for input purposes. The most important of these techniques include the following:

(a) hardware constraints, e.g. necessitating the use of a key to engage the terminal, or placing the terminal in a location to which access is carefully restricted;

(b) the allocation of identification numbers to authorised terminal operators, with or without the use of passwords: these are checked by the mainframe computer against stored tables of authorised numbers and passwords.

(c) using operator characteristics such as fingerprints, width of fingers, width of hand, etc., as a means of identification by the mainframe computer: this identification may easily be carried out by special devices at the terminal;

(d) restricting the access to particular programs or master files held in the mainframe computer to designated terminals: this arrangement may be combined with those indicated above;

(e) in top-security systems, the authority to allocate authorities such as those indicated above (i.e. determination of passwords, nominating selected terminals) will *itself* be restricted to senior personnel other than intended users;

(f) a special file may be maintained in the central processor which records every occasion on which access is made by particular terminals and operators to central programs and files: this log will be printed out at regular intervals, e.g. the end of each day, or on request by personnel with appropriate authority.

10.3   Real-time systems

In some computer applications a buffer store of input data will be held by the central processor prior to accessing the master files; in such cases input from remote terminals may be checked by special scanning programs before main processing commences.

However, in real-time systems action at the terminal causes an immediate response in the central processor, whenever the terminal is on-line. Security against unauthorised input and access outlined in section 10.2 above is therefore even more important in real-time systems because:

(a) the effect of the input (whether keyed in on the keyboard typewriter or via punch cards, paper tape, etc.) instantaneously updates the files held in the processor;

(b) edit-checks on the input are likely to be under the control of the terminal operator.

11.0   THE AUDIT IMPACT OF MINI-COMPUTERS

The majority of large audit firms now employ staff whose abilities are commensurate with the tasks imposed by large-scale computer processing. On the other hand, the vast majority of smaller audit firms are unprepared for the EDP revolution, and it is they who are most likely to feel the repercussions of their ignorance of modern methods of data processing.

I say this advisedly, particularly in view of the advent of mini-computers which are now well within the financial reach of all but the smallest of business entities. Many auditors erroneously regard these streamlined little objects as little more than advanced forms of book-keeping machines, but nothing could be further from the truth; they are in every sense computers. Indeed, it could almost be said that their particular attributes render them potentially far more dangerous, from the security viewpoint, than their large mainframe counterparts. These attributes include:

(a) flexibility in application;

(b) adaptability through simple programming;

(c) extremely robust hardware, so that little caution is necessary on the matters of atmospheric sensitivity (which, in practice, usually means that the more important fire and flood precautions, standby arrangements, etc., are equally ignored—no smoking restrictions, for example);

(d) ease of input access, often by terminal;

(e) few technical staff requirements;

(f) visual display unit (VDU) output screens.

As a result, the mini-computer installation is often viewed by staff as being an "open house", and all and sundry "get in on the EDP act". So simple is its operation that it could, for an entire processing run, remain under the sole control of one person—an obvious security hazard. Such matters as controlled access, physical precautions, secrecy of output, authorisation of program changes, logging of use, care of files and the innumerable other security measures, as vital in a mini-computer establishment as in any other, become secondary considerations and eventually fade entirely. That is, of course, until such neglect results in the inadvertent destruction of unsupported master files, or a power failure reveals the deficiency of standby facilities, to mention but two of a range of untoward consequences, of varying degrees of seriousness for the entity concerned. A mini-computer can all too easily result in a maxi-disaster!

In such a case it may prove difficult for the auditor, having continuously acquiesced in what amounts to a flagrant disregard for basic internal control criteria, to establish his own freedom from culpability in the matter, especially if outside losses result. In short, if this section sounds like a warning, it is meant to. Liability can no longer be regarded purely in the light of the basic statutory reporting duty, and data processing methods do not alter principles of law or established standards of professional competence.

12.0   FUTURE DEVELOPMENTS

It is generally observable that the unprecedented technological strides in hardware development over the past twenty years are now likely to be transferred to the field of software, particularly in the form of:

(a) versatile manufacturer's "packages" (programs for particular applications, e.g. stock control) which may be purchased together with the computer, or at any later stage; and

(b) high-level programming languages, the most sophisticated of which are almost indistinguishable from straightforward English, which enable users to write their own programs after a short training period: this is made possible by the use of special "compiler" programs, which, by being run together with the high-level language programs (which are held on punched cards or paper tape or other machine-sensitive device), translate the latter into machine language (binary).

In America, computer audit programs are being mass-produced as packages, and are designed to cover a wide range of normal audit testing routines.

Major advances are also to be witnessed in the efficiency and ingenuity of computer peripherals. Some of these carry implications which auditors will not be able to ignore, e.g. "on-line" cathode ray output, which provide virtually instantaneous output responses to input keyed in. The general development in on-line, "real-time" configurations is bound to cause the auditor to carry out much of his work in parallel with actual processing.

13.0   SUMMARY OF INTERNAL CONTROL AREAS

Several references have been made, throughout this chapter to specific areas of internal control. Students may therefore find it helpful to refer to Fig. 22, which summarises all the control divisions already discussed.

14.0   CONCLUSIONS

Figs 23 and 24 emphasise the essential differences in the control structures of manual and EDP systems respectively, from the point of view of:

    (a) the nature of controls; and

    (b) the location of controls:

The overriding message, implicit throughout this chapter, is that the auditor's conventional attitudes require a radical reassessment when faced with data processing by computer. The changes required apply to virtually the whole of the audit procedures, despite the fact that the overall objectives remain identical, i.e. to assess and report on the view presented by the accountants which purport to reflect the results of business activities, during the period under review.

With EDP, the *means* whereby the accounting results are finally determined are totally different from the means traditionally utilised in manual (or even machine-accounting) systems. Consequently, the internal controls which are required in EDP systems are correspondingly different, and will appear unfamiliar to those trained to assess systems on the basis of conventional criteria.

15.0   MICROFILMING THE RECORDS

The Companies Act 1985, section 722, permits accounting records to be in any form, but specifies that where they are not in the form of bound books there must be adequate precautions in force to prevent destruction or falsification, and to facilitate its discovery.

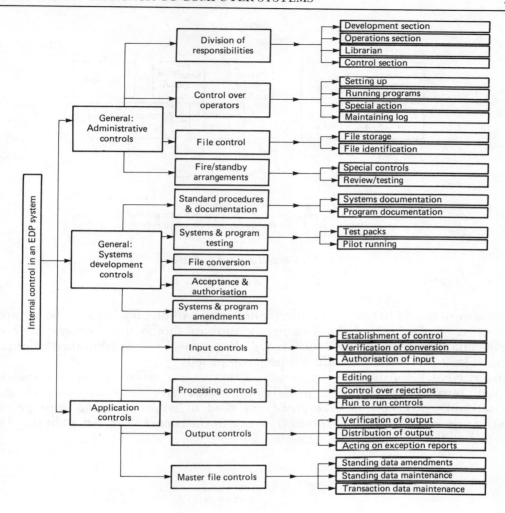

Fig. 22. *EDP systems—internal control areas.*

As a result of the increased cost of storage and the Companies Act 1985, a number of companies have turned to the use of microfilm for storing their accounting records.

15.1 Internally and externally generated documents

There are basically two different categories of documents—*internally* generated documents, e.g. copy sales invoices, goods inwards notes, etc. and those *externally* generated, e.g. purchase invoices. Generally speaking microfilm copies of internally generated documents are satisfactory evidence for audit purposes—subject, of course, to the adequacy of the controls in force. It is felt, however, that no matter how good the control procedures relating to externally generated documents, the possibility of their being altered does exist and that it would be extremely difficult, if not impossible, to detect an alteration from an examination of a microfilm copy. (There is also the

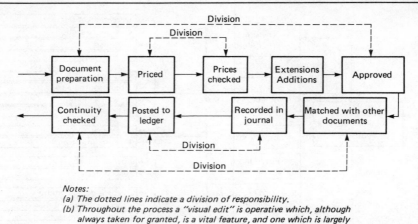

Notes:
(a) The dotted lines indicate a division of responsibility.
(b) Throughout the process a "visual edit" is operative which, although always taken for granted, is a vital feature, and one which is largely lost in EDP systems.

Fig. 23. *Manual system controls.*

possibility of failure to microfilm information which might, for instance, be printed or written on the back of the document.) Auditors should therefore give serious consideration to insisting that "third party" documents be retained in their original form, at least until after the audit has been completed.

In any event, before he can even consider accepting microfilm copies of documents for audit purposes, the auditor must satisfy himself as to the internal control over the microfilming process. *These controls will need to ensure that the appropriate information is recorded at the correct time and in the correct form.* An audit may be required on the microfilm process itself.

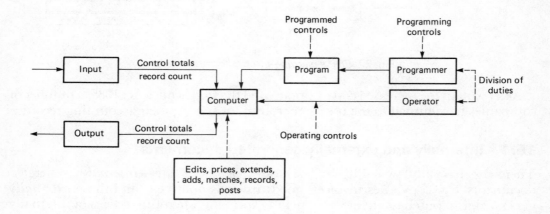

Note
"Visual editing" is virtually limited to the left-hand side of the diagram (original input and final output). It is difficult, if not impossible, to directly monitor the activities on the right of the diagram.

Fig. 24. *EDP system control*

15.2 Microfilm controls

These are similar to controls instituted over computer input and processing, and would be expected to include the following additional matters:

(a) A policy should be formally recorded and approved by senior management, setting out the documents, which may be destroyed. All such destructions should be properly authorised in accordance with this policy.

(b) It is important for audit purposes that the company should arrange for the microfilming to be done under adequate supervision (for example by the internal audit department or other responsible official independent of the microfilming personnel) and the external auditors should carry out such tests of the above procedures as they consider necessary.

(c) Special registers should be maintained, using batch numbers to record and control the documents microfilmed and destroyed respectively.

(d) Indexing and the retrieval controls should ensure that the company is able to refer quickly and easily to any microfilms of documents.

(e) A complete set of back-up films should be maintained at a different location from that of the originals.

In order that the auditors may have access to the microfilm records, a reader would have to be made constantly available to them during the audit.

15.3 Audit planning

It is essential that auditors liaise with their clients before a microfilm system is installed, otherwise they may find, too late, that essential records have been destroyed. It is also important that no records should be destroyed before the audit report is signed, but should clients consider this necessary, it should take place only after discussion with the auditors, and this may necessitate audit visits on a more regular basis.

PROGRESS TEST 11

1. Distinguish between general controls and application controls. (4.1)

2. What is the principal method of file retention where magnetic tape is in use? (5.4)

3. List four methods by which input could be controlled clerically. (7.1)

4. What do you understand by reasonableness checks? (7.5(c))

5. Distinguish between controls round the machine and through the machine. (8.3)

6. List the principal CAATs. (8.8)

7. How may access to terminals be controlled? (10.2)

CHAPTER TWELVE
Audit Management

Note

From time to time questions appear in the professional examinations on problems of controlling the audit from the point of view of the auditing firm itself. In this context students will find the Guidelines (on "planning" and "controlling") to the Operational Standard of particular benefit.

1.0   OBJECTIVES OF AUDIT MANAGEMENT

The effective management of the audit involves three objectives:

    (a) ensuring that the auditing practice operates profitably;

    (b) providing a high level of service to clients, and

    (c) taking all reasonable steps towards avoiding liability.

These objectives which are sometimes in mutual opposition are usually achieved in two ways:

    (a) by effective audit planning; and

    (b) by instituting procedures for quality control.

2.0   AUDIT PLANNING

Planning the audit, especially a large audit, involves close liaison with the client company's financial director and his staff. As much of the work as possible should be completed at the interim stage, leaving the final audit clear for such matters as verification of assets and liabilities, the final review of the accounts and checks that disclosure requirements have been complied with.

Where joint audits are undertaken, planning the allocation of work between the two firms ought to take place several months before it is due to be performed. Similarly, the external auditors should be in close touch with the internal audit staff in order to avoid unnecessary overlap of work and at the same time to ensure that, between them, all detailed audit procedures are satisfactorily completed.

Most client companies have a detailed programme of work leading up to the final preparation of their annual accounts, and the auditor should be provided with the details of this programme for his own purposes. This is especially useful in connection with routine matters such as:

    (a) stock verification;

    (b) cash count;

    (c) securities count;

    (d) debtor circularisation.

By careful planning at all stages of the audit, the auditing firm can ensure, as far as possible, *the availability of the right number of each grade of staff required on the audit team, at every stage of the audit.*

3.0 QUALITY CONTROL PROCEDURES

3.1 Standardisation of documentation

The detailed content of all audit files should, as far as possible, be predetermined, and their completion ensured by the use of standard indices. The permanent file, for example, will include details of:

    (a) the history and nature of the business;

    (b) copies of the memorandum and articles;

    (c) sets of previous accounts for two or three years;

    (d) extracts of essential contents of documents such as long-term contracts, leases, insurance policies and title deeds;

    (e) extracts from previous years' accounts indicating the trend of business, divisional results, key ratios, etc.;

    (f) a copy of the original letter of engagement and any amendment thereto.

It is even more important that the current audit file should be complete and, for the duration of the audit in question, certain documents of a permanent nature (e.g. internal control questionnaire) will be transferred to the current file.

The standard content of the current file (including documents effectively in use for longer than one audit period) should be incorporated in the standard index, and the following documents will obviously be included:

    (a) current draft accounts and supporting schedules;

    (b) the detailed audit programme;

(c)   the internal control questionnaire (ICQ);

(d)   the internal control evaluation (ICE);

(e)   flow-diagrams;

(f)   letters of weakness (more than one may be issued during the audit);

(g)   the letter of representation;

(h)   standard confirmations from:

(i)   the bank, re all account balances and securities held for safe security;

(ii)   finance companies and others re loans/mortgages;

(iii)   warehouses/agents, re goods held at docks awaiting clearance or for re-export, goods held by others on a sale or return basis and goods held by consignees;

(iv)   members of staff re loans;

(v)   foreign agents and associated firms, re client assets held abroad;

(vi)   circularisation of debtors;

(i)   checklists of:

(i)   Companies Act requirements—including 1985 Act formats, details of directors' emoluments, loans to officers, quasi-loans, credit transactions and material interests of directors in contracts (CA 1985); proper accounting records;

(ii)   SSAPs (noting particularly the date from which operative);

(iii)   Stock Exchange requirements for listed companies;

(iv)   contents of the directors' report;

(v)   requirements under other statutes and regulations relating to, e.g., building societies, friendly societies, solicitors, etc.

One of the most important checklists is that which relates to the audit report itself, of which the following is a specimen:

Technical content

	Yes	No	Not applicable
(a) Have all the explanations and information necessary for the purposes of the audit been obtained—with particular reference to certificates and confirmations from third parties, including subsidiary auditors?			
(b) Have proper accounting records been kept and proper returns received from any branches not visited?			

	Yes	No	Not applicable
(c) Are the accounts in agreement with the records and returns?			
(d) Do the accounts give a *true* view of the result for the period and the state of affairs at the balance sheet date?			
(e) Do the accounts give not only a true but also a *fair* view?			
(f) Do the accounts comply with the requirements of the Companies Act 1985?			
(g) Are details of the following items included in the audit report to the extent that they are not properly disclosed in the accounts:			
(i) directors' emoluments, pensions, and compensation for loss of office?			
(ii) loans and quasi-loans to officers?			
(iii) chairman's emoluments?			
(iv) emoluments of highest paid director (other than chairman)?			
(v) directors' emoluments waived?			
(vi) the number of directors and employees whose emoluments fall within specified statutory bands?			
(vii) material contracts and other transactions with directors required to be disclosed under CA 1985?			
(h) Where appropriate, do the group accounts show a true and fair view of the group position and comply with the requirements of the Companies Act 1985?			
(i) Where appropriate, does the audit report include any qualifications contained in the reports of subsidiary auditors to the extent that the qualifications are material in the context of the group accounts as a whole?			
(j) Have questionnaires, sent to subsidiary auditors, been duly completed and returned to our satisfaction?			

	Yes	No	Not applicable

(k) Do the accounts include a funds statement which complies with SSAP 10?

(l) If answer to (k) is "no" and turnover is greater than £25,000, have we included a suitable qualification?

(m) Does the audit report refer, in appropriate terms, to all significant departures from other Accounting Standards?

(n) Does the drafting of our audit report accord with the requirements of the 1980 Auditing Standards?

(o) Have the accounts been approved and signed by the directors before the audit report is signed?

(p) Have all outstanding queries been satisfactorily resolved?

(q) Have we, in the conduct of our audit and the drafting of our report, complied with the 1980 Auditing Standards?

(r) Have we examined the directors' report under the Companies Act 1985, s. 237, and if so are we satisfied that it is consistent with financial statements? If not, have we disclosed lack of consistency in our report?

(s) If our report is qualified and a dividend declared, have we stated whether the qualification is material for determining whether dividend is legal (CA 1985)?

Possible clerical errors

(a) Does the audit report refer to the correct accounting reference date and period?

(b) Does the report state correctly whether the company has made a profit or a loss for the period? (It is preferable for the report to use the word "results".)

(c) Are the references in the report to page numbers in the accounts correct?

(d) Is the audit report correctly addressed?

	Yes	No	Not applicable

(e) Has a partner, not in any way involved with the audit in question:
   (i) independently read the draft auditor's report and approved its technical content and the suitability of the wording relating to any departures from the clean "short-form" report?
   (ii) reviewed the above checklist?

3.2 Standardisation of audit techniques

The standardisation of documentation is only a partial contribution towards establishment and maintenance of quality control. It is most important that all audit staff should be familiar with the use of the audit techniques as practised by the firm. This has specific application to:

(a) use of standard symbols in flow-charting techniques;

(b) guidelines governing the use of statistical sampling techniques (e.g. where this method may or may not be appropriate);

(c) procedures for observation of physical stocktaking;

(d) action to be taken on discovery of internal control weaknesses and/or compensating controls;

(e) setting materiality limits;

(f) use of computer-assisted audit techniques.

3.3 Review of quality control

The maintenance of auditing standards requires constant vigilance and many firms appoint partners to a committee (sometimes referred to as "post-audit review" committee). It is the responsibility of this committee:

(a) to determine the level of audit testing required in particular circumstances;

(b) to determine the appropriate techniques to be used by staff;

(c) to disseminate up-to-date information to staff at all appropriate levels;

(d) to organise suitable training courses, the content of which should be geared to the level of staff attending;

(e) to monitor constantly standards operating in every office which carries the firm's name: staff suggestions based on field tests and general feed-back should be fully taken into account in this connection.

Some major international firms have taken the review a degree further by arranging unexpected visits to branch offices in any part of the world with a view to inspecting accounts/working paper files/audit reports, etc. as a means of assessing the extent to which the local office is consistently applying the firm's predetermined standards. These are usually known as "peer" reviews.

The ultimate in peer reviews arises where one major firm invites another firm to undertake a review of its standards and methods on a completely independent basis. In the United States, the Securities and Exchange Commission has recently requisitioned such a review in the case of one major firm and it is the intention of the SEC that this form of review should operate more widely.

PROGRESS TEST 12

1. What are the advantages of effective audit management? (3.0)

2. List three methods of controlling quality by auditing firms. (3.0)

CHAPTER THIRTEEN

Specialised Audits and Investigations

1.0 INSURANCE COMPANIES—THE SPECIAL AUDIT DIFFICULTIES

The specific audit problems which arise in such circumstances relate to four main areas:

(a) ascertainment of debtors and creditors;

(b) unearned premiums;

(c) unexpired risks;

(d) outstanding claims.

Consequently, any examination question on such an audit would require the answer to deal with these four areas in particular, and the following notes are therefore relevant.

1.1 Ascertainment of debtors and creditors

Insurance companies rarely maintain their personal ledgers in such a way as to produce directly a separate list of debtors and creditors, since their ledgers frequently reflect the section of the market from which the business originates, e.g. brokers, re-insurers, direct policyholders, etc.; hence it is possible that both debtor and creditor balances will exist in one ledger, sometimes for the same person. Nor is the legal position clear in relation to the right of set-off between the debit and creditor balances with the same person; it is therefore vital for the auditor to ensure that the company applies a consistent approach in establishing the separate amounts of debtors and creditors, especially since circularisation procedures are generally inappropriate.

1.2 Unearned premiums

An unearned premium represents the appropriate proportion of a premium during the year under review, which is applicable to a later accounting period. Once again, it is important that a consistent approach is adopted and that the accounts declare the bases selected by the insurance company, under the heading of accounting policies, since a number of variations are in fact possible.

1.3   Unexpired risks

This amount represents the "carry forward" to the next accounting period in circumstances where it appears that insurance business undertaken in the period under review is unprofitable; it is thus similar to the provision for future losses on long-term contracts in the construction industry. The chief audit difficulty is that a considerable element of judgment enters the computation of such unexpired risks and the auditor will be required to form an opinion on the need for such a provision and, if one exists, whether the sum provided is adequate.

1.4   Outstanding claims

Such claims may be classified between those which:

(a)   have been notified and agreed, but are still outstanding at the balance sheet date;

(b)   have been notified before, but not yet agreed, at the balance sheet date; and

(c)   have arisen but which have not yet been notified to the company by the balance sheet date.

A good deal of estimation is needed with regard to claims in categories (b) and (c) above, and audit procedures will therefore include a review of the claims files in order to appraise the company's estimates.

It will also be necessary to compare the average cost of outstanding claims for each class of business with current experience. Finally, the auditor should examine statistical elements comparing past estimates with actual results, and should employ the use of "market intelligence" wherever available.

2.0   CONTEMPORARY BANKING PROBLEMS—THE AUDIT APPROACH

Note
Audit problems in connection with banks and insurance companies fall within the published syllabus. Most basic audit considerations will be obvious from an examination of the accounts of such an institution; however, examiners now appear to require more than a superficial description of audit procedures, and this note therefore describes the considerations which auditors should bear in mind when taking into account contemporary problems in the banking sector.

2.1   Introduction and background

The difficulties encountered by the fringe banking sector during the 1970s are widely known, and a number of lessons have now, it is hoped, been learnt. In essence, the disasters were attributable to the banks' speculative involvement with property development companies to whom vast amounts of finance were allocated, on the ill-conceived basis that property prices would continue to spiral upwards indefinitely.

Until a property development is complete no income is received, and consequently many of the banks who lent on the strength of future prospects were obliged to "roll up" their interest charges (i.e. compound them and add them to the capital), even though they were themselves paying interest rates on the money market of as high as 15% to 20%.

When the upward trend in property prices reached its peak and began to move into reverse, a large number of speculative development projects came to an immediate halt, often bringing bankruptcy to the building contractors involved; thus the waiting game began and in the unsettled state of the property market even the giants were at a loss as to the valuation of their portfolio in the annual accounts—hence the proliferation of qualifications in the auditors' reports.

The above chain of events inevitably led to "lifeboat" operations by the clearing banks under the auspices of the Bank of England. Now that much of the dust has settled, revealing a drastically pruned property sector and a fringe banking fraternity still licking its wounds, the "senior citizens" of the City establishments are considering ways of avoiding a similar catastrophe.

2.2   Critical review of bank's trading position

The Bank of England, in particular, is tightening up its supervisory role and thus aiding the health of the banking industry as a whole. Recent legislation involves a licensing system for banks, and it is likely that there will in future be continued supervision.

The Bank of England is currently seeking a good deal of detailed information from individual banking institutions; this is to be sought once a year from the clearers, but more frequently from the smaller banks. The range of questions being asked is wide, and accords closely with the kind of questions which the banks' auditors should be asking. It is therefore worth examining some of the enquiries in detail:

(a)   When looking at a bank's profit and loss account it is important to discover precisely what proportions of the bank's profits are derived from the hard core of sustainable business, and how much from sources of income which, if not speculative, are at least uncertain. For example, the auditor should examine the proportions of income derived from the following three sources:

   (i)   net interest margins between lending and borrowing;

   (ii)   dealing profits derived from the bank's investment portfolio;

   (iii)   fees and commissions.

(b)   Although auditing a prior period, auditors should discuss current problems with the bank's management to discover whether profits are being made in the current period.

(c)   Enquiries should be made as to whether such projected profits take into account suspended interest "rolled up", bad debt provisions, and any other decline in the realisable value of assets.

(d) The auditors should enquire when such provisions were last reviewed and how frequently reviews are made.

Enquiries along these lines would indicate some of the background detail of a bank's trading account, and establish the trend of its business; such enquiries would also show whether the bank is essentially profitable or is relying upon dealing or windfall profits and therefore at risk.

2.3   Normal or abnormal?

Given the versatility which banking institutions now require in order to remain viable, it is not always a simple matter to distinguish between normal and abnormal events. For example, in relation to interest received and paid, the following questions are relevant:

(a) Are net interest margins positive, particularly in relation to the funding of the bank's fixed assets?

(b) How much interest is being suspended, and on what proportion of the total loan portfolio?

In relation to questions such as these there is little collective experience as to what should be regarded as normal or abnormal respectively.

2.4   Further enquiries

Further enquiries should be aimed at establishing:

(a) the areas in which a bank is dealing, e.g.:

  (i) investments;

  (ii) certificates of deposit;

  (iii) foreign exchange;

  (iv) commodities;

  (v) land and property;

(b) the fee-earning activities of the bank, for example in respect of:

  (i) loan commitments;

  (ii) acceptances;

  (iii) portfolio management;

  (iv) corporate advisory work.

2.5   Conclusion

The insight into the strength of the institution being audited which the above approach is bound to give, will prove to be invaluable in assessing its viability. A thorough investigation along these lines will also provide indications of great benefit to management, particularly in alerting the latter to the danger signals which may be thrown up by their own management accounts before it is too late to take remedial action.

3.0 JOINT AUDITS

This is a situation often encountered in practice and concerning which there is a surprising amount of confusion, especially with regard to the respective responsibilities and duties of the audit firms involved. The situation is often complicated in practice by the fact that one of the firms of joint auditors acts for the client company in an accountancy capacity.

Auditors accepting an appointment to act jointly with another firm should be cognisant of the following factors:

(a) Responsibility, which clearly could lead to liability, is in no way reduced in such an arrangement, although clearly damages would be apportioned in relation to the incidence of any negligence proved. Apportionment of blame in such circumstances is extremely difficult and it would clearly be unwise to rely upon this form of protection.

(b) It is essential that there should be a full and mutual exchange of information between the two firms acting jointly, and planned co-ordination of the duties which each respectively agrees to undertake. Otherwise, the risk is that the client company, far from having the assurance of extra protection given by the overlapping of certain procedures, may find that lack of co-ordination between the auditors leads to a number of important areas not being adequately covered.

(c) It is clearly prudent that on the occasion of each audit the duties and responsibilities undertaken by each firm should be set out in writing and mutually exchanged.

(d) Although the other firm is already undertaking extensive accountancy work for the client company, this should not in any way minimise the firm's audit responsibilities, despite the difficulty in maintaining an independent view of work which they themselves have carried out. The circumstances therefore place an additional burden on the firm invited to act jointly and the latter should therefore elicit assurances that the execution of accounting functions will not be regarded as a substitute for pure auditing.

4.0 SOLICITORS' ACCOUNTS RULES

4.1 Introduction

The statutory provisions for regulating the handling of clients' money (and accounting therefor) and trust money are contained in the following:

(a) the Solicitors Act 1974;

(b) the Solicitors' Accounts Rules 1975;

(c) the Solicitors' Trust Account Rules 1975;

(d) the Solicitors' Accounts (Deposit Interest) Rules 1975;

(e) the Accountant's Report Rules 1975.

4.2 Purpose of the rules

The rules are intended:

(a) to require a solicitor to keep clients' money separate from his own money;

(b) to ensure that a solicitor keeps adequate records of his transactions so that his books show money received and paid and balance held on account of each client;

(c) to ensure that money of each client is clearly distinguished from that of other clients, and from other money passing through a solicitor's accounts.

Rule 12 of the Solicitors' Accounts Rules 1975 gives the Council of the Law Society power to order the inspection of accounts of individual solicitors to ascertain whether the rules have been complied with.

4.3 Broad effect of rules

Money received by a solicitor which does not belong to him must be dealt with:

(a) through his client account if he receives it in connection with his practice;

(b) either through client account, or separate trust bank account opened for the particular trust if it is money subject to a trust of which the solicitor is sole trustee or co-trustee only with a partner, clerk or servant;

(c) through his client account if it is subject to any other trust of which he is trustee.

4.4 Points to note

(a) Cheques on a client bank account should be signed by the solicitor. Only in exceptional circumstances, e.g. illness or unavoidable absence on business or holiday, should this practice be departed from. The practice of signing cheques in blank and leaving them with an employee is clearly unwise and to be deprecated.

(b) A solicitor must not treat himself as a client. Nor may he finance a client out of his (the solicitor's) money held in a client account.

(c) Money received by a solicitor as trustee may be paid into a client bank account.

(d) A solicitor can withdraw his own money from a client bank account only by transfer to his office bank account or a cheque drawn in his own favour.

(e) A cheque or draft received on behalf of a client and endorsed over in the ordinary course of business would not pass through the solicitor's client bank account but it should nevertheless be recorded in his books as a transaction on behalf of the client.

(f) Drawing against a cheque before it is cleared could result in the account held for a particular client going negative, i.e. another client's money being used to make the payment. If this occurs the solicitor will have committed a breach of the rules. Even if the solicitor on discovery of the breach immediately pays the appropriate amount from his own resources into client account, the accountant may still decide to qualify his report.

(g) Where money is received on account of costs:

    (i) it must be paid into the solicitor's office account if the costs have been incurred and a bill of costs has been delivered to the client;

    (ii) it must otherwise be paid into client account.

4.5 Accountant's Report Rules 1975

General principles

Every solicitor who handles clients' money shall produce annually a report by a qualified accountant that the solicitor has complied with the Solicitors' Accounts Rules. Note that:

(a) a report is required once in every year;

(b) this is a separate matter from the issue to a solicitor of his annual practising certificate.

Neither the Solicitors Act nor the Accountant's Report Rules requires a complete audit of the solicitor's accounts. Nor do they require the preparation of a profit and loss account or balance sheet.

Qualification of accountant

To be qualified to give a report the accountant must be an English, Scottish or Irish Chartered Accountant or a Certified Accountant. He must not be a partner, clerk or servant of the solicitor and he must not have been disqualified by the Council of the Law Society.

Examination of books and accounts

The accountant is not in the normal case required to check and vouch each and every item in the books or bank statements. But if the general examination and detailed tests disclose evidence that the rules have not been complied with, the accountant must pursue a more comprehensive investigation.

For the purpose of giving an accountant's report an accountant must:

(a) ascertain from the solicitor particulars of all bank accounts (excluding trust banking accounts) kept or operated by the solicitor in connection with his practice;

(b) examine the book-keeping system in every office of the solicitor to see that the system complies with Rule 11 of the Solicitors' Accounts Rules 1975, and that:

    (i) there is an appropriate ledger account for each client;

    (ii) the ledger accounts show separately from other information particulars of all clients' money received, held or paid on account of each client;

    (iii) transactions relating to clients' money and other money dealt with through a client account are recorded in the solicitor's books so as to distinguish such transactions relating to any other money;

(c) make test checks of postings to clients' ledger accounts from records of receipts and payments of clients' money;

(d) make test checks of the casts of such accounts;

(e) compare a sample of lodgments and payments from the client account, as shown in the bank statements with the solicitor's records of receipts and payments of clients' money;

(f) enquire into and test check the system of recording costs and of making withdrawals in respect of costs from the client account;

(g) satisfy himself by test examination of documents that the financial transactions (including those giving rise to transfers between ledger accounts) are in accordance with the Solicitors' Accounts Rules 1975, and that entries in the clients' ledger accounts reflect the transactions in a manner which complies with those rules;

(h) extract (or check the extraction of) all clients' ledger balances at not fewer than two dates selected by the accountant; and at each date compare the total shown by the ledger accounts with the cash book balance on client account; and reconcile the cash book balance with that confirmed direct to the accountant by the bank. In June 1979 the Law Society agreed to modify this rule so that a *test* check of the extraction *only* is required if:

    (i) the solicitor uses a computerised or mechanised system which automatically produces an extraction of all client balances; and

    (ii) a satisfactory system of internal control is in operation,

but in all other cases it is necessary for the accountant to extract or check the extraction of *all* balances, regardless of the existence of an efficient system of internal control;

(i) make a test examination to ascertain whether payments from client account have been made on any individual account in excess of the money held on behalf of that client;

(j) peruse the office ledger, cash accounts and bank statements to see whether clients' money has not been paid into a client account.

"Accountant not required..."
The accountant is not required:

(a) to extend his enquiries beyond the information contained in the relevant documents, supplemented by such information and explanations as he may obtain from the solicitor;

(b) to enquire into stocks, shares, other securities of documents of title held by the solicitor on behalf of clients;

(c) to consider whether the books of account of the solicitor were properly written up in accordance with the rules at any other time than that at which his examination took place.

A blank specimen of the accountant's report is shown in Fig. 25.

4.6 Solicitors Accounts (Deposit Interest) Rules 1975

Where a solicitor holds or receives for an account of a client money which, having regard to the circumstances (including the amount and length of time held) ought in fairness to the client to have earned him interest, the solicitor must either deposit the money in a separate account and pass over to the client any interest earned, or pay to the client out of his own money a sum equivalent to the interest which would have been earned if the money had been separately deposited. In general this rule applies where the sum involved exceeds £500 and at the time of its receipt was unlikely to be reduced to less than £500 within two months.

The Law Society will adjudicate in disputes if so requested.

5.0 INVESTIGATIONS

5.1 Introductory note

Auditing and investigations have a good deal in common. However, whereas auditing is practised in accordance with precise disciplines, usually under statutory regulation, the nature of investigations will vary depending upon the circumstances. Investigations are usually undertaken to obtain information of a specialised nature.

Despite the wide variety of investigations, they may be classified under the following general heads:

(a) reports in prospectuses;

(b) investment decisions:

    (i) purchase of shares in company;

   (ii) purchase of a share in partnership;

  (iii) loans;

(c) fraud;

(d) back duty;

(e) under the Companies Act, on behalf of the Department of Trade and Industry.

THE ACCOUNTANT'S REPORT RULES 1975

NOTE:— In the case of a firm with a number of partners, carbon copies of the Report may be delivered provided section 1 below is completed on each Report with the name of the individual solicitor.

(a) BLOCK CAPITALS.

1. Solicitor's Full Name *(a)* _____

(b) NOTE:— All addresses at which the Solicitor(s) practise(s) must be covered by an Accountant's Report or Reports. If an address is not so covered the reason must be stated.

2. Firm(s) Name(s) and Address(es) *(b)* _____

3. Whether practising alone or in partnership _____

(c) NOTE:— The period(s) must comply with Section 34(1) of the Solicitors Act 1974, and the Accountant's Report Rules 1975.

4. Accounting Period(s) *(c)*

    Beginning .... Ending ....

    Beginning .... Ending ....

ACCOUNTANT'S REPORT

In compliance with Section 34 of the Solicitors Act 1974, and the Accountant's Report Rules 1975, made thereunder, I have examined to the extent required by Rule 4 of the said Rules the books, accounts and documents produced to me in respect of the above practice(s) of the above-named solicitor.

1. In so far as an opinion can be based on this limited examination I am satisfied that during the above-mentioned period(s) he has complied with the provisions of the Solicitors' Accounts Rules 1975, except so far as concerns:—

Delete sub-paragraph(s) not applicable.

    (a) certain trivial breaches due to clerical errors or mistakes in book-keeping, all of which were rectified on discovery and none of which, I am satisfied, resulted in any loss to any client;

    (b) the matters set out in the First Section on the back hereof, in respect of which I have not been able to satisfy myself for the reasons therein stated;

    (c) the matters set out in the Second Section on the back hereof, in respect of which it appears to me that the solicitor has not complied with the provisions of the Solicitors' Accounts Rules 1975.

2. The results of the comparisons required under Rule 4 (1) *(f)* of the Accountant's Report Rules 1975, at the dates selected by me were as follows:—

    (i) at ....

Delete (a) or (b) as appropriate.

    (a) the figures were in agreement;

    (b) there was a difference computed as follows:—

                                                 £

        Liabilities to clients as shown by clients' ledger accounts   ...

        Cash held in client account after allowance for outstanding cheques and lodgments cleared after date   ...   .

                                                 £

    (ii) at ....

Delete (a) or (b) as appropriate.

    (a) the figures were in agreement;

    (b) there was a difference computed as follows:—

                                                 £

        Liabilities to clients as shown by clients' ledger-accounts   ...

        Cash held in client account after allowance for outstanding cheques and lodgments cleared after date   ...   .

                                               £

Fig. 25. *The accountant's report.*

3. *(a)* Having retired from active practice as a solicitor the said . . . .
. . . . ceased to hold client's money
. . . .

(b) Having ceased to practise under the style of . . . .
. . . .
the said . . . .

ceased to hold client's money under that style on . . . .

Particulars of the accountant:—

> Full name . . . .
> Qualifications . . . .
> Firm Name . . . .
> Address . . . .
> . . . .
> Date . . . . Signature . . . .

To The Secretary,
   The Law Society,
      The Law Society's Hall,
         113 Chancery Lane, London WC2A 1PL.

FIRST SECTION
Matters in respect of which the accountant has been unable to satisfy himself and the reasons for that inability:—

SECOND SECTION
Matters (other than trivial breaches) in respect of which it appears to the accountant that the solicitor has not complied with the provisions of the Solicitors' Accounts Rules 1975:—

5.2   General procedures

Most investigations involve a detailed examination of accounts covering a period of one or more years, and the subsequent interpretation of those accounts in accordance with the purpose of the investigation. The following general procedures would normally be appropriate:

(a) decide upon the number of years to be covered;

(b) obtain copies of the detailed accounts for each of those years;

(c) note any qualifications in the reports of auditors;

(d) consider detailed information in the accounts for each year in conjunction with available supporting schedules and working papers;

(e) adjust the accounts for:

    (i) income and expenditure not applicable in future;

    (ii) likely future income and expenditure, not previously applicable;

    (iii) amounts at which assets and liabilities should be included in the accounts in accordance with the purpose of the examination;

(f) consider trends and ratios after the accounts have been adjusted, for example:

    (i) closing stock: cost of sales;

    (ii) debtors: sales;

    (iii) purchases: creditors;

    (iv) gross profit: sales;

    (v) net profit: sales;

    (vi) current assets: current liabilities;

    (vii) fixed assets: shareholders' equity;

(g) draw conclusions from the examination, in anticipation of preparation of a report;

(h) draft a report to the client.

5.3   Reporting rules

Certain reporting rules should be carefully observed and these may be summarised as follows:

(a) the *subject* of the report should be immediately apparent from the main heading and subsequent headings;

(b) the *conclusions* reached from the investigation should be clearly set out in the body of the report;

(c) *detailed calculations and statistics* used in reaching the conclusions may be referred to in the body of the report but should be included in *appendices* attached;

(d) all detailed workings and notes should be *preserved* indefinitely since the conclusions may be subsequently contested, possibly in the course of litigation, and it is obviously dangerous to rely upon memory in such circumstances;

(e) the report should take into account the level of *accounting knowledge* of the parties to whom it is addressed; an unduly sophisticated report would run the risk of being misunderstood.

5.4 Special points to note

With reference to the need to adjust accounts, as mentioned in section 5.2(e) above, the investigator should adjust an existing figure only if the grounds for doing so are reasonably certain. It would, for example, be reasonable to make adjustments in the following circumstances:

(a) The investigator may be aware of the company's shortage of working capital causing it to rely heavily on expensive external finance such as debt-factoring services. The prospective purchaser, on the other hand, may be prepared to inject additional funds, thus saving substantially on *credit-servicing* charges previously incurred.

(b) Similarly, in such straits it may not have been possible to take full advantage of *cash discounts* when settling trade liabilities, nor of trade discounts through bulk purchasing.

(c) The company's results may have been adversely affected by persistently *loss-making subsidiaries,* which the future management could either sell off or operate more efficiently.

It is important for the investigator to look beyond the accounts under review, and the co-operation of the company's accounting staff and auditors will normally be necessary. Examples of such enquiries are:

(a) *Analysis of sales.* Clearly not all of the company's products will be equally profitable and it is important to know their respective grades of success.

(b) *Research and development.* The contribution which such expenditures has made to earnings must be assessed. The investigator should ascertain the R & D effort on the most and least successful products respectively prior to marketing, and thereby determine whether profits are in fact being enhanced by such expenditure.

(c) *Present management policy.* This may be inadequately reflected in the recorded results of past years owing to recently instituted changes; clearly it is important to assess the future impact of such policies, e.g. the selling off of loss-making subsidiaries and superfluous assets, sale-and-lease-back arrangements on freeholds, or writing off of capital or R & D expenditure unlikely to be recouped.

(d) *The tax position.* There are few business decisions that do not have tax implications. If, for example, the company being reviewed is in the same industry, set-off of profits and losses arising in the future will be possible.

(e) *External factors.* Since many investigations will require future projections to be based on past results, it is not sufficient to confine enquiries to the accounts themselves. The investigator's horizons must extend to *external factors,* and he is bound to consider the following all-important matters:

  (i) staff loyalty;

  (ii) customer goodwill;

  (iii) length of current leases;

  (iv) expiry dates of major contracts and production patents;

  (v) the age and general condition of the stocks;

  (vi) the soundness of the trade debts;

  (vii) the condition and estimated future useful life of the major fixed assets, and their estimated replacement cost;

  (viii) the likely effect of forthcoming legislation, fiscal and otherwise, which may affect the profitability of the business;

  (ix) roads and building plans within the district (the conversion of a road into a motorway can halve the custom of a shopping site);

  (x) general economic and fiscal prognostications which may affect trade.

5.5 Prospectus reports

All accountants' reports in prospectuses are required by the Quotations Department of the Stock Exchange to include:

(a) a disclosure of the balance sheet at the end of the last accounting period reported upon;

(b) the funds statements (or consolidated funds statements in the case of a holding company) in summarised form at the end of each previous accounting period reported on, and at the beginning of the first such period.

The information regarding profits and losses must be disclosed as follows. In respect of each of the years reported on (normally five years):

(a) sales, specifying method of arriving at sales;

(b) total cost of goods sold;

(c) other income (non-trading);

(d) share of profits of associated companies;

(e) profit before tax and extraordinary items;

(f) taxation on profits, including basis;

(g) minority interests in profits;

(h) extraordinary items (less any tax attributable thereto);

(i) profit attributable to shareholders after tax and extraordinary items;

(j) preference dividends;

(k) profit attributable to equity;

(l) dividends on equity.

The accounting policies followed in determining the profits and losses must be disclosed, as well as any other matters which appear to be relevant for the purpose of the report.

Other Stock Exchange rules are as follows:

(a) a period of more than six months between date of final accounts reported on and the date of prospectus would normally be unacceptable;

(b) significant departures from the Accounting Standards approved by the accountancy bodies must be disclosed and explained;

(c) the report should state that the profits or losses have been arrived at on defined bases in accordance with approved Accounting Standards, and after making such adjustments as are considered appropriate;

(d) reports containing significant qualifications are normally unacceptable: any reservations expressed must also indicate the extent and materiality of such reservations;

(e) reference in the report to the reports or valuations of other experts (e.g. valuers) which are not reproduced in the prospectus, should include their names, addresses and professional qualifications (the usual statement of consent as per section 61 of the Companies Act 1985, must cover such references in the form and context in which they are included);

(f) the rules make provision for a statement in standard form of all adjustments made in arriving at the figures of profits or losses (giving reasons therefor) signed by the reporting accountants, to be available for inspection by the public.

Finally, reporting accountants are required to submit a letter to the Quotations Department on the following four matters:

(a) *stocks and work in progress:* adequacy of records—proper ascertainment—acceptable bases—consistently applied;

(b) *depreciation and amortisation:* whether provisions are reasonable, having regard to assets which the company has not depreciated; and where a revaluation has been carried out, whether depreciation charged in the report has been based on revalued figures;

(c) *deferred taxation:* disclosure of material differences between amounts on which depreciation will be charged and amounts on which capital allowances will be obtained (where this is the case and there is no provision for deferred tax, this will have to be disclosed and explained under "accounting policies");

(d) *accounting policies:* confirmation that these are in accordance with approved Standards.

A typical accountants' report is reproduced below.

Letter from the joint reporting accountants
The Directors
Sonic Sound Audio Holdings plc   **14th January 1986**

Gentlemen,

We have reviewed the accounting policies applied and the calculations made in preparing the forecast of profit before taxation of Sonic Sound Audio Holdings plc and subsidiaries ("the group") (for which you, as directors, are solely responsible) for the year ending 31st October 1986, set out in the prospectus dated 14th January 1986. The principal assumptions made by you upon which the forecast of profit before taxation is based are set forth in the said prospectus. The forecast of profit before taxation includes results shown by unaudited management accounts for the period ended 3rd January 1986.

Our review indicated that the forecast of profit before taxation, so far as the accounting policies and calculations are concerned, has been compiled on the basis of the assumptions made by you referred to above and is presented on a basis consistent with the accounting policies normally adopted by the group.

Yours faithfully,

Arthur Andersen & Co   Halpern and Woolf
Chartered Accountants   Chartered Accountants

Accountants' report
The following is a copy of a report received from Arthur Andersen & Co, the joint reporting accountants, and Halpern and Woolf, the auditors and joint reporting accountants.

The Directors
Sonic Sound Audio Holdings plc

The Partners
Earnshaw, Haes & Sons   14th January 1986

Gentlemen,

We have audited the balance sheet of Sonic Sound Audio Holdings plc ("the company") at 1st November 1985, and the related statements of profits and retained earnings and source and application of funds for the years ended 31st October 1982, 1983, 1984 and 1st November 1985, in accordance with approved Auditing Standards.

The company was incorporated on 21st September 1981, under the name of Astor Hi-Fi Ltd and commenced trading on 5th November 1981. The company's name was changed to Sonic Sound Audio Holdings Ltd on 8th January 1986 and to Sonic Sound Audio Holdings plc on 12th January 1986.

Halpern and Woolf have reported on each of the above four years. The financial information presented below is based on the audited accounts, after reflecting the change in the basis of accounting for deferred taxation which is explained further in note 4.

In our opinion, the financial information, which has been prepared under the historical cost convention and is shown below, gives a true and fair view of the state of affairs of the company at 1st November 1985, and of the profits and source and application of funds for each of the four years referred to above, on a consistent basis.

We have also reviewed the entries giving effect to the post balance sheet transactions described in notes 10 and 11, and in our opinion these entries have been properly applied to the balance sheet of the company at 1st November 1985, which has then been combined with the audited balance sheet of Sonic Sound Audio Ltd at 1st November 1985, to arrive at the pro-forma group balance sheet at 1st November 1985.

Accounting policies
The significant accounting policies adopted in arriving at the financial information set out in this report are as follows:

(a) *Basis of preparation:* The financial information has been prepared under the historical cost convention. Until 31st October 1984, the company prepared its accounts as at 31st October. Subsequently, the company has prepared its accounts to the close of business on the Saturday nearest to 31st October.

(b) *Interest in subsidiary company:* At 1st November 1985, the company had one dormant subsidiary which had never traded. No consolidated accounts have been prepared because, in the opinion of the directors, they would be of no real value to the members in view of the insignificant amounts involved. The interest is stated at cost in the company's balance sheet.

(c) *Stock:* Stock is stated at the lower of cost on a first-in, first-out basis, and net realisable value.

(d) *Deferred taxation:* Deferred taxation is provided to the extent that the directors believe that the related liabilities have a reasonable probability of materialising in the foreseeable future, to allow for the effect of items of income and expense being attributed for tax purposes to years different from those in which the credits or charges are recorded in the accounts. Deferred taxation is computed using the liability method whereby timing differences are tax effected at the rate of corporation tax at the balance sheet date.

(e) *Sales:* Sales represent invoiced value, excluding value added tax.

(f) *Licence income:* Licence income represents the gross amount receivable under the terms of the licences.

(g) *Fixed assets:* Fixed assets are stated at cost. Depreciation is provided on a straight-line basis at annual rates based on the estimated economic lives of the assets as follows:

(i) leasehold property—over the residual term of the lease;

(ii) furniture, fixtures, fittings and equipment—10%;

(iii) motor vehicles—25%.

Statements of profits and retained earnings

| | | *Years ended* | | | |
	Note	*1st November 1985* £	*31st October 1984* £	*31st October 1983* £	*31st October 1982* £
Sales		2,601,136	2,123,962	1,080,210	623,467
Cost of sales		1,900,152	1,585,244	795,029	461,350
Gross trading profit		700,984	538,718	285,181	162,117
Licence income, gross		227,858	188,370	131,477	52,219
		928,842	727,088	416,658	214,336
Selling and other expenses	2	536,065	475,299	241,761	160,027
		392,777	251,789	174,897	54,309
Exceptional item	3	88,691	—	—	—
Profit before taxation		304,086	251,789	174,897	54,309
Taxation	4	—	—	—	—
Net profit		304,086	251,789	174,897	54,309
Retained earnings, brought forward		480,995	229,206	54,309	—
Retained earnings, carried forward		785,081	480,995	229,206	54,309
Earnings per share	5	5.07p	4.20p	2.91p	0.91p

Balance sheets

| | | 1st November 1985 | |
| | | | Pro-forma Group |
	Note	*Company* £	*(Note 11)* £
Fixed assets, net	6	243,459	294,670
Interest in subsidiary company	7	145	145
		243,604	294,815
Current assets:			
Stock	8	1,101,754	1,101,754
Debtors and prepaid expenses		259,926	213,616
Cash		11,860	11,860
		1,373,540	1,327,230
Current liabilities:			
Creditors and accrued expenses		776,699	782,994
Bank overdraft	9	29,407	29,407
		806,106	812,401

Balance Sheets

Net current assets		567,434	514,829
Non-current portion of exceptional item	3	(20,957)	(20,957)
Net assets		790,081	788,687
Shareholders' funds:			
Share capital	10	5,000	537,500
Retained earnings		785,081	251,187
		790,081	788,687

Statement of source and application of funds

	1st November 1985	31st October 1984	31st October 1983	31st October 1982
	Years ended			
SOURCE OF FUNDS:				
Operations:				
Net profit for the year	304,086	251,789	174,897	54,309
Add/(deduct) items not involving the movement of funds				
Depreciation	33,392	32,448	29,488	12,573
Surplus on disposal of fixed assets	(6,226)	(2,329)	(2,580)	(285)
Total fund from operations	331,252	281,908	201,805	66,597
Sale proceeds of fixed assets	30,787	9,964	28,823	8,494
Shares issued	—	—	—	5,000
Non-current portion of exceptional item	20,957	—	—	—
	382,996	291,872	230,628	80,091
APPLICATION OF FUNDS:				
Capital expenditure	105,693	85,117	153,821	73,377
Interest in subsidiary	—	—	—	145
Increase in working capital, as shown below	277,303	206,755	76,807	6,569
	382,996	291,872	230,628	80,091
INCREASE/(DECREASE) IN WORKING CAPITAL:				
Stock	348,107	331,703	218,472	203,472
Debtors and prepaid expenses	46,598	84,238	104,286	24,804
Creditors and accrued expenses	(64,602)	(349,779)	(185,992)	(176,326)
Movement in net liquid funds, as shown below	(52,800)	140,593	(59,959)	(45,381)
	277,303	206,755	76,807	6,569
INCREASE/(DECREASE) IN NET LIQUID FUNDS:				
Cash	(23,393)	14,165	20,868	220
Bank overdraft	(29,407)	126,428	(80,827)	(45,601)
	(52,800)	140,593	(59,959)	(45,381)

Notes

1. FORMATION OF COMPANY

The company was incorporated on 21st September 1981 under the name of Astor Hi-Fi Ltd and commenced trading on 5th November 1981. The company's name was changed to Sonic Sound Audio Holdings Ltd on 8th January 1986 and to Sonic Sound Audio Holdings plc on 12th January 1986.

2. SELLING AND OTHER EXPENSES
Selling and other expenses include:

	1985 £	1984 £	1983 £	1982 £
Depreciation	33,392	32,448	29,488	12,573
Interest expense	25,268	10,798	10,945	8,479
Directors' emoluments	54,058	54,100	27,555	19,830

3. EXCEPTIONAL ITEM
Following a settlement with a former director whereby his existing consultancy contract was terminated, the company entered into a new agreement on 23rd December 1985, which provided for payments over the next five years. The company has accrued at 1st November 1985 for the discounted present value of its commitment under this agreement.

4. TAXATION
(a)   The contingent liability calculated at 52% in respect of deferred taxation at 1st November 1985 amounted to:

	£
Corporation tax on the excess of the net book value of assets eligible for tax allowances over the corresponding tax written-down value of such assets	67,000
Stock relief	470,000
Other timing differences	(37,000)
Taxation losses carried forward	(103,000)
	397,000

Following the release by the Inland Revenue on 14th November 1985 of the Consultative Document on the Proposals for Stock Relief, the directors believe that the contingent liability relating to stock relief will not materialise.

(b) In the audited accounts prior to those for the year ended 31st October 1984, the company's policy was to make full provision for deferred taxation liabilities. During 1984 this policy was changed and, in accordance with SSAP 15 of the Accounting Standards Committee, provision is now only made for tax liabilities which the directors believe have a reasonable probability of materialising in the foreseeable future. The effect of this change has been to eliminate the need for a provision in respect of deferred taxation. The prior years' accounts have been restated accordingly.

5. EARNINGS PER SHARE
Earnings per share have been calculated by dividing the net profit for each year by 6,000,000, being the number of shares which will be in issue after the completion of the transactions described in notes 10 and 11 and after the issue of an additional 625,000 shares by way of the prospectus dated 14th January 1986.

6. FIXED ASSETS

(a)   Fixed assets of the company at 1st November 1985 comprise:

	Cost	Accumulated depreciation	Net book value
Leasehold property	13,254	1,043	12,211
Furniture, fixtures, fittings and equipment	200,514	42,402	158,112
Motor vehicles	98,231	25,095	73,136
	311,999	68,540	243,459

(b) Capital commitments: At 1st November 1985, the company had capital commitments which had been authorised by the board amounting to approximately £175,000.

7. INTEREST IN SUBSIDIARY COMPANY

At 1st November 1985, the company had the following wholly-owned subsidiary, which is incorporated in Great Britain. The company has not traded.

	Date of incorporation	Issued capital	Advances
Sonic Sound Audio (Export) Ltd	13th May 1982	£100	£45

8. STOCK

Stock comprises finished goods held for resale. Certain suppliers have reserved title over the goods supplied until payment. At 1st November 1985 the total value of such supplies included in stock was £155,067.

9. BANK OVERDRAFT

At 1st November 1985, the company had an overdraft facility of £215,000, secured primarily by way of a fixed and floating charge on the company's assets. On 5th January 1986 the group was granted an overdraft facility of £500,000, secured by way of a debenture on the group's assets. This facility replaces the previous facility.

10. SHARE CAPITAL

At 1st November 1985, the share capital of the company was as follows:

Authorised, issued and fully-paid Ordinary Shares of £1 each   5,000

At an Extraordinary General Meeting held on 23rd December 1985, resolutions were passed to sub-divide each Ordinary Share of £1 into Ordinary Shares of 10p each and to increase the authorised share capital from £5,000 to £1,000,000 by the creation of 9,950,000 Ordinary Shares of 10p each. In addition, 625,000 10p shares were issued on renounceable letters of allotment at 80p each as consideration for the acquisition of Sonic Sound Audio Ltd, as described in note 11.

   At an Extraordinary General Meeting held on 30th December 1985, a resolution was passed to make a bonus issue of 94 Ordinary Shares at 10p each for each registered Ordinary Share of 10p each by capitalisation of £470,000 (£437,500 from share premium account and £32,500 from retained earnings). An additional 4,700,000 shares were issued as a result of this resolution.

11. PRO-FORMA GROUP BALANCE SHEET

Sonic Sound Audio Ltd was incorporated on 10th June 1982, and was dormant until July 1985 when it signed an agreement to acquire a leasehold interest in three shop units in the new EMI Centre in Tottenham Court Road. Between July and December 1985, it entered into licences (including one licence granted to Sonic Sound Audio Holdings plc) in respect of those premises and had the units fitted out. Trading commenced on 10th December 1985. At 1st November 1985, Sonic Sound Audio Ltd had capital commitments which had been authorised by its board amounting to approximately £275,000.

On 23rd December 1985, and with effect from 2nd November 1985, the company acquired the entire issued share capital of Sonic Sound Audio Ltd from Messrs Lionel and Sidney Astor. The entries giving effect to this transaction and those described in note 10 have been applied to the balance sheet of the company at 1st November 1985, which has then been combined with the audited balance sheet of Sonic Sound Audio Ltd at 1st November 1985 to arrive at the pro-forma group balance sheet at 1st November 1985.

The £501,394 ascribed by the directors to intangibles, principally licences, arising from this transaction has been written off in the pro-forma group balance sheet.

12. LEASE COMMITMENTS

Under various leases expiring between 1987 and 2010, the group is committed to current annual rentals totalling £215,900. There are rent reviews every five years under most of the leases, the next significant review being in 1988.

13. PENSION ARRANGEMENTS

At 1st November 1985, only one employee was covered by a company pension scheme. The company's contribution in 1985 amounted to £413. There is no past service liability.

14. DIVIDENDS

No group company has declared or paid any dividend during the four years ended 1st November 1985.

15. AUDITED ACCOUNTS

No audited accounts have been prepared in respect of any period since 1st November 1985.

Yours faithfully,

Arthur Andersen & Co   Halpern and Woolf
Chartered Accountants   Chartered Accountants

5.6 The APC Guideline: Prospectuses

In 1984 the APC issued a draft guideline entitled "Prospectuses and the Reporting Accountant" from which the following extracts have been taken.

Introduction

1.   A prospectus is an invitation to the public to subscribe for, or to purchase, shares or debentures in a company. There are a variety of circumstances in which prospectuses may be issued, the most common of which are those where a company is seeking admission to the Stock Exchange's Official List or its Unlisted Securities Market (the "USM"). The form and content of a prospectus may vary according to the circumstances in which it is issued.

2.   This guideline has been written in the context of a prospectus issued by a company seeking admission to the Stock Exchange's Official List or its USM. However, in the absence of specific provisions to the contrary, the general principles embodied in this guideline should also be followed whenever an accountant is requested to prepare a report for inclusion in any other prospectus, such as those issued in connection with an over the counter market, or other similar documents such as placing documents and those issued in connection with schemes of arrangement and substantial acquisitions and realisations.

3.   The minimum contents for a prospectus to be issued by a company seeking a listing on the Stock Exchange are laid down in ss. 56, 57, 62 and 66 and the Third Schedule to the Companies Act 1985, and in chapter 3 and Sched. 11 to the Stock Exchange's "Admission of Securities to Listing" (the "Yellow Book"). It is essential that a reporting accountant should be familiar with these provisions and this guideline should be read in conjunction with them. Reference should also be made to the Prevention of Fraud (Investments) Act 1958. Where an accountant's report is required in connection with a prospectus or similar document which is not subject to the Yellow Book, best practice dictates that its provisions are applied wherever possible.

4.   Sections 56, 57 and 66 of the Companies Act 1985 and the Third Schedule to that Act deal with the matters and reports to be set out in a prospectus. In certain circumstances, when companies are about to be listed, those requirements may be waived by a Stock Exchange "certificate of exemption", on the grounds that compliance with the fourth schedule would be unduly burdensome, and replaced by specific requirements of the Stock Exchange.

5.   The 1985 Act requires the prospectus to be produced by the directors of the company issuing the shares or debentures, and they must collectively and individually accept full responsibility for the completeness and accuracy of the information given in the document. The prospectus will include a considerable amount of information on the company's financial affairs and will also include reports by "experts", one of whom is the reporting accountant. A merchant bank or broker will usually be sponsoring the issue and will take the lead in organising

the preparation of the prospectus and in obtaining the various reports which the prospectus is required to contain.

6.   The purpose of the accountant's report is to give possible investors financial information, relating to the company concerned, which will assist them in making a decision as to whether to invest in it. The Yellow Book sets out the minimum information to be included in the accountant's report. The report is required to include an expression of opinion as to whether or not the financial information gives a true and fair view of the company's (or group's) state of affairs at the latest balance sheet date and of the profits and losses and sources and applications of funds for the preceding five years, or for the period since incorporation if that is a shorter period. Any other matters which the reporting accountant considers pertinent should also be dealt with in his report.

7.   As an alternative to applying to the Stock Exchange's Official List, a company may apply to the Stock Exchange for admission to the USM. The Stock Exchange requirements for the USM are contained in its publication "The Stock Exchange—Unlisted Securities Market" (the "Green Book"). The main differences, from the Stock Exchange requirements, for the listed market are that for the USM:

   (a)   the company must normally have been trading for three years (five years for full listing);

   (b)   a minimum of 10% of the equity must normally be in public hands when dealing starts (25% for full listing);

   (c)   there are no lower limit requirements of market capitalisation for USM entry (usually £500,000 for full listing);

   (d)   where no marketing of new shares is to take place, companies can come to the USM without any obligation to present an accountant's report, although in practice such a report is often required by the sponsors to the introduction.

8.   Whenever a prospectus is being issued, a reporting accountant may be required to write a detailed report, for the merchant bank, broker or other institution sponsoring the prospectus, which covers various aspects of the company's business, including its management, profit record, assets and liabilities, and prospects. This type of report, commonly referred to as a "long form" report, is outside the scope of this guideline.

9.   In addition to his duty to prepare an accountant's report, a reporting accountant is required by the Yellow Book to examine and report on the accounting policies and calculations for any profit forecast included in the prospectus. Guidance on this responsibility is given in the Statement entitled "Accountants' Reports on Profit Forecasts" issued in 1978 by the accountancy bodies, and hence is not dealt with in this guideline.

Procedures

10.   The reporting accountant should carry out procedures such as those discussed below and should obtain relevant and reliable evidence sufficient to enable him to form an opinion on the financial information reported on.

PLANNING, CONTROLLING AND RECORDING

11.   The reporting accountant will either be the company's auditor or another accountant who must act with the auditor for the purposes of the work on the prospectus. The extent of the work which the reporting accountant will need to carry out in relation to his report may be significantly influenced by two important considerations:

(a)   whether all financial statements to be reported upon have previously been subjected to audit; and

(b)   whether the reporting accountant himself audited the financial statements on which the report is to be based.

Where the auditor also acts as reporting accountant, it is desirable for the partner in charge of the audit to involve another partner in the prospectus work, so as to provide a fresh view of the matter reported on. This will encompass the work described in paras 15 to 19.

12.   Where material financial information has not been audited it will usually be necessary to carry out additional work, before it can be included in the accountant's report, in order to ensure that it can provide a satisfactory basis for his opinion. The extent of the additional work should be planned in detail and, even if he is not carrying out the detailed work himself, the reporting accountant should be closely involved in its planning.

13.   Additional work will normally be required, for example, where the latest financial period reported on by the company's auditors ended more than six months before the date of the prospectus (or nine months in the case of a transaction on the USM) and thereby the Stock Exchange's normal requirement regarding the maximum period of time between the date of the figures to be reported upon and the date of the report will not have been satisfied. In these circumstances an audit of financial statements drawn up to an interim date will normally be required. Additional work will also be required where financial information has been a constituent part of audited financial statements without having been the specific subject of an audit opinion, e.g. the results of a single division or branch of a large company.

14.   The reporting accountant will need to control and record his work. This will involve the direction and supervision of his staff and the review of their work, and the preparation of working papers setting out the procedures carried out by the reporting accountant and his staff, the documents reviewed and the conclusions reached.

EVIDENCE

15.   The reporting accountant, in order to form an opinion as to whether the figures incorporated within his report give a true and fair view, will review and discuss with management the features and trends of the results during the relevant period, thereby enabling him to acquire the detailed understanding necessary for the purposes of providing a meaningful presentation in his report.

16.   The reporting accountant should also review the audit working papers relating to the period to be covered by his report, and he should pay particular attention to any difficult or contentious points which came to light during the course of the audit and to the manner in which they were settled. Where the reporting accountant was not the auditor of the financial statements being reported upon, he will need to liaise with the auditor so as to be able to make full use of his working papers. He should also seek information from the auditor about the latter's examination of important matters and he should seek clarification from the auditor of any significant matters arising from the reporting accountant's discussions with management.

17.   In carrying out his review of the working papers, the reporting accountant should seek to assure himself that the audit conclusions reached with regard to the relevant financial statements were supported by adequate audit evidence, and that the audit work was in accordance with good practice and with approved Auditing Standards. With the benefit of the hindsight generally available to the reporting accountant, he should assess the extent to which he is able to rely on audit work already performed and determine the further procedures which he considers necessary. It must be emphasised, however, that the fact that an audit has previously been carried out does not alleviate the burden of responsibility for the opinion given by the reporting accountant.

18.   In addition, the reporting accountant should undertake a general assessment of the company's accounting systems and records relating to the period to be covered by his report in order to determine their reliability as sources of evidence. This work should pay particular attention to difficult or contentious points which have come to light during the course of his discussions with management and to other matters critical to the ascertainment of profit, and therefore to his report, such as evidence concerning the physical existence and basis of valuation of stocks and work-in-progress. This work will be particularly important where he is unable to obtain the assurance he seeks from his review of audit working papers.

19.   If the reporting accountant cannot satisfy himself as to the results in all material respects by the procedures outlined above, he may need to undertake detailed audit procedures relating to earlier years. Where it is impracticable for him to repeat auditing procedures relating to earlier years, his reservations should appear in his report. If he believes his reservations to be fundamental, he should not allow his name to be associated with the prospectus. However, if additional assurance is required by the reporting accountant only in respect of the latest

period under review, then it may still be possible to arrange for supplementary audit procedures in the relevant areas to be carried out.

REVIEW OF FINANCIAL STATEMENTS

20. The reporting accountant will need to review the relevant financial statements to determine, *inter alia*, whether any adjustments are required thereto for the purposes of his report. A practical approach may be to carry out this review of financial statements concurrently with a review of the audit working papers (see para 16 above). The review of financial statements should include consideration of whether:

   (a) relevant material events, which may have taken place subsequent to the time of preparation and audit of the financial statements, require adjustments to ensure that they are accounted for in the correct period;

   (b) material expenditure or revenue of a non-recurring nature may have arisen in circumstances which require it to be eliminated from normal operations and disclosed separately as an extraordinary or exceptional item; and

   (c) material changes in accounting policies may have been applied during the period covered by the report, and may therefore require adjustments in order to provide valid comparisons between financial statements prepared on a consistent basis.

21. In carrying out his review of the financial statements, the reporting accountant will need to give special attention to any matters which have given rise to qualified audit reports. He will also need to consider carefully the significance of any such qualifications on his own report. In the case of a quantified qualification, it may be possible to make adjustments to the reported results to eliminate the need to qualify the accountant's report. However, in the case of a fundamental qualification, giving rise to an adverse opinion or to a disclaimer of opinion, or in the case of an unquantified qualification, there may be instances where it will not be possible to express an opinion that a true and fair view is given.

22. The reporting accountant will need to review the appropriateness of all the accounting policies, as well as their compliance with accounting standards and the consistency of their application. It is essential to ascertain that all the financial statements encompassed by the accountant's report are set out on the basis of current accounting policies.

23. Since the introduction of SSAP 16 the Stock Exchange has required listed companies subject to that standard to publish current cost profit and loss statements for the latest two years beginning on or after 1st January 1980 and the latest current cost balance sheet, and the relevant information is also required in the accountant's report. The reporting accountant will have to review the working papers supporting the current cost statements to ensure that they are in accordance with accounting standards. The current cost accounts should be adjusted as appropriate for the purpose of the accountant's report.

24. Analytical review will assist the reporting accountant in determining whether adjustments need to be made to any of the annual financial statements. Explanations of trends, ratios and other statistics should help to indicate whether or not items have been recorded within the correct accounting period. In particular, "abnormal" items should be highlighted and dealt with accordingly in the analytical review of trading results. Key areas which will be covered by review procedures will include sales trends and gross and net profit margins, as any material fluctuations need to be adequately explained if the reporting accountant is to obtain confidence for his report.

Adjustments to reported figures

25. Whilst it will frequently not be the case, as indicated earlier, it may be necessary for the reporting accountant to adjust some of the reported figures in the financial statements of the five year period. This matter is referred to in chapter 3 of the Yellow Book which states: "In making a report ... the accountants should make such adjustments (if any) as are in their opinion appropriate for the purposes of the report ..." In addition, the reporting accountant is required to prepare a statement known as a "statement of adjustments", showing how the audited profit and loss accounts, balance sheets and source and application of funds statements have been adjusted in order to arrive at the figures included in his report. This statement is submitted separately from his report and must be made available for inspection.

26. Adjustments should be made only if their effect is material and, in particular, where:

    (a)   the financial statements of the various years need to be adjusted so that accounting policies are applied consistently from year to year;

    (b)   there has been a fundamental error;

    (c)   post balance sheet events of an "adjusting" nature have occurred;

    (d)   the trend of results would be misleading for any other reason.

    In considering whether an adjustment is required it is essential to bear in mind that the accountant's duty is to report on past profits or losses and not to attempt to forecast results in future conditions. For example, it would not normally be appropriate to adjust past profits or losses where the future charge for directors' remuneration was expected to differ materially from that of the past. The report should, however, indicate that there has been a change in the level of directors' remuneration.

27. The Yellow Book does not specify any particular format for the statement, and therefore the format most appropriate to the circumstances should be adopted. The statement of adjustments should include details of, and the reasons for, the adjustments sufficient to reconcile the figures from the audited financial statements with the figures included in the accountant's report. Where current cost and historical cost accounts are involved, separate statements of adjustments should be prepared. The statement of adjustments must be submitted in draft to

the Quotations Department of the Stock Exchange at least ten days before publication of the accountant's report, and should be on display in its final form at the time of issue of the prospectus, and filed with the Registrar of Companies.

28.   The reporting accountant will have to consider for each problem area whether an adjustment or mention by way of note might be appropriate. One important area is where a company or business has been acquired or disposed of during the period, as it will be necessary to consider how the effect of the change in the group's operations can most appropriately be shown. Except where merger accounting is adopted, the acquisition or disposal of companies or businesses is not normally a reason to make adjustments to the audited financial statements for the years prior to the acquisition or disposal, which should remain as originally reported. However, where the acquisition or disposal is material, its effect should be disclosed within the accountant's report, and the most appropriate presentation of the results of the group as constituted at the date of the report may be by way of note setting out separately the relevant figures in respect of the acquisition or disposal.

Reporting

REPORTING ACCOUNTANT'S REPORTS

29.   Chapter 3 of the Yellow Book sets out the Stock Exchange's requirements for a reporting accountant's report to the directors of a company and to the issuing house. When shares are being offered to members of the public for the first time, the principal contents of the report should be as follows:

(a)   profits, losses, dividends and earnings per share of the company (or group if it has subsidiaries) in respect of each of the five immediately preceding completed financial years;

(b)   movements on reserves not reflected in the statement of profits and losses;

(c)   the balance sheet of the company and, in the case of a group, the consolidated balance sheet at the end of the last accounting period reported upon or, in the case of an unincorporated business being acquired, the assets and liabilities of the business;

(d)   the source and application of funds statements of the company (or group if it has subsidiaries) in respect of each previous accounting period forming the basis of the report;

(e)   accounting policies, and

(f)   any other matters which appear to be relevant for the purpose of the report.

Reference should be made to chapter 3 of the Yellow Book for the details required under each heading.

30.   The reporting accountant should make such changes to the presentation of information contained in the audited financial statements as he considers necessary, in order to ensure that matters of particular importance in the context of the prospectus are set out prominently.

31.   The financial information described in para 29 above is required where practicable to be computed in compliance with the accounting standards applicable to the last of the five years, adjustments being made to the earlier years' figures if necessary. If it is not practicable to make such adjustments, and if the effect of the change of policy is material, the policies adopted in the earlier and later years, and the effect of the change in the year of change, should be stated.

32.   If the accountant's report refers to reports, confirmations or opinions of other experts, the names and professional qualifications of the parties concerned should be stated. Their consent to the references, in the form and context in which they appear, will be required.

33.   The report should be addressed to the directors of the company and to the issuing house or sponsoring broker. The following form of wording may be appropriate for the opinion section of the report:

> "We have examined the financial information presented below for ... (the 'Company') and its subsidiaries for the five years to ... in accordance with approved Auditing Standards. The Company and its subsidiaries are referred to as the 'Group'. (XYZ & Co have acted as the Company's auditors throughout the relevant period.) The financial information set out under 'historical cost information' and 'current cost information' is based on the audited financial statements of the Company and the Group after making such adjustments as we consider appropriate.
>
> In our opinion the financial information shown under 'historical cost information' below gives, under the historical cost convention (which has been modified by the revaluation of certain assets), a true and fair view of the results and source and application of funds of the Group for five years ended ... and of the state of affairs of the Company and the Group at that date.
>
> In our opinion the abridged supplementary current cost financial statements for the ... years ended ... which are set out under 'current cost information' below have been properly prepared in accordance with the policies and methods set out in the notes thereto to give the information required by Statement of Standard Accounting Practice No. 16."

34.   If the reporting accountant has reservations on any material matters, then his report must be qualified. All reasons for the qualification should be stated, together with the amounts involved if this is relevant and practical. The Auditing Standard "Qualifications in Audit Reports" should be followed. In practice a material qualification which casts doubt on the reported trend of profits or the balance sheet figures may cause the prospectus not to be issued.

35.   In that the financial information contained in an accountant's report does not constitute full accounts within the meaning of the Companies Act 1985, a statement will be required to the effect that full accounts have been delivered to the Registrar of Companies and that such accounts have been reported on by the auditor with or without qualification.

36. Financial and other information is contained throughout a prospectus and not only in the accountant's report. Whilst the reporting responsibility of the reporting accountant does not extend beyond his own report, he should consider the document as a whole and should be party to all the principal discussions concerned with the drafting of a prospectus. He should only give consent to the publication of the prospectus containing his report in circumstances where he is satisfied with the form and context in which his report is to appear in the published document. Guidance on the form of his letter of consent is included in paras 38 and 39 below.

37. As well as containing matters of fact, a prospectus will commonly deal with matters of opinion, full understanding of which entails professional advice from other specialists such as surveyors, lawyers and actuaries. In these circumstances, the reporting accountant should be satisfied that the substance of this advice has been properly reflected in the prospectus and, as with his own report, included only with the consent of the professional firms concerned.

LETTERS OF CONSENT

38. Under s.11 of Part A of the Yellow Book and s.61 of the Companies Act 1985, if a prospectus contains any statement purporting to be made by an expert, the expert must have given and not withdrawn his written consent to the issue of the prospectus, with the statement included in its existing form and context. A statement to the effect that he has so given and not withdrawn his consent must be made in the prospectus. This requirement applies to the reporting accountant's report.

39. An appropriate form of letter to the directors and to any issuing house or sponsoring broker may be as follows:

> "We hereby consent to the issue of the document dated ... issued in connection with the placing of ... shares of ..., containing our report and the references thereto in the form and context in which they appear, and we attach a copy of the document intialled by us for the purposes of identification."

It will be noted that the reporting accountant is giving consent to the issue of the prospectus as a whole, not just to the inclusion in it of his report, and in this connection reference should be made to the guidance offered in para 36 above.

40. It should also be noted that a reporting accountant will not be liable under ss.67, 68 and 69 of the Companies Act 1985 (as extended by s.78(2) of that Act to prospectuses of companies incorporated outside Great Britain) for the issue of a prospectus containing an untrue statement purporting to be made by him if, *inter alia*, before allotment thereunder, on becoming aware that the statement is untrue, he withdraws his consent in writing to the issue of the prospectus and gives reasonable public notice of the withdrawal and of the reasons therefor.

Associated reports not intended for publication

REPORTS ON WORKING CAPITAL REQUIREMENTS

41.   Sched. II of Part A of the Yellow Book also requires that the directors of the company state that in their opinion the company's working capital is sufficient for the requirements of the business or, if not, how it is proposed to provide the additional working capital thought by the directors to be necessary. It is customary for the directors and the issuing house to ask the reporting accountant to review and report to them on the cash flow forecast prepared for this purpose and this may include a request for a report on the assumptions on which it is based.

42.   Generally, the approach to such an assignment involves obtaining and reviewing the forecasts prepared by management of the company concerned and comparing the cash flow shown by these forecasts with the facilities and resources available, or to become available, to the company. The extent of the facilities and resources available should be confirmed directly to the reporting accountant by the appropriate third party.

43.   The forecasts should normally cover at least one year from the date of the relevant document and should include forecasts of profit, cash flow and financial position at the end of the period together with detailed assumptions used in their preparation. The reporting accountant will be required not only to check the arithmetical accuracy of the forecasts and that they are properly derived from the assumptions, but also that the assumptions are reasonable based on historical experience of the company and management's intentions for the future. The degree of review required will in part depend on management's historical accuracy in forecasting and on the surplus of resources over the estimated cash flow requirements. The statement entitled "Accountants' Reports on Profit Forecasts" issued in 1978 by the accountancy bodies provides guidance in this area.

44.   The report should clearly identify the information on which the opinion is based. It should only be issued after the reporting accountant has satisfied himself as to the care with which all the directors have considered that information as they, the directors, have sole responsibility for the statement as to the adequacy of working capital.

The form of report will normally be that, in the opinion of the reporting accountant:

(a)   the directors' statement has been made with due care and the forecast is properly compiled on the footing of the underlying assumptions; or

(b)   it is reasonable for the directors to make their statement.

LETTERS REGARDING BORROWINGS AND OTHER MATTERS

45.   Sched. II of Part A of the Yellow Book requires that there should be shown, in relation to the company and its subsidiaries:

(a)   particulars of the loan capital (including term loans) outstanding, or created but unissued, and of all mortgages or charges, or an appropriate negative statement;

(b)   particulars (as at the latest practicable date) or other borrowings or indebtedness in the nature of borrowings, including bank overdrafts and liabilities under acceptances (other than normal trade bills) or acceptance credits, hire purchase commitments, or guarantees or other material contingent liabilities, or, if there are no such liabilities, a statement to that effect.

In setting out borrowings, inter-company liabilities within the group should normally be disregarded, a statement to that effect being made where necessary. As regards bank indebtedness, where practicable it is recommended that cash book figures should be shown and that they should be reconciled to bank confirmations to ensure there is no unusual pattern of transactions around the relevant date.

46.   The date at which borrowings and bank indebtedness are stated will usually be other than the accounting year-end date. Thus the reporting accountant will generally have less evidence on which to support the establishment of the correct figure for borrowings than would be the case at the year-end. In these circumstances, he will have to place significant reliance on management as to the identification of those parties from whom there are outstanding borrowings. These should be substantiated by direct confirmation from the lenders of the amounts outstanding at the relevant date.

47.   As with working capital, it is customary for the issuing house and the directors to ask the reporting accountant to review and report on the above figures. However, the reporting accountant should where appropriate include in his report reference to the fact that he has placed reliance on management as to the completeness of the amounts shown as borrowings.

48.   The issuing house may also request letters on other financial matters. For instance, where a major acquisition has taken place since the balance sheet date, or is envisaged at the time the prospectus is prepared, it is common practice for the prospectus to include a pro-forma balance sheet setting out a combination of assets and liabilities of the new or enlarged group, together with a statement of the basis on which it has been prepared. The reporting accountant will normally be expected to review the pro-forma balance sheet and report to the issuing house that the directors of the company have properly prepared it in accordance with the basis stated.

5.7   Purchase of a business

It is well known that accounts may be manipulated in a number of ways and the investigating accountant should be wary of the following common methods of doing so:

(a) Stocks may be overstated by:

    (i) double-counting of certain items;

    (ii) over-valuation;

    (iii) inflation due to manipulation of cut-off.

(b) Sales may be overstated by:

    (i) treating goods issued on sale-or-return or consignment as sales;

    (ii) ante-dating post balance sheet copy-sales invoices;

    (iii) creating fictitious documents for credit sales;

    (iv) inflating cash sales by feeding the till from an external source.

(c) Purchases may be understated by:

    (i) post-dating or suppressing year-end invoices;

    (ii) paying for goods from an external or private source;

    (iii) treating goods purchased as held on consignment or sale or return.

(d) Expenditure levels may require adjustment owing to:

    (i) necessary expenditure having been deferred deliberately;

    (ii) inadequate management remuneration having been charged;

    (iii) cash discounts not taken owing to lack of working capital;

    (iv) trade discounts not taken owing to inability to buy in bulk.

5.8   Purchase of shares in a company

Consideration must be given to:

(a) the amounts at which any transfers of shares in the company have recently taken place;

(b) whether the shares to be acquired comprise a majority or minority holding: in the latter case dividend policy will not be able to be dictated, and shares should be valued on the basis of distributions in previous years;

(c) the company's articles to discover whether any resolutions require more than, say, a two-thirds majority, in which case the actual size of the prospective holding will influence the purchase price: holdings exceeding 10% and 25% respectively may also be significant under the terms of the articles.

5.9   Purchase of a share in a partnership

The special procedural points are to ascertain:

(a) the likely reasons for wishing to admit a new partner;

(b) the details of the partnership deed (if there is one), or if not, the existing arrangements regarding:

    (i) profit sharing;

    (ii) preparation and audit of accounts;

    (iii) ascertainment of individual shares on a dissolution or death/retirement of existing partner, including valuation of goodwill;

    (iv) dealing with disputes between partners on accounting matters;

    (v) potential liability in the event of an unexpected failure, particularly where strong risk elements are implicit in the nature of the partnership business;

(c) details of insurance cover, especially professional indemnity;

(d) the extent to which an incoming partner may be liable for partnership debts incurred prior to his admission;

(e) the manner in which the change of partnership is to be dealt with for taxation purposes;

(f) the general economic and trading outlook for the partnership business.

5.10 Loans

Ascertain:

(a) the purpose for which the loan is required;

(b) the adequacy for the purpose of the amount being sought—a borrower will often consider the *least* that the business requires, and even a minor downturn in trade will cause the borrowing requirements to increase;

(c) the adequacy of any underlying security and the ease with which it may be realised;

(d) the proposed arrangements for payment of interest and the period over which repayment is to be completed.

5.11 Fraud

Most defalcations involve loss of cash, and it would be necessary in such cases to carry out the following procedures:

(a) ascertain the level of authority and nature of duties of the defaulting employee;

(b) cast and vouch cash book, and obtain certificates of opening and closing balances from the bank;

(c) check cash book against bank statements, paying particular attention to dates of lodgments to ascertain whether receipts were banked without delay;

(d) examine original pay-in slips at the bank and compare with counterfoils, since this may reveal the practice known as "teeming and lading";

   (e) circularise debtors positively;

   (f) note any apparently irregular cash payments;

   (g) examine cancelled cheques and compare names of payees with details of cash book and invoices;

   (h) obtain duplicates of missing vouchers;

   (i) vouch all amounts shown as partners' or directors' drawings or loans;

   (j) vouch and cast petty cash book;

   (k) confirm names of all employees shown on wages lists with chief accountant or other senior official and amounts payable to them;

   (l) if defaulter had access to all books, all postings should be checked and a trial balance extracted;

   (m) confirm all bad debts written off, discount allowances and returns;

   (n) check order book against sales day book or copy-sales invoices to detect any sales which have been wholly unrecorded;

   (o) cash sales should be verified against whatever evidence may be available;

   (p) vouch purchase invoices with purchase day book, and see that none has been passed through twice;

   (q) obtain duplicates of all missing vouchers;

   (r) compare creditors' statements against purchase ledger balances;

   (s) check goods inwards book or order book against invoices to ensure that the latter relate to bona fide purchases.

(See also Chapter 10, section 2.3.)

5.12 Back duty investigations

Back duty investigations are carried out over a specified number of years in order to establish whether complete and accurate returns of taxable income have been made by the taxpayer to the revenue authorities.

   Procedures will normally involve the setting out of capital statements at the beginning and end of the period in question wherever records of transactions are materially incomplete. The following statement demonstrates how income from a source unaccounted for may be approximately determined.

Statement of reconciliation of capital

			£
Total wealth of taxpayer, wife and dependants at the commencement of the investigation period			xx.xxx

		£	
Add: Known sources of earned income declared		xx.xxx	
Known sources of unearned income declared		xx.xxx	
Profits on sales			
investments		xx.xxx	
rights issues		xx.xxx	
other issues		xx.xxx	
Capital increase from			
gifts		xx.xxx	
legacies		xx.xxx	
life policies matured		xx.xxx	
life policies surrendered		xx.xxx	
windfall gains		xx.xxx	
other items (specify)		xx.xxx	
		xx.xxx	

	£		
Less: Known expenditure accounted for, and compatible with taxpayer's standard of living	xx.xxx		
Losses on sales of			
investments	xx.xxx		
other assets	xx.xxx		
Capital decreases			
gambling losses	xx.xxx		
gifts	xx.xxx		
other losses (specify)	xx.xxx		
(see note)		xx.xxx	
Surplus/deficiency		xx.xxx	xx.xxx
"Notional" total wealth at the close of the period			xx.xxx
Actual total wealth at the close of the period, as disclosed			xx.xxx
Discrepancy due to undisclosed source of income			£xx.xxx

Note
"Other losses" will include assets worn out or discarded.

In the course of collecting the information required for the above capital statement, the following procedural points should be noted:

(a) the investigation relates to the income and expenditure of the taxpayer in his private as well as business capacity;

(b) enquiries must extend to his wife and his dependants;

(c) all sources of potential information which may be relevant must be tapped, such as bank statements, deposit receipts, brokers' notes, insurance policies, interest and dividend counterfoils etc.;

(d) receipts and payments should be traced through to source and destination respectively; small items should not be overlooked since they may indicate the existence of assets previously undisclosed, e.g. a charge for storing a fur coat, or valuable in the "strongroom" of a bank;

(e) the amount of insurance cover should be ascertained since this indicates the approximate value of the underlying assets;

(f) the final report on the back duty investigation should clearly refer to deficiencies in information and the assumptions and estimates which it has therefore been necessary to make.

5.13   Investigations under the Companies Act 1985

The Companies Act 1985 provides for the appointment of inspectors to investigate a company's affairs in certain circumstances. Section 431 provides that the Department of Trade and Industry may make such an appointment on the application:

(a) in the case of a company having a share capital, either of not less than two hundred members or of members holding not less than one-tenth of the shares issued;

(b) in the case of a company not having a share capital, of not less than one-fifth in number of persons on the company's register of members;

(c) of the company (CA 1985, s.43)

Under section 432 of the 1985 Act the Department of Trade and Industry must appoint inspectors to investigate a company's affairs if:

(a) the company by ordinary resolution (prior to the 1985 Act a *special* resolution was required); or

(b) the court by order,

declares that the company's affairs ought to be investigated.

The Department of Trade and Industry may also make such an appointment if it appears to them that there are circumstances suggesting:

(a) that the company's business is being or has been conducted with intent to defraud its creditors or the creditors of any other person, or otherwise for a fraudulent or unlawful purpose, or in a manner oppressive to any part of its members, or that it was formed for any fraudulent or unlawful purpose; or

(b) that persons concerned with the company's formation or the management of its affairs have in connection therewith been guilty of fraud, misfeasance or other misconduct towards it or towards its members; or

(c) that the members of the company have not been given all the information with respect to its affairs which they might reasonably expect.

Security for the costs of investigation were increased from £100 to £5000 by the Companies Act 1985. Inspectors appointed under either section 431 or 432 have power to investigate the affairs of any other body corporate which is or has at any relevant time been the company's subsidiary or holding company, or a subsidiary of its holding company, or a holding company of its subsidiary. The following is a summary of the major provisions:

Examination of officers and access to books, documents etc.

The inspector has power to examine on oath all *past and present* officers and agents (including bankers, solicitors and auditors) of the company and it shall be their duty to attend before him when required to do so. If any such officer or agent refuses to produce any book or document or to answer any question put to him, the inspector may certify his refusal, whereupon the court may enquire into the case, and, after hearing witnesses for and against the alleged offender, may punish him as for contempt of court (section 434 of the 1985 Act).

Section 43A of the 1985 Act enables inspectors who consider that any other person is or may be in possession of information concerning the company's affairs, to require that person to produce books and documents in his possession relating to the company and to give all reasonable assistance with the investigation.

It also enables the inspector to require a past or present director of a company or its subsidiary or holding company under investigation to produce to him all documents in his possession or under his control relating to his bank account, provided that the inspector thinks on reasonable grounds that payments have been made into or out of the account in respect of:

(a) undisclosed directors' remuneration; or

(b) substantial contracts between companies and their directors or connected persons which by s. 232 of the Act should have been disclosed in the accounts and were not so disclosed; or

(c) transactions between recognised banks and their directors which do not meet the disclosure requirements of s. 233 of the Act, or particulars of which were not included in the register of transactions provided for by s. 343 of the Act; or

(d) acts or omissions which constituted misconduct, whether fraudulent or not, towards the company or its subsidiary or holding company or its members under investigation.

This subsection does not extend to investigations under s.442 of the Act.

Note that since the decision of the House of Lords in *R.* v. *IRC, ex parte Rossminster* (1980) it seems clear beyond doubt that the requirement that the inspector must think "on reasonable grounds" is to be objectively construed—i.e. there must exist reasonable grounds in fact, and it is not sufficient that the inspector honestly believes in the reasonableness of objectively unreasonable grounds.

Copies of the report

The inspector must report to the Department of Trade and Industry, who must forward a copy of the report to the company, and a further copy shall, in the case of an investigation under section 431, at the request of the applicants, be delivered to them. Where the inspection is under section 432, a copy of the report must be furnished to the court. If the Department think fit they may furnish a copy of the report to any other person who is a member of the company or of any body corporate dealt with in the report of whose interests as a creditor of the company or any other body corporate appear to the Department to be affected (section 437 of the Act).

Section 437 of the Act provides that where inspectors were appointed by order of the court under s. 432 of the Act, the Secretary of State is to furnish a copy of the report to the court and may if he thinks fit forward a copy to the company's registered office and provide a copy on request and payment of a fee to:

(a) any member of the company under investigation;

(b) any person whose conduct is referred to in the report;

(c) the auditors concerned;

(d) the applicants for the investigation; and

(e) any other person whose financial interest appears to the Secretary of State to be affected by matters dealt with in the report.

Section 437 of the Act provides that a copy of the inspectors' report shall be admissible as evidence of the inspectors' opinion provided it is certified by the Secretary of State to be a true copy.

Civil proceedings and winding up

Under section 438 of the Companies Act 1985, if it appears to the Department of Trade and Industry, from any report made under section 437 of the Act, that civil proceedings ought in the public interest to be brought by any body corporate, they may themselves bring such proceedings in the name and on behalf of that body corporate.

If it appears to the Department of Trade and Industry that it is expedient to do so, the Department may present a petition for the winding-up of the company (section 440 of the Companies Act 1985).

Proceedings for fraud and misconduct etc.

If, from the report, it appears that any body corporate dealt with by the report ought, in the public interest, to bring proceedings for the recovery of damages in respect of any fraud, misfeasance or other misconduct in connection with the promotion, formation or management of that body corporate, or for the recovery of any of its property which has been misapplied, the Department of Trade and Industry may bring proceedings for that purpose in the name of the body corporate (section 438 of the Companies Act 1985).

Investigation procedures

The procedure to be followed by the accountant appointed to conduct such an investigation must be determined by the terms of his instructions, but in most cases a very detailed examination of the company's books and records will be necessary. Particular attention must be paid to the certification of the existence of assets, the nature of the liabilities contracted by the company, dealings with subsidiaries, and the manner in which the profits or losses disclosed by the published accounts have been arrived at.

Discovering financial interests

Under section 442 of the Act the Department of Trade and Industry may appoint one or more competent inspectors to investigate and report on the membership of any company and otherwise with respect to the company for the purpose of determining the true persons who are or have been financially interested in the success or failure (real or apparent) of the company or able to control or materially to influence the policy of the company.

An application for an investigation under this section may be made to the Department by members of the company in the same way as under section 431 of the Act.

Section 443 of the Act extends the power of the Department of Trade and Industry when carrying out an investigation under s. 442 of the Act of the ownership of a company, to any person whom the inspector reasonably believes to possess information relevant to the investigation.

Section 443 of the Act provides that the Secretary of State may, if he thinks there is good reason for not divulging part of a report, omit that part from disclosure. He may cause the Registrar to keep a copy of the report with that part omitted, or in the case of any other such report, a copy of the whole report.

Officers and agents of bodies being investigated have a duty to assist the inspectors, who may make interim reports to the Department, and on the conclusion of their investigation, shall make a final report to the Department.

Dealings in shares and options

The investigation powers of the Department of Trade and Industry were considerably extended by the Companies Act 1967. Under section 446 of the 1985 Act, where it appears to the Department that contraventions may have occurred of the requirements regarding dealings by directors and their families in share options, or the obligation of directors to notify the company of interest in its shares, or the granting by directors to members of their families of the right to subscribe for shares or debentures of the company, they may appoint one or more inspectors to carry out such investigations as will enable them to discover whether such contraventions have taken place, and to report thereon to the Department.

Overseas companies operating in UK

The investigation powers of the Department of Trade and Industry are further extended by section 453 of the Companies Act 1985 to apply to all bodies corporate outside Great Britain which are carrying on business in Great Britain, or have at any time carried on business therein as if they were companies registered under the 1985 Act.

Production of evidence

The 1985 Act is extremely far reaching, and is concerned with the inspection of companies' books and papers. Under section 447 the Department of Trade and Industry, "if they think there is good reason to do so", may require virtually any company formed or carrying on business in the United Kingdom to produce books or papers—or any person having possession of them to do so (but without prejudice to any lien they may have).

Penalties

The Department of Trade and Industry may take extracts and require explanations (a power extended to all investigations), refusal being punishable by three months' imprisonment and/or a £200 fine maximum, and such statements may be admitted in evidence against such officers. If hindrance is suspected, the Department may obtain a warrant to search premises and to take away or safeguard documents; anyone obstructing this is liable to the same penalty. Such information, however, is to be kept confidential, unless the Department needs to use it for civil or criminal proceedings, or winding-up action or for appropriate publication of an inspector's report.

The standard penalties under the 1985 Act for summary conviction or conviction on indictment apply equally to improper disclosure of such information and the destruction of falsification of documents or false statements. Solicitors' privileged communications are safeguarded as is bankers' information, except in regard to the person being investigated.

Extension of powers to require information

Section 444 of the 1985 Act extends the Department of Trade and Industry's powers to require information as to persons interested in shares or debentures, to any person having or being able to obtain such information. The section previously applied only to persons interested in shares or debentures or who had acted as solicitor or agent in respect thereof.

Power to impose restrictions on shares or debentures

Under s. 445 of the Act the power to impose restrictions is no longer confined to cases where the difficulty in discovering relevant facts is due wholly or mainly to the unwillingness of the persons concerned to assist in the investigation.

Purported agreements to transfer either shares which are subject to a restriction on transfer, or rights to be issued with unissued shares which are similarly subject, are void.

An aggrieved party may apply to the court for an order that the restrictions be lifted, and such an order may be made if the court is satisfied that the relevant facts have been disclosed to the company and that no unfair advantage accrued to any person as a result of a failure to make disclosure, or the shares are to be sold and the court or the Secretary of State approves the sale (see next paragraph).

The court may direct that any shares which are subject to restrictions under s. 454 of the 1985 Act be sold, subject to the court's approval of the terms of sale, and such restrictions may be lifted in consequence.

Disclosure of information obtained from certain investigations

Section 449 of the Act provides that information obtained under ss. 447 or 448 of the Act may be made available to inspectors appointed to conduct formal inspections under ss. 431, 432 or 446 of the Act, for the purposes of cross-examination of any person in the inspection.

Professional privilege

Section 732 of the Act extends privilege from the disclosure of information requirements to barristers and advocates as well as to solicitors, save in so far as the name of the lawyer's client is concerned, and to extend the privilege to matters in the hands of the client.

Investigation by the Department of Trade and Industry on liquidator's report

The Department has power under s. 632 of the Act to investigate cases where it appears to the liquidator of a company in voluntary winding-up that any present or past officer of the company has committed a criminal offence in relation to the company. By s. 632 of the Act the Department, where a liquidator's report is referred to it by the Director of Public Prosecutions or the Lord Advocate for further enquiry, may exercise all the powers available to inspectors under the general inspection provisions of s. 431 or s. 432 of the Act.

5.14   An investigations case study

Note

In view of the fact that all the investigations referred to in this chapter will have many features in common, with special reference to the interpretation of financial statements, the following illustration will be found instructive, and should be worked through in detail.

Mr Funds has been approached by Expansion Ltd, with a view to his lending the company £50,000 for five years at an interest rate of 12%.

Mr Funds has been given the following summarised information from the company's accounts.

Balance sheets as on 31st December

	1983 £	1984 £	1985 £
Share Capital	50,000	50,000	50,000
Revenue reserves	35,000	38,000	40,000
6% debentures	32,000	24,000	16,000
	£117,000	£112,000	£106,000
Fixed assets:			
Leasehold property	12,000	9,000	6,000
Plant machinery	44,000	35,000	28,000
	56,000	44,000	34,000

Current assets:

Stock and work in progress	64,000	62,000	72,000
Debtors	54,000	55,000	60,000
Development expenditure	19,000	22,500	26,000
	137,000	139,500	158,000

Current liabilities:

Creditors	27,000	28,000	30,000
Corporation tax	12,000	11,000	11,000
Bank overdraft (secured)	37,000	32,500	45,000
	76,000	71,500	86,000
Net current assets	61,000	68,000	72,000
	£117,000	£112,000	£106,000

Profit and loss accounts for the year ended 31st December

	1983	1984	1985
	£	£	£
Sales	325,000	335,000	360,000
Cost of sales: materials, labour and direct factory costs	227,000	238,000	260,000
Gross profit	98,000	97,000	100,000
Other costs (see note (a))	68,000	69,000	71,000
Operating profit	30,000	28,000	29,000
Corporation tax	12,000	11,000	11,000
Dividends paid	15,000	15,000	15,000
Retention	£3,000	£2,000	£3,000

Notes

    (a) Other costs include:

	1983	1984	1985
	£	£	£
Rent	2,000	2,000	2,000
Depreciation	10,000	10,500	11,000
Amortisation	3,000	3,000	3,000
Directors' salaries	24,000	24,500	25,000
Bank interest	3,500	3,250	4,250

(b) The acquisitions and disposals of fixed assets during the three-year period have been relatively insignificant.

(c) Depreciation at 10% and amortisation is provided on a straight-line basis designed to write off the assets over their useful life.

Mr Funds is told the following, as to the reason for the need for further capital and by way of general explanation:

(a) Provided that a discount of 10% is given and an additional month's credit is allowed on the additional business, firm orders can be obtained which would enable the unit turnover to be increased by 50% over the 1985 figures.

(b) To enable the additional business to be handled, the directors would propose to rent an adjacent factory building of 6,000 square feet at a rental of £9,000 a year, thereby increasing the total available space to 18,000 square feet. The liability for rates is estimated at 50p per square foot.

(c) The cost of additional plant and machinery is estimated at £100,000.

(d) The company is a private one, the share capital being held by the widows of the two founder members. The directors, because they have no shareholdings, are remunerated on an incentive basis based on turnover.

(e) In reply to a question asked by Mr Funds, the directors replied that they would not anticipate that the overhead expenses would rise very much as a result of the additional turnover.

You are required to prepare notes as the basis for your report to Mr Funds on the proposition, using only the information given and deductions and inferences which may reasonably be drawn therefrom. Your supporting schedules should include:

(a) a cash budget forecast to the year ended 31st December 1986, showing the projected year-end position;

(b) notes to the cash budget, showing the basis of your computations;

(c) forecast assets position at 31st December 1986; and

(d) forecast trading results for the year to 31st December 1986.

Since you are advising Mr Funds on the basis of information supplied by *others*, your notes should also reflect your criticisms of the data supplied, and the assumptions on which it is based.

Make any calculations to the nearest £500.

5.15 Case study solution: notes for report to Mr Funds

Investment criteria

1. Mr Funds has asked us to advise him on the proposal to invest £50,000 in Expansion Ltd for a fixed term of five years at a rate of 12%. We do well to begin by reminding ourselves of the three usual investment criteria: income; growth; security.

2. The *income* appears to be reasonable. The total equity interest is £90,000 and a

dividend of £15,000 appears to be perennially paid, giving a rate of 16⅔%. The rate offered to Mr Funds is somewhat less, but (assuming the security proves to be adequate) this is to be expected where no risk is involved. As far as *growth* is concerned, this consideration does not apply in an investment of this nature, the principal, rate and term all being fixed. What, then, of the *security*? This remains to be discovered.

Error in data

3.   The perceptive reader will have noticed the error in the data provided. Does the build-up of reserves reconcile with disclosed annual profits? In 1984 a profit of £2,000 is shown—yet the revenue reserves have increased by £3,000, as revealed by the 1983 and 1984 balance sheets respectively. The profit for 1982, we are told, is £3,000. The balance sheet as on 31st December 1985 shows revenue reserves at £40,000, i.e. only £2,000 higher than at the previous 31st December. So there is a compensating error of £1,000 over the two years.

In practice it is often necessary to go back to source and query errors in the basic information. Don't assume automatically that it is *you* who have got it wrong!

Cash budget

4.   A cash budget, based on the forecasts supplied, will show us how our bank balance might fare at the end of 1986.

5.   The preparation of the budget, however, requires a number of assumptions to be made, some of greater significance than others. The first item of information given to Mr Funds, concerning the means of securing a 50% increase in turnover, contains ambiguous wording. It is uncertain as to whether the discount of 10% would need to be given on *all* future sales, or only on the *additional* future sales effected after the implementation of the new policy. Either of the two possibilities could be intended, since a clear distinction is made between new and existing business as far as the additional month's credit is concerned: the latter is to apply, we are told, to the *additional* business only—but what of the 10% discount? That is less clear.

6.   The idea of operating a sales organisation which allows:

(a) a 10% discount; and

(b) an extra month's credit,

on certain orders only, the distinction being based entirely on whether classified as "new" or "existing" business, could only have been conceived in a dream world.

7.   Undoubtedly increased sales would be derived, in part at least, from existing customers; is it seriously suggested that they would co-operate in supporting this meaningless distinction? Even if it is intended that the special terms are to apply to *new* customers only, existing customers would very soon learn the score and Expansion Ltd could well lose more business than it now hopes to gain.

8. In view of the farcical nature of this policy, if taken literally, we shall proceed with our investigation on the only realistic basis possible—i.e. that the special terms are to apply to *all* future business placed after the new era of "expansion" has dawned! (See cash budget attached.)

9. Although the bank overdraft at 31st December 1985 is secured (we are not told what the security is), it is most unlikely that the bank would readily accede to so substantial an increase in the sum projected which, if the security is a floating charge on the company's assets, would have the effect of watering it down considerably.

Bank position

10. Unless the security is in the form of specific tangible assets, such as freeholds, whose realisable worth is not dependent upon the successful operation of the business, the bank would be very much concerned with:

    (a) the period of normal trading over which the overdraft might be reduced to nil; and

    (b) the likely worth of the underlying assets, assuming the need for a quick realisation.

The gradual reduction of the overdraft through normal trading very much depends on the *profitability* of that trading, and we shall look at that question in a moment. As to the worth of the assets on a forced realisation, the projected balance sheet as on 31st December 1986 would include the items shown in Supporting Schedule (C).

Realisable value of assets

11. We are not told the nature of the company's business and the type of plant it uses. What the plant (even the new plant) and the stocks would realise on a forced sale is an open question, although the debts should be collectible on the whole, provided the company's credit control policy is sufficiently cautious during the period of expansion.

Development expenditure

12. The development expenditure which has been carried forward is an intangible which must obviously be ignored for security assessment purposes. Indeed, we must question the justification for not writing off this expenditure in the first place. We do not know the nature of the company's business and are thus unaware of the importance of this expenditure in securing the company's future place in its market. What we *do* know, however, is that the development expenditure carried forward (over several years, possibly):

    (a) is equal to over half the revenue reserves, and rising annually;

    (b) has been greater than the ploughback over the last two accounting periods.

13. We are given no indication of any development expenditure having been written off, and our investigation at this stage would have to include a thorough appraisal of the true worth of what is being annually carried forward. As a matter

of policy, expenditure of this nature ought to be written off progressively, even if it bears fruit in the form of new products and sophistication and improvement of existing ones. Unless the £26,000 capitalised represents:

(a) saleable "know-how"; or

(b) expenditure on new products which have now reached a marketable stage with every prospect of producing a satisfactory revenue return,

there is no justification whatever in perpetuating what amounts to a manipulation of the company's results in continuing to carry these sums forward. Even if possibility (b) above is applicable, a write-off over reasonably few years should commence.

Overhead expenses

14. We are told (item 5) that the directors "would not anticipate that the overhead expenses would rise very much as a result of the additional turnover". Our cash budget, on the basis of available information on variable costs, assumed that the latter would rise in proportion to the new production levels anticipated, but (so-called) fixed overheads were assumed to rise only where specifically indicated, as in the case of renting new factory premises.

15. The hope that fixed overheads will remain near-static in the face of rising production levels is all very well within certain bounds, but a surge in production of such dramatic proportions as that anticipated by the directors would certainly cause some sympathetic increase in fixed costs. Expansion's fixed costs are considerable; and there is little doubt that at the new heights of anticipated production the additional administrative burden might be very costly. None the less, no projected figures have been built into our Schedules.

Future projects

16. We have already considered the security for the overdraft, because clearly this has a bearing on the security for the loan from Mr Funds, repayment of which, it appears, is not to be preferential within the specific terms of the loan itself.

17. Our projections have so far extended only to 31st December 1986 (see Schedule (C) attached), and although the book value of assets at that date will, it seems, be adequate from both the banks' and Mr Funds' viewpoints, what will the picture be like in five years when the loan is due for repayment? Although it is impossible to answer this now, it is worth considering, as a guide, the projected trading results for 1986. (See Schedule (D) attached.)

18. These projections hardly foretell a rosy future for Expansion Ltd. The estimated realisable value of its plant and machinery, including that purchased during 1986, will be little indeed. The possible value of stocks and debtors in 1991 is of academic interest, since some other saving plan will be needed to avoid recurring future losses.

Plant and machinery

19. Two additional points arise in connection with the plant and machinery. Firstly,

during 1985 its written-down value has decreased by only £7,000 although £11,000 depreciation has been charged. This suggests that net additions of £4,000 have taken place during the year, and any item which exceeds the company's annual ploughback can hardly be described as "relatively insignificant" (see note (b) of question).

20. Secondly, the annual depreciation charge is 10%, calculated on a straight-line basis, and the £11,000 depreciation charge therefore suggests that the present written-down value of £28,000 will be completely written off in the next two to three years, based on an original cost of £110,000 (£11,000 × 10). The important message in this is that Expansion Ltd will, during the period while Mr Funds' loan is outstanding, have to replace its *existing* plant at an approximate outlay of £200,000, assuming that the replacement costs of the plant in question have increased in general sympathy with other price levels since their original purchase. Severe cash problems are therefore bound to crystallise when the plant replacement falls due.

The lease

21. To drive the point home finally, we should note that the lease has only one year to run after 1986. Even assuming the lease to be renewable at a rent similar to that presently obtaining on the adjacent site currently under consideration, the additional charges will be considerable, and no sums appear to have been set aside in previous periods to offset this increase, which is calculated as follows:

		£
12,000 sq. feet renewable at (per annum)		18,000
Less		
Present rental (per annum)	2,000	
Present annual amortisation	3,000	
		5,000
Additional charge (per annum)		£13,000

This makes the future trading prospects even sadder than the forecasts already prepared, and by this stage in our investigation it seems obvious that Mr Funds was approached to stave off a disaster which it is now not too difficult to predict.

22. An interesting feature of the estimate trading results shown above is that even the *gross* profit is lower than that for 1985. The 1986 gross profit is shown as £100,000; under the new proposals this would be nominally increased by £50,000, but then reduced by £54,000 representing 10% discount on sales, not previously allowed, resulting in gross profit of only £96,000—a fact which in itself warns strongly against implementation of the "expansionist" plans ("contractionist" in reality!).

Conclusion

23. Unless further enquiry into the company's trading circumstances brings to light information of an altogether different nature, Mr Funds would be ill advised to

risk his money for what is, in any case, an unexceptional return. Nor would we have much difficulty in persuading him of this view in a well-drafted report, incorporating our reasons and supporting data.

24. It seems clear that Expansion Ltd is about to enter a period of financial difficulty, due to the following:

    (a) Limited bank finance, the bank being primarily concerned with tangible security in the form of property and other saleable fixed assets (rather than current trading items, such as stocks and debtors). In fact, had the approach to Mr Funds been successful, it is likely that the £50,000 would have been spent on new assets which, in turn, would have provided the security for further bank finance, rather than as security for Mr Funds himself.

    (b) The additional period of credit extended to customers is not matched by a sympathetic move by the company's suppliers. Indeed, cash flow difficulties are likely to cause Expansion Ltd to lose out on discounts from suppliers in return for prompt payment.

    (c) The company's future seems to be dependent on development expenditure being incurred, and it is doubtful if the development budget will be able to match its needs. Indeed, the estimated trading results for 1986 (see Schedule (D) attached) assume no additional write-off of development expenditure, a fact which masks even greater losses than those projected. By this stage there can be little justification for continuing to regard this item as a valuable asset in the balance sheet.

    (d) The additional sales revenue projected by the directors is unlikely to produce a satisfactory return for the effort involved, due largely to the gratuitous 10% discount to be given. Gross margins on existing business are slender at around 27%, and the proposed discount will have the effect of reducing the gross profit to below its present level (see paragraph 22 above).

25. Not wishing to conclude on an altogether negative note, our final observation relates to the soundness of the proposition put to Mr Funds in the first place. All that has been said is based upon a request for £50,000, and it may well be that, in requesting as low a sum as seemed to the directors to be compatible with survival, they have fallen into the oldest trap of all—that of asking for far too little!

26. Depending, of course, on the resources which Mr Funds has available for the purpose, we should urge him to consider a very much more substantial investment than the £50,000 requested, as an alternative to an outright refusal. Provided adequate security could be arranged (by no means an insuperable problem) a larger cash input would:

    (a) enable the company to strengthen its market position without resorting to crippling giveway techniques;

    (b) allow for adequate ploughback for development of its product range;

    (c) facilitate the replacement of outmoded plant with more efficient, economical and technologically superior machines; and

(d) allow for natural expansion into new premises if desired, especially on the expiry of the existing lease.

27. This is an altogether different proposal—and obviously the subject of another case study! But we can see that perhaps the real problem with Expansion Ltd is that it has had an easy ride to date, making moderate profits, and never had to face the type of problem which now looms on the not-too-distant horizon. It would not be altogether unfair to suggest that in drafting their proposal to Mr Funds, the directors have displayed the most common of all management defects—quite simply, lack of vision!

5.16 Case study solution: supporting schedules

(A) Cash budget—forecast to year ended 31st December 1986

RECEIPTS

	£	£	£
Collection of debts outstanding at 31st December 1985			60,000
Sales revenue received (1982 total + 50%)		540,000	
Less 10% discount		54,000	
		486,000	
Less estimated debtors at 31st December 1986 (3 months)			
× £486,000 (see note 1)		121,500	
			364,500
			424,500
Proposed loan from Mr Funds			50,000
			474,500

PAYMENTS

	£	£	£
Settlement of creditors at 31st December 1986		30,000	
Payments to creditors (see note 2)		345,000	
"Other costs"— 1985	71,000		
Less amortisation and depreciation	14,000		
debenture interest saved on debentures redeemed (480) say,	500		
	14,500		
		56,500	
Repayment of debentures		8,000	
Purchase of additional fixed assets		100,000	
Additional rent charge		9,000	
Additional rates charge (6,000 sq. ft × 50p)		3,000	
Interest on loan to Mr Funds		6,000	
Additional directors' remuneration		9,000	
			566,500

Deficit on year to 31st December 1986
   (excluding additional bank interest)   92,000
Overdraft at 31st December 1985   45,000

                                                  137,000
Additional bank interest (see note 3)   8,500
Projected overdraft at 31st December 1983   £145,000

(B) Cash budget notes

NOTE 1
The ratio of sales to debtors indicated by the 1985 accounts is 360,000:60,000, which gives an average period of credit of two months. We are told that under the new proposals it will be necessary to give an extra month's credit.

NOTE 2
The cost of sales is calculated as follows:

	£
1985 cost of sales	260,000
50% increase (assuming all costs are variable)	130,000
Cost of sales	390,000
Less: creditors at 31st December 1986 (1985 figure + 50%)	45,000
Cash paid to creditors	£345,000

We are obliged to assume that creditors at 31st December 1983 are *trade* creditors in the absence of any other information.

NOTE 3
The bank interest charge for the year is based on a fluctuating balance overdrawn, of which we have no details. It is therefore necessary to estimate the 1986 charge by comparing the 1985 charge with the amount overdrawn at 31st December 1983. Thus:

$$4,250 \times \frac{137,000}{45,000} = \qquad\qquad 12,939 \,(\text{approx.})$$

	£
Less: 1985 charge	4,250
Additional charge for 1986	8,689
(say)	£8,500

NOTE 4
It is not possible from the figures supplied to discover the exact basis of the directors'

remuneration, and so the increase has been estimated in our cash flow projections. It seems that such remuneration has been approximately 7% of turnover in the past, and this rate is therefore assumed for the expanded turnover, net of discounts.

NOTE 5

It is assumed that debentures will continue to be redeemed at the rate of £8,000 per annum.

(C) Estimated assets position—31st December 1986

	£	£
Fixed assets:		
Leasehold property		3,000
Plant and machinery (see note)		107,000
		110,000
Current assets:		
Stock and work in progress (1985 plus 50%)	108,000	
Debtors (as previously calculated)	121,500	
Development expenditure (assuming no further increase)	26,000	
		255,500
		£365,500

Note

		£
Plant and machinery:		
Written-down value at 31st December 1985		28,000
Less: depreciation (same as for 1985—presumably 10% on cost which is not disclosed; and assuming no disposals in 1986)		11,000
		17,000
Additional plant purchased	100,000	
Less: 10% depreciation	10,000	
		90,000
		£107,000

(D) Estimated trading results for the year to 31st December 1986

	£	£
Sales (1985)	360,000	
Add: 50% increase	180,000	
	540,000	
Less: 10% discount	54,000	
		486,000
Cost of sales (1985)	260,000	
Add: 50% increase	130,000	
		390,000
Gross profit		96,000

Less: expenses—	
"Other costs" (1985)	71,000
Additional rent	9,000
Additional rates	3,000
Additional depreciation	10,000
Additional bank charges, previously calculated	8,500
Interest on loan to Mr Funds	6,000
Additional directors' remuneration	9,000
	116,500

Less: debenture interest saved on debentures redeemed (say)	500	
		116,000
Projected trading loss for 1986		£20,000

(N.B. No development expenditure has been written off.)

6.0   REPORTS ON PROFIT FORECASTS

6.1   Introductory note

During the late 1960s the City Panel on Takeovers and Mergers was set up in order to regulate procedures in the City in connection with bid situations. This was partly due to a measure of adverse publicity surrounding instances of totally inaccurate forecasting, as a result of which bid prices were unrealistic.

One of the first major tasks of the Panel was the establishment of the City Code on Takeovers and Mergers, which has been in use in its present form since April 1968, and is periodically updated in the light of experience.

There is no doubt that the work of the Panel has played a major role in regulating the sensitive relationships which arise in the course of takeover bids, but it remains questionable as to whether the Panel's structure and scope will remain adequate in the future. One of the criticisms of the present system is that the Panel lacks the power of legal sanction; the only threat which it can levy against delinquent operators is the suspension of membership of the relevant body, e.g. the Issuing Houses Association. It is argued by many, including a number in government posts, that an equivalent of the Securities and Exchange Commission (SEC) in the USA is an essential requirement for this country, the SEC having wide reaching statutory powers in the spheres of both civil and criminal law.

6.2   The accountant's role

Under the rules of the Code, *profit forecasts* made by directors in any bid situation form part of the public documents available for inspection, and these must be examined by the company's auditors and confirmed by them as fulfilling certain basic criteria.

The Code requires the accounting bases and calculations of forecasts to be examined and reported on, and any document containing such forecasts must also include the accountant's report, together with a statement that the accountant has given and has not withdrawn his consent to publication. Forecasts are subject to substantial inherent uncertainties, and therefore cannot be confirmed or verified in the same way as the results of completed accounting periods. The assumptions upon which the directors have based their forecasts must be clearly stated, and the reporting accountants (auditors) must examine and report upon the accounting bases and calculations of those forecasts.

6.3 Preliminary points

Prior to accepting instructions to report in connection with profit forecasts, the reporting accountant is advised to reach agreement with the directors on the following preliminary points:

(a) the time available to the accountant for the preparation of his report should not be so limited that, having regard to the company's circumstances, it would be plainly impossible for sufficient information to be obtained to enable the accountant properly to exercise such professional judgment as may be required;

(b) it must be clearly established that the accountant's responsibility is confined to the accounting bases and calculations for the forecasts and does not extend to the assumptions on which the directors have based their forecasts;

(c) since forecasts are subject to increasing uncertainty the further forward they extend, accountants should not normally undertake to review and report on forecasts which relate to more than the current accounting period and (provided a sufficiently significant part of the current year has elapsed) the next accounting period;

(d) it must be established that the reporting accountant cannot relieve the directors of their own responsibility for profit forecasts which may be disclosed to, and relied upon by, outside parties.

6.4 Detailed work in profit forecasts

In the course of his review of profit forecasts the reporting accountant should consider the following:

(a) the general character and recent history of the company's business with particular reference to its main products, markets, customers, suppliers, labour force, and trend of results;

(b) the accounting policies normally adopted in preparing the company's annual accounts and the fact that these have been consistently applied in the preparation of the profit forecasts;

(c) whether or not the preparation of the forecasts is consistent with the economic, commercial, marketing and financial assumptions which the directors have stated to be the underlying bases;

(d) the company's general procedures in the preparation of forecasts; in particular the accountant will wish to ascertain whether forecasts are regularly prepared for management purposes and if so, the degree of accuracy and reliability normally achieved; he will also wish to discover the extent to which the forecast results of expired periods are supported by reliable interim accounts, and how the forecasts take account of any material exceptional items;

(e) matters of general concern include the adequacy of provisions made for foreseeable losses and contingencies, and the adequacy of working capital as indicated by properly prepared cash flow forecasts.

6.5   Main matters to be stated in accountant's report

The report should be addressed to the directors, and should:

(a) indicate in general terms the work carried out, i.e. review of accounting bases and calculations on which profit forecasts are based;

(b) ensure specific identification of the forecasts and the documents to which the report refers;

(c) if an audit of estimated results for expired periods has not been carried out, include a statement to that effect;

(d) express an opinion as to whether forecasts are properly compiled on the basis of assumptions made by the board, and the figures presented on bases consistent with normal practices;

(e) qualify the report if appropriate (qualifications may be necessary on grounds of substantial restrictions of time).

6.6   Specimen report

An accountant's report on the accounting bases and calculations for profit forecasts might in appropriate circumstances, where there are no grounds for qualification, read as follows:

TO THE DIRECTORS OF X LTD

We have reviewed the accounting bases and calculations used for the period forecasts of X Ltd (for which the directors are solely responsible) for the periods ... set out on pages ... of this circular. The forecasts include results shown by audited interim accounts for the period ... In our opinion the forecasts, so far as the accounting bases and calculations are concerned, have been properly compiled on the basis of the assumptions made by the board set out on page ... of this circular, and are presented on a basis consistent with the accounting practices normally adopted by the company.

7.0   BUILDING SOCIETY AUDITS

7.1   Background

Recent years have seen the collapse of a number of building societies, with or without a fraudulent ingredient. The two most recent collapses were the Wakefield and Grays, which have a good deal in common. A brief analysis of Grays may therefore be instructive. This fraud, which resulted in a loss of over £7 million, included a fair amount of sensational matter. It lasted for over fifty years and was brought to a conclusion by the suicide of the chairman and secretary of the society, Mr Harold Jaggard, at the age of 79.

7.2 Legal requirements

The governing legislation is the Building Societies Act 1962, and it will be seen from the following extracts that there are strong similarities between building societies and companies legislation:

Section 87

(a) The auditors of a building society shall make a report to the members on the accounts examined by them, and on every balance sheet and every revenue and appropriation account laid before the society at the annual general meeting during their tenure of office.

(b) The auditors' report shall be read before the building society at the annual general meeting and shall be open to inspection by any member.

(c) The report shall state whether the balance sheet and revenue and appropriation account are properly drawn up in accordance with the requirements of the Act and the regulations made thereunder and whether, in the opinion of the auditors, they give a true and fair view:

  (i) in the case of the balance sheet, of the state of the building society's affairs as at the end of its financial year; and

  (ii) in the case of the revenue and appropriation account of the income and expenditure of the building society for its financial year.

(d) It shall be the duty of the auditors of a building society in preparing this report under this section to carry out such investigations as will enable them to form an opinion as to the following matters, that is to say:

  (i) whether the society has kept proper books of account and proper records of the matters referred to in subsection (1) of section 27 of the Act;

  (ii) whether the society has maintained a satisfactory system of control over its transactions and records, and, in particular, whether the requirements of paragraph (*b*) of subsection (1) and subsection (3) of section 76 of the Act have been complied with; and

  (iii) whether the balance sheet and revenue and appropriation account are in agreement with the books of account and records of the society.

  and if the auditors are of opinion that the society has failed to keep proper books of account or proper records of the matter referred to in subsection (1) of section 27 of the Act, or to maintain a satisfactory system of control over its transactions and records, or if the balance sheet and revenue and appropriation account are not in agreement with the books of account and records of the society, the auditors shall state that fact in their report.

(e) Every auditor of a building society:

  (i) shall have a right of access at all times to the books, accounts, records and vouchers of the society and to all other documents relating to its affairs including the deeds relating to property mortgaged to the society; and

  (ii) shall be entitled to require from the officers of the society such information and explanations as he thinks necessary for the performance of the duties of the auditors.

(f) If the auditors fail to obtain all the information and explanations which, to the best of their knowledge and belief, are necessary for the purposes of their audit, they shall state that fact in their report.

(g) The auditors of a building society shall be entitled:

  (i) to attend any general meeting of the society and to receive all notices of, and other communications relating to, any general meeting which any member of the building society is entitled to receive; and

  (ii) to be heard at any meeting which they attend on any part of the business of the meeting which concerns them as auditors.

Section 91

(a) The auditors of a building society shall make a report on the annual return which shall be annexed to the annual return made to the Chief Registrar of Friendly Societies.

(b) Regulations under section 86 of the Act may provide that the auditors of a building society shall not be required in their report on the annual return to deal with such of the matters to be contained in the annual return as may be prescribed by the regulations for the purposes of this subsection.

(c) The auditors' report on the annual return shall (without prejudice to any provision of the Act requiring any other information to be contained therein) contain statements as to the following matters, that is to say:

  (i) whether in their opinion the annual return is properly drawn up in accordance with the requirements of the Act and regulations made thereunder; and

  (ii) whether the annual return gives a true and fair view of the matters to which it is to be addressed (other than those with which the auditors, by virtue of regulations made in pursuance of the last preceding subsection, are not required to deal); and

  (iii) whether the annual return is in agreement with the books of account and records of the society.

7.3   Cash receipts and payments

As a background to analysing the Grays fraud it is necessary to note that the chief sources of receipts by cash and cheque are:

(a) deposits received;

(b) mortgage repayments, comprising:

    (i) capital; and

    (ii) interest;

(c) mortgage redemptions (final).

The following are the major payments:

(a) interest on deposits;

(b) mortgage advances to vendors or their solicitors;

(c) payments to the building society's own solicitors (fees) and insurance premiums.

7.4   The nature of the Grays fraud

The Department of Trade and Industry report on Grays noted that the chairman was:

(a) misappropriating cash received;

(b) teeming and lading to cover up the deficiency;

(c) "plugging the gap" by misallocating mortgage redemption cheques which, by their nature, usually comprise substantial amounts.

The Grays fraud was based on the simple principle that a certain ratio of liquidity was needed on a day-to-day basis and that other sums, over and above this ratio, were therefore susceptible to misappropriation. This principle applies in banks—there is little chance that under normal circumstances all depositors would wish to draw out their money on one day. The chairman of Grays simply ensured that the society's predictable cash requirements were always available. We now know what he did with the remainder, although the exact nature of his personal expenditure has not been established. He was a heavy gambler, and there were rumours of other "extra-mural activities"—but we need not go into this here.

7.5   The cover-up

He was able to cover up the fraud:

(a) by making the book entries (over which he had complete control) appear to reflect the actual transactions, i.e. as if the cash was present in the society's account;

(b) by controlling his co-directors, to whom board minutes were never circulated, and who clearly had little conception of the nature of their own statutory duties: they always "rubber stamped" mortgage redemptions, but they never checked that the payments had actually been received and banked;

(c)   by hiring staff who were incapable of appreciating what he was doing or how his position in the company would naturally allow the exercise of a free hand, especially in relation to the manipulation of cash assets and supporting records;

(d)   by maintaining a handwritten recording system despite the fact that the society's assets approached £10 million;

(e)   by effectively controlling the audit function.

7.6   The audit

(a)   Tests carried out by the Grays' auditors were always carried out in an identical sequence. The society's records were therefore presented to the auditors in the same sequence, and this enabled the chairman to alter records after audit inspection. Incidentally, figures were always presented to the auditors in pencil, and as a result of subsequent alterations crosscasts *appeared* to agree but in fact did not.

(b)   The audit staff were clearly incompetent to understand the purpose of their tests. They were conducted mechanically, each state of the audit being pursued in isolation from all other stages. The audit staff appear to have acted under the chairman's control, and it was subsequently discovered that many of the tests laid down were never performed.

(c)   The partner responsible for the audit clearly did not know what was actually going on. For example, he did not know that:

   (i)   all incoming mail was opened by the chairman personally;

   (ii)   mortgage redemption cheques were always handed to the chairman personally;

   (iii)   the year-end summaries contained post-audit erasures and did not crosscast.

(d)   The audit partner did know that cash was not banked daily but, in his view, overcame this weakness by occasionally counting the cash. Unfortunately, however, such cash counts were never conducted on a surprise basis.

7.7   Summary of the Grays situation

(a)   The accounting procedures were never subjected to review.

(b)   Internal control procedures as a whole were never subjected to review, either by the board or by the auditors.

(c)   Neither the board nor the auditors had any real idea of the possibilities open to the chairman, nor of his ability to override such controls as purported to exist.

7.8 Department of Trade and Industry recommendations

The inspectors recommended as follows:

(a) strengthening the powers and procedures available to the Registrar of Building Societies concerning the review of societies' operations and the effectiveness of their auditors;

(b) provision by building society auditors of a more explicit and detailed report as part of the annual return;

(c) it is good practice for the auditors to meet the board, or the appropriate committee, at least once a year to discuss the accounts, the accounting procedures and the internal control: it is recommended that the auditors should confirm in their report that this has been done;

(d) that the ability and knowledge of building society directors in general should be enhanced, and that they should be required to resign and seek annual re-election upon reaching the age of 70 (as is the case under the Companies Act);

(e) the law should be changed to ensure that the chairman of a building society should not also act as chief executive;

(f) there should be at least two executive directors on every building society board.

Finally, the inspectors recommended that they should be able to apply to the court for an order to compel witnesses to attend. The Grays inspectors were unable to compel certain witnesses (e.g. bookmakers, whose co-operation would have been necessary to ascertain more accurately the personal expenditure of the chairman) to answer their questions. Such a power exists, of course, under the Companies Act 1985, but this does not extend to building societies.

7.9 Institute Guidelines

Some years ago the Institute of Chartered Accountants in England and Wales issued guidelines on the audit of building society accounts. The appropriate extracts are as follows:

Limitations in the Rules
The rules and policy of the society may impose limitations as to:

(a) types of property which may be accepted as security;

(b) proportion of the value of the security which may be advanced;

(c) overall limit on the amount which may be advanced either per property, per borrower or over a stated period;

(d) types of additional security which may be accepted and any special conditions;

(e) the competent persons who are eligible to value properties;

(f) advances on properties in course of erection;

(g) rates of interest and repayment terms.

Records of advances

The records maintained by the society in respect of advances should include the following which are hereafter referred to as the "advance records", irrespective of the form they may take in any particular society:

(a) offers of advances and by whom authorised;

(b) security for advances, survey report, solicitors' report on title, and status reports;

(c) name and address of borrower;

(d) terms;

(e) records of compliance with any conditions;

(f) board approval;

(g) acceptance or withdrawal of applications.

The auditors' examination

The auditors have a statutory duty to carry out such investigations as will enable them to form an opinion whether the foregoing requirement has been complied with. Particular points to consider in examining the system include:

(a) the procedure for checking deeds on receipt from the solicitors to see that they are complete, in accordance with the "advance records", correctly executed and stamped;

(b) the maintenance of a record showing the location of all the deeds and the dates of any changes in the locations of any of them;

(c) the procedure for ensuring that the deeds are received from the society's solicitors without undue delay; solicitors frequently need to submit documents to the Land Registry and as there is often a delay of some months at the Registry it is important that the society should have an established follow-up procedure, to ensure that the receipt of deeds from the solicitors is not delayed longer than is necessary for registration to be completed;

(d) the authority required for any temporary release of deeds from their normal custody and proper control for their prompt return;

(e) whether there is a continuous independent check (which some large societies maintain) of the deeds against the "advance records" or the borrowers' ledger accounts;

(f) the necessity for satisfactory cross-reference between the "advance records", the cash book, the borrowers' ledger accounts and the deeds;

(g) the procedure for release of deeds on redemption of a mortgage; on premature redemption the discharge of a mortgage will usually have to be completed by the society and passed, with the title deeds, to the society's solicitors some time before the redemption money is received and there should therefore be an established follow-up procedure.

Examining the deeds

When examining the deeds the auditors' purpose should be to ascertain whether:

(a) the mortgage is in the name shown in the "advance records", unless it is a "transfer of equity" in which case the mortgage would be in the name of the original mortgagor while the name in the "advance records" should be that of the transferee in the new document of title;

(b) there is a document of title to the property under mortgage and the society's solicitors have been satisfied as to the borrower's title;

(c) the amount of the advance as stated in the mortgage deed is not less than that shown on the "advance records";

(d) the mortgage deed is stamped, properly signed and witnessed and is *prima facie* in order;

(e) the property is adequately insured, the premium is paid up to date and the society's interest as mortgagee is endorsed on the insurance policy.

Shares and deposits

(a) An indication is given below of matters which the auditors will need to consider when assessing the system and deciding what tests they should apply in order to satisfy themselves on the records of shares and deposits. An effective confirmation of balances is a most important safeguard and the auditors should either carry out or supervise the carrying out of a test confirmation at least once a year.

(b) Shares may consist of subscription shares and paid-up shares; there are also term shares where the shareholder will not normally require repayment until after a specified period of years. Interest on shares or deposits may be credited to the account instead of being paid. The following should be covered by the society's system to ensure proper control:

(i) responsible custody of unused share and deposit pass-books, receipt forms and share certificates;

(ii) instructions to the staff as to the making of entries in pass-books, and the issue of receipts;

(iii) withdrawal terms, notice, specimen signatures;

(iv) authorisation of withdrawals by ledger department or against pass-book;

(v) records of deaths, marriages, powers of attorney and transmission of shares and deposits (direct transfers from one account to another should not be permitted: transfers should be entered in a journal so that all such entries may be verified);

(vi) comparison of the balance shown in the pass-book with that shown in the ledger account; this may be carried out continuously by retaining pass-books for comparison before return or by periodical circularisation of depositors or shareholders requesting them to send in their pass-books for the purpose. It is desirable that the society's system should provide for special arrangements to deal with withdrawals from accounts where correspondence has been returned unanswered or trace has otherwise been lost of depositors or shareholders.

Cash

The handling of cash is always accompanied by possibilities of error and misappropriation, concealed by "teeming and lading", manipulation of dormant accounts and other devices. This problem is of special importance to auditors of building societies because of the large extent of cash transactions, but it does not involve audit considerations which differ in principle from those encountered in many other businesses. In assessing the system and testing its effectiveness the auditors will need to apply rigorously their professional techniques. Discrepancies revealed by surprise cash counts or by searching tests "in depth" will call for exhaustive investigation.

"Window dressing"

Auditors should examine transactions which have the effect of showing as on the balance sheet date a state of affairs (particularly the society's liquidity) which is materially better than it was during the year and shortly after. Items requiring particular attention are:

(a) large deposits received shortly before the year end and repaid shortly after;

(b) large mortgage repayments received shortly before the year end and re-advanced on the same property shortly after;

(c) unusual delay until after the year end in making payments in accordance with applications received for withdrawals of shares or deposits;

(d) an abnormal year-end accumulation of commitments for advances followed by the making of the advances shortly after the year end;

(e) the significance of the items in bank reconciliation statements.

The report of the auditors

Where the auditors have no reservations to make in respect of any of the matters specified in section 87 a suitable form of report would be:

REPORT TO THE AUDITORS TO THE MEMBERS OF THE . . . . BUILDING SOCIETY
The foregoing balance sheet and revenue and appropriation account are properly drawn up in accordance with the requirements of the Building Society Act 1962, and the regulations made thereunder. In our opinion they give respectively a true and fair view of the state of the society's affairs as on . . . . . and of its income and expenditure for the financial year ended on that date.

If the auditors are unable to report in those terms or find it necessary to report on any of the matters referred to in subsection (4) or (5) of section 38 their report should be factual, specific and as brief as is consistent with conveying the essential points.

Note

The above accords with the content of the APC guideline on Building Society audits.

8.0   REPORTING ON THE ACCOUNTS OF ESTATE AGENTS

8.1   Legal background

The affairs of estate agents are now governed by the Estate Agents Act 1979. Estate agents who are members of the Royal Institution of Chartered Surveyors (RICS) will also be subject to that body's regulations. Auditors with estate agent clients will need to be concerned with the Estate Agents Act 1979 and/or RICS Members' Accounts Regulations.

The RICS regulations set out in detail the work which the reporting accountant must do. The Estate Agents Act provides for the Secretary of State to make parallel regulations but these have not yet appeared. The Act itself requires those carrying out estate agency work to maintain a "client" bank account, to have insurance cover for clients' money and to account for interest on client deposits.

In the absence of detailed accounts regulations under the Estate Agents Act, this section sets out the work which should be done under the RICS regulations, as set out in advice given to CCAB members by the APC in *True & Fair*.

8.2   Instructions

Before doing any work you will need confirmation of your instructions. These instructions will describe any work which you are to do beyond that required by the Estate Agents Act or the RICS regulations. They may or may not require you to express an opinion on the accounts but in any event you should ensure that the accounts (which may be used for the admission of future partners and for submission to the Inland Revenue) comply with current best practice as far as possible within your terms of reference.

8.3   Handling clients' funds

The RICS regulations which relate to work which an accountant is required to perform before signing an accountant's report give an indication of the minimum work which is necessary in relation to clients' funds. Such work includes:

(a) examination of client ledger accounts to ensure that particulars of all clients' money received, held or paid on account of each client is separately identified;

(b) checks of postings to the clients' ledger accounts from receipts and payments records;

(c) comparison of a sample of payments and receipts shown on the bank statements with the records of receipts and payments of clients' money;

(d) test checks and enquiries into the system of recording costs and making transfers in respect of costs from the clients' account;

(e) examination of relevant documentation to ensure that legitimacy of transfers between accounts and of other financial transactions;

(f) checks of the balances on the clients' ledger accounts and agreeing the total with the balance on the clients' account;

(g) reconciliation of the clients' bank balance;

(h) checks to ensure that the total of the clients' account balances agree with the balance on the clients' bank account;

(i) tests to ensure that monies have not been incorrectly omitted from the clients' account.

A detailed examination of the RICS regulations will be necessary where the estate agent is a member of the RICS to ensure compliance with the specific regulations.

8.4   Accounts with building societies

The chances are that your client will have an agency with a building society. As such he is acting as a branch office of the building society and may receive monies as regular instalments of mortgage payments or regular deposits in a building society investment account. If he receives the money in the form of a cheque he will probably be required by the building society to pay the money into a bank for the credit of the building society concerned. If this is done the money probably will not enter his own books of account.

Alternatively, the estate agent may receive the money in cash. If this is the case he should pay it into a separate bank account and reconcile this with his ledger account. He will be required to make returns to the building society on a regular basis to record these transactions.

The estate agent may also make payments out to a building society investor, to a specified limit. He may hold a float from the building society for this purpose and these transactions again will be accounted for in the regular returns to the building society.

Your tests should include checks on all these transactions to ensure that any monies received by the estate agent are properly recorded and paid over to the building society.

8.5   Accounts with insurance companies

Your estate agent client may also act as an agent for an insurance company collecting insurance premiums on its behalf. You should check that these transactions are recorded properly and that any commissions payable by the insurance company to the estate agent for his agency services are made in accordance with this agency agreement. Reconciliations of bank accounts maintained for these purposes and ledger accounts will be necessary and you should ensure that the regular returns made by the estate agent to the insurance company are in agreement with your client's records.

8.6   Fee income

Many of an estate agent's transactions are abortive and do not lead to income. There is a risk therefore, that successful transactions may be overlooked and on occasions never billed. Such errors may be concealed in the accounts because it is accepted practice for an estate agent to offer "competitive commissions" for particular types of work including that connected with his appointment as a vendor's sole agent. Audit tests to ensure the completeness of billings should include an examination of "confirmatory letters" which establish the amount of the fee to be charged. Similarly, attention should be paid to the accounting policies for commissions and fee income so that profit is not taken too early on work that cannot be billed until completion takes place, or too late if completion has already taken place.

8.7   Management letters

The efficient running of an estate agent's practice and your ability to work fast and effectively are substantially affected by the quality of your client's book-keeping. The book-keeping entries are probably more complicated than many practitioners suspect and the specialised nature of an estate agent's work requires the same care and attention afforded to any other specialist job. Particular care is needed when your work is in respect of only one area of your client's activities. So when your work on the accounts is completed it must make sense to assist your client all you can by submitting a constructive and concise management letter.

9.0   THE AUDIT OF INVESTMENT COMPANIES

The comments below relate to any company holding investments in securities whether or not for the purpose of trading in those securities and whether or not the company is called a "trust".

Incidentally, despite the name, investment trusts are in fact limited liability companies, subject to the requirements of the Companies Act. They are not trusts in the sense that they are governed by a trust deed, as in the case with unit trusts for example, and in fact, in many cases, the word "trust" appears in the name of the company purely for historical reasons.

Many investment companies obtain "approved" status for taxation purposes, by complying with certain legal requirements, the most important being that their shares are publicly quoted, that they do not retain more than 15% of their income from shares and securities and that they do not distribute surpluses on the realisation of their investments. The effect of "approval" is that the company suffers a lower than normal tax charge on all or some of its income.

9.1   Audit work

As well as the usual audit work needed to enable the auditor to express an opinion on the accounts, some specific audit points are set out below:

Review of internal control
The auditor will, as usual, need to acquire a knowledge of the accounting system and, if he wishes to rely on it, the system of internal control. He will need to evaluate such controls and to carry out compliance tests in order to decide on the extent to which his

substantive tests can be reduced in the light of such reliance. The most important areas where control is of fundamental importance are:

(a) portfolio valuation;

(b) purchase/sale of investments;

(c) accounting for income;

(d) title/custody of investments.

Investments

Verification of the existence of investments included in the balance sheet will involve either:

(a) a "count" at the balance sheet date, or at some other date if the system of control is sufficient to enable the auditor to verify movements in the intervening period; or

(b) direct confirmation of investments held by an external custodian. The adequacy of a confirmation in such circumstances will be assessed having considered the status of the custodian, in addition to the client company's own system of monitoring of and control over the actions of the custodian.

The auditors will need to confirm the company's proper title to the investments, that there is no lien on them and that they are registered in the company's name or the name of an authorised nominee company. Routine audit tests will need to be performed on the accuracy and completeness of the investment lists, on the prices used in calculating the values of investments and on the reconciliation of investment control accounts.

Surpluses and deficiencies on investment transactions

The accounting treatment of realised and unrealised surpluses on the sale and valuation of investments should be set out in the memorandum and articles of association. SSAP 6, "Extraordinary Items and Prior Year Adjustments", identifies investment trust companies as special cases. Accordingly, surpluses or deficiencies which are not dealt with in the profit and loss account must be shown either in the balance sheet or in the notes to the accounts.

Income

During the course of his review of internal control the auditor should have obtained information on the client's policy with regard to accounting for income. Dividends received and interest on investments are normally credited to revenue on one of the following bases:

(a) date dividend paid;

(b) date dividend declared;

(c) date investment is quoted "ex-dividend";

(d) time apportionment (for fixed interest securities).

The auditor should verify both the accuracy and the completeness of the income from investments, in conjunction with his balance sheet work, by reference to an outside share information service. It should be remembered that SSAP 8, "The Treatment of Taxation under the Imputation System in the Accounts of Companies", refers specifically to the treatment of taxation credits on investment income and disclosure of material tax credits on franked investment income.

Taxation

In respect of corporation tax, if the company has computed its taxation charge/ liability on the basis of approved status, in this respect the auditor should:

(a) confirm that the requirements for approved status have been and are being complied with; and

(b) check that the correct taxation rate for investment trust companies is being used.

Stock exchange requirements

If the investment company is a public quoted company, in addition to his normal review in respect of Stock Exchange requirements for such companies, the auditor will need to review the special Stock Exchange requirements in respect of investment companies.

Companies Act 1985

The effect of any dividend must not be to reduce the assets of the company to below $1\frac{1}{2}$ times the aggregate of its liabilities (CA 1985, s. 265).

10.0 THE AUDIT OF CLUBS

10.1 Introduction

The term "club" embraces a variety of institutions. Well known examples are local sports clubs and working men's clubs, some of which may be registered under the Friendly Societies and Industrial and Provident Societies Acts. The following does not deal with proprietary clubs where ownership is divorced from membership and which are run for profit.

10.2 Definition

A club may be defined as a society of persons associated for the promotion of a common object or objects, other than for gain. In many cases the clubs' assets belong to the members. Often they may be vested in trustees who hold the accounts for the benefit of the members. An individual pays a subscription and fulfils certain conditions to become a member and, in so doing, effectively enters into a contract with each and every member, the rules of the club being the terms of that contract.

10.3 Reporting

Before any work is undertaken, the terms of reference should be clarified, and recorded in a letter of engagement. It should be clearly agreed, for example, whether or not an audit report is to be given (perhaps because of statutory requirements or the club's constitution). If it is, it should be clearly agreed whether or not the report is to be on a true and fair view basis. The work necessary to support the report can then be determined. When reporting on friendly or industrial and provident societies, the statement on auditing, "Auditors' Reports—Registered Friendly Societies and Industrial and Provident Societies", should be referred to. Otherwise the normal principles of auditing will apply to reporting and operational matters.

10.4 Requirements of relevant acts

Clubs registered under either the Friendly Societies Act 1974 or the Industrial and Provident Societies Act 1965 are required to:

(a) keep proper books of account with respect to their transactions and their assets and liabilities;

(b) establish and maintain a satisfactory system of control of their books of account, their cash holdings, and their receipts and payments;

(c) appoint a qualified accountant or accountants to audit accounts and balance sheet for each year of account, and to report as to whether the revenue account gives a true and fair view of the income and expenditure and surplus or deficit, and the balance sheet shows a true and fair view of the state of affairs of the club.

In the case of industrial and provident societies, these requirements are set out in the Friendly and Industrial and Provident Societies Act 1961 and in the case of friendly societies in the Friendly Societies Act 1974.

Let us now consider the controls which are necessary for most clubs.

10.5 The need for control

Whether an audit is required for statutory purposes or because the constitution of the club requires it, the main problems are similar. How do you control cash and stock? These areas are hard enough to control in a limited liability company when you have full-time paid employees. The problem is exaggerated in most clubs because the majority of the workers are volunteers and the committee or committees running the club are made up again of volunteers, but without the powers or professionalism of, say, a board of directors. The biggest psychological problem to be overcome is the fear of hurting someone's feelings. This matter is often not faced and, as a result, control is non-existent.

When the problem is faced, it has to be done diplomatically or resignations may result. In the financial and stock control areas volunteers with adequate abilities and the available time are scarce and frequently the small size of managerial staff and its voluntary nature render the division of duties difficult.

10.6 Major control areas

The major areas where control is needed in most clubs are:

Receipts

The sources of cash are often many and varied. Subscriptions and joining fees are easy enough to control, but there may also be income from social functions, vending machines, the hire of the club and its facilities, a bar or restaurant, local authority subsidies or grants. Unusual or non-recurring receipts will cause particular problems.

Expenditure

Particularly difficult are those expenses which are paid by cash from receipts. Unless the receipts are controlled, it will be impossible to verify the expenditure, particularly when payments are for such items as casual labour. Many staff at clubs work on a casual basis and may be paid daily in cash. Many of these people have full-time jobs and as such the club could be faced with significant liabilities, particularly for PAYE, unless deductions are properly made.

Stocks

The size of this problem depends on the number of stock lines and the accuracy of both the analysis of the cash and the purchases.

10.7 Types of control

The following suggestions are not comprehensive but are probably appropriate to most clubs:

(a) the use of an active committee to review receipts and expenditure, and any available managerial information, monthly;

(b) intelligent analytical review of periodic management information may detect irregularities at an early stage;

(c) monitoring margins against expected margins for each area of income, and the investigation of all variances;

(d) ensuring that there are always two signatories for all cheques, and that nobody signs a cheque without its supporting documentation: no cheques should ever be signed blank, and wherever possible payment should be made by cheque rather than cash;

(e) ensuring that all invoices of cash expenditure are authorised by the head of the relevant committee (or at least someone other than the person handling the cash), and marked as to date paid;

(f) the use of an analysis cash register so that each source of income can be identified;

(g) the use of meters, registers or number sequence wherever possible;

(h) keeping records of all gifts, abnormal wastage, sundry payments or receipts, and ensuring this information tallies with the reconciliations;

(i) controlling stocks by regular stocktaking and where appropriate the use of a professional stocktaker to provide a shortage report (a schedule of opening and closing stocks at selling prices, sales value of purchases, sale proceeds and shortages);

(j) reconciling membership records and subscriptions;

(k) banking cash takings intact;

(l) regular counts of cash.

In conclusion, where a true and fair opinion is to be expressed, two important general points can be made with regard to controls in clubs. Firstly, clearly the auditor must be satisfied with the club's internal controls to give a "clean" opinion, or he must express his dissatisfaction with material inadequacies, in his report. Secondly, when auditing clubs, the emphasis will probably be on substantive tests and analytical reviews rather than compliance testing.

11.0   THE AUDIT OF FRIENDLY SOCIETIES (U26)

11.1   Governing legislation

FRIENDLY, INDUSTRIAL AND PROVIDENT SOCIETIES ACT 1968 AND FRIENDLY SOCIETIES ACT 1974

The statutory requirements in these Acts govern the accounts, the audit and the appointment of auditors. The requirements concerning the qualifications of, and restrictions placed upon, auditors are similar to those laid down in the Companies Act—except that, like the Building Societies Act 1962, the *employer* of an officer or servant of the society may not act as auditor.

The Acts permit societies to prepare annual accounts in any form provided they give a true and fair view of the matters specified in the Acts. Societies are under an obligation to send accounts and annual reports to the Registrar of Friendly Societies, containing such particulars as he prescribes. An annual return must include the revenue account and the balance sheet, and may also include additional accounts which must be covered by the auditor's report. Accounts may not be included in the annual return unless they have been audited.

The annual return must be made up to 31st December, and sent to the Registrar no later than the 31st May.

The auditor's report on the balance sheet must state whether it shows a true and fair view of the assets and current liabilities, and of the resulting balance of the funds.

Although auditors are not specifically required to deal with the question of actuarial solvency (a matter required to be covered by the accounts), disclosure of actuarial information in relation to the solvency of the Society is an essential requirement of a "true and fair view". Auditors shall therefore qualify their reports:

(a) where inadequate information is given in the financial statements, or

(b) where there is reason to believe that the fund is actuarially insolvent.

11.2   Audit report

In an unqualified audit report, the following would be a suitable form:

AUDITORS' REPORT TO THE MEMBERS OF THE XYZ FRIENDLY SOCIETY
In our opinion the foregoing revenue account, balance sheet, statement of source and application of funds and the notes thereon, which have been prepared under the historical cost convention (as modified by the revaluation of certain assets), give a true and fair view of the assets and current liabilities of the society, and the resulting balance of its funds at 31st December 19 ..., the income and expenditure of the society for the year ended on that date, and comply with the requirements of the Friendly Societies Act 1974.

11.3   Group accounts (industrial and provident societies)

An industrial and provident society with subsidiaries has an additional obligation to prepare group accounts, and to submit them for audit to the society's auditors. The auditors are required to report to the society on the group accounts, and the latter, together with the report, must be sent to the Registrar together with the annual return. The report drafted above may be suitably debated to meet the requirements of a situation in which group accounts are involved.

PROGRESS TEST 13

1. What should an auditor keep in mind in relation to his appointment as a joint auditor? (3.0)

2. What work must an accountant carry out on the records of solicitors under the Accountant's Report Rules? (4.0)

3. State the main matters to be contained in the accountant's report on a profit forecast. (6.0)

4. What are the main items included in the accountants' report in a prospectus? (5.5)

5. What are the main sources of receipts and payments by building societies? (8.4)

6. What are the most important areas of control in relation to an investment company? (9.0)

7. What special points should be borne in mind when making adjustments for investment investigations ? (9.0)

8. State the types of control which would be appropriate to the operation of a club. (10.0)

APPENDIX 1

Index to Examination Questions and Suggested Answers

Examination Questions

Introduction to auditing

1. You have been invited to give a short presentation to some new students in your office on the subject of audit working papers. Prepare your notes for the presentation setting out:

    (a) the reasons for preparing working papers;

    (b) the contents of working papers; and

    (c) the criteria you would use to judge the quality of working papers.

2. You are a partner in an accountancy practice which has been formally appointed as auditors to Move-it plc, a listed company engaged in national and international road haulage. You are drafting an engagement letter and are required to:

    (a) set out the reasons why it is desirable to write such a letter; and

    (b) list the main items that you would include therein.

Internal control

3. You are a member of a team of auditors preparing to undertake the audit of a medium-sized manufacturing company which has been acquired during the year by a holding company, for which your firm acts as auditor. You have been asked to list, in question form, the matters which you would regard as significant in relation to the internal control system for additions to and disposals of plant and machinery.

4. You have recently been appointed auditor of a company which manufactures a range of products from basic components. What matters would you consider to be of particular importance when examining the company's system of internal control over the movement of components?

5. Set out clearly the matters which the statutory auditors should consider before deciding how far they may rely upon the work performed by the internal audit section of a large public company.

Assessment of internal control

6. Many practising firms of auditors now use standardised pre-printed forms, to be completed in the course of ascertaining and evaluating their clients' internal control systems. In addition to the usual standard questionnaires, an overall assessment is often made with the assistance of an internal control evaluation (ICE).

(a) Set out part of the section of ICE dealing with purchases and creditors in a form currently adopted. You should include one "control question", and the criteria to be considered prior to answering it.

(b) What particular advantages arise from the use of ICEs?

7. You are compiling the internal control questionnaire at the commencement of your audit of AB Ltd. Explain the significance of the following questions and state how you would obtain the information, detailing any independent verification you would carry out.

(a) Is the client's organisation chart (showing the functions and responsibilities of senior officials) properly amended to date?

(b) Are all staff required to take an annual holiday?

(c) Are journal entries authorised by a responsible official?

(d) Are statements rendered to customers by the ledger clerk without reference to the cashier?

(e) Are travelling expenses passed for payment by a responsible official other than the cashier?

8. Your client, Adam plc, owns and operates three large departmental stores in London, Birmingham and Manchester. Each store has more than 22 departments.

You are at present preparing your audit plan and you are considering carrying out detailed audit tests on a rotational basis. You consider that all departments within the stores should be covered over a period of five years but that more frequent attention should be given to those where the "audit risk" demands it. You are required to detail the factors which you would consider in order to evaluate the audit risk.

Verification

9. Your client, Hepplewhite Ltd, is a company which manufactures fertilisers from raw materials obtained from approximately 300 suppliers. The company does not specifically record the terms and conditions of trade with its suppliers. Part of the audit plan states that work is to be carried out to establish whether there are any amounts due to trade creditors which may be secured by the reservation of legal title. You are required to:

(a) describe the audit procedures required to comply with the audit plan;

    (b) draft a suitable note to be included in the financial statements, assuming that the procedures disclose the existence of a material number and amount of creditors, so secured; and

    (c) comment on the recent case law concerning this subject.

10. You are the auditor of Sheraton Ltd, the year end of which is 30th November. You are currently planning the 1985 audit and want to incorporate procedures which will ensure that, in finalising its financial statements, the company has complied with SSAP 17, on post balance sheet events. You are required to:

    (a) detail the procedures that you would incorporate into the audit plan; and

    (b) describe the types of events, as defined in the Standard, and their accounting treatment.

11. Set out the information you would normally expect to find recorded in the plant register of a large manufacturing company and describe the functions of the register of which you, as auditor, would normally expect to make use in the course of your verification procedures.

12. Your client, Combiners Ltd, is a long-established company which deals in agricultural machinery, and its year end is 31st October. You are engaged on that part of the audit relating to the valuation of stock, particularly the second-hand items.

From your past experience you are aware that over half of the company's stock consists of second-hand items which have been acquired by trade-in against sales of new machinery. Over 90% of the value of the second-hand stock is represented by approximately 500 high-value items such as combine harvesters and tractors. Some of these items may be held in stock for at least two or three years and, indeed, may end up being scrapped.

It is the company's policy to generate profit from the sale of new machinery rather than the second-hand items. Consequently, when the salesmen are negotiating the sales of new pieces of machinery, they may often buy in second-hand items at a trade-in cost which is in excess of estimated realisable value at that time.

Sales of machinery take place almost entirely in the spring and summer months. Any renovation work that is carried out on the trade-in purchases is undertaken by the company.

The company maintains a used machinery stock register which records trade-in costs, estimated realisable value at the time of trade-in, and subsequent renovation costs.

The audit has to be completed by 31st January each year and, for simplicity, the company evaluates the stock of second-hand machinery by totalling the trade-in cost of items held in stock, adding the actual renovation costs in respect thereof, and then writing down the resultant figure by 50%.

You are required to:

    (a) outline the resulting audit problems arising from this method of valuation; and

    (b) outline the audit work to be undertaken to satisfy yourself that the valuation of second-hand stocks produces an acceptable result.

Note: Marks will be awarded for displaying a knowledge of auditing principles involved rather than for a knowledge of the agricultural industry.

Ignore taxation.

13. You are the auditor of a large manufacturing company and have included the observation of your client's year-end stocktaking in your verification programme. Detail five factors which you would carefully consider prior to accepting the valuations based on the physical inventories, on the grounds that the amount at which the stocks are stated in the balance sheet could be materially affected thereby.

14. Prepare a post balance sheet review checklist which will be introduced by your firm as a standard working paper.

15. Department of Trade and Industry inspectors, reporting on Pergamon Press in 1972, were critical of the non-disclosure of "related party transactions".

(a) Why might related party transactions require special attention by the auditor?

(b) Name five persons/organisations which, in your opinion, might be included within a definition of "related parties" for this purpose.

(c) Suggest four types of transaction which may indicate the existence of related parties.

16. (a) What circumstances might indicate that an enterprise is no longer a going concern?

(b) What audit procedures would you employ to satisfy yourself that an enterprise has sufficient cash resources to meet its needs as they arise?

Auditors and the Companies Act

17. The Companies Act 1985 contains certain provisions which are of general significance to the auditor. You are required to:

(a) identify the topics concerned; and

(b) discuss the audit implications thereof.

18. (a) What qualifications are required of an auditor under the Companies Act 1985?

(b) What powers are vested in such an auditor?

19. State the matters to which you would direct your attention when reviewing a company's statutory books and registers as part of your audit.

20. (a) Explain each of the fundamental accounting concepts that you, as auditor, would expect to be adopted in the preparation of financial accounts on which you are reporting and which are intended to show a true and fair view.

(b) If there has been a departure from one of the concepts in the accounts on which you are reporting, what information is required to be given in the audit report?

Considerations affecting audit reports

21. When accountancy or audit work is undertaken for sole traders and partnerships, as distinct from corporate bodies, professional responsibility is governed by the instructions of the particular client rather than by statute.

(a) What are the most important matters which accountants and auditors in professional practice should consider when associating their names with the accounts of these clients?

(b) Set out the form of an accountant's report which you would use where you have been asked to prepare the accounts but not to audit them.

22. It is customary for the auditor of the parent company in a group to issue detailed questionnaires to the auditors of subsidiaries, in connection with the accounts and audit of those subsidiaries.

(a) State briefly why these questionnaires are issued.

(b) List eleven specific issues (five relating to accounting policies and six to the scope of the audit) normally covered in the questionnaires regarding the accounts and the audit respectively.

23. Your firm acts as auditors of Wiseguys National Bakeries Ltd. The finance director has prepared financial statements of the company for the year to 30th September 1985, which show a pre-tax profit of £450,000. You have been advised that the board of directors has approved the financial statements and decided that no amendments should be made thereto.

As partner responsible for the audit you have noted the following matters during your review of the financial statements and the audit working papers:

(a) The freehold property, which was included at cost in previous years' balance sheets, has now been restated at a professional valuation of £1,250,000 carried out during the year. You are satisfied with the valuation, the relevant figures have been correctly adjusted and the necessary information disclosed in the notes to the accounts.

(b) No depreciation has been provided on the company aircraft which is stated at the cost to the company when it was acquired on 1st October 1984 for £900,000. The directors' reasons for not providing depreciation are fully explained in the notes to the accounts and you concur with their decision.

(c) As in previous years, you have been unable to carry out any practical audit procedures to confirm the value of trade marks which have been included in the balance sheet at £800,000 ever since they were valued by the directors in 1982.

(d) An amount of £45,000 due from a customer in respect of sales during the year is included in debtors but, from information made available to you, you conclude that no part of this debt will be recovered. No provision has been made against this amount.

(e) The financial statements do not disclose the fact that a director was indebted to the company for an amount of £22,000 during a period of six weeks commencing 1st February 1985.

(f) A substantial claim was lodged against the company, arising from a major breach of contract and alleged damage to a customer's business. No provision has been made for legal costs or compensation payable as it is not possible to determine with reasonable accuracy the amounts, if any, which may become payable. A full explanation of the circumstances is given in the notes to the accounts.

You are required to write a letter to the directors explaining how you propose to deal with the above matters in your audit report. Write as from a firm, using a fictitious name and address. Marks will be awarded specifically for style as well as for content.

Statistical sampling

24. You are required to present the arguments for and against the use of statistical sampling in auditing, and reach a conclusion on the subject.

25. For many years auditors have known that statistical sampling techniques might usefully be applied to their own procedures in certain circumstances but not in others.

(a) Describe the conditions which should be present before such techniques may be applied to a population of items subject to audit scrutiny.

(b) Apart from the obvious advantages of enabling the results of the auditor's tests to be assessed, quantified and expressed in a scientific way, a further advantage is that it imposes certain disciplines over the conduct of the audit procedures themselves.

Tabulate and explain these disciplines.

The liability of auditors

26. It has become apparent in recent years that the responsibilities of an auditor of a limited company may no longer be regarded as residing within the strict confines of his relationship with the shareholders to whom he nominally reports. To what extent:

(a) have decided legal cases indicated a responsibility to parties with whom the auditor has no contractual relationship?

(b) might it be held that the auditor has a legal responsibility towards shareholders and others who based investment decisions on accounts which he has audited?

27. Summarise the legal basis of an auditor's liability under common law and statute.

Your answer should deal with both civil and criminal liability and should make appropriate reference to decided cases.

28. Past-it Ltd, an engineering company, went into creditor's voluntary liquidation in February 1986 with total assets, estimated to realise £764,000, and total estimated liabilities of £946,000. The liquidator has recently commenced proceedings against the company's auditors for alleged negligence, and the auditors' solicitors have approached you, as an independent expert, to advise on the auditors' position.

The last audited financial statements were for the period to 30th June 1985 and were signed by the auditors without qualification, on 16th September 1985. It is alleged that the financial statements, which showed fixed assets and deferred expenditure of £192,000, current assets of £734,000 and total liabilities of £796,000, contained the following inaccuracies and omissions:

(a) Improvements to leasehold premises, costing £54,000 in July 1984, had been capitalised and were being amortised over the life of the twenty-five-year lease. These premises were vacated in October 1985 and placed on the market. No tenant could be found and the liquidator ultimately surrendered the lease to the landlord.

(b) Deferred expenditure in the balance of £34,000 represented the balance of pure and applied research and development costs incurred two years previously. It was to have been written off over the following eight years, being the remaining period estimated by the directors over which the relevant product was expected to be sold, although production of that product ceased in July 1985.

(c) Credit notes totalling £17,000 were raised in August, September and October 1985 in respect of sales of faulty goods to customers, which had been included in debtors at 30th June 1985, against which no provision had been made.

(d) Prior to 30th June 1985 the company had guaranteed advances of £61,000 by its bankers to another company also under the control of the directors. The bankers enforced the guarantee in January 1986. No mention of the guarantee was made in the financial statements.

(e) In August 1985 the company implemented a decision to make more than half of the employees redundant, giving rise to redundancy payments of £27,000 which were not provided for in the balance sheet as at 30th June 1985, but which were disclosed in notes to the financial statements.

(f) Outgoings on entertaining and publicity costs had amounted to approximately £30,000 per annum in recent years and approximately 50% represented "reimbursements" from petty cash to each of the three directors for which no vouchers were available.

Before deciding whether or not to instruct you further, the solicitors would like to discuss the foregoing information with you. You are required to prepare notes for a meeting with the auditors' solicitors:

(a) commenting on the treatment of each of these six matters within the financial statements; and

(b) indicating whether or not the auditors may have been negligent.

The audit approach to computer systems

29. You have been asked by your firm to compile a standard "internal control checklist", in question form, suitable for use on each computer audit assignment. Prepare the section of the checklist which covers the input controls over transactions and master data.

30. As technological improvements extend the speed and capability of computer processing, auditors are obliged to reply to an increasing extent on controls over input and output. Describe four methods of ensuring the validity and accuracy of computer input.

31. (a) Explain, giving an example, what you understand by the term "audit trail".

   (b) Explain carefully the developments in data processing which have resulted in the auditor often finding that the audit trail has been lost.

   (c) Provide one typical example of a situation in which such developments have resulted in absence of audit trail.

   (d) Describe two audit techniques which may be employed to overcome the loss of audit trail where data is processed by computer.

32. Explain the stages in the development of a new computer application, from feasibility study through to the implementation of the program, indicating the points at which consultation with the external auditor is advisable.

33. (a) What is a "computer audit program"?

   (b) Describe three applications of such a program, in connection with the verification of assets or liabilities.

34. (a) Explain why the computerisation of a company's data processing methods necessarily alters its systems of internal control.

   (b) What factors, arising from this change, would you, as auditor, expect the company's administrative controls to take into account?

   (c) How would the change affect your approach to the audit?

35. (a) What difficulty does an "on line, real-time" computer system present for the auditor, and how may this be overcome?

   (b) Mention the practical requirements that should be borne in mind in establishing a system of internal control for applications processed at a service bureau.

36. The usual implication of on-line computer systems is that the user can have direct access to the master files within the system, through the medium of a terminal. You are required to:

    (a)   describe the potential control weaknesses, specific to on-line systems; and

    (b)   detail the methods that can be adopted to overcome these weaknesses.

37. Fleabite Enterprises Ltd, your client company, has decided to utilise the data processing facilities of a local computer bureau for most of its major accounting routines, and the managing director has sought your advice on the control procedures which, in your opinion, should be adopted by Fleabite when the new arrangement comes into effect. Prepare a summary for the managing director of the controls which you regard as most important under such arrangement dealing specifically with:

    (a) transmission of data to bureau;

    (b) master file amendments;

    (c) error correction routines and re-submissions;

    (d) output;

    (e) security and reconstruction.

Briefly indicate any special considerations applicable to the control areas (a) to (e) above.

38. In computer systems which employ the use of remote terminals for input purposes, it is clearly important for controls to ensure that only valid data is input.

    (a) Mention six typical techniques which may be used to control the use of terminals for input purposes.

    (b) Explain briefly why such input controls are even more important in "real-time" systems.

39. The exposure in 1973 of the massive fraud by officers of the Equity Funding Corporation of America highlighted the danger for auditors of placing too much reliance on computer output, without investigating the means by which that output is produced. These two different approaches to the audit of EDP systems are often expressed as "round the machine" and "through the machine" respectively. Clearly explain the difference between these two audit approaches and set out the dangers inherent in the "round the machine" approach.

40. Your client, Change-it Ltd, is a company engaged in the wholesaling of electrical components and its year end is 31st August. It has expanded steadily over the last five years and the current turnover is approaching £4 million. Pre-tax profits are forecast to be in the region of £200,000 in the current financial year.

Until recently all the accounting records were maintained on a mechanical system. Stock records were kept manually on a card system.

The directors decided to install a mini-computer and purchase a software package designed specifically for wholesalers. The system went live in April 1985, with all the accounting and stock recording systems being transferred, although the intention is to continue running the mechanised and manual systems in parallel until 31st July 1985.

You have in the past operated a systems-based audit and in fact you carried out some compliance testing in January of this year which proved to be satisfactory.

You are required to detail the particular matters to which you would give attention following the introduction of the mini-computer, and to state how these would be likely to affect your work on the audit for the year to 31st August 1985.

Audit management

41. It is generally accepted that if auditors are to provide their clients with a satisfactory service, while taking all reasonable steps towards avoiding liability, it is essential that "quality control procedures" should be instituted. The establishment of such procedures will normally result in the standardisation of certain aspects of audit work.

(a)   Name four audit techniques or procedures in the case of which, in your opinion, standardisation would be appropriate.

(b)   The maintenance of quality control is usually the responsibility of a sub-committee of audit partners. Mention five specific responsibilities which, in your view, fall within the scope of this committee's work.

42. (a)   State what you understand by the term "audit planning" and explain its importance in the light of present conditions.

(b)   Outline the problems which may be encountered in implementing audit planning, and make suggestions as to how these might be overcome.

Specialised audit situations and investigations

43. (a)   What are the requirements of the City Code on Take-overs and Mergers with regard to the accountant's report on profit forecasts in a bid situation?

(b)   Outline:

(i)   the preliminary considerations to be borne in mind by the accountant before accepting instructions to report on profit forecasts; and

(ii)   the main points to be considered by the accountant in the course of his review of such forecasts.

44. A client whom you have known for several years is interested in the purchase of a business which will involve his full-time participation and will provide him with a modest but secure return on his investment. He has been advised by his agents that a small, well-established shop selling newspapers, cigarettes, tobacco and confectionery in West London is on offer for sale, and he has accordingly asked you to carry out an investigation.

(a)   Set out the steps you would take prior to commencing your detailed enquiries.

(b)   Describe the work you would carry out in connection with the accounts of the business.

    (c)   Specify any other matters which will call for your investigation prior to submitting a final report to your client.

45. Set out briefly the requirements of the Quotations Department of the Stock Exchange on accountants' reports in prospectuses, with specific regard to the following matters:

    (a)   independence of reporting accountants;

    (b)   age of figures reported on;

    (c)   Accounting Standards and the computation of profits;

    (d)   qualified audit reports;

    (e)   trend of profits;

    (f)   other expert opinions.

46.   (a)   Why is it invariably necessary for a company's accounts to be adjusted prior to their inclusion in the auditor's report in a prospectus?

        (b)   Mention three instances in which such adjustments would normally be necessary.

        (c)   Without entering any amounts, provide a statement of profits and losses for inclusion in the auditor's report in a prospectus, in a form acceptable to the Quotations Department of the Stock Exchange under current regulations.

47. Mr W. Minge is the managing director of Eternal Optimists Ltd., a client company of which you have recently been appointed auditor. He has requested you to audit the three-year profit forecasts which the chief accountant has prepared for the purpose of circularising these amongst the company shareholders. Describe seven matters on which you would initially seek clarification from Mr Minge, prior to commencing work on this assignment.

48. As auditor of a secondary banking concern, you are mindful of the severe financial difficulties which many such institutions have faced in recent years. Indicate concisely the main lines of enquiry which you would pursue in the course of your review of the bank's accounts, in order to assess its financial strength as a going concern.

49. A client is considering the purchase of a retail shop on his local High Street, and has requested that you undertake an investigation into this matter on his behalf. Set out in suitable sequence:

    (a)   the general procedures which you would follow in conducting this investigation;

    (b)   the adjustments to the past accounts of the business which it may be necessary for you to make;

    (c)   the matters *beyond the accounts* concerning which it would normally be necessary to make enquiries;

(d) the general rules of reporting which you would observe when finally presenting your recommendations to your client.

50. You have recently been appointed auditor of one of the colleges of an old and established university.

(a) List eight sources of revenue which you would expect to be disclosed in the accounts.

(b) Mention four internal controls which you would expect to be operative, in relation to the college's revenues.

(c) Describe five audit tests which you would apply to the accounts submitted to you for audit.

51. Your client is proposing to form a company specialising in the provision of tuition for professional law examinations, and is about to approach his bank concerning the finance which will be necessary to support the venture during its first two years. He is not certain how the information to be presented to the bank manager should be prepared, and has requested your assistance. Set out the matters, both general and financial, which, in your view, are likely to be of particular concern to the bank manager prior to making his decision, and which should therefore be included in your client's presentation.

General questions

52. "Pre-war audits were commonly criticised on the grounds that too often they were basically merely 'ticking' audits whereas what was needed were 'thinking' audits. Present-day audits still remain essentially ticking audits, and the only apparent difference is that it is now the auditor's own working papers that get ticked rather than the client's records." Discuss this statement.

53. The following quotation is taken from a recent issue of a leading management journal:

"The traditional statutory audit is largely governed by formal regulation and accounting convention. Few managements would regard it as a worthwhile service: it is far too 'past-oriented' for that. Those that regard the official audit as little more than an expensive but legally necessary evil are not unduly cynical, for their view is undoubtedly based on experience. Until formal auditing training and education are extended, the expertise required for the operations audit must be found elsewhere."

(a) What, in your view, is meant by the author's criticism that the statutory audit is too "past-oriented"?

(b) Indicate, with specific reference to the present difficulties facing management, three ways in which auditors could be of more constructive use than, in the opinion of the author quoted, they are at present.

(c) Explain what you understand by the "operations audit", mentioning seven of the most important areas which it would normally cover.

54. "No matter how full and detailed a company's annual report and accounts may be, these attributes are of less importance to the modern shareholder than promptness and frequency of reporting." Discuss this statement and suggest the main practical problems which would face the auditor of a limited company if asked to report to shareholders on interim accounts.

55. You are the auditor of Growing Ltd. which commenced trading on 1st June 1984 as mini-computer distributors. You have completed the audit for the year ended 31st May 1985. The company commenced business selling new computers and spares only, with a total staff of five, and during the course of the first year extended its activities into the sale of second-hand computers, and the servicing and hire of computers, with a total staff at the end of the year of twenty, including an accounts department of three.

Basic systems of internal control were not in evidence in all areas until after the end of the first year. You qualified your report in respect of the first year by making reference to the reliance placed upon management assurances.

Following the end of the second financial year to 31st May 1986 you have contacted the client with a view to planning the audit for that year and you have established from information provided by the company accountant, who joined the company in January 1986, that the total number of staff had increased to over fifty by May 1986, and that sales have broadly doubled every three months. During the course of the year, as additional staff have been taken on, the basic systems of internal control have developed and altered to meet the needs of the rapidly expanding business.

You are required to:

(a) detail the problems, specifically relating to the circumstances outlined, that you might anticipate in carrying out the audit with the objective of producing an unqualified audit report; and

(b) outline the approach to the audit.

56. You are required to present the arguments for and against the contention that it is essential to a true and fair view that information about finance leases is given by capitalisation of the rights and obligations within financial statements, of lessees, and to reach a conclusion on the matter.

57. Your firm has recently accepted appointment as auditor to Forget-me-Not Ltd, a company whose directors adopt an informal management style in running its affairs. You are the partner responsible, and have just commenced the audit for the year ended 31 March 1985. The company has grown rapidly in the field of marketing packaged computer software, and is currently expanding into several related activities. Its turnover has increased from £1,850,000 to £3.1m over the 12 months to 31 March 1985. The accounts for the year ended 31 March 1984, audited by your predecessor, showed pre-tax profits of £325,000.

Meetings of the directors take place frequently but irregularly, based on need, but in response to questions from you on minutes governing the matters described below, the managing director, who is also company secretary, has stated that although these matters were discussed fully and agreement on them reached at the relevant meetings, the directors are "far too busy to bother with such trifling formalities as official minutes", especially since they all trust each other implicitly, the company is obviously highly successful, and the previous auditors never even raised the subject. In the circumstances he therefore considered that "minutes would not be worth the paper they were written on", and he had "more urgent matters on which to concentrate his energies if the company was to reach the USM by late 1986". As a concession to your obvious concern, he has, however, agreed to create the minutes for each of the meetings held during the year to March 1985, have them duly signed by the chairman, and to present them to you within the next few days.

The matters specifically raised by you included the following:

(i) the formal appointment of your firm as auditors and acceptance of your engagement terms;

(ii) the contractual terms governing the employment of two recently appointed senior executives responsible for marketing and finance respectively;

(iii) receipt of a loan of £750,000, repayable over four years, with interest at 3.5% over base rate, secured by way of a floating charge on the company's assets;

(iv) directors' performance-related bonuses, the determination of which awaits finalisation of the accounts you are auditing;

(v) a claim by a customer for £150,000 damages, including consequential losses, arising from the sale to the customer of computer programs which, it is alleged, were totally useless for the purposes intended.

You are required to write a letter to the managing director of Forget-me-Not Ltd, advising him concisely:

(a) why board minutes are necessary;

(b) why his concession to create the minutes of meetings held during the year is useless for audit purposes;

(c) what conditions must in future be fulfilled if board minutes are to provide acceptable audit evidence;

(d) what practical steps can now be taken to rectify the present situation as far as possible;

(e) what audit purposes would have been served by the existence of valid minutes in respect of each of the five matters listed above.

58. For four years your firm has been acting as auditor to Rising Sunset Retailers' Ltd, a company with 25 branches of similar size spread throughout the UK. Turnover for the year ended 31 December 1984 was in excess of £50m, pre-tax profits were £3.5m, and net assets were £21m. The audit report was signed without qualification on 28 March 1985 by the partner responsible for the assignment.

The partner concerned has been telephoned by the client company's finance director and informed that the accounts clerk responsible for sales ledgers at the Colchester branch was found to be diverting company funds into his own account by means of a "teeming and lading" fraud, apparently executed without collusion.

The finance director has instituted investigations which have now revealed that during 1984 some £110,000 of receipts from customers were diverted in this way.

Investigations designed to ascertain losses, if any, in earlier years are still in progress. The finance director has requested that the audit partner attend a meeting with him to discuss the matter, and has laid emphasis on your firm's responsibility for failing to detect the fraud at an earlier stage.

The Colchester turnover during 1984 was £1.8m, its results showed a profit of £11,000, and its net assets at the year end were £970,000. Although branch visits for audit purposes are organised by rotation, members of the audit staff did in fact visit Colchester.

As partner responsible for technical standards and file reviews, it is necessary for you to assess your firm's responsibility in the matter, and to brief the audit partner in anticipation of his forthcoming meeting.

You are required to summarise

(a) the information you would require (giving your reasons) from the audit files themselves, assuming they meet your firm's prescribed standards;

(b) the information which should be sought from the finance director at the meeting;

(c) notes for the audit partner's use at the meeting, on the basis that the audit appears from the files to have been performed in accordance with approved Auditing Standards. (For the purpose of compiling these notes you may make factual assumptions regarding information obtained from the files under (a) above.)

59. (a) Summarise the matters to which auditors should have regard when considering a client company's accounting policies and their disclosure.

(b) Department of Trade Inspectors, reporting in 1978 on Court Line, the travel group, which failed shortly after issuing accounts declaring a pre-tax profit of £4.7m, criticised its directors for selecting accounting policies which had the effect of presenting the company's results and financial position in the most favourable possible light. The following were included in the company's accounting policies:

(i) Proportions of charter revenues, ranging in individual cases from 10% to 50% of the charter hires from contracts negotiated prior to year-end for flights subsequent to that date, are included in profit before taxation. The proportions so included comprise cancellation fees and deposits not refundable to the charterers in the event of their cancellation of the contracts.

(ii) The previous policy of charging the cost of major surveys of ships against results of the succeeding five years has been changed, and after charging the relevant proportion against profits of the current year the balance brought forward from the previous year has been charged as an extraordinary item.

(iii) In the case of hotels in the Caribbean, cost includes the cost of original furniture and equipment, together with such additions as are considered to be material improvements. No depreciation is charged either on buildings or furniture and equipment. Replacements are charged to revenue as and when incurred. Depreciation provided in previous years has been released in these accounts as an extraordinary item to give effect to this change in policy.

(iv) The initial costs of introducing new aircraft services, including the costs of training aircrew and engineering personnel prior to the introduction and operation of aircraft, are in the main charged against profits of succeeding financial years by 10 equal annual instalments. Interest on a fixed loan to finance the purchase of aircraft and spares is dealt with similarly.

You are required to state whether, in your opinion, each of the policies quoted represents currently acceptable accounting practice, as regards both content and formulation. In each case you should give reasons for your opinion and, where appropriate, suggest preferable alternatives.

60. With current advances in electronics technology, computer security is a matter of increasing concern to computer users and auditors alike. Since by the time appropriate security measures are introduced the technology for which they were designed has already been superseded, management is often exposed to risks whose severity may be insufficiently appreciated.

You are required to identify six current computer security hazards, and in each case to describe the practical steps towards improved security which auditors should recommend to their clients.

Suggested Answers to Examination Questions

1. (a) The Auditing Guidelines give the following reasons for the preparation of audit working papers:

   (i) The reporting partner needs to be able to satisfy himself that work delegated by him has been properly performed. The reporting partner can generally only do this by having available to him detailed working papers prepared by the audit staff who performed the work.

   (ii) Working papers provide, for future reference, details of problems encountered together with evidence of work performed and conclusions drawn therefrom in arriving at the audit opinion.

   (iii) The preparation of working papers encourages the auditor to adopt a methodical approach.

   (b) As set out in the Auditing Guidelines audit working papers will typically contain:

   (i) information which will be of continuing importance to the audit, for example, memorandum and articles of association;

   (ii) audit planning information;

   (iii) the auditor's assessment of the enterprise's accounting system and his review and evaluation of its internal controls;

   (iv) details of the audit work carried out, notes of errors or exceptions found and action taken thereon, together with the conclusions drawn by the audit staff who performed the various sections of the work;

   (v) evidence that the work of the audit staff has been properly reviewed;

   (vi) records of the relevant balances and other financial information, including analyses and summaries supporting the financial statements;

(vii) a summary of significant points affecting the financial statements and the audit report, showing how these points were dealt with.

(c)   The criteria for judging the quality of working papers are that:

(i) audit working papers should always be sufficiently complete and detailed to enable an experienced auditor with no previous connection with the audit to ascertain from them what work was performed and to support the conclusions reached;

(ii) in the case of questions of principle or judgment, the papers should make it clear what facts were known at the time the auditor reached his conclusion and enable a demonstration that, based on those facts, the conclusion was reasonable.

Tutorial Note

There are regular questions similar to this which are drawn directly from the Auditing Standards and Guidelines. In such cases it is considered that most marks will be obtained by answering direct from those documents.

2.   (a)   An engagement letter should be written for the following reasons:

(i) The letter should define clearly the extent of the auditor's responsibilities, and thus minimise the possibility of misunderstanding between management and auditor. This is beneficial to both client and auditor.

(ii) The letter serves to formalise the basis of the auditor's appointment which, although required by statute, is a contractual arrangement between auditor and client company. The letter indicates the auditor's acceptance of the appointment and, if duly acknowledged, the client's acceptance of its terms by covering such matters as the purpose and scope of the engagement, the form of report, and the basis of charging fees. The letter achieves this objective, and also that of identifying the directors' responsibility.

(iii) The letter is an incidental aid to the ethical rules which govern the acceptance of assignments previously undertaken by other firms. Once an engagement letter is sent, there can be no doubt that professional work has been offered and accepted.

(b)   Engagement letters should include the following items:

(i) scope of audit function under statute, and the corresponding duties of the directors in relation to financial statements, accounting records, and internal control;

(ii) reporting duties, indicating the difference between the prescribed contents of a clean and qualified report respectively, including matters covered by SSAPs;

(iii) reference to the auditing standards which govern audit work and reports, outlining the nature and purpose of the tests normally conducted in the course of an audit: the need to obtain relevant and reliable evidence should be mentioned, as well as the relationship between the level of testing and the quality of internal controls in force;

(iv) the fact that weaknesses in the system will be drawn to the attention of management periodically;

(v) the responsibility of management for prevention and detection of errors and fraud, and that audit work will nevertheless be planned with a view to having a reasonable expectation of detecting material mis-statement resulting from such irregularities;

(vi) the periodic request for formal representations from managements confirming information received in the course of the audit;

(vii) the requirement that all statements to be issued together with the published accounts will have to be reviewed by the auditor;

(viii) availability of a range of services additional to the audit (as appropriate for a plc), such as the provision of taxation advice and general financial consultation;

(ix) the basis upon which professional fees will normally be charged, and the practice of billing at suitable intervals;

(x) a request that, subject to any further clarification that might be needed, the letter should be duly acknowledged as being in accord with the client's understanding of the engagement.

3. (a) Who is responsible for preparation of annual plant and machinery budget?

(b) Who authorises the purchase of plant? What are the limits to their authority?

(c) Are requests for permission to incur capital expenditure on plant made in a formal manner?

(d) Is authorisation evidenced (e.g. board minute)?

(e) Is work of a capital nature undertaken by company's own employees properly recorded and authorised?

(f) How is such work valued? Are overhead expenses included?

(g) Whose responsibility is the allocation of expenditure between capital and revenue?

(h) What basis and records are used for this procedure, and what evidence remains?

(i) Who compares actual expenditure with the amount authorised?

(j) What action is taken if budgeted expenditure is exceeded?

(k) What system exists to record authorised purchases not yet made, and authorised orders placed?

(l) Who authorises expenditure on overhauls and what evidence exists?

(m) How and by whom is the sale or scrapping of machinery authorised?

(n) What is the company's policy with regard to disposal of machinery?

(o) What plant transactions take place between companies in the group?

(p) Are "arms length" values used in such transactions, and how are inter-company profits dealt with in the accounts?

(q) What authority is required before plant and machinery can be removed from the company's premises?

(r) Who reconciles cash proceeds with the written authority for disposals?

Tutorial Note:
The above questions may be summarised in key questions for internal control evaluation:

(a) Can the company incur unauthorised capital expenditure?

(b) Can plant and machinery acquired be omitted from or incorrectly recorded in the fixed asset records?

(c) Can plant and machinery be sold without authorisation or without being recorded?

(d) Where the company constructs its own plant and machinery can the amounts capitalised be incorrectly stated?

4. The following matters would be regarded as of particular importance when examining the system of internal control over the movement of components.

(a) *Material inwards:* Consider whether:

   (i) a minimum re-order level has been specified for all types of components;

   (ii) requisitions for further supplies may be made by specified employees in the stores only;

   (iii) requisitions are made out on standard forms and authorised by the foreman or other responsible official prior to transmission to purchasing department;

   (iv) goods are ordered only on the company's standard order forms;

   (v) details are checked against the original requisition and authorised by the purchasing manager prior to the order being despatched to supplier;

   (vi) orders are placed with an authorised list of suppliers only for the purpose of obtaining the most suitable discount and delivery terms;

   (vii) unfulfilled orders are regularly reviewed and follow-up procedures instituted;

    (viii) goods received are thoroughly checked against copy orders for quantity, specification and price prior to being admitted to stores;

    (ix) such admission is properly signified and the accounts department advised; and

    (x) the stores records are promptly written up.

(b)   *Stores issued to production:* Consider whether:

    (i) requisitions from stores are made out on standard forms and authorised by the production manager;

    (ii) the costing department is promptly advised of all issues to production; and

    (iii) the stores records are promptly adjusted to reflect all issues to production.

(c)   *The stock records:* the stock records covering components should be sufficiently detailed and should disclose the following:

    (i) the exact description and specification including identifying code of the item in stock;

    (ii) dates of all receipts and issues;

    (iii) names of suppliers and, in the case of stores issued to production, the particular department should be specified;

    (iv) quantities of receipts and issues with or without nominal sterling values (according to the company's circumstances);

    (v) a perpetual balance thrown out each time a movement takes place—this will enable impromptu checks to be made comparing physical stocks with stores ledger balances; and

    (vi) the minimum re-order quantity should be indicated on each card.

5. Before deciding how far he may rely upon the work of the internal audit section, the statutory auditor should carefully consider:

(a)   the degree of independence of the internal auditor from those whose responsibilities he is reviewing;

(b)   the number of suitably qualified and experienced staff employed in the section;

(c)   the scope, extent, direction and timing of the tests made by the internal auditors; any terms of reference expressed in writing should be carefully examined and internal audit programmes critically scrutinised;

(d)   the evidence available of the work done by the internal auditors and of the review of that work;

(e)   the extent to which management takes action based upon the reports of the internal audit section.

Careful and diplomatic enquiries along the lines indicated above should enable the statutory auditors to assess the effectiveness of the internal audit section and the extent to which they may rely on their work.

6.(a)

SECTION: PURCHASES	INTERNAL CONTROL EVALUATION First evaluation on . . . . 19 . .			Subsequent evaluations
CONTROL QUESTION	Criteria	Answer to control question	Might error be material?	on 19 . . on 19 . . on 19 . .
CAN LIABILITIES BE SET UP FOR GOODS (OR SERVICES) WHICH ARE EITHER NOT AUTHORISED OR NOT RECEIVED?	(1) Segregation of duties (purchasing, receiving, inventory, ledger-keeping, payment) (2) Issue and authorisation of requisitions (3) Issue and authorisation of official purchase orders (4) Proper receipt and inspection of goods and the issue of sequentially numbered goods-received notes (5) Procedures for dealing with short-delivered or damaged goods (6) Independent matching of invoices with purchase orders and goods-received notes and proper clearing of missing, unmatched and disputed items (7) Safeguards against the re-use of documents or the use of duplicators (8) Procedures to check freight, insurance charges, against the relevant purchases (9) Control over direct deliveries to customers (10) Effective supervision			

(b)   The chief advantage of the ICE is that it focuses the attention of audit staff on the matters most fundamental to control in the area being reviewed, by means of the control question. Most standard internal questionnaires lack this feature. Other advantages are:

(i)   material and non-material errors are distinguished;

(ii)   the list of criteria provides a ready guide to the matters to be considered before reaching a conclusion on the adequacy of the system;

(iii)   the completed ICE assists in planning the extent of the detailed audit tests to be carried out, and enables a "letter of weakness" to be drawn up for the information of management.

7.   (a)   The significance of the question is twofold. Firstly, it enables the auditor to obtain important information to help him to determine the appropriate officials, and their levels of responsibility, at the time of verifying the authority for transactions. Secondly, it is also necessary for members of the staff to understand the levels of authority within their own organisation.

The information could be obtained from either the secretary of the company or the chief accountant, though in certain organisations it may be necessary to obtain this information from a director of the company.

The accuracy of the organisation chart would be checked during the course of the audit, when the auditor would need to ensure that transactions are, in practice, authorised by those shown on the organisation chart as being responsible for them.

(b) One of the important forms of internal check is the rotation (where practicable) of duties. Hence the importance of this question is that, when members of staff are on holiday, their work has to be carried out by others. This constitutes an important check on their work, as suspicious discrepancies may be revealed along with other obvious weaknesses such as non-compliance with company procedures.

It would be normal to obtain this information from the company's personnel officer, or in his absence the company secretary.

The auditor could check the information so obtained by looking through the payroll records ("holiday pay") to ascertain whether an annual holiday has, in fact, been taken by each member of the company's staff.

(c) A journal records the reason for entries in the books of accounts, and without proper authorisation for journal entries by a responsible official, incorrect entries may be made resulting in serious consequences. Without the proper use of "authorised journal vouchers" incorrect adjustments to various ledgers could be made, or capital and revenue charges could be manipulated.

The chief accountant would be able to inform the auditor of matters relating to the journal, and in addition should provide a list of officials who have the authority to make journal entries.

The auditor should examine and test journal entries, verify that entries can only be made by an authorised person, and also that they are initialled by the person making them.

(d) One of the important principles of internal control is the segregation of authority, and the importance of this question is based on the separation of the cashier's duties and those responsible for issuing statements. In order to prevent fraud, it is important to ensure that those having custody over remittances (cash) should not have access to statements and ledger accounts.

The information may be obtained from a procedural flow-chart or by an examination of the company's counting procedures. The auditor should verify the system by observing company procedures in practice.

(e) This question is similar to (d), in that it is aimed at finding out whether there is proper division of responsibility between the cashier and the official responsible for authorising travelling expenses. The absence of such a segregation of duties would enable a dishonest cashier to draw cash on the basis of fictitious expenses which he has entered in the books.

The chief accountant would be able to supply the information (though it would also show up on a detailed organisation chart). Independent verification by examination of vouchers for travelling expenses would show who had authorised these for payment.

8. Audit risk is related to materiality. Materiality is in turn related to size (amount) and incidence. Thus, high-value items may have a low incidence, and vice versa. Low-value items should never therefore be neglected, since in total they may well be material.

Bearing this in mind, the following factors should be considered when assessing audit risk attaching to each department:

    (a)   concerning goods:

        (i) the materiality of individual items sold by the department;

       (ii) the ease with which they may be removed without authority;

      (iii) previous records of losses due to theft or otherwise unexplained disappearances of goods;

      (iv) the presence and effectiveness of store detectives, closed circuit TV surveillance, etc.;

       (v) the frequency of stocktaking; whether or not by surprise; the independence of the stocktakers; the results of comparisons between stocks counted and recorded stock levels;

      (vi) obsolescence risks and perishability of type of stocks held;

    (b)   concerning cash:

        (i) the system governing control over cash takings, and its effectiveness in practice;

       (ii) the ease and frequency of reconciliations between cash and goods; and previous known discrepancies in excess of predetermined reasonable margins;

      (iii) frequency of bankings; security arrangements; and independence of staff performing banking functions;

      (iv) nature of control features incorporated in sales documentation and sales recording system, e.g. whether it facilitates independent proof of sales and cash totals; special features, such as point-of-sale computer terminals which guarantee correct billings;

       (v) separation of staff duties relating to handling of goods and cash respectively;

      (vi) independent, double-check of initial cash floats;

    (c)   general matters:

        (i) quality of supervision over departmental activity and internal authority limits;

       (ii) enforcement of head office rules, e.g. against local purchasing;

      (iii) presence of interim audit and results of any internal audit work already conducted;

(iv) results of own compliance tests conducted at the interim stage;

(v) arrangements for rotation and segregation of duties interdepartmentally and within departments;

(vi) evidence of statistical norms, e.g. sales mix variations within departments;

(vii) quality, loyalty and general calibre of sales staff, from past records.

9. (a)

(i) Since Hepplewhite Ltd does not specifically record terms, the auditors should ascertain what steps the directors (or others responsible for purchasing) have taken to identify those suppliers who have reserved title to goods pending settlement.

(ii) Based on (i) above and other work, quantify the secured liability to suppliers as at the balance sheet date, including goods not yet invoiced at that date.

(iii) Where suppliers have clearly laid down conditions of sale, these should be examined and the secured liability correctly stated in the notes to the accounts. This should also be done in respect of creditors identified by auditors as having included reservation of title in their terms.

(iv) Where the secured liabilities to suppliers are material, ensure that they are stated as being secured in the accounts; and ensure that the relevant accounting policy is disclosed in the accounts.

(v) Obtain formal representation from directors that either there are no material liabilities of this nature, or that the full amount is disclosed in the accounts.

(vi) Identify those suppliers whose terms refer specifically to the position relating to materials which are no longer in their original condition due to manufacturing processes. Consider the implications for client's liability of any legal advice the board may have received in relation to the "tracing" principle involved in such cases, including the question of who is responsible for insuring the goods.

(b) "Hepplewhite purchases goods from certain suppliers on terms which give those suppliers the right to reclaim the goods if they are not paid for, subject to legal interpretation. The total amount of such purchases which are included in creditors at 31st December 19xx is £167,902. At the date the directors approved the accounts all such liabilities had been settled."

(c) Although there have been recent case law developments, these do not appear to have fundamentally altered the principle established in the *Romalpa* case (1976), in which it was held that a seller may validly reserve title to goods, to other goods produced from them, and possibly to the proceeds from resale of those goods, unless and until they have been paid for by the immediate buyer. The clause used in the case was tortuously worded but extremely effective, because the buyer was treated as agent for the seller until all the goods (aluminium) were paid for, provided the goods remained identifiable.

In *Borden* v. *Scottish Timber Products*, however, the Appeal Court reversed a decision of the lower court, and held that the resin bought for making chipboard, had, by the time it was incorporated in the chipboard, completely changed its character, and was therefore irrecoverable for practical purposes. The resin no longer existed, and the court said it was untenable to claim the retention of title to something which no longer existed.

In the *Monsanto* case (1979), the seller included a term seeking to retain "equitable and beneficial" ownership of the Acrilan which it sold. Monsanto (the seller) lost, however, when the judge said the clause did not bestow any legal ownership—which, he held, had passed on delivery. He said that the clause gave Monsanto an equitable interest, which should have been registered at Companies House under section 95 (now section 396) of the Companies Act 1948 (now 1985). As it had not been so registered, Monsanto had no priority over other creditors.

It seems, therefore, that the simple stipulation that ownership will not pass until the goods are paid for is the most likely to be effective. If "tracing" rights are sought, separate agreement (based on legal advice) should be entered into.

10. (a) The following procedures in the audit plan should ensure that Sheraton Ltd has complied with SSAP 17:

   (i) Examine entries in accounting and management records following the year end, with the following matters specifically in mind:

     (1) accuracy in implementation of year-end cut-off arrangements;

     (2) independently confirmed information from customers and suppliers to support year-end balances;

     (3) any unusual journal entries;

     (4) payment of liabilities outstanding at year-end;

     (5) comparisons between business activity levels before and after year-end, respectively.

  (ii) Examine profit forecasts, cash-flow projections and other significant management data, such as budgets or divisional sales forecasts, etc.

 (iii) Examine areas of business of known high risk and susceptibility to external events, such as raw material price changes.

 (iv) Examine post balance sheet minutes of directors' and members' meetings, and of management meetings where appropriate.

  (v) Consider externally derived information which has a bearing, including that based on audits of other clients in same trade, news reports, etc. Discussions should be held with management on market conditions, cost variations, loss of business, cancellation of orders, disputes with staff and customers/suppliers.

(vi) Consider treatment in accounts of known contingencies, and then likely out-turn in the light of latest information and predictions.

(vii) Obtain suitably worded representations from directors, including information on contingencies such as legal matters still unresolved.

(viii) Ensure that, in respect of all material matters mentioned above, working papers adequately reflect supporting information; details of enquiries; replies given by management; own reservations on outcome of unresolved areas.

(ix) Ensure compliance in financial statements with all Companies Act requirements and SSAPs.

(x) Ensure, in relation to SSAP 17, that the accounts properly distinguish between adjusting and non-adjusting events, as defined.

(xi) Ensure that directors have visibly approved the financial statements and directors' report *before* signing the audit report.

(xii) Consider the effect on financial statements of events coming to notice between date of signing audit report and AGM, and the appropriate action to be taken in such circumstances.

(b) *Adjusting events* are those which provide additional evidence relating to conditions existing at the balance sheet date, and which require changes in amounts to be reflected in the financial statements. Their separate disclosure is not normally required, since they simply provide additional evidence of the accuracy and reliability of items appearing in the financial statements.

Non-adjusting events are those which arise *after* the balance sheet date and concern conditions which did *not* exist at that time; they result in no changes of amount of items in the statements. Where material, their disclosure will be required by way of note to ensure that financial statements are not misleading. In this regard, all matters should be considered which are necessary to enable users of the statements to assess the financial position. Notes should explain the event, and estimate its effect, where possible.

(Some matters which actually affect the going concern status of the company, such as a post balance sheet deterioration in business, may have to be treated as adjusting events.)

11. Information normally included in the plant register of a large manufacturing company would be as follows:

(a) description of plant;

(b) serial number;

(c) manufacturer;

(d) cost;

(e) location;

(f)   new or second-hand;

(g)   date of installation;

(h)   production department;

(i)   rate of depreciation;

(j)   additions or modification details;

(k)   how disposed of;

(l)   date of disposal;

(m) sale proceeds.

Functions of a plant register record are as follows:

(a)   It establishes accountability over each plant item. Without this detailed record it would be difficult to determine whether items have been dismantled, scrapped or sold without appropriate authorisation or correct accounting treatment. The record also facilitates the periodical inventory of plant assets.

(b)   It provides the means whereby depreciation charges may be accurately determined. It also provides information for the adjustment of annual depreciation charges for assets sold, retired or become fully depreciated. It also facilitates comparisons with taxation allowances and hence the calculation of deferred taxation transfers.

(c)   The register provides information on original costs and accumulated depreciation so that appropriate accounting entries may be made on disposal. Such information would be virtually unobtainable in the absence of the plant register.

12.   (a)   Secondhand machinery: audit problems on valuation:

(i)   The method adopted is arbitrary, and in any one accounting period could give rise to a stock valuation which is very materially incorrect. (Global method is in conflict with SSAP 9.)

(ii) The method does not represent a change of policy, and it appears to have been accepted by auditors in the past; this makes it considerably more difficult to persuade management to change to an acceptable method now.

(iii) During the period between 31st October and 31st January virtually no sales take place. Therefore no post balance sheet transactions can be used to test accuracy of valuations. (Pressure on audit completion within three months is further problem.)

(iv) Since the quantities involved amount to more than half the total stocks, and comprise 500 high-value items, the sums are almost certainly material, and as such would normally demand audit consideration on an individual rather than collective basis.

(v) Since items are in stock for two or more years, and may even be eventually scrapped, there appears to be no satisfactory method of comparing valuations with actual proceeds within a reasonable time-span; it is also questionable whether these stocks justify inclusion in "current assets". It is essential that items acquired more than one year previously (i.e. in an earlier period) should be considered individually for further write-down. This does not appear to be happening.

(vi) Since the "trade-in cost" is often known to be in excess of estimated realisable value (ERV), the valuation starting point is too high; the arbitrary 50% reduction may thus prove to be quite insufficient.

(vii) Renovation costs are added. How is this determined? Compliance with SSAP 9 requires that a proportion of workshop overheads should also feature in this costing, to ensure that stock is valued at the amount which a sale would need to cover to ensure *full* recovery.

(viii) The stock register will be useful to auditors only if accurately cross-referenced to records of purchases and sales; in any case it will give audit problems since it does not appear to record whether *further* maintenance and/or renovation work is needed before item is sale-worthy; nor does it show ERV at the balance sheet date; nor subsequent write-downs, if any. (It is hoped that it records renovation costs on an individual basis.)

(ix) The auditors lack the expertise needed to estimate future ERV.

(b) The auditors should perform their own valuation tests for comparison with the method adopted by the company, as follows (in respect of suitable sample):

(i) Determine (from past records, company policy etc.) the *normal* discount level allowed on cash sales of new machinery, and adjust the "trade-in cost" or part-exchange item to reflect this (usually a downward adjustment to arrive at *real* cost).

(ii) Add actual renovation costs, including overhead allocation.

(iii) Estimate date of realisation on basis of market intelligence and/or past averages for the class of machine, and calculate DCF factor back to present value. If these results show significant differences from the company's arbitrary method, insist on adjustment to accounts, or qualify audit report.

(iv) Perform tests on suitable sample of items sold during period, and compare proceeds with register valuations. If significantly lower, consider the need to adjust valuation of unsold items (as determined by company, or in point (iii) above) to effect such reduction.

(v) Inspect unsold stocks, and observe physical count; where age and condition indicate likelihood of scrapping, ensure write-down is effected accordingly.

  (vi) Perform analytical review, including comparison with amounts and ratios of earlier periods.

  (vii) Compare balance sheet values of individual items in stock with sale prices of similar items of similar age, advertised in trade journals.

13. The following factors could materially affect the accuracy of the figures appearing in the company's balance sheet for stock, and each consequently merits the careful consideration of the auditor:

  (a) *Cut-off procedure.* This should be explicitly laid down in a form which may be readily understood by personnel within the accounts department as well as those involved in the physical stocktaking. Unless this is achieved, it is unlikely that the company's records of purchases and sales towards the end of the financial period could be accurately reconciled with physical stocks in hand on the stocktaking date.

  (b) *Slow-moving items.* These may normally be discovered by reference to the usual turnover period. The ratio of stock in hand to cost of sales should provide a useful indicator.

  (c) *Items subject to deterioration.* The risk of deterioration would apply particularly in the case of goods susceptible to atmospheric variations such as humidity, temperature etc.

  (d) *Obsolescence.* Goods which may be classified as obsolete may prove difficult to identify, but circumstances may arise in certain trades, e.g. fashion, where a large volume of goods would have to be valued well below cost having become obsolete for purposes of sale.

  (e) *Goods received from/issued to agents or consignors/consignees.* Great care must be taken to ensure that the final inventory totals reflect the ownership of such items rather than their physical location, since grossly inaccurate results would otherwise follow.

14. Client . . . . Period of account . . . .

Post balance sheet review checklist

	Review by	Date to which review extends	Working paper reference
1. Review receivables records for collection of outstanding balances and credit notes issued and adjustments.			
2. Review payables records and unpaid invoice files for evidence of liabilities not recorded in the balance sheet.			

3. Review cash receipts records for evidence of:

    (a) significant sales of fixed assets or investments;

    (b) realisations of debtors' balances;

    (c) loan issues or repayment proceeds;

    (d) any unusual items.

4. Review cash payments records for evidence of:

    (a) liabilities not included in the balance sheet;

    (b) acquisitions of subsidiaries, fixed assets or investments;

    (c) any other unusual items.

5. Review journal entries.

6. Read minutes of directors and any other important management committees for matters which will materially affect the financial position of the company.

7. Inspect the register of charges.

8. Review interim financial reports.

9. Discuss with management as to whether, since the balance sheet date there have been any developments involving matters of significance affecting the company's state of affairs at the balance sheet date or the results of the year.

15. (a) Related party transactions require special attention and scrutiny by the auditor since the terms and conditions of these transactions may be unduly favourable to one of the parties.

    Depending upon the circumstances and materiality of the transactions concerned, the auditor may wish to consider the adequacy of the disclosure of these transactions in the accounts. For example, the Companies Act 1985 requires disclosure of significant contracts (as adjudged by the directors) in which directors have a material interest, but apart from such statutory provisions the auditor may take the view that the disclosure of related party transactions is required to enable the financial statements to show a true and fair view.

(b) The following might be included within the definition of related parties:

     (i) organisations under common control with the client company (regarding "control" as the power to direct management and policy through ownership, contract or otherwise);

    (ii) shareholders with substantial holdings of voting shares (exceeding, say, 10%);

   (iii) the executive directors and their immediate families;

   (iv) associated companies;

    (v) any other party which has the ability to prevent the company from pursuing its own interests independently.

(c) The following types of transaction may indicate the existence of related parties:

    (i) borrowing/lending at rates of interest substantially higher/lower than current market rates;

   (ii) sales/purchases of assets at prices substantially different from those currently ruling;

   (iii) straightforward exchange of assets in a manner which masks the underlying value of the assets exchanged;

   (iv) granting of loans with no scheduled repayment terms.

Tutorial Note

"Related party transactions" is a popular examination topic and will presumably eventually be the subject of accounting and auditing standards; a background paper was published early in 1980 by the APC.

16. (a) The following are symptoms which might indicate that an enterprise is no longer a going concern:

    (i) loan repayments are falling due in the near future;

   (ii) high or increasing debt to equity ratios existing;

   (iii) increasing dependence upon short-term finance;

   (iv) an inability to take advantage of discounts, suppliers enforcing cash terms, or the time taken to pay creditors is increasing;

    (v) substantial losses are occurring, or the rate of profitability is declining;

   (vi) purchases are being deferred, thereby reducing stocks to dangerously low levels;

   (vii) capital expenditure is being switched to leasing agreements;

   (viii) a company is in an exposed position in relation to future commitments, such as long-term assets financed by short- or medium-term borrowings;

    (ix) a company has a net deficiency of assets, or its ratio of current assets to current liabilities is declining;

    (x) a company is near to its present borrowing limits, with no sign of a reduction in requirements;

    (xi) collection from debtors is slowing down;

    (xii) rapid development of business creates a dangerous overtrading situation;

    (xiii) there is substantial investment in new products, ventures or research which are not yet successful;

    (xiv) there is reliance on a limited number of products, customers or suppliers;

    (xv) there is evidence of reductions or cancellations of capital projects;

    (xvi) there is heavy dependence on an overseas holding company (for finance or trade).

(b)   Evidence of the presence of any of the above factors necessitates the auditor satisfying himself that the enterprise has sufficient cash resources to meet its needs. The auditor should:

    (i) compare the client's cash flow forecast with the overdraft or other loan facilities available for up to twelve months from the accounting date;

    (ii) enquire into and obtain written evidence of any steps the client is taking to correct its decline in fortunes;

    (iii) in the case of a subsidiary company, obtain written confirmation from the holding company that it intends its subsidiary to continue in business and will not withdraw loan facilities.

Tutorial Note

This remains an important and extremely relevant topic. You might like to consider what grounds led Westward Television's auditor to qualify the July 1979 accounts which were published in January 1980 subsequent to the announcement of the impending loss of its franchise.

17. (a) The following topics, within the provisions of the Companies Act 1985, are of general significance to auditors:

    (i) disclosure requirements governing the particulars, and amounts involved, relating to loans to directors, quasi-loans to directors of public companies and connected persons, and provisions of guarantees and security by public companies in connection with loans etc.;

    (ii) disclosure requirements concerning loans to persons who are officers, other than directors;

    (iii) transactions between companies and their directors requiring prior approval in general meeting for transfer to or from the company of material non-cash assets;

(iv) supporting documentation and procedures applicable to the conversion of a private to a public company; requiring a balance sheet and statement from auditors;

(v) valuation reports by an expert: these are required on the issue by a public company of shares for consideration other than cash, and on transfers of non-cash assets to a public company by a member;

(vi) prohibition of insider dealings;

(vii) definition of "Companies Act", and reference thereto in report;

(viii) determination of the amounts which may legitimately be paid by way of dividend.

(b) In relation to items (i) to (iii) in (a) above, certain specific audit responsibilities are laid down in the Act. Section 237 requires the disclosure in the audit report of all matters in contravention of the prohibitions against loans, quasi-loans, guarantees and provision of security (as already outlined in (a) above), to the extent not disclosed in the accounts. The same section requires disclosure of the amounts involved, as well as particulars.

Whether or not a specific audit duty is laid down, unless auditors are thoroughly familiar with these provisions concerning transactions and loans, they will not be in a position to state, whether in their opinion, the financial statements comply with the Companies Act.

Under (a) (iv) above, when a private company is converted to a public company, the auditors are required to prepare a written statement that in their opinion the net assets are not less than the share capital and undistributable reserves. The accompanying balance sheet must be supported by an audit report carrying no qualification which is material for determining the above net assets position.

The "expert", whose valuation report is required under (a) (v) above, does not have to be the auditor but in many cases the auditor will be appointed for this purpose—especially since the Act requires the valuer to have the same qualifications, and independent position, as the auditor. The valuation report required on the transfer of shares in exchange for non-cash consideration must include the nominal value and premium, if any; a description of the non-cash consideration; the method of valuation, and statement that it is:

(i) reasonable; and

(ii) worth no less than the amount treated as paid up.

Although auditors are not named as insiders (see (a) (vi) above) it is obvious that their duties bring them into contact with price-sensitive information, and they are hence barred from acting on it in share dealings, or from passing it to others. This has been covered by professional ethics rules for some time, but nevertheless highlights the caution with which such information must now be guarded—not only by auditors, but also by their staff acting as their agents.

The rules for determining divisible profits ((a) (viii) above) are covered by an onerous "blanket" requirement that if dividends are paid out of profits as shown in accounts to which a qualified audit report is attached, the auditors must state in writing whether in their opinion the qualification is material for the purpose of determining the legitimacy of the dividends. This may cause exceptional difficulties in cases where auditors are unable to quantify the effect of their qualification, for example where no depreciation has been charged on buildings, or where the directors' valuation of goodwill cannot easily be substantiated.

18. (a)   The auditor of a company must either be a member of a body of accountants recognised by the Department of Trade and Industry or be authorised by the Department of Trade and Industry to act as an auditor for some other reason.

        The bodies of accountants whose members are recognised by the Department of Trade and Industry as being qualified to act as auditors are:

    (i) the Institute of Chartered Accountants in England and Wales;

    (ii) the Institute of Chartered Accountants of Scotland;

    (iii) the Institute of Chartered Accountants in Ireland;

    (iv) the Chartered Association of Certified Accountants (incorporated by royal charter).

The other reasons for which a person may be recognised as an auditor of a company by the Department of Trade and Industry are:

    (i) he has obtained similar qualification outside the UK;

    (ii) he has obtained adequate knowledge and experience in the course of his employment by a member of one of the bodies of accountants mentioned above; and

    (iii) he has practised in Great Britain as an accountant before 6th August 1947.

A person is also qualified for appointment as auditor of a private company or unquoted public company provided that:

    (i) he is authorised by the Department of Trade and Industry as having been in practice as an accountant throughout the twelve months to 3rd November 1966; and

    (ii) he was on that date appointed auditor of an exempt private company under the Companies Act 1948; and

    (iii) the holding company is also a private company or unquoted public company.

  (b)   The following powers are vested in the auditor:

    (i) he has right of access, at all times, to the books and accounts and vouchers of the company;

    (ii) he shall be entitled to require from officers of the company such information and explanations as he thinks necessary for the performance of the duties of the auditor;

(iii) he shall be entitled to attend any general meeting of the company, receive all notices of and communications relating to any general meeting, which a member of the company is entitled to receive, and be heard at any general meeting on any part of the meeting's business which concerns the auditors.

19. The auditor should direct his attention to the following matters when reviewing a company's statutory books and registers:

(a) Share register:

    (i) the register is properly maintained and kept up to date;

    (ii) any changes in the shareholdings of directors, required to be disclosed in the annual report and accounts, are correctly reflected in the register of directors' shareholdings;

    (iii) substantial holdings (greater than 5%) of shares in a public company have been notified to the Council of the Stock Exchange and the Registrar of Companies;

    (iv) new issues of shares are supported by appropriate entries in the directors' minutes and accounting records, with special reference to cash received, share capital account, and share premium account where applicable;

    (v) the Companies Act 1985 requirements on shares issued for consideration other than cash and purchase by a company of its own shares (if applicable) have been complied with fully and correctly reflected in the register.

(b) Register of debenture holders (if kept):

    (i) ensure that debentures issued and/or redeemed during the financial year have been minuted by the directors and correctly recorded in the accounting records, with reference to cash receipts and payments, and relevant nominal ledger accounts;

    (ii) ensure that interest paid during the year accords with the amount of debenture outstanding as per the register;

    (iii) assuming the debentures are secured on specific assets or by way of floating charge on the assets, ensure that such security is noted in the financial statements, and reflected the company's register of charges.

(c) Register of directors' shareholdings:

    (i) ensure that changes are duly reflected in the minutes of the meetings of directors;

    (ii) ensure that the holdings of directors are properly disclosed in the company's annual return and in the annual report and accounts.

(d)   Register of directors and secretary: ensure that this reflects the up-to-date position taking into account any changes during the year, duly authorised in the minutes of the meetings of directors.

(e)   Directors' minute book:

    (i)   This should contain the original minutes of every meeting of the directors held during the year under review, and these should have been approved at the successive board meeting as accurately reflecting all business transacted, as evidenced by the signature of the chairman, and dated.

    (ii)   The auditor's use of the directors' minutes is extensive, since these minutes represent the highest level of internal evidence available, affecting all matters outside of the routine day-to-day business transactions of the company, such as capital commitments, share issues, changes of business location; and legal claims.

The auditor will refer to the minutes on the company's financial position, and which may indicate the existence of liabilities and contingencies not otherwise evidenced in the company's accounting records but which should nevertheless be incorporated appropriately in the financial statements.

(f)   members' minute book: the minutes of the meeting of *members* of the company will be examined by the auditor to ensure that all matters on the agenda of such meetings have been duly approved by the appropriate majority, as required under the Companies Act and under the company's own articles of association. The auditor will be specifically concerned with:

    (i)   the approval by the members of the annual financial statements;

    (ii)   the reappointment of directors retiring by rotation;

    (iii)   the authorisation given to the directors by the members to determine the auditor's remuneration;

    (iv)   the approval by the members of the dividend proposed by the directors; and

    (v)   where applicable, the ratification of the appointment of the auditors.

(g)   Register of charges:

    (i)   ensure that the charges included accord with details on the company's annual return, submitted to Companies House for filing;

    (ii)   ensure that the register of charges is up to date and that any guarantees or other indemnities entered into in respect of bank loans, overdrafts etc. secured by way of floating charge on the company's assets, or by way of specific charge on identifiable assets, are correctly reflected, and duly noted in the financial statements as required by the Companies Act.

(h)   Memorandum and articles of association:

      (i) ensure that the company's trading activities and contracts entered into are not in breach of its objects clause;

      (ii) ensure that the company's borrowings do not exceed the borrowing limits as specified in the memorandum and articles;

      (iii) ensure that all provisions in the articles have been satisfactorily observed at all material times, with reference to such matters as notice of meetings, retirement and re-appointment of directors, quorum at meetings, procedural matters affecting meetings, and transfer or sale of shares in the company.

20. (a) The fundamental accounting concepts which should be adopted in the preparation of financial statements intended to show a true and fair view are set out in Statement of Standard Accounting Practice 2, and incorporated in Part 2 of Schedule 4 to the Companies Act 1985. These are as follows:

      (i) *Going concern.* The company shall be presumed to be a going concern. This means that at the date on which the audit report to the members is signed it is believed that the company will continue to be financially viable for the foreseeable future. Such belief therefore justifies, for example, the carry forward of the value of assets not yet written off.

      (ii) *Consistency.* The company's accounting policies shall be applied consistently from one financial period to the next. This ensures that the financial statements of successive periods may be used for the purpose of making valid comparisons. An unwarranted change of accounting policy, or a change whose effect is not adequately disclosed, will render such comparison misleading.

      (iii) *Prudence.* Items included in financial statements shall be determined on a prudent basis. In particular: only profits realised at the balance sheet date shall be included in the profit and loss account; and all liabilities and losses which have arisen or are likely to arise in respect of the period reported on shall be reflected in the financial statements, including those which become apparent after the balance sheet date but before the financial statements are approved.

      (iv) *Accruals.* All income and charges which relate to the financial period in question shall be reflected in the financial statements without regard to the time of receipt or payment. Without this concept financial statements would be prepared on a receipts and payments basis, which would be misleading since accrued income and accrued charges, due for settlement after the balance sheet date, would consequently be disregarded.

The Companies Act 1985 includes a fifth "accounting principle" (the "aggregation" principle) which is that the amount of each individual asset or liability included within the aggregate amount shall be determined separately, i.e. the Act does not permit the "set-off" of an asset against a liability.

(b) Under the Companies Act 1985 the directors of a company are permitted to depart from the concepts set out above if it appears to them that there are special reasons for so doing; but the notes to the accounts must give:

    (i) particulars of the departures;

    (ii) the reasons for them; and

    (iii) the effect of such departures.

The content of the audit report in such circumstances will be determined by the adequacy of the disclosure in the notes to the accounts, as indicated above. If the auditor fully concurs with the necessity for departing from a concept, and is satisfied with the prominence and content of the explanatory note, he may wish to give special emphasis to the note which explains and quantifies the effect of the departure, so that the attention of readers of the accounts is drawn thereto.

If the auditor disagrees with the necessity for departing from any of these concepts, he would:

    (i) draw attention to the explanatory note;

    (ii) give the reasons for disagreeing with it; and

    (iii) qualify his opinion on the financial statements in terms which comply with the Auditing Standard on "Qualifications in Audit Reports", giving an "except" opinion or an adverse opinion, depending on whether the effect of the departure is material or fundamental respectively.

21. (a) It is important that any misunderstanding as to the responsibility of accountants for work done for sole traders or partnerships should be avoided. Care must therefore be taken in the way accountants associate their names with accounts not prepared under statute. Practical matters to be borne in mind are as follows:

    (i) Clients should be made aware of the scope of the work which is accepted by the accountant and a suitably worded "letter of engagement" should be sent to the client in which the relevant details are set out; an additional copy would normally be provided for the client to acknowledge by signature and return. The letter will make clear the degree of responsibility which the accountant is prepared to accept in relation to the accounts as well as indicating the broader terms of reference, e.g. the nature of work to be undertaken.

    (ii) A report should always be appended to the accounts whether these have been audited or simply prepared. The report should make clear the extent of responsibility accepted for accounts which have merely been prepared (but not audited)—an opinion should be given only on audited accounts.

    (iii) Where accounts have been prepared but not audited, the report should be headed "Accountant's Report" and worded so that the association of the name with the accounts cannot be misunderstood. It is also desirable that the report should specifically state that the accounts have not been audited.

(iv) As far as possible in the absence of an audit, accountants should ensure that accepted accounting principles are complied with in the accounts which they prepare and, where this has not been done, this should be made clear in the accounts.

(v) Where certain items in the accounts are based on estimates, as is often necessary where the records are deficient, such estimated items should be thus described. It is vital that accountants should not allow their names to be associated with accounts (even though unaudited) which they believe present a misleading view.

(vi) Care should be taken that any reference in the accounts or elsewhere to accountants' fees does not describe them as audit fees.

(vii) Where a non-statutory audit is carried out, normal audit principles and standards would apply. Consequently, reports should state that the accounts have been audited and whether in the opinion of the auditors they present a true and fair view subject to any necessary reservations.

(viii) Accounts prepared with or without audit should always be approved by a client before the report is signed. Wherever possible, the client should be asked to sign a declaration on the face of the copy of the accounts retained by the accountant, indicating the client's approval of the accounts and confirming that all relevant records and information necessary for their preparation have been made available.

(b)   Where an accountant has been asked to prepare accounts but not to audit them, a suitable form of report would be as follows:

"Accountants' Report

In accordance with instructions given to us, we have prepared, without carrying out an audit, the annexed accounts from the accounting records of XXX & Co, and from information and explanations supplied to us for the purpose."

22. Under present companies legislation, the auditors of the parent company are legally responsible for the expression of opinion as to whether the accounts of the group show a true and fair view as regards members of the holding company. Since the group accounts incorporate the accounts of the subsidiaries which have not necessarily been audited by the parent company auditors, it is normal practice for the parent company auditors to make the enquiries referred to in the question.

The specific issues normally covered in the inter-firm questionnaires are as follows:

(a)   *Accounting policies:*

(i) disclosure of movements on share capital and reserves;

    (ii) details of long- and medium-term liabilities including repayment dates, premium on repayments, interest rates, security;

    (iii) trade creditors and accrued liabilities including details of provision as distinct from accrual;

    (iv) outstanding hire purchase liabilities;

    (v) contingent liabilities;

    (vi) taxation including details of items in dispute and deferred taxation;

    (vii) fixed assets including details of inter-company purchases and sales;

    (viii) consistency of depreciation rates;

    (ix) stock and work in progress with particular reference to company procedures on stock control and stocktaking;

    (x) bases of valuation;

    (xi) trade debtors;

    (xii) the basis of computing provision for bad and doubtful debts;

    (xiii) deferred revenue expenditure;

    (xiv) consistency of accounting policies.

  (b) *Scope of audit:* the following questions would normally be asked:

    (i) Internal control: was the system of internal control in operation reviewed during the year? If not, when was it last reviewed? Give details of any material weakness which you have drawn to the attention of the management during the year, and attach a copy of any letter of weakness sent to the company.

    (ii) Books of account; do you consider the company's accounting records to be entirely satisfactory? If not give details.

    (iii) Detailed audit procedures: have these included:

      (1) inspection of documents of title for assets?
      (2) attendance to observe stocktaking?
      (3) check of cut-off procedure?
      (4) overall tests of trading account items?
      (5) confirmation that stock and work in progress are properly valued?
      (6) circularisation of a sample of trade debtors?
      (7) obtaining certificate from company's bankers as to balance at the year end?
      (8) verification of all liabilities?
      (9) obtaining a letter of representation from the company? If so, attach a copy.

23.
                                                          K. Arthur & Co
                                                          Castle House
                                                          67–70 Knights Road
                                                          London EC1

N. Cyril Esq
Finance Director
Wiseguys National Bakeries Ltd
Wiseguys House
Woodley Industrial Estate
Woodley
BEDS   5th November 1985

Dear Mr Cyril,

Financial statements—year ended 30th September 1985
Thank you for your letter dated 1st November 1985 and copy of the minutes of your board meeting at which the above financial statements were approved. I note also that it was resolved that no amendments should be made to the statements as approved.

I must nevertheless point out that there are certain matters which we have noted during our review of the financial statements and, subject to further discussions, these may well require suitable reference in our audit report when this is finalised in due course. These matters are accordingly listed below.

FREEHOLD PROPERTY
In past years this property has been shown in the statements at its original cost, whereas it is now restated at £1,250,000, as professionally valued during the year. In the first paragraph of our audit report we shall therefore note that the financial statements have been prepared under the historical cost convention, as modified by the revaluation of the company's freehold property.

DEPRECIATION ON AIRCRAFT
We have already discussed with you your decision that no depreciation should be provided on the company aircraft, and have advised you that we fully concur with this decision. Since the reasons for not providing depreciation, as well as the auditors' concurrence therewith, are fully detailed in the notes, we do not believe that any reference to this matter will be required in our report.

VALUE OF TRADE MARKS
In view of the materiality of the valuation originally attributed to trade marks by the directors in 1982, and the practical impossibility of applying audit procedures to verify this value, we are obliged as in previous years to note our uncertainty in this regard. This will be dealt with in a separate paragraph of our report, in which we shall state that:

(a)   the trade marks have been valued by the directors at £800,000 in 1982 and included in the balance sheet at this figure;

(b)   as in previous years, we have been unable to carry out any procedures to confirm that this valuation is justified;

(c)   we are therefore uncertain as to whether the company's assets and reserves have accordingly been overstated; and

(d)   we have qualified our report in the two previous years on the grounds of the same uncertainty.

We shall follow this by saying that, subject to this reservation, a true and fair view is given of the state of the company's affairs.

DOUBTFUL DEBT PROVISION

It is our belief that no part of the debt of £45,000 due from XYZ Ltd will be recovered by the company. Since the financial statements which the directors have approved include no provision against this debt, it will be necessary for us to state that:

(a)   no provision has been made against an amount of £45,000 owing by a customer;

(b)   we believe such amount to be irrecoverable; and

(c)   in our opinion, except for the failure to make such provision, a true and fair view of the state of the company's affairs and its results is given by the financial statements.

LOAN TO A DIRECTOR

Since the director's indebtedness of £22,000, which subsisted during a six-week period, has not been disclosed in the financial statements in accordance with the provisions of the Companies Act 1985, we are obliged under sections 233 and 237 of the same Act to include in our report a statement giving the required particulars. These particulars include:

(a)   the name of the director;

(b)   the fact of his indebtedness; and

(c)   the amount due (including any interest), i.e. £22,000.

Our report will conclude with a statement of our opinion that the financial statements, except for the information specified above, comply with the Companies Act 1985, so far as that Act applies to the financial statements.

ALLEGED BREACH OF CONTRACT

Because of the uncertainty concerning the amount of compensation (possibly including costs) which it appears will be payable following the major breach of your contract with LMN Ltd, it will be necessary for our report to:

(a)   refer to the explanatory note in the financial statements in which this contingent liability is disclosed;

(b)   refer to the uncertainty; and

(c)   express our opinion that subject to any adjustment of profits which may ultimately be required when the outcome of the litigation is known, the financial statements give a true and fair view, etc.

FINAL FORM OF REPORT

Should you and your co-directors wish to discuss these matters with me, please do not hesitate to let me know. If it is believed that, in the light of the above, amendments to the approved accounts should now be made in order to avoid the necessity for us to qualify our report as indicated above, it will, of course, be necessary for the board to re-approve the amended financial statements.

If, on the other hand, the board is adamant that no amendments should be made, we shall let you have a draft of the final formulation of our report, incorporating the various matters referred to in this letter.

Yours sincerely,

for K. Arthur & Co

24. (a)   Arguments in favour of the use of statistical sampling in auditing:

   (i)   The auditor is forced to assess the reliability required from his tests before commencing them. The process of evaluating the sources of assurance and risk respectively is therefore accorded its due importance.

   (ii)   Important considerations cannot be "glossed over", such as deciding what constitutes an "error" for the purposes of the test, and the level of errors to be regarded as acceptable.

   (iii)   The imposition of a discipline with a mathematical basis lends greater credibility to audit conclusions, especially where the results of a test indicate that more extensive testing is necessary in order to reach a valid conclusion.

   (iv)   The use of statistical sampling for determining sample sizes is accompanied by the use of random selection techniques for selecting sample items; this gives assurance that the conclusions are not based on a biased selection.

   (v)   These techniques enable sample results to be expressed in a manner which highlights the level of risk associated therewith; the fact that the auditor cannot *guarantee* any result is therefore evident from a correctly drafted conclusion.

   (vi)   In view of its scientific basis, statistical sampling will normally prescribe smaller sample sizes than the exercise of subjective judgment; this represents a saving of time.

(b)   Arguments against the use of statistical sampling in auditing:

   (i)   By its nature, auditing depends on intuitive skills, and does not therefore lend itself to the use of scientific skills.

   (ii)   Properly designed statistical schemes require an inordinate length of time to be set up, possibly including the manual prenumbering of batches of documents to facilitate selection; during this time much representative sampling could in any event have been conducted with reasonable assurance of validity.

(iii) Very small sample sizes depend for validity on rigid adherence to sampling disciplines, even a minor breach might invalidate the conclusions.

(iv) To avoid the dangers under (iii) above, a clear grasp of the mathematical principles is needed, and not all members of the audit team may possess this.

(v) An unwitting bias in the selection process may invalidate conclusions based on very small samples.

(vi) The method may be inappropriate in many common conditions, e.g. where population items are not homogeneous in nature or materiality, or where they are not easily identifiable or accessible.

(c) Conclusion: provided the auditor is mindful of the attendant risks and pitfalls, sound use can be made of statistical sampling techniques, especially where:

(i) large populations of homogeneous items are being tested;

(ii) internal controls are reasonably sound;

(iii) members of the audit team possess the necessary skills, and have been thoroughly trained in the use of the methods and applications adopted by the audit firm.

25. (a) Whatever method of sampling an auditor employs, he relies on his own judgment for the final test of acceptability of recorded evidence. Statistical sampling has nevertheless substantial advantages in terms of reliability. The conditions which should be present before statistical sampling methods may be used are as follows:

(i) The population must be sufficiently large for the mathematical laws of probability to apply in a meaningful way.

(ii) The accounting or data processing system which produces the records under examination must be sufficiently reliable. Although this level of reliability (just as the size of population under (i) above) cannot be objectively quantified, it is clear that statistical sampling techniques cannot be used in a chaotic state of affairs, since then each item scrutinised would be representative only of itself, and it would therefore be impossible for valid conclusions about the population to be drawn on the strength of a sample.

(iii) All items within a particular population must be homogeneous, i.e. they must all fall within the same "category". Homogeneity, for this purpose, would relate to materiality (thus ensuring comparable significance) and also to the manner of recording (including the internal checks applicable thereto).

(iv) On a practical level, items within the population must be both identifiable and accessible. If this requirement is not met, the execution of the sampling method may prove to be impossible—after all, the validity of any sample depends upon each item within the population standing an equal chance of being selected for examination. This requirement often presents practical problems, e.g. where no sequential numbering system exists or, where it does exist, documents have been re-sorted and filed for another purpose.

(b) The disciplines referred to may be explained as follows:

  (i) the need for the auditor to predetermine the degree of reliability which he requires (i.e. that the sample size is representative of the population);

  (ii) the need for him to predetermine the degree of certainty (normally shown as +/- percentage points) for the assumption that the number of errors discovered in the sample applies. proportionately to the unsampled portion of the population as well;

  (iii) the need for the auditor to define in advance precisely what constitutes an "error";

  (iv) the need to predetermine the level of errors which he will regard as acceptable (i.e. non-material) for the purposes of the particular test;

  (v) the need to take appropriate special action should the sample test disclose an unsatisfactory result (e.g. a level of errors which exceeds that defined under (iv) above);

  (vi) for the sample to be valid, the selection of items within it must be made by entirely random methods, preferably with the use of random number tables: this has the advantage of avoiding any element of personal bias in the auditor's selections.

26. (a) Although there is nothing in the statute book at the present time which specifies a legal responsibility on the part of the auditor outside of his relationship with the shareholders to whom he reports the courts have made it clear that liability may extend to others who have relied upon the work of an auditor, albeit without any contractual relationship subsisting.

It was decided some twenty years ago in the case of *Candler* v. *Crane, Christmas & Co* that there could be no liability in the absence of a fiduciary or contractual obligation, even though the auditors (in that case acting as accountants) knew that a potential investor depended upon accounts specially (and negligently) prepared for the purpose of assisting the investment decision.

This decision—a majority of two to one in the House of Lords—was heavily criticised and in 1963 was specifically overruled. The House of Lords in the case of *Hedley Byrne & Co* v. *Heller & Partners Ltd* held that financial liability could in fact arise where third parties have relied upon the expertise and competence of a person or firm acting in a professional capacity.

Subsequent cases in this country and overseas have followed the *Hedley Byrne* decision, although it would appear that the negligent opinion or statement must be issued in the context of the ordinary business of the party issuing it in order for liability to arise (*Evatt* v. *Citizens & Mutual Life Assurance Co*).

(b)   Counsel's opinion (obtained by the Institute of Chartered Accountants) on the practical application of the *Hedley Byrne* case has suggested that an investment decision based on a negligently prepared report in a prospectus or other document of offer would probably give rise to liability. The broad rule suggested by counsel was that the reliance must have given rise to specific financial loss within a context known to the negligent party at the time.

Counsel's opinion did, however, state that financial liability was unlikely in the case of reliance by shareholders or others who have suffered loss as a result of an investment decision based on accounts prepared for stewardship purposes, albeit negligently. The reason given by counsel was that the stewardship context does not extend to a basis for investment decisions. Since, however, it is *ipso facto* true that stewardship accounts are used for this purpose (there being no other readily available information on which such decisions may be based) it is unlikely that any current decision in the courts would concur with the opinion of counsel in this report. This view has been proved correct in the legal decision *Jeb Fasteners Ltd* v. *Marks Bloom & Co* (1981), where the auditors were held responsible even though they had no prior knowledge that their report was to be relied on for an investment purpose.

27. COMMON LAW

The auditor is subject to the common law in being required to carry out his duties under contract with reasonable care and skill. What is reasonable will vary according to developments within the profession and the interests of those which it serves.

The usual charge against auditors in common law proceedings is in respect of the tort of negligence and considerable body of case law has been built up both in this country and abroad. It is clear that at the present time the range of liability is wider than has ever been the case previously.

The particular branch of auditor's liability for negligence which has attracted much attention is that which concerns injured third parties. Leading cases are *Candler* v. *Crane, Christmas & Co* (1954) and *Hedley Byrne & Co Ltd* v. *Heller & Partners Ltd* (1963). The pre-1981 position would seem to have been that third party plaintiff would have to establish:

(a)   that there had in fact been negligence;

(b)   that the defendant party knew that the statement, document, balance sheet, report, etc. containing the negligent mis-statement was being prepared for the specific purpose which gave rise to the action; that it was likely to be relied upon by the injured party; and that the loss/injury clearly flowed from the mis-statement.

The 1981 case of *Jeb Fasteners Ltd* v. *Marks, Bloom & Co* has, however, shown that negligent work is actionable if it was *reasonable* to foresee that it might be relied upon by a third party, even though the defendant has no knowledge of such reliance at the time. This was upheld on appeal in June 1982.

LIABILITY UNDER STATUTE

This may be civil or criminal.

Civil proceedings against auditors may arise under section 631 of the Companies Act 1985 in respect of misfeasance or breach of trust, the company being in process of liquidation.

Criminal statutory law may affect auditors under sections 624–630 of the Companies Act 1985. The auditor has been held to be an officer of the company for the purposes of the winding-up penalty sections aforementioned (*R. v. Schacter* (1960)). Auditor's liability may additionally arise under sections 12 and 13 of the Prevention of Fraud (Investments) Act 1958, and sections 15–20 of the Theft Act 1968, which consolidates all previous Larceny Acts and Falsification of Accounts Acts. Under all of the above sections, with the exception of those in Prevention of Fraud (Investments) Act, where it is merely to prove criminal recklessness, a successful prosecution would have to establish a state of moral turpitude, i.e. wilful intent to deceive.

28. Notes for meeting with auditor's solicitors:

ACCOUNTING TREATMENT

AUDIT NEGLIGENCE

(a) Acceptable provided expected useful life of improvements is at least twenty-five years. If not, write-off period should have been less. If intention to vacate was known prior to approval of accounts, improvements should have been written off, or circumstances fully noted.

(a) Was intention to vacate in October known prior to 16th September? If so, was it minuted? Did auditors examine these minutes? If not minuted, was it covered by representation letter? Is there documentation on file to show why auditors allowed twenty-five-year write-off? (Possible negligence depends on answers to these questions.)

(b) Accounting treatment not acceptable, since SSAP 13 does not allow research expenditure to be carried forward. Write-off period (total ten years) appears excessive in any case. Post balance sheet discontinuance of product is adjusting event under SSAP 17, and complete write-off therefore required.

(b) For reasons given on left, audit report should have been qualified. Negligence therefore probable.

(c) Post balance sheets events should have indicated the need for most of these adjustments, and accounts

(c) Negligence probable, since returns of faulty goods should have been picked up by:

should have reflected credit notes known; provision should have been made for returns likely, for similarly faulty goods. Adjusting events under SSAP 17.

(d) The Companies Act requires the disclosure of all contingent liabilities and an indication of their nature, if material, by way of note to the accounts. Although the loan may not be prohibited (assuming Past-It Ltd is not a "relevant company" under the 1985 Act) disclosure of the loan is required under s. 232 of the 1985 Act, since it is a transaction in which the directors have an interest. Under SSAP 18, provision is required if it is likely that contingency will materialise. This should have been known to the directors in view of their connection with, and control over, other company.

(e) Whether or not this should be treated as adjusting or non-adjusting depends on when the decision was reached, and when conditions deteriorated to the point that it became obvious that drastic action of this nature was unavoidable. On the face of it, treatment as a non-adjusting event, duly noted, seems acceptable, but this depends in turn whether going concern status should have been seen to be threatened. If decision was pre-year end, full provision for redundancy payments should have been made.

(f) Proportion of expenditure unsupported by vouchers is too high to be credible, since it is normally possible to obtain vouchers for such items. More

(i) post balance sheet tests, or
(ii) letter of representation, or
(iii) debtor confirmations.

Only deliberate concealment by directors may constitute defence.

(d) Auditors failed to qualify report on non-disclosure of contingent liability required under both SSAP 18 and Companies Act. The Act requires disclosure of such items in the auditors' report (i.e. material transactions in which the directors have an interest) if not adequately disclosed in the accounts. Therefore negligence seems probable, especially since auditors should have examined the returns of directors' shareholdings and representations covering holdings in other companies, as a means of identifying related party transactions.

(e) Negligence depends on the resolution of matters referred to at left. The scale of redundancies suggests that a substantial part of the business, at least, was not a going concern at 30th June 1981, and that full provision should therefore have been made, or the audit report suitably qualified.

(f) Auditors appear to have accepted material item without any of the supporting evidence which might reasonably have been expected. Even directors' representations in likely to be directors' remuneration at rate of £5,000 per annum on average per director. In absence of evidence to contrary, accounts should be adjusted accordingly, and full provision made for PAYE liability on such remuneration as cannot be justified or substantiated as genuine expenses.

such circumstances would be insufficient, unless there is corroborative evidence available—e.g. confirmation to auditors from persons entertained, etc. Negligence probable.

Notes

(a) *It is assumed that the sums involved were material in relation to accounts. They are material in relation to the deficiency of £182,000.*

(b) *Negligence, if established on all or any of the matters referred to, would not necessarily result in liability. Liquidator would have to establish a connection between the negligence and the financial loss to creditors, and this seems possible in the circumstances outlined; otherwise liability might be limited to no more than audit fee plus costs. Negligent accounting treatment (and/or inadequate disclosure) does not automatically imply cause of loss to creditors on liquidation.*

29. Audit of computer systems internal control checklist:

SECTION: INPUT CONTROLS—TRANSACTIONS AND MASTER DATA

	Tick Yes No	No answers ref. to weakness letter	Initials	Date of review
1. Are the user department personnel adequately trained in their duties and is there an up-to-date instruction manual or procedure guide available?				
2. Are control totals generated in the user department adequate for subsequent checking purposes? Specifically:				
(i) Are source documents batched, each batch being separately controlled?				
(ii) Are batch totals held in a register and input for each run agreed with the DP control section to confirm that all input has entered the computer system?				
(iii) Is access to the register suitably restricted?				

	Tick Yes No	No answers ref. to weakness letter	Initials	Date of review
(iv) Does the system ensure that no input could be accidentally lost or intentionally extracted or inserted without detection?				
3. Are input documents serially numbered, and is there either a manual or computer check on the sequence of numbers?				
4. Is adequate control exercised over unused supplies of source documents?				
5. Is all coding on source documents double-checked within the user department?				
6. Is there a proper system for processing exceptional transactions which are not catered for by the computer system?				
7. Are source documents filed in a manner that enables them to be retrieved without undue difficulty?				
8. Are source documents retained for a sufficient period should it be necessary for a file to be re-created?				
9. Does the computer system include a procedure so that it can be reviewed by the user department before processing commences?				

30. The following are four usual methods of ensuring the validity and accuracy of computer input:

(a) *Document count.* The number of invoices, vouchers, etc. being processed in a particular batch are counted before processing begins, normally with the assistance of serial numbering. Once processing begins, the computer will verify the number of documents and the same total will be printed as part of the output.

(b) *Hash total.* This total is the result of adding up all the code numbers of items being processed in a particular run, and therefore has no significance beyond its control function. The hash total can be printed by the computer at intermediate or final processing stages and therefore acts as a check that no data has been lost.

(c) *"Data-scan" program.* This is a small program by means of which the computer edits the input. Such a program will automatically pick up code numbers which are invalid owing to the presence of the wrong number of digits, numbers outside of specified parameters, or an incorrect balance between alpha and numeric digits.

(d) *Control totals.* Where data is machine-listed before the source documents are passed for punching, sterling control totals appearing on the pre-lists may be compared with totals created after punching and verification is complete. Discrepancies would indicate either that data had been lost during punching or that punching errors had taken place.

31. (a) The "audit trail" is the visible means whereby the auditor may trace a business transaction through all the stages in which it features in the records of the business. For example sequentially numbered copy sales invoices would normally be listed in a register or daybook and subsequently filed either in numerical or chronological sequence. In either case, it would be possible, by reference to the number or the date, to trace a particular invoice from the daybook to the original on file or vice versa.

(b) Developments in third generation computer technology have resulted in substantial increases in the speed and ease by which data may be processed. Consequently there is a strong disincentive to leaving a visible trail or record of all information which has been processed (even though this would enable the auditor to perform his tasks, as it were, "around" the computer) since this necessitates the use of a line printer and other peripheral equipment which, by contrast with the speed of the computer itself, is extremely slow. Thus, instead of the creation of comprehensive "hard copy" which was prevalent with first and second generation computers, management have come to rely heavily on reporting by exception, and such reliance is inevitably complementary to the loss of the audit trail.

(c) Technological developments described in (b) above have resulted in the production of instantaneous analyses, balances and sub-totals (e.g. on a cathode ray display) without a permanent record being retained. The copy sales invoices referred to in (a) above, for example, may have been totalled for the purpose of ascertaining sales for the period in question, without a listing or other means of independently establishing the total being retained. Moreover, the invoices themselves may well have been re-sorted for the purpose of, say, analysing sales geographically. In the circumstances, it would be extremely difficult for the auditor:

  (i) to verify the figure of total sales; or

  (ii) to locate a particular copy invoice after the re-sorting operation.

(d) In certain cases, it is equally important for the management and for the auditor alike to maintain a permanent record of the stages in processing data, particularly where large amounts are involved and possibilities of misappropriation are considerable. In such circumstances the auditor may prevail upon the directors to ensure that visible records are produced regardless of the effect this might have on total processing time. In other circumstances, however, the loss of audit trail will need to be overcome by CAATs, such as:

(i) *The use of test packs.* As has been indicated, management by exception normally results in a loss of trail and the auditor may employ the use of test packs in order to establish the correct functioning of the controls which are alleged to reside in the normal computer programs. A series of fictitious transactions make up the test pack; some may be based on transactions known to have taken place in the past, while others may be deliberately contrived in order to test the controls, e.g. a test pack on wages would include overtime claims of varying amounts from normal to abnormal to absurd. The data in the test pack is then processed following usual routines existing elsewhere; the results are then carefully scrutinised by the auditor.

(ii) *Special computer programs for auditors.* Specially devised interrogation programs are now available by means of which the auditor may obtain a print of any information contained in the client's master files, suitably presented according to the criteria applicable. Thus, such a program would be of use to the auditor when he is assessing the adequacy of a general provision for bad debts, since it will enable him to obtain a complete printout of the debtor balances specially stratified according to the size of the amounts outstanding. Alternatively, or additionally, the balances can be stratified according to the "age" of the debts. Similar advantages obviously arise in the examination of a stock inventory where it is necessary to pay particular attention to apparently slow-moving items. Many of the programs now available also include routines for performing methodical editing and statistical functions such as the construction of a statistical sampling test involving the use of computer-generated random numbers.

Auditors may also use exception reporting for audit purposes by asking for programs to include exception reports in the form of a print-out useful for audit tests.

32. Before a new computer application can be implemented, a feasibility study must be undertaken by personnel both technically qualified and thoroughly familiar with the company's processing requirements. Their work at this stage will be so directed that a decision may be made on whether the ultimate benefit likely to accrue from the new application is feasible from an economic point of view as well as being technically possible.

Assuming a project to be feasible on the basis of the initial investigation, the management objectives for the new application should be carefully drawn up in detail and passed to a team of systems analysts for the next stage towards implementation. The analysts' function is threefold:

(a)   to draw up plans of the system currently in operation;

(b)   to appraise the existing system in consultation with the department heads involved in order to ascertain those aspects which are regarded as essential for purposes of control or general management information, and which must therefore be incorporated in any new system being designed.

(c)   to discover in which respects information currently processed is inadequate owing to clerical and other practical limitations, since the provision of further data hitherto unobtainable may well be within the scope of the program being designed.

It is with particular reference to these three analytical functions that the external auditor should be consulted and given sufficient time to weigh up the consequences for the audit of the revised systems currently in preparation. There may for example be instances where the audit trail would be unnecessarily lost in the construction of a system by those unmindful of the auditor's requirements, and also where "exception reports" can be built in to assist the auditor.

The final stage of the analysts' work will involve the diagrammatic representation of the desired system, incorporating all the requirements of the various interested user departments and external auditors. These charts (known as block diagrams) will be passed to the programming department whose task it is to write computer programs, using an appropriate high-level language, which will give effect to the specifications prescribed. In certain cases, it will be necessary to refer back to the analysts, e.g. where the particular hardware available is incapable of providing all the statistical data desired.

During the course of program preparation "pilot runs", testing programming efforts to date, will be undertaken and errors coming to light will be corrected. Once programs have been written which comply with the original requirements, a period of parallel running will be entered into. During this period, a certain amount of information held in the existing format (e.g. conventional machine-processed ledger accounts) will be converted into computer format; current transactions affecting this data will then be processed by computer, using the new programs, in parallel with conventional machine processing. Results will be compared and all differences thoroughly investigated, usually necessitating reference back to the programming department so that appropriate amendments to the programs can be made.

After the successful conclusion of parallel running the new system will take over processing completely and the conventional processing methods will be discontinued. Prior to the final decision being made, it is once again advisable that the examples of the print-out which he will encounter during the conduct of his audit be presented to the external auditor for approval.

33.   (a)   A computer audit program is a software "package" which has been specially developed for the purpose of interrogating computer files. It is necessary for details of the hardware, e.g. capacity of computer memory, to be taken into account as well as details of the layout of data fields used in the master files, prior to the utilisation of the computer audit program. This program enables a wide variety of information to be extracted from computer files in a format significant for the purpose of the user.

(b) In connection with the verification of assets and liabilities the computer audit program may be used as follows:

(i) *Debtors.* Information can be extracted from debtor file so as to provide stratification according to size of amount; age; balances which exceeded credit limits ("exceptions reporting").

(ii) *Stock in trade.* The computer audit program will provide an analysis of stock according to age; materiality of individual items; items classified as defective.

(iii) *Fixed assets register.* Information can be extracted from this register to give details of fixed assets movements during the current accounting period, i.e. acquisitions and disposals. It will also highlight changes in depreciation rates on individual plant items and assets on which no depreciation has been charged at all.

34. (a) The computerisation of data processing methods would inevitably affect the system of internal control for the following reasons:

(i) Computers are capable of processing and recording large volumes of transactions at considerable speed and these transactions would normally be dealt with in batches rather than as individual items. It is therefore likely that these batches would form individual units of control.

(ii) Amendments to "standing data", e.g. price lists, rates of pay, names and addresses of customers, etc. would not be made clerically but would have to be accumulated for processing by the computer at pre-determined times.

(iii) The details of ordinary transactions have to be converted into a form intelligible to the computer; the conversion process would have to be carefully controlled and the computer can itself be used for "editing" the data.

(iv) The most fundamental way in which internal controls are affected by computerisation is their removal from those departments preparing and using the data, and their transfer to the EDP department, on which great reliance has therefore to be placed. This gives rise to the need for special controls on computer processing such as "tolerance" checks within the programs themselves, and the need to separate the functions of data preparation, programming and processing from one another.

(b) The auditor would expect the company's administrative controls to take the following factors into account:

(i) The company's files, in magnetic form, incorporate data in a highly concentrated form with little to distinguish one file from another apart from the labelling methods employed.

(ii) The physical hazards which are inseparable from EDP. For example, atmospheric conditions have to be carefully controlled with regard to temperature, humidity and dust; care must be taken to avoid files coming in contact with an electronic or magnetic field; as all materials are highly inflammable, suitable fire precautions must be taken in the form of asbestos linings and fire alarms.

(iii) The need for standby arrangements whereby vital processing can continue by agreement with another user of similar equipment in the event of breakdown, e.g. due to power cuts.

(iv) Division of responsibilities among computer personnel to ensure that development staff are not involved with day-to-day computer processing and that the duties of supervisors and file librarian should not overlap the duties of other personnel.

(v) File security and re-creation; a clear policy is needed with regard to the retention of files after they have been superseded by more up-to-date versions, in case current master files are inadvertently destroyed. Methods such as "grandfather/father/son" in the case of magnetic tapes, and "dumping" in the case of discs are obvious examples.

(c) (i) Computerisation would affect the audit approach fundamentally by making a conventional or historical audit difficult if not impossible. Audit procedures would need to be contemporary to ensure that operating controls are being enforced.

(ii) Improvements in computer processing speeds have resulted in "management by exception" techniques whereby complete print-outs of the results of processing runs are not available. This often leads to a loss of "audit trail" whereby computer-generated totals, analyses and balances lack supporting background data. In consequence, in such cases, techniques for auditing "through the computer", particularly the use of "test packs", must be developed.

(iii) To the extent that fundamental controls lie within computer programs, the auditor is obliged to give considerable emphasis to the strength of corresponding clerical controls on input and output within the user departments, and to make use of systems of "auditing round the computer" (e.g. matching input to output) wherever possible.

35. (a) The main audit problem presented by "on-line, real-time" systems is caused by the absence of customary source documents that can normally be used in audit tests. This could be overcome by the auditor by persuading the management that the presence of an audit trail is essential in order to achieve effective internal control; the computer could maintain a chronological or numerical file of events being processed as they occur.

(b) The practical requirements needed to establish internal control for service bureau applications are as follows:

(i) clearly defined liaison between bureau and user;

(ii) systems testing of all clerical procedures at the user company;

(iii) file conversion checking procedures;

   (iv) controls over physical movements of data, possibly assisted by microfilm;

   (v) planned rejection procedures and documentation covering identification of errors; correction and re-submission procedures;

   (vi) output distribution controls;

  (vii) clerical controls to verify accuracy of output;

 (viii) check of program functioning;

   (ix) controls over maintenance of master files.

36.   (a) Potential control weaknesses—on-line systems:

   (i) The master files are remote from the terminals, and these may be read or updated without an adequate audit trail remaining—or, in some cases, without *any* record remaining.

  (ii) Dependence on controls is sometimes subject to risk, due to controls being computer-based, such as the retention of a "buffer" store of all keyed-in inputs held in the central processor before accessing the master files. Computer-based controls may be subject to the very risks the controls are allegedly guarding against.

  (iii) The effect of keyed-in input is to update instantaneously the centrally held files.

  (iv) Any edit-checks on input are often under the control of the terminal operators themselves.

  (v) Unauthorised access can, in the case of input, corrupt standing data by adding or removing data, and introduce or amend transaction data, such as false discounts. Similar risks apply to the issue of unauthorised output and to the general possibility of file corruption or sabotage.

  (vi) Programs themselves can be corrupted or sabotaged.

  (b) Methods to overcome these weaknesses:

   (i) Hardware controls, such as the use of key, magnetic strip, badge or card needed to engage the terminal; locating terminal in restricted access area; use of closed circuit TV surveillance.

  (ii) Use of identification codes for authorised terminal operators, with the possible use of passwords. These may be checked by main-frame computer against stored tables of authorised codes and/or passwords, and should be periodically varied.

  (iii) "Voice prints" or other operator characteristics may be used, including "hand geometry", such as finger-length ratios, thumbprints etc., for all purposes of operator identification in high-security environments.

  (iv) Access to specific programs or files may be permitted, while others may be classified as "forbidden" to access by operators below certain grades. Similarly, specifically designated terminals may have exclusive access to key files.

(v) Authority to allocate access etc., may itself be restricted in top-security systems, only the most senior personnel having such discretion.

(vi) A security file at the central processor may be used for logging each occasion on which access takes place, the log disclosing the identification of terminal, operator, the files accessed, updated, etc. The log is inspected by senior security personnel only.

37. Data processing at computer bureau: summary of controls to be instituted by Fleabite Enterprises Ltd.

(a) Transmission of data to bureau:

(i) document count;

(ii) transaction count;

(iii) control totals, e.g. batches, sterling values.

Special considerations: Additional controls are needed if data conversion is performed by Fleabite. Controls must be established at the point where the bureau takes over responsibility for the data.

(b) Master file amendments:

(i) routine print-out of all changes;

(ii) control count of master records;

(iii) control total of all master file contents;

(iv) control over pre-numbered amendment/input slips;

(v) strict amendment/authorisation procedures.

Special considerations: Regular file reviews should include periodic print-outs of selected data. Special file analysis and interrogation programs should be used.

(c) Error correction routines and re-submissions:

(i) planned procedures at user and bureau locations for identifying input errors;

(ii) programs to provide detailed error print-out, identifying all errors not detected at input;

(iii) client-controlled error log;

(iv) correction and review of re-submissions.

Special considerations: Re-submissions should be given prior approval by liaison personnel at client, after investigation into cause.

(d) Output:

(i) approved distribution list;

(ii) surprise test packs for control purposes;

(iii) control over action on exception reports;

(iv) periodic print-outs, e.g. ledger balances or plant schedules.

Special considerations: Controls should ensure that all exception reports are received. Auditor should be invited to participate in planning and execution of test pack, with facility to compile his own limited test data.

    (e)   Security and reconstruction:

        (i)   microfilming of source documents transmitted to bureau;

       (ii)   provision by client for file construction on basis of "worst case" loss;

      (iii)   ensure bureau capability for routine reconstruction;

      (iv)   security supervision over all client files retained at bureau.

Special considerations: Assurances should be periodically obtained from bureau liaison personnel in connection with last two provisions above, and arranging for periodic reconstruction test checks.

38.   (a)   Typical techniques employed to control the use of terminals for input purposes include:

        (i)   hardware constraints, e.g. necessitating the use of a key to engage the terminal and/or placing the terminal in a location to which access is carefully restricted;

       (ii)   the allocation of identification numbers to authorised terminal operators, with or without the use of passwords: these are checked by the main-frame computer against stored tables of authorised numbers and passwords;

      (iii)   using operator characteristics such as finger-prints, widths of fingers, width of hand, etc. as a means of identification by the main-frame computer: this identification may easily be carried out by special devices at the terminals (e.g. laser scanner);

      (iv)   restricting access to particular programs or master files held in the main-frame computer to designated terminals: this arrangement may be combined with those indicated above;

       (v)   in top-security systems, the authority to allocate authorities such as those indicated above (i.e. determination of password, nominating selected terminals) will itself be restricted to senior personnel other than intended users;

      (vi)   a special file may be maintained in the central processor which records every occasion on which access is made by particular terminals and operators to central programs and files: this log will be printed out at regular intervals, e.g. the end of each day, or by request by personnel with appropriate authority.

    (b)   The input controls outlined above are even more important in real-time systems because:

        (i)   the effect of the input (whether keyed in on the key-board typewriter or via punch cards, paper tape, etc.) instantaneously updates the files held in the central processor.

(ii) edit-checks on the input are likely to be under the control of the terminal operator.

39. THE "ROUND THE MACHINE" APPROACH

Such an audit tends to ignore the procedures which take place within the computer programs and concentrates on initial input and final output, usually on a selective basis.

The auditor checks the validity of the input; that it is properly authorised and clerically controlled in batches with suitable control totals; and that it has been correctly coded.

The final output will be compared in detail with source documents and clerical control totals as a means of checking accurate processing.

THE "THROUGH THE MACHINE" APPROACH

The approach is no less thorough than that described above in connection with the audit of input and output; however, it includes a thorough examination of the computer's own processing to ensure that:

(a) all input finds its way into the machine;

(b) unusual conditions in the input cannot cause processing errors;

(c) computer operators cannot cause irregularities in processing and in the final reports to be distributed; and

(d) controls within the computer programs are as effective in practice as they may appear to be in theory.

The following are the dangers inherent in the "round the machine" approach:

(a) attempts by the auditors to verify output against original input may be frustrated by the input having been re-sorted for another purpose; thus making it virtually impossible for individual items to be traced;

(b) the "round the machine" approach normally follows the pattern of the historical audit and whereas the conclusion regarding operating controls may be valid for programs currently in force, these conclusions would lack validity in respect of periods prior to the introduction of major program changes;

(c) as processing speeds are improved through technical innovation, management becomes increasingly reluctant to produce voluminous "hard copy" for the sake of providing an audit trail: thus as "management by exception" becomes prevalent, auditors will find that insufficient data is produced to justify the "round the machine" approach;

(d) fraudulent members of staff will find it a relatively straightforward matter to present the auditors with output that carries all appearances of authenticity but which has in fact been manufactured purely in anticipation of the audit tests;

(e) the "round the machine" approach is often adopted for no better reason than that the auditor lacks the technical competence to investigate machine processing while it is taking place: such an attitude ignores the fact that a thorough audit always requires a technical knowledge appropriate to the data processing methods employed, no matter how satisfactory the clerical controls in the "user" departments may appear to be. This is important since the scope for manipulating within computer programs is virtually limitless, and it is becoming increasingly difficult for the auditor to justify an approach which does not use the computer itself as a prime audit tool.

40. (a) Matters requiring particular attention following introduction of mini-computer:

  (i) the extent to which parallel run is highlighting significant deficiencies in hardware, programs, and operating systems;

  (ii) the likelihood of achieving satisfactory results by 31st July (date of end of parallel run); it would seem to be sensible to persuade management to continue manual and mechanised systems for a further month, to balance sheet date;

  (iii) the adequacy of systems documentation; the audit trail provided on the new system; the control procedures, including fire and back-up precautions; the adaptation of standard software to the needs of Change-it Ltd; staff training and competence;

  (iv) the concentration of stock and accounting records in the computer department, and consequent risks of breakdown without reconstruction ability; collusion between computer staff due to lack of independent checking by user department;

  (v) possible ease of access to computer and EDP records, especially if accompanied by use of on-line terminals; controls must take this into account;

  (vi) audit files must be fully updated to include complete documentation of new system, specimen forms, etc., and details of effect on existing controls; also, effect on audit procedures and programmes;

  (vii) locations in which back-up files and source documents are retained, to ensure facility of audit tests and reconstruction potential in a "worst case" loss eventuality.

(b) The factors listed above are likely to affect audit work as follows:

  (i) If the stock records on the manual system are abandoned before the year end, the physical stocks should be checked by staff (and observed by auditors) against computer records with special care on 31st August.

  (ii) Auditors will have to execute a series of tests to ensure that the transfer to computer format of all accounting records has been reliably accomplished. These tests should include a suitable selection of transactions devised by the auditor for "through the machine" verification, especially where controls are located in the program.

(iii) The auditor should submit a "letter of weakness" indicating any areas of special concern in which the new system appeared to be susceptible to abuse or manipulation. The matters identified in (a) (iv) and (v) above have special application here.

(iv) The audit staff employed will have to study the system documentation on file, and ensure that they have a thorough and comprehensive grasp of the new system and the changes occasioned thereby. Where, for example, VDU displays are used for output, and print-out is not retained, audit work may have to be performed at the time, rather than at a later date. Audit staff will have to be selected on the basis of EDP skills and experience.

(v) Since processing of records is now being performed by computer, auditors will have to place far greater emphasis on the accuracy and completeness of *input*, by testing make-up of batch totals, sequence checks, document counts, etc., and noting evidence of validation and authorisation.

(vi) Reliability of debtor and creditor records should be confirmed by direct circularisation.

(vii) Since clerical staff may not yet have settled into the new system (which may in any case be subject to modification), compliance testing may prove to be unproductive. The emphasis during the first audit should therefore be on substantive testing. All systems changes (in procedures or programs) must carry proper authorisation, evidence of which the auditor must examine.

41. (a) The following techniques/procedures would normally be standardised in the pursuit of quality control:

(i) methods to be adopted by audit staff in determining and assessing the quality of internal control procedures, with specific reference to such matters as compliance tests, documentation and the use of standard symbols in flow-charting;

(ii) the issue of guidelines governing the use of sampling methods particularly as to those situations in which the use of statistical tables and graphs might be appropriate;

(iii) standard procedures to be adopted by staff when observing year-end asset verification by client staff, e.g. physical stocktaking; securities/ cash counting;

(iv) reporting action to be taken by audit staff on discovering internal control weaknesses (with or without the existence of compensating controls).

(b) The following five responsibilities normally fall within the scope of the audit review committee:

(i) the issue of guidelines in determining the level of audit testing required in particular circumstances, depending upon the efficiency or otherwise of internal control procedures;

(ii) the determination and establishment of appropriate audit techniques to be followed by staff:

(iii) the dissemination of up-to-date information to staff at all appropriate levels relating to current legislation and current professional developments;

(iv) the organisation of regular training courses, the contents of which should be geared to the level of staff attending: all audit staff should be required to attend appropriate courses on a regular basis;

(v) the constant monitoring of standards operating in all offices carrying the firm's name: in this connection, the review committee should take into account suggestions from staff based on field tests as well as general "feed-back" on the operation of audit procedures in practice.

42. (a) The Auditing Standard requires that the auditor should adequately plan his work as it:

(i) establishes the intended means of achieving the objects of the audit;

(ii) assists in the direction and control of the work;

(iii) helps to ensure that attention is devoted to critical aspects of the audit; and

(iv) helps to ensure that the work is completed expeditiously.

"Audit planning" involves the forecasting of audit personnel requirements covering all grades of staff necessary for the satisfactory flow of audit work arising during the period covered by the plan. The procedures which would be involved in audit planning include:

(i) reviewing matters raised in the audit of the previous year which may have continuing relevance;

(ii) assessing the effects of any changes in legislation or accounting practice affecting the financial statements;

(iii) reviewing interim accounts and consulting with management of the client;

(iv) identifying any significant changes in accounting procedures;

(v) considering the timing of significant phases in the preparation of the financial statements;

(vi) considering the extent to which analyses and summaries can be prepared by the client's staff;

(vii) considering the relevance of any work to be carried out by the client's internal auditors.

Such planning is especially important today since many client companies have so expanded their activities as to require audit work to be phased over the calendar year in order to achieve a satisfactory appraisal of its activities and accounts. The growth in multinational companies has led to an increase in the auditors' concern over their overseas activities, particularly where local auditors are acting independently for subsidiaries; this situation creates an additional need for careful audit planning.

    (b)   The problems in implementing audit planning are as follows:

        (i)   education and training arrangements within the profession involve substantial periods of study leave;

       (ii)   many clients have financial year ends which coincide and this places a burden on the staff at certain times of the year particularly with regard to physical verification of stocks and the counting of securities;

      (iii)   a well-planned audit requires staff of varying grades at distinct phases of the audit while ensuring overall supervision throughout;

      (iv)   difficulties within the client organisation on the preparation of accounts are often unpredictable.

These and several other problems may best be overcome by:

        (i)   close liaison with the client's senior accounting staff;

       (ii)   co-operation with the internal auditors on sharing the working load on routine audit matters;

      (iii)   entering into arrangements with tutorial organisations to standardise study leave arrangements as far as possible;

      (iv)   adopting techniques such as critical path analysis for audit purposes so that all predictable requirements may be graphically represented for ease of future planning.

43. The City Code requires that where profit forecasts are included in any documents addressed to shareholders in connection with an offer, the assumptions upon which the directors have based their forecast must be stated; furthermore, the accounting bases and calculations for the forecasts must be examined and reported on by the company's auditors or consultant accountants. It also requires that documents containing the forecasts must also include the accountants' report.

    (a)   Prior to accepting instructions to report in connection with profit forecasts, the reporting accountant is advised to reach agreement with the directors on the following preliminary points:

        (i)   The time available to the accountant for the preparation of his report should not be so limited that, having regard to the company's circumstances, it would be plainly impossible for sufficient information to be obtained to enable the accountant properly to exercise such professional judgments as may be required.

       (ii)   It must be clearly established that the accountant's responsibility is confined to the accounting bases and the calculations for the forecasts and does not extend to the assumptions on which the directors have based their forecasts.

(iii) Since forecasts are subject to increasing uncertainty the further forward they extend, accountants should not normally undertake to review and report on forecasts which relate to more than the current accounting period and (provided a sufficiently significant part of the current period has elapsed) the next accounting period.

(iv) It must be established that the reporting accountant cannot relieve the directors of their own responsibility for profit forecasts which may be disclosed to and relied upon by outside parties.

(b) The following are the main points to be considered by the reporting accountant in the course of his review of profit forecasts:

(i) the general character and recent history of the company's business with particular reference to its main products, markets, customers, suppliers, labour force and trend of results;

(ii) the accounting policies normally adopted in preparing the company's financial statements and the fact that these have been consistently applied in the preparation of the profit forecasts;

(iii) the accountant must satisfy himself that the preparation of the forecasts is consistent with the economic, commercial, marketing and financial assumptions which the directors have stated to be the underlying bases;

(iv) the company's general procedures in the preparation of forecasts; in particular the accountant will wish to ascertain whether forecasts are regularly prepared for management purposes and if so, the degree of accuracy and reliability normally achieved; he will also wish to discover the extent to which the forecast results for expired periods are supported by reliable interim accounts, and how the forecasts take account of any material exceptional items;

(v) matters of general concern including the adequacy of provisions made for foreseeable losses and contingencies, the adequacy of working capital as indicated by properly prepared cash flow forecasts.

44. (a) (i) Ascertain precise terms of reference, e.g. the sum available for investment, the minimum return expected on the investment, the number of years' accounts which the client expects the investigator to examine.

(ii) Establish a basis for negotiation between the client and the proprietor of the business for sale, in order to ensure maximum co-operation.

(iii) If the accounts of the business have been subject to audit, obtain consent to contact auditors so that supporting schedules of accounts may be available if required.

(b)   (i) Eliminate from each set of accounts examined items of income and expenditure which will not apply in future, e.g. rents received from a subsidiary source, interest on investments, interest paid on an overdraft which will not be necessary after the purchase.

    (ii) The accounts must be adjusted to bring charges and income into line with future circumstances. For example, the lease may shortly be due for renewal at a higher rent; the management charge may, in the past, have been unrealistically low.

    (iii) Scrutinise the accounts for indications of "window dressing" pending the sale of the business, for example avoidance of expenditure on necessary repairs.

    (iv) Examine the accounts for any evidence of deliberate manipulation, e.g. inflation of cash sales by introducing money from a private source; conversely, the payment for trade purchases out of private resources. The trading account ratios would provide the obvious intimation of such manipulation having taken place. In particular, the closing stock valuation should be supported by detailed inventories, and in view of the likely materiality of the sums involved an independent valuation might be advisable.

    (v) The accounts as now adjusted should be re-drafted as a more realistic basis for determining the purchase consideration.

(c)   Prior to preparing final recommendations attention should be given to:

    (i) local development plans for the area which may affect the future of the site in question;

    (ii) the need to introduce a restrictive covenant into the sale contract to avoid the present proprietor setting up business in opposition in the immediate vicinity;

    (iii) the loyalty of staff presently employed.

45. Stock Exchange requirements on the matters specified:

(a)   The reporting accountant should be independent both of the company and any other company concerned to the same degree as is required of auditors under the Companies Act.

(b)   Listing would not normally be granted where the latest financial period reported on is more than six months out of date.

(c)   Prospectus reports must be prepared in conformity with Accounting Standards. Significant departures must be disclosed and explained. Reporting accountants must include the basis adopted for the computation of profits. This normally states that profits or losses have been arrived at on defined bases in accordance with Accounting Standards approved by the accountancy bodies and after making such adjustments as are considered appropriate.

(d) Reports containing significant qualifications relating to profits or losses or the balance sheets included therein would not normally be acceptable to support application for listing.

(e) In the body of the prospectus there should be included an explanation of the trend of profits dealing particularly with the effects of changes in financing and of the acquisition of subsidiaries.

(f) Where the reporting accountants refer to reports or opinions of other experts the names, addresses and professional qualifications of such persons or firms should be stated in the report, and such expert reports and opinions should be supported by the usual consents.

46. (a) It is invariably necessary for a company's accounts to be adjusted prior to their inclusion in a prospectus report since the purpose of such a report is quite different from that of the company's published accounts presented to its shareholders.

Published accounts are prepared by a company's directors for presentation to committed investors, i.e. shareholders, in order to acquaint them with the results of the company's activities during the latest complete year of stewardship. Information included in prospectus reports is addressed to potential investors in such a way as to enable them to form an opinion on the likely prospects of the company in question under future trading conditions, so far as the latter may be assessed.

It is therefore necessary for the information in published accounts to be represented so as to facilitate this purpose. As far as possible, therefore, the adjustments to the published accounts should take future conditions into consideration.

(b) The following are three instances in which such adjustments would normally be necessary:

(i) Specific items of income or expenditure which have arisen in the past in the ordinary course of business, and which it is known will not arise in the future, should be eliminated. An example would be charges for debenture interest when it is known that the debentures are to be repaid out of the proceeds of the issue.

(ii) Changes in accounting policy during the five-year period reported on. For the sake of comparability, the accounts for the years affected by the change should be adjusted so that the same basis of accounting is applied throughout.

(iii) In certain cases, foreign branches or subsidiary companies may have been nationalised or sequestrated during the period reported on; amounts reflecting the activities of these units should be eliminated for all periods reported on.

(c) Since 1st October 1973, the Quotations Department of the Stock Exchange has required the profit and loss account section of prospectus reports to take the following form:

	Year 1	Year 2	Year 3	Year 4	Year 5
(i) Sales (state the basis)					
(ii) Costs of goods sold					
(iii) Other income (non-trading)					
(iv) Group's share of profit from associated companies					
(v) Profit before taxation and extraordinary items					
(vi) Taxation (state the basis)					
(vii) Minority interests					
(viii) Extraordinary items (net of any tax effect)					
(ix) Shareholders' undistributed profit after taxation and extraordinary items					
(x) Dividends on preference share capital					
(xi) Undistributed equity interest in profits					
(xii) Dividends on equity share capital					

47. The following are the matters on which initial clarification should be sought, prior to commencing work on the profit forecasts:

(a) whether the forecasts have been prepared within the context of a takeover situation in which case the rules of the City Code on Takeovers and Mergers would have to be complied with and the auditor's report on the forecasts worded accordingly;

(b) whether the request from Mr Minge was part of the terms of the auditor's appointment, in which case it would be necessary to ascertain precisely what work was expected in relation to the audit of these forecasts by reference to the letter of engagement;

(c) depending upon the replies to the above queries, it would be necessary to point out to Mr Minge that this assignment was of a non-statutory nature and that the responsibility for the accuracy of the forecasts rested entirely with the company's management;

(d) the auditor should ascertain whether the circularisation of forecasts amongst shareholders was a normal procedure, or whether these have been prepared for some specific purpose of which the auditor would require full details;

(e) it should be pointed out that the forecasts range further into the future than most auditors would be prepared to comment on: the professional bodies have recommended that an opinion on forecasts should be limited to the current financial year or, in cases where the financial year has largely lapsed, the next financial year, and particularly in current economic conditions, forecasts ranging further than that would be far too speculative from the audit point of view.

(f)   the auditor should ascertain whether all the directors have agreed to the auditing of forecasts or whether Mr Minge is acting independently of the rest of the board;

(g)   any limitations as to the time available for this assessment; any opinion would have to be carefully qualified if time constraints prevented the auditor conducting a sufficiently comprehensive review.

In general, it may be observed that "audit" in relation to long-term forecasts is perhaps the wrong word, implying a degree of certainty which cannot in practice be achieved.

The auditor should ensure that the terms of his engagement are clearly set out in writing by exchange of letters and these terms should make it clear that an audit, by its nature, relates to historical data. The forecasts remain an expression of the views of the company's directors and the investigating work must necessarily be confined to tests on the underlying assumptions and accounting bases on which the forecasts rest.

48. In order to assess the financial strength of the bank, the following lines of enquiry should be followed. These enquiries would show whether the bank is genuinely profitable, as opposed to relying upon dealing or windfall profits, and therefore at risk.

PROFIT AND LOSS ACCOUNT

It is important to discover what proportions of the bank's profits are derived from sustainable business, as opposed to sources of income which, even if not speculative, are at least uncertain. In particular, the proportion derived from the following three source should be closely examined:

(a)   net interest margins between lending and borrowing;

(b)   dealing profits derived from the bank's investment portfolio;

(c)   fees and commissions.

CURRENT SITUATION

Auditors should discuss current problems with the bank's management to discover whether profits are being made in the current trading period (i.e. after the period subject to audit). Enquiries should be made as to:

(a)   whether such projected profits take into account suspended interest "rolled up", bad debt provisions, and any other falls in the realisable value of assets;

(b)   when such provisions were last reviewed, and how frequently reviews are made; and

(c)   the current values of any securities held as collateral against losses and advances.

INTEREST RECEIVED AND PAID

In relation to interest received and paid, the following questions are relevant:

(a)   Are net interest margins positive, particularly in relation to the funding of the bank's own fixed assets?

(b)   How much interest is being suspended, and on what proportion of the total loan portfolio?

GENERAL

Further enquiries should be aimed at establishing:

(a)   the areas in which a bank is dealing, e.g.:

  (i)   investments;

  (ii)   certificates of deposit;

  (iii)   foreign exchange;

  (iv)   commodities;

  (v)   land and property.

(b)   The fee-earning activities of the bank, for example in respect of:

  (i)   loan commitments;

  (ii)   acceptances;

  (iii)   portfolio management;

  (iv)   corporate advisory work.

(c)   The liquidity ratios, to ensure that all reasonably expected withdrawals by depositors can be met without embarrassment. The borrowing facilities available to the bank are relevant here.

Such enquiries will enable the auditor to assess the extent of the bank's dependence upon activities which may be subject to abnormal risk at the time of his review.

49.   (a)   The following are the general procedures to be followed when conducting an investigation into the purchase of a business:

  (i) Ascertain from client the precise terms of reference and confirm them in writing. In particular ascertain the number of years to be covered in the course of the investigation, the purchase price being sought, the funds which the client has available and the maximum amount which he is prepared to spend, and whether it is the client's intention to become involved in an executive capacity.

  (ii) Obtain copies of the detailed accounts for each of the years to be covered.

  (iii) Note any qualifications in the reports of auditors

  (iv) Consider detailed information in the accounts for each year in conjunction with available supporting schedules and working papers.

   (v) Make adjustments to the accounts for past years bearing in mind the likely future conditions of the business.

  (vi) Consider trends and ratios after the accounts have been adjusted, for example closing stock: cost of sales; debtors: sales; purchases: creditors; gross profit: sales; net profit: sales; current assets: current liabilities; and fixed assets: shareholders' equity.

 (vii) Draw conclusions from the examination, in anticipation of the report.

(viii) Draft a report to the client.

(b)   The specific matters for which it may be necessary to adjust the past accounts of the business are as follows:

   (i) past income and expenditure not applicable in the future;

  (ii) likely future income and expenditure not previously applicable;

 (iii) realistic present values for all assets and liabilities and depreciation thereon;

 (iv) savings through discounts not previously taken owing to working capital shortages;

  (v) expenditure deferred by the previous proprietor in anticipation of the sale of the business.

(c)   The investigator would normally enquire beyond the accounts in respect of the following matters:

   (i) staff loyalty and availability of suitable staff;

  (ii) customer goodwill, considering the need to enter into restrictive covenants with the former proprietor;

 (iii) length of current leases;

 (iv) the age and general condition of the stocks;

  (v) the soundness of the trade debts;

 (vi) the condition and estimated future useful life of the major fixed assets, and their estimated replacement cost;

 (vii) the likely effect of forthcoming legislation, fiscal and otherwise, which may affect the profitability of the business;

(viii) road and building plans within the district (conversion of a roadway into a motorway can halve the custom of a shopping site);

 (ix) general economic and fiscal prognostications which may affect trade.

50. (a)   The auditor would expect the following sources of revenue to be disclosed in the accounts:

(i) student tuition fees;

(ii) funds received from governmental agencies and local government;

(iii) government grants and contracts for specific research and other programmes or projects;

(iv) gifts and private grants received for education and other purposes, including student aid and bursaries; this includes grants from trusts;

(v) endowment income, both unrestricted for general purposes and restricted for specific projects;

(vi) sales and services of individual departments such as film rentals and scientific or literary projects;

(vii) activities organised by education departments: such activities are carried on primarily for the training of students, e.g. food technology, dairy farming, etc.;

(viii) income from investments and gains on the sale of investments of unrestricted available funds.

(b) The following are four major internal controls:

(i) budgetary control over all recorded revenues, including regular comparisons with budget estimates and independently carried out analysis of significant variations;

(ii) control over revenues by recording them on a consistently adopted accruals basis and comparing them regularly with previous year, as adjusted (e.g. for new investment);

(iii) independent control over issues of credits, allowances, scholarships, and any other adjustments to normal revenue flows;

(iv) strictly applied procedures for receiving and acknowledging all gifts and grants.

(c) Five audit tests which should be applied to the accounts submitted for audit are as follows:

(i) review each divisional revenue account and make comparison with the prior period and the budget estimates; determine the reasons for any significant variations;

(ii) compare revenues with appropriate statistical reports relating to enrolment, occupancy of halls of residence, meals served, etc. prepared by departments or individuals not involved with the revenue-recording or cash-receiving functions;

(iii) review and examine the data underlying gifts, grants and bequests, including documentation, correspondence, acknowledgments and notifications of grant awards; governing board minutes; and compare by type and nature with amounts from prior periods;

    (iv) examine gross margin percentages relating to the auxiliary activities of the college unions, college stores and other services such as college hairdressers, cinemas, etc., and compare with prior-year periods and budget estimates;

    (v) test records and revenues relating to sporting events including record of ticket sales, ticket numbers, free tickets and contracts with other institutions.

51. The following matters would be of principal concern to the bank manager in the circumstances described.

GENERAL:

    (a) the background and professional standing of the promoters of the company;

    (b) the viability of the concern in the light of current and future legal education requirements;

    (c) the size of the available market;

    (d) the quality of the tuition to be offered by the new company in comparison with that already available;

    (e) the availability of suitably located premises at an economic rent, possessing permission for educational use.

FINANCIAL

Since it would appear that bank finance will be required to support the venture during its first two years, the bank manager will be most concerned about the company's cash position during, say, years one, two and three; estimated cash budgets will therefore be more significant than any estimates of profitability. Basically two sets of schedules would be required:

    (a) estimates, set out month by month, from courses and variable expenses directly related thereto such as lecturers' fees and test marking expenses;

    (b) estimates, once again set out monthly, of fixed costs likely to be incurred from the inception of the school: these expenses would cover:

       (i) administrative salaries, including directors' salaries;

      (ii) establishment expenses, e.g. rent and rates; premium on the lease;

     (iii) costs of decorating and refurbishing to meet classroom requirements;

     (iv) costs of office furniture, typewriters etc.;

      (v) initial and regular advertising, direct mail and design of stationery;

     (vi) costs of writing and printing manuals, tests, etc. to be used in conjunction with the classes;

    (vii) repairs and maintenance;

(viii) interest charges on the finance which it is hoped the bank will extend.

A suitable margin for unforeseen contingencies should also be allowed in the estimates.

The submission to the bank manager should therefore set out the net monthly cash flow, being the difference between the estimated cash revenue (net of variable costs) and the estimated fixed costs.

52. Changes in auditing techniques have increased rapidly during the last decade. Not so many years ago it would have been the expected procedure to "tick" one's way through an audit. An audit was prepared and books and records were ticked, as this was what the client expected.

During the post-war era, however, changes in procedure came about. The professional bodies issued auditing recommendations; internal control question-naires, statistical sampling, and flow-charting came into being. These "thinking" techniques are the result of higher standards set by the profession. Increases in costs and overheads have also forced the auditor to resort to thinking techniques.

The basic principles now adopted by an auditor when commencing audit are:

(a) critically review the client's system of accounting and internal control;

(b) ascertain that the system properly and accurately records all transactions;

(c) determine whether he can rely on the system.

The auditor evaluates the system of internal control by means of internal control questionnaires or flow-charts in order to ascertain the strengths and weaknesses of the system and from the effectiveness or otherwise of the system will be able to design the audit programme and level of tests. This illustrates how auditing techniques have changed for the better. More "thinking" is done before carrying out a test. The principle of test checking also results in less ticking, and more planning.

Each year at the actual commencement of an audit, the auditor will review the systems according to his working paper and test to see that such systems are operative, amending his records where necessary—his own records will be ticked.

The greater responsibilities reposed in the auditor as a result of the Companies Act 1985, compliance with the disclosure requirements under the Act, the Stock Exchange Listing Agreement, and Statements of Standard Accounting Practice all call for further working papers to confirm compliance, and these need to be "ticked".

As auditing develops, more time will be spent by the auditor in ticking his own working papers instead of his client's records.

The change from "ticking" to "thinking" audits does indicate that the auditor is keeping abreast of the ever-changing scene and that the reasons for carrying out a particular test have been seriously considered so that the auditor can perform a more efficient audit.

53. (a) Particularly in times of economic crises, managements of many concerns require information which is accurate, up to date, and adequately presented for the purposes of making major decisions. When industry is riding on the crest of a wave this problem is less critical, and at such times management information systems might be viewed purely as supplementary or "back-up" for policies which virtually run themselves.

At the present time, however, the statutory audit often takes place only annually (and after the formal accounts have been completed), and the work of the external auditor may be viewed with some cynicism by those managements who seek performance data on a monthly, weekly or even daily basis. It is their view that the external auditor should possess the expertise which would enable him to fulfil a more vital role for the benefit of management, and to them forecasts are more significant than last year's performance.

(b)   Auditors could be of more constructive use to management in the following ways:

   (i) View the company's needs in terms of a much briefer cycle than the financial year (e.g. monthly), as suggested in (a) above.

   (ii) Prepare reports, by arrangement, on matters outside statutory requirements. Many companies lack the size and manpower to accommodate separate departments for budgetary control, costing and internal audit purposes. The external auditor could meet this deficiency by monitoring regularly prepared statistical data and issuing regular reports, particularly where danger signs were apparent.

   (iii) Auditors could be especially vigilant over those areas in which the company was particularly vulnerable, for example, over liquidity. In recent months many small- and medium-sized companies have been forced into liquidation through cash-flow problems which remained undetected by their financial advisors; such managements often confuse liquidity and profitability and their auditors are ideally placed for highlighting the essential differences.

It is suggested, in other words, that the statutory auditor should move outside of the narrow confines of his company law duties, if the audit is ever to be seen as a useful influence in the realm of management. Auditors are, in fact, not unaware of this need but do not wholly fulfil the requirement at present.

(c)   The "operations audit" is the title usually given to the all-embracing review of a company's operations, the need for which is referred to above. The size of the operations audit programme is, however, flexible and it takes place in phases, normally:

   (i) gathering information;

   (ii) analysing information collected;

   (iii) drawing conclusions on opportunities for improvement, and reporting.

Some of the most important areas which it would normally cover are as follows:

   (i) management of plant and machinery, e.g. measures adopted for preventive maintenance of machinery, to minimise lost production;

   (ii) management of labour resources, e.g. personnel policies, recruitment methods, training facilities and staff welfare;

(iii) production purchasing, e.g. maintenance of register of authorised suppliers;

(iv) pricing policy and its relationship to costs;

(v) assessment of research and development programmes, e.g. effectiveness with which pure research expenditure is controlled;

(vi) reputation and corporate image, e.g. relationships with shareholders, customers and the community;

(vii) assessment of financial return including appraisal of return on investors' fund and profit forecasts.

54. There is a good deal of truth in the statement quoted in the question, for the following reasons:

(a) The rapidity of events which affect businesses often render annual accounts ineffective for the purpose of making investment decisions—annual accounts often describe a situation which it is too late to do anything about.

(b) The company's management may have been subject to several internal changes which have a material effect on the general efficiency of the manner in which the business is conducted. Shareholders should be acquainted with the effect of these changes at the earliest possible moment.

(c) In distinction to (b) above, the business may be affected by external economic changes over which the management has little control, e.g. fluctuations in the price and scarcity of the company's raw materials; industrial labour relations, etc. Once again, it is important that the effect of such changes should be reported more frequently than is normally the case today.

The following are the main practical problems which would face the auditor of a limited company if asked to report to shareholders on interim accounts:

(a) There is at the present time no statutory provision for such an audit and there might be difficulty in establishing a sound legal basis for this work, especially having regard to the seasonal nature of many business activities.

(b) Although interim audits often take place, audit firms are carefully staffed to cater for annual reports to shareholders; the undertaking of additional quarterly or half-yearly audits will materially increase the staffing requirement and it may prove difficult in practice to allocate staff of the right calibre for this work.

(c) If promptness of reporting is one of the prime objectives, the amount of time available for the interim audit may be distinctly limited; this in turn may limit the effectiveness of the audit and will require such limitations to be declared in the audit report. A further consequence is that the value of the audit report might be down-graded in the eyes of the recipients.

    (d)   The shareholders of private and public companies respectively have very different requirements. Any proposals to report on an interim basis would have to take these differences into account and, in the case of quoted companies, would have to be negotiated with the Council of the Stock Exchange.

55. Growing Ltd—possible audit problems:

    (a)   If a clean report is to be given, independently originated evidence must replace the management assurances given in previous period. This may be feasible for assets, but undisclosed liabilities and contingencies may be difficult to detect, e.g. to suppliers for goods, parts and second-hand items, and warranties.

    (b)   No track record exists, and analytical review will have no background data for comparative purposes.

    (c)   The majority of staff members are new and untried, and of unknown reliability.

    (d)   No definitive system of operation or control has been in force for a long period, and hence checking procedures will have to be especially comprehensive.

    (e)   The expansion in activity, involving spare second-hand computers etc., will mean that stock control is difficult, and records thereof unreliable. High-value items are small and portable, and extensive pilferage therefore possible. The auditors will lack the technical expertise to identify items of specialised equipment.

    (f)   It seems clear that the period of exceptional growth has taken place without any contact or involvement with auditors. There will inevitably be areas of weak, possibly non-existent, controls. Compliance testing will not be feasible due to the absence of a system sufficiently understood and well established.

    (g)   The speed of growth suggests severe accompanying risks in the area of financial control, e.g. overtrading; the inability to meet liabilities when falling due; the granting of generous discounts to stimulate sales; the servicing of computers for cash which staff may be misappropriating; and general circumstances prevailing which are not conducive to the procurement of the high bank overdrafts which may be required.

    (h)   The period prior to January 1982 may have been haphazardly documented, and the accountant may be left with a backlog.

The approach to the audit is entirely conditioned by the matters already outlined in (a) to (h) above, and cannot therefore be separated therefrom. In particular, the best audit approach should be circumspect, taking nothing on trust, yet flexible in responding to the situation as the audit staff find it in practice. The following further matters are relevant:

    (a)   Management assurances previously given should be compared with the out-turn of events in the second year to assess their reliability. Any discrepancies should be brought firmly to the attention of the management.

(b) Levels of testing must be high enough to ensure that reliable conclusions are drawn therefrom, especially since little audit assurance is likely to be derived from:

   (i) internal controls; and

   (ii) "reasonableness" tests and analytical review of the draft accounts.

A large proportion of all recorded transactions will therefore have to be examined and verified.

(c) Quality of staff should be assessed carefully, due to pressurised recruitment policy and continuously altered clerical and authorisation procedures, especially pre-January.

(d) Comparisons between the key financial ratios (gross margins, stock/turnover, sales/debtors, liquidity, etc.) of Growing Ltd and other clients in the same trade, or other available marketing statistics, should be made.

(e) Each operational area (i.e. new machine sales, second-hand sales, service, hire) should be separately assessed and reviewed for reliable accounting and control procedures.

(f) Circularisation of debtors and creditors; observation of physical stocktaking procedure and reconciliation of stock levels with records of stock movements and purchase/sale invoices, are obvious and indispensable audit procedures.

(g) The reliability of senior management must be assessed from previous business experience and their ability to control the rapid growth to date.

56. Arguments in favour of capitalisation of finance leases:

(a) The work of the Accounting Standards Committee for a dozen years has been concerned with the need for the true and fair view to reflect the underlying commercial substance of transactions, rather than their legal form. The real substance of finance leasing is a method of permanent acquisition and financial statements should therefore disclose this by capitalisation.

(b) Treatment of what are in effect, capital repayments and interest payments as "rent" has the effects of:

   (i) avoiding disclosure of the value of assets whose use contributes to trading profits; and

   (ii) avoiding disclosure of the true level of external funding required to sustain business activities.

Gearing ratios are consequently misleading. (When Court Line went into liquidation after showing a £4.7 million profit, it was discovered that "off balance sheet" finance in the form of finance leases amounted to over £20 million.) Those approached for further finance may thus be seriously misled by current financial statements.

(c)   Hire purchase of capital assets is invariably treated as an acquisition; to regard payment under a finance lease as "rent" is therefore to use a completely inconsistent method for recording a transaction of an essentially similar nature.

(d)   Accounting treatment should reflect the intent in the minds of the parties. Assets held and used under finance leases are intended to be retained for the whole of their estimated useful lives, and should therefore be distinguished from, say, plant which is hired for a relatively short period and then returned to its owners.

Arguments against capitalisation of finance leases:

(a)   The revenue authorities may choose to follow a revised accounting treatment, and dismantle the whole tax-benefit structure which now allows the lessee to deduct "rentals" from profits, and the lessor to claim capital allowance. This might in turn be disastrous economically, because of the effect on the companies manufacturing the capital goods (i.e. if tax advantages to their customers are removed).

(b)   The calculations involved in capitalising leases are too complicated for small companies. In the USA (FAS 13) the Standard applies only to large companies.

(c)   Capitalisation of leases may cause many companies to be in breach of their borrowing limits, since the present value of future rentals would be disclosed as a liability.

(d)   If companies are compelled to bring leases into their balance sheets, as recommended in ED 29, they may be discouraged from investing in capital equipment, again with a deterimental effect on industry and the economy.

(e)   Only the strict legal position should be used in accounting treatment. Interpreting "substance" is too subjective a basis to be valid. Where would this line of reasoning end?

One can conclude that all the arguments "against" listed above have been shown to be without foundation; even the Revenue authorities have said that implementation of ED 29 would not of itself lead to a fiscal change. The arguments against capitalisation have been produced by representatives of the leasing industry itself, and can therefore hardly claim to be objectively conceived. The more powerful argument of "substance over form" used by the ASC should therefore prevail against those who seek to use financial statements to dissemble reality. The ASC has stated also that simple calculation methods will be made available to small companies.

57. The formalities of the letter are in this instance omitted to save space, though these would count towards marks awarded.

(a)   (i) Section 382, CA 1985, requires that minutes of directors' meetings shall be kept and prescribes penalties for failure to do so.

(ii) For the avoidance of subsequent doubt and dispute by the directors (present and future) the minutes, having been accepted by all who were present as an accurate and fair record of all that transpired, and evidenced to that effect by the Chairman's signature in their presence, carry the highest internal authority for the conduct of the company, its directors and servants.

(iii) If properly filed and indexed they facilitate easy reference to detailed and complex policy decisions.

(iv) In the light of above it is clear that they are useful to auditors and will hence save management time on audit queries and hence on audit costs.

(v) Minutes create a welcome discipline for directors' meetings, thus enabling dates of future meetings to be recorded in advance, and also facilitating preparation for forthcoming meetings. They also clear up misunderstandings as to what was in fact agreed.

(vi) They concentrate on decisions concerning non-routine matters which, by their nature, will often by very material, and for which they may constitute the only available evidence.

(b) The retrospective creation of a collection of minutes is useless since:

(i) they are based on memory, which can be highly selective, if not inventive;

(ii) not having been read following the meeting they purport to describe, by those purported to have been present, they cannot be regarded as a reliable record of what transpired.

(c) Procedures—minutes as acceptable audit evidence:

(i) draft minutes must be circulated following meeting (1) to all who were present;

(ii) at next meeting (2) minutes of meeting (1) are approved, with agreed alterations if necessary, and approval evidenced;

(iii) at meeting (3) minutes of meeting (2), which include approval of minutes of meeting (1), will be approved, and so on, until the final board meeting before completion of audit, at which the financial statements will be approved by directors with the auditors in attendance.

There is therefore a "chain of authenticity" which must not be broken if the minutes of *any* of the meetings affected are to constitute reliable audit evidence.

(d) Practical steps:

(i) the auditor should prepare a full schedule of all matters (including the five listed) in respect of which board minutes are required and would naturally be expected in a well-directed company;

(ii) the schedule should be presented to the directors for consideration at the next board meeting, when consensus should be reached with regard to each of them in turn;

(iii) the board's agreement on each item on the schedule should be documented, signed by each director, and formally minuted for future reference;

(iv) the procedures for minutes of meetings outlined under (c) above should be implemented forthwith.

(e) The matters listed—use of minutes by auditors:

(i) this would have assured the auditors that their appointment is valid and binding on themselves and on the company; also that terms of engagement had been circulated to directors, understood by them, and approved;

(ii) this would have clarified the executives' responsibilities as determined and understood by the board, and would therefore enable the auditors to assess the effect of these appointments, particularly that of the financial executive, on the internal controls in force; it would also have reduced the risk of misunderstandings regarding remuneration packages, and enabled the auditor to consider the accuracy of the charge in the accounts in respect of their employment, and of the disclosures thereof in the notes;

(iii) the minutes would have established the extent of discussion which preceded the decision to borrow; whether the directors had considered alternative, less onerous, forms of finance; whether any other potential sources had turned the application down and, if so, on what grounds; the extent of any guarantees given in addition to the floating charge; and also assist the auditors to confirm that the financial statements reflect the correct charges for interest, and comply fully with the format classifications in the balance sheet under CA 1985;

(iv) minutes would have revealed the agreement of all directors to the bonus scheme itself as well as to the method of calculating bonuses by reference to performance. This would have assisted the auditors to check the calculations and hence to verify the adequacy or otherwise of the amounts provided for in the accounts in respect of bonuses, as well as the accuracy of the classification of directors' emoluments; it would also have assisted the auditors to ensure that the accounts properly reflected the taxation consequences of the method of determining and paying bonuses, especially if these were needed to rectify any directors' current account debit balances;

(v) minutes might have revealed the directors' assessment of the seriousness of the claim and of the likelihood of its success; they would have shown whether any directors expressed minority opinions on how to handle the claim, and whether a similar problem might be brewing in other quarters; they might have included reference to verbal opinions obtained from solicitors. All of this would have assisted auditors to determine the correctness of the treatment of what is obviously a material claim in the financial statements, in terms of both adequacy of provision or disclosure of contingency.

58. (a) Information required from files:

(i) Engagement letter: did we make it clear that our tests are designed to give a reasonable expectation of discovering fraud which is *material* in relation to the financial statements?

(ii) Were weakness/management letters sent in which
—the risk of teeming and lading was specifically mentioned?
—the finance director was advised that branches should not maintain autonomous sales ledgers because of this very risk, and hence that sales ledger accounting should operate centrally?

(iii) Whether analytical procedures were performed on Colchester results and, if so, their details; in particular, whether these highlighted
—the inconsistency between Colchester and the other branches,
—the explanations given for this,
—whether this inconsistency existed in earlier periods.

(iv) By what rotational means branches are selected for audit, and how Colchester in particular came to be selected (i.e. by random selection or specific intention, possibly based on results of analytical tests already mentioned).

(v) Materiality criteria used for determining high/low value items, high/low risk factors, and sample sizes for substantive testing of transactions and balances; how effectively these materiality criteria were translated into sampling plans; and whether the findings were validly interpreted.

(vi) Concerning the Colchester financial statements:
—the breakdown between cash and credit sales at branch,
—analysis of net assets to determine average level of debtors.

(vii) Internal control procedures at Colchester regarding:
—receipt of remittances,
—promptness of banking,
—credit and cash discount terms extended,
—returns of goods from customers,
—bad debt write-offs,
—credit control in general.

(b) Information required from client:

(i) the means by which the fraud was perpetrated and covered up;

(ii) how it came to light;

(iii) whether any confessions have been made by the clerk, and whether these appear reliable;

   (iv) whether the police have been notified and charges pressed;

   (v) whether any arrangements have been made for recovery of losses, or some of them, from the clerk;

   (vi) date of clerk's appointment, details of job description, his background experience, and whether the usual references, appropriate to an accounting appointment requiring honesty and integrity, were sought and taken up;

   (vii) whether similar occurrences could be happening at other branches, and whether our assistance in connection with special enquiries is required.

(c) Notes for meeting with finance director:

   (i) enquire regarding matters (i) to (vii) under (b) above, and note replies;

   (ii) past management letters have drawn attention to the relevant weaknesses, but make it clear that the risk is not material for audit purposes;

   (iii) the Colchester inconsistencies revealed by analytical procedures were raised with finance director who gave plausible explanations, including returns of defective goods caused by warehouse damage; prompt settlement by customers claiming cash discounts; and severe bad debt losses—i.e. the very methods used by clerk for covering up the fraud;

   (iv) engagement letter clearly relates our concern with fraud to materiality. We used 0.5% of turnover as materiality limit (ML) for company = £250,000, and our audit procedures reflected this throughout. The losses due to fraud were not material for substantive testing purposes, nor in relation to company profits (3.1%);

   (v) both the financial statements and the audit opinion would have been entirely unaffected by discovery of fraud *prior* to approval of financial statements by directors.

59. (a) *Accounting policies:*

   (i) Ensure that accounting policies conform with Accounting Standards or that departures are justified in the circumstances to give true and fair view.

   (ii) Ensure that all policies are appropriate to nature of business.

   (iii) Ensure that all companies in group have adopted the policies prescribed by the holding company.

   (iv) Ensure that the policies applied are consistent with those applied in earlier years, and that there is adequate justification for any policy changes, the effect of which must be disclosed in financial statements as prior-year adjustments.

(v) Ensure that policies disclosed in financial statements are those which all companies in group have actually applied in preparing those statements.

(vi) Ensure that formulation of policies is clear, concise yet full, accurate and unlikely to be misinterpreted or misunderstood.

(b) *Court Line policies:*

(i) Formulation, although cumbersome, conveys the policy reasonably clearly. Policy not acceptable since receipts, although not refundable, have not been *earned.* Cancellation fees treated as current revenue may not even be covered by deposits received. Although deposits not refundable if charterer cancels, would be refundable if cause of non-performance attributable to hirer or external factors. Policy conflicts with acceptable principles of revenue recognition, and any deposits received should be treated as income received in advance, and included in creditors.

(ii) Policy description unacceptably vague, and meaning remains doubtful. No valid reason given for change of policy, or even what new policy is. Quoted policy explains only treatment of balance brought forward, which is unacceptable. Even if change of policy valid, effect should be treated as prior-year adjustment. Probable motivation to avoid any effect on EPS by treatment as extraordinary item.

(iii) Formulation deceptive. Fact that change of policy is involved is concealed until very end. Effect is to credit all past accumulated depreciation to current year's results. New policy not acceptable since depreciation charges are significant on such assets as buildings, furniture and equipment, and new basis (charging all replacements to revenue when cost is incurred) accords with cash-flow accounting, but not with accrual accounting, which recognises revenue in period to which costs and benefits relate, irrespective of when these costs and benefits manifest in cash terms. Policy therefore conflicts with SSAP 12 and CA 1985. Assets should be written off over expected useful economic life.

(iv) Costs and benefits of introducing new services and training are matched over too long a period (i.e. 10 years is unrealistically optimistic). Impossible for any management to be sure that:
—services introduced will be profitable;
—they will be operating for as far ahead as 10 years;
—crew and other staff being trained will remain with company, operating same services, for ensuing 10 years.
A two-year deferral of write-off would be more realistic and acceptable. The last sentence of policy is vague. What does "similarly" mean? If taken literally means interest is written off over 10 years irrespective of loan term, which is not acceptable. Finance charges are time-related and should be written off as they are incurred.

60. (a) Password security. If intended to restrict access, staff should be required to be more disciplined. Password codes are often attached to terminals; sometimes complete password lists are left in unlocked drawers.

Recommendations to clients:

—Change passwords periodically but not predictably.

—Instil stricter discipline.

—Use easily memorable phrases (e.g. "time flies") to avoid the need to write down password codes.

—Change system to voice or fingerprint recognition, and abolish passwords altogether.

(b) Control over input. Excessive reliance on manually created batch or other user-based input controls results in delays if performed properly, or in high input error rates if corners are cut.

Recommendations to clients:

—Write adaptable application software for checking input at entry stage against

 (i) normal paramater values

(ii) user-produced control data.

—Query unusual data with originating department as soon as it is highlighted by the program.

—Produce exception reports for subsequent comparison with those normally produced at processing stage.

(c) Scrambling of sensitive data during processing. Encryption of sensitive data takes place too close to processing, by which time it may have been seen or copied by unauthorised personnel.

Recommendations to clients:

—Encryption should feature as *early* as possible, especially when highly sensitive data relates to very material sums, e.g. electronic funds transfer internationally, when destination is featured in original input.

—Encryption should be preceded by a message authentication device, operated independently of the data source and destination.

—Unscrambling at output destination should again be preceded by message authentication device, and should take place *after* output has left DP centre.

(d) Software integrity. Software is used to authenticate messages, perform key accounting calculations, authorise asset movements, etc. The consequences of fraudulent or corrupted codes in programs used for such purposes could be disastrous.

Recommendations to clients:

—Identify those source programs which, if manipulated, could cause potentially substantial losses through fraud or other irregularity.

—Arrange for codes in programs to be checked regularly, without warning, by personnel independent of operators, programmers, and analysts.

—Use test-packs specially created for this purpose and record results for subsequent reference.

(e) Data security. Highly confidential information is held on both current and non-current files. Tapes can easily be removed. Security guards do not search employees.

Recommendations to clients:

—Identify data on file which could be exploited if in the wrong hands.

—Classify it according to a security hierarchy, which incorporates codes indicating data held on behalf of others (banks, computer bureaux, finance companies, stockbrokers).

—Apply appropriate encryption routines to sensitive data to ensure it is non-recognisable.

—Ensure compliance with Data Protection Act 1984.

(f)   Database security. In a database only small proportion of stored data is accessed daily or weekly. Some customer records may not be accessed for months. In the meanwhile, stored data may have inadvertently or deliberately been corrupted, and this may even have reached back-up files.

Recommendations to clients:

—Remind staff to check accuracy of standing data accessed from database.

—Institute system of routine checking of database accuracy on sample basis, performed regularly.

—At prescribed (but longer) intervals, perform database dump and delete obsolete data, checking right through for accuracy.

—Investigate unauthorised changes.

Index